Attention, Space and Action

Studies in Cognitive Neuroscience

Edited by

GLYN W. HUMPHREYS
School of Psychology, University of Birmingham

JOHN DUNCAN
MRC Cognition and Brain Sciences Unit, Cambridge

and

ANNE TREISMAN
Department of Psychology, Princeton University

*Orginating from contributions
to a Discussion Meeting
of the Royal Society of London*

OXFORD
UNIVERSITY PRESS

OXFORD
UNIVERSITY PRESS

Great Clarendon Street, Oxford OX2 6DP

Oxford University Press is a department of the University of Oxford
and furthers the University's aim of excellence in research, scholarship,
and education by publishing worldwide in

Oxford New York

Athens Auckland Bangkok Bogotá Buenos Aires Calcutta
Cape Town Chennai Dar es Salaam Delhi Florence Hong Kong Istanbul
Karachi Kuala Lumpur Madrid Melbourne Mexico City Mumbai
Nairobi Paris São Paulo Singapore Taipei Tokyo Toronto Warsaw

and associated companies in Berlin Ibadan

Oxford is a registered trade mark of Oxford University Press
in the UK and in certain other countries

Published in the United States
by Oxford University Press, Inc., New York

Chapters 1,15–18 © Oxford University Press, 1999
Chapters 2–14 © The Royal Society, 1999

The moral rights of the author have been asserted

Database right Oxford University Press (maker)

First published 1999

A catalogue record for this book is available from the British Library

Library of Congress Cataloging in Publication Data

Attention, space, and action: studies in cognitive neuroscience
edited by Glyn W. Humphreys, John Duncan, and Anne Treisman,
"Drawn from papers reported to two linked meetings, a discussion
meeting of the Royal Society . . . and a meeting at the Novartis
Foundation . . . held in November 1997" – Pref.
Includes bibliographical references and index.

1. Attention – Congresses.   2. Cognitive neuroscience – Congresses.
3. Visual perception – Congresses.   I. Humphreys, Glyn W.
II. Duncan, John, Dr.   III. Treisman, Anne.   IV. Royal Society
(Great Britain)   V. Novartis Foundation for Gerontological Research.
[DNLM: 1. Visual Perception congresses.   2. Attention congresses.
3. Cognition congresses.   WW 105 A883 1999]
QP405.A865 1999   612.8'4–dc21   99–10686

ISBN 0 19 852469 2 (Hbk)
ISBN 0 19 852468 4 (Pbk)

Typeset by Newgen Imaging Systems (P) Ltd., Chennai, India
Printed in Great Britain
on acid-free paper by
Bookcraft (Bath) Ltd,
Midsomer Norton, Avon

Preface

The chapters in this book are drawn from papers reported to two linked meetings, a discussion meeting of the Royal Society on 'Brain mechanisms of selective perception and action' and a meeting at the Novartis Foundation on 'The control of attention', held in November 1997. These meetings enabled us to bring together leading figures in the cognitive neuroscience of attention, in an attempt to integrate recent work relating processes of selection to representations of space and action. We wish to thank both the Royal Society and the Novartis Foundation for their support. We also thank Janet Clifford for her help in seeing the manuscripts into print.

Edgbaston   G. W. H.
Cambridge   J. D.
Princeton   A. T.
August 1998

Contents

Section 4   Visual attention and action   199

Section 5   The control of attention   249

Contributors

Alan Allport   Department of Experimental Psychology, University of Oxford, Oxford OX1 3UD, UK.

Claus Bundesen   Center for Visual Cognition, Psychological Laboratory, University of Copenhagen, Njalsgade 90, DK 2300 Copenhagen S, Denmark.

Neil Burgess   Institute of Cognitive Neuroscience, Department of Anatomy, University College London, Gower Street, London WC1E 6BT, UK.

Maurizio Corbetta   Departments of Neurology, Radiology, Anatomy and Neurobiology, McDonnell Center for the Study of Higher Brain Function, Washington University, 660 South Euclid Avenue, St. Louis, MO 63110, USA.

Robert Desimone   Laboratory of Neuropsychology, NIMH, 49 Convent Drive, Building 49, Bethesda, MD 20892-4415, USA.

James G. Donnett   Institute of Cognitive Neuroscience, Department of Anatomy, University College London, Gower Street, London WC1E 6BT, UK.

Jon Driver   Institute of Cognitive Neuroscience, Department of Psychology, Alexandra House, University College London, Gower Street, London WC1E 6BT, UK.

John Duncan   MRC Cognition and Brain Sciences Unit, 15 Chaucer Road, Cambridge CB2 2EF, UK.

Christopher D. Frith   Wellcome Department of Cognitive Neurology, Institute of Neurology, 12 Queen Square, London WC1E 3BG, UK.

Steven A. Hillyard   Department of Neurosciences, University of California San Diego, La Jolla, California 92093-0608, USA.

George Houghton   Centre for Perception, Attention and Motor Sciences, School of Psychology, University of Wales, Bangor, Gwynedd LL57 2DG, Wales.

Louise A. Howard   Centre for Perception, Attention and Motor Sciences, School of Psychology, University of Wales, Bangor, Gwynedd LL57 2DG, Wales.

Glyn W. Humphreys   Cognitive Science Research Centre, School of Psychology, University of Birmingham, Edgbaston, Birmingham B15 2TT, UK.

Kathryn J. Jeffery   Institute of Cognitive Neuroscience, Department of Anatomy, University College London, Gower Street, London WC1E 6BT, UK.

Makato Kusunoki   Nihon University, School of Medicine, Department of Physiology, 30-1 Oyaguchi Kamimachi Itabashi-ku, Tokyo 173, Japan.

Steven J. Luck   Department of Psychology, University of Iowa, Iowa City, IA 522422-1407, USA.

Eleanor A. Maguire   Wellcome Department of Cognitive Neurology, Institute of Neurology, University College London, 12 Queen Square, London WC1E 3BG, UK.

Tom Manly   MRC Cognition and Brain Sciences Unit, 15 Chaucer Road, Cambridge CB2 2EF, UK.

Earl K. Miller   Department of Brain and Cognitive Sciences and the Center for Learning and Memory, Massachusetts Institute of Technology, Cambridge, MA 02139, USA.

A.D. Milner   Department of Psychology, University of St. Andrews, St. Andrews, Fife, KY16 9JU, UK.

Akira Murata   Nihon University, School of Medicine, Department of Physiology, 30–1 Oyaguchi Kamimachi Itabashi-ku, Tokyo 173, Japan.

John O'Keefe   Institute of Cognitive Neuroscience, Department of Anatomy, University College London, Gower Street, London WC1E 6BT, UK.

Geraint Rees   Wellcome Department of Cognitive Neurology, Institute of Neurology, 12 Queen Square, London WC1E 3BG,UK.

Ian H. Robertson   Department of Psychology, Trinity College Dublin, Dublin, Ireland.

Hideo Sakata   Nihon University, School of Medicine, Department of Physiology, 30-1 Oyaguchi Kamimachi Itabashi-ku, Tokyo 173, Japan.

Gordon L. Shulman   Department of Neurology, McDonnell Center for the Study of Higher Brain Function, Washington University, 660 South Euclid Avenue, St. Louis, MO 63110, USA.

Charles Spence   Department of Experimental Psychology, University of Oxford, Oxford OX1 3UD, UK.

Masato Taira   Nihon University, School of Medicine, Department of Physiology, 30-1 Oyaguchi Kamimachi Itabashi-ku, Tokyo 173, Japan.

Yuji Tanaka   Nihon University, School of Medicine, Department of Physiology, 30-1 Oyaguchi Kamimachi Itabashi-ku, Tokyo 173, Japan.

Steven P. Tipper   Centre for Perception, Attention and Motor Sciences, School of Psychology, University of Wales, Bangor, Gwynedd LL57 2DG, UK.

Anne Treisman   Department of Psychology, Princeton University, Princeton, New Jersey 08544-1010, USA.

Ken-ichiro Tsutsui   Nihon University, School of Medicine, Department of Physiology, 30-1 Oyaguchi Kammimachi Itabashi-ku, Tokyo 173, Japan.

Edward K. Vogel   Department of Neurosciences, University of California San Diego, La Jolla, California 92093-0608, USA.

Robert Ward   Centre for Perception, Attention and Motor Sciences, School of Psychology, University of Wales, Bangor, Gwynedd LL57 2DG, Wales.

Glenn Wylie   Department of Experimental Psychology, University of Oxford, Oxford OX1 3UD, UK.

1

Introduction

Glyn W. Humphreys, John Duncan, and Anne Treisman

Abstract

Over the past 15 years or so there have been substantial and important developments in the cognitive neuroscience of selective perception and action. We review the role played in these developments by the component disciplines of experimental psychology, neuropsychology, electrophysiology, mathematical and computational modelling, and functional imaging. We argue that interdisciplinary work in this field has played a major part in advancing our understanding, and that there are benefits to be gained from gathering converging evidence at different levels of analysis. We discuss the relations between these arguments and the chapters presented in book.

The world is full of objects. Some may be static, others not. Some may be partially occluded, others standing alone. Some may emit sounds, others not. Some we may be touching (hands resting on a table), others out of reach. At a sensory level, the means by which the world comes to be organized into objects is a far from trivial problem, since stimulus information is typically ambiguous as to which local parts of a scene 'belong' together. It is also unclear how different forms of sensory information combine—does each sense operate independently, or is information integrated in forms of multi-modal representation (Driver and Spence, this volume)? Furthermore, the behavioural responses we are equipped to make are inherently limited. We may only name one object at a time; we can reach at most to two objects. The information available to our senses needs to be selected, so that only relevant parts of the world are represented for action. Scenes may be parsed in different ways according to our intended behaviour. Perception and action may be linked through processes of selective attention (Milner, this volume; Tipper *et al.*, this volume).

These are exciting times in the study of selective attention. For many years the topic has been studied primarily at a psychological level. More recently, however, progress has been made by linking theories and experimental procedures from psychology to the techniques of neuroscience. This has allowed us to begin to understand how perceptual processing in the brain is modulated by selective attention, and how selective perceptual processing relates to action.

In this Introduction, we ask what has been and what can be gained by inter-disciplinary research in this field. We suggest that there is much. Psychology launched the scientific study of attention, making seminal contributions to both theoretical issues and methodology, but we suggest that progress has accelerated since the findings and ideas developed through behavioural techniques have been complemented by the contributions of cognitive neuroscience. We consider first the contribution of psychology, before proceeding to review some of the developments facilitated by neuroscientific techniques.

1.1 Contributions of psychology

(i) Research questions

Perhaps one of the most important past and continuing contributions of psychology to understanding selective perception and action is in helping to establish the research questions. In many respects psychology sits at a vital level in neuroscience, since it typically provides a functional analysis of either whole system or sub-system behaviour, without necessarily having to be concerned with the details of how a functional system may be implemented in the brain. When we conduct a psychological experiment, we are concerned with either how a whole motivated individual, or some designated processing system in the individual (e.g., his or her object recognition system) responds under a set of circumstances. Experiments are designed to elucidate the functional nature of the processing systems underlying the behaviour—the form(s) of representation involved, how representations are activated, how they interact or are shielded from outside influence, their time course, how access to the representations may be controlled—and any information gained can be used to define the way in which a system needs to operate at a level above that of the neuronal hardware. Marr (1982), writing on the topic of visual perception, argued that theories need to be defined at different levels of analysis to provide an over-arching account of intelligent behaviour. He distinguished between *computational, algorithmic* and *hardware* levels of analysis. A computational account would provide a set of constraints on understanding how a given behaviour may be realised irrespective of whether this is done by biological organism or a computer. An algorithmic account would specify the nature of the processing algorithm used to generate the behaviour by the particular organism involved. A hardware account deals with how the algorithm is implemented in the organism (e.g., how object recognition is realised in a brain). Marr argued that theories at each of these levels could help constrain understanding at the others. Most relevant for our present purposes, a theory that details a particular algorithm used by human beings may be useful in guiding the search for the structures mediating that algorithm at a neuronal level. Psychological studies can help to specify the functional algorithms involved in selective perception and action. In so doing, these studies not only constrain neuroscientific research but they also provide much of the framework for research at a hardware level.

Examples of how psychology has provided the framework for the analysis of selective perception and action can be illustrated by outlining the questions that continue to direct neuroscientific research, and which are addressed in this book: is selection early (affecting perceptual processes) or late (affecting post-perceptual processing and action) (see Hillyard, Vogel and Luck, and Rees and Frith, for evidence on early selection, and Tipper *et al.* for evidence of effects on action)? Is selection constrained by limited processing resources or by the need for coherence in action (see Treisman for an argument concerned limited processing resources, Duncan for arguments about mechanisms of providing coherent perceptual information for action)? Is there a single, central processing limitation (the 'bottleneck') or several (possibly even many) (see Allport and Wylie, Duncan)? Does selection utilise excitatory or inhibitory processes (Tipper *et al.*)? What factors control attention—bottom-up (exogenous) signals or top-down (endogenous) signals, and how might different control mechanisms interact (Driver and Spence, Miller, Ward)? Is selection location-based or object-based, or both (Corbetta and Shulman, Humphreys, Treisman)? Even, what is the relation between selective attention and consciousness (Milner)? Neuroscientific research may ultimately suggest different answers from those generated by behavioural analyses, but it remains the case that the questions were initially framed by psychological study.

(ii) Paradigms

A second way in which psychology has fostered the development of the field has been through the design of many of the basic paradigms that have been used to study selective attention, typically using situations that limit the variables affecting performance. Many paradigms can be listed: dichotic listening, dual task interference, spatial cueing, priming and cost-benefit analysis, task switching and visual search being examples that have provided tests of when selective processing is required (and how efficiently it operates). Through these paradigms, basic phenomena have been generated that have become the daily fare of attention researchers: flanker interference, inhibition of return, negative priming, visual marking, switch costs, attentional blink—phenomena that can be isolated and subject to further manipulation to help us better understand the underlying mechanisms. Using these paradigms and phenomena, psychologists have discovered (not without pain!) the necessary controls that must be imposed to gain uncontaminated measures of selection (to minimise order effects, effects of changes with practice and/or strategy, effects of context, range effects etc.). These paradigms and phenomena can now be seen adapted in functional imaging studies, in experiments using visual evoked responses, even in studies using single cell recording techniques (as in analogues of visual search tasks), to evaluate attentional mechanisms at a neuronal level.

Of course, much remains open in this behavioural-level research, as it does at the neural level. Nevertheless we increasingly see agreement over broad principles of how selection must operate—agreement that supersedes some of the initial dichotomies made by theorists (early vs. late selection being one notorious example), to provide often a more complex but deeper account (not *whether* selection is early or late-acting, but *when* it is and *what* are the consequences). Such convergence is also gradually leading to the development of detailed quantitative theoretical accounts that integrate a wide range of attentional phenomena—an example of which is the 'Theory of Visual Attention' proposed here by Bundesen. This broad understanding at the behavioural level provides a general framework guiding neuroscientific analysis.

In respect of the development of converging theories, the problem of attention is perhaps highly suited to the new multidisciplinary attack of current cognitive neuroscience. There is a growing wealth of neuroscientific evidence that in itself begins to constrain higher-level psychological theories. Moreover, we believe this evidence is important not only for understanding attention in its own right, but more pertinently for understanding how selection influences basic processes in perception and action. We would go so far as to argue that perception and action cannot be comprehended properly without considering how they are modulated by attention.

1.2 Contributions from neuroscience

As we have noted, much of the current excitement in attention research comes from the application of new neuroscientific techniques for measuring and localising the activity of the animal (human and non-human) brain, in some cases in real time. This allows us to begin to see some convergence between questions addressed through physiological as well as psychological analysis. We highlight points illustrating aspects of this convergence.

(i) Temporal ordering

ERP and MEG recordings can provide on-line measures of the time course of mental events, tapping otherwise hidden stages between the presentation of the physical stimulus and the behavioural response; they may even demonstrate degrees of processing of stimuli when explicit behavioural responses cannot be made (e.g., as in studies of implicit stimulus processing in patients with unilateral neglect, or in studies of the 'attentional blink'; for work on neglect see Vallar *et al.* 1991; Viggiano *et al.* 1995; for work on the attentional blink see Luck *et al.* 1996). By providing a fine-grained analysis of the temporal parameters of processing, these techniques can throw light on several issues concerning the time at which attention impacts on information processing. An excellent example of this is the work of Hillyard and colleagues on changes in early components of the ERP waveform under varying attentional conditions, suggesting that different selection criteria may operate in different ways (some amplifying attended signals, some suppressing unattended signals), and over contrasting time courses (Hillyard *et al.*, this volume). Though this work may not be able to answer whether there are multiple modes of selection or a single mode implemented over a varying time course according to the task set, it certainly provides constraints on psychological accounts of selection. Here more detailed information on the time course of processing helps provide concrete demonstrations of the modulatory role of attention on perception.

(ii) Localisation of function

Do we learn anything about the functional organisation of information processing, at a psychological level, from knowing where in the brain attention effects are apparent? After all, functional levels of description may be provided independent of the hardware used to implement the information processing system. Already, however, we see that knowing where an effect arises in the brain provides an important extra source of information for our theorising at a functional level, since we may know something about the function of a given neuronal region from other studies (e.g., analysing single cell recordings or the effects of brain lesions). Knowing that attention influences an ERP component arising in extra-striate cortex, for example, tells us something about the stage and kind of visual process affected, due to converging evidence on the forms of processing operating in that brain region (see Hillyard *et al.*, this volume).

A similar point can be made from studies of functional brain imaging using PET and fMRI. Rees and Frith (this volume), for instance, report evidence using fMRI showing that activity in the human equivalent of cortical area V5, driven by motion signals, is modulated by the processing load imposed on a task performed to stationary stimuli at fixation. Under high load conditions, activity in V5 is reduced (though it operates under low load conditions). There is considerable converging evidence that V5 is involved in the perceptual analysis of motion (see Zeki 1993). The fMRI evidence, then, suggests that processing load can modulate perceptual analysis in the brain, supporting theories at a psychological level (e.g., Lavie 1995). Interestingly, this research also points to a methodological shift in the way we may go about studying attention using functional imaging techniques. By using stimulus markers known to influence particular brain regions, we can assess whether attention impacts on those regions and from this derive an account of how attention influences perception and action.

Another approach stressing localisation of function is to evaluate whether the same brain areas are recruited in tasks that, putatively, involve particular psychological processes. From positive evidence here it may be argued that a common functional operation is involved in the different tasks. An example of this is provided in Corbetta and Shulman's chapter in this volume. Corbetta and Shulman report that the same area of the parietal lobe is implicated in switching attention in space (under conditions of spatial cueing) and in search tasks requiring the detection of targets defined by conjunctions of form and colour, features that may need to be bound together. From this, they argue that a common process is involved in these conditions—the shifting of attention in space either to follow spatial cues or to bind features together at one location at a time (see Treisman, this volume, also for this argument). Again, neuroscientific procedures can provide answers pitched at a functional level of description.

Studies of single cell activity (see Desimone, Duncan, Miller, O'Keefe *et al.*, Sakata *et al.*, this volume) can be said to provide the best evidence we have on both the time course and neural localisation of processing. The well-known studies of Moran and Desimone (1985) and of Chelazzi *et al.* (1993) give some of the strongest indications to date of the modulatory role of attention at different points in the visual processing pathway, and of the time taken for such effects to emerge. The studies also contrast attention to spatial properties of stimuli with attention to non-spatial properties of stimuli such as colour and shape, indicating that attention might be called to object properties as well as to space. Thus they speak to functional as well as physiological issues, such as the relations between space-based and object-based selection.

(iii)   Dissociative methodology

Neuropsychological studies have a long-standing relation with functional accounts of information processing (see Shallice 1988, for example). Now through improved accuracy in localisation techniques and through the application of functional imaging, these studies can provide extra constraints on localisation of function (see (ii) above). It is possible to assess with great accuracy where a common lesion site might lie across a set of patients, though problems due to the sheer size of naturally occurring lesions will always be with us. However, in addition to addressing localisation issues, these studies can also provide what may be counter-intuitive insights into the nature of information processing, by showing how processing breaks down after selective brain lesion. Examples of this in the present volume come from the papers of Humphreys and Milner. Humphreys describes forms of unilateral neglect, where patients fail to select stimuli presented on one side of space. He suggests that contrasting forms of neglect can emerge, even in the same patient, because space is represented differently within an object and between separate objects. These representations of space can be selectively affected by lesions to different brain sites. Milner describes differences between the effects of brain lesions on perceptual judgements and on action where, for example, visual information can be used for action but not for perceptual judgements. Apparently visual processing may be segregated according to the uses to which it is put. The dissociations apparent in these different patients might well not have been proposed from studies of normal observers, where intact systems may interact to produce integrated behaviour. In such cases, the brain lesions may prise the integrated processes apart, so that we witness their operation in relative isolation.

Treisman demonstrates a yet different use of neuropsychological data. She reports data associating impaired spatial localisation with poor binding of visual information (e.g., when the colour and shape of several letters have to be reported). From this, Treisman argues that attention to spatial location plays an important (even crucial) role in binding together visual properties of whole objects. This finding, of poor binding coinciding with impaired localisation, is predicted by Treisman's Feature Integration Theory, and so in this sense cannot be said to be counter-intuitive. Nevertheless, it provides a striking real-life example of deficits when visual selection becomes limited by brain insult. The need for theories of vision to deal with the problem of selection is illustrated in the clearest terms.

Neuropsychological studies deal with nature's accidents. Such studies can be complemented by research examining the effects of lesioning in non-human animals, where more precise neural sites can be targeted, often to reveal selective patterns of deficit. Research at a single-cell level can be linked to what is often more wide-spread damage in human neuropsychological cases and so likely to reflect impairments to larger functional sub-systems.

(iv)   Theoretical concepts

Neuroscientific studies of selective perception and action are not only providing new methods, however; they also contribute directly to the development of theoretical concepts. For example, concepts developed at the single cell level can be used to provide a framework for understanding effects at the behavioural level; thus behavioural theories now propose competing neural populations, synaptic change for associative learning, population coding, winner-take-all networks, attentional receptive fields etc. (see Duncan, Tipper *et al.*, this volume for illustrations). In each case, models become linked more closely to underlying physiological concepts. The field is moving towards models in which broad theoretical principles at the level of behaviour are integrated with corresponding accounts at the level even of single neurons.

In some examples, hypotheses generated from the properties of single neurons are being used directly to predict patterns of behaviour and its breakdown following brain lesion. This is perhaps most apparent in the study of cross-modal influences on selection and action. Single cell studies have shown how the responses of cells to one sensory signal are modified by the alignment of the receptors with receptors from a second modality—one example being cells whose response to visual stimulation depends on the position of this input relative to some body part, such as the hand or arm (see Anderson *et al.* 1997; Graziano and Gross 1993). Such results can provide a framework for understanding deficits in selective attention and action in humans—as when cross-modal extinction is found to be modified by the position of a visual stimulus with respect to the hand of the patient (e.g., di Pellegrino *et al.* 1997; Ladavas *et al.*, in press). The physiological data suggest ways in which supra-modal representations of space become established, with subsequent implications for understanding how attentional operations are modulated. This topic is taken up by Driver and Spence here.

Increasingly, single cell recording research helps to provide an account of the operation of large-scale processing networks in the brain. For example, single cell studies conducted whilst monkeys perform visual search tasks have suggested that several brain sites may, in combination, serve the selection of targets from distractors enabling actions to be directed to targets (see Desimone, Duncan, this volume). The 'set' for the task may involve activation maintained within the pre-frontal cortex (Desimone, Miller, this volume), which feeds back in a top-down fashion to 'prime' other areas concerned with visual processing. In this way, selection is a property of a network of areas, which act in an integrated way to optimise the processing of behaviourally relevant information.

1.3   This book

The chapters in this book are organised into five broad topic areas covering what we believe are key issues in current studies of selective perception and action. These are: *visual selective attention, attention and perceptual integration, spatial representation and attention, visual attention and action,* and *the control of attention.*

In the first section, on *Visual selective attention,* there are four chapters. Desimone begins with an analysis of single cell recording data showing how properties of cells in multiple cortical regions are modulated by attention. According to Desimone, attention serves to bias the competition that arises when multiple signals fall within the receptive field of a single cell. As we hinted above, Desimone proposes that one major source of this bias is top-down activation from working memory structures located in pre-frontal cortex. In this chapter, Desimone shows how single cell research can be allied to an over-arching theoretical framework that can provide a functional account of whole-system behaviour. In the following chapter, Hillyard *et al.* use recordings from event-related brain potentials to provide converging evidence for attentional modulation of early visual processing. They suggest that attentional effects are produced by changes in the gain control of activation in extrastriate visual areas, and that there is both suppression of unattended inputs and facilitation of attended ones. The techniques used by Hillyard and colleagues also provide information on the time course of these modulatory effects on information processing in the brain. In the third chapter in this section, Bundesen presents a mathematical model of visual attention as a unified account of how people select information from multi-element displays. This model conceptualises selection in terms of competition between elements in the visual field; elements may group in various ways, and competition is based on the activation of memory templates that specify the criteria for the selection task. This framework is similar to that offered by Desimone and also by Duncan (this volume), but couched at a level abstracted from physiological mechanism. In the fourth chapter Rees and Frith summarise recent data acquired using functional imaging procedures (PET and fMRI) to suggest that selective attention changes the gain control and bias signal mechanisms of sensory processes. They also show how these new neuroscientific techniques can be used to address long-standing psychological questions, such as whether there are early effects of attention on perception.

The second section deals with *Attention and perceptual integration*. In the first chapter, Treisman presents her Feature Integration Theory, which holds that attention is required in order to bind together the features of objects, in the context of neuropsychological evidence showing that feature binding can be disrupted following damage to the parietal cortex, a brain region implicated in shifts of attention (Corbetta and Shulman, this volume) and in spatial localisation (e.g., Ratcliff and Davies-Jones 1972; Ungerleider and Mishkin 1982). In the second chapter, Duncan proposes an Integrated Competition hypothesis, in which stimuli compete for neural representation in multiple separate brain systems (see also Desimone, Bundesen, Section 1, this volume). Integration of this competition across systems produces a unified state of 'attention' to the same dominant object with its multiple properties and implications for action. The third chapter, by Driver and Spence, is concerned with how stimuli from different modalities interact in perception and action. They use evidence from physiological studies to guide hypotheses, and, using evidence from audition and touch as well as vision, they illustrate the important role of cross-modal interactions in attention.

In Section 3, three chapters are included on the topic of *Spatial representation and attention*. The first, by O'Keefe *et al.*, begins with single cell recording work that assesses forms of spatial representation used for navigation by the rat. These authors consider not only the particular types of information used to represent space, but also the involvement of one particular brain structure, the hippocampus, in this process. Their findings are consistent with converging data on activation of the hippocampus in humans during spatial navigation tasks, using functional imaging techniques. The second chapter, by Humphreys, addresses the ways in which information about objects and information about space interact in human vision. Neuropsychological data are used along with evidence from experimental psychology to argue for the existence of different forms of spatial representation, some concerned with the relations between parts within objects and some with the relations between independent visual objects. These different forms of spatial representation are linked to different constraints on visual selection (e.g., on the number of visual elements that may be represented and used concurrently for action). Corbetta and Shulman, in the final chapter in the section, use PET evidence to argue for a form of interaction between spatial vision (in the dorsal cortex) and object vision (in the ventral cortex) in which visual processing is biased by attention to areas of the visual field containing objects. They propose that this biasing operation involves regions of parietal and frontal cortex that are closely related to oculomotor processes. These results mesh with those of Treisman, who argues for feature binding by attention to space.

Section 4 deals with *Visual attention and action*. Sakata *et al.* first report evidence on cells in the parietal cortex that respond to the sight of three-dimensional objects. Though this area of cortex has classically been linked to the coding of visual space, these results indicate that it (also?) mediates the visual guidance of hand actions by three-dimensional object features. Neuropsychological evidence on the different ways in which visual information is used for perception and action is reviewed by Milner in the following chapter, using data from a variety of syndromes including visual agnosia and unilateral neglect. One important role for attention is to enable actions to be made in a coherent manner when there are many objects in the environment. The third chapter in the section, by Tipper *et al.*, deals with how visual information is selected when actions are made to objects. These authors argue for a role of action-based representations which can be selectively activated or inhibited according to task demands and the presence of other stimuli in the environment. Such representations are conceptualised in terms of population coding of neurons for directing action in space.

The final section deals with the processes involved in *The control of attention*. Much of the work on selective perception and action over the past twenty years has focused on the effects of particular attentional operations on performance, as indicated by research questions such as: does attention affect early or late-acting processes? and, is attention necessary for feature binding? In this analysis, the question of how attentional operations are themselves controlled has remained somewhat in the background. However, to understand how selective perception and action comes about, we must be clear about how attentional operations are set up in the first place. How are task instructions set into place? How are the task goals maintained and brought to bear on bottom-up activation generated by sensory input? Miller begins with a review of physiological studies aimed at examining the properties of cells in the pre-frontal cortex and their role in the control of behaviour. Miller argues that the pre-frontal cortex not only maintains information over the intermediate term (in the absence of the stimulus), but it is also involved in selecting behaviourally relevant information when several stimuli are subsequently presented (via top-down activation of earlier cortical regions; see also Desimone, Duncan, this volume). In addition, cells in the pre-frontal cortex can become tuned to task-specific rules, and so may play a part in implementing goal-based strategies in both perception and action. The next chapter, by Allport and Wylie, provides a behaviour-level analysis of goal-based control processes. They use the paradigm of 'task switching' to examine how we impose rules for particular tasks and overcome previous rules that have been used for other, recently completed tasks. There are large costs in processing efficiency when we have to switch from one task to perform another. Allport and Wylie argue that at least part of these costs can result from components of the previous task which remain activated involuntarily, sometimes until the stimulus for the second task is presented (and even when participants are instructed to prepare for the new task). The different components that carry over from one task-set to another can also be decomposed to provide a fine-grained analysis of the control structures involved in task performance. The ability to implement task goals is contingent on maintenance of the appropriate goal state across time. In the third chapter, Robertson and Manly review neuropsychological and functional imaging studies of sustained attention, including the ability to maintain a task-set in an effective state. They note evidence for a sustained attention system located within the right hemisphere, and suggest that this system may help maintain selected representations over time. They also argue that deficits in a sustained attention system can interact with spatial biases in selection, to generate at least some of the problems associated with the syndrome of unilateral neglect. Here again the idea of a large-scale cortical network devoted to different components of selection (maintenance of task goals, selection of stimuli from one side of space, priming of action to one side of space etc.) may be useful for understanding behaviour. The final chapter, by Ward, outlines a computational model that tries to capture some of the ways in which a large-scale cortical network might operate to produce both selective perception and action. This model uses an interactive activation and competition framework, with extensive feed back as well as feed forward connections, and separate components for computing where a stimulus is and what its visual properties are. Ward shows how some of the temporal dynamics of human grasping and pointing responses can emerge within such an interactive system, and also how damage to different components can produce selective disorders of pointing but not grasping and vice versa. Such a model is able to simulate dissociations of the type reported by Milner (this volume), in which an action task (e.g., grasping) may be spared even when perceptual judgements are severely impaired. Ward's model uses separable representations, so that there are selective break downs in performance, yet, in the normal case, behaviour emerges from interactions between processing components. The properties of such interactive, dynamic systems seem well worth exploring in close relation to neuroscientific studies aimed at delineating the properties of the component representations.

Overall, the papers in the book provide examples of the broad yet converging set of techniques that characterise current cognitive neuroscience. Many issues remain to be debated concerning the nature of attentional processes in the brain, but the papers here offer the promise of a future convergence—a convergence helped no doubt by research pitched at different levels of analysis.

References

Anderson, R. A., Snyder, L. H., Bradley, D. C. and Xing, J. 1997 Multimodal representation of space in the posterior parietal cortex and its use in planning movements. *Ann. Rev. Neurosci.* **20**, 303–30.

Chelazzi, L., Miller, E. K., Duncan, J. and Desimone, R. 1993. A neural basis for visual search in inferior temporal cortex. *Nature* **363**, 345–7.

di Pellegrino, G., Ladavas, E. and Farne, A. 1997. Seeing where your hands are. *Nature* **388**, 730.

Graziano, M. S. A. and Gross, C. G. 1993. A bimodal map of space: Somatosensory receptive fields in the macaque putamen with corresponding visual receptive fields. *Exp. Brain Res.* **97**, 96–109.

Ladavas, E., di Pellegrino, G., Farne, A. and Zeloni, G. In press. Neuropsychological evidence of an integrated visuo-tactile representation of peripersonal space in humans. *J. Cog. Neurosci.*

Lavie, N. 1995. Perceptual load as a necessary condition for selective attention. *J. Exp. Psych.: Hum. Perc. and Perf.* **21**, 451–68.

Luck, S. J., Vogel, E. K. and Shapiro, K. L. 1996. Word meanings can be accessed but not reported during the attentional blink. *Nature* **383**, 616–18.

Marr, D. 1982. *Vision.* San Francisco: W. H. Freeman.

Moran, J. and Desimone, R. 1985. Selective attention gates visual processing in the extrastriate cortex. *Science* **229**, 782–4.

Ratcliff, G. and Davies-Jones, G. A. B. 1972. Defective visual localisation in focal brain wounds. *Brain* **95**, 49–60.

Shallice, T. 1988. *From neuropsychology to mental structure.* Cambridge: Cambridge University Press.

Ungerleider, L. G. and Mishkin, M. 1982. Two cortical visual systems. In *Analyses of visual behavior* (eds J. Ingle, M. A. Goodale and R. J. W. Manfield), pp. 549–86. Cambridge, MA: MIT Press.

Vallar, G., Sandroni, P., Rusconi, M. L. and Barbieri, S. 1991. Hemianopia, hemianesthesia and spatial neglect: A study with evoked potentials. *Neurol.* **41**, 1918–22.

Viggiano, M. P., Spinelli, D. and Mecacci, L. 1995. Pattern reversal visual evoked potentials in patients with hemineglect syndrome. *Brain and Cog.* **27**, 17–35.

Zeki, S. 1993. *A vision of the brain.* Oxford: Blackwells.

Section 1

Visual selective attention

2

Visual attention mediated by biased competition in extrastriate visual cortex

Robert Desimone

Abstract

According to conventional neurobiological accounts of visual attention, attention serves to enhance extrastriate neuronal responses to a stimulus at one spatial location in the visual field. However, recent results from recordings in extrastriate cortex of monkeys suggest that any enhancing effect of attention is best understood in the context of competitive interactions among neurons representing all of the stimuli present in the visual field. These interactions can be biased in favour of behaviourally relevant stimuli as a result of many different processes, both spatial and nonspatial and both bottom–up and top–down. The resolution of this competition results in the suppression of the neuronal representations of behaviourally irrelevant stimuli in extrastriate cortex. A main source of top–down influence may derive from neuronal systems underlying working memory.

2.1 Introduction

A typical visual scene contains many different objects, not all of which can be fully processed by the visual system at any given time. Thus, attentional mechanisms are needed to limit processing to items that are currently relevant to behaviour (for examples, see Broadbent 1958; Neisser 1967; Treisman 1969; Bundesen 1990; Tsotsos 1990; Allport 1993; Desimone and Duncan 1995; Duncan 1996). Probably the dominant neurobiological hypothesis to account for attentional selection is that attention serves to enhance the responses of neurons representing stimuli at a single behaviourally relevant location in the visual field (see Colby 1991, for a review). This enhancement model is closely related to older 'spotlight of attention' models in psychology, in which visual attention serves to limit processing to a single locus of variable size in the visual field. According to this classical view, a behaviourally relevant object in a cluttered field is found by rapidly shifting the spotlight from one object in the scene to the next, until the sought-for object is found. Attention essentially serves as an internal eye that can shift its focus from one location to another. Because all visual attention is inherently spatial according to this view, even objects defined by their shape or colour must be found by examining candidate objects with the serially scanning spotlight, unless the object is so distinctive that it 'pops out' and automatically attracts the attentional spotlight. The neurobiological spotlight hypothesis has the advantage of both simplicity and a clear relation to the neuronal enhancement effects seen in the oculomotor system for stimuli that are the targets of eye movements; indeed, a common corollary to the enhancement hypothesis is that the control signals for attentional selection derive from structures involved in oculomotor control.

On the basis of behavioural, neuropsychological, and neurophysiological data, we have developed an alternative model for attentional selection, which we term 'biased competition'

(Desimone *et al.* 1990; Desimone and Duncan 1995; Desimone 1996; Duncan 1996; Luck *et al.* 1997; Chelazzi *et al.* 1998). According to this account, any enhancing effect of attention on neuronal responses is best understood in the context of competition among all of the stimuli in the visual field for control over behaviour. The psychological aspects of this model are more fully described elsewhere (Desimone and Duncan 1995; see Duncan, this volume) and will not be considered here. In this review, we will first briefly outline the neurobiological aspects of the model as it applies to attentional selection in the 'ventral stream' of extrastriate cortex, which is the network of cortical visual areas that is important for object recognition in primates (see Ungerleider and Mishkin 1982; Ungerleider and Haxby 1994; Ungerleider 1995). We will then review some of the neurophysiological evidence that led to the development of the model.

There are five main tenets in the biased competition model as it applies to visual processing in cortex. The first is that objects in the visual field compete for the responses of cells in visual cortex. For example, if two stimuli are presented simultaneously within the visual field, they will initially activate their neuronal representations in parallel throughout the extrastriate visual areas. If both are independent objects, and if a local region of cortex receives inputs from both of them, neuronal responses in that region will be determined by a competitive interaction between the two stimuli. On average, these interactions will be mutually suppressive.

The second tenet is that competitive interactions are strongest in a given cortical area when competing stimuli activate cells in the same local region of cortex. Thus, in visuotopically organized areas in which neurons have restricted receptive fields, competitive interactions between two stimuli will be strongest when the two stimuli fall within the same receptive field.

The third tenet is that these competitive interactions can be biased in favour of one stimulus in a cluttered field by virtue of many different mechanisms, rather than by a single overall 'attentional control' system. Such mechanisms include both 'bottom-up', or stimulus-driven, influences (e.g. one stimulus has greater novelty or has a higher contrast than another) and 'top-down' feedback mechanisms (e.g. one stimulus has greater behavioural relevance than another). Increases in feedback bias are frequently accompanied by increases in the maintained activity of visual cortical neurons or by an increase in sensory-evoked responses, but these effects are not invariable.

The fourth tenet is that the feedback bias is not purely spatial, i.e. it is not limited to cells with receptive fields at a single locus in the visual field. Thus, processing can be biased in favour of stimuli possessing a specific behaviourally relevant colour, shape, texture, and so on, in parallel throughout the visual field, in addition to biases in favour of stimuli occupying a specific relevant spatial location. In this view, the search for an object with a specific shape in a scene, for example, does not necessarily require a serially scanning neural selection process. This is consistent with recent psychological accounts of attention, which posit at least some top-down parallel selection of candidate objects throughout the visual field (see, for example, Duncan and Humphreys 1989; Treisman and Sato 1990; Wolfe *et al.* 1989; Grossberg *et al.* 1994).

Finally, the fifth and perhaps most speculative tenet of the model is that a main source of the 'top-down' biasing inputs to ventral stream areas in extrastriate cortex derives from structures involved in working memory, specifically prefrontal cortex. We will now consider some of the neurophysiological evidence that bears on the model.

2.2 Visual search

Some of the strongest support for the model comes from studies of neurons in inferior temporal (IT) cortex of macaque monkeys, studied while the monkeys performed a visual search task (Chelazzi *et al.* 1993, 1998). IT cortex is a high-order visual processing area in the ventral stream crucial for object recognition. Monkeys and humans with lesions of IT cortex are severely impaired in object recognition (see Desimone and Ungerleider 1989). Consistent with this role in object recognition, IT neurons have extremely large receptive fields that are typically bilateral and include the centre of gaze, and they have complex stimulus specificities, such as selectivity for shape, colour and texture (Desimone and Gross 1979).

In these studies, the monkeys were rewarded for finding a target object in an extrafoveal array of stimuli, similar to finding a 'face in a crowd' (Chelazzi *et al.* 1993, 1998). A schematic representation of the task is shown in figure 2.1*a*. At the start of each trial, a cue stimulus was presented at the centre of gaze, followed by a blank delay period of either 1.5 or 3 s. The monkey was required to maintain fixation throughout the cue and delay period. At the end of the delay, an array of one to five stimuli was presented extrafoveally, and the monkey was rewarded for making a saccadic eye movement to the target stimulus matching the cue. The location of the target stimulus on a given trial was random—the monkey had to find it based on non-spatial features such as shape or colour. On some 'target-absent' trials, none of the stimuli in the array matched the cue, and the monkey was rewarded for simply maintaining fixation. The stimuli were digitized pictures of complex objects, which are the sort of stimuli that typically elicit selective responses from IT neurons. We made no attempt to understand why a cell either did or did not respond to a particular stimulus; it was only necessary that a cell responded selectively. The question we asked was how the target stimulus may be found, based on the responses of the cells.

Because the receptive fields of IT neurons are extremely large, they would typically include both the cue stimulus at the centre of gaze as well as all the extrafoveal locations where the stimuli in the array were presented. If a cell were equally responsive to all the stimuli in the array present throughout these large fields, this would complicate the interpretation of any target-selection effects on the responses. We therefore needed a way to 'label' a cell's responses to the different stimuli, to test the effects of selecting one of the stimuli as a target. To do this, we used a strategy that we had used previously in a study of spatial selective attention in visual cortex (Moran and Desimone 1985). Each cell was first tested with a large set of visual stimuli while the monkey performed a simple fixation task. On the basis of the responses to this set, one stimulus was chosen as a 'good' stimulus for the cell (i.e. would elicit a strong response when presented alone) and one or more stimuli were chosen as 'poor' stimuli for the cell (i.e. would elicit little or no response when presented alone). The choice arrays for the search task would then comprise one good stimulus and one or more poor stimuli. Because only the good stimulus in the array was effective in driving the cell, we could test the response to only the good stimulus in the array on trials when it was the target compared with trials when the same good stimulus was a distractor (i.e. when the poor stimulus was the target).

The results are shown in figure 2.1*b,c*, which shows the average response of a population of individually recorded IT neurons on target-present trials in which a two-stimulus choice array was presented in the contralateral visual field. As shown in figure 2.1*b*, at the time of the presentation of the cue, cells responded better in trials when the cue was the good stimulus for the cell than when it was the poor stimulus. This was expected because the cue stimuli were chosen on the basis of the cells' selective responses to them.

Following the response to the cue, there were three critical time periods in the trial. The first critical period was the delay interval after the cue, where the monkey gazed at a blank screen, awaiting the choice array. During this delay (figure 2.1*b*), most cells maintained a higher firing rate when their good stimulus was the cue than when their poor stimulus was the cue. This higher maintained activity was not simply a prolonged sensory after discharge to the good stimulus because the difference in delay activity was eliminated in control blocks of trials, where the same stimuli were presented but the monkey did not perform the search task. Furthermore, in some sessions the same cue was used for several consecutive trials in a block, and, in these blocks, the

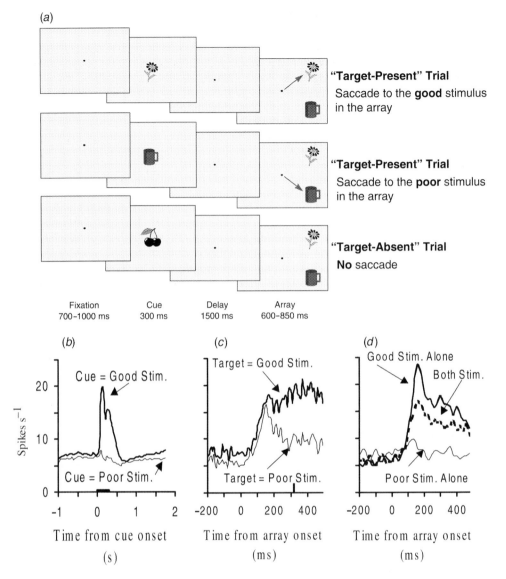

Fig. 2.1 Responses of neurons in IT cortex in a visual search task, with search arrays confined to the contralateral visual field. (*a*) Schematic representation of the task. A cue stimulus was presented at the start of the trial, followed by a delay, and then an array of stimuli. In target-present trials, the array contained a target matching the cue, and the monkey was rewarded for making a saccade to it. In some trials the cue-target was a good stimulus for the cell (top row), and in other trials it was a poor stimulus for the cell (middle row). In target-absent trials, the array did not contain a target, and the animal was rewarded for maintaining fixation during the presentation of the stimulus array. Relative locations of the good and poor stimulus in the array varied randomly from trial to trial. (*b*) Response of a population of 88 individually recorded IT neurons at the time of the cue presentation. Trials with a given cue were run in blocks. Cells showed higher maintained activity both before and after the cue presentation on trials when the cue was a good stimulus for the cells. (*c*) When the choice array was presented, the same cells shown in *b* initially responded well, regardless of which stimulus was the target. By 170 ms after stimulus onset, responses diverged dramatically depending on whether the target was the good or poor stimulus for the cell. This target-selection effect occurred well in advance of the saccade to the target, indicated by the small vertical bar on the horizontal axis. (*d*) In target-absent trials, the response to the good and poor stimulus together was smaller than the response to the good stimulus alone. Adapted from Chelazzi *et al.* (1998).

maintained activity of the cells was higher at the start of the trial, preceding the good cue, than it was preceding the poor cue. This can be seen in the population histogram of figure 2.1*b*, which shows the results from the blocked-cue trials. Thus, the animal's expectation of a behaviourally relevant stimulus caused a chronic elevation of activity in cells representing that stimulus. Together, the results argue for some type of feedback activation, or bias, in favour of cells selective for a feature of the cue-target stimulus on a given trial.

The next critical time period was when the choice array was presented. As shown in figure 2.1*c*, the initial population response to the array was the same, regardless of whether the good or poor stimulus was the target. Thus, several stimuli appearing in the visual field initially activate their cortical representations in parallel, consistent with the biased competition model.

The last critical time period began about 200 ms after the onset of the array, when responses to the array diverged dramatically depending on which stimulus was the target. When the good stimulus was the target, the response to the good stimulus in the array remained high until the time of the eye movement, which is indicated by the small vertical bar on the horizontal axis in figure 2.1*c*. Following the eye movement, activity increased somewhat, owing to the shift of the good stimulus to the foveal part of the retina, which is the most sensitive portion of IT receptive fields. In contrast, when the poor stimulus was the target, the response to the (now irrelevant) good stimulus in the array became strongly suppressed over the course of approximately 100 ms. Similar results were found with larger arrays. In principle, the suppression began long enough in advance of the eye movement (at least 100 ms) to be the signal to the oculomotor system to make the eye movement to the target. With selection of the target, cells responded as though the irrelevant distractors had been filtered from the visual field. Thus, the resolution of competition results in a suppression of cells representing behaviourally irrelevant stimuli. The temporal dynamics of the suppressive effects are consistent, even at a quantitative level, with the predictions of a computational implementation of biased competition during search (Usher and Nieber 1996).

Together, these physiological results illustrate some of the basic components of the biased competition model, including a bias in favour of cells representing the relevant stimulus, an initial parallel activation of cortical representations by several stimuli in the visual field, and the ultimate suppression of response to the behaviourally irrelevant distractors. An examination of the results from trials with a single stimulus in the choice array as well as from trials in which the target was absent from the array allowed us to ask more detailed questions about the nature of the competitive interactions, which are described in the next section.

(a) Competitive interactions

Several lines of evidence strongly suggested that a main effect of target selection is to bias an underlying suppressive interaction between the stimuli in the choice array. First, we compared the response to the two-stimulus arrays when the target was absent (target-absent trials in figure 2.1*a*) to the response to the good and poor stimuli presented alone, with stimuli contained within the contralateral visual field. Figure 2.1*d* shows the population histograms for this comparison, which reveal a suppressive influence of the poor stimulus in the array on the response to the good stimulus. The response to the two-stimulus array was intermediate between the responses to either stimulus alone. Other studies have also reported that the response to two stimuli in the RF of an IT neuron are smaller than the response to either stimulus alone (Richmond *et al.* 1983; Sato 1989; Miller *et al.* 1993*a*; Rolls and Tovee 1995), supporting the idea of a competitive interaction.

Next, we compared the responses to the individual stimuli presented alone with the response to the two-stimulus array on target-present trials. These data showed that, by the time the eye movement was made, the effect of selecting the good stimulus as the target in the two-stimulus array was to eliminate the suppressive effect of the poor stimulus. That is, by the time of the eye movement, the response to the good stimulus had become about equal to the response to the good stimulus presented alone. Conversely, the effect of selecting the poor stimulus as the target in the two-stimulus array was to nearly eliminate the excitatory influence of the good stimulus. That is, by the time of the eye movement, the response to the array when the poor stimulus was selected as a target had been reduced almost to the level of the response to the poor stimulus presented alone. These results strongly argue against a model for selection based purely on enhancement. Rather, the main effect of attentional selection in this study appears to be a modulation of the underlying competitive interaction between the stimuli in the visual field.

Interestingly, a somewhat different picture emerged when we examined the data from trials where the two stimuli in the choice array were positioned on opposite sides of the vertical meridian, in opposite hemifields. In this case, whichever stimulus was in the contralateral visual field appeared to dominate the cell's response to the two-stimulus array, and this dominant effect was largely unaffected by selecting either stimulus as a target. Other studies have found significant attentional effects with this configuration, but the effects are smaller than when stimuli compete within the same hemifield (Sato 1988; R. Desimone, unpublished observations). Apparently, anatomical connections that cross the midline are at a great competitive disadvantage compared with those that originate within the same hemisphere. Again, these attentional results are inconsistent with a simple attention-enhancement model; rather, they indicate that attentional selection is strongly linked to the underlying anatomy that subserves competitive interactions between stimuli in the visual field.

The effects of target selection in visual search are not confined to temporal lobe areas. In preliminary experiments, we have found very similar results in area V4 (Chelazzi and Desimone 1994), a visuotopically organized area that projects to IT cortex and forms part of the ventral stream for object recognition (Zeki 1971; Van Essen and Zeki 1978; Desimone *et al.* 1980; Gattass *et al.* 1988; Baizer *et al.* 1991). Neurons in area V4 have restricted receptive fields and respond selectively to stimulus form and colour (Zeki 1973, 1983, 1996; Desimone and Schein 1987; Schein and Desimone 1990; Gallant and Van Essen 1996).

We found that, as in IT cortex, stimuli that are contained within the receptive field of a V4 neuron appear to engage in suppressive interactions, which are strongly modulated by attentional selection (Chelazzi and Desimone 1994). Independent of target selection, the presence of a poor stimulus in the receptive field has a suppressive effect on the response of a V4 neuron to a good stimulus in the receptive field, and this suppressive effect is reduced as the poor stimulus is moved further away, well outside the receptive field. If a good and a poor stimulus are paired in a search array contained within the receptive field and the animal selects the good stimulus as the target, the cells give a good initial response and continue to respond well until the time of the eye movement. In contrast, with the same pair of stimuli, the response of the cell to the good stimulus is initially strong but soon becomes greatly suppressed on trials when the poor stimulus is the target. If the poor stimulus is moved well outside the receptive field, these attentional effects are reduced in magnitude. Thus, consistent with the biased competition model, competitive interactions are strongest when competing stimuli activate cells in the same local region of cortex with similar receptive fields. Because the attentional feedback biases this underlying competitive interaction, the attentional effects are stronger with nearby stimuli as well.

These data on attentional modulation of V4 responses in visual search are also in general agreement with those of Motter (1994), who has also reported attentional effects not limited to a single spatial location in V4. In Motter's study, the animal was presented with a large array of coloured stimuli and was cued to attend to all stimuli of a given colour, which varied from trial to trial. The responses of V4 cells were larger when the cued colour matched the colour of a stimulus in the receptive field, even though the monkey had not been cued to attend specifically to the receptive field location. Although Motter did not study competitive interactions between the stimuli in the array, such interactions are likely to have been present owing to the density of stimuli in the vicinity of the receptive field.

2.3 Spatially directed attention

From the point of view of the competition model, attentional selection of a stimulus on the basis of its spatial location should involve neuronal mechanisms that are qualitatively similar to those for selection by non-spatial stimulus features. Thus, spatial selection should involve a feedback bias in favour of a stimulus that is behaviourally relevant because of its location, and this bias should then modulate an underlying competitive interaction among the attended and unattended stimuli in the visual field. This is precisely what has been found in studies of spatial attention in ventral stream areas, and a recent study indicates that the same principle may hold in some dorsal stream areas as well (see next paragraph).

Moran and Desimone (1985) and Luck and co-workers (1997) studied spatial attention in ventral stream areas. In these studies, two stimuli were typically presented simultaneously in the visual field, and the animal was rewarded for performing a task (e.g. matching-to-sample or target detection) on the stimulus at one of the locations, while ignoring the stimulus at the irrelevant location. One of the stimuli was placed within the receptive field, and the other was placed at a variable location, either inside or outside the receptive field. The animal was cued as to the relevant location at the start of each block of trials, and the relevant location was switched between blocks. As in the visual search studies, one stimulus in the pair was typically chosen to be a good stimulus for the cell and the other was chosen to be a poor stimulus. By using this strategy, one could measure the neuronal response to the good stimulus in the receptive field when it was attended on one set of trials, compared with when the same stimulus was an irrelevant distractor on a different set of trials.

(a) Feedback bias

With a single stimulus inside the receptive field, the effects of any feedback bias during spatially directed attention may be observed independently of any effects of the bias on competitive inter-actions. When one stimulus was located inside the receptive field of a cell in either V2 or V4 and another stimulus was located outside, Luck and co-workers (1997) found that the maintained firing rate of the cells was higher when attention was directed to the location inside the receptive field than when attention was directed outside. As shown in figure 2.2, the increase in firing rate began at the start of the trial, before any stimulus was presented, and thus was owing strictly to the animal expecting a relevant stimulus at the receptive field location. This is very similar to the elevation in maintained firing rate found by Chelazzi and co-workers (1993) during visual search, where IT cells showed higher maintained firing rates if the animal was attending to a stimulus with a preferred, non-spatial, feature for the cell. As in the visual search experiment, this increase in firing rate during spatial attention is consistent with the idea of feedback biasing activity in favour of the behaviourally relevant stimulus.

The spatial resolution of this feedback bias for spatial location is also very high. Luck and co-workers (1997) measured the maintained firing rate when the animal directed its attention to

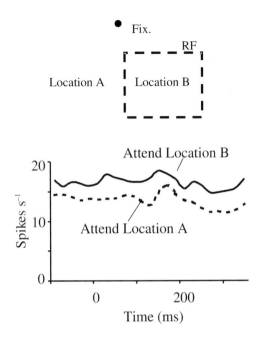

Fig. 2.2 Maintained activity of V4 neurons varies according to the locus of spatial selective attention. Top: schematic representation of stimulus configuration. While the animal maintained its gaze on a fixation spot (Fix.), stimuli were presented asynchronously at two locations in the visual field. One location was within the receptive field (RF, 'Location B') of the neuron (dashed box) and the other was outside ('Location A'). The animal was cued to perform a discrimination task on the stimulus at one location, and the task-relevant location was varied across blocks of trials. The task is described in greater detail in Luck *et al.* (1997). Bottom: summed activity of 26 individually recorded V4 neurons in trials with the attended location inside against outside the receptive field. The maintained activity was higher when the animal was attending to the receptive field location. The data are time-locked (time = 0) to the presentation of the stimulus outside the receptive field. Thus, although the animal was attending to the receptive field location during this time, no stimulus was actually present within the receptive field. Adapted from Luck *et al.* (1997).

one of two locations within the RF of cells in V4, one closer to the 'hot spot' of the receptive field than the other (i.e. elicited higher firing rates to the same stimulus). The maintained firing rate was higher when attention was directed to the location closer to the hot spot, indicating that the resolution of the mechanism responsible for the increase in firing rate has a resolution finer than the dimensions of the receptive field. This fine spatial resolution of the feedback is presumably related to the ability of cells to distinguish between attended and unattended stimuli located simultaneously within the receptive field, described here.

In addition to increasing maintained neuronal activity, other studies suggest that the bias in favour of the relevant location also increases the sensitivity of cells to stimuli presented at that location, although this increase in sensitivity may not always result in stronger sensory responses. Spitzer and co-workers (1988) found that attention to a stimulus within the receptive field of cells in V4 increased the cells' selectivity for orientation and colour and also caused an increase in the gain in the response by about 20%, compared with when the animal attended to a stimulus outside the receptive field. However, this increase in the magnitude of the response to the attended stimulus was found only when the animal performed a difficult task. Likewise, a preliminary study has shown that attention to a stimulus in V4 specifically increases the contrast sensitivity of cells (Reynolds *et al.* 1996; Reynolds and Desimone 1997), i.e. cells responded to the attended stimulus as though its contrast had been increased. This increase in contrast sensitivity with attention was found predominantly with low-contrast stimuli, because the responses of many V4 cells were already saturated at high stimulus contrast even in the absence of attention (Reynolds *et al.* 1996). An overall increase in response with attention in V4 has recently been confirmed in a preliminary study by McAdams and Maunsell (1997). Differences in task-difficulty, contrast-saturation effects, or both factors together may explain why several other studies have failed to detect the effects of feedback bias on the gain or sensitivity of cells to a single stimulus in the receptive field of V4 cells (Moran and Desimone 1985; Haenny *et al.* 1988; Maunsell *et al.* 1991; Motter 1993; Luck *et al.* 1997).

In summary, a bias in favour of an attended stimulus inside a V4 receptive field causes an increase in sensitivity, or excitability, which may become manifest as a change in maintained activity and/or sensory-evoked responses. However, these attentional effects with a single stimulus inside the receptive field are variable and have, at best, a rather modest effect on the absolute magnitude of firing rate in prestriate areas such as V2 and V4. As described below, strong, consistent effects of attention occur when these biases in favour of the relevant stimulus influence the competition between stimuli in the visual field.

(b) Effects of attention on competition

Similar to what was found in the visual search experiment in IT cortex, attention has a large effect on responses when two stimuli compete within the same receptive field. When two stimuli are located within the receptive field of cells in V2 or V4, and the animal attends to one of them, the cell's response is predominantly determined by the attended stimulus (Moran and Desimone 1985; Luck *et al.* 1997). If the good stimulus for the cell is attended, the response is strong. If the poor stimulus is attended, the response to the good stimulus in the receptive field is greatly suppressed. Figure 2.3 shows the effects of attention on competition between two stimuli in the receptive field for a population of V4 cells. Comparable effects are found in IT cortex, although the receptive fields of IT cells are much bigger and the attentional effects generalize over a larger portion of the visual field than in V2 and V4 (Moran and Desimone 1985). As predicted by the biased competition model, a preliminary study in areas V2 and V4 indicates that attention serves to modulate the suppressive interaction between two or more stimuli within the receptive field (Reynolds *et al.* 1994, 1995).

Interestingly, during spatially selective attention, the onset of suppression for an unattended stimulus often occurs earlier in the neuronal response than was found in the visual search task. In the visual search task, the onset of suppression for the unattended stimulus began as early as 170 ms in the population response. However, in one study of spatial attention in V4, attentional effects were found at the very onset of the response (Luck *et al.* 1997), 50 ms after stimulus onset, and other studies have found an onset of suppression shortly after the onset of the visual response, in the range of 90–120 ms (J. Moran and R. Desimone, unpublished data; J. Reynolds and R. Desimone, unpublished data). It is possible that this difference is owing to the nature of the feedback bias, which may be more accurately targeted to all cells with the same receptive field in a small portion of a visuotopically organized area than to cells that share a common selectivity for shape or colour but which are widely distributed throughout the cortical area.

A somewhat different account of the effects of attention has been advanced by Connor and colleagues (1996) who have studied the effects of spatially directed attention in V4. In their experiment, the animal's attention was directed to one of several large stimuli in the shape of rings immediately outside the classical receptive field of the cell. They then measured the response to a probe stimulus presented at a variable location within the receptive field. They found that the response to the probe stimulus at a given location in the receptive field was typically greatest

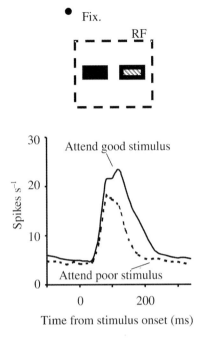

Fig. 2.3 Stimulus-evoked responses in V4 vary according to the locus of spatial attention. Top: schematic representation of stimulus configuration. While the animal maintained its gaze on a fixation spot (Fix.), two stimuli were presented simultaneously within the receptive field (RF, dashed box). One of the stimuli was a good stimulus for the cell (i.e. would activate the cell well if presented alone), and the other was a poor stimulus for the cell (i.e. would not activate the cell very well if presented alone). The animal was cued to perform a discrimination task on the stimulus at one location or the other, and the task-relevant location varied across blocks of trials. Bottom: average response of 29 individually recorded V4 neurons to the pair of stimuli when either the good or poor stimulus was attended. The response to the good stimulus was suppressed when the animal attended to the poor stimulus of the pair. Adapted from Luck *et al.* (1997).

when attention was directed to a nearby ring on the same side of the receptive field as the probe than when it was directed to a more distant ring on the opposite side of the receptive field. The authors interpreted this effect as a shift in the receptive field sensitivity profile towards the locus of attention. A related notion that the receptive field shrinks around the locus of attention was originally proposed to account for the effects of attention in V4 (Moran and Desimone 1985; Desimone *et al.* 1989). Neither idea is strictly incompatible with the competition model because, according to the model, attentional modulation of competition may lead to changes in the apparent size or profile of the receptive field. The empirical question is whether the apparent shift in receptive field profile in the study by Connor and colleagues (1996) is actually owing to an attentional modulation of a competitive interaction between the ring stimulus and the probe. Competition from stimuli outside the receptive field borders is likely to be strongest when the stimuli are both large and numerous, as in the study by Connor and co-workers (1996).

(c) Biased competition in the dorsal stream

Evidence that some type of biased competition may operate in the dorsal stream of visual areas important for spatial vision has recently been reported by Treue and Maunsell (1996). They made recordings from cells in MT and MST in monkeys trained to attend to one of two stimuli moving in opposite directions in the visual field. Cells in both MT and MST are often highly selective for the direction of motion of a stimulus, although receptive fields are much larger in MST than MT. Treue and Maunsell used the same strategy that had been used in V4 and IT cortex to study attentional selection of one of two competing stimuli in the receptive field. They chose one stimulus to be a good stimulus for the recorded cell (moving in its preferred direction) and the other to be a poor stimulus (moving in the opposite direction). They compared the response to the good stimulus when it was attended to when it was an irrelevant distractor. When both stimuli were in the same receptive field of cells in either MT or MST, the response of the cell was almost completely determined by the attended stimulus, similar to what has been found in V2, V4, and IT cortex. The response was good when the animal attended to the stimulus moving in the preferred direction of the cell and poor when it attended to the stimulus moving in the opposite direction. The competition model predicts that this attentional modulation of responses should be correlated with a competitive interaction between the two stimuli in the receptive field, but this has not yet been tested in MT and MST. Much smaller effects of attention were found when one of the two stimuli was moved outside the receptive field, presumably reducing local competitive interactions in these areas. This inverse dependence of the attentional effects on the spatial separation between the stimuli is inconsistent with any simple enhancement model of attention but is similar to what was found in V2 and V4. Groh and co-workers (1996) have recently reported that they have failed to replicate strong attentional effects in MT using a different task and different stimuli from those used by Treue and Maunsell (1996), raising the possibility that the attentional modulation of a particular visual area will be stimulus- or task-specific (see Richmond and Sato 1987; Spitzer and Richmond 1991; Corbetta *et al.* 1991).

It seems likely that some form of biased competition works in other dorsal stream areas as well. Several studies have shown that responses to a stimulus in the receptive field of cells in posterior parietal cortex are larger when the animal attends to it than when it ignores it (Lynch *et al.* 1977; Robinson *et al.* 1978, 1995; Bushnell *et al.* 1981; Steinmetz *et al.* 1994; Steinmetz and Constantinidis 1995; Colby *et al.* 1996). This is the traditional 'enhancement' effect of attention. However, there is at least some suggestive evidence for competitive interactions between targets and distractors in structures associated with the dorsal stream, in addition to the traditional enhancement for stimuli chosen as targets.

In the frontal eye fields (FEF), an oculomotor structure closely associated with the dorsal stream, Schall and colleagues (Schall and Hanes 1993; Schall *et al.* 1995) have found that the response to a distractor stimulus within the receptive field of visual cells is suppressed when the animal plans to make an eye movement to a target stimulus outside the receptive field. However, this suppression of the distractor response is much greater when the target stimulus is located just beyond the receptive field borders than when it is in a more distant location, consistent with some type of competitive interaction.

Likewise, in the superior colliculus, another oculomotor structure, Basso and Wurtz (1997) have found that the activity of build-up cells in the intermediate layers is suppressed by the presence of several stimuli in the visual field. The suppression ceases when a stimulus inside the cell's movement field is chosen as a target. Suppression is also reduced by increasing the probability that the stimulus in the movement field of a cell will be chosen as a target. Basso and Wurtz interpreted the suppressive effects of several stimuli in the visual field to mean that collicular responses are reduced by target uncertainty, i.e. that the suppressed responses reflect the reduced likelihood that a stimulus in a given cell's movement field will be the target of an eye movement. An alternative view is that target uncertainty *per se* is not computed. Rather, the response suppression may be owing to mutually inhibitory interactions among cells activated throughout the visual field map of the colliculus (or an upstream structure). These interactions would then be modulated by feedback to the colliculus, biasing the interactions in favour of cells at the target location. Competition between stimuli is likely to take place at all levels of the nervous system, from stimulus to response.

2.4   Attention, memory, and prefrontal cortex

Attention is often thought of as the gateway to memory, as we typically remember little about stimuli we ignore. However, the reverse is also true—mechanisms for learning and memory play a critical role in selecting which stimulus we will attend to in a crowded scene. Attention may be directed preferentially to novel stimuli, to recognized stimuli, to stimuli with learned behavioural relevance, and so on. In fact, some of the neuronal mechanisms for memory and attention are so intertwined that one may question whether they are even distinguishable (Desimone *et al.* 1994; Ungerleider 1995; Desimone 1996). Here, we will focus on the role of neuronal mechanisms for working memory, as those are the ones most likely to be involved in many of the attentional experiments described so far in this review.

Working memory in monkeys typically refers to any type of short-term memory in which specific information is kept actively 'on-line' for up to several seconds and then discarded (see Baddeley (1986), for a review of human studies). In one type of working memory task, known as matching-to-sample, the monkey is shown a sample stimulus at the start of the trial, followed by a sequence of one or more test stimuli. Delay intervals intervene between all of the stimulus presentations, and the monkey is rewarded for signalling when a test stimulus matches the sample. Working memory is required to solve such a task when small stimulus sets are used, because the relevance of a particular stimulus changes from trial to trial—a stimulus used as the sample on one trial will temporarily have great behavioural relevance but will become behaviourally irrelevant in another trial in which it is a nonmatching stimulus.

Neurons in IT cortex of monkeys performing the matching-to-sample task often show stimulus-specific activity during the delay interval following the sample (Fuster and Jervey 1981; Miyashita and Chang 1988; Miller *et al.* 1993*a,b*, 1996; Vogels and Orban 1994). If the sample stimulus is a good stimulus for the cell, the maintained activity during the delay is high, whereas if the sample is a poor stimulus the maintained delay activity is low. Furthermore, in a version of the task that is particularly demanding of working memory, the response of an IT neuron to a given test stimulus is enhanced if it matches the sample (Miller and Desimone 1994). Both the higher maintained activity and enhanced responses suggest that some IT cells are sensitized, or biased, to respond preferentially to the behaviourally relevant (matching) choice stimulus in a trial.

This biasing of IT neurons in a working memory task is remarkably similar to the biasing effects on neuronal responses found throughout extrastriate cortex during visual search and spatially directed attention. Indeed, there is every reason to expect that they should be similar, because in both types of tasks the animal must use information held flexibly in working memory to guide its selection of stimulus or response when confronted with a choice. The difference is that in many working memory tasks the choice stimuli are distributed in time, whereas in visual search the choice stimuli are distributed in space. Because the functional requirements for this feedback to visual cortex are the same in both working memory and attention tasks, it is reasonable to assume that it derives from the same sources.

There are several reasons to suspect that a main source of top-down feedback to visual cortex during both working memory and attention is prefrontal cortex (see Desimone and Duncan 1995). One main reason is that prefrontal cells seem to have the appropriate properties. In working memory tasks, prefrontal cells show stimulus-specific delay activity (Fuster 1973, 1995; Niki and Watanabe 1976; Funahashi *et al.* 1989, 1993*a,b*; Sawaguchi *et al.* 1988*a,b*; Wilson *et al.* 1993; di Pellegrino and Wise 1993; Miller *et al.* 1996; Rao *et al.* 1997). Thus, if at the start of a behavioural trial animals are shown a brief cue that specifies the critical information that they need to solve the task on that trial, some prefrontal cells will show high cue-specific activity that persists for as long as that information is important. Cells in the dorsolateral portion of prefrontal cortex tend to have delay activity that is specific for a remembered location in space, whereas cells on the ventral convexity of prefrontal cortex tend to have delay activity that is specific for a particular complex object (Wilson *et al.* 1993), and many cells in both regions have delay activity that is specific for both object and place (Rao *et al.* 1997). If this maintained activity were fed back to the appropriate cells in extrastriate cortex, prefrontal cortex would be in a position to bias extrastriate activity in favour of a relevant object at either a specific spatial location or with a specific shape, colour, and so on. Furthermore, delay activity in prefrontal cortex is not disrupted by intervening or distracting stimuli, unlike delay activity in IT cortex (Miller *et al.* 1996). Brain imaging studies indicate that both prefrontal cortex and extrastriate visual areas are activated during both visual stimulation and the delay periods of working memory tasks, but prefrontal activity is more closely linked to the delay period whereas extrastriate activity is more closely linked to the visual stimulation (Courtney *et al.* 1997).

Both behavioural and anatomical data also suggest that feedback from prefrontal cortex plays an important role in attention and working memory. Lesions or deactivation of prefrontal cortex impair performance on working memory tasks in monkeys (Mishkin 1957; Bauer and Fuster 1976; Mishkin and Manning 1978; Fuster *et al.* 1985; Sawaguchi and Goldman-Rakic 1991; Funahashi *et al.* 1993*a*; Schindy *et al.* 1994), and cooling a small part of prefrontal cortex causes delay activity in IT cortex to become less selective (Fuster *et al.* 1985). Anatomical studies reveal that prefrontal cortex has reciprocal connections with virtually all extrastriate cortical areas and is, therefore, in a position to directly influence visual cells throughout all areas except for primary visual cortex (Barbas 1988; Barbas and Pandya 1989; Ungerleider *et al.* 1989; Webster *et al.* 1994). Finally, it makes sense for the feedback to extrastriate visual cortex in working memory and attentional selection tasks to come from structures such as prefrontal cortex that are not purely visual. Behavioural relevance and expectations are often established by the behavioural context, which is itself defined by abstract and multimodal sources of information. A hypothetical representation of the interaction between prefrontal and IT neurons during visual search is shown in figure 2.4.

Despite this suggestive evidence, the definitive experiments to test the role of prefrontal feedback to extrastriate cortex have not yet been done. Several cortical regions share at least some key properties with prefrontal cortex (see, for example, Suzuki *et al.* 1997), and it may be overly simplistic to think of a single cortical region providing most or all of the top-down feedback to extrastriate visual areas, even in well-defined tasks of working memory and attention. Furthermore, the behavioural relevance of a stimulus will often be defined not only by the contents of working memory but also by affective state and long-term learned associations, which probably involve different neural systems. How these many potential sources of feedback target the specific visual cells representing behaviourally relevant stimuli remains perhaps the most mysterious aspect of attention.

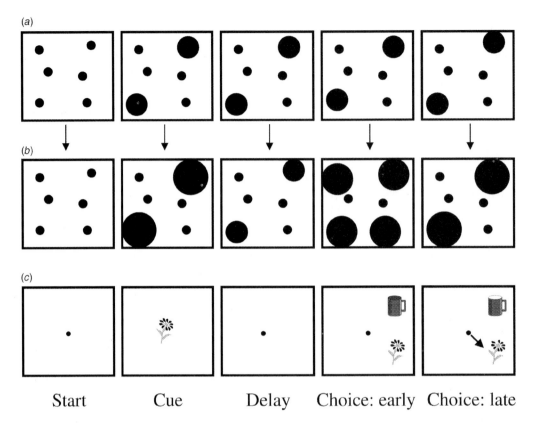

Start   Cue   Delay   Choice: early Choice: late

Fig. 2.4 Possible interaction between prefrontal and IT cortex during visual search. (*a*,*b*) Each box represents the activity in a hypothetical population of prefrontal or IT neurons. Each dot represents a population of cells, and the size of the dot represents the level of activity. (*c*) Representation of stimuli used in the task. When the cue is presented, the prefrontal cells that represent the features of the cue develop a high state of maintained activity which persists for the duration of the trial. This activity is fed back to IT cortex, biasing activity in favour of cells selective for features of the stimulus used as the cue and target. When the choice array is presented, cells in IT cortex are initially activated if they are selective for a feature of any stimulus in the array. Cells representing different stimuli engage in mutually suppressive interactions, which are biased in favour of cells representing the target. By late in the choice period, cells representing non-target stimuli are suppressed. About 100 ms after the onset of suppression, the eye movement to a target (arrows) is initiated.

Acknowledgements

I thank my collaborators on the attentional experiments: L. Chelazzi, J. Duncan, S. Hillyard, S. Luck, J. Moran, E. Miller, T. Pasternak, J. Reynolds and H. Spitzer. L. Ungerleider provided valuable comments on the manuscript.

References

Allport, D. A. 1993 Attention and control: have we been asking the wrong questions? A critical review of twenty-five years. In *Attention and performance XIV* (eds D. E. Meyer and S. Kornblum), pp. 183–218. Cambridge, MA: MIT Press.

Baddeley, A. D. 1986 *Working memory*. Oxford University Press.

Baizer, J., Ungerleider, L. and Desimone, R. 1991 Organization of visual inputs to posterior parietal and inferior temporal cortex in the macaque. *J. Neurosci.* **11**, 168–90.

Barbas, H. 1988 Anatomic organization of basoventral and mediodorsal visual recipient prefrontal regions in the rhesus monkey. *J. Comp. Neurol.* **276**, 313–42.

Barbas, H. and Pandya, D. N. 1989 Architecture and intrinsic connections of the prefrontal cortex in the rhesus monkey. *J. Comp. Neurol.* **286**, 353–75.

Basso, M. A. and Wurtz, R. H. 1997 Modulation of neuronal activity by target uncertainty. *Nature* **389**, 66–9.

Bauer, R. H. and Fuster, J. M. 1976 Delayed-matching and delayed-response deficit from cooling dorso-lateral prefrontal cortex in monkeys. *J. Comp. Physiol. Psychol.* **90**, 293–302.

Broadbent, D. E. 1958 *Perception and communication*. London: Pergamon Press.

Bundesen, C. 1990 A theory of visual attention. *Psychol. Rev.* **97**, 523–47.

Bushnell, M. C., Goldberg, M. E. and Robinson, D. L. 1981 Behavioral enhancement of visual responses in monkey cerebral cortex. I. Modulation in posterior parietal cortex related to selective visual attention. *J. Neurophysiol.* **46**, 755–72.

Chelazzi, L. and Desimone, R. 1994 Responses of V4 neurons during visual search. *Soc. Neurosci. Abstr.* **20**, 1054.

Chelazzi, L., Miller, E. K., Duncan, J. and Desimone, R. 1993 A neural basis for visual search in inferior temporal cortex. *Nature* **363**, 345–7.

Chelazzi, L., Duncan, J., Miller, E. K. and Desimone, R. 1998 Responses of neurons in inferior temporal cortex during memory guided visual search. (Submitted.)

Colby, C. L. 1991 The neuroanatomy and neurophysiology of attention. *J. Child Neurol.* **6**, 90–118.

Colby, C. L., Duhamel, J.-R. and Goldberg, M. E. 1996 Visual, presaccadic, and cognitive activation of single neurons in monkey lateral intraparietal area. *J. Neurophysiol.* **76**, 2841–52.

Connor, C. E., Gallant, J. L., Preddie, D. C. and Van Essen, D. C. 1996 Responses in area V4 depend on the spatial relationship between stimulus and attention. *J. Neurophysiol.* **75**, 1306–8.

Corbetta, M., Miezin, F. M., Shulman, G. L. and Petersen, S. E. 1991 Selective and divided attention during visual discriminations of shape, color, and speed: functional anatomy by positron emission tomography. *J. Neurosci.* **11**, 2383–402.

Courtney, S. M., Ungerleider, L. G., Keil, K. and Haxby, J. V. 1997 Transient and sustained activity in a distributed neural system for human working memory. *Nature* **386**, 608–11.

Desimone, R. 1996 Neural mechanisms for visual memory and their role in attention. *Proc. Natn. Acad. Sci. USA* **93**, 13 494–9.

Desimone, R. and Duncan, J. 1995 Neural mechanisms of selective visual attention. *A. Rev. Neurosci.* **18**, 193–222.

Desimone, R. and Gross, C. G. 1979 Visual areas in the temporal cortex of the macaque. *Brain Res.* **178**, 363–80.

Desimone, R. and Schein, S. 1987 Visual properties of neurons in area V4 of the macaque: sensitivity to stimulus form. *J. Neurophysiol.* **57**, 835–68.

Desimone, R. and Ungerleider, L. G. 1989 Neural mechanisms of visual processing in monkeys. In *Handbook of neuropsychology*, vol. II (eds E. Boller and J. Grafman), pp. 267–99. Amsterdam: Elsevier.

Desimone, R., Fleming, J. and Gross, C. G. 1980 Prestriate afferents to inferior temporal cortex: an HRP study. *Brain Res.* **184**, 41–55.

Desimone, R., Moran, J. and Spitzer, H. 1989 Neural mechanisms of attention in extrastriate cortex of monkeys. In *Dynamic interactions in neural networks: models and data* (eds M. Arbib and S. Amari), pp. 169–82. New York: Springer.

Desimone, R., Wessinger, M., Thomas, L. and Schneider, W. 1990 Attentional control of visual perception: cortical and subcortical mechanisms. *Cold Spring Harb. Symp. Quant. Biol.* **55**, 963–71.

Desimone, R., Miller, E. K. and Chelazzi, L. 1994 Interaction of neural systems for attention and memory. In *Large-scale theories of neuronal function* (eds C. Koch and J. Davis), pp. 75–91. Cambridge, MA: MIT Press.

di Pellegrino, G. and Wise, S. P. 1993 Primate frontal cortex: visuospatial vs. visuomotor activity, premotor vs. prefrontal cortex. *J. Neurosci.* **13**, 1227–43.

Duncan, J. 1996 Cooperating brain systems in selective perception and action. In *Attention and performance XVI* (eds T. Inui and J. L. McClelland), pp. 549–78. Cambridge, MA: MIT Press.

Duncan, J. and Humphreys, G. W. 1989 Visual search and stimulus similarity. *Psychol. Rev.* **96**, 433–58.

Funahashi, S., Bruce, C. J. and Goldman-Rakic, P. S. 1989 Mnemonic coding of visual space in the monkey's dorsolateral prefrontal cortex. *J. Neurophysiol.* **61**, 331–49.

Funahashi, S., Bruce, C. J. and Goldman-Rakic, P. S. 1993a Dorsolateral prefrontal lesions and oculomotor delayed-response performance—evidence for mnemonic scotomas. *J. Neurosci.* **13**, 1479–97.

Funahashi, S., Chafee, M. V. and Goldman-Rakic, P. S. 1993b Prefrontal neuronal activity in rhesus monkeys performing a delayed anti-saccade task. *Nature* **365**, 753–6.

Fuster, J. M. 1973 Unit activity in prefrontal cortex during delayed-response performance: neuronal correlates of transient memory. *J. Neurophysiol.* **36**, 61–78.

Fuster, J. M. 1995 *Memory in the cerebral cortex*. Cambridge, MA: MIT Press.

Fuster, J. M. and Jervey, J. P. 1981 Inferotemporal neurons distinguish and retain behaviorally relevant features of visual stimuli. *Science* **212**, 952–5.

Fuster, J. M., Bauer, R. H. and Jervey, J. P. 1985 Functional interactions between inferotemporal and prefrontal cortex in a cognitive task. *Brain Res.* **330**, 299–307.

Gallant, J. L., Connor, C. E., Rakshit, S., Lewis, J. W. and Van Essen, D. C. 1996 Neural responses to polar, hyperbolic, and cartesian gratings in area V4 of the macaque monkey. *J. Neurophysiol.* **76**, 2718–39.

Gattass, R., Sousa, A. P. and Gross, C. G. 1988 Visuotopic organization and extent of V3 and V4 of the macaque. *J. Neurosci.* **8**, 1831–45.

Groh, J. M., Seidemann, E. and Newsome, W. T. 1996 Neurophysiology: neural fingerprints of visual attention. *Curr. Biol.* **6**, 1406–9.

Grossberg, S., Mingolla, E. and Ross, W. D. 1994 A neural theory of attentive visual search: interactions of boundary, surface, spatial, and object representations. *Psychol. Rev.* **3**, 470–89.

Haenny, P. E., Maunsell, J. H. R. and Schiller, P. H. 1988 State dependent activity in monkey visual cortex. II. Retinal and extraretinal factors in V4. *Exp. Brain Res.* **69**, 245–59.

Luck, S. J., Chelazzi, L., Hillyard, S. A. and Desimone, R. 1997 Neural mechanisms of spatial selective attention in areas V1, V2 and V4 of macaque visual cortex. *J. Neurophysiol.* **77**, 24–42.

Lynch, J. C., Mountcastle, V. B., Talbot, W. H. and Yin, T. C. 1977 Parietal lobe mechanisms for directed visual attention. *J. Neurophysiol.* **40**, 362–89.

McAdams, C. J. and Maunsell, J. H. R. 1997 Spatial attention and feature-directed attention can both modulate responses in macaque area V4. *Soc. Neurosci. Abstr.* **23**, 2062.

Maunsell, J. H. R., Sclar, G., Nealey, T. A. and DePriest, D. 1991 Extraretinal representations in area V4 of the macaque monkey. *Vis. Neurosci.* **7**, 561–73.

Miller, E. K. and Desimone, R. 1994 Parallel neuronal mechanisms for short-term memory. *Science* **263**, 520–2.

Miller, E. K., Gochin, P. M. and Gross, C. G. 1993a Suppression of visual responses of neurons in inferior temporal cortex of the awake macaque monkey by addition of a second stimulus. *Brain Res.* **616**, 25–9.

Miller, E. K., Li, L. and Desimone, R. 1993b Activity of neurons in anterior inferior temporal cortex during a short-term memory task. *J. Neurosci.* **13**, 1460–78.

Miller, E. K., Erickson, C. A. and Desimone, R. 1996 Neural mechanisms of visual working memory in prefrontal cortex of the macaque. *J. Neurosci.* **16**, 5154–67.

Mishkin, M. 1957 Effects of small frontal lesions on delayed alternation in monkeys. *J. Neurophysiol.* **20**, 615–22.

Mishkin, M. and Manning, F. J. 1978 Non-spatial memory after selective prefrontal lesions in monkeys. *Brain Res.* **143**, 313–23.

Miyashita, Y. and Chang, H. S. 1988 Neuronal correlate of pictorial short-term memory in the primate temporal cortex. *Nature* **331**, 68–70.

Moran, J. and Desimone, R. 1985 Selective attention gates visual processing in the extrastriate cortex. *Science* **229**, 782–4.

Motter, B. C. 1993 Focal attention produces spatially selective processing in visual cortical areas V1, V2 and V4 in the presence of competing stimuli. *J. Neurophysiol.* **70**, 909–19.

Motter, B. C. 1994 Neural correlates of attentive selection for color or luminance in extrastriate area V4. *J. Neurosci.* **14**, 2178–89.

Neisser, U. 1967 *Cognitive psychology.* New York: Appleton-Century-Crofts.

Niki, H. and Watanabe, M. 1976 Prefrontal unit activity and delayed response: relation to cue location versus direction of response. *Brain Res.* **105**, 79–88.

Rao, S. C., Rainer, G. and Miller, E. K. 1997 Integration of what and where in the primate prefrontal cortex. *Science* **276**, 821–4.

Reynolds, J. and Desimone, R. 1997 Attention and contrast have similar effects on competitive interactions in macaque area V4. *Soc. Neurosci. Abstr.* **23**, 302.

Reynolds, J., Chelazzi, L., Luck, S. and Desimone, R. 1994 Sensory interactions and effects of selective spatial attention in macaque area V2. *Soc. Neurosci. Abstr.* **20**, 1054.

Reynolds, J., Nicholas, J., Chelazzi, L. and Desimone, R. 1995 Spatial attention protects macaque V2 and V4 cells from the influence of non-attended stimuli. *Soc. Neurosci. Abstr.* **21**, 1759.

Reynolds, J., Pasternak, T. and Desimone, R. 1996 Attention increases contrast sensitivity of cells in macaque area V4. *Soc. Neurosci. Abstr.* **22**, 1197.

Riches, I. P., Wilson, F. A. and Brown, M. W. 1991 The effects of visual stimulation and memory on neurons of hippocampal formation and the neighboring parahippocampal gyrus and inferior temporal cortex of the primate. *J. Neurosci.* **11**, 1763–79.

Richmond, B. J., Wurtz, R. H. and Sato, T. 1983 Visual responses of inferior temporal neurons in the awake rhesus monkey. *J. Neurophysiol.* **50**, 1415–32.

Robinson, D. L., Goldberg, M. E. and Stanton, G. B. 1978 Parietal association cortex in the primate: sensory mechanisms and behavioral modulations. *J. Neurophysiol.* **41**, 910–32.

Robinson, D. L., Bowman, E. M. and Kertzman, C. 1995 Covert orienting of attention in macaques. II. Contributions of parietal cortex. *J. Neurophysiol.* **74**, 698–712.

Rolls, E. T. and Tovee, H. J. 1995 The responses of single neurons in the temporal visual cortical areas of the macaque when more than one stimulus is present in the receptive field. *Exp. Brain Res.* **103**, 409–20.

Sato, T. 1988 Effects of attention and stimulus interaction on visual responses of inferior temporal neurons in macaque. *J. Neurophysiol.* **60**, 344–64.

Sato, T. 1989 Interactions of visual stimuli in the receptive fields of inferior temporal neurons in awake macaques. *Exp. Brain Res.* **77**, 23–30.

Sawaguchi, T. and Goldman-Rakic, P. S. 1991 D1 dopamine receptors in prefrontal cortex: involvement in working memory. *Science* **251**, 947–50.

Sawaguchi, T., Matsumura, M. and Kubota, K. 1988*a* Delayed response deficit in monkeys by locally disturbed prefrontal neuronal activity by bicuculline. *Behav. Brain Res.* **31**, 193–8.

Sawaguchi, T., Matsumura, M. and Kubota, K. 1988*b* Dopamine enhances the neuronal activity of spatial short-term memory task in the primate prefrontal cortex. *Neurosci. Res.* **5**, 465–73.

Shindy, W. W., Posley, K. A. and Fuster, J. M. 1994 Reversible deficit in haptic delay tasks from cooling prefrontal cortex. *Cerebr. Cortex* **4**, 443–50.

Schall, J. D. and Hanes, D. P. 1993 Neural basis of saccade target selection in frontal eye field during visual search. *Nature* **366**, 467–9.

Schall, J. D., Hanes, D. P., Thompson, K. G. and King, D. J. 1995 Saccade target selection in frontal eye field of macaque. I. Visual and premovement activation. *J. Neurosci.* **15**, 6905–18.

Schein, S. and Desimone, R. 1990 Spectral properties of V4 neurons in the macaque. *J. Neurosci.* **10**, 3369–89.

Spitzer, H. and Richmond, B. J. 1991 Task difficulty: ignoring, attending to, and discriminating a visual stimulus yields progressively more activity in inferior temporal neurons. *Exp. Brain Res.* **83**, 340–8.

Spitzer, H., Desimone, R. and Moran, J. 1988 Increased attention enhances both behavioral and neuronal performance. *Science* **240**, 338–40.

Steinmetz, M. A. and Constantinidis, C. 1995 Neurophysiological evidence for a role of the posterior parietal cortex in redirecting visual attention. *Cerebr. Cortex* **5**, 448–56.

Steinmetz, M. A., Connor, C. E., Constantinidis, C. and McLaughlin, J. R. 1994 Covert attention suppresses neuronal responses in area 7a of the posterior parietal cortex. *J. Neurophysiol.* **72**, 1020–3.

Suzuki, W., Miller, E. K. and Desimone, R. 1997 Object and place memory in the entorhinal cortex. *J. Neurophysiol.* **78**, 1062–1081.

Treisman, A. M. 1969 Strategies and models of selective attention. *Psychol. Rev.* **76**, 282–99.

Treisman, A. and Sato, S. 1990 Conjunction search revisited. *J. Exp. Psychol.* **16**, 459–78.

Treue, S. and Maunsell, J. H. R. 1996 Attentional modulation of visual motion processing in cortical areas MT and MST. *Nature* **382**, 539–41.

Tsotsos, J. K. 1990 Analyzing vision at the complexity level. *Behav. Brain Sci.* **13**, 423–69.

Ungerleider, L. G. 1995 Functional brain imaging studies of cortical mechanisms for memory. *Science* **270**, 769–75.

Ungerleider, L. G., Gaffan, D. and Pelak, V. S. 1989 Projections from inferior temporal cortex to prefrontal cortex via the uncinate fascicle in rhesus monkeys. *Exp. Brain Res.* **76**, 473–84.

Ungerleider, L. G. and Haxby, J. V. 1994 'What' and 'where' in the human brain. *Curr. Opin. Neurobiol.* **4**, 157–65.

Ungerleider, L. G. and Mishkin, M. 1982 Two cortical visual systems. In *Analysis of visual behavior* (eds X. Ingle, M. A. Goodale and R. J. W. Mansfield), pp. 549–86. Cambridge, MA: MIT Press.

Usher, M. and Niebur, E. 1996 Modeling the temporal dynamics of IT neurons in visual search: a mechanism for top-down selective attention. *J. Cogn. Neurosci.* **8**, 311–27.

Van Essen, D. C. and Zeki, S. M. 1978 The topographic organization of rhesus monkey prestriate cortex. *J. Physiol.* **277**, 193–226.

Vogels, R. and Orban, G. A. 1994 Activity of inferior temporal neurons during orientation discrimination with successively presented gratings. *J. Neurophysiol.* **71**, 1428–51.

Webster, M. J., Bachevalier, J. and Ungerleider, L. G. 1994 Connections of inferior temporal areas TEO and TE with parietal and frontal cortex in macaque monkeys. *Cerebr. Cortex* **4**, 470–83.

Wilson, F. A. W., O'Scalaidhe, S. P. and Goldman-Rakic, P. S. 1993 Dissociation of object and spatial processing domains in primate prefrontal cortex. *Science* **260**, 1955–7.

Wolfe, J. M., Cave, K. R. and Franzel, S. L. 1989 Guided search: an alternative to the feature integration model for visual search. *J. Exp. Psychol.* **15**, 419–33.

Zeki, S. M. 1971 Cortical projections from two prestriate areas in the monkey. *Brain Res.* **34**, 19–35.

Zeki, S. M. 1973 Colour coding in rhesus monkey prestriate cortex. *Brain Res.* **53**, 422–7.

Zeki, S. M. 1983 The distribution of wavelength and orientation selective cells in different areas of monkey visual cortex. *Proc. R. Soc. Lond.* B **217**, 449–70.

Zeki, S. M. 1996 Are areas TEO and PIT of monkey visual cortex wholly distinct from the fourth visual complex (V4 complex)? *Proc. R. Soc. Lond.* B **263**, 1539–44.

3

Sensory gain control (amplification) as a mechanism of selective attention: electrophysiological and neuroimaging evidence

Steven A. Hillyard, Edward K. Vogel and Steven J. Luck

Abstract

Both physiological and behavioral studies have suggested that stimulus-driven neural activity in the sensory pathways can be modulated in amplitude during selective attention. Recordings of event-related brain potentials indicate that such sensory gain control or amplification processes play an important role in visual-spatial attention. Combined event-related brain potential and neuroimaging experiments provide strong evidence that attentional gain control operates at an early stage of visual processing in extrastriate cortical areas. These data support early selection theories of attention and provide a basis for distinguishing between separate mechanisms of attentional suppression (of unattended inputs) and attentional facilitation (of attended inputs).

3.1 Introduction

In 1990, Corbetta and his colleagues published a groundbreaking study in which they used positron emission tomography (PET) to examine the effects of selective attention on neural activity (Corbetta *et al.* 1990). In this experiment, subjects viewed arrays of moving bars and judged whether successively presented arrays were the same or different. Selective attention was manipulated by instructing the subjects to report size changes in one trial block, colour changes in a second block, velocity changes in a third block, or a change in any of these features in a fourth block. It was found that blood flow was increased in specific cortical regions when a single feature was attended compared with when attention was divided among all three features. Furthermore, different cortical regions were affected for each feature type, such that attending to a given feature appeared to increase blood flow in cortical regions that were specialized for the sensory processing of that feature. For example, attending to stimulus velocity caused an increase in blood flow in the region of the human homologue of areas MT and MST, which studies in both humans and monkeys have shown to be important for motion perception (Zeki *et al.* 1991; Newsome *et al.* 1995; Tootell *et al.* 1995).

Corbetta and associates (Corbetta *et al.* 1990, 1991) suggested that a possible mechanism for these feature-specific changes in regional cerebral bloodflow (rCBF) may involve a 'sensory enhancement', whereby incoming visual information in primed (attended) sensory pathways would trigger stronger and more selective neuronal responses with a higher signal-to-noise ratio than in unprimed pathways. This idea has been expressed more generally in terms of an 'amplification' of neuronal activity within sensory processing areas, such that attended information elicits larger sensory-evoked responses than ignored information (Posner and Driver 1992; Posner and Dehaene 1994). This amplification mechanism is applicable to a wide variety of attentional manipulations. For example, just as attending to motion and ignoring colour is proposed to yield an amplification of activity within motion-processing areas (Corbetta *et al.* 1991), attending to the visual modality and ignoring the auditory modality should lead to a widespread amplification across visual cortex, and attending to the left visual field and ignoring the right visual field should lead to a retinotopically organized amplification of activity corresponding to the left visual field.

The concept of sensory amplification or 'gain control' may be traced to early studies of attentional influences on evoked electrical responses in the sensory pathways in animals (Hernandez-Peon *et al.* 1956; Hernandez-Peon 1966; Oatman and Anderson 1977). In these experiments, the amplitudes of sensory-evoked responses were found to be enlarged when the animal's attention was directed towards a stimulus and reduced when attention was directed elsewhere. These effects were interpreted as reflecting a sensory 'gating' or 'filtering' process whereby unattended inputs were blocked or suppressed (i.e. their gain was reduced) in relation to attended inputs. Contemporaneous theories of attention derived from behavioural studies were based on similar concepts of filtering or attenuation (Broadbent 1958; Treisman 1969).

Subsequent electrophysiological experiments in humans have examined the evoked or event-related potentials (ERPs) that can be recorded non-invasively from the scalp as subjects engage in attention-demanding tasks. The surface recorded ERPs represent the summated electric field arising from populations of nerve cells activated by a stimulus. ERP waveforms consist of a sequence of voltage deflections or components that register the time-course of sensory-evoked activity patterns with a millisecond level of resolution. Early ERP experiments in both auditory and visual modalities showed that stimulus-evoked potentials from cortical sensory areas are strongly modulated by attention, with larger amplitudes for attended stimuli in relation to unattended stimuli (Hillyard *et al.* 1973; Eason 1981; Harter and Aine 1984; Hillyard and Muente 1984). These effects were also interpreted in terms of a sensory gain control mechanism that acts to increase or decrease the magnitude of stimulus-evoked neural activity according to the amount of attention allocated to that input (see, for example, Hillyard and Mangun 1987). If this gain control simply affected the magnitude of the overall stimulus-driven response in a particular brain region without changing the time-course or patterning of the neural activity, this would be reflected in the associated ERP as an amplitude change without any modification of waveform, as shown in figure 3.1. In this paper we will use the terms 'gain control' and 'amplification' interchangeably to refer to this type of attentional modulation of sensory-evoked activity. Gain control processes have been inferred in a wide range of attention experiments using diverse methodologies including ERPs and neuromagnetic recordings (Hillyard *et al.* 1995), PET (Corbetta *et al.* 1991; Heinze *et al.* 1994; O'Leary *et al.* 1996), single unit neurophysiology (see, for example, Luck *et al.* 1997), and behavioural psychophysics (Hawkins *et al.* 1990; Hikosaka *et al.* 1993; Tsal *et al.* 1994).

Although sensory amplification seems to be involved in a wide range of stimulus selection processes, Desimone and his colleagues (Chelazzi *et al.* 1993; Desimone and Duncan 1995; Luck *et al.* 1997) have identified another general type of attentional mechanism that could also account for attention-related changes in blood flow observed in PET experiments such as those of Corbetta (1990, 1991). Specifically, attending to a feature such as velocity may cause a 'bias signal' to be sent from higher attentional control areas to the sensory areas specialized for motion-processing, and this bias signal might increase tonic neural activity without necessarily modulating sensory-evoked neural responses. This sort of tonic bias would be consistent with cognitive models of attention in which the selection of attended information is achieved by comparing incoming sensory information with an 'attentional template' that specifies the features that are relevant for the current task (Duncan 1981, 1992). The attentional template might be instantiated by an increase in the baseline firing rates of the neurons that normally code stimuli containing the attended feature, and such an increase in baseline firing would be expected to cause an increase in regional cerebral blood flow (rCBF) and thus greater PET activation. In fact, tonic biases might

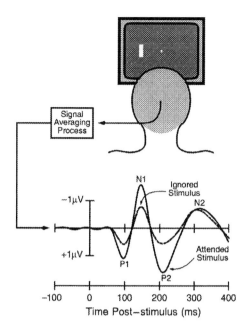

Fig. 3.1 Schematic diagram of a typical ERP attention experiment. The subject fixates the central cross and attends to either the left or right visual field. Bars are flashed to the left and right fields in a rapid, randomized sequence, and the subject responds to occasional targets (e.g. slightly smaller bars) in the attended field. The EEG is recorded during this task, and a signal-averaging process is used to extract the ERPs elicited by the individual stimuli from the ongoing EEG. The ERP elicited by a visual stimulus typically consists of early sensory-evoked components including the P1 and N1 waves, followed by higher-level cognitive components such as the N2 and P3 waves. ERPs shown here are in response to left field stimuli. The early sensory-evoked components are typically found to be larger when a stimulus is presented at an attended location as compared with an unattended location.

lead to even larger changes in PET activation than amplifications of sensory responses, because the amplification effects would be confined to the relatively brief period of sensory-evoked activity whereas the bias effects would be sustained over longer time intervals.

Several studies of single unit activity in monkeys have demonstrated that attending to a feature or a location may lead to long-lasting, sustained changes in neural activity (Fuster and Jervey 1982; Funahashi *et al.* 1989; Chelazzi *et al.* 1993; Luck *et al.* 1997). In the example shown in figure 3.2, recordings were obtained from an area V4 neuron while the monkey attended either to a location inside or outside of the neuron's receptive field. For 80% of the neurons, the baseline firing rate was elevated when attention was directed inside versus outside of the receptive field, with an average increase in firing rate of 30% over the entire population. This effect could be seen prior to the sensory response evoked by a stimulus presented inside the neuron's receptive field (figure 3.2a), and it could also be seen in periods without any sensory response, such as when a stimulus was presented outside the neuron's receptive field (figure 3.2b). The transient response elicited by the presentation of a stimulus inside this neuron's receptive field was not influenced by attention (figure 3.2a). This is a clear example of a bias effect in the absence of an amplification effect. Note that, given the size of this bias effect and its widespread occurrence across the population of neurons, this sort of attention effect would presumably lead to a substantial change in blood flow in a PET or functional magnetic resonance imaging (fMRI) experiment.

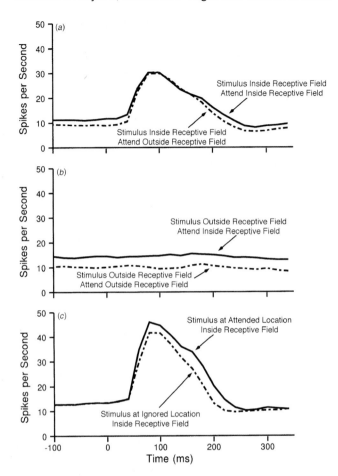

Fig. 3.2 Averaged post-stimulus histograms of neural activity recorded from individual neurons in area V4 of the macaque monkey (Luck *et al.* 1997). Stimulus onset is at time zero. (*a*) Sensory responses elicited by a stimulus presented inside the receptive field when this location was attended compared with when attention was directed to a location outside the receptive field. In this case, attention modulated baseline firing rates but did not influence the stimulus-elicited response. (*b*) Neural activity recorded when a stimulus was presented outside the receptive field. Again, attention can be seen to modulate the spontaneous activity of the neuron. (*c*) Sensory responses elicited by a stimulus presented inside the receptive field when this location was attended compared with when attention was directed to another location inside the receptive field. In this case, attention clearly modulated the stimulus-elicited response. No effects of attention can be observed in the prestimulus period, however, because attention was always directed inside the receptive field in this condition.

These same experiments also showed modulations of transient sensory-evoked responses by attention under some conditions, as well as changes in sustained neural activity. For example, when both the attended and ignored locations fell within the receptive field of the neuron being recorded, the neuron's response to a stimulus was larger when the stimulus was presented at the attended location than at the ignored location (figure 3.2c). It should also be noted that there were no sustained shifts in baseline activity under these conditions owing to the fact that the monkey always attended inside the receptive field, thus making it impossible to compare attend-inside with attend-outside conditions.

Several single unit experiments have demonstrated the existence of both amplification effects and sustained bias effects (Chelazzi *et al.* 1993; Miller and Desimone 1994; Luck *et al.* 1997), and it is clear that the two are not mutually exclusive. These mechanisms are conceptually quite distinct, however, and undoubtedly exert very different influences on sensory processing. For example, while a neural firing bias may well correspond to the establishment of a search template, the amplification of sensory-evoked activity may improve the signal–noise ratio of attended inputs and hence increase the discriminability of those signals (Hawkins *et al.* 1990; Luck *et al.* 1994). Another well-known attention effect on neural activity is the re-routing of attended inputs into specialized processing circuits for further analysis; the activation of these separate attention-specific neural populations is associated with 'endogenous' ERP components as opposed to the sensory-evoked components that are subject to amplification effects (Hillyard *et al.* 1995).

In the following sections, we discuss how attention-related amplification has been assessed with electrophysiological techniques, as well as a recent proposal for separating amplification and bias effects through measures of rCBF. We conclude with a discussion of how the general concept of amplification or sensory gain control can be subdivided into more specific mechanisms of attentional suppression and enhancement.

3.2   Visual–spatial attention: evidence for an early gain control mechanism

It is well established that directing attention to the location of a stimulus can lead to more rapid and accurate discrimination of the information contained in that stimulus (reviewed in LaBerge 1995). A long-running debate still continues, however, concerning the mechanism of these spatial attention effects. Some authors have proposed that stimuli falling within the 'spotlight' of attention are processed more efficiently at early sensory levels (Hawkins *et al.* 1990; Reinitz 1990; Luck *et al.* 1996) and that this early facilitation takes the form of an amplification of perceptual information arising from attended locations (Posner and Dehaene 1994). Alternatively, it has been hypothesized that spatial selection acts at late, post-perceptual levels through the selective biasing of decision or response processes in favour of attended-location stimuli (Sperling and Dosher 1986; Shiu and Pashler 1995).

ERP data recorded during spatial attention tasks have provided useful evidence with respect to this theoretical controversy. Paying attention to the location of a stimulus produces a characteristic pattern of changes in the ERP waveform, which is exemplified in a study by Mangun and colleagues (Mangun *et al.* 1993). As shown in figure 3.3*a*, this study presented briefly flashed stimuli in random order to four locations in the visual field. Subjects attended to the flashes at one of the locations on each run, ignoring the flashes at the other three locations. Figure 3.3*b* shows the ERP recorded for the flashes at one location (lower left-field) when they were attended (solid line) and when other locations were attended (dashed line). Directing attention to the location of these flashes produced amplitude increases in its early evoked ERP components recorded over the posterior visual cortex, including the positive P1 (latency 80–100 ms) and the negative N1 (140–190 ms) waves.

There are several features of this P1–N1 amplitude enhancement suggesting that it reflects an attentional mechanism of early sensory gain control or amplification. The finding that the increment in P1 amplitude with attention has exactly the same scalp topography as the unattended P1 itself (figure 3.3*c*) supports the hypothesis that attention acts to amplify the neural response

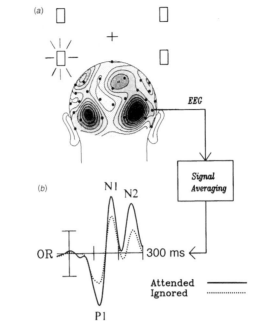

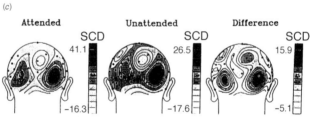

Fig. 3.3 Amplitude modulation of early visual ERP components in the spatial attention experiment of Mangun *et al.* (1993). (*a*) Subjects fixated the centre cross while stimuli (flashed rectangles) were presented one at a time to the four quadrants in random order at intervals of 250–550 ms. Subjects attended to stimuli in only one quadrant during each run. ERPs were recorded from 30 scalp sites, and the map of scalp current density (SCD, the second spatial derivative of voltage) for the P1 component elicited by the lower left stimulus is shown on the schematic head. (*b*) ERP waveforms to lower left flashes when these flashes were attended (solid line) and ignored (dotted line). (*c*) SCD maps for the P1 component in response to lower left stimuli when attended and unattended, and for the attended minus unattended difference wave. Note that the contralateral occipital current source does not change in position with attention. SCD scale values are in microvolts per square metre.

that is automatically evoked by that particular stimulus even when it is not attended. In contrast, an attention mechanism that involved activation of a separate neural population that was not activated by unattended stimuli would typically (though not inevitably) produce an altered voltage topography. Furthermore, the finding that the incremented ERP has the same phasic waveform as the unattended ERP strongly favours a gain control process as opposed to either a tonic bias or the activation of a separate neural population.

The idea that spatial attention operates in humans by controlling the gain of sensory-evoked responses was put forward many years ago (Eason 1981; Harter and Aine 1984; Hillyard and Muente 1984) and has received considerable support since then (reviewed in Mangun and Hillyard

1995; Hillyard *et al.* 1996). Important new evidence has come from studies that varied stimulus luminance while recording ERPs in a spatial attention task (Johannes *et al.* 1995; Wijers *et al.* 1997). The rationale for these studies was as follows: if the principal effect of attention is to amplify sensory-evoked activity in the visual pathways, then manipulations of the physical stimulus (such as luminance changes) that affect the latency, waveform or scalp topography of the corresponding ERPs should have a similar influence on the attention-produced enhancements of those ERPs. In particular, the attended and unattended waveforms should remain precisely superimposed in time (as in figure 3.3*b*), even though their latencies may be affected by changes in stimulus luminance, and the amplified portion of the ERP should maintain a similar scalp distribution to that of the ERP to the same stimulus when unattended (as in figure 3.3*c*).

Exactly this pattern of results was observed by both Johannes *et al.* (1995) and Wijers *et al.* (1997) for the P1 attention effect, thereby providing strong support for a sensory gain control mechanism at this early level. The effects of attention on the subsequent N1 component were more complicated, however, probably because the N1 consists of summated negative potentials arising from several different cortical sources (see next paragraph), not all of which may be influenced in the same way by attention. Whereas Wijers *et al.* found that the enhancements of N1 amplitude with attention fit the pattern of sensory gain control, Johannes *et al.* observed that the enhanced N1 negativity could be dissociated in time from the unattended N1 waveform, suggesting that attention had initiated activity in a separate neural population.

An amplification of the evoked P1–N1 components has been observed in a number of spatial attention tasks, including situations of sustained attention to randomized stimulus sequences as in figure 3.3 and in trial-by-trial cueing tasks where each individual stimulus was preceded by a cue that informed the subject of its most probable location. In such cueing tasks stimuli at precued (valid) locations generally evoked enlarged P1 and/or N1 components in association with speeded reaction times and/or improved target detectability relative to when the stimuli occurred at uncued or unexpected locations (Heinze *et al.* 1990; Mangun *et al.* 1993, 1995; Anllo-Vento 1995; Eimer 1997). This correspondence between behavioural improvement and ERP enhancement reinforces the concept of an amplification mechanism that gives inputs from attended locations an improved signal–noise ratio (Hawkins *et al.* 1990) and supports the view that these ERP modulations actually reflect sensory information that is used for perceptual judgements.

3.3   Localization of early attention effects

Several recent studies have used ERP source localization techniques to investigate the anatomical level(s) of the visual pathways at which the amplification of attended inputs takes place. These studies have found that the earliest ERP component (termed the 'C1'), which has an onset latency of 50–60 ms, does not show any significant change with spatial attention (Mangun *et al.* 1993; Gomez *et al.* 1994; Johannes *et al.* 1995; Clark and Hillyard 1996; Wijers *et al.* 1997). As shown in figure 3.4, the C1 component has maximal amplitude over the parieto-occipital scalp near the midline and remained invariant when attention was shifted to and from the location of the evoking stimulus. In contrast, the P1–N1 components over the lateral occipital scalp showed the usual amplitude modulations with attention, as did the N1 waves recorded over parietal, occipital, and frontal scalp sites. Dipole modelling of the C1 voltage topography points to a neural generator in primary visual cortex (figure 3.5*a*) (Gomez *et al.* 1994; Clark and Hillyard 1996; Johannes *et al.* 1998), and the C1 varies in polarity according to stimulus position in the visual field in a manner consistent with the retinotopic organization of the striate cortex within the calcarine fissure (Mangun *et al.* 1993; Clark *et al.* 1995). These ERP data suggest that visual processing

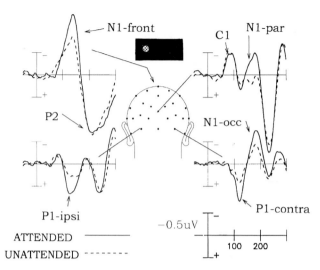

Fig. 3.4 Visual ERPs recorded from four different scalp sites in response to left-field stimuli in a spatial attention task (Clark and Hillyard 1996). Small circular checkerboards were flashed in random order to the left and right visual fields while subjects attended to the stimuli in one visual field at a time. When the left field stimuli were attended (solid lines), the P1 and N1 components were enlarged in relation to when right-field flashes were attended (dashed lines). The earlier C1 component was unaffected by attention.

at the level of the striate cortex is not affected by spatial attention. There is some evidence from animal neurophysiological (Motter 1993) and human neuroimaging (Worden and Schneider 1996; Shulman *et al.* 1997) studies, however, which suggests that attention may influence striate cortex activity under certain conditions.

The amplitude modulation of the P1 component starting about 80 ms post-stimulus appears to represent the earliest effect of spatial attention on visual processing. Attempts to localize the neural generators of this P1 modulation by using scalp current density mapping and dipole modelling have indicated a source in ventral–lateral extrastriate cortex (Mangun *et al.* 1993; Gomez *et al.* 1994; Johannes *et al.* 1995; Clark and Hillyard 1996; see figure 3.5b). Given the ambiguities inherent in calculating the intracranial sources of neural activity based on scalp recordings, however, several recent studies have combined ERP recording with PET to take advantage of the anatomical information provided by this blood flow imaging technique. The first experiment of this type (Heinze *et al.* 1994) required subjects to attend to either the right or left side of a bilateral stimulus display, with ERP recordings taken in one session and PET during a second session. Dipole modelling of the P1 enhancement over the hemisphere contralateral to the attended visual field indicated a generator source in the fusiform gyrus of the ventral extrastriate cortex. This calculated source corresponded very closely to the zone of increased regional cerebral blood flow (rCBF) revealed by PET, which strongly suggested that this ventral extrastriate region was the site of the early attentional gain control reflected in the P1 amplitude modulations.

To explore further the anatomical bases of this early P1 attention effect, Mangun *et al.* (1997) compared ERP and PET localizations during the symbol matching task used by Heinze and co-workers (1994) and during a less demanding dot detection task. As seen in figure 3.6a (also see plate section), PET revealed two foci of rCBF increase during the symbol task in the hemisphere contralateral to the attended visual half-field, the first in the posterior fusiform gyrus as was found by Heinze *et al.* and a second, smaller focus in ventral–lateral extrastriate cortex of the middle

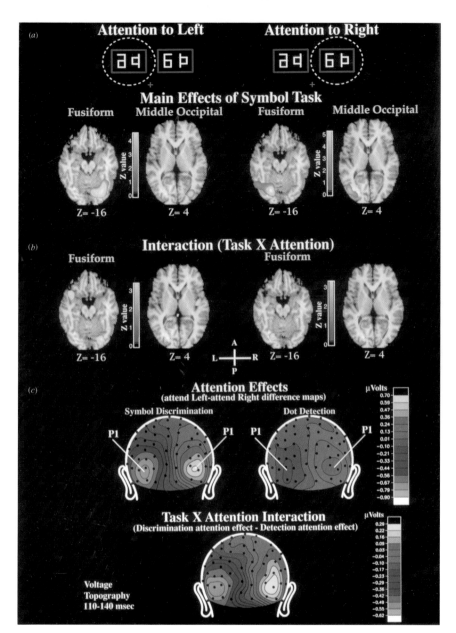

Fig. 3.6 (a) Top row shows examples of bilateral symbols used as stimuli in the study by Mangun *et al.* (1997). In different runs subjects attended to the right or left side of the displays, which were presented in rapid, randomized order. Brain sections show that attention to the left-field stimuli produced PET activations in the right fusiform and middle occipital gyri, while attention to the right produced corresponding activations in the left hemisphere. Note that left side of the images corresponds to left side of brain. (b) Visual cortex activations were greater for the symbol discrimination task than for a simpler dot detection task only in the contralateral fusiform gyrus. (c) Topographical voltage maps of the attention effect on the PI component (110–140 ms latency) elicited by the bilateral stimuli. Maps represent P1 voltage distributions in attend left minus attend right conditions. Lower head shows that the PI attention effect was greater for attend-symbol than for attend-dot conditions, as was the fusiform gyrus activation shown in *b*.

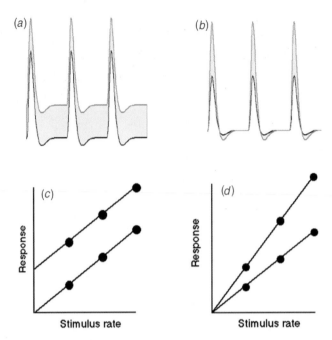

Fig. 5.1 Theoretical illustration of bias and gain control mechanisms of attention. (*a, b*) Schematic illustration of how stimulus-evoked neural activity (red) might be modulated (*grey*) by an attentional signal. The form of this modulation could take the form of (*a*) an additive bias signal or (*b*) a true modulation of stimulus-evoked responses alone (*c, d*), varying the rate at which stimuli are presented produces a relation between the total evoked response (integrated over time) and the frequency of presentation. The attentional effects (*a, b*) can now be distinguished by their effects on intercept (*a, c*) or slope (*b, d*) of this relation, respectively.

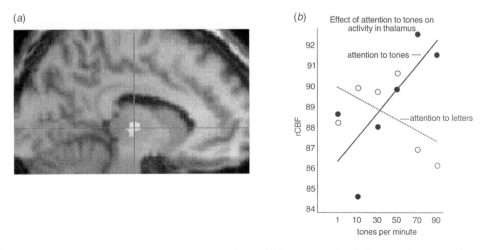

Fig. 5.2 Modulation of thalamic rCBF by attention. (*a*) The area in the thalamus where attention to the auditory signals significantly modulates the correlation between cerebral blood flow and presentation rate is shown superimposed on a saggital slice of the average structural MRI of the six subjects. (*b*) Cerebral blood flow in the thalamus plotted as a function of tone presentation rate for when subjects attend to the tones and when subjects attend to the visual signals.

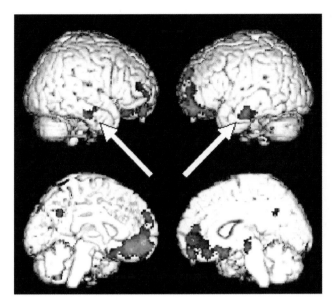

Fig. 5.3 Decreases in cerebral blood flow correlated with rate. Areas that show significant decreases in regional cerebral blood flow with increasing stimulus presentation rate are rendered on a canonical T1-weighted structural MRI placed in the anatomical space of Talairach and Tournoux. The areas deactivated include medial frontal structures and bilateral areas of inferior temporal cortex (arrowed).

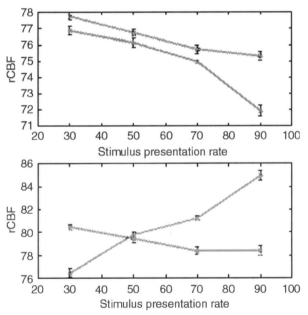

Fig. 5.4 Two modulatory effects of attention on rCBF. (*a*) Cerebral blood flow in left inferotemporal cortex (see Figure 5.3) plotted as a function of stimulus presentation rate, separately for attention to visual conjunctions (red line) compared with individual features (green line). There is a significant difference in the intercept of these two lines, but no significant difference in slope. This represents an additive effect of attention that is constant across presentation rates (cf. Figure 5.1*a*). (*b*) Cerebral blood flow in the left premotor cortex plotted as a function of stimulus presentation rate, separately for attention to visual conjunctions (red line) compared with individual features (green line). There is a significant difference in the slope of these two lines. This effect represents an interaction between stimulus rate-evoked changes in rCBF and attention (cf. Figure 5.1*b*).

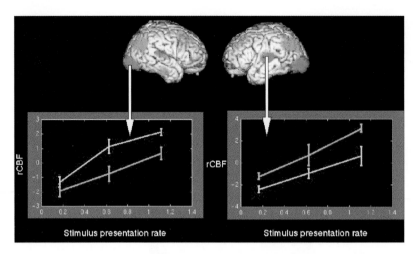

Fig. 5.5 Right and left lateral views of areas where changes in rCBF show significant positive (red) or negative (green) correlations with presentation rate. Activations are rendered on a canonical T1-weighted MRI image in the Talairach and Tournoux anatomical space. Below visual (left) and auditory (right) cortex are plotted the relation between rCBF and presentation rate, as a function of attention to visual (yellow line) or auditory signals (blue line).

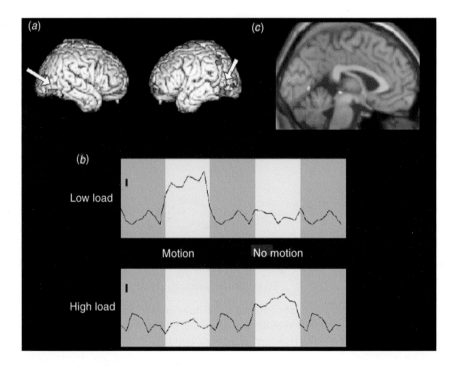

Fig. 5.6 Modulation of ignored motion processing by attentional load. (a) Lateral views of the left hemisphere of a T1-weighted volume rendered image plotted in the Talairach and Tournoux space. Areas where brain activity showed an interaction between motion and processing load are shown in red. The left V5 complex is indicated by arrows. (b) Mean activity and replications of each condition taken from the left V5 complex. Baseline conditions (dark grey) alternate with experimental conditions (light grey shading). The scale bar represents 0.1% BOLD signal change. (c) Activation in the superior colliculus due to the interaction of motion processing and perceptual load (sagittal slice from same image as (a)).

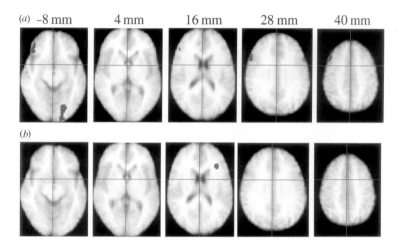

(a) -8 mm　　4 mm　　16 mm　　28 mm　　40 mm

(b)

Fig. 7.4 Significant bloodflow differences ($p < .05$, corrected for multiple comparisons) between leftward and rightward attention. (a) Greater flow in leftward attention; (b) the reverse. Each series shows horizontal brain slices progressing from bottom (left) to top (right) of the brain, after averaging between subjects and normalization to the standard space of Talairach and Tournoux (1988). Standard z levels of each slice are shown at the top of the figure; within each slice, the left of the brain appears on the left. Significant differences are show in red on the mean of the 14 subjects' normalized magnetic resonance images (MRIs). Analyses conducted using standard SPM software (Friston *et al.* 1995). Adapted with permission from Vandenberghe *et al.* (1997*b*).

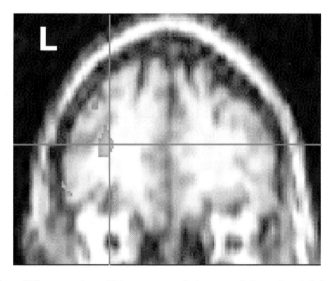

Fig. 7.5 Bloodflow differences ($p < .001$ uncorrected), between leftward and rightward attention for a single subject from the study of Vandenberghe *et al.* (1997*a*). Differences (orange-yellow) shown on coronal slice from subject's individual MRI, normalized to standard space of Talairach and Tournoux (1988) and taken at $y = 42$ mm to show prefrontal cortex. Crosshair marks maximum activation in inferior frontal sulcus. Other details as in figure 7.4.

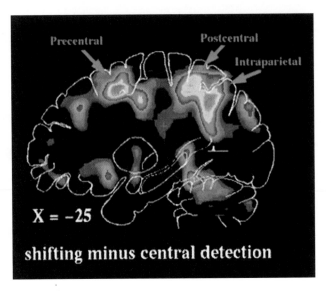

Fig. 11.2 Sagittal PET section, 25 mm left of midline, of group ($n = 24$) subtraction image between shifting attention and central detection with peripheral distractors tasks.

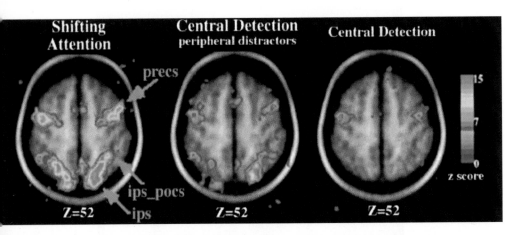

Fig. 11.3 Group fMRI activity superimposed on anatomical MRI during shifting attention, central detection with peripheral distractors, and central detection tasks in the left visual field. In the fixation control common to all tasks, the array of boxes was displayed, no stimuli were presented, and subjects maintained fixation on the central box. Transverse section, $z = 52$. Abbreviations: precs, precentral sulcus; ips_pocs, intraparietal sulcus–postcentral sulcus; ips, intraparietal sulcus.

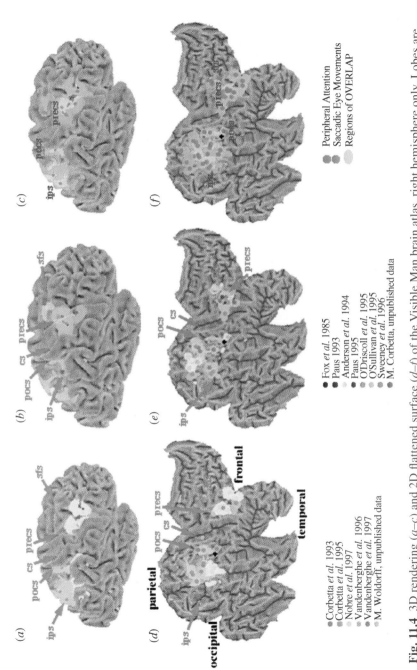

Fig. 11.4 3D rendering (*a–c*) and 2D flattened surface (*d–f*) of the Visible Man brain atlas, right hemisphere only. Lobes are indicated in 2D surface. Sulci are indicated as follows: sfs, superior frontal sulcus (s.); precs, precentral s.; cs represents central s.; pocs, postcentral s.; ips, intraparietal s. (*a, d*): areas of activation during peripheral attention. (*b, e*): areas of activation during saccadic eye movements. (*c, f*): anatomical overlap of areas active during peripheral attention and saccadic eye movements.

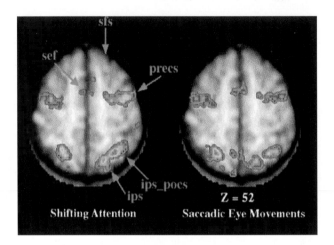

Fig. 11.5 Group (*n* = 5) fMRI activity superimposed on anatomical MRI during shifting attention and saccadic eye movement tasks in left visual field. A fixation control was common to both tasks. Anatomical regions as in figures 11.3 and 11.4. Abbreviations as in figure 11.3, and sef, supplementary eye field.

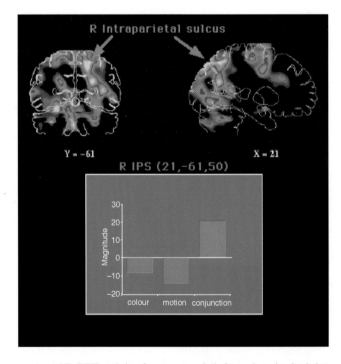

Fig. 11.6 Top: group (*n* = 17) PET activity from coronal (left) and sagittal (right) sections in the right intraparietal sulcus during visual search for targets defined by a conjunction of colour and motion speed. The control conditions is passive viewing of the same display. Bottom: magnitude of blood flow responses (in PET counts) in the feature (colour, motion) and conjunction conditions for the intraparietal region maximally activated in the shifting attention task (figure 11.1).

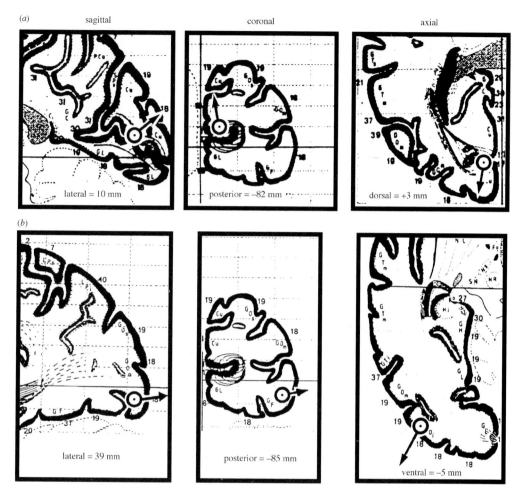

Fig. 3.5 Projections of dipoles representing the estimated sources of the C1 and P1 components onto brain sections of the Talairach and Tournoux (1988) atlas. Best-fit dipole locations were calculated from scalp voltage topographies using the algorithm developed by Scherg 1990. (*a*) The dipole corresponding to C1 was localized to primary visual cortex near the calcarine fissure. (*b*) The dipole corresponding to the P1 attention effect (attended minus unattended P1 voltage distribution) was localized to ventral–lateral extrastriate cortex. Data from Clark and Hillyard (1996).

occipital gyrus. Only the fusiform activation showed an increase for the more difficult symbol task relative to the dot detection task (figure 3.6*b*), however, and this was paralleled by an increased contralateral P1 amplitude in the symbol task (figure 3.6*c*). This ERP–rCBF correlation provides further evidence that the P1 attention effect is generated primarily in or near the fusiform gyrus.

A combined ERP–PET study by Woldorff and co-workers (1997) suggested that the amplification of visual evoked activity reflected in the P1 wave takes place in retinotopically organized visual cortex. They found that when stimuli were presented to the lower visual fields, below the horizontal meridian, that spatial attention produced an increase in rCBF in dorsal extrastriate occipital cortex of the contralateral hemisphere; the associated P1 attention effect was also

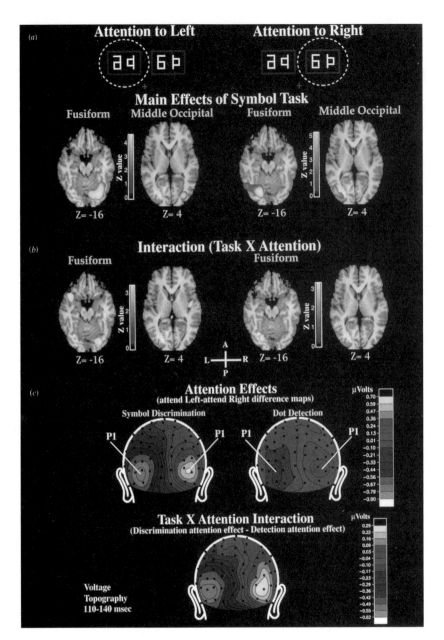

Fig. 3.6 (*a*) Top row shows examples of bilateral symbols used as stimuli in the study by Mangun *et al.* (1997). In different runs subjects attended to the right or left side of the displays, which were presented in rapid, randomized order. Brain sections show that attention to the left-field stimuli produced PET activations in the right fusiform and middle occipital gyri, while attention to the right produced corresponding activations in the left hemisphere. Note that left side of the images corresponds to left side of brain. (*b*) Visual cortex activations were greater for the symbol discrimination task than for a simpler dot detection task only in the contralateral fusiform gyrus. (*c*) Topographical voltage maps of the attention effect on the P1 component (110–140 ms latency) elicited by the bilateral stimuli. Maps represent P1 voltage distributions in attend left minus attend right conditions. Lower head shows that the P1 attention effect was greater for attend-symbol than for attend-dot conditions, as was the fusiform gyrus activation shown in *b*. (See colour plate section)

localized by dipole modelling to the same dorsal region. This contrasted with the more ventral PET and ERP localizations obtained by Heinze and co-workers (Heinze *et al.* 1994) and Mangun *et al.* (1997), in whose studies stimuli were presented to the upper visual fields. Such a pattern of results would be expected if spatial attention affected evoked neural activity in retinotopically organized visual areas such as V2, V3–VP, or V4, which have been recently mapped in humans (Sereno *et al.* 1995; DeYoe *et al.* 1996).

No evidence for attentional modulation of short-latency evoked activity in primary visual cortex (V1) was obtained in any of these combined PET–ERP studies nor in a spatial attention study that used a novel optical imaging technique (Gratton 1997). These studies thus offer no support for the hypothesis that visual transmission from the lateral geniculate to striate cortex is under the control of spatial attention (Crick 1984). However, the short latency of the extrastriate P1 attention effect (onset at 70–80 ms) and its apparent retinotopic properties indicate that the initial amplification of attended-location inputs takes place in posterior extrastriate cortex in areas where only elementary visual features are represented. This PET–ERP evidence thus provides strong evidence for 'early selection' theories of attention, according to which sensory inputs to attended locations are enhanced at early levels of visual processing prior to full stimulus identification and recognition (reviewed in LaBerge 1995). This early amplification process seems to be applied to all stimuli presented to attended locations, whether they are task relevant or not (Heinze *et al.* 1990; Luck *et al.* 1993) and augments their signal-to-noise ratio so that they may be processed more effectively at higher levels of object and pattern recognition.

3.4   Pet evidence for amplification?

The co-localization of ERP and rCBF modulations during spatial attention to common cortical areas provides evidence that both measures are reflecting the same gain control processes in the same extrastriate cortical regions. It is important to note, however, that these PET data *per se* do not provide unequivocal evidence for a gain control mechanism of attention. The pattern of PET changes observed in the spatial attention tasks reviewed here, like those reported by (Corbetta *et al.* 1991) in tasks involving attention to non-spatial features (colour, shape, movement), consisted of enhanced rCBF in specific sensory areas under conditions of increased attention relative to control conditions. As discussed, such a pattern could be produced by a tonic biasing of baseline neural firing rather than an amplification of sensory-evoked responses.

Recently, it has been suggested that PET data could be used to distinguish between attentional mechanisms of gain control over sensory input versus tonic biasing of neural activity by studying how rCBF changes vary as a function of stimulus repetition rate (Rees *et al.* 1997). The reasoning is illustrated in figure 3.7. As repetition rate increases, more stimulus-evoked responses will occur during the PET imaging period, leading to a greater PET (rCBF) response. If attention simply adds a bias signal but does not influence the actual sensory responses, then the increase in rCBF will be independent of the stimulation rate, as shown in figure 3.7*a*. However, if attention amplifies the sensory response to each stimulus, then the number of amplified responses will increase as more stimuli are presented during the PET imaging period, and the effect of attention will, therefore, be greater at higher stimulation rates. This is illustrated in figure 3.7*b*. In other words, changes in gain will influence the slope of the stimulation-rate function, whereas changes in bias will only influence the intercept. When Rees and colleagues applied this reasoning to a visual search experiment, they concluded that attention acted to modulate the gain of responses in the precuneus, the left cerebellum, and the premotor cortex, whereas attention added a bias signal to activity in the left inferior temporal gyrus and the right cerebellum.

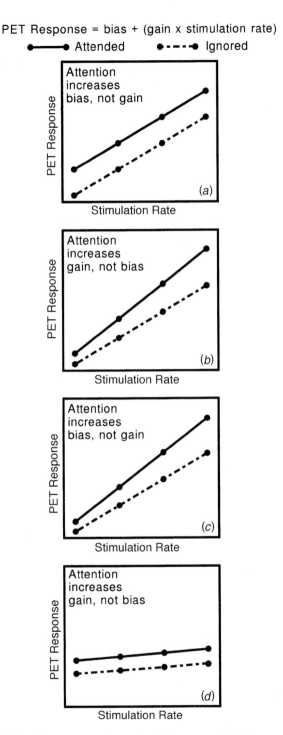

Fig. 3.7 Hypothetical relations between attention, stimulation rate, and PET response (rCBF). (*a*) In this case attention adds a bias signal, and the bias signal and the single-stimulus sensory response are assumed to be unaffected by stimulation rate. Because more stimuli are presented during the data acquisition interval, the PET response will increase as the stimulation rate increases. The effect of adding a constant bias signal will appear as a shift in the intercept of the stimulation rate function. (*b*) In this case, attention

The validity of this approach for distinguishing the two types of modulatory effects of attention would appear to depend on several assumptions that are open to question. In particular, this approach assumes that the effects of attention on bias and gain are constant across stimulation rates and that the neural responses elicited by individual stimuli also remain constant with changes in stimulation rate. There are many ways in which these assumptions might be expected to be violated, however, and we will consider two particularly likely and problematic scenarios. First, it is likely that different attentional strategies will be employed when the stimulation rate increases, owing both to the need for increased perceptual selectivity under conditions of high load (Lavie 1995) and to the increased ease of maintaining an attentional template when the relevant stimuli occur more frequently. These factors could lead to progressive increases in an attentional bias signal at higher stimulation rates and, therefore, a steeper slope in the stimulation-rate function, even if attention did not influence the gain of the sensory response (figure 3.7c). Second, it is well-known that sensory-evoked responses to repeated stimuli often exhibit decreased amplitudes at higher stimulation rates owing to refractory or fatigue effects (Naatanen 1992). As shown in figure 3.7d, this could lead to a shallow slope in the function relating blood flow to stimulation rate, because the increase in the number of stimuli presented during the PET imaging period would be partly offset by the decreased size of the neural response to each stimulus (this function could also be nonlinear, flat, or even declining). If attention then increased the gain of sensory responses by a constant factor but did not affect their refractory properties, this amplification effect could lead to a change in intercept rather than a change in slope. Additional nonlinearities might arise if there were ceiling effects on total neuronal activity that would prevent the divergence of the two curves in figure 3.7b or if the function relating increased neural activity to increased blood flow were nonlinear. Even more complex interactions could be envisaged if the bias signals from attentional control areas acted not only to change tonic firing rates in the target brain areas but also affected the sensory gain factor, which seems like a reasonable possibility. A final type of complication could ensue if the attentional process led to a reorganization of cellular firing patterns within a brain region rather than simple additive or multiplicative effects. In this latter case different neuronal subpopulations may be affected in opposing ways, making the net influence on rCBF difficult to predict.

Because of this multiplicity of confounding factors that may perturb the relation between neuronal responses (manifested in rCBF changes) and stimulation rate as a function of attention, it is difficult to accept the proposal that diverging curves (such as in figure 3.7b) are uniquely associated with a gain control mechanism and parallel curves (figure 3.7a) with a bias mechanism. Indeed, the example given by Rees and colleagues (Rees *et al.* 1997) of diverging response slopes that was interpreted as indicating a sensory gain change (their figure 1d) does not seem to be straightforward, as the slope of the function in one of the attention conditions appears to be close

---

increases the sensory gain without any bias signal, and the single stimulus sensory responses are assumed to be unaffected by stimulation rate. Because the response to each individual stimulus is increased by attention, the effect of attention on the PET response will be larger at higher stimulation rates. (c) In this case, attention adds a bias signal without influencing gain, as in a, but the size of this bias signal is assumed to increase as the stimulation rate increases (owing, for example, to increased attentional requirements at high stimulation rates). The result is a greater slope for the attended stimuli, as in b. (d) In this case, attention increases the sensory gain without any bias signal, as in b, but the single stimulus sensory responses are assumed to decrease as the stimulation rate increases (owing to neural fatigue). This causes the slope of the stimulation rate function to be very shallow, and there is no change in slope for the attended stimuli compared with the ignored stimuli.

to zero. In such a case, increasing the gain *per se* would not seem capable of producing a line of steeper slope. Given these complexities in interpreting the PET data, it appears that gain control and bias mechanisms can be distinguished (at least for the present) more clearly by means of ERP, neuromagnetic, or single unit recordings where time-course and waveform information are also available.

3.5 Attentional costs and benefits

Although the concept of sensory gain control or amplification appears to be a useful first approximation for describing the effects of attention on perceptual processes, it is clearly not the whole story. In particular, electrophysiological studies have provided evidence that the suppression of inputs at unattended locations and the facilitation of signals at attended locations may be done by separate mechanisms, associated with attentional costs and benefits, respectively. In addition, the facilitative mechanism seems to be preferentially engaged in situations where task-relevant stimuli must be discriminated rather than simply detected.

As was shown in figures 3.1 and 3.3, the P1 and N1 waves are typically larger in amplitude for attended-location stimuli than for unattended-location stimuli. A simple explanation for this pattern of results is that the sensory gain is increased for the attended location at an early stage and that this effect propagates forward to increase the amplitudes of the subsequent ERP components. However, several studies have now shown that the P1 and N1 attention effects are dissociable and reflect qualitatively different aspects of attention. An example of this is shown in figure 3.8*a*, which illustrates the results of a spatial cueing experiment (Luck *et al.* 1994). In this experiment, each trial consisted of a spatial cue followed by a brief luminance-increment target and a pattern mask. The subject's task was to report the presence or absence of the luminance-increment target at the masked location. In most of the trials, a single location was cued and the target–mask complex appeared at the cued location; these were called 'valid' trials. In a small percentage of trials, a single location was cued but the target–mask complex appeared at an uncued location; these were called 'invalid' trials. In yet a third type of trial, cues were pointed toward all possible target locations and the target–mask complex was equally likely to appear at any of these locations; these were called 'neutral' trials. In neutral trials attention was presumably unfocused or broadly focused, which provided a baseline condition that made it possible to distinguish between suppressive and facilitatory attention effects. Specifically, larger ERP amplitudes on valid trials than on neutral trials would indicate a relative facilitation of processing at the attended location, whereas smaller amplitudes on invalid trials than on neutral trials would indicate a relative suppression of processing at the ignored locations.

Several patterns of data were possible in this experiment. For example, attention may operate simply to increase the sensory gain at the attended location, which would result in larger P1 and N1 waves on valid trials than on neutral trials, with no suppression in invalid trials relative to neutral trials. Alternatively, attention may decrease the gain at the ignored locations, resulting in decreased P1 and N1 amplitudes in invalid trials relative to neutral trials. As shown in the bar graphs of figure 3.8*a*, however, neither of these patterns was observed. Instead, the P1 and N1 waves (both recorded over the occipital scalp) showed completely different attention effects: the P1 wave was reduced in invalid trials relative to neutral trials with no additional enhancement in valid trials, whereas the N1 wave was enhanced in valid trials relative to neutral trials with no additional reduction in invalid trials. In other words, the P1 wave exhibited only suppression at the ignored locations (associated with behavioural 'costs'; i.e. reduced target detectability), whereas the N1 wave exhibited only facilitation at the attended location (associated with behavioural 'benefits'; i.e. improved target detectability). This pattern of results is not compatible with the hypothesis of an early, single stage modulation of sensory gain but rather indicates that attention may have qualitatively different effects at different stages of processing.

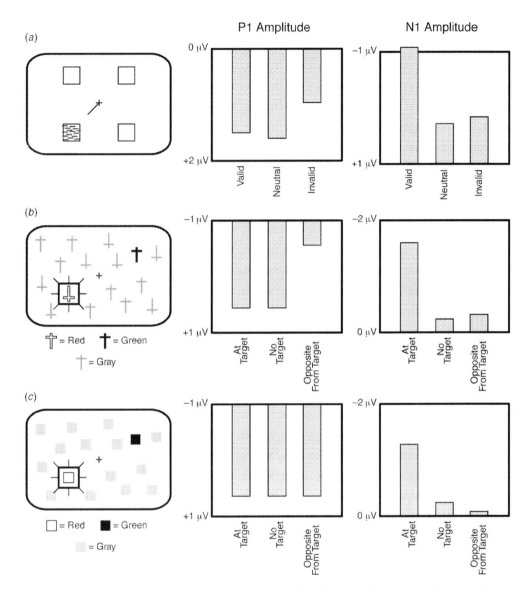

Fig. 3.8 Dissociations between the P1 and N1 attention effects in a spatial cueing experiment and two visual search experiments. (*a*) Stimuli and ERP results from spatial cueing experiment of Luck *et al.* (1994). Each trial began with an arrow cue, followed 200–500 ms later by a luminance target and pattern mask. P1 and N1 components were elicited at occipital sites by target-mask complex under three modality conditions. (*b*) Stimuli and ERP amplitudes in conjunction search experiment of Luck and Hillyard (1995). Subjects reported orientation of 'T' in designated target colour. P1 and N1 components were elicited by irrelevant probe square that either surrounded the target, surrounded a 'T' opposite to the target, or occurred in the absence of a target. (*c*) Same as *b*, but subjects only had to report the presence or absence of the target colour.

To assess the generality of this dissociation between the P1 and N1 waves during spatial attention, we did an analogous manipulation of attention using a very different task, namely visual search (Luck and Hillyard 1995). As illustrated in figure 3.8b, the stimuli in this experiment were arrays of 16 upright and inverted Ts, 14 of which were grey and two of which were different colours (selected at random from red, green, blue, or violet). At the beginning of each trial block, subjects were instructed to attend to one of the colours and to press one of two buttons for each stimulus array to indicate whether the T drawn in the attended colour was upright or inverted, if it was present at all (they were instructed to press neither button if the attended colour was absent). Because the ERP elicited by the visual search arrays reflected the processing of all of the items in the array, it was not possible to use these ERPs to assess the processing of stimuli at attended and ignored locations. Instead, a task-irrelevant 'probe' square was presented around one of the coloured Ts in each array, and the ERP elicited by this probe stimulus was used as a measure of sensory processing at the probed location. In some trials, the probe was presented at the location of the attended-colour T (the target); because we assume that attention was directed to the location of the target, this trial type is analogous to a valid trial in a cueing paradigm. In other trials, the probe was presented at the location of a coloured T on the opposite side of the array from the attended target (analogous to an invalid trial). In a third type of trial, the attended colour was absent and one of the two irrelevant-colour Ts was probed; because attention was presumably unfocused or diffusely focused on these trials, these were analogous to neutral trials. The probe was presented 250 ms after the onset of the search array to provide time for attention to be allocated to the location of the target.

As shown in the bar graphs of figure 3.8b, the same pattern of P1 and N1 attention effects was obtained in this visual search experiment as in the cueing experiment illustrated in figure 3.8a. The N1 component was enhanced for probes presented at the location of the target compared with probes presented on target-absent trials, but there was no suppression of the N1 when the probe was presented at a location in the opposite hemifield from the target. In contrast, the P1 component was suppressed when the probe was presented at a location in the opposite hemifield from the target compared with probes presented on target-absent trials, but there was no enhancement of P1 amplitude when the probe was presented at the location of the target compared with probes presented on target-absent trials. This provides additional evidence that the P1 reflects a suppression of processing at ignored locations whereas the N1 reflects a facilitation of processing at attended locations.

It could be argued that it does not matter whether the gain is increased at attended locations or decreased at ignored locations; in either case, the result is a larger signal for attended locations relative to ignored locations. Indeed, this would be true if attention merely controlled the gain of sensory processing (and if neural responses were not bounded by maximum and minimum firing rates). However, there is increasing evidence that the N1 enhancement observed at attended locations may reflect more than a simple increase in sensory gain. This derives from two additional dissociations that have been observed between the P1 and N1 attention effects. First, when the visual search paradigm shown in figure 3.8b was changed so that subjects had only to indicate the presence or absence of the attended colour, the P1 attention effect was eliminated while the N1 effect remained (Luck and Hillyard 1995). This is shown in figure 3.8c. Second, in a series of cueing experiments, Mangun and Hillyard (1991) found that the N1 attention effect was eliminated when subjects performed a simple-RT task in which they pressed a single button as fast as possible when they detected the target, regardless of its identity. The N1 effect returned, however, when the subjects performed a choice-RT task in which they were required to quickly press one of two buttons to indicate whether the target was a tall bar or a short bar. The P1 attention effect was present in both the simple- and choice-RT tasks. On the basis of these results, it was proposed that the P1 attention effect does reflect a reduction in sensory gain that attenuates potentially interfering information from ignored locations, whereas the N1 attention effect reflects the application of a limited-capacity discriminative process to stimuli at the attended location (Luck 1995).

This hypothesis for P1 is based on observations suggesting that the P1 attention effect occurs primarily under conditions that might lead to interference. For example, when a subject performs a difficult luminance detection task, noise from other locations might impair performance. Similarly, when a subject must respond as quickly as possible to the appearance of a stimulus, a low motor-response threshold will be established, and it is necessary to suppress noise that might otherwise trigger a spurious motor response. Suppression of irrelevant inputs will also be useful in a conjunction discrimination task such as that shown in figure 3.8b, because it is necessary to avoid combining the form of a distractor item with the colour of the target item. These are all conditions under which the P1 wave is modulated by attention. In contrast, no P1 suppression was observed in a simple feature detection task (figure 3.8c) (Luck and Hillyard 1995), presumably because simple, suprathreshold features can be identified with very little interference from concurrently presented distractor items (Treisman 1988, 1996). Thus, several lines of evidence suggest that the P1 attention effect reflects a suppression of processing (i.e. a gain reduction) at unattended locations that serves to mitigate interference between attended and unattended information.

The proposal that the N1 attention effect reflects the application of a limited-capacity discriminative process to the attended location was initially based on the finding that this effect was present when subjects performed discriminations, but not when they performed simple-reaction time (RT) tasks (Mangun and Hillyard 1991). More recent evidence for this hypothesis is considered in §3.6.

3.6 A limited-capacity discriminative process

The ERP correlates of discriminative processing were examined some years ago by Ritter and colleagues with foveally presented stimuli (Ritter et al. 1983, 1988). The logic behind these experiments was straightforward; if the same stimulus was presented during a simple-RT task and during a choice-RT task, then the use of discriminative mechanisms in the choice-RT task would lead to additional ERP activity that could be visualized by comparing the ERPs elicited during the simple- and choice-RT conditions. When Ritter and co-workers (1983, 1988) made this comparison, they found a greater negativity during the choice-RT task that included several distinct phases, the earliest of which coincided in time and scalp distribution with the occipitotemporal N1 wave. Ritter and colleagues termed this entire negative component the 'NA' wave and proposed that it was an index of a pattern discrimination and recognition process.

In a recent series of experiments, we examined more closely the early phase of the NA—which coincides with the N1 wave and is here termed the N1 discrimination effect—to evaluate the hypothesis that it truly reflects a perceptual discrimination process and to determine its relation to the attention-related modulations of the N1 wave described here. Before describing these experiments, however, it is necessary to distinguish between two difrent varieties of N1 attention effects. The N1 wave can be observed at both anterior and posterior scalp sites, but it peaks 30–60 ms earlier at anterior sites. Both the anterior and posterior N1 waves are larger for attended-location stimuli than for unattended-location stimuli, but these effects are differentially influenced by several experimental manipulations (Luck et al. 1990). It is the posterior N1 attention effect that we propose reflects the application of a discriminative process to attended-location stimuli (Luck 1995).

Figure 3.9a illustrates the basic N1 discrimination effect. When subjects performed either a colour discrimination task or a letter discrimination task, there was a greater negativity in the N1

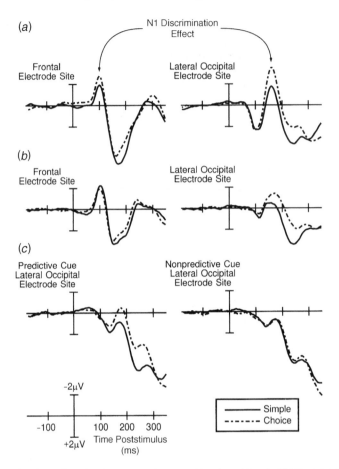

Fig. 3.9 N1 discrimination effect in three experiments (Vogel and Luck 1997). (*a*) ERPs elicited at anterior and posterior electrode sites by non-target stimuli in a simple-RT task and a choice-RT task. An N1 discrimination effect can be seen at both the anterior and posterior electrode sites. (*b*) ERPs elicited at anterior and posterior electrode sites by non-target stimuli in a simple-count task and a choice-count task. An N1 discrimination effect can be seen only at the posterior electrode site. (*c*) ERPs elicited at posterior electrode sites by non-target stimuli when preceded by a predictive cue (left) or a nonpredictive cue (right). An N1 discrimination effect can be seen only when the cue was predictive.

latency range than when the subjects performed a simple-RT task with the same stimuli. This effect was present at both anterior and posterior scalp sites. However, it is possible to explain this effect in terms of differences in motor preparation rather than the application of a discriminative process. Because the subjects knew what response was to be made even before stimulus onset in the simple-RT task but not in the choice-RT task, they may have begun preparing the response before stimulus onset in the simple-RT task. This early preparation would probably be associated with negative 'motor potentials' arising from the motor cortex that began earlier in the simple-RT condition and added extra negativity to the measured N1 wave.

Several experiments were aimed at distinguishing motor-preparatory from sensory-discriminative influences on the N1 wave (Vogel and Luck 1997). In one experiment, differences in anticipatory activity were minimized by using a highly variable interstimulus interval, making it difficult for the subjects to anticipate the onset time of the stimuli. In addition, differences in motor activity were eliminated by requiring subjects to silently count the stimuli rather than making overt motor responses to them. In the 'simple-count' condition, subjects silently counted the number of stimuli that were presented in a trial block and reported this number at the end of the block. In the 'choice-count' condition, subjects counted the number of stimuli containing the colour red rather than counting all of the stimuli. The primary difference between the tasks was the requirement of colour discrimination in the choice-count condition. As shown in figure 3.9*b*, there was a greater negativity in the N1 latency range for the choice-count condition than for the simple-count condition, and this effect was restricted to posterior, occipitotemporal scalp sites. On the basis of these results and other similar findings, we concluded that the anteriorly distributed N1 discrimination effect is probably attributable to differential motor preparation but that the posteriorly distributed N1 difference does indeed reflect the engagement of a visual discrimination process.

Once motor preparatory activity had been eliminated, the scalp distribution of the N1 discrimination effect was found to be similar to the scalp distribution of the posterior N1 attention effect, with a maximum at occipitotemporal electrode sites. To provide further evidence that these effects reflect the same underlying neurocognitive process, we examined the N1 discrimination effect in a spatial cueing experiment. If this effect reflects a limited-capacity process that can be allocated to a single location in the visual fields, then it should be present only when the target location is known in advance. This hypothesis was tested in an experiment with four conditions: simple-predictive, simple-nonpredictive, choice-predictive, and choice-nonpredictive. In the predictive conditions, a cue at the beginning of each trial indicated (with 100% reliability) the location at which the subsequent target would be presented; in the nonpredictive conditions, a cue was presented but was not correlated with the location of the subsequent target. Figure 3.9*c* compares the simple-RT and choice-RT tasks for the predictive and nonpredictive conditions. A significant N1 discrimination effect was observed for the predictive condition, but not for the nonpredictive condition. Thus, both the N1 discrimination effect and the N1 attention effect are present only when the subject knows the location of the to-be-discriminated stimulus. We, therefore, tentatively conclude that these effects reflect the same underlying neural and cognitive mechanisms and that spatial attention operates, in part, by controlling the allocation of a limited-capacity discriminative process to attended-location signals. This may well involve both gain control–amplification of the evoked N1 generators plus the engagement of specialized discriminative neural activity that extends beyond the N1 latency range.

3.7 Conclusion

As we have outlined here, recent studies using the methods of cognitive neuroscience have refined and extended the decades-old notion of attentional gain control in several ways. First, these methods have allowed amplification mechanisms to be differentiated from bias mechanisms, even when both mechanisms operate in the same brain regions and in the same tasks. Second, they have identified the neural loci at which amplification occurs, demonstrating that sensory gain control mechanisms operate in extrastriate areas of visual cortex, but not in striate cortex. These data strongly support 'early selection' models of visual attention. Third, these studies have distinguished between different subcategories of gain-control mechanisms, indicating the existence of separable mechanisms for suppressing unattended sources of information and for enhancing the processing of attended sources. Further work is needed to decipher the specific neural codes that represent perceptual information and to delineate the neural circuitry that exerts attentional control over perceptual experience.

Acknowledgements

We thank our many colleagues who have contributed to the studies reviewed here, including L. Anllo-Vento, L. Chelazzi, V. Clark, R. Desimone, S. Fan, C. Gomez, S. Hackley, J. Hansen, H. Heinze, H. Hinrichs, R. Mangun, T. Muente, T. Picton and M. Woldorff. Supported by Grants from NIMH (MH25594 and MH56877), NIH (NS17778), ONR (N00014-93-I-0942), and the McDonnell-Pew Program in Cognitive Neuroscience (95-38).

References

Anllo-Vento, L. 1995 Shifting attention in visual space: the effects of peripheral cueing on brain cortical potentials. *Int. J. Neurosci.* **80**, 353–70.

Broadbent, D. E. 1958 *Perception and communication.* New York: Pergamon.

Chelazzi, L., Miller, E. K., Duncan, J. and Desimone, R. 1993 A neural basis for visual search in inferior temporal cortex. *Nature* **363**, 345–7.

Clark, V. P. and Hillyard, S. A. 1996 Spatial selective attention affects early extrastriate but not striate components of the visual evoked potential. *J. Cogn. Neurosci.* **8**, 387–402.

Clark, V. P., Fan, S. and Hillyard, S. A. 1995 Identification of early visually evoked potential generators by retinotopic and topographic analyses. *Hum. Brain Mapp.* **2**, 170–87.

Corbetta, M., Miezin, F. M., Dobmeyer, S., Shulman, G. L. and Petersen, S. E. 1990 Attentional modulation of neural processing of shape, color, and velocity in humans. *Science* **248**, 1556–9.

Corbetta, M., Miezin, F. M., Dobmeyer, S., Shulman, G. L. and Petersen, S. E. 1991 Selective and divided attention during visual discriminations of shape, color, and speed: functional anatomy by positron emission tomography. *J. Neurosci.* **11**, 2383–402.

Crick, F. 1984 Function of the thalamic reticular complex: the searchlight hypothesis. *Proc. Natn. Acad. Sci. USA* **81**, 4586–90.

Desimone, R. and Duncan, J. 1995 Neural mechanisms of selective visual attention. *A. Rev. Neurosci.* **18**, 193–222.

DeYoe, E. A., Carman, G. J., Bandettini, P., Glickman, S., Wieser, J., Cox, R., Miller, D. and Neitz, J. 1996 Mapping striate and extrastriate visual areas in human cerebral cortex. *Proc. Natn. Acad. Sci. USA* **93**, 2382–6.

Duncan, J. 1981 Directing attention in the visual field. *Percept. Psychophys.* **30**, 90–3.

Duncan, J. and Humphreys, G. W. 1992 Beyond the search surface: visual search and attentional engagement. *J. Exp. Psychol. Hum. Percept. Perf.* **18**, 578–88.

Eason, R. G. 1981 Visual evoked potential correlates of early neural filtering during selective attention. *Bull. Psychon. Soc.* **18**, 203–6.

Eimer, M. 1997 Attentional selection and attentional gradients: an alternative method for studying transient visual-spatial attention. *Psychophysiology* **34**, 365–76.

Funahashi, S., Bruce, C. J. and Goldman-Rakic, P. S. 1989 Mnemonic coding of visual space in the monkey's dorso-lateral prefrontal cortex. *J. Neurophysiol.* **61**, 331–49.

Fuster, J. M. and Jervey, J. P. 1982 Neuronal firing in the inferotemporal cortex of the monkey in a visual memory task. *J. Neurosci.* **2**, 361–75.

Gomez, C. M., Clark, V. P., Luck, S. J., Fan, S. and Hillyard, S. A. 1994 Sources of attention-sensitive visual event-related potentials. *Brain Topogr.* **7**, 41–51.

Gratton, G. 1997 Attention and probability effects in the human occipital cortex: an optical imaging study. *NeuroReport* **8**, 1749–53.

Harter, M. R. and Aine, C. J. 1984 Brain mechanisms of visual selective attention. In *Varieties of attention* (eds R. Parasuraman and D. R. Davies), pp. 293–321. London: Academic Press.

Hawkins, H. L., Hillyard, S. A., Luck, S. J., Mouloua, M., Downing, C. J. and Woodward, D. P. 1990 Visual attention modulates signal detectability. *J. Exp. Psychol. Hum. Percept. Perf.* **16**, 802–11.

Heinze, H. J., Luck, S. J., Mangun, G. R. and Hillyard, S. A. 1990 Visual event-related potentials index focused attention within bilateral stimulus arrays. I. Evidence for early selection. *Electroencephalogr. Clin. Neurophysiol.* **75**, 511–27.

Heinze, H. J. (and 11 others) 1994 Combined spatial and temporal imaging of brain activity during visual selective attention in humans. *Nature* **372**, 543–6.

Hernandez-Peon, R. 1966 Physiological mechanisms in attention. In *Frontiers in physiological psychology* (ed. R. W. Russell), pp. 121–47. New York: Academic Press.

Hernandez-Peon, R., Scherrer, H. and Jouvet, M. 1956 Modification of electrical activity in the cochlear nucleus during attention in unanesthetized cats. *Science* **123**, 331–2.

Hikosaka, O., Miyauchi, S. and Shimojo, S. 1993 Focal visual attention produces illusory temporal order and motion sensation. *Vis. Res.* **33**, 1219–40.

Hillyard, S. A. and Muente, T. F. 1984 Selective attention to color and locational cues: an analysis with event-related brain potentials. *Percept. Psychophys.* **36**, 185–98.

Hillyard, S. A., Hink, R. F., Schwent, V. L. and Picton, T. W. 1973 Electrical signs of selective attention in the human brain. *Science* **182**, 177–9.

Hillyard, S. A., Mangun, G. R., Woldorff, M. G. and Luck, S. J. 1995 Neural systems mediating selective attention. In *The cognitive neurosciences* (ed. M. S. Gazzaniga), pp. 665–81. Cambridge, MA: MIT Press.

Hillyard, S. A., Anllo-Vento, L., Clark, V. P., Heinze, H. J., Luck, S. J. and Mangun, G. R. 1996 Neuro-imaging approaches to the study of visual attention: a tutorial. In *Converging operations in the study of visual selective attention* (eds A. K. M. Coles and G. Logan), pp. 107–38. Washington, DC: American Psychological Association.

Johannes, S., Muente, T. F., Heinze, H. J. and Mangun, G. R. 1995 Luminance and spatial attention effects on early visual processing. *Cogn. Brain Res.* **2**, 189–205.

Johannes, S., Knalmann, U., Mangun, G. R., Heinze, H. J. and Munte, T. F. 1998 The visual C1 component: scalp topography, dipole sources, and effects of luminance and spatial attention. In *Mapping cognition in time and space* (eds H. J. Heinze, T. F. Muente, G. R. Mangun and H. H. Scheich). Boston, MA: Birhauser. (In the press.)

LaBerge, D. 1995 Computational and anatomical models of selective attention in object identification. In *The cognitive neurosciences* (ed. M. S. Gazzaniga), pp. 649–61. Cambridge, MA: MIT Press.

Lavie, N. 1995 Perceptual load as a necessary condition for selective attention. *J. Exp. Psychol. Hum. Percept. Perf.* **21**, 451–68.

Luck, S. J. 1995 Multiple mechanisms of visual-spatial attention: recent evidence from human electrophysiology. *Behav. Brain Res.* **71**, 113–23.

Luck, S. J. and Hillyard, S. A. 1995 The role of attention in feature detection and conjunction discrimination: an electrophysiological analysis. *Int. J. Neurosci.* **80**, 281–97.

Luck, S. J., Heinze, H. J., Mangun, G. R. and Hillyard, S. A. 1990 Visual event-related potentials index focused attention within bilateral stimulus arrays. II. Functional dissociation of P1 and N1 components. *Electroencephalogr. Clin. Neurophysiol.* **75**, 528–42.

Luck, S. J., Fan, S. and Hillyard, S. A. 1993 Attention-related modulation of sensory-evoked brain activity in a visual search task. *J. Cogn. Neurosci.* **5**, 188–95.

Luck, S. J., Hillyard, S. A., Mouloua, M., Woldorff, M. G., Clark, V. P. and Hawkins, H. L. 1994 Effects of spatial cuing on luminance detectability: psychophysical and electrophysiological evidence for early selection. *J. Exp. Psychol. Hum. Percept. Perf.* **20**, 887–904.

Luck, S. J., Hillyard, S. A., Mouloua, M. and Hawkins, H. L. 1996 Mechanisms of visual-spatial attention: resource allocation or uncertainty reduction. *J. Exp. Psychol. Hum. Percept. Perf.* **22**, 725–37.

Luck, S. J., Chelazzi, L., Hillyard, S. A. and Desimone, R. 1997 Neural mechanisms of spatial selective attention to areas V1, V2, and V4 of macaque visual cortex. *J. Neurophysiol.* **77**, 24–42.

Mangun, G. R. and Hillyard, S. A. 1991 Modulations of sensory-evoked brain potentials indicate changes in perceptual processing during visual-spatial priming. *J. Exp. Psychol. Hum. Percept. Perf.* **17**, 1057–74.

Mangun, G. R. and Hillyard, S. A. 1995 Attention: mechanisms and models. In *Electrophysiology of mind–event-related potentials and cognition* (eds M. D. Rugg and M. G. H. Coles), pp. 40–85. Oxford University Press.

Mangun, G. R., Hillyard, S. A. and Luck, S. J. 1993 Electrocortical substrates of visual selective attention. In *Attention and performance XIV* (eds D. Meyer and S. Kornblum), pp. 219–43. Cambridge, MA: MIT Press.

Mangun, G. R., Hopfinger, J., Kussmaul, C. L., Fletcher, E. and Heinze, H. J. 1997 Covariations in ERP and PET measures of spatial selective attention in human extrastriate visual cortex. *Hum. Brain Mapp.* **5**, 1–7.

Miller, E. K. and Desimone, R. 1994 Parallel neuronal mechanisms for short-term memory. *Science* **263**, 520–2.

Motter, B. C. 1993 Focal attention produces spatially selective processing in visual cortical areas V1, V2 and V4 in the presence of competing stimuli. *J. Neurophysiol.* **70**, 909–19.

Naatanen, R. 1992 *Attention and brain function.* Hillsdale, NJ: Lawrence Erlbaum.

Newsome, W. T., Shadlen, M. N., Zohary, E., Britten, K. H. and Movshon, J. A. 1995 Visual motion: linking neuronal activity to psychophysical performance. In *The cognitive neurosciences* (ed. M. S. Gazzaniga), pp. 401–14. Cambridge, MA: MIT Press.

Oatman, L. C. and Anderson, B. W. 1977 Effects of visual attention on tone burst evoked auditory potentials. *Exp. Neurol.* **57**, 200–11.

O'Leary, D. S., Andreason, N. C., Hurtig, R. R., Hichwa, R. D., Watkins, G. L., Boles Ponto, L. L., Rogers, M. and Kirchner, P. T. 1996 A positron emission tomography study of binaurally and dichotically presented stimuli: effects of level of language and directed attention. *Brain Lang.* **53**, 20–39.

Posner, M. I. and Dehaene, S. 1994 Attentional networks. *Trends Neurosci.* **17**, 75–9.

Posner, M. I. and Driver, J. 1992 The neurobiology of selective attention. *Curr. Opin. Neurobiol.* **2**, 165–9.

Rees, G., Frackowiak, R. and Frith, C. 1997 Two modulatory effects of attention that mediate object categorization in human cortex. *Science* **275**, 835–8.

Reinitz, M. T. 1990 Effects of spatially directed attention on visual encoding. *Percept. Psychophys.* **47**, 497–505.

Ritter, W., Simson, R. and Vaughan, H. G. 1983 Event-related potential correlates of two stages of information processing in physical and semantic discrimination tasks. *Psychophysiology* **20**, 168–79.

Ritter, W., Simson, R. and Vaughan, H. G. 1988 Effects of the amount of stimulus information processed on negative event-related potentials. *Electroencephalogr. Clin. Neurophysiol.* **69**, 244–58.

Scherg, M. 1990 Fundamentals of dipole source potential analysis. In *Auditory evoked magnetic fields and potentials. Advanced audiology*, vol. 6 (eds F. Grandori, M. Hoke and G. L. Romani), pp. 40–69. Basel: Karger.

Sereno, M. I., Dale, A. M., Reppas, J. B., Kwong, K. K., Belliveau, J. W., Brady, T. J., Rosen, B. R. and Tootell, R. B. H. 1995 Borders of multiple visual areas in humans revealed by functional magnetic resonance imaging. *Science* **268**, 889–93.

Shiu, L. P. and Pashler, H. 1995 Spatial attention and vernier acuity. *Vis. Res.* **35**, 337–43.

Shulman, G. L., Corbetta, M., Buckner, R. L., Raichle, M. E., Fiez, J. A., Miezin, F. M. and Petersen, S. E. 1997 Top-down modulation of early sensory cortex. *Cerebr. Cortex* **7**, 193–206.

Sperling, G. and Dosher, B. A. 1986 Strategy and optimization in human information processing. In *Handbook of perception and human performance*, vol. 1 (eds L. K. K. R. Boff and J. P. Thomas), pp. 2–65. New York: Wiley.

Talairach, J. and Tournoux, P. (eds) 1988 *Co-planar stereotaxic atlas of the human brain: 3-dimensional proportional system: an approach to cerebral imaging.* New York: Thieme Medical Publishing Inc.

Tootell, R. B. H., Reppas, J. B., Kwong, K. K., Malach, R., Born, R. T., Brady, T. J., Rosen, B. R. and Belliveau, J. W. 1995 Functional analysis of human MT and related visual cortical areas using magnetic resonance imaging. *J. Neurosci.* **15**, 3215–30.

Treisman, A. 1969 Strategies and models of selective attention. *Psychol. Rev.* **76**, 282–99.

Treisman, A. 1988 Features and objects: the Fourteenth Bartlett Memorial Lecture. *Q. J. Exp. Psychol.* **40**, 201–37.

Treisman, A. 1996 The binding problem. *Curr. Opin. Neurobiol.* **6**, 171–8.

Tsal, Y., Shalev, L., Zakay, D. and Lubow, R. E. 1994 Attention reduces perceived brightness contrast. *Q. J. Exp. Psychol.* A **47**, 865–93.

Vogel, E. K. and Luck, S. J. 1997 ERP evidence for a general-purpose visual discrimination mechanism. *Soc. Neurosci. Abstr.* **23**, 158.

Wijers, A. A., Lange, J. J., Mulder, G. and Mulder, L. J. M. 1997 An ERP study of visual spatial attention and letter target detection for isoluminant and nonisoluminant stimuli. *Psychophysiology* **34**, 553–65.

Woldorff, M. G. (and 10 others) 1997 Retinotopic organization of the early visual-spatial attention effects as revealed by PET and ERPs. *Hum. Brain Mapp.* **5**, 280–6.

Worden, M. and Schneider, W. 1996 Visuospatial attentional selection examined with functional magnetic resonance imaging. Soc. *Neurosci. Abstr.* **22**, 1856.

Zeki, S., Watson, J. D. G., Lueck, C. J., Friston, K. J., Kennard, C. and Frackowiak, R. S. J. 1991 A direct demonstration of functional specialization in human visual cortex. *J. Neurosci.* **11**, 641–9.

4

A computational theory of visual attention

Claus Bundesen

Abstract

A computational theory of visual attention is presented. The basic theory (TVA) combines the biased-choice model for single-stimulus recognition with the fixed-capacity independent race model (FIRM) for selection from multi-element displays. TVA organizes a large body of experimental findings on performance in visual recognition and attention tasks. A recent development (CTVA) combines TVA with a theory of perceptual grouping by proximity. CTVA explains effects of perceptual grouping and spatial distance between items in multi-element displays. A new account of spatial focusing is proposed in this article. The account provides a framework for understanding visual search as an interplay between serial and parallel processes.

4.1 Introduction

This article describes and further develops a computational theory of visual attention. The theory is based on a race model of selection from multi-element displays and a race model of single-stimulus recognition. In race models of selection from multi-element displays, display elements are processed in parallel, and attentional selection is made of those elements that first finish processing (the winners of the race). Thus, selection of targets (elements to be selected) instead of distractors (elements to be ignored) is based on processing of targets being faster than processing of distractors. In race models of single-stimulus recognition, alternative perceptual categorizations are processed in parallel, and the subject selects the categorization that first completes processing.

The first race models of selection from multi-element displays appeared in the 1980s (see Bundesen 1987; Bundesen *et al.* 1985; also see Bundesen 1996). The most successful among the models was the fixed-capacity independent race model (FIRM) of Shibuya and Bundesen (1988). In this model, a stimulus display is processed as follows. First an attentional weight is computed for each element in the display. The weight is a measure of the strength of the sensory evidence that the element is a target rather than a distractor. Then the available processing capacity is distributed across the elements in proportion to their weights. The amount of processing capacity that is allocated to an element determines how fast the element can be encoded into visual short-term memory (VSTM). Finally the encoding race between the elements takes place. The elements that are selected (i.e., stored in VSTM) are those elements whose encoding processes complete before the stimulus presentation terminates and before VSTM has been filled up.

In a generalization of FIRM called TVA (Theory of Visual Attention; Bundesen 1990), selection depends on the outcome of a race between possible perceptual categorizations. The rate at which a possible categorization ('element x belongs to category i') is processed increases with (a) the strength of the sensory evidence that supports the categorization, (b) the subject's bias for assigning stimuli to category i, and (c) the attentional weight of element x. When a possible categorization completes processing, the categorization enters VSTM if memory space is available there. The span of VSTM is limited to about four elements. Competition between mutually incompatible categorizations of the same element is resolved in favour of the first-completing categorization.

TVA accounts for many findings on single-stimulus recognition, whole report, partial report, search, and detection. Recently the theory has been extended by Gordon Logan (1996). The extended theory, CTVA (CODE Theory of Visual Attention), combines TVA with a theory of perceptual grouping by proximity (van Oeffelen and Vos 1982). CTVA explains a wide range of spatial effects in visual attention.

The formal assumptions of TVA and CTVA are presented in the first main section of this article (§4.2). The presentation includes a new account of spatial focusing, which provides a framework for understanding visual search as an interplay between serial and parallel processes. The following main sections of the article treat applications of the theory to single-stimulus recognition (§4.3) and selection from multi-element displays (§4.4).

4.2 General theory

(a) Basic TVA

In TVA, both visual recognition and attentional selection of elements in the visual field consist in making perceptual categorizations. A perceptual categorization has the form 'element x has feature i', or equivalently, 'element x belongs to category i'. Here element x is an object (a perceptual unit) in the visual field, feature i is a perceptual feature (e.g., a certain colour, shape, movement, or spatial position), and category i is a perceptual category (the class of all elements that have feature i).

A perceptual categorization is made if and when the categorization is encoded into visual short-term memory (VSTM). When the perceptual categorization that element x belongs to category i has been made (i.e., encoded into VSTM), element x is said to be selected and element x is also said to be recognized as a member of category i. Thus, attentional selection of element x implies that x is recognized as a member of one or another category. Element x is said to be retained in VSTM if and when one or another categorization of the element is retained in VSTM.

Once a perceptual categorization of an element completes processing, the categorization enters VSTM, provided that memory space for the categorization is available in VSTM. The capacity of VSTM is limited to K different elements, where K is about 4 (cf. Sperling 1960). Space is available for a new categorization of element x, if element x is already represented in the store (with one or another categorization) or if less than K elements are represented in the store (cf. Luck and Vogel 1997). There is no room for a categorization of element x if VSTM has been filled up with other elements.

Consider the time taken to process a particular perceptual categorization, 'element x belongs to category i'. This processing time is a random variable that follows a certain distribution. In TVA, the distribution is defined by specifying the instantaneous tendency (probability density) that the processing completes at time t, given that the processing has not completed before time t. This instantaneous tendency (hazard rate) is a measure of the speed at which the perceptual categorization is processed. In TVA, the measure is called the v-value of the perceptual categorization that x belongs to i, $v(x, i)$, and $v(x, i)$ is determined by two basic equations. By equation 4.1,

$$v(x, i) = \eta(x, i)\beta_i \frac{w_x}{\sum_{z \in \mathcal{S}} w_z}, \tag{4.1}$$

where $\eta(x, i)$ is the instantaneous strength of the sensory evidence that element x belongs to category i, β_i is a perceptual decision bias associated with category i, $\mathcal{S}$ is the set of all elements in the visual field, and w_x and w_z are attentional weights of elements x and z, respectively.

By equation 4.1, both perceptual decision biases and attentional weights multiply strengths of sensory evidence, but they do so in very different ways. Parameter β_i multiplies not only $\eta(x, i)$, but every η-value of which perceptual category i is the second argument. Parameter w_x (or $w_x/\Sigma_{z \in S} w_z$) multiplies not only $\eta(x, i)$, but every η-value of which element x is the first argument. Thus, decision bias parameters are used for manipulating classes of v-values (processing speeds) defined in terms of perceptual categories (values of i), whereas weight parameters are used for manipulating classes of v-values defined in terms of perceptual elements (values of x). In this sense, perceptual decision biases and attentional weights are complementary parameters.

The attentional weights are derived from perceptual processing priorities. Every perceptual category is associated with a certain processing priority (pertinence value). The processing priority associated with a category is a measure of the current importance of attending to elements that belong to the category. The weight of an element x in the visual field is given by

$$w_x = \sum_{j \in \mathcal{R}} \eta(x, j)\pi_j, \qquad (4.2)$$

where $\mathcal{R}$ is the set of all perceptual categories, $\eta(x, j)$ is the instantaneous strength of the sensory evidence that element x belongs to category j, and π_j is the perceptual processing priority of category j.

By equation 4.2, perceptual processing priorities can be used for manipulating attentional weights. The attentional weight of an element depends on the perceptual features of the element, and π_j determines the importance of feature j in setting the attentional weights of elements.

By equations 4.1 and 4.2, v-values can be expressed as functions of η, β, and π-values. When η, β, and π-values are kept constant, processing times for different perceptual categorizations are assumed to be stochastically independent.

In most applications of the theory to experimental data, η, β, and π-values have been assumed to be constant during the presentation of a stimulus display. When η, β, and π-values are constant, v-values are also constant. The v-values were defined as hazard rates, and when these are kept constant, categorization times become exponentially distributed. The v-value of the perceptual categorization that element x belongs to category i becomes the exponential rate parameter for the processing time of this perceptual categorization.

(b)   Filtering and pigeonholing

(i) Filtering

Basic TVA contains two mechanisms of selection: filtering and pigeonholing (cf. Broadbent 1970). The filtering mechanism is represented by perceptual processing priorities and attentional weights derived from processing priorities. Consider how the mechanism works. Suppose one searches for something that belongs to a particular category, say, something that is red. Selection of red elements in the visual field is favoured by letting the processing priority of the class of red elements be high. For, equation 4.2 implies that if the processing priority (the π-value) of red is increased, then the attentional weight of an element x gets an increment which is directly proportional to the strength of the sensory evidence that the element is red. Thus, if the priority of red is increased, then the attentional weights of those elements that are red increase in relation to the attentional weights of any other elements. By equation 4.1 this implies that the v-values for perceptual categorizations of red elements increase in relation to the v-values for perceptual categorizations of other elements. Thus, the processing of red elements is speeded up in relation to the processing of other elements so that the red ones get a higher probability of winning the processing race and becoming encoded into VSTM.

(ii) Pigeonholing

The pigeonholing mechanism is represented by perceptual bias parameters. Consider how the mechanism works. Suppose one wishes to categorize objects with respect to colour. One can prepare oneself for categorizing elements in the visual field with respect to colour by giving higher values to perceptual bias parameters associated with colour categories than to other perceptual bias parameters. For, equation 4.1 implies that if the perceptual bias parameter (the β-value) for a particular category is increased, the tendency to classify elements into that category gets stronger: The v-values for perceptual categorizations of elements as members of the category are increased, but other v-values are not affected.

(iii) Combined filtering and pigeonholing

Consider how filtering and pigeonholing can be combined. To be specific, consider a partial-report experiment. Let the stimulus displays consist of mixtures of red and black digits, and let the task be to report as many as possible of the red digits and ignore the black ones. A plausible strategy for doing this task is as follows. In order to select red rather than black elements, the processing priority of the class of red elements is set high, but other processing priorities are kept low. The effect is to speed up the processing of red elements in relation to the processing of black elements. In order to perceive the identity of the red digits rather than any other attributes of the elements, 10 perceptual bias parameters, one for each type of digit, are set high, but other perceptual bias parameters are kept low. The effect is to speed up the processing of categorizations with respect to digit types in relation to the processing of other categorizations. The combined effect of the adjustments of priority and bias parameters is to speed up the processing of categorizations of red elements with respect to digit types in relation to the processing of any other categorizations.

(iv) Processing priorities versus decision biases

Processing priorities (π-values) and decision biases (β-values) are different concepts. A perceptual system in which processing priorities can be varied independently of decision biases is inherently more powerful than a system in which the two are bound to covary (Bundesen 1990, pp. 525–6). For example, when the task is to report the identity of the red digits from a mixture of red and black digits, the ideal observer should set π high for red and β high for each of the 10 types of digits, but π-values for the 10 types of digits should be zero. When π is high for red but not for types of digits, then the attentional weights of the black digit distractors may be close to zero. But if π were high for both red and types of digits, performance should deteriorate because the black digit distractors would get appreciable attentional weights.

Consider the consequences of setting β high for red, when π is high for red. If both π and β are high for red, then any red element (relevant or irrelevant to the current task) will tend to be categorized with respect to colour and take up storage space in VSTM, regardless of whether the identity of the element has been determined. Because storage capacity is limited, this may be detrimental to performance. However, if the number of elements in the display is less than storage capacity K, then no loss should be incurred by letting β-values be high.

Basic TVA is neutral on whether all types of perceptual categories can be given positive-valued processing priorities (rather than having priority values fixed at zero). There is evidence to suggest that only a subset of the class of perceptual categories can have positive priorities. For example, both individual letters and short multiletter words are assumed to be perceptual categories, and both letters and words can be associated with positive biases (β-values). Furthermore, demonstrations of automatic attention attraction to particular types of individual letters (after extended consistent training in detecting these letters; cf. Shiffrin and Schneider 1977) suggest that individual letter types can be associated with positive processing priorities. However, a recent study by Bundesen *et al.* (1997) suggests that the initial allocation of attention to items in a visual display may be insensitive to words.

Bundesen *et al.* (1997) presented subjects with briefly exposed visual displays of words, which were short, common first names. In the main experiment, each display consisted of 4 words: 2 names shown in red and 2 shown in white. The subject's task was to report the red names (targets), but ignore the white ones (distractors). On some trials the subject's own name appeared as a display item (target or distractor). Presentation of the subject's name as a distractor caused no more interference with report of targets than did presentation of other names as distractors. Apparently, visual attention was not automatically attracted by the subject's own name.

If priority learning could occur for visual words, so that a visual word could attract attention automatically, one would expect a subject's attention to be attracted automatically by his or her own name (cf. Moray 1959). The contrast between findings with single letters and digits and findings with multiletter words suggests that visual attention can be attracted by individual alphanumeric characters, but not by shapes as complex as multiletter words. Multiletter words may be too complex in shape to have positive processing priorities.

(c) CTVA

Logan (1996) has proposed a theory that integrates space-based and object-based approaches to visual attention (see also Bundesen 1998; Logan and Bundesen 1996). The theory was made by linking TVA together with van Oeffelen and Vos' (1982, 1983) COntour DEtector (CODE) theory of perceptual grouping by proximity. The integrated theory is called the CODE Theory of Visual Attention (CTVA).

(i) Perceptual grouping

In the theory of van Oeffelen and Vos (1982, 1983), grouping by proximity is modeled as follows (see figure 4.1). First, each stimulus item is represented by a distribution centered on the position that the object occupies in one- or two-dimensional space. Van Oeffelen and Vos originally used normal distributions, but Compton and Logan (1993) found that Laplace distributions worked just as well. Thus, in the one-dimensional case (e.g., a linear array of items positioned along a u-axis),

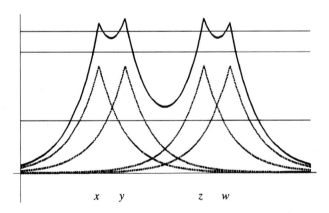

Fig. 4.1 Perceptual grouping by proximity. Laplace distributions (broken curves) and a CODE surface (solid curve) are shown for four items (x, y, z, and w) arrayed in one dimension. Thresholds applied to the CODE surface are shown by crossing horizontal lines. The low threshold includes all four items in one group. The middle threshold generates two groups with two items in each. The high threshold separates all four items.

item y may be represented by the Laplace distribution

$$f_y(u) = \tfrac{1}{2} \lambda_y \exp(-\lambda_y |u - \theta_y|) \qquad (4.3)$$

with scale parameter λ_y and position parameter θ_y. Second, a CODE surface is constructed by summing the distributions for different items over space, and a threshold is applied to the CODE surface, cutting off one or more above-threshold regions. A perceptual group is defined as an above-threshold region of space, that is, a region for which the code surface is above the threshold. In terms of TVA, a perceptual group is the same as an element in the visual field.

Groups of different sizes can be defined by raising and lowering the threshold. A low threshold produces a small number of groups with many items in each group. A high threshold produces a large number of groups with few items in each. The smaller groups are nested within the larger groups, so the grouping is hierarchical.

(ii) Spatial focusing

To link CODE to TVA, Logan (1996) assumed that the distribution for an item is a distribution of information about the features of the item. Thus, in equation 4.3, $f_y(u)$ is the density of information about features of y at spatial position u. Logan further assumed that TVA samples information from one or more above-threshold regions of the CODE surface and no information at all from the remaining regions. Here I propose a revision of this assumption.

At any point in time, there is a certain set of elements (above-threshold regions) in the visual field that forms the focus of attention, $\mathcal{F}$. The focus of attention is also called the field of spatial attention (cf. Logan and Bundesen 1996). Processing of elements in the focus of attention is faster than processing of elements outside the focus of attention, because effective η-values for elements in the focus of attention are greater than effective η-values for elements outside the focus of attention. Formally the effect of attentional focusing at $\mathcal{F}$ is to multiply η-values for any element x by an attenuation factor $a_\mathcal{F}(x)$ such that

$$a_\mathcal{F}(x) = \begin{cases} 1 & \text{if } x \in \mathcal{F} \\ k & \text{if } x \notin \mathcal{F}, \end{cases} \qquad (4.4)$$

where $0 \le k < 1$. If $a_\mathcal{F}(x) = 1$, processing of x is said to be unattenuated.

Spatial focusing of attention is assumed to be constrained as follows. First, the focus of attention, $\mathcal{F}$, can be widened to encompass all elements in the visual field. That is, $\mathcal{F}$ can be set equal to S.

Second, the focus of attention, $\mathcal{F}$, can be restricted to any element x found in VSTM. If $\mathcal{F}$ is restricted to x, and x is a group with several members, then the members of x are processed in parallel. Thus, when the focus of attention is directed to a particular perceptual group, a parallel search through the group is performed, and if focusing is strong (so that $a_\mathcal{F}(x) \approx 0$ for $x \notin \mathcal{F}$), then the search may occur without any noticeable effects of elements outside the focus of attention.

Finally, if a perceptual group x is found in VSTM, and element y is a member of the group, then the focus of attention, $\mathcal{F}$, can be narrowed down to element y. Thus, a serial search through a perceptual group x represented in VSTM can be performed by shifting $\mathcal{F}$ around among the members of the group. If the members of x themselves are perceptual groups with several members, then the search through x consists in a series of parallel searches through subsets of x.

(iii) Feature catch

The amount of information in a given above-threshold region of the CODE surface about a feature from a particular stimulus item is called the feature catch from that item in the given above-threshold region (see figure 4.2). It equals the area or volume of the distribution for the

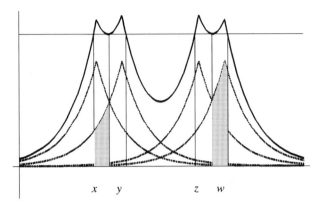

Fig. 4.2 Feature catch. Laplace distributions (broken curves) and a CODE surface (solid curve) are shown for items x, y, z, and w. A threshold (horizontal line) applied to the CODE surface generates four above-threshold regions (separated by vertical lines). The feature catch from item y in the above-threshold region formed by item x [i.e., $c(x, y)$] equals the shaded area to the left. The feature catch from item w in the above-threshold region formed by item w [i.e., $c(w, w)$] equals the shaded area to the right.

item that falls within the limits of the above-threshold region. The feature catch is positive for all items in the display, but it decreases as the spatial distance of the item from the given region is increased.

Suppose a threshold is applied to the CODE surface for a multi-element display so that each item in the display forms a separate above-threshold region. Let x and y be items in the display, that is, above-threshold regions of the CODE surface. The catch in the x region of features extracted from the y region, $c(x, y)$, is a measure of the likelihood of sampling features stemming from item y in the processing of item x. In the one-dimensional case,

$$c(x, y) = \int_{\text{region } x} f_y(u)\, du, \tag{4.5}$$

where $f_y(u)$ is given by equation 4.3, and the integration is done over the above-threshold region formed by item x (cf. figure 4.2).

(iv) Effective η-values

Both spatial focusing of attention and feature catch relations in the display modulate the information input to TVA. Formally this is represented by replacing η-values $\eta(x, i)$ by effective η-values $\eta_e(x, i)$ in equations 4.1 and 4.2 of TVA. The effective η-value for the categorization that item x is a member of category i (i.e., x has feature i) is given by

$$\eta_e(x, i) = a_{\mathcal{F}}(x) \sum_{y \in \mathcal{S}} c(x, y)\eta(y, i), \tag{4.6}$$

where $\mathcal{S}$ is the set of all items in the display, and $a_{\mathcal{F}}(x)$ and $c(x, y)$ are given by equations 4.4 and 4.5 respectively. By the summation in equation 4.6, the effective evidence that item x has feature i depends upon the evidence that item y has feature i to the extent that features stemming from item y are caught in the above-threshold region formed by item x.

Substituting $\eta_e(x, i)$ for $\eta(x, i)$ in equations 4.1 and 4.2 of TVA yields the CTVA equations

$$v(x, i) = \eta_e(x, i)\beta_i \frac{w_x}{\sum_{z \in \mathcal{S}} w_z} \tag{4.1'}$$

and

$$w_x = \sum_{j \in \mathcal{R}} \eta_e(x, j)\pi_j. \qquad (4.2')$$

Thus, CTVA becomes identical to TVA when $\eta_e(x, i) = \eta(x, i)$ for every element x and every perceptual category i. This is the case when (i) $\mathcal{F} = \mathcal{S}$ (i.e., the focus of attention coincides with the set of items in the display) and (ii) $c(x, x) = 1$ for every item x, but $c(x, y) = 0$ when x is different from y. For example, in many partial-report experiments, it seems plausible that (a) the focus of attention encompasses all items in the display and (b) interitem distances are so long that feature catches from adjacent items can be neglected. In such cases, an analysis based on CTVA reduces to an analysis based on TVA. Thus, CTVA can be viewed as a generalization of TVA, and TVA can be viewed as a special case of CTVA.

4.3   Applications I. Single-stimulus recognition

(a)   Biased-choice model

TVA has been applied to experimental findings from a broad range of paradigms concerned with single-stimulus recognition and selection from multi-element displays. For single-stimulus recognition, the theory provides a simple derivation of a classical model of effects of visual discriminability and bias: the biased-choice model of Luce (1963).

Consider a single-stimulus recognition experiment with n distinct stimuli and n appropriate responses, one for each stimulus. On each trial, one of the n stimuli is exposed, and the subject attempts to identify the stimulus by giving the appropriate response. The presentation of the stimulus continues until the subject responds. With a single element x in the visual field, equation 4.1 implies that for every perceptual category i,

$$v(x, i) = \eta(x, i)\beta_i.$$

Assume that η and β-values are constant during the period of stimulus exposure. Then the processing time of the perceptual categorization that x belongs to i is exponentially distributed with a rate parameter equal to the v-value, $v(x, i)$. Suppose the subject's choice among the n responses is based on the winner of the processing race between n corresponding perceptual categorizations, one for each response. Then the probability that the subject chooses the ith response can be written and rewritten as follows:

$$P = \int_0^\infty v(x, i) \exp[-v(x, i)t] \prod_{\substack{j=1 \\ j \neq i}}^n \exp[-v(x, j)t] \, dt$$

$$= \int_0^\infty v(x, i) \exp\left[-\sum_{j=1}^n v(x, j)t\right] dt$$

$$= \frac{v(x, i)}{\sum_{j=1}^n v(x, j)}$$

$$= \frac{\eta(x, i)\beta_i}{\sum_{j=1}^n \eta(x, j)\beta_j}.$$

The last expression for P is identical to the basic representation of choice probabilities in the biased-choice model of Luce (1963).

The biased-choice model has been successful in explaining many experimental findings on effects of visual discriminability and bias in single-stimulus recognition. For example, in a thorough test of 10 mathematical models of visual letter recognition against data from a letter confusion experiment, Townsend and Ashby (1982) found that the biased-choice model consistently provided the best fits.

(b)   Processing time distributions

The derivation of the biased-choice model presented above presupposes that v-values are constant during stimulus exposure, which means that processing times are exponentially distributed. The biased-choice model can also be derived on the weaker assumption that the v-values are mutually proportional functions of time (cf. Bundesen 1990, footnote 4; Bundesen 1993). However, the available evidence suggests that the strong assumption that v-values are constant during stimulus exposure is true to a first approximation.

To test the assumption that v-values are constant over time, Lisbeth Harms and I investigated single-letter recognition as a function of the exposure duration of the stimulus. Our subjects were presented with one stimulus letter (a randomly chosen consonant) on each trial. The letter appeared at one of 12 equiprobable positions that were equally spaced around the circumference of an imaginary circle centred on fixation. Exposure duration was varied from 10 ms up to 200 ms, and the stimulus was followed by a pattern mask. The subject's task was to report the identity of the stimulus letter, but refrain from guessing.

Figure 4.3 shows the observed proportion of correct reports as a function of the exposure duration of the stimulus letter for each of the 3 subjects. Smooth curves show least squares fits to the data by the exponential distribution function

$$F(t) = \begin{cases} 0 & \text{for } t < t_0 \\ 1 - \exp[-v * (t - t_0)] & \text{for } t \geq t_0, \end{cases}$$

where $F(t)$ is the probability that the stimulus is correctly identified as a function of exposure duration t, parameter v is the constant v-value of the correct categorization of the stimulus, and parameter t_0 is the minimum effective exposure duration. As can be seen, the exponential distribution function provided reasonable approximations to the data.

4.4   Applications II. Selection from multi-element displays

(a)   Applications of TVA

Bundesen (1990) applied TVA to experimental findings from a broad range of paradigms stemming from a number of different research traditions. The findings included effects of object integrality in selective report (e.g., Duncan 1984), number and spatial position of targets in studies of divided attention (Posner *et al.* 1978; Sperling 1960, 1967; van der Heijden *et al.* 1983), selection criterion and number of distractors in studies of focused attention (Estes and Taylor 1964; Treisman and Gelade 1980; Treisman and Gormican 1988), joint effects of numbers of targets and distractors in partial report (Bundesen *et al.* 1984; Bundesen *et al.* 1985; Shibuya and Bundesen 1988), and consistent practice in search (Schneider and Fisk 1982). Two of these applications are described below.

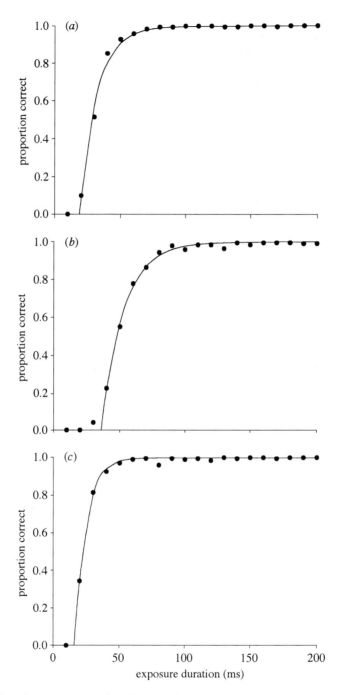

Fig. 4.3 Proportion of correct reports of the identity of a single, postmasked stimulus letter as a function of the exposure duration of the letter. (Individual data for 3 subjects: Subjects EA [top panel], MK [middle panel], and AO [bottom panel]. Theoretical fits are indicated by smooth curves.)

(i) Partial report

Shibuya and Bundesen's (1988) fixed-capacity independent race model (FIRM) for selection from multi-element displays can be derived as a special case of TVA. Basically, the notion of a fixed processing capacity (C) can be derived from the normalization of attentional weights assumed in equation 4.1 (see Bundesen 1990, pp. 524–5). The remaining parameters of FIRM are the storage capacity of VSTM (K), the ratio between the attentional weight of a distractor and the attentional weight of a target (α), and the minimum effective exposure duration (t_0).

Although FIRM has only four free parameters (C, K, α, and t_0), the model has provided highly accurate accounts of effects of the number of targets, the number of distractors, and the exposure duration on the number of targets that can be reported from briefly presented displays. To illustrate, figure 4.4 shows a fit to observed frequency distributions of scores for a subject tested by Shibuya and Bundesen (1988). The subject was required to report as many digits as possible from briefly presented mixtures of digits (targets) and letters (distractors) followed by pattern masks. Let F_j ($j = 1, 2, \ldots$) be the relative frequency of scores of j or more (correctly reported targets). Each panel in the figure shows F_1, F_2, etc., as functions of exposure duration for a given combination of number of targets T and number of distractors D. Hence, within each panel, the distance in the direction of the ordinate between 1 and F_1 equals the relative frequency

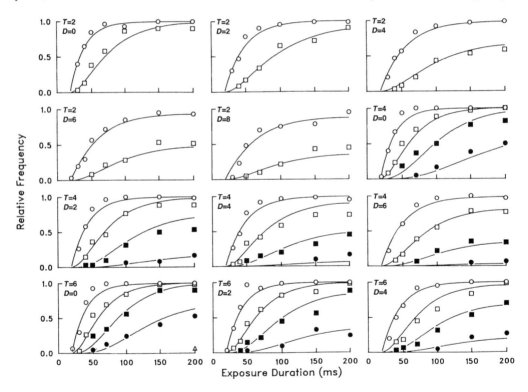

Fig. 4.4 Relative frequency of scores of j or more (correctly reported targets) as a function of exposure duration with j, number of targets T, and number of distractors D as parameters in the experiment of Shibuya and Bundesen (1988). (Data for Subject MP. Parameter j varies within panels; j is 1 [open circles], 2 [open squares], 3 [solid squares], 4 [solid circles], or 5 [triangle]. T and D vary between panels; their values are indicated on the figure. Smooth curves represent a theoretical fit to the data. For clarity, observed frequencies less than 0.02 are omitted from the figure. From Shibuya and Bundesen (1988, p. 595). Copyright 1988 by the American Psychological Association.)

of scores of exactly 0, the distance between F_1 and F_2 equals the frequency of scores of exactly 1, and so on. The theoretical fit is shown by smooth curves, which were generated by FIRM with processing capacity C at 49 elements per second, storage capacity K at 3.7 elements, weight ratio α at 0.40, and minimum effective exposure duration t_0 at 19 ms.

(ii) One-view search

Figure 4.5 illustrates an application of TVA to a case of highly efficient visual search studied by Treisman and Gelade (1980, Experiment 1, feature search condition). In this case, subjects searched for a target that was equally likely to be a blue element (a blue T or a blue X) or an S (a brown S or a green S). The distractors were brown Ts and green Xs, and the display was exposed until a positive ('target present') or negative ('target absent') response was made.

The reaction time data in figure 4.5 are fitted by two straight lines, one for positive and one for negative responses. The fit was made on the assumption that positive responses were based on positive categorizations, whereas negative responses were made by default when a temporal deadline d was reached, but no positive categorization had been made (deadline model of one-view search). A positive categorization was assumed to be a categorization of the form 'x is blue' or 'x is an S', and processing priorities (π-values) and decision biases (β-values) were assumed to be high for blue and S, but low for any other perceptual categories.

For any deadline d, there is a certain probability r of missing a target, because the deadline may be reached before a positive categorization has been made even if a target is present in the display. Consistent with error rates observed by Treisman and Gelade, the deadline d was assumed to increase with display size in such a way that the miss rate r was kept constant.

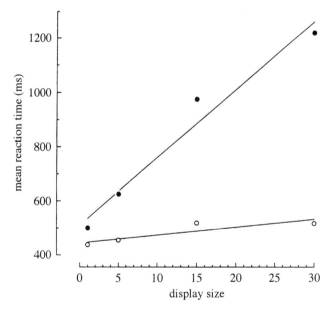

Fig. 4.5 Positive and negative mean reaction times as functions of display size in feature search condition of Treisman and Gelade (1980, Experiment 1). (Group data for 6 subjects. Positive reaction times are shown by open circles, negative reaction times by solid circles. A theoretical fit is indicated by unmarked points connected with straight lines. The observed data are from Treisman and Gelade (1980, p. 104). The figure is from Bundesen (1990, p. 535). Copyright 1990 by the American Psychological Association.)

The assumptions left four free parameters: r, the ratio α/C, a positive base reaction time a, and a negative base reaction time b (cf. Bundesen 1990, pp. 534–5). The least squares fit shown in figure 4.5 was obtained with r at 0.0002, α/C at 2.93 ms, a at 448 ms, and b at 536 ms. The estimate for α/C seems plausible; it is consistent with a hypothesis that, say, $C = 49$ elements/s (as in the fit shown in figure 4.4) and $\alpha = 0.14$.

(b)   Applications of CTVA

(i)   Spatial effects

Logan (1996) applied CTVA to many findings of effects of perceptual grouping and spatial distance between items on reaction times and error rates in visual attention tasks. The findings included effects of grouping (Prinzmetal 1981) and effects of distance between items (Cohen and Ivry 1989) on occurrence of illusory conjunctions, effects of grouping (Banks and Prinzmetal 1976) and effects of distance between items (Cohen and Ivry 1991) in visual search, and effects of distance between target and distractors in the flankers task (Eriksen and Eriksen 1974). Effects of distance between items on occurrence of illusory conjunctions and effects of distance in the flankers task were explained by the assumption that the feature catch factor for a particular item in a region around another one increases if the distance between the two items is decreased. The finding that conjunction search is slowed down when distances between items are decreased was explained by assuming that the threshold applied to the CODE surface is raised in order to prevent formation of illusory conjunctions when distances between items are decreased.

Logan and Bundesen (1996) reanalysed the data of Mewhort et al. (1981) on location errors in the bar-probe partial-report task introduced by Averbach and Coriell (1961). In this task, the subject is presented with an array of items and instructed to report a single one, which is the item adjacent to a bar marker (probe). A response is required on each trial. When the bar probe is presented at various delays relative to the array, decay functions similar to those observed in the partial-report paradigm of Sperling (1960) are observed.

Mewhort et al. (1981) distinguished correct reports from two types of errors: location errors in which the subject reports a distractor that has been presented in the array and item errors in which the subject reports an item that has not been presented in the array. In the standard Averbach and Coriell condition, Mewhort et al. found a nearly perfect trade-off between correct reports and location errors. As probe delay increased, the frequency of correct reports decreased, but the frequency of location errors increased in a compensatory fashion. Thus, the frequency of item errors remained nearly constant over probe delays. Mewhort et al. also analysed the spatial distribution of location errors and found that they primarily came from items immediately adjacent to the target. These results led Mewhort et al. to conclude that decay in sensory memory (iconic memory; Neisser 1967) after the offset of a stimulus display is a decay of location information rather than item information.

According to the reanalysis by Logan and Bundesen (1996), attention is spread evenly over the stimulus array until the bar probe is presented (i.e., all items in the array have the same attentional weight). When attention is reallocated in response to the probe, all attentional weight is concentrated on the target (i.e., attentional weights of distractors are set to zero). Processing of the target is speeded up once attention is concentrated on the target, so the frequency of correct reports is inversely related to probe delay. Also, the longer the time that the array is processed with equal attention to each item and the shorter the time the array is processed with attention concentrated on the target, the greater the probability that VSTM will contain distractors from the array without containing the target. Hence, assuming that distractor items in VSTM are reported with greater probability than items not in VSTM, the frequency of location errors must increase with probe delay. Thus, the trade-off between correct reports and location errors found by Mewhort *et al.* is perfectly compatible with the traditional assumption that sensory memory decay reflects the loss of item information rather than the loss of location information proposed by Mewhort *et al.*

The finding that location errors primarily come from items immediately adjacent to the target was also explained by CTVA. The finding is predicted by the assumption that attention is focused on an above-threshold region of the CODE surface at the location of the target, where feature catch factors are particularly high for items adjacent to the target.

Logan and Bundesen (1996) presented detailed quantitative fits of CTVA to the data of Mewhort *et al.* (1981). Other spatial effects in the partial-report paradigm were explained at a qualitative level. These effects included Snyder's (1972) finding that errors in a single-target partial-report task with selection based on colour were likely to be correct reports of items adjacent to the target; Fryklund's (1975) finding that performance in a multitarget partial-report task was better when the targets were clustered together than when they were spread at random throughout the display; and Merikle's (1980) finding that performance in a multitarget partial-report task was better when the targets formed a row than a column if the display was organized (by proximity) as a set of rows, whereas performance was better when the targets formed a column than a row if the display was organized as a set of columns. The findings of Fryklund (1975) and Merikle (1980) were explained by noting that in CTVA, intrusions from near neighbours on the feature catch of an attended target tend to generate correct reports when the near neighbours are targets, but errors when the near neighbours are distractors.

(ii) Many-view search

Many experiments on visual search have yielded positive and negative mean reaction times that are essentially linear functions of display size with a positive-to-negative slope ratio of about $1:2$ (cf. Grossberg *et al.* 1994). For example, in Experiment 1 of Treisman and Gelade (1980), conjunction search for a green T among brown Ts and green Xs generated a positive reaction time function with a slope constant of 29 ms per item, a negative reaction time function with a slope constant of 67 ms per item, and a slope ratio of 0.43. In Experiment 2 of Treisman and Gelade (1980), search for a red O among green Os and red Ns generated a positive reaction time function with a slope constant of 21 ms per item, a negative function with a slope constant of 40 ms per item, and a slope ratio of 0.52. Nearly the same positive and negative slope constants and a slope ratio of 0.53 were found by Treisman and Gormican (1988) as means across 37 conditions of feature search with low target–distractor discriminability.

Wolfe (1994) and his associates examined 708 sets of positive (target present) and negative (target absent) search slopes from subjects tested on a wide variety of different search tasks in their laboratory. Among these 708 sets, 167 had positive slopes greater than 20 ms per item. This subset showed a (harmonic) mean positive-to-negative slope ratio of 0.50. Another 187 had positive slopes less than 5 ms per item. For this subset, the (harmonic) mean positive-to-negative slope ratio was 0.53.

The pattern of approximately linear reaction time functions with positive-to-negative slope ratios of about $1:2$ suggests search with (overt or covert) reallocation of attention (many-view search). The pattern conforms to predictions from simple self-terminating serial models in which attention is shifted from element to element until a target has been found (respond present) or the display has been searched exhaustively, but no target has been found (respond absent; cf. Treisman and Gelade 1980). The pattern also conforms to predictions from the assumption that attention is shifted among groups (subsets) of elements in the display so that processing is parallel within groups but serial between groups, and shifting is random (blind) with respect to the distinction between target and distractors (cf. Pashler 1987; Treisman and Gormican 1988; also see Bundesen and Pedersen 1983; Duncan and Humphreys 1989; Treisman 1982). (The guided search model of Wolfe *et al.* (1989) and Cave and Wolfe (1990) predicts slow serial search with a 1 : 2 slope ratio when activations caused by targets and distractors are identically distributed so that the serial order in which items are scanned is independent of their status as targets compared with distractors. However, when target activations are stronger than distractor activations, search is guided by the activations so that any target in the stimulus display is likely to be among the first items that are scanned. Thus, when search becomes guided, both the positive search slope and the positive-to-negative slope ratio should decrease. The results of Wolfe's (1994) study of 708 sets of search slopes went counter to this prediction. To accommodate the results, Wolfe (1994) suggested a modification of the guided search model based on the assumption that as signal strength increases, the mean of the distribution of target activations increases, but the standard deviation of the distribution decreases (an inverted Weber's law).)

In TVA, reallocation of attention is assumed to be slow, but serial search through a display should occur when the time cost of shifting (reallocating) attention is outweighed by gain in speed of processing once attention has been shifted (cf. Bundesen 1990, pp. 536–7). Serial search is based on selection by location. Specifically, serial search is performed by first using a spatial selection criterion for sampling elements from one part of the display, then (with or without eye movements) shifting the selection criterion to sample elements from another part of the display, and so on, until a target has been found or the entire display has been searched exhaustively.

CTVA also assumes that serial search is based on selection by location, but in CTVA selection by location is 'special' (cf. Nissen 1985; also see Bundesen 1991). Selection by criteria other than location must be done by filtering, that is, by raising the processing priority (say, π_j) of the class of elements to be selected. By equations 4.2 and 4.2', the attentional weight of an element is a sum of weight components, one for each perceptual category, and the effect of increasing π_j is to increment the weight component that corresponds to category j. The summation (addition) of weight components permits efficient search for feature disjunctions (e.g. search for elements that are blue or *S*-shaped; Treisman and Gelade 1980, Experiment 1), but not for conjunctions.

By contrast, selection by location can be done by spatial focusing, that is, by restricting the focus of attention $\mathcal{F}$ to a perceptual group at the target location. The effect is to attenuate effective η-values for elements outside the target location by multiplication with a factor $k < 1$. If $k \approx 0$, and if feature catches from elements outside the target location are negligible, then a parallel search through the members of the perceptual group at the target location should be just as efficient as it would have been if no elements had been presented outside the target location.

Thus, in CTVA, a parallel search for a target defined by a feature, f, can be restricted to a perceptual group at a certain location with no loss in efficiency. If the perceptual group is the set of elements with feature g, then the process as a whole is a search for a feature conjunction of f and g (for examples, see Egeth *et al.* 1984; Kaptein *et al.* 1995).

If target–distractor discriminability is high with respect to feature f, and the processing priority (π-value) is high for feature f, and only for feature f, then the distractor-to-target weight ratio α must be low. In this case, the perceptual group can be rapidly searched for an element with feature f by processing the group in parallel in accordance with the deadline model of one-view search. When processing is done in accordance with the deadline model, the time taken to process the perceptual group varies directly with weight ratio α (cf. Bundesen 1990, pp. 534–5). In the limiting case in which $\alpha = 0$, the search time is independent of the number of elements in the search set. Hence, if feature g defines a strong perceptual group, and detection of feature f is easy ($\alpha \approx 0$), then search for a conjunction of f and g should show little effect of display size (for examples of fast conjunction search, see Nakayama and Silverman 1986; Wolfe *et al.* 1989).

Our considerations of the implications of CTVA suggest a simple explanation for the frequently observed pattern of positive and negative search reaction times that are essentially linear functions of display size with a wide range of slopes but positive-to-negative slope ratios of 1 : 2. Such search functions can be explained by assuming that the stimulus displays are processed by shifting the focus of attention $\mathcal{F}$ among groups of elements so that processing is parallel within groups but serial between groups. The parallel processing of members of the same group can be done in accordance with the deadline model of one-view search, so that the time taken to process a group varies with target-distractor discriminability. But the shifting among groups is random (blind) with respect to the distinction between target and distractors, and it is this randomness that generates the 1 : 2 slope ratios.

4.5 Concluding remarks

TVA (Bundesen 1990) provides a unified account of single-stimulus recognition and selection from multi-element displays. It integrates the biased-choice model for single-stimulus recognition (Luce 1963) with the fixed-capacity independent race model for selection from multi-element displays (Shibuya and Bundesen 1988). Mathematically the theory is tractable, and it organizes a large body of experimental findings on performance in visual recognition and attention tasks. CTVA (Logan 1996) combines TVA with a theory of perceptual grouping by proximity (van Oeffelen and Vos 1982). The combined theory explains a wide range of effects of perceptual grouping and spatial distance between items on performance in attention tasks. It also provides a useful framework for describing visual search as an interplay between serial and parallel processes.

Acknowledgements

The reported research was supported by grants from the Danish Ministry of Education and Research and the International Human Frontier Science Program Organization. Thanks are due to Jon Driver and John Duncan for constructive comments on the draft.

References

Averbach, E. and Coriell, A. S. 1961 Short-term memory in vision. *Bell System Technical Journal* **40**, 309–28.

Banks, W. P. and Prinzmetal, W. 1976 Configurational effects in visual information processing. *Perception and Psychophysics* **19**, 361–7.

Broadbent, D. E. 1970 Stimulus set and response set: Two kinds of selective attention. In D. I. Mostofsky (ed.), *Attention: contemporary theory and analysis* (pp. 51–60). New York: Appleton-Century-Crofts.

Bundesen, C. 1987 Visual attention: Race models for selection from multielement displays. *Psychological Research* **49**, 113–21.

Bundesen, C. 1990 A theory of visual attention. *Psychological Review* **97**, 523–47.

Bundesen, C. 1991 Visual selection of features and objects: Is location special? A reinterpretation of Nissen's (1985) findings. *Perception and Psychophysics* **50**, 87–9.

Bundesen, C. 1993 The relationship between independent race models and Luce's choice axiom. *Journal of Mathematical Psychology* **37**, 446–71.

Bundesen, C. 1996 Formal models of visual attention: A tutorial review. In A. F. Kramer, M. G. H. Coles and G. D. Logan (eds), *Converging operations in the study of visual selective attention* (pp. 1–43). Washington, D.C.: American Psychological Association.

Bundesen, C. 1998 Visual selective attention: Outlines of a choice model, a race model and a computational theory. *Visual Cognition* **5**, 287–309.

Bundesen, C. and Pedersen, L. F. 1983 Color segregation and visual search. *Perception and Psychophysics*, **33**, 487–93.

Bundesen, C., Pedersen, L. F. and Larsen, A. 1984 Measuring efficiency of selection from briefly exposed visual displays: A model for partial report. *Journal of Experimental Psychology: Human Perception and Performance* **10**, 329–39.

Bundesen, C., Shibuya, H. and Larsen, A. 1985 Visual selection from multielement displays: A model for partial report. In M. I. Posner and O. S. M. Marin (eds), *Attention and performance XI* (pp. 631–49). Hillsdale, NJ: Lawrence Erlbaum.

Bundesen, C., Kyllingsbæk, S., Houmann, K. J. and Jensen, R. M. 1997 Is visual attention automatically attracted by one's own name? *Perception and Psychophysics* **59**, 714–20.

Cave, K. R. and Wolfe, J. M. 1990 Modeling the role of parallel processing in visual search. *Cognitive Psychology* **22**, 225–71.

Cohen, A. and Ivry, R. 1989 Illusory conjunctions inside and outside the focus of attention. *Journal of Experimental Psychology: Human Perception and Performance* **15**, 650–63.

Cohen, A. and Ivry, R. B. 1991 Density effects in conjunction search: Evidence for a coarse location mechanism of feature integration. *Journal of Experimental Psychology: Human Perception and Performance* **17**, 891–901.

Compton, B. J. and Logan, G. D. 1993 Evaluating a computational model of perceptual grouping by proximity. *Perception and Psychophysics* **53**, 403–21.

Duncan, J. 1984 Selective attention and the organization of visual information. *Journal of Experimental Psychology: General* **113**, 501–17.

Duncan, J. and Humphreys, G. W. 1989 Visual search and stimulus similarity. *Psychological Review* **96**, 433–58.

Egeth, H. E., Virzi, R. A. and Garbart, H. 1984 Searching for conjunctively defined targets. *Journal of Experimental Psychology: Human Perception and Performance* **10**, 32–9.

Eriksen, B. A. and Eriksen, C. W. 1974 Effects of noise letters upon the identification of a target letter in a nonsearch task. *Perception and Psychophysics* **16**, 143–9.

Estes, W. K. and Taylor, H. A. 1964 A detection method and probabilistic models for assessing information processing from brief visual displays. *Proceedings of the National Academy of Sciences, USA* **52**, 446–54.

Fryklund, I. 1975 Effects of cued-set spatial arrangement and target-background similarity in the partial-report paradigm. *Perception and Psychophysics* **17**, 375–86.

Grossberg, S., Mingolla, E. and Ross, W. D. 1994 A neural theory of attentive visual search: Interactions of boundary, surface, spatial, and object representations. *Psychological Review* **101**, 470–89.

Kaptein, N. A., Theeuwes, J. and van der Heijden, A. H. C. 1995 Search for a conjunctively defined target can be selectively limited to a color-defined subset of elements. *Journal of Experimental Psychology: Human Perception and Performance* **21**, 1053–69.

Logan, G. D. 1996 The CODE theory of visual attention: An integration of space-based and object-based attention. *Psychological Review* **103**, 603–49.

Logan, G. D. and Bundesen, C. 1996 Spatial effects in the partial report paradigm: A challenge for theories of visual spatial attention. In D. L. Medin (ed.), *The psychology of learning and motivation* (Vol. 35, pp. 243–82). San Diego, CA: Academic Press.

Luce, R. D. 1963 Detection and recognition. In R. D. Luce, R. R. Bush and E. Galanter (eds), *Handbook of mathematical psychology* (Vol. 1, pp. 103–89). New York: Wiley.

Luck, S. J and Vogel, E. K. 1997 The capacity of visual working memory for features and conjunctions. *Nature* **390**, 279–81.

Merikle, P. M. 1980 Selection from visual persistence by perceptual groups and category membership. *Journal of Experimental Psychology: General* **109**, 279–95.

Mewhort, D. J. K., Campbell, A. J., Marchetti, F. M. and Campbell, J. I. D. 1981 Identification, localization, and 'iconic memory': An evaluation of the bar probe task. *Memory and Cognition* **9**, 50–67.

Moray, N. 1959 Attention in dichotic listening: Affective cues and the influence of instructions. *Quarterly Journal of Experimental Psychology* **11**, 56–60.

Nakayama, K. and Silverman, G. H. 1986 Serial and parallel processing of visual feature conjunctions. *Nature* **320**, 264–5.

Neisser, U. 1967 *Cognitive psychology*. New York: Appleton-Century-Crofts.

Nissen, M. J. 1985 Accessing features and objects: Is location special? In M. I. Posner and O. S. M. Marin (eds), *Attention and performance XI* (pp. 205–19). Hillsdale, NJ: Lawrence Erlbaum.

Pashler, H. 1987 Detecting conjunctions of color and form: Reassessing the serial search hypothesis. *Perception and Psychophysics* **41**, 191–201.

Posner, M. I., Nissen, M. J. and Ogden, W. C. 1978 Attended and unattended processing modes: The role of set for spatial location. In H. L. Pick and E. Saltzman (eds), *Modes of perceiving and processing information* (pp. 137–57). Hillsdale, NJ: Lawrence Erlbaum.

Prinzmetal, W. 1981 Principles of feature integration in visual perception. *Perception and Psychophysics* **30**, 330–40.

Schneider, W. and Fisk, A. D. 1982 Degree of consistent training: Improvements in search performance and automatic process development. *Perception and Psychophysics* **31**, 160–8.

Shibuya, H. and Bundesen, C. 1988 Visual selection from multielement displays: Measuring and modeling effects of exposure duration. *Journal of Experimental Psychology: Human Perception and Performance* **14**, 591–600.

Shiffrin, R. M. and Schneider, W. 1977 Controlled and automatic human information processing: II. Perceptual learning, automatic attending, and a general theory. *Psychological Review* **84**, 127–90.

Snyder, C. R. R. 1972 Selection, inspection, and naming in visual search. *Journal of Experimental Psychology* **92**, 428–31.

Sperling, G. 1960 The information available in brief visual presentations. *Psychological Monographs* **74** (11, Whole No. 498).

Sperling, G. 1967 Successive approximations to a model for short-term memory. *Acta Psychologica* **27**, 285–92.

Townsend, J. T. and Ashby, F. G. 1982 Experimental test of contemporary mathematical models of visual letter recognition. *Journal of Experimental Psychology: Human Perception and Performance* **8**, 834–64.

Treisman, A. M. 1982 Perceptual grouping and attention in visual search for features and for objects. *Journal of Experimental Psychology: Human Perception and Performance* **8**, 194–214.

Treisman, A. M. and Gelade, G. 1980 A feature-integration theory of attention. *Cognitive Psychology* **12**, 97–136.

Treisman, A. M. and Gormican, S. 1988 Feature analysis in early vision: Evidence from search asymmetries. *Psychological Review* **95**, 15–48.

van der Heijden, A. H. C., La Heij, W. and Boer, J. P. A. 1983 Parallel processing of redundant targets in simple visual search tasks. *Psychological Research* **45**, 235–54.

van Oeffelen, M. P. and Vos, P. G. 1982 Configurational effects on the enumeration of dots: Counting by groups. *Memory and Cognition* **10**, 396–404.

van Oeffelen, M. P. and Vos, P. G. 1983 An algorithm for pattern description on the level of relative proximity. *Pattern Recognition* **16**, 341–8.

Wolfe, J. M. 1994 Guided search 2.0: A revised model of visual search. *Psychonomic Bulletin and Review* **1**, 202–38.

Wolfe, J. M., Cave, K. R. and Franzel, S. L. 1989 Guided search: An alternative to the feature integration model for visual search. *Journal of Experimental Psychology: Human Perception and Performance* **15**, 419–33.

5

How do we select perceptions and actions? Human brain imaging studies

Geraint Rees and Christopher D. Frith

Abstract

The selective nature of human perception and action implies a modulatory interaction between sensorimotor processes and attentional processes. This chapter explores the use of functional imaging in humans to explore the mechanisms of perceptual selection and the fate of irrelevant stimuli that are not selected. Experiments with positron emission tomography show that two qualitatively different patterns of modulation of cerebral blood flow can be observed in experiments where non-spatial visual attention and auditory attention are manipulated. These patterns of modulation of cerebral blood flow modulation can be described as gain control and bias signal mechanisms. In visual and auditory cortex, the dominant change in cerebral blood flow associated with attention to either modality is related to a bias signal. The relation of these patterns of modulation to attentional effects that have been observed in single neurons is discussed. The existence of mechanisms for selective perception raises the more general question of whether irrelevant ignored stimuli are nevertheless perceived. Lavie's theory of attention proposes that the degree to which ignored stimuli are processed varies depending on the perceptual load of the current task. Evidence from behavioural and functional magnetic resonance imaging studies of ignored, visual-motion processing is presented in support of this proposal.

5.1 Introduction

Humans have a remarkable ability to attend selectively to one out of many competing streams of information (Cherry 1957; Broadbent 1958). Selection of a stream can be made not only on the basis of modality, but also within a single modality. Furthermore, subjects can attend to a subset of information within a single stream. Such a process, of selecting from among many incident stimuli, is the clearest manifestation of selective attention. This paper will discuss the nature of attentional selection; in particular, the neural mechanisms underlying selective processing and the fate of rejected stimuli. Initially we present a selective review of neurophysiological studies suggesting that there are two different types of extra-retinal signal involved in selection in the visual modality. We then describe functional imaging experiments in humans that suggest that changes in regional cerebral blood flow (rCBF) follow a similar pattern. Finally we discuss recent functional imaging evidence that the degree to which rejected stimuli are nevertheless processed depends on attentional load.

5.2 Mechanisms of selection

(a) Single neuron

Moran and Desimone (1985) investigated whether responses of single cells in visual areas differed depending on whether or not a monkey was attending to a stimulus. In primary visual cortex, there was no difference, but in area V4 the response to an irrelevant stimulus was reduced by about two-thirds. Furthermore, this attenuation only occurred when both attended and unattended stimuli were located simultaneously within the receptive field (RF) of the neuron. When the unattended stimulus was outside the receptive field and the attended stimulus inside it, no modulation of neural responses was observed. In inferotemporal cortex (IT), attenuation was always observed, as the receptive fields in this area are large and cover most of the visual field. The effects of attention are invariably seen when both relevant and irrelevant stimuli are presented simultaneously, but effects are also seen when stimuli are presented sequentially, suggesting that competition takes place in both space and time (Luck *et al.* 1997). Desimone and Duncan (1995) argued that these findings were compatible with a 'biased competition' model of attention, where objects in the visual field compete for processing at the receptive field level. The role of top-down selective influences is to bias the processing at a cellular level towards one stimulus or the other. The results of Moran and Desimone (1985) are consistent with this as they show that attention only has an effect when relevant and irrelevant stimuli are competing for the cell's response. According to the 'biased competition' model, perceptual selection is a two-stage process (Desimone and Duncan 1995). Initially, top-down signals bias activity in neurons representing the relevant object or location. Consistent with this, elevations of baseline firing rates are seen in V4 neurons whenever attention is directed towards their receptive field (Luck *et al.* 1997); similarly in IT, neurons show elevated activity in the delay period of a delayed match-to-sample task (Chelazzi *et al.* 1993). These findings are consistent with an extrinsic 'bias' signal. In the second stage of perceptual selection, neurons that have received a bias signal gain an advantage in their competitive interactions (mediated through local intrinsic connections) with other neurons. Consistent with this, attention to non-spatial features of objects influences not only baseline (spontaneous) firing rates but also modulates stimulus-evoked responses (Haenny *et al.* 1988; Ferrera *et al.* 1994; Luck *et al.* 1997). Thus it seems that there are at least two different mechanisms at a single-cell level that might mediate selective attention. In visual cortex, elevations in baseline firing rate and modulation of stimulus-evoked activity are two mechanisms that appear to operate.

(b)   Electrophysiological

Electrophysiological studies in humans are discussed elsewhere in this volume (Hillyard *et al.*, this volume) and will not be reviewed in detail. The most important finding from event-related potential (ERP) studies is that components arising very soon after the presentation of a stimulus clearly differ as a function of whether the stimulus is attended or ignored (Hillyard *et al.* 1995). The visually evoked component P1 is smaller when a stimulus is ignored because of its location. When selection is based on stimulus attributes other than location, such as colour, an additional component is superimposed on the N1 and P1. This colour selection component is substantially reduced when the stimulus is in an ignored spatial location, suggesting that the location and colour selection are organized hierarchically with location-selection dominant (Mangun *et al.* 1993). The location of the generators of these components in early sensory processing areas suggests that the mechanism of selection not only operates very soon after stimulus presentation but also very early in the anatomical hierarchy of processing areas (Woldorff *et al.* 1993). It is difficult to relate these ERP findings to the single cell data, because stimuli in ERP studies are frequently presented alone to aid interpretation of the resultant waveforms. Furthermore, where ERP attention effects have been seen as a function of competition between relevant and irrelevant stimuli, the stimulus conditions have never led to the simultaneous presence of attended and ignored stimuli inside a single receptive field in extrastriate cortex.

(c)   Functional imaging

In humans, functional imaging studies have shown that attention to different attributes of visually presented stimuli changes evoked activity in areas of cortex concerned with processing those attributes. For example, attention to the colour of visual stimuli changes evoked activity in cortical area V4, compared with attention to the motion of identical visual stimuli (Corbetta *et al.* 1990,

1991). Similarly, attention to visual motion modulates the stimulus-evoked activity in cortical area V5 (Büchel and Friston 1997; O'Craven *et al.* 1997). These functional imaging experiments have demonstrated the general principle that attention modulates functionally segregated and stimulus-specific regions of visual cortex, but have not provided any insight into the mechanism of such processes. The reason for this lies in the experimental design; typically, investigators have compared a state where the subject attends to a certain aspect of a display with a state where the subject receives identical visual stimulation but does not attend. The difference in activity between these two states has been attributed to the effects of attention. However in light of the preceding discussion it can be seen that such a difference between 'attend' and 'no attend' conditions necessarily conflates both additive and interactive (stimulus-evoked) components of attention. Intuitively this can be seen by imagining doing the experiment again but without using a stimulus. Would comparing 'attend' and 'no attend' reveal a difference in evoked activity (that could be produced by a change in baseline firing rates or bias signal), or is such a difference contingent on stimulus-evoked activity (a true modulatory effect of attention)? Such a thought experiment serves to illustrate the theoretical point that to characterize the effects of attention by using functional imaging requires an experimental manipulation of stimulus-evoked activity that is independent of the experimental manipulation of attention. The independent manipulation of attention and stimulus-evoked activity allows the separate characterization of attentional effects owing to modulation of the stimulus-evoked activity *per se*, or owing simply to changes in baseline activity independently of that evoked by the stimulus. Note that the requirement for a measure of stimulus-evoked activity independent of the attentional manipulation is largely a consequence of the time over which functional imaging measurements are acquired (of the order of seconds) relative to the time-scale over which the neuronal effects are manifest (of the order of milliseconds). This means that in any given trial, both stimulus-evoked activity and baseline activity are lumped together. To separate the effects of attention on each requires some independent manipulation of stimulus-evoked activity.

Frith and Friston (1996) proposed that such an independent measure of stimulus-evoked activity might be elicited by varying the rate of presentation of visual and auditory stimuli. The basis for this proposal is the observation that cerebral blood flow in primary sensory, primary motor and higher order association cortices increases with increasing stimulus presentation (Price *et al.* 1992; Frith and Friston 1996; Rees *et al.* 1997c; Sadato *et al.* 1997). The most likely interpretation of these results is that each stimulus produces a transient increase in blood flow such that the total increase in blood flow is directly related to the number of stimuli presented during the scan. This means that the slope of the line relating activity to presentation rate is an index of the amount of transient activity associated with the presentation of a single stimulus. Attention can now be investigated by studying how the slope or intercept of this line varies with the direction of attention (figure 5.1; also see plate section). A change in slope implies a true modulatory effect of attention; the amount of activity associated with each stimulus presentation is directly changed. On the other hand, a change in intercept implies that the activity associated with each stimulus presentation is unchanged, but instead a 'bias' signal, constant across different presentation rates, is added. This pattern implies that there may be activity in an area even in the absence of stimulus presentation.

The approach outlined here relies on measuring the relation between rCBF and a stimulus variable (presentation rate), and then examining how a manipulation of attention changes this relation. Certain assumptions are implicit in this approach that should be made clear. Most impor-tantly, the assumption is made that within an area, the gain control or bias signal factor is constant across different presentation rates. If this assumption is incorrect then the measured changes in rCBF, although remaining a correct description of the effects of attention on rCBF, will be falsely attributed to a single underlying mechanism. In other words our approach makes the simplifying

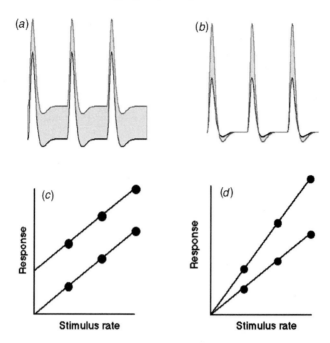

Fig. 5.1 Theoretical illustration of bias and gain control mechanisms of attention. (*a,b*) Schematic illustration of how stimulus-evoked neural activity (red) might be modulated (grey) by an attentional signal. The form of this modulation could take the form of (*a*) an additive bias signal or (*b*) a true modulation of stimulus-evoked responses alone (*c,d*), varying the rate at which stimuli are presented produces a relation between the total evoked response (integrated over time) and the frequency of presentation. The attentional effects (*a, b*) can now be distinguished by their effects on intercept (*a, c*) or slope (*b, d*) of this relation, respectively. (See colour plate section)

assumption of a unitary neurobiological mechanism of attention with a constant gain control or bias signal across the range of presentation rates studied. In our initial experiments a restricted range of presentation rates is used for this reason.

5.3 Imaging the mechanisms of selection

In this section we will review the three functional imaging experiments that have used a manipulation of stimulus presentation rate to characterize attentional effects. All have used positron emission tomography (PET), and this may be important as there is evidence that the functional magnetic resonance imaging (fMRI) signal dependency on rate of presentation of stimuli may be nonlinear, showing saturation as presentation rate increases (Binder *et al.* 1994; Rees *et al.* 1997*c*). These nonlinearities may be owing to stimulus habituation and would obscure or alter the interpretation of attentional effects in the approach we have outlined (Hillyard *et al.*, this volume). In the data presented here, obtained with PET, the relation between rCBF and presentation rate is linear throughout.

(a) Does attention change the relation between rCBF and presentation rate?

Frith and Friston (1996) correlated changes in cerebral blood flow with rate of presentation of simple tones to identify brain regions where auditory signals elicited a transient response. They compared one condition, where participants were asked to attend to the tones and ignore visual signals (single letters) presented at the same time, with another where participants were asked to attend to the visual signals and ignore the tones. They found that activity in the right thalamus was strongly correlated with the rate of presentation of the tones only when subjects attended to the auditory signals (figure 5.2; also see plate section). When attention was directed to the visual signals there was no correlation between cerebral blood flow and the presentation rate of the tones. In other words, the effect of attention in this area was to modulate the stimulus-evoked transient response produced by a single tone. Such an effect is similar to the conception of auditory

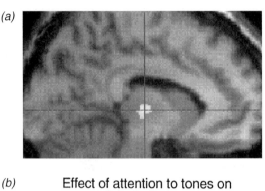

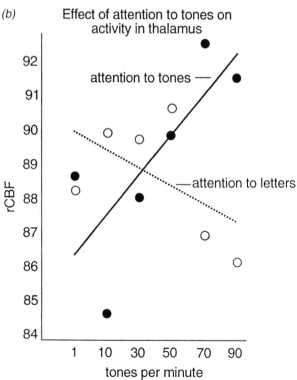

Fig. 5.2 Modulation of thalamic rCBF by attention. (*a*) The area in the thalamus where attention to the auditory signals significantly modulates the correlation between cerebral blood flow and presentation rate is shown superimposed on a saggital slice of the average structural MRI of the six subjects. (*b*) Cerebral blood flow in the thalamus plotted as a function of tone presentation rate for when subjects attend to the tones and when subjects attend to the visual signals. (See colour plate section)

attention as a 'gain control'. This experiment showed that PET is in principle able to detect one of the two types of attentional influence predicted on theoretical and empirical grounds here.

(b) Can gain and bias effects of attention on cerebral blood flow be distinguished?

The paradigm used by Frith and Friston (1996) used two very different streams of information and the items within stream to be monitored were highly distinguishable. Competition between stimuli would be expected to be minimal and, consistent with this, the participants found the task extremely easy. This study did not find any additive effects of attention on cerebral blood flow that would be consistent with a bias signal and it is possible that this was owing to the lack of competition between stimuli. We (Rees *et al.* 1997*a*) therefore extended this approach by using only a single visual stream, presented at a relatively fast rate and with unfamiliar abstract stimuli. Participants viewed a continuous stream of simple visual shapes (ellipses) that were oriented either horizontally or vertically and coloured red, green or blue. Participants were asked to attend to the visual stimuli and to classify them as targets or nontargets on the basis either of a single feature (for example, colour or orientation), or on the conjunction of features (colour and orientation together). We identified areas where there was a correlation between rate of presentation of the visual stimuli and cerebral blood flow, suggesting that task-related signals elicited a transient response in these areas. Several areas showed a positive correlation with rCBF, notably areas of extrastriate cortex and motor cortex contralateral to the hand that subjects used to make their responses. However, it was more interesting that several areas also showed a robust negative correlation with increasing presentation rate, including bilateral areas of inferior temporal cortex (figure 5.3; also see plate section). This pattern of changes in rCBF suggests that stimulus presentation is associated with a transient relative decrease in rCBF in inferior temporal cortex. The functional status of task-related

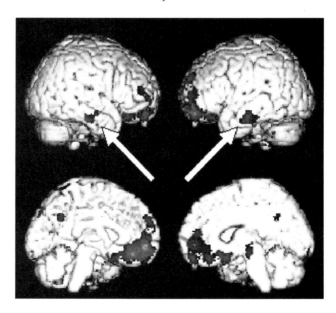

Fig. 5.3 Decreases in cerebral blood flow correlated with rate. Areas that show significant decreases in regional cerebral blood flow with increasing stimulus presentation rate are rendered on a canonical T1-weighted structural MRI placed in the anatomical space of Talairach and Tournoux. The areas deactivated include medial frontal structures and bilateral areas of inferior temporal cortex (arrowed). (See colour plate section)

decreases in haemodynamic activity has been controversial and often attributed to increases in cerebral blood flow in the control condition. The parametric design of this experiment, however, makes this explanation untenable and this pattern of blood flow changes suggests that regional decreases in rCBF may be functionally important. How might such changes in cerebral blood flow be reflected in underlying neuronal activity? The changes observed by using functional imaging techniques represent the overall rCBF response to changes in neural activity occurring in a population of several tens of thousands of neurons. The relation between responses observed with single cell electrophysiology and changes in rCBF may therefore be complex, but our results limit the number of possible explanations. First, it could be that each stimulus evokes a transient decrease in overall neural activity in this area, accounting for the progressive fall in cerebral blood flow as presentation rate increases. However neurons in this area in monkey generally show increases in activity in response to stimulus presentation. An alternate possibility is that as rate increases, the amount of overall neural activity evoked by each stimulus becomes smaller or present for a shorter period of time. However, to give rise to a negative slope in the relation between rCBF and presentation rate, the magnitude of such a reduction would have to more than offset the increase in activity caused by merely increasing the presentation rate. Furthermore, such an effect must be caused by a neural mechanism specific to inferior temporal cortex, as other areas (for example, visual cortex) show increasing cerebral blood flow with increasing rate. This suggests that the decrease in cerebral blood flow in inferior temporal cortex is not caused by a general mechanism such as habituation of neuronal responses, but that there may be more specific mechanisms mediating such a decrease in activity.

Changes in cerebral blood flow owing to attending to conjunctions as opposed to features influenced the relation between rCBF and presentation rate in a number of areas. Activity in the left precuneus, premotor cortex and cerebellum showed an interaction effect, with a change in the slope of the line relating cerebral blood flow to presentation rate as a function of attention (figure 5.4; also see plate section). This type of effect is identical to the attention effect seen in the thalamus by Frith and Friston (1996). However, areas in the left inferior temporal cortex, and in the right cerebellar hemisphere showed an additive effect of attention with no change in the slope of the line relating rCBF to presentation rate. Taken together, these findings indicate that the operation of attention appears to result in two qualitatively different patterns of modulation of evoked haemodynamic activity, in keeping with our theoretical predictions. We will now discuss the effects of attention to conjunctions in inferior temporal cortex in more detail.

In one of the areas in inferior temporal cortex that showed a decrease in activity as presentation rate increased, there was a change in activity due to attending to conjunctions as opposed to features. The change in activity took the form of a decrease in activity in the conjunction task that was constant across all presentation rates (figure 5.4). This change in activity must be owing to the different attentional demands of the conjunction task, as the visual stimuli were the same across all tasks. In contrast to the attentional modulation seen by Frith and Friston (1996), this modulation takes the form of a baseline shift that is independent of the correlation of cerebral blood flow with stimulus presentation rate. In other words, the slope of the relation between cerebral blood flow and stimulus presentation rate is unchanged by attention, but the intercept is changed, consistent with a bias signal. The direction of the attentional effect is negative, decreasing evoked activity in inferior temporal cortex. We suggest two possible explanations for this type of effect. An explanation based on the feature integration theory (Treisman and Gelade 1980) would suggest that in the feature task, any relevant feature should trigger a correct response. However, in the conjunction task the separate features of the relevant conjunction will tend to evoke false alarms. They will therefore need to be inhibited, so that responses are made only to the correct conjunctions. In other words, more inhibition is required in the conjunction task giving rise to a lower overall evoked rCBF in inferior temporal cortex. An alternate explanation

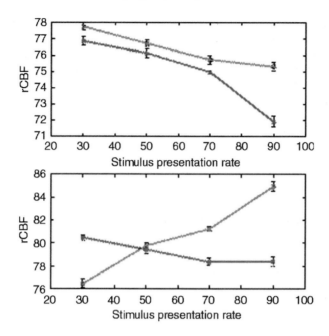

Fig. 5.4 Two modulatory effects of attention on rCBF. (*a*) Cerebral blood flow in left inferotemporal cortex (see figure 5.3) plotted as a function of stimulus presentation rate, separately for attention to visual conjunctions (red line) compared with individual features (green line). There is a significant difference in the intercept of these two lines, but no significant difference in slope. This represents an additive effect of attention that is constant across presentation rates (cf. figure 5.1*a*). (*b*) Cerebral blood flow in the left premotor cortex plotted as a function of stimulus presentation rate, separately for attention to visual conjunctions (red line) compared with individual features (green line). There is a significant difference in the slope of these two lines. This effect represents an interaction between stimulus rate-evoked changes in rCBF and attention (cf. figure 5.1*b*). (See colour plate section)

may be that conjunctions are coded in inferior temporal cortex as higher order combinations of single features. A hierarchical coding scheme would mean that fewer cells are selective for conjunctions compared with individual features. In such a scheme fewer cells would therefore need to be biased to give rise to selectivity for conjunctions as opposed to features. Overall neural activity evoked by feature selectivity would therefore be higher than for conjunctions, giving rise to a lower rCBF in the conjunction condition. Convergent functional imaging evidence supports the proposal that less activity is evoked in human inferotemporal cortex during the identification of conjunctions as opposed to individual visual features (Elliott and Dolan 1997). These authors showed a decrease in rCBF in left inferior temporal cortex when participants perform a visual delayed match to sample task on the basis of conjunctions of colour and form compared with individual features. The location of the area in left inferotemporal cortex identified by Elliott and Dolan (1997) is very close to that identified by Rees *et al*. 1997*a*, suggesting a common effect related to the identification of visual conjunctions of colour and form in both paradigms.

Relating the functional imaging findings in inferior temporal cortex to the neurophysiological data in monkeys is more difficult. Cells in inferotemporal cortex in monkeys show a range of different response properties. In delayed match-to-sample tasks, both cue-related activity in delay periods and enhanced responses to target stimuli matching a previous cue are seen. The presence of delay-related activity has been suggested as a neural correlate of an attentional bias signal (Desimone and Duncan 1995). Our functional imaging data is consistent with an additional signal associated with attention in inferior temporal cortex, independent of, and additive to, transient stimulus-evoked activity. However, whereas the activity of single cells shows an additive increase in activity, the functional imaging data shows an additive decrease in rCBF when conjunctions are compared with features. In other words, the response at the relatively coarse spatial scale detected by functional imaging is not the same as that recorded in a small number of single cells within this area. Intuitively this may seem plausible; for every cell that shows cue specificity and elevated delay-related activity within a single trial, most of the population will not show elevated delay-related activity. At a population level, the aggregate neuronal dynamics will therefore not necessarily bear a straightforward relation to the changes in firing rate of a single cell. Indeed, it is possible that although individual neurons show an increase in firing rate due to attention, the overall level of activity in a population of neurons may decrease if, for example, local interactions lead to suppression of activity. However, the relation of single cell activity to that of populations of cells in this area has not been explored experimentally in detail, so such a mechanism remains speculative.

(c)   How does attention modulate rCBF in visual and auditory cortex?

The two previous experiments suggest that the effects of attention in human cortex are expressed in two different patterns of changes in cerebral blood flow. However, the modulatory effects that we observe are located relatively distant from extrastriate cortex, and may reflect the relatively abstract nature of the stimuli used. In the first experiment where there was relatively little competition between stimuli, only changes in stimulus-evoked activity were observed, whereas when there was more competition in the second experiment both changes in stimulus-evoked activity and changes compatible with a bias signal were seen. We therefore undertook a further experiment similar in conception to Frith and Friston (1996) in using both visual and auditory streams of information. However, to increase competition both within and between streams not only did presentation rate vary in both streams, but the stimuli and manipulations were the same in auditory and visual streams, decreasing their discriminability. In this study we attempted primarily to clarify the nature of attentional effects on extrastriate and auditory cortex. Participants were scanned while being presented with two concurrent streams of information, visual and auditory. They saw single letters presented at fixation, or single letters spoken binaurally through insert earphones. The letters varied both in their identity, and in their physical characteristics (grey-scale intensity or volume respectively). In separate PET scans, participants were asked to attend either to the visual stream, or to the auditory stream and to press a button whenever a target appeared. In separate scans, the target was defined either on the basis of its identity or on its intensity (grey-scale or volume, depending on which stream was attended). We correlated changes in rCBF with changes in presentation rate of the targets, and studied how this relation changed in auditory and extrastriate cortex as a function of the direction of attention to visual or auditory streams. In both extrastriate and auditory cortex, directing attention to the appropriate modality produced a change in activity that was independent of the relation between stimulus presentation rate and cerebral blood flow (figure 5.5; also see plate section). In other words, the dominant attentional mechanism in both visual and auditory cortex in this study was an additive effect. This is not the only response property in extrastriate cortex, as a small area of right fusiform cortex showed an interaction between the attended modality and the relation between presentation rate and cerebral blood flow. Therefore it seems that, as already mentioned, PET is not in principle insensitive to changes in attention that directly modulate stimulus-evoked rCBF. Rather it seems that the dominant mechanism may be changes in rCBF in an area that are independent of, and additive to, stimulus-evoked rCBF.

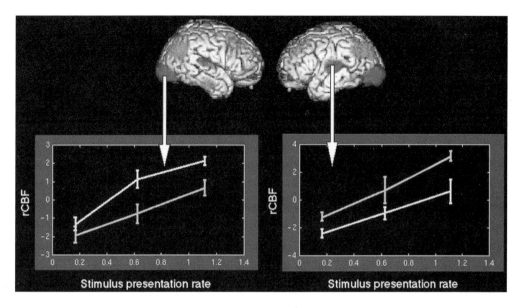

Fig. 5.5 Right and left lateral views of areas where changes in cerebral blood flow show a significant positive (red areas) or negative (green areas) correlation with stimulus presentation rate. The activations are rendered on a canonical T1-weighted MRI image placed in the standard anatomical space of Talairach and Tournoux. Below visual (left) and auditory (right) cortex are plotted the relation between cerebral blood flow and stimulus presentation rate, as a function of attention to the visual signals (yellow line) or the auditory signals (blue line). In both cases there is an additive effect of attention, with no interaction between attention and stimulus presentation rate. (See colour plate section)

The relation between these findings and the neurophysiological data concerning neural responses in monkey ventral stream processing is worth noting. Neurons in V4 and IT show changes in both stimulus-evoked activity and baseline firing rates as a function of attention. Changes in stimulus-evoked activity, if mirrored in changes in rCBF, would be expected to produce changes in the slope of the relation between rCBF and presentation rate. However, it seems that in the present study the dominant pattern of attentional modulation in extrastriate cortex takes the form of a change in the baseline activity, irrespective of presentation rate. There is therefore a discrepancy between the single cell and human data. The imaging experiments reviewed here suggest that PET is not in principle insensitive to the detection of attentional modulation of stimulus-evoked activity, so is it possible that a difference in paradigms may account for the discrepancy? In monkeys, attentional modulation of stimulus-evoked activity is seen only when both target and distractor are within a single receptive field. However, changes in baseline firing rates caused by attention are seen regardless of whether target and distractor are in the same receptive field, or presented sequentially at different times (Luck *et al.* 1997). Changes in the baseline firing rate may reflect a top-down signal that gives a competitive advantage to a stimulus at an attended location. This signal may bias one local population of cells over another, explaining why it is seen regardless of the positions of target and distractor within the receptive field (unlike the more local competition effects). The coexpression of stimulus-evoked and baseline shift activity within a single population of cells may explain the apparent discrepancy between single cell studies, where attentional effects are typically only seen when stimuli are placed within a single RF, and functional imaging studies. In such studies, including those reviewed here, stimuli have often been widely placed in locations expected to be in different receptive fields, or presented at different times. Over extended periods of time, with a relatively large interstimulus interval, changes in baseline firing rate might be expected to dominate the observed changes in rCBF. This explanation of the discrepancy is speculative, for there are many other respects in which functional imaging and electrophysiological paradigms are very different. However, our results presented here suggest that functional imaging techniques may be primarily sensitive to baseline shift activity. More closely analogous experiments done in both monkeys and humans may resolve this issue.

5.4 Discussion

The data reviewed in §5.3 show that two qualitatively different patterns of modulation of rCBF can be observed by using functional imaging techniques in experiments where non-spatial visual and auditory attention is manipulated. These patterns of modulation can be described as gain control and bias signal mechanisms. It is not yet clear whether these changes in cerebral blood flow can be directly identified with changes in baseline neural firing rates and modulation of stimulus-evoked activity by attention that have been observed in single neurons.

5.5 The control of attention

If regions of visual cortex show patterns of evoked neural and haemodynamic activity that can be interpreted as the effects of perceptual selection on stimulus-evoked activity, is it reasonable to seek evidence for structures involved in the control of attention? Some authors have argued that the multiplicity of definitions and dissociation of different types of behavioural effect due to attention makes the concept of a single attentional system untenable (Allport 1993). Nevertheless, considerable progress has been made in establishing the importance of parietal cortex in the shifting of spatial attention (see, for example, Corbetta *et al*. 1995). The experiments discussed in this paper all used non-spatial attentional tasks, where structures other than parietal cortex may be involved. Rees and co-workers (1997*a*) found that a single area of right prefrontal cortex, probably Brodmann area 8 (BA8), was activated by the conjunction task relative to the feature tasks. This area showed no correlation between stimulus presentation rate and cerebral blood flow, and so may be involved in establishing an attentional 'set', irrespective of rate and therefore independent of stimulus-evoked activity. This is compatible with the observation that ablation of this area in monkeys causes specific deficits in tasks involving a conjunction of visual and auditory inputs (Petrides and Iversen 1976, 1978). BA8 is well placed to be a source of modulatory influence, receiving connections from a wide range of cortical areas (Barbas and Mesulam 1985; Cavada and Goldman Rakic 1989). However, the homologies between monkeys and humans in this area of dorsolateral prefrontal cortex are not exact. For example, this area in monkeys contains the frontal eye fields, whereas in humans consistent functional imaging evidence suggests that the frontal eye fields are located in a more posteromedial location, in BA6 (Paus 1996). BA8 involvement in an attentional task was also shown by Rees and Frith in the experiment discussed in §5.3c. Activity in right BA8 showed two different patterns. In one part of BA8, activity showed an interaction between the direction of attention to visual or auditory modalities, and the direction of attention within that modality (toward identity or intensity targets). Such a modulatory interaction would be expected if this area was involved in the control both of the between-modality direction of attention and the attentional 'set' within modality. In another part of BA8 that partly overlapped with the first area, evoked activity also showed a significant interaction between rate of presentation and the between-modality direction of attention. This is a surprising observation, as Rees and colleagues (1997a) found no effect of stimulus presentation rate in this area. However, the range of presentation rates used in this study was much greater than by Rees *et al.* (1997a) and the cerebral blood flow in this area depends not only on the presentation rate, but on the context of whether attention is directed to auditory or visual signals. Further studies will be needed to clarify the nature of presentation rate effects in both sensorimotor and 'attentional' areas of cortex. However the present results are consistent with a role for right prefrontal cortex in the direction of these attentional effects.

5.6   The fate of rejected stimuli

The discussion so far has considered the consequences for stimulus processing of choosing to attend to a particular stimulus attribute or part of the visual scene. The converse question can also be addressed by functional imaging experiments; namely, what is the fate of rejected stimuli? Behavioural research in this area has ranged widely over a variety of tasks in both auditory and visual modalities. In general, when subjects are asked to focus on certain stimuli and ignore others, it seems that only relatively large changes in the physical properties of the rejected stimuli result in spontaneous reports (Cherry 1957). However, in other circumstances it seems that the rejected stimuli can be extensively processed and influence behaviour as measured by indirect methods such as reaction time or evoked potentials (for a review, see Neill *et al.* 1995). It has not been clear why different paradigms produce such different results and there has been a long-standing debate about attention theory as to whether perception is dependent on attention (implying that ignored stimuli are not processed) or whether perception is independent of attention (implying that ignored stimuli are fully processed). Evidence from behavioural, electrophysiological and functional imaging experiments has been advanced to support one or other position, without consensus or resolution (Kahneman and Treisman 1984; Johnston and Dark 1986; Hillyard *et al.* 1987; Corbetta *et al.* 1991).

Lavie's theory (Lavie 1995) provides a theoretical resolution to this debate. She proposes that capacity for perception is limited, but within those limits perception proceeds automatically. So although limited capacity means that we cannot perceive everything, within those limits we are unable to stop perceiving whatever we can. The critical determinant of whether irrelevant stimuli can be ignored is therefore the degree to which the task we are engaged in exhausts available capacity. If the processing load of the task exhausts available capacity, irrelevant stimuli will not be perceived. However, if the target processing load is low, attention will inevitably spill over to the processing of irrelevant stimuli. In other words, we will only be successful in ignoring irrelevant stimuli if the task we are engaged in exhausts available capacity. This will occur only under conditions of high load. In her account, the selective nature of perception is contingent not simply on the existence of limited processing resources, but on the ability to allocate less than the available capacity if the task does not demand it. Note that the concept of processing load relates to increasing the number of items in a display, their similarity, or the degree of processing required for each item. This concept is related to the idea of competition elaborated by Desimone and Duncan (1995). However in Lavie's (1995) theory, it is different task requirements (high and low load) that produce differential competition for limited processing resources and hence differential processing of irrelevant stimuli.

A re-examination of the experimental data relating to the processing of irrelevant stimuli in the light of Lavie's theory is now possible (Lavie and Tsal 1994). Many of the tasks that show little evidence that irrelevant stimuli are processed are difficult, demanding tasks such as dichotic listening. In contrast, the behavioural evidence that irrelevant stimuli do indeed undergo processing is often gathered by using relatively austere paradigms with a limited number of items or low processing load. Furthermore, behavioural experiments specifically addressing Lavie's theoretical predictions show that irrelevant stimuli interfere more with behavioural responses under conditions of low load compared with high load conditions, suggesting a greater degree of processing (Lavie and Tsal 1994). The evidence therefore suggests that selective perception is dependent on attention only under conditions of high load.

5.7   Imaging the fate of rejected stimuli

Investigating whether irrelevant stimuli are processed or not in a behavioural study requires an indirect measure of stimulus processing. Most often, this has been achieved by noting how indirect stimuli modulate or interfere with the primary task the subject is undertaking. Functional imaging offers the opportunity to circumvent the need for an indirect measure. fMRI allows non-invasive visualization of the evoked haemodynamics related to the processing of sensory signals (Kwong et al. 1992). If an irrelevant stimulus is known to activate a region of the brain functionally distinct from the areas activated by stimuli relevant to the task, then potentially this allows direct experimental observation of whether processing of the irrelevant stimuli has occurred. In the experiments reviewed here, there is some evidence to suggest that processing of irrelevant stimuli may occur. For example, Frith and Friston (1996) observed that there was a correlation between cerebral blood flow and the rate of presentation of tones in auditory cortex, even when subjects were attending to visual stimuli and attempting to ignore the auditory stimuli. Similarly in areas of extrastriate cortex, there is a correlation between letter presentation rate and cerebral blood flow even when subjects are attending to auditory information and ignoring the visual information. These observations suggest that processing of ignored auditory and visual stimuli may nevertheless take place under certain conditions. However, although these observations are suggestive, they fall short of a specific examination of the processing of irrelevant stimuli in the light of theories such as that of Lavie.

In collaboration with Lavie, we did a specific test of the predictions of her theory, that irrelevant stimuli are only processed under conditions of low load (Rees et al. 1997b). We used radial visual motion as an irrelevant stimulus. Visual motion is known to activate a functionally distinct cortical area, V5, whose location has been demonstrated in previous imaging studies (Zeki et al. 1991; Watson et al. 1993). Activation of V5 by moving as opposed to static irrelevant stimuli should allow us to determine whether processing of irrelevant motion has taken place. To modulate processing load, we used a linguistic task where subjects saw single words and monitored for the occurrence of targets. In both high and low load conditions, the subjects saw exactly the same physical stimuli, but the target criterion varied. Under low load conditions, targets were the words written in upper case letters; under high load conditions, targets were bisyllabic words. Activity evoked by the presence of irrelevant visual motion in the periphery of the display (compared with a static irrelevant stimulus) was significantly greater under conditions of low load (compared with high load) in several areas. In accordance with the predictions of Lavie's theory, an interaction between motion-related signals and perceptual load was seen bilaterally in V5 complex (see figure 5.6; also see plate section). Under conditions of low load, there was a significant activation in these areas produced by moving dots; under conditions of high load the activation was reduced to baseline. In support of these results, a convergent behavioural experiment, modelled on those previously reported by Chaudhuri and Shulman (Chaudhuri 1991; Shulman 1991, 1993), showed

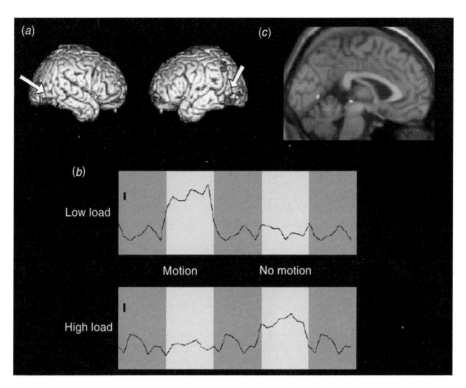

Fig. 5.6 Modulation of ignored motion processing by attentional load. (a) Lateral views of the left hemisphere of a T1-weighted volume rendered anatomical image that conforms to the stereotactic space of Talairach and Tournoux. On this image are superimposed in red the areas from where brain activity in the group of subjects showed the predicted interaction between the effects of visual motion and linguistic processing load. The locations of the left V5 complex is indicated by the arrows. (b) Mean activity over all subjects and replications of each experimental condition taken from the left V5 complex. Activity during baseline periods (dark grey shading) is shown alternating with that during experimental conditions (light grey shading). The scale bar represents a value of 0.1% BOLD signal change. (c) Activation in the superior colliculus produced by the interaction of motion processing and perceptual load, displayed on a sagittal slice from the same T1 canonical image as in *a*. (See colour plate section)

that the motion after-effect (which is thought to be contingent on V5 activity (Tootell *et al.* 1996) was significantly shorter under conditions of high load (figure 5.7).

An interesting aspect of the findings of Rees and co-workers (1997*b*) is that a large number of areas outside V5 showed a modulation of motion-related signals by attentional load. In particular, areas very early in the anatomical hierarchy of visual processing, close to the V1–V2 border and in the superior colliculus (SC), showed such a pattern of modulation (figure 5.6). The involvement of the superior colliculus is particularly interesting in the light of an ablation study in monkeys (Desimone *et al.* 1990). Removal of the superior colliculus led to impairment in a visual discrimination task, but only under conditions where the unaffected part of the visual field contained a competing item. This suggests that the SC is sensitive to competition between stimuli. However, our results were obtained by manipulating the attentional load, rather than by changing the display in any way. Taken together, the work on monkeys and humans suggest that greater competition

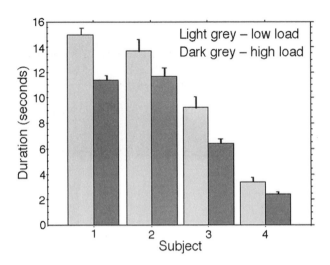

Fig. 5.7 The mean duration of the motion after-effect for four subjects, measured after 32 s performing either low or high perceptual load tasks from the experiment described in the text. In each case there is a significant ($p < 0.05$, one-tailed) reduction in the motion after-effect under conditions of high perceptual load compared with low load.

for attention may occur either as a consequence of increasing the number of visual items, or with more processing for the same items.

5.8 Conclusion

The experiments reviewed here suggest the feasibility of using functional imaging techniques to address directly the nature of the modulation of brain activity produced by attention. Variation of stimulus presentation rate provides a powerful way to characterize transient stimulus-evoked activity and to study the modulatory effects of attention. Such studies suggest that the effects of attention on rCBF are expressed in two different ways (bias and gain signals), and provide intriguing but incomplete parallels with single cell neurophysiological data. Further exploration of the assumptions underlying our approach and of the relation between changes in single cell activity and rCBF will enhance our understanding of these mechanisms. Finally, we have shown how specific cognitive theories about the operation of attention can be tested by using convergent fMRI and behavioural data, and demonstrated that stimuli that are ignored may nevertheless be perceived under certain circumstances.

Acknowledgements

This work was funded by The Wellcome Trust. The experiments reviewed here were done in close collaboration with K. Friston and N. Lavie. We thank our colleagues at the Wellcome Department, particularly R. Frackowiak, O. Josephs, R. Turner and the radiography staff.

References

Allport, A. 1993 Attention and control: have we been asking the wrong questions? A critical review of twenty-five years. In *Attention and performance. 14. Synergies in experimental psychology, artificial intelligence, and cognitive neuroscience* (eds D. E. Meyer and S. Kornblum), pp. 183–218. Cambridge, MA: MIT Press.

Barbas, H. and Mesulam, M. M. 1985 Cortical afferent input to the principalis region of the rhesus monkey. *Neuroscience* **15**, 619–37.

Binder, J. R., Rao, S. M., Hammeke, T. A., Frost, J. A., Bandettini, P. A. and Hyde, J. S. 1994 Effects of stimulus rate on signal response during functional magnetic resonance imaging of auditory cortex. *Brain Res. Cogn. Brain Res.* **2**, 31–8.

Broadbent, D. E. 1958 *Perception and communication*. London: Pergamon Press.

Büchel, C. and Friston, K. J. 1997 Modulation of connectivity in visual pathways by attention: cortical interactions evaluated with structural equation modelling and fMRI. *Cerebr. Cortex* **7/8**, 768–78.

Cavada, C. and Goldman Rakic, P. S. 1989 Posterior parietal cortex in rhesus monkey. II. Evidence for segregated corticocortical networks linking sensory and limbic areas with the frontal lobe. *J. Comp. Neurol.* **287**, 422–45.

Chaudhuri, A. 1991 Modulation of the motion aftereffect by selective attention. *Nature* **344**, 60–62.

Chelazzi, L., Miller, E. K., Duncan, J. and Desimone, R. 1993 A neural basis for visual search in inferior temporal cortex. *Nature* **363**, 345–7.

Cherry, C. 1957 *Human communication*. London: Wiley.

Corbetta, M., Miezin, F. M., Dobmeyer, S., Shulman, G. L. and Petersen, S. E. 1990 Attentional modulation of neural processing of shape, color, and velocity in humans. *Science* **248**, 1556–9.

Corbetta, M., Miezin, F. M., Dobmeyer, S., Shulman, G. L. and Petersen, S. E. 1991 Selective and divided attention during visual discriminations of shape, color, and speed: functional anatomy by positron emission tomography. *J. Neurosci.* **11**, 2383–402.

Corbetta, M., Shulman, G. L., Miezin, F. M. and Petersen, S. E. 1995 Superior parietal cortex activation during spatial attention shifts and visual feature conjunction. *Science* **270**, 802–5.

Desimone, R. and Duncan, J. 1995 Neural mechanisms of selective visual attention. *A. Rev. Neurosci.* **18**, 193–222.

Desimone, R., Wessinger, M., Thomas, L. and Schneider, W. 1990 *Cold Spring Harb. Symp. Quant. Biol.* **55**, 963.

Elliott, R. and Dolan, R. 1998 The neural response in short-term visual recognition memory for perceptual conjunctions. *NeuroImage* **7**, 14–22.

Ferrera, V. P., Rudolph, K. K. and Maunsell, J. H. 1994 Responses of neurons in the parietal and temporal visual pathways during a motion task. *J. Neurosci.* **14**, 6171–86.

Frith, C. D. and Friston, K. K. 1996 The role of the thalamus in 'top down' modulation of attention to sound. *NeuroImage* **4**, 210–5.

Haenny, P. E., Maunsell, J. H. and Schiller, P. H. 1988 State dependent activity in monkey visual cortex. II. Retinal and extraretinal factors in V4. *Exp. Brain Res.* **69**, 245–59.

Hillyard, S. A., Woldorff, M., Mangun, G. R. and Hansen, J. C. 1987 Mechanisms of early selective attention in auditory and visual modalities. *Electroencephalogr. Clin. Neurophysiol.* **39**, 317–324.

Hillyard, S. A., Mangun, G. R., Woldorff, M. G. and Luck, S. J. 1995 Neural systems mediating selective attention. In *The cognitive neurosciences* (ed. M. Gazzaniga), p. 665. Cambridge, MA: MIT Press.

Johnston, W. A. and Dark, V. J. 1986 Selective attention. *A. Rev. Psychol.* **37**, 43–75.

Kahneman, D. and Treisman, A. 1984 Changing views of attention and automaticity. In *Varieties of attention* (eds R. Parasuraman and D. R. Davies), pp. 29–61. London: Academic Press.

Kwong, K. K., Belliveau, J. W., Chesler, D. A., Goldberg, I. E., Weiskoff, R. M., Poncelet, B. P., Kennedy, D. N., Hoppel, B. E., Cohen, M. S., Turner, R. *et al.* 1992 Dynamic magnetic resonance imaging of human brain activity during primary sensory stimulation. *Proc. Natn. Acad. Sci. USA* **89**, 5675–9.

Lavie, N. 1995 Perceptual load as a necessary condition for selective attention. *J. Exp. Psychol. Hum. Percept. Perf.* **21**, 451–68.

Lavie, N. and Tsal, Y. 1994 Perceptual load as a major determinant of the locus of selection in visual attention. *Percept. Psychophys.* **56**, 183–197.

Luck, S. J., Chelazzi, L., Hillyard, S. A. and Desimone, R. 1997 Neural mechanisms of spatial selective attention in areas V1, V2, and V4 of macaque visual cortex. *J. Neurophysiol.* **77**, 24–42.

Mangun, G. R., Hillyard, S. A. and Luck, S. J. 1993 Electrocortical substrates of visual selective attention. In *Attention and performance*, vol. 14 (eds D. Meyer and S. Kornblum), pp. 219–43. Cambridge, MA: MIT Press.

Moran, J. and Desimone, R. 1985 Selective attention gates visual processing in the extrastriate cortex. *Science* **229**, 782–4.

Neill, W. T., Valdes, L. A. and Terry, K. M. 1995 Selective attention and the inhibitory control of cognition. In *Interference and inhibition in cognition* (eds F. N. Dempster and C. J. Brainerd), pp. 207–61. San Diego, CA: Academic Press.

O'Craven, K. M., Rosen, B. R., Kwong, K. K., Treisman, A. and Savoy, R. L. 1997 Voluntary attention modulates fMRI activity in human MT-MST. *Neuron* **18**, 591–8.

Paus, T. 1996 Location and function of the human frontal eye-field: a selective review. *Neuropsychologia* **34**, 475–83.

Petrides, M. and Iversen, S. D. 1976 Cross-modal matching and the primate frontal cortex. *Science* **192**, 1023–24.

Petrides, M. and Iversen, S. D. 1978 The effect of selective anterior and posterior association cortex lesions in the monkey on performance of a visual-auditory compound discrimination test. *Neuropsychologia* **16**, 527–37.

Price, C., Wise, R. J. S., Ramsay, S., Friston, K. J., Howard, D., Patterson, K. and Frackowiak, R. S. J. 1992 Regional response differences within the human auditory cortex when listening to words. *Neurosci. Lett.* **146**, 179–82.

Rees, G., Frackowiak, R. and Frith, C. 1997*a* Two modulatory effects of attention that mediate object categorization in human cortex. *Science* **275**, 835–8.

Rees, G., Frith, C. D. and Lavie, N. 1997*b* Modulating irrelevant motion perception by varying attentional load in an unrelated task. *Science* **278**, 1616–19.

Rees, G., Howseman, A., Josephs, O., Frith, C. D., Friston, K. J., Frackowiak, R. S. J. and Turner, R. 1997*c* Characterizing the relationship between BOLD contrast and regional cerebral blood flow measurements by varying the stimulus presentation rate. *NeuroImage* **6**, 270–8.

Sadato, N., Ibanez, V., Campbell, G., Deiber, M. P., Le Bihan, D. and Hallett, M. 1997 Frequency-dependent changes of regional cerebral blood flow during finger movements: functional MRI compared to PET. *J. Cerebr. Blood Flow Metab.* **17**, 670–9.

Shulman, G. L. 1991 Attentional modulation of mechanisms that analyze rotation in depth. *J. Exp. Psychol. Hum. Percept. Perf.* **17**, 726–37.

Shulman, G. L. 1993 Attentional effects on adaptation of rotary motion in the plane. *Perception* **22**, 947–61.

Tootell, R. B., Reppas, J. B., Dale, A. M., Look, R. B., Sereno, M. I., Malach, R., Brady, T. J. and Rosen, B. R. 1996 Visual motion aftereffect in human cortical area MT revealed by functional magnetic resonance imaging. *Nature* **375**, 139–41.

Treisman, A. M. and Gelade, G. 1980 A feature-integration theory of attention. *Cogn. Psychol.* **12**, 97–136.

Watson, J. D., Myers, R., Frackowiak, R. S., Hajnal, J. V., Woods, R. P., Mazziotta, J. C., Shipp, S. and Zeki, S. 1993 Area V5 of the human brain: evidence from a combined study using positron emission tomography and magnetic resonance imaging. *Cerebr. Cortex* **3**, 79–94.

Woldorff, M. G., Gallen, C. C., Hampson, S. A., Hillyard, S. A., Pantev, C., Sobel, D. and Bloom, F. E. 1993 Modulation of early sensory processing in human auditory cortex during auditory selective attention. *Proc. Natn. Acad. Sci. USA* **90**, 8722–6.

Zeki, S., Watson, J. D., Lueck, C. J., Friston, K. J., Kennard, C. and Frackowiak, R. S. 1991 A direct demonstration of functional specialization in human visual cortex. *J. Neurosci.* **11**, 641–9.

Section 2

Attention and perceptual integration

6

Feature binding, attention and object perception

Anne Treisman

Abstract

The seemingly effortless ability to perceive meaningful objects in an integrated scene actually depends on complex visual processes. The 'binding problem' concerns the way in which we select and integrate the separate features of objects in the correct combinations. Experiments suggest that attention plays a central role in solving this problem. Some neurological patients show a dramatic breakdown in the ability to see several objects; their deficits suggest a role for the parietal cortex in the binding process. However, indirect measures of priming and interference suggest that more information may be implicitly available than we can consciously access.

6.1 The binding problem

The binding problem in perception deals with the question of how we achieve the experience of a coherent world of integrated objects, and avoid seeing a world of disembodied or wrongly combined shapes, colours, motions, sizes and distances. In brief, how do we specify what goes with what and where? The problem is not an intuitively obvious one, which is probably a testimony to how well, in general, our brains solve it. We simply are not aware that there is a problem to be solved. Yet findings from neuroscience, computer science and psychology all imply that there is.

There is considerable evidence that the visual system analyses the scene along a number of different dimensions in various specialized modules. Both anatomical and physiological evidence (reviewed, for example, by Cowey (1985) and Zeki (1993)) suggests the existence of several maps of the visual scene laid out in different visual areas of the brain. Recordings from single or multiple neurons in animals have shown different specializations. Ungerleider and Mishkin (1982) distinguished a dorsal pathway, coding motion and space, and a ventral pathway, coding colour, shape and other features in extrastriate areas and eventually objects in area IT. Consistent with this inferred modularity, localized brain damage in human patients leads to selective losses in perceptual abilities. For example, colour vision can be lost in achromatopsia, without any impairment in shape or motion perception (Meadows 1974; Damasio *et al.* 1980); the ability to perceive motion can also be independently lost in akinetopsia, resulting in perception of frozen stills (Zihl *et al.* 1983; Zeki 1991); so can the ability to discriminate orientations or simple shapes (Goodale and Milner 1992). Finally, in humans with intact brains, positron emission tomography (PET) and functional magnetic resonance imaging (fMRI) have shown focal activity shifting to different brain areas as subjects are asked to respond to different aspects of the same displays—the shapes, colours and directions of motion (see Corbetta *et al.* 1991; Gulyas and Roland 1991; Sereno *et al.* 1995).

These findings, suggesting that specialized areas code different aspects of the visual scene, raise the question of how we get from dispersed brain representations to the unified percepts that we experience. If the world contained only one object at a time, this need not be a problem: there is nothing to demand that a unitary percept must depend on a unitary localized neural code.

However, the binding problem is raised in a more acute form when we realize two facts: first, that we typically do not look at scenes with only one object in them. The world around us is a crowded place, full of objects. Second, receptive fields in many of the specialized visual areas are quite large—up to $30°$ in temporal areas. Beyond the earliest stages of visual processing, single neurons respond across areas that would certainly hold several objects in crowded displays. If two objects with potentially interchangeable properties are detected by the same units, the potential for miscombining is present. For example, if a unit responding to red is active at the same time as a unit responding to motion, we need some way of distinguishing whether their receptive fields contain a moving red object, or a moving green object together with a stationary red object.

Which mechanisms could resolve this ambiguity? One possibility is that single units directly code conjunctions of features at earlier levels where receptive fields are small enough to isolate single objects. Certainly most cells in both early and late visual areas are selective along more than one dimension. Tanaka (1993) has shown single units in area IT that respond to relatively complex combinations of features. But in these experiments the animals were typically shown one object at a time, so the binding problem did not arise. The cells in IT could be coding the output of the binding process. There must be limits to the use of direct conjunction coding as a solution to the binding problem. We can see an essentially unlimited number of arbitrary conjunctions, immediately, the first time we are shown them. A purple giraffe with wings would look surprising but it would not be invisible. There are certainly too few neurons to code individually the combinatorial explosion of arbitrary conjunctions that we are capable of seeing.

A suggestion that is currently arousing interest in both neuroscience and computer modelling is that binding might depend on synchronized neural activity. Units that fire together would signal the same object. Gray *et al.* (1989) and Singer and Gray (1995) have collected evidence showing the presence of stimulus-dependent synchrony between units in quite widely separated areas of the brain. It is an interesting hypothesis, but I don't think it solves the same binding problem that I raised at the beginning of this paper. Synchrony is a possible way of holding on to the solution, of tagging the units that are responding to the same object once they have been identified, but we still need a way of finding which those are. The Gestalt psychologists identified a number of perceptual cues, such as collinearity, proximity, similarity, which determine perceptual grouping within dimensions such as colour, orientation and common motion. Facilitatory connections between cells responding to the same or related features within dimensions might mediate this grouping by helping to synchronize their firing across different locations (see, for example, Hummel and Biederman 1992), but risk also leading to false bindings when different objects share the same features. Furthermore, they would not bind the different features like orientation, motion, and colour, that happen to belong to the same object. This paper suggests a possible mechanism for binding across dimensions through shared locations, and also for using similarity to bind within dimensions across locations.

6.2   A role for spatial attention?

Psychologists have been interested for many years in a spatially selective mechanism of visual attention. For example, Posner (1980) showed that giving a spatial cue, such as a momentary brightening of one of two frames, would speed responses to a target object that subsequently appeared in that frame, even when the subject's eyes remained fixated centrally. We use the analogy of a 'window' of attention for this unitary, spatially selective mechanism. Other experiments have investigated visual search by asking subjects to find a target object in a display of nontargets (we call them distractors). We measure how long it takes to find the target as a function of how many distractors there are in the display. In some search tasks, the search time increases linearly with the number of distractors, as though subjects used a serial process of checking objects to find the target. Perhaps the same attention window must be centred on each object in turn. There is evidence that the attention window can be scaled—its size can adjust to fit the objects or groups of objects that are relevant to the task. For instance, in a display containing a global letter made of smaller local letters, we can attend to the global letter or to any one of the local ones, and it takes time to switch between these two states (Navon 1977; Ward 1982). In search, we process homogeneous groups of items in parallel (Treisman 1982).

Some years ago, I suggested that spatially selective attention may play a role in binding (Treisman and Gelade 1980; Treisman 1988). The idea, a very simple one, was that we code one object at a time, selected on the basis of its location at an early level where receptive fields are small. By temporarily excluding stimuli from other locations, we can simply bind whatever properties are currently attended. Figure 6.1 shows the model I proposed to relate the early parallel stages of vision to later attentional stages. It includes a master map of locations, that registers the locations of regions without giving access to the features that define them—for example whether they represent discontinuities in luminance, colour, depth or motion—and a separate set of feature maps. The feature maps contain two kinds of information: a 'flag' signalling whether the feature

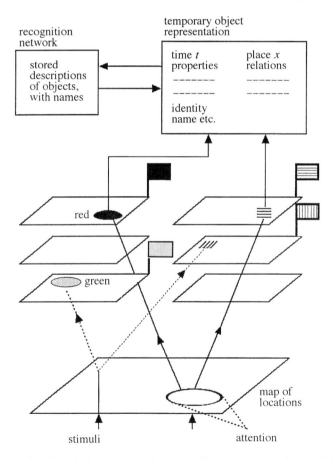

Fig. 6.1 Model suggesting the relation between feature coding, spatial attention and binding in object perception.

is present anywhere in the field, and some implicit information about the current spatial layout of the feature. Not all tasks require binding. If a task can be done simply by checking the flag for the presence of activity within a single feature map, it should not depend on attention. So, for example, the information that there is something red out there can be accessed directly from the feature maps, but the location of the red thing and its other features cannot.

The hypothesis is that locating and binding the features requires retrieval of their connections to the master map of locations. To put 'what' and 'where' together, an attention window moves within the location map and selects from the feature maps whatever features are currently linked to the attended location, temporarily excluding the features of all other objects from the object perception level. The attended features can then be entered, without risk of binding errors, into the currently active object representation where their structural relations can be analysed. At the instant shown in the figure, the information explicitly available would be a detailed specification of the object currently in the attentional window, plus the fact that green and vertical are present elsewhere. There might also be surviving representations of previously attended objects, although, surprisingly, there is some evidence that the bindings are lost as soon as attention is withdrawn (Wolfe 1998). Once a unitary object has been set up, it can be matched to stored models and identified, and actions such as reaching or grasping it can be programmed.

6.3   Evidence from illusory conjunctions

Next, I will outline some behavioural evidence that seems consistent with this hypothesis. Perhaps the most dramatic comes from a patient who seems to have severe problems in binding features (Friedman-Hill *et al.* 1995; Robertson *et al.* 1997). They illustrate what can happen when binding breaks down. We showed R.M. some very simple displays containing just two coloured letters selected from T, X, and O in red, blue, or yellow, and asked him to tell us the first letter he saw (figure 6.2). The exposure durations ranged from 0.5 to 10 s. In some sessions, even with exposures as long as 10 s, he made binding errors, reporting one letter in the colour of the other, in more than 35% of trials. He reported a feature that was not in the display in less than 10% of trials. If he were guessing, these two kinds of errors would be equally likely, as there was always one other colour or shape in the display and one not presented, so we can infer that one-quarter to one-third of his responses were binding errors. Clearly something had gone very wrong with his ability to bind. He had lost the ability that we all rely on to see stable well-integrated objects,

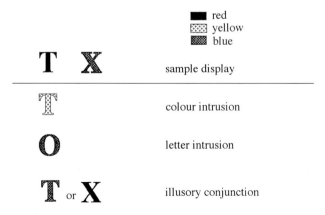

Fig. 6.2   Stimuli used to test feature binding in patient R.M.

and he now lives in a troubling world in which the binding problem is one he must constantly confront. I will return later to discuss other aspects of his perceptual problems.

Are there any conditions in which normal people have similar problems? As the hypothesis was that spatial attention is involved, we tried to prevent people from focusing attention by giving them a brief presentation and requiring them to spread their attention globally over the whole display (Treisman and Schmidt 1982). In one experiment, the displays contained four shapes varying in colour, size, shape, and format (filled or outline) arranged at the corners of a square, flanked on each side by two smaller black digits (figure 6.3*a*). Subjects were asked to give priority to noting the digits and to report them first. In addition they were to report all the features they could of the shape in one of the four locations, cued by a bar marker which appeared 200 ms after the display. The prediction is that they too should then make binding errors, putting features together in the wrong conjunctions. Subjects did in fact make many conjunction errors recombining the shape,

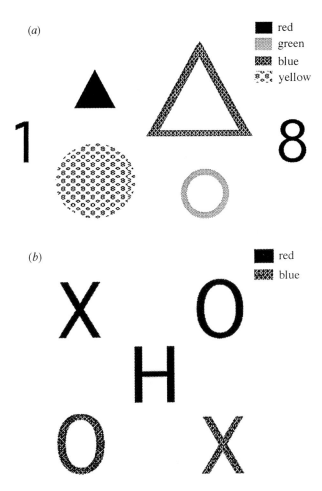

Fig. 6.3 (*a*) Display illustrating task to test the role of attention in binding in normal subjects. The task is to report the identity of the two digits first and then as many features as are confidently seen for the object in the cued location, indicated by the bar marker. (*b*) Display illustrating same–different matching task that reveals binding errors without a load on memory.

size, format and colour. These occurred in 18% of trials, compared with only 6% intrusion errors. Again, we would expect equal numbers of each if subjects were guessing or misperceiving the individual features. Instead they seemed to form illusory conjunctions recombining features that in fact characterized separate objects. In another experiment with coloured letters, there were more than 30%. We called these errors 'illusory conjunctions', implying that they are real perceptual illusions. Having frequently experienced them myself, although I had not expected to, I do think they are real illusions. Some are seen with high confidence. Also several subjects reported seeing coloured digits—even though they were not asked to report the colour of the digits and in fact had been told that they would always be black. Some binding errors may arise in memory; for example, a subject might remember seeing some red but forget where it was. But we still get a substantial number of illusory conjunctions when the task is simply to report whether there are two identical items in a display like that in figure 6.3b, where you can recombine the colour of the red H with the shape of the blue O to create an illusory red O, matching the one that is actually present.

Can we tie these binding errors more closely to the fact that we prevented subjects from focusing attention? In the experiment I described, where the relevant item was cued only after the display, subjects had no time to focus down to each coloured shape in turn in the brief exposures we gave them (around 200 ms). Using the same displays with another group of subjects, we cued the relevant item 150 ms before the display, and allowed subjects to ignore the digits, so that they could focus attention on the target item. We matched the overall accuracy by using a briefer exposure. As predicted, the binding errors disappeared: there were about as many intrusions (10% compared with 12%), which means that all the errors could be accounted for as misperceptions of the target feature or guesses. So it does seem that spatial attention plays a role specifically in the binding process.

In other experiments we have recorded similar errors that recombine parts of shapes, like lines and Ss that recombine to form dollar signs in displays like those in figure 6.4a,b, even when the lines must be taken from apparently holistic perceptual units like triangles (figure 6.4c). We get illusory arrows from lines and angles (figure 6.4d), but not illusory triangles (figure 6.4e), at least not until we add some circles to the display (figure 6.4f; Treisman and Paterson 1984). The explanation we proposed here is that triangles have the extra visual feature, closure, that also has to be present in the display before an illusory triangle can be generated.

The theory predicts that illusory conjunctions are created on the basis of the flags that signal the presence of particular features. If this is the case, the number of binding errors should not be affected by the similarity of the objects on other attributes. This is what we found. Differences in the shape or size of the objects made little difference to the probability of a binding error involving colour, as though the features are detected independently of each other and then bound. In generating the resulting percept, the spatial distribution of colour is selected to fit the shape with which it has been bound, whether correctly or erroneously.

Some researchers (see, for example, Cohen and Ivry 1989) have shown spatial proximity effects on illusory conjunctions, such that features are more likely to be wrongly bound if they are close in space than if they are distant. Cohen and Ivry suggested that features have 'coarse' location tags that are preattentively available. Proximity effects on binding errors could be a problem if we assume that locations are not available within the feature maps. However, it is very difficult to distinguish coarse coding of location from the idea that attention can rapidly zoom in to define a general area (like the upper left quadrant), but that it takes longer to focus more finely on one of two adjacent items. When the task prevented this zooming in by focusing attention narrowly at the fovea, our normal subjects showed no more illusory conjunctions between adjacent than between distant items (Treisman and Schmidt 1982). The Balint's patient, R.M., showed no effect

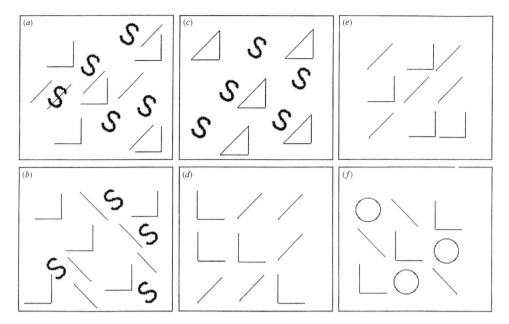

Fig. 6.4 Examples of displays used to look for illusory conjunctions of parts of shapes. Subjects report illusory dollar signs in 6.3*a*, illusory arrows in 6.3*b*, and illusory triangles in 6.3*d* but not 6.3*c*.

of distance on his binding error rates, consistent with the suggestion (§6.5) that he had lost his map of locations.

Another prediction is that the number of binding errors should also be independent of the number of instances of particular features because the claim is that all we have before the binding has occurred is information about the presence of features (the 'flags' in figure 6.1), not their individual instantiations. In an experiment (A. Treisman, unpublished data), we varied the number of instances of particular features in a display of four bars varying in orientation, format (filled, outline or dotted) and colour. To minimize memory errors, we cued subjects immediately after the display whether to report the digits (on 20% of trials) or one of the bars (on 80% of trials), giving high priority to accuracy in reporting the digits whenever they were cued. In displays with three instances of one feature (e.g. red) and only one of another (e.g. green), we found little difference in the number of illusory conjunctions involving migrations of the feature with three instantiations and of those with only one. The ratio was 1.5 : 1 rather than the 3 : 1 ratio that would be predicted if individuated tokens of the features were migrating. For example, in figure 6.5, reports of an illusory red bar in panels (*a*) and (*b*) were made on 15% and 10% of trials respectively, although there are three times as many red objects in panel (*a*). In another experiment varying just colour and orientation the ratio was even lower, 1.2 : 1. Note that to the extent that the amount of red present affects the chance of detecting it, quite apart from the number of instances of red, we would expect the ratio to exceed 1 : 1.

The evidence from illusory conjunctions supports four claims: (i) that features are separately coded, otherwise they could not recombine; (ii) that the binding problem is therefore a real one; (iii) that focused attention is involved in solving it; and (iv) that attention is not required for the

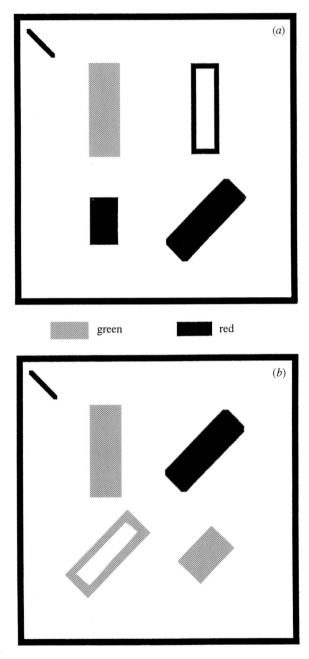

Fig. 6.5 Examples of displays to test whether feature tokens or feature types migrate when binding errors are formed. In reporting the colour of the cued bar, the token hypothesis predicts three times as many illusory migrations of red in *a* as in *b*.

simple detection of separate features (although it is often attracted by the prior detection of a unique feature).

6.4   Visual search and binding

Search tasks offer another source of information on the role of attention in binding. We can define a target so that it either does or does not require binding. In displays of green Xs and brown Ts, a target specified only by a conjunction of features, for example a green T, should require focused attention to each item in turn, whereas a target specified by either of two unique features, a blue letter or a curved letter, should not involve binding and might therefore be detected independently of attention. If attention must be focused on each item in turn to find conjunction targets, we predict a linear increase in search times with the number of items in the display. This is what we found (Treisman and Gelade 1980). On the other hand, feature targets, signalled by flags on the feature maps, showed no effect of the number of items. They simply popped out of the displays.

In some conjunction search tasks, there are other strategies besides the serial scan with focused attention, that can be used. We and others (see, for example, Treisman 1988; Wolfe *et al.* 1989; Nakayama 1990; Treisman and Sato 1990) have shown that when the target features are known in advance and when the relevant features are highly discriminable, subjects can use a feature-based grouping strategy to bypass the binding process. Essentially in looking for a red O among red Xs and blue Os, they may inhibit any location that contains blue and any location that contains an X. The red O would then emerge unscathed, without any need to bind distractor features. In the model, this would be implemented by reverse connections between the feature maps and the location map, selectively inhibiting all locations that contain unwanted features, and leaving only the target location to be checked (see figure 6.6).

6.5   Evidence from parietal lesions

So far this paper has been mostly behavioural. The model was developed from perceptual experiments. Can we tie it more closely to the brain? A classic experiment by Moran and Desimone (1985) seems consistent with the idea that attention selects by narrowing an attention window around the relevant object. Recording from cells in monkeys' area V4, they showed receptive fields essentially shrinking to exclude an unattended object when it fell into the same receptive field as the object to which the animal was trained to attend. What areas might control the attentional window? The parietal lobes are certainly involved in spatial attention. Unilateral damage to one parietal lobe produces a marked attentional deficit in the contralateral area of space. Particularly with right parietal damage, patients often show severe neglect of the left side of the visual field or the left side of an object. Investigations involving the patient I described earlier, who had such severe binding problems, may lead to a greater understanding of the brain areas involved. R.M. was unfortunate enough to suffer two successive strokes which destroyed both his parietal lobes, one after the other. He has normal acuity, contrast sensitivity, colour vision, stereopsis, and visual fields as tested formally by an ophthalmologist. However, he was left with a severe set of perceptual disabilities, some of which I've already outlined. Our hypothesis is that the master map of locations depends on parietal function. If this is correct, we can predict the set of deficits that the model would predict from his lesions.

1. Like any other theory, it would predict severe difficulties in conscious access to spatial information. The ability to point, reach for, or verbally label locations would be lost.

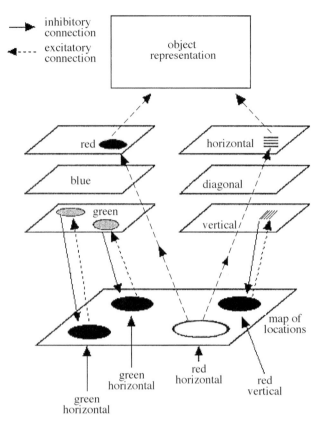

Fig. 6.6 Modified model to allow control of selective attention from one or more feature maps as well as through a serial scan by a spatial window.

2. If individuating objects depends on binding them to separate locations, only one should be visible at a time.
3. If space is the medium in which attention binds features, there is a risk of illusory conjunctions whenever more than one object is present.
4. Conjunction search should be abnormally difficult or impossible; however, in feature search tasks, there should be no difficulty in detecting the presence of a target feature, even when it is embedded in several nontargets, as feature detection does not depend on binding.

I have already described data from R.M. confirming prediction 3—the illusory conjunctions. It is important to note that R.M. has no difficulty in binding the features of single objects presented sequentially. When we presented two coloured letters successively for 3 s each (instead of simultaneously for a total of 10 s), the estimate of binding errors was 0. So R.M. does not have a general deficit in binding features or a memory problem in remembering them; his difficulty is specifically in the ability to bind simultaneously presented features to the correct objects.

We tested R.M. on prediction 4, and found a dramatic difference in his ability to do the tasks. The target was a red X. In the feature search condition, the distractors differed either in shape (red Os) or in colour (blue Xs). In the conjunction search task, he looked for a red X among red Os and blue Xs. He had no difficulty with the feature targets. He detected the unique colour or shape in almost every trial, and independently of the number of items in the display, but he was unable to do the conjunction search, even with displays of only three to five items. He took up to 5 s and had error rates of 25%.

What about the first two predictions? These are the classic symptoms that Balint described in 1909. The spatial difficulties and the inability to see more than one object (simultanagnosia) are usually assumed to be separate and unrelated deficits, except that they co-occur with parietal damage. However, feature integration theory suggests that the simultanagnosia may actually be caused by the loss of space, simply because attention uses space to bind features to objects. R.M. did show severe deficits in his ability to localize. We asked him to report whether an X was at the top, bottom, left or right of the screen, or whether it was to the right, left, above or below an O. He was at chance in judging the relative locations of a widely separated X and O on the computer screen, and only slightly better at saying whether a single X was at the top, bottom, left or right of the screen. He seemed to have lost his representation of space almost completely. The confusion was not with the meaning of the words: he performed almost perfectly when asked to localize a touch on his back as up or down, or left or right. His somatosensory spatial functions were intact, and his spatial difficulties were specific to the visual modality.

R.M. also conformed to the second prediction. His simultanagnosia was as striking as his localization failures, at least in the early days after his stroke. When we held up two objects, say, a comb and a pair of scissors, he typically saw only one of them. When we asked him to count dots in displays of one to five, in an early session he saw at most two dots, even when we presented five. In later sessions, he guessed higher numbers but was still very inaccurate. We think he switched to attending more globally, to the group of dots as a whole, but this made him unable to access any individual dot and count it. R.M.'s simultanagnosia makes his normal performance in feature search all the more surprising. At a time when he could typically see only one or two objects, he had no difficulty detecting a unique colour or shape, regardless of how many other items were present.

An intriguing incident throws more light on R.M.'s perceptual experience. One morning he told us he had found a good way to improve his vision. With the help of his granddaughter, he had made a tube through which he looked at whatever he wanted to see more clearly. For someone suffering from simultanagnosia, one would think that a tube restricting the angle of vision would be the last thing they needed. However, on reflection, it makes more sense. If the damage to his brain prevents the normal binding of features without preventing their detection at early levels of visual processing, the features of different objects should tend to coalesce into a single object, producing confusing mixtures of several features in the one object that is seen. R.M. did complain of such illusions. For example, he said 'When I first look at it, it looks blue and it changes real quick to red. I see both colours coming together . . . Sometimes one letter is going into the other one. I get a double identity. It kind of coincides.' His descriptions sound as though he has no perceptual space in which to separate the letters and bind colours to shapes. The tube he invented may have helped by restricting the early detection of features to those of a single object. Essentially, he constructed an external window of attention to supplement a defective internal window. The findings with R.M. are consistent with the predictions that follow if he has lost the location map that controls spatial attention.

Further support for a parietal role, both in shifting spatial attention and in binding, comes from two recent studies of PET activation by Corbetta, Petersen and others (Petersen *et al.* 1994; Corbetta *et al.* 1995; see also Corbetta, this volume). They compared activation in a conjunction search task, and in a task that required active shifting of attention between locations to track a target. They found similar activation in the superior parietal cortex in both tasks, consistent with the prediction that the binding process required in conjunction search does involve scanning with spatial attention, and that the parietal area is involved in its control. Ashbridge and co-workers (1997) found that transcranial magnetic stimulation to the right parietal lobe slowed conjunction search but left feature search unaffected. Taken together, these data suggest that we need an explicit representation of space for accurate conscious binding of features to objects. Thus, the dorsal parietal pathway interacts with the ventral pathway in mediating the perception of simultaneously presented objects. There might be 're-entrant' connections from the parietal lobes, perhaps via the pulvinar, to selected locations in visual areas V1 or V2.

6.6   Binding in feature search

Having shown a possible link between the model and the brain, I will describe next some further behavioural findings with normal subjects that led us to elaborate the theory. One challenge to the feature integration account of search came from a suggestion that the pattern of linearly increasing search times with increasing number of distractors might result when targets are difficult to discriminate from distractors because they are similar to them, and when the distractors are sufficiently different from each other to prevent good grouping and segregation from the target (Duncan and Humphreys 1989). This could account for the difficulty of conjunction search, in which the target shares one or other feature with all the distractors while the two distractor types differ in both features from each other. It also predicts that search for feature targets could be equally difficult if they closely resemble the distractors, although no feature binding should be involved. One can certainly get steep and linear search functions with targets defined by a small unidimensional difference (see, for example, Treisman and Gormican 1988). However, the critical question is what counts as a feature for the visual system. The answer must be determined empirically. The challenge led to some further research which pointed to a new version of the binding problem that might explain these data.

When I drew the model in figure 6.1, I put in three feature maps per dimension, mainly because drawing 50 was beyond my artistic capabilities. But there is some evidence that the visual system does use coarse coding, representing different values on each dimension by ratios of activity in only a few separate populations of detectors (for example, vertical, diagonal and horizontal, for orientation, or red, green, blue and yellow for colour). Stimuli differing only slightly along a single dimension would not activate separate populations of feature detectors and would not be expected to pop out. They would pose a somewhat different binding problem—binding to location—so that the small differences in activation between areas containing only distractors and an area containing the target as well could be discriminated.

We have observed large asymmetries in search difficulty with many different pairs of stimuli, depending on which is the target and which the distractors (Treisman and Gormican 1988). A tilted line pops out among vertical lines, a curved line among straight ones, a circle with a gap among closed circles, an ellipse among circles, whereas the reverse pairings—a vertical line among tilted ones, a straight line among curves, a closed circle among circles with gaps, and a circle among ellipses—give search that is much slower and seems to require focused attention to each item in turn. The targets that pop out behave as though they have a unique perceptual feature, like a red dot among green dots, whereas the others do not. We also find a marked search asymmetry when we compare search for a shape with an added feature (like a Q among Os) and search for a shape that lacks the same feature (like an O in a display of Qs, Treisman and Souther (1985)). Note that detecting an O among Qs also requires binding. To find the one circle which lacks a tail, we must locate all the tails and bind them to the Qs. On the other hand, to find a Q among Os, we can simply check for the presence of a tail anywhere in the display. There is no need to bind the tail to know that a Q is present. In this example, the same discrimination poses very different problems for the visual system, depending on whether or not the task requires binding.

Can we find an analogy in the case of the search asymmetries with apparently unidimensional stimuli like the targets defined by orientation or curvature? Here is where the coarse coding of features becomes relevant. A slightly tilted line might be coded by activity mainly in the detectors for vertical, with some additional activity in the diagonal detectors, just as a Q can be described as an O plus an extra tail. A slightly curved line could be coded as basically straight, plus some additional activity in detectors for curvature. The hypothesis is that the presence of this extra activity is detected without any need to bind it to the object, and this is enough to signal that the target is present. On the other hand, when the target is the one vertical line in a display in which all the lines but one are slightly tilted, both vertical and tilted detectors would be active everywhere except in the one location where the vertical target leaves the tilt detectors silent.

If this hypothesis is correct, we should be able also to prevent pop-out for a tilted target by turning its detection into a task that requires binding. The assumption is that a tilted target pops out among verticals because of the additional unique activity it evokes in the detectors for diagonals. If we now mix diagonal distractors with the vertical ones, activity in the vertical and diagonal detectors must be bound together to identify the target by its particular ratio of activation levels in the two detector populations. This changes the task into search for a conjunction target, and we should expect to switch from parallel pop-out to serial search with focused attention. Similarly a purple target will pop out among either blue or red distractors alone, but among a mixture of blue and red distractors it will require binding of activity in blue and red detectors that share the same location and should therefore depend on serial attentive scanning. I tested search for purple targets tilted $27°$ in displays of blue vertical bars and pink bars tilted $63°$, and found that search indeed looked serial, even though the colour and orientation of the target were objectively unique in the display and easily discriminable from either type of distractor alone (Treisman 1991). Furthermore, when we briefly flashed displays with the same stimuli, subjects made a large number of false alarms, detecting illusory targets. They saw far more illusory conjunctions in these displays in which I suggest that within-dimension binding is required than in displays where the target, although equated for similarity, was defined by a colour and orientation that would be directly coded by standard feature detectors, for example a blue vertical bar among purple and turquoise bars tilted $27°$ left and right. Thus, coarse coding by ratios of firing in different populations of feature detectors does seem to create another kind of binding problem.

The features that are preattentively detected are probably not those of the retinal image. Enns and Rensink (1991) and He and Nakayama (1992), have shown rapid or parallel detection of simple three-dimensional (3D) features of surfaces and illumination. The shading that results from 3D shape can produce segregation of a group of convex objects among concave ones, assuming lighting from above (Ramachandran 1988). This segregation is much clearer than with supposedly simpler black and white patterns. Although these might seem like conjunctions of shape and texture or luminance, the critical question is whether they are directly sensed by separate populations of neural detectors. Lehky and Sejnowski (1988) showed that simple neural networks, when trained to respond to gradients of shape from shading, evolve hidden units (i.e. units intermediate between the input and the output units) that look very similar to the simple cells that Hubel and Wiesel (1968) identified in area V1 and that have normally been assumed to be bar or grating detectors. The features that are directly coded by the visual system may actually be features that characterize 3D surfaces. It seems harder to find plausible candidates for featurehood in the geometric line arrangements of the cubes whose 3D orientations define the target in some of Enns and Rensink's (1991) experiments. However, what they find are asymmetries of search rather than the flat search functions associated with pop-out. Search is much faster for some target–distractor combinations

Table 6.1 Visual search studies

Serial search (attention required)	Parallel search (automatic pop-out)
Conjunction targets (e.g. green T in green Hs and brown Ts)	Feature targets (e.g. blue or S in green Hs and brown Ts)
Os in Qs	Qs in Os
Vertical line in tilted lines	Tilted line in vertical lines
Straight line in curved lines	Curved line in straight lines
Parallel lines in converging lines	Converging lines in parallel lines
Circle with gap in closed circles	Closed circle in circles with gaps
Purple bar tilted 27° in blue 0° (vertical) bars and red bars tilted 63°	Blue 0° (vertical) bar in purple bars tilted 27° left and turquoise bars tilted 27° right

than for others but not usually parallel unless shading is also present. Table 6.1 summarizes the results I have described on search and binding.

6.7   Implicit processing of conjunctions

For the last part of the paper, we move to another line of research which opens up issues in three new directions: so far I have discussed binding under a fairly narrow definition: it has been measured by conscious reports rather than by implicit indices; it has been manifested in immediate perceptual tests rather than in memory; and finally the information has concerned only stimulus features and locations, not the binding of actions to perceived events. Yet these are also aspects of a more general binding problem. We need to retain bindings in memory after the objects disappear, and we need to bind appropriate responses to the objects we identify. The experiments I have been pursuing recently extend the research in these three directions by comparing implicit with explicit measures of visual memory and specifying the choice of which object requires a response. The results have surprised us, and seem to have important implications for a more general understanding of binding.

First the question whether any implicit binding can be revealed, which we are unable to access consciously. There is increasing evidence that explicit reports may not exhaust all the information available to the visual system. Understanding what makes some information accessible and some not is an intriguing challenge. In particular, it is important to determine whether binding imposes a real computational limitation, or whether it is just a problem for conscious representation?

First, we did get a few surprising results with the patient R.M., when we used indirect measures to probe for implicit information about locations. We presented the word 'UP' or 'DOWN' at the top or bottom of a vertical rectangle. In any given trial, the semantics of the word and its location could be consistent (e.g. the word UP in the upper location), or inconsistent (e.g. the word UP in the lower location). R.M. read the words rapidly and correctly (note that binding was not necessarily involved in this reading task because the two words to be discriminated differed in all their letters and also in length), but his response times were 142 ms slower when the word was in an inconsistent location. So the locations interfered with his reading at a time when he was at chance in voluntarily locating the words. We were also able to show unconscious priming of spatial selection by a cross-modal cue although R.M. was unable voluntarily to select the cued item. We presented two visual letters, one on each side of the screen, at the same time as tapping his right or left shoulder. When we asked him to name the letter on the side that we had tapped, he was at chance, but when we simply asked him to name the first (or only) letter he saw, he reported significantly more from the tapped side. It seems that some implicit representation of space remains despite the loss of parietal function, perhaps in extrastriate areas of the ventral pathway, although this information is not consciously accessible. Finally, Egly and colleagues (1995) ran another experiment that also revealed implicit information about the spatial distribution of elements. Their displays consisted of a global letter made of local letters. When asked what he saw, R.M. never reported the global letter. He seemed to see only one of the local letters. Yet when asked to classify the local letter as one of two possible targets, he was significantly slower when the global letter was inconsistent with the local ones than when it was consistent. Again, he seemed to have implicit information—this time about the whole, even though he could only respond to a part.

DeSchepper and I have explored implicit visual processing in normal subjects as well. We found indirect evidence that fairly complex patterns can be registered, bound and stored implicitly without conscious attention. However, it is important to add that this seems to be true only for one unattended object. When more are added, the evidence for implicit binding disappears (Neumann and DeSchepper 1992). The measure we used is known as negative priming. Subjects are typically shown two objects and asked to respond to one of the two, selected by some simple distinguishing feature like its colour. So, for example, Tipper and Cranston (1985) asked subjects to name pictures of familiar objects selecting the red one in each overlapped pair. Their responses were slower when the unattended green object on one trial became the attended red one on the next, relative to when two new objects were shown. A plausible account was that subjects inhibited the green object to avoid naming it instead of the red. When it then became the relevant object, on the next trial, they had to overcome the inhibition. As a result, the response was slightly delayed. This negative priming implies: (i) that subjects formed and retained a memory trace of the picture, even when it was the unattended member of a pair; and (ii) that an action tag was bound to the memory, specifying whether it should be responded to or ignored.

DeSchepper and I wondered whether novel patterns would also produce negative priming. If so, this would be evidence that a representation of their shape was formed, even in the absence of attention. We used overlapped pairs of 270 nonsense shapes that the subjects had never seen before, similar to those in figure 6.7 (DeSchepper and Treisman 1996). The task was to decide whether the green shape on the left matched a single white shape to the right of the display, ignoring the red shape. We gave subjects some practice with a set of 12 shapes that we used repeatedly, and then we introduced new shapes mixed with the old. We found a clear negative priming effect of about 30 ms, which was actually larger on the first trial in which a new shape was presented than it was for the familiarized shapes. Subjects apparently set up a new representation for the unattended as well as the attended shape and attached an inhibitory action tag to it, specifying that it should be rejected. On the other hand, they had no conscious memory at all for the unattended shape. Their recognition was at chance, even when probed immediately after a pair was presented. We infer that attention is needed at the time of encoding if objects are to be explicitly retrieved.

Can we say any more about the nature of these implicit memory traces? How detailed and specific are they? How well bound are their parts and properties? With two other students, Alex Kulczycki and Xuexin Zhang, I asked what happens if we change either a feature or a component of the unattended prime before presenting it again as the attended probe (Zhang et al. 1996). In one experiment, we either kept the size the same, or changed it to larger or smaller. Surprisingly, when we changed the size, the result was not inhibition but facilitation. Subjects were slightly quicker to respond to the previously unattended shape when its size was changed than to respond to a new shape. In another experiment, we presented only half of the prime shape combined with half a new shape, to see if the inhibition was attached only to the whole or separately to each component

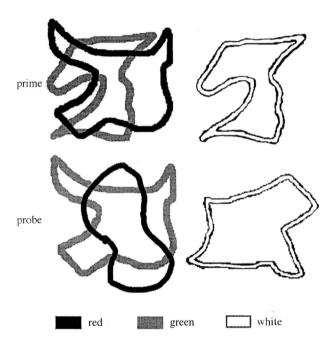

| ■■■ red | ▨▨ green | ☐ white |

Fig. 6.7 Examples of a prime and a probe trial testing negative priming with novel nonsense shapes. Subjects attended to the green shape in each trial and decided whether it matched the white one. They ignored the red shape, which on negative priming trials, reappeared as the attended shape in green, resulting in slower responses.

part. Figure 6.8 shows three successive trials in which subjects matched the two outside shapes and ignored the central shape. Two trials later, half of the first ignored central shape appeared as half of the relevant outside shapes, combined with half of the second ignored shape. We got negative priming as usual when the shapes were identical, but again there was facilitation when we recombined two previously unattended halves from two different trials to form a new whole, and also when we presented only half the prime shape combined with a new half shape. Khurana and co-workers (1994) looked at negative priming for faces and got a similar result: when the prime and the probe face were identical, they got inhibition, but when they reversed the contrast on the probe trial, they got facilitation.

Thus, the action tag that produces negative priming seems to be bound to a very specific conjunction of shape with size or contrast and of the parts of a shape with each other. But in addition we form a more abstracted representation which is size and contrast-invariant, and which may have separate articulated parts. This representation is not linked to the specific responses required in the context in which it was seen, and it can facilitate later perception of similar or related objects.

We wondered how long these implicit memory traces for novel unattended shapes would linger in our subjects' brains. So we looked for negative priming, not only in the next trial, but after 10, 100 or 200 intervening trials with up to 400 different intervening shapes. To our considerable surprise, we found that the inhibition was undiminished 200 trials later. The binding here seems quite persistent even though it is formed in a single unattended trial. We also tested intervals of a day, a week and a month and found significant priming even at those long delays, but with some indication of a shift from inhibition to facilitation. The survival of these memory traces for novel shapes in our experiments suggests a surprising combination of visual plasticity and

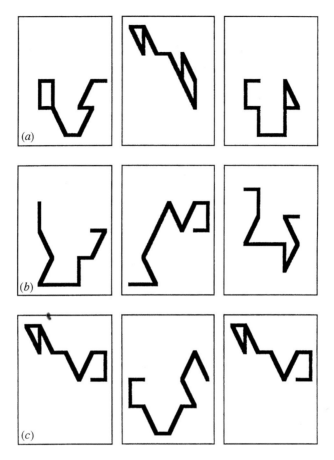

Fig. 6.8 Examples of two prime trials and a probe trial. The task was to decide as quickly as possible whether the shapes in the two outside positions were the same or different. The third (probe) trial recombines two previously unattended half primes to form the attended shape. Instead of negative priming, facilitation was observed relative to a new shape that had not been previously presented.

persistence. The newly formed representations remain available, separate and distinct from each other, for days or even weeks. If we had to speculate about where the representations are formed and stored, the temporal lobes in the ventral pathway seem a likely neural basis. Single unit recordings in monkeys, and brain imaging studies in humans, suggest that this is the area where objects are perceptually coded and form the memory traces that mediate subsequent priming. For explicit memory, on the other hand, the hippocampus and adjacent cortical areas are likely to be involved.

6.8 Conclusions

It is time to try to pull things together, both the different results described here, and their relation to the different view of attention proposed by Duncan (this volume). The results on tasks requiring explicit binding, both from normal subjects and from the patient R.M., suggested that attention is needed to bind features together, and that without attention, the only information recorded is the presence of separate parts and properties. Yet both the negative priming results in normals and the interference from global letters in R.M. suggest that there are conditions in which wholes are registered automatically, without attention or conscious awareness.

I think there is no real contradiction between these results. Binding failures typically occur with high load displays when several objects must be processed under high time pressure. When there is only one unattended object, its features must belong together, so there should be no problem determining what goes with what. Indeed, when the number of unattended objects in a negative priming task was increased from one to two or three, Neumann and DeSchepper (1992) found that negative priming disappears. Attention here plays a different role: the unattended object may be suppressed to prevent response conflict and to ensure that conscious experience is coherent and consistent with our behavioural responses.

The patient R.M. makes binding errors with only two objects present because he is unable to separate them spatially to select one for attention and ignore the other. His implicit knowledge about locations that he cannot consciously locate may come from the ventral pathway where it is not normally accessible for conscious perception. As Humphreys (this volume) suggests, spatial relations within objects may be coded by separate systems from the spatial relations between objects. The arrangement of parts within an object may be coded holistically in order to identify the object rather than to relate the two parts as separate entities in space. We might explain the spatial Stroop interference shown by R.M., if his ventral pathway coded the rectangle together with its word as a consistent or inconsistent whole. In the location naming task, on the other hand, R.M. was asked to relate the position of the word as an object to the rectangle as another object, presumably requiring the use of his damaged parietal lobes to label these between-object relations.

The hypothesis outlined in this chapter about the role of attention in binding appears to conflict with Duncan's view of attention as integrated competition between objects (Desimone and Duncan 1995; Duncan, this volume; see also Bundesen, this volume). In Duncan's language, attention is a state into which the system settles through global competition between objects for dominance over experience and action, rather than a selective process that helps create those objects. He denies the need for any external selective mechanism. However, for the features of the same object to cooperate in competition with others and to benefit from each other's ascendancy in the competition, it seems as though they would already need to be bound. Duncan's suggestion is that binding is achieved through detectors directly coding conjunctions of pairs of attributes. An alternative is that the competition postulated in Duncan's framework could arise at a later level than the binding mechanism proposed here, and could have evolved to determine selection for the control of actions. Attention need not be a unitary process simply because a single word is used in everyday language.

One of the findings supporting Duncan's account is the long duration that he and his colleagues observed for the 'attentional blink' (the interference with detecting a second target caused by detecting the first in a rapid visual sequence of items (Duncan *et al.* 1994)). The interference lasts for about 500 ms after the first target has been detected, suggesting an 'attentional dwell time' of half a second rather than the 60 or so milliseconds implied when one interprets the slope of search times against the number of items simultaneously presented as a serial scanning rate. However, there are a number of ways of reconciling these findings. One is that scanning items that are simultaneously present and unmasked may allow some parallel preprocessing to occur at the same time as the serial attentional binding, whereas each item in a sequential display interrupts the processing of its predecessor and must itself be processed from scratch. With a presentation rate of 150 ms instead of 90 ms per item, we found little evidence of a blink, suggesting that when the processing is not interrupted by the early onset of a new item or mask, an upper limit to the dwell time is 100–200 ms rather than 500 ms. Another contrast with most attentional blink experiments is that processing in search displays is serial across distractors, not targets, if it is serial at all. Processing of targets is likely to take longer than processing of distractors, as it requires commitment to a response. Finally, if processing in search is serial across pairs or small groups of homogeneous distractors rather than single items, observed slopes of 60 ms per item would imply dwell times of 120 or 180 ms (Treisman and Sato 1990), reducing the apparent discrepancy between sequential and simultaneous presentation.

As must be clear, this is work in progress and there is much that is not yet understood. The use of implicit priming measures opens new perspectives. The intriguing dissociations that we and others are finding between conscious experience and indirect priming suggest that the binding problem may be intimately bound up with the nature of consciousness, but that is a story that I think no one is yet ready to tell.

Acknowledgements

This work was supported by NSF, grant numbers SBR-9511633 and SBR-9631132. I thank D. Kahneman for helpful comments on the manuscript.

References

Ashbridge, E., Walsh, V. and Cowey, A. 1997 Temporal aspects of visual search studied by transcranial magnetic stimulation. *Neuropsychologia* **35**, 1121–31.

Cohen, A. and Ivry, R. 1989 Illusory conjunctions inside and outside the focus of attention. *J. Exp. Psychol. Hum. Percept. Perf.* **15**, 650–63.

Corbetta, M., Miezin, F., Dobmeyer, S., Shulman, G. and Petersen, S. 1991 Selective and divided attention during visual discrimination of shape, colour and speed: functional anatomy by positron emission tomography. *J. Neurosci.* **11**, 2383–402.

Corbetta, M., Shulman, G. L., Miezin, F. M. and Petersen, S. E. 1995 Superior parietal cortex activation during spatial attention shifts and visual feature conjunction. *Science* **270**, 802–5.

Cowey, A. 1985 Aspects of cortical organization related to selective attention and selective impairments of visual attention. In *Attention and performance XI* (eds M. P. and O. Marin), pp. 41–62. Hillsdale, NJ: Erlbaum.

Damasio, A., Yamata, T., Damasio, H., Corbetta, J. and McKee, J. 1980 Central achromatopsia: behavioral, anatomic, and physiologic aspects. *Neurology* **30**, 1064–71.

DeSchepper, B. and Treisman, A. 1996 Visual memory for novel shapes: implicit coding without attention. *J. Exp. Psychol. Learn. Mem. Cogn.* **22**, 27–47.

Desimone, R. and Duncan, J. 1995 Neural mechanisms of selective visual attention. *A. Rev. Neurosci.* **18**, 193–222.

Duncan, J. and Humphreys, G. W. 1989 Visual search and stimulus similarity. *Psychol. Rev.* **96**, 433–58.

Duncan, J., Ward, R. and Shapiro, K. 1994 Direct measurement of attentional dwell time. *Nature* **369**, 313–15.

Egly, R., Robertson, L. C., Rafal, R. and Grabowecky, M. 1995 Implicit processing of unreportable objects in Balint's syndrome. Los Angeles: Psychonomic Society Abstracts.

Enns, J. and Rensink, R. A. 1991 Preattentive recovery of three-dimensional orientation from line drawings. *Psychol. Rev.* **98**, 335–51.

Friedman-Hill, S. R., Robertson, L. C. and Treisman, A. 1995 Parietal contributions to visual feature binding: evidence from a patient with bilateral lesions. *Science* **269**, 853–5.

Goodale, M. A. and Milner, A. D. 1992 Separate visual pathways for perception and action. *Trends Neurosci.* **15**, 20–5.

Gray, C. M., Konig, P., Engel, A. and Singer, W. 1989 Oscillatory responses in cat visual cortex exhibit inter-columnar synchronization which reflects global stimulus properties. *Nature* **338**, 334–7.

Gulyas, B. and Roland, P. E. 1991 Cortical fields participating in form and colour discrimination in the human brain. *NeuroReport* **2**, 585–8.

He, Z. J. and Nakayama, K. 1992 Surfaces versus features in visual search. *Nature* **359**, 231–3.

Hubel, D. H. and Wiesel, T. N. 1968 Receptive fields and functional architecture of monkey striate cortex. *J. Physiol.* **195**, 215–43.

Hummel, J. E. and Biederman, I. 1992 Dynamic binding in a neural network for shape recognition. *Psychol. Rev.* **99**, 480–517.

Khurana, B., Smith, W. C., Baker, M. T. and Huang, C. 1994 Face representation under conditions of inattention. *Invest. Ophthalmol. Vis. Sci.* **35**(Suppl. 4), Abstract No. 4135.

Lehky, S. R. and Sejnowski, T. J. 1988 Network model of shape-from-shading: neural function arises from both receptive and projective fields. *Nature* **332**, 154–5.

Meadows, J. C. 1974 Disturbed perception of colours associated with localized cerebral lesions. *Brain* **97**, 615–32.

Moran, J. and Desimone, R. 1985 Selective attention gates visual processing in the extra-striate cortex. *Science* **229**, 782–4.

Nakayama, K. 1990 The iconic bottleneck and the tenuous link between early visual processing and perception. In *Vision: coding and efficiency* (ed. C. Blakemore), pp. 411–22. Cambridge University Press.

Navon, D. 1977 Forest before trees: the precedence of global features in visual perception. *Cogn. Psychol.* **9**, 353–83.

Neumann, E. and DeSchepper, B. G. 1992 An inhibition-based fan effect: evidence for an active suppression mechanism in selective attention. *Can. J. Psychol.* **46**, 1–40.

Petersen, S. E., Corbetta, M., Miezin, F. M. and Shulman, G. L. 1994 PET studies of parietal involvement in spatial attention: comparison of different task types. *Can. J. Exp. Psychol.* **48**, 319–38.

Posner, M. I. 1980 Orienting of attention. *Q. J. Exp. Psychol.* **32**, 3–26.

Ramachandran, V. S. 1988 Perceiving shape from shading. *Sci. Am.* **259**, 76–83.

Robertson, L., Treisman, A., Friedman-Hill, S. and Grabowecky, M. 1997 The interaction of spatial and object pathways: evidence from Balint's syndrome. *J. Cogn. Neurosci.* **9**, 254–76.

Sereno, M. I., Dale, A. M., Reppas, J. B., Kwong, K. K., Belliveau, J., Brady, T. J., Rosen, B. R. and Tootell, R. B. H. 1995 Borders of multiple visual areas in humans revealed by functional magnetic resonance imaging. *Science* **268**, 889–93.

Singer, W. and Gray, C. M. 1995 Visual feature integration and the temporal correlation hypothesis. *A. Rev. Neurosci.* **18**, 555–86.

Tanaka, K. 1993 Neuronal mechanisms of object recognition. *Science* **262**, 685–8.

Tipper, S. P. and Cranston, M. 1985 Selective attention and priming: inhibitory and facilitatory effects of ignored primes. *Q. J. Exp. Psychol.* A **37**, 591–611.

Treisman, A. 1982 Perceptual grouping and attention in visual search for features and for objects. *J. Exp. Psychol. Hum. Percept. Perf.* **8**, 194–214.

Treisman, A. 1988 Features and objects: the Fourteenth Bartlett Memorial Lecture. *Q. J. Exp. Psychol.* A **40**, 201–37.

Treisman, A. and Gelade, G. 1980 A feature integration theory of attention. *Cogn. Psychol.* **12**, 97–136.

Treisman, A. and Gormican, S. 1988 Feature analysis in early vision: evidence from search asymmetries. *Psychol. Rev.* **95**, 15–48.

Treisman, A. and Paterson, R. 1984 Emergent features, attention and object perception. *J. Exp. Psychol. Hum. Percept. Perf.* **10**, 12–21.

Treisman, A. and Sato, S. 1990 Conjunction search revisited. *J. Exp. Psychol. Hum. Percept. Perf.* **16**, 459–78.

Treisman, A. and Schmidt, H. 1982 Illusory conjunctions in the perception of objects. *Cogn. Psychol.* **14**, 107–41.

Treisman, A. and Souther, J. 1985 Search asymmetry: a diagnostic for preattentive processing of separable features. *J. Exp. Psychol. Gen.* **114**, 285–310.

Ungerleider, L. G. and Mishkin, M. 1982 *Two cortical visual systems*. Cambridge, MA: MIT Press.

Ward, L. 1982 Determinants of attention to local and global features of visual forms. *J. Exp. Psychol. Hum. Percept. Perf.* **8**, 562–81.

Wolfe, J. M. 1998 Inattentional amnesia. In *Fleeting memories* (ed. V. Coltheart). Cambridge, MA: MIT Press.

Wolfe, J. M., Cave, K. R. and Franzel, S. L. 1989 Guided search: an alternative to the feature integration model for visual search. *J. Exp. Psychol. Hum. Percept. Perf.* **15**, 419–33.

Zeki, S. M. 1991 Cerebral akinetopsia (visual motion blindness). *Brain* **114**, 811–24.

Zeki, S. 1993 *A vision of the brain*. Oxford: Blackwell.

Zihl, J., von Cramon, D. and Mai, N. 1983 Selective disturbance of movement vision after bilateral brain damage. *Brain* **106**, 313–40.

7

Converging levels of analysis in the cognitive neuroscience of visual attention

John Duncan

Abstract

Experiments using behavioural, lesion, functional imaging, and single neuron methods are considered in the context of a neuropsychological model of visual attention. According to this model, inputs compete for representation in several visually responsive brain systems—sensory and motor, cortical and subcortical. Competition is biased by advance priming of neurons responsive to current behavioural targets. Across systems competition is integrated such that the same, selected object tends to become dominant throughout. The behavioural studies reviewed concern divided attention within and between modalities. They implicate within-modality competition as one main restriction on concurrent stimulus identification. In contrast to the conventional association of lateral attentional focus with parietal lobe function, the lesion studies show attentional bias to be a widespread consequence of unilateral cortical damage. Although the clinical syndrome of unilateral neglect may indeed be associated with parietal lesions, this probably reflects an assortment of further deficits accompanying a simple attentional imbalance. The functional imaging studies show joint involvement of lateral prefrontal and occipital cortex in lateral attentional focus and competition. The single unit studies suggest how competition in several regions of extrastriate cortex is biased by advance priming of neurons responsive to current behavioural targets. Together, the concepts of competition, priming and integration allow a unified theoretical approach to findings from behavioural to single neuron levels.

7.1 Introduction

In any normal visual environment, filled with a complex clutter of overlapping objects and surfaces, three aspects of the attentional problem are immediately evident. First is limited attentional capacity: at any given moment, only a small fraction of the total visual input is actively taken up and used in the control of behaviour. In this sense objects compete to be processed. Second is top-down control or selectivity based on relevance to behaviour: given attentional competition, it is important to deal selectively with those particular objects of relevance to current concerns. Third is integration (Treisman, this volume; Treisman and Gelade 1980): generally speaking, behaviour directed to some chosen object—e.g. reaching to pick up a specified object from a table—will require that several separate properties of that object (shape, location, orientation and so on) be selected and processed together.

Much is now known of the many regions of the primate brain that are concurrently activated by visual input. In the posterior cerebral cortex these include several 'visual areas', specialized for different purposes and in part for the processing of different visual attributes such as shape, motion, and spatial position (Zeki 1978; Desimone and Ungerleider 1989). In anterior cortex, visually driven activity is also seen in several more 'motor' areas, including frontal eye fields, premotor cortex and so on. Also included should be subcortical structures, including the superior colliculus and several nuclei of the thalamus. In this paper, the problems of competition, integration and top-down control are considered in light of this widely distributed brain activity.

One conventional view is that selective visual attention is the province of spatial processing structures, in particular the parietal lobe (see, for example, De Renzi 1982). According to a simple version of this view, each parietal lobe is predominantly responsible for directing attention to the contralateral side of stimulus space, though a number of more sophisticated versions have also been proposed (see, for example, Mesulam 1981; Posner *et al.* 1984). In this paper I present a somewhat different view, the integrated competition hypothesis (Desimone and Duncan 1995; Duncan 1996; Duncan *et al.* 1997*a*), and experiments bearing on it from levels of normal and impaired human behaviour to functional neuroimaging and single unit electrophysiology.

7.2 Integrated competition hypothesis

The integrated competition hypothesis rests on three general principles.

1. As already detailed, many brain systems are concurrently activated by visual input. Our hypothesis suggests that, in many and perhaps most of these systems, processing is competitive: enhanced response to one object is associated with decreased response to others. For example, responses to different objects may be mutually inhibitory.

   At the behavioural level, we take competition to be reflected in the interference that generally occurs when a person must divide attention between different objects in a visual scene. Many previous experiments have detailed properties of this interference, which occurs whether objects are presented at widely separate locations or overlapping at the point of fixation (Duncan 1984; Vecera and Farah 1994), and whether the person is asked to identify similar aspects of the two attended objects, e.g. their shapes or locations, or dissimilar aspects, e.g. the shape of one object and the location of another (Duncan 1993*a,b*; for a partial exception, see Duncan and Nimmo-Smith 1996).

2. Top-down priming of neural activity biases competition towards objects of relevance to current behaviour (Walley and Weiden 1973; Harter and Aine 1984). A good example is the partial report experiment, in which an array of letters (or other objects) is displayed, usually so briefly as to prohibit eye movements. Subjects are asked to identify some of these letters while disregarding others. Consider a subject who is asked to read only the red letters. We propose that, in extrastriate systems coding colour, neurons selective for red inputs are preactivated or primed by this instruction. A largely equivalent possibility is that neurons selective for other colours are deactivated or inhibited. Red letters in the display thus activate primed neurons, and are at a competitive advantage.

   Physiological evidence for such priming will be considered in a later section (see also Desimone, this volume). For the present, the key point is that selective priming gives top-down attentional control its required flexibility. In different behavioural contexts, inputs of any kind might in principle be the most relevant. Returning to the partial report experiment, the instructed selection rule can be based on location (e.g. report only letters from a specified row; see Sperling 1960), on assorted object properties (e.g. report only letters of a specified colour, size, or direction of motion; see von Wright 1968), or even on more complex categorizations (e.g. report letters while ignoring digits; Merikle 1980; Duncan 1983). In all these cases, there is evidence for preferential target processing; in particular, performance depends more on the number of targets than the number of non-targets in a display (Duncan 1980; Bundesen *et al.* 1985; Shibuya 1993). Thus, many different visual properties can be used to direct attention or assign limited processing capacity to objects of relevance to current behaviour. According to our hypothesis, such control is implemented by differential patterns of neural priming, very likely in different extrastriate regions coding the multiple properties of visual input.

3. Competition, finally, is integrated between components of the sensorimotor network (see, for example, Farah 1990; Mesulam 1990). As an object gains dominance in any one system, responses to this same object are supported elsewhere. Various network models have been proposed to account for how such integration might occur (see, for example, Phaf *et al.* 1990). For present purposes, the key point is that the network as a whole tends to cascade into a state in which the same object is dominant throughout. In this way its numerous properties are made concurrently available for control of different aspects of behaviour.

Such integration is a functional requirement if whole object selection is to be achieved starting from task-specific, local patterns of neural priming. Returning to partial report, very different priming patterns will doubtless be established by instructions to read red letters, or small letters, or letters in a particular row; in each case, however, the final result must be selective processing of the desired shapes and their names. Integration is also reflected in a robust behavioural result: for many pairs of dimensions, two simultaneous discriminations concerning the same object can be made without loss of accuracy (Duncan 1984, 1993*a,b*; Duncan and Nimmo-Smith 1996; see also Lappin 1967; Kahneman and Henik 1977; Treisman *et al.* 1983). While distinct objects compete to be processed, different properties of the same object become available together for report and control of behaviour.

According to the integrated competition hypothesis, attentional functions such as competition and priming are not the specific province of some particular part of the sensorimotor network, such as the parietal lobe. Rather they reflect distributed states of the network as whole. The remainder of this paper presents four lines of experimental work done in the context of this general view. A first set of experiments addresses the domain of attentional competition at the behavioural level. It suggests a substantial modality-specific element to limited processing capacity. A second set of experiments shows lateral attentional imbalance to be a rather common consequence of unilateral brain lesions, irrespective of parietal involvement. Such imbalance may be only one component of the clinical picture of 'unilateral neglect' associated with parietal lesions. A third set of experiments uses functional imaging to implicate joint, competitive activity of occipital and prefrontal cortex in lateral attentional focus. The final experiments detail attentional competition in single neurons of the extrastriate cortex of the macaque, and consider the role of such neurons in top-down attentional control.

7.3 Behavioural studies

A key aspect of the integrated competition hypothesis is competition between concurrent visual representations. In large part, we take such competition to occur in the several extrastriate regions coding different properties of the visual input. A natural prediction might be that competition will be very much weaker when inputs occur in different sensory modalities, and thus are represented in very different sensory systems. Data in support of this prediction were obtained in an early study by Treisman and Davies (1973). Recently, we have extended their methods to provide detailed measurements of attentional competition time-locked to the presentation of critical target stimuli within and between modalities (Duncan *et al.* 1997*b*).

A first experiment used auditory stimuli. In each trial, the subject heard two brief speech streams, spoken concurrently over headphones by two different voices, one high and one low. The impression was of two centrally located voices speaking rapidly and simultaneously for a period of a few seconds. Each stream consisted of a series of non-targets—the syllable 'guh' repeated at a rate of 4 s^{-1}—with a single target word embedded somewhere within it. In any given trial, the first target occurred unpredictably in either the high- or the low-voice stream; the second occurred in the other stream following an interval (stimulus onset asynchrony or SOA) of between 125 and 1375 ms. The task was simply to identify targets, ignoring non-targets. In focused attention conditions, subjects listened only to one voice, high or low for a whole block of trials, and thus identified only one word per trial. In divided attention conditions, subjects listened to both voices and identified both targets in each trial. In all cases, the indication of which target or targets had been heard was made after the whole stimulus sequence had finished.

Results are shown in figure 7.1a. In this figure, the accuracy of identifying the first target in any given trial is shown at negative SOA, while second target data appear at positive SOA. Data at -125 ms, for example, show performance for a first target presented 125 ms before a second. Comparison of focused and divided attention shows two results. First, there was an overall loss of accuracy in the divided attention case. Several factors may contribute to a general difficulty in preparing and executing two concurrent tasks (Pashler 1994); these are not our main concern here. Of more interest is the second finding in the divided attention condition: when one target was followed within a few hundred milliseconds by another, the accuracy of identifying both (in particular the second) was decreased. Interference between targets presented close together in time is a common result in experiments of this sort (Broadbent and Broadbent 1987; Raymond et al. 1992; Duncan et al. 1994; see also Ostry et al. 1976; Duncan 1980). A time-course of a few hundred milliseconds is typical of such interference. Subjectively, attention is committed to the first target and is then unavailable for the second.

The visual case was examined in a second experiment. With one complication, events and timing were copied closely from the auditory study. The complication concerns event streams, which were designed so that, even in focused attention conditions, it would always be optimal to keep the eyes fixated on the centre of the display. Each event in the 'horizontal stream' was a pair of letter strings, flashed briefly and simultaneously to the left and right of fixation. For non-targets, both letter strings were rows of three 'x's. For targets, one string (at random either left or right) was a three-letter word to be identified. As before, events (flashes) followed one another in rapid succession, at a rate of 4 s^{-1}. The 'vertical stream' was similar, except that the components of each flash appeared one above and one below fixation. As for high and low voices in the auditory study, horizontal and vertical streams were presented concurrently for a period of a few seconds. Overall, therefore, the subject saw rows of 'x's flashing rapidly and concurrently in all four screen locations, with one target presented at some time during the trial to left or right of the fixation point, and another above or below. Again, the divided attention case (identify both targets) was compared with focused attention controls (identify only the horizontal target in some trial blocks, only the vertical target in others). Results, shown in figure 7.1b, were very much as before. In the divided attention condition, again, there was substantial interference when successive targets occurred within an interval of a few hundred milliseconds.

The results of auditory and visual studies are remarkably similar. Does this indicate some common, general limit on the capacity to process concurrent stimulus events? The answer is provided in the third experiment, in which concurrent targets came from separate sensory modalities. For this experiment, the high voice stream of the auditory experiment was combined with the horizontal stream of the visual experiment. Again each stream contained a single target, with details of timing and procedure exactly as before. Results are shown in figure 7.1c. Again there was

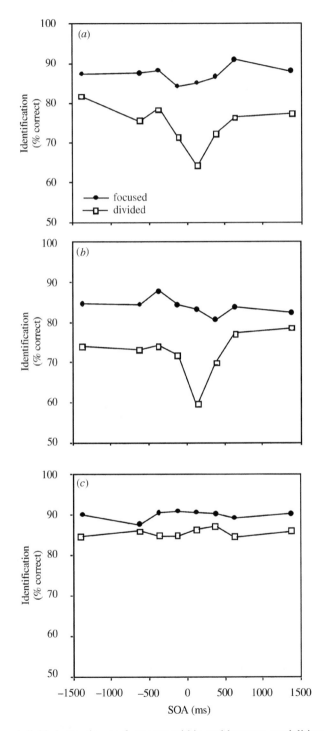

Fig. 7.1 Focused and divided attention performance within and between modalities: (*a*) auditory; (*b*) visual; (*c*) mixed modality. Score is per cent correct target identification as a function of between-target interval. Adapted with permission from Duncan *et al.* (1997*b*).

a general loss of accuracy associated with the requirement to perform two tasks at once. This time, however, there was absolutely no interference time-locked to target presentation. Under the circumstances of this experiment, directing attention to a target in one modality left concurrent processing in a different modality undisturbed.

In our experiments, all stimuli were located close to the central or straight-ahead position. Auditory stimuli were presented binaurally over headphones, while visual stimuli were all presented within about 2° of central fixation. A somewhat separate issue arises in experiments with large angular separations between inputs in different modalities. As one example, Driver and Spence (1994) presented concurrent auditory and visual stimuli from speakers–screens positioned approximately 30° to left and right of body midline. Under these circumstances, concurrent identification of the two inputs was much better when they originated on the same side. The results are strongly reminiscent of our proposal that the same selected input tends to become dominant throughout the sensorimotor network. When inputs arise from widely separate locations, there is a clear preference for auditory and visual systems to converge to work on the same general area of space (Kinsbourne 1987). Similar results in other studies suggest spatial integration of visual, auditory, postural, tactile, and even motor systems (see Driver, this volume; Morais 1978; Robertson and North 1994; Driver and Grossenbacher 1996). When all inputs are close to central, however, our results show substantial independence in the processing of visual and auditory targets. Under these circumstances, the results imply that the principal basis for attentional competition lies in modality-specific sensory systems.

7.4 Lesion studies

Lesion studies provide a principal motivation for the conventional association of visual attention with the parietal lobe. In the human, parietal lesions (in particular on the right) are often associated with a clinical picture of hemispatial or contralateral neglect. Such neglect is manifest in a general tendency to disregard the side of space opposite to the lesion. Examples include failure to complete the left half of drawings, or to mark left-sided targets when asked to cross out lines in a jumbled spatial array (Bisiach and Vallar 1988).

For several reasons, neglect has often been considered to reflect attentional bias. Particularly relevant is an element of the disorder termed extinction: in some cases, contralesional inputs are only disregarded in the presence of simultaneous, competing inputs on the unaffected or ipsilesional side (Bender 1952; Karnath 1988). Such results strongly imply lateral bias in the normal process of attentional competition.

A recent study, done in collaboration with the groups of Claus Bundesen in Copenhagen and Glyn Humphreys in Birmingham, suggests a different perspective (Duncan *et al.*, in press). In combination with others, our findings suggest that extinction or lateral bias may be a very widespread consequence of unilateral brain injury. The gross clinical disorder associated with right parietal lesions arises through combination of this general lateral bias with one or more further impairments, in some cases influencing both sides of space. In our experiments, several methods are combined to measure distinct components of attentional impairment. Here, I shall give just a brief description of two aspects of the results.

To measure extinction or lateral bias we use a standard divided attention method. In single target control trials, the patient is asked to identify letters flashed singly to left or right of fixation. In divided attention trials, letters are flashed simultaneously to left and right, and the patient must identify both. Displays are too brief to permit eye movement, and central fixation is monitored at the start of each trial. For individual patients, exposure duration is adjusted to bring accuracy into a suitable range to avoid ceiling and floor effects.

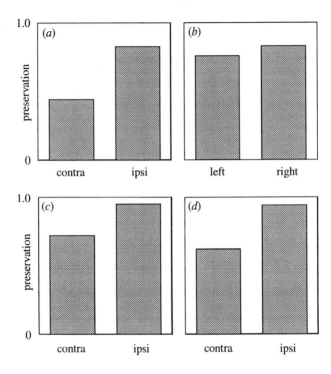

Fig. 7.2 Divided attention performance for three patient groups and matched controls: (*a*) right parietal; (*b*) control; (*c*) right other; (*d*) left occipitotemporal. Preservation score (proportion correct in divided attention divided by proportion correct in single target controls) is shown separately for contralesional (contra) and ipsilesional (ipsi) visual fields. For controls the corresponding separation is simply left compared with right field.

Results for several subject groups appear in figure 7.2. For letters in each visual field we calculate a preservation score reflecting how well accuracy is maintained in divided attention. This score is simply proportion correct in divided attention trials divided by proportion correct in single target controls. A score of zero in the contralesional field, for example, would indicate complete extinction by an accompanying ipsilesional target.

In figure 7.2*a* are shown mean results for a group of six patients with lesions of the right parietal lobe, in some cases extending into adjacent areas. The results show a typical extinction pattern; while letters on both sides suffer in divided attention (preservation score less than 1.0), this cost is carried predominantly by the contralesional (left-sided) items. Controls (seven subjects, figure 7.2*b*) show no such result; though mean data suggest a slight tendency for poorer preservation on the left, this was weak and inconsistent across individuals. These are exactly the results that would be predicted by the conventional parietal lobe hypothesis.

One reason for doubting this hypothesis comes from small groups of patients with other posterior lesions. In figure 7.2*c* are shown mean results for two patients with right posterior lesions not involving the parietal lobe. Figure 7.2*d* shows results for a single patient with an occipitotemporal lesion in the left rather than the right hemisphere (Duncan 1996). In both cases there is the standard extinction result, with preservation scores close to 1.0 for the ipsilesional field, but substantially lower for the contralesional field.

In fact, our results are in line with several other studies showing that extinction can arise after many different kinds of cortical and subcortical lesions (for examples, see Bender 1952; Desimone *et al.* 1990; Vallar *et al.* 1994). These are very much the results to be expected according to the integrated competition hypothesis. Once a part of the sensory input becomes dominant in any region of the sensorimotor network, it will tend to capture control of that network as a whole. Given that many different unilateral lesions may weaken the local representation of contralateral space, the common result should be a generalized competitive disadvantage for that side.

If lateral bias alone is not sufficient to explain the effects of right parietal lesions, what additional factors are involved? Our second set of data concerns total capacity or rate of processing visual input. For this measurement, arrays of five letters were flashed for varying durations in left or right visual field. Subjects simply reported as many as possible. To eliminate lateral bias within

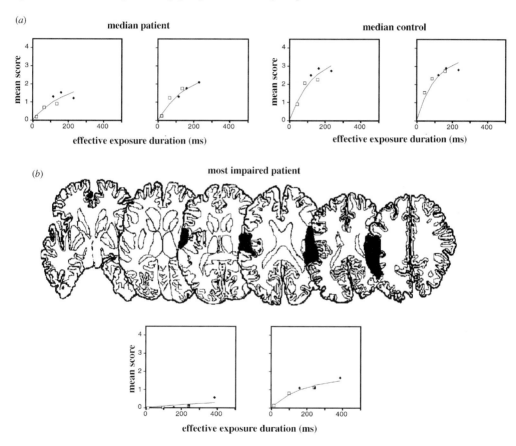

Fig. 7.3 (*a*) Whole report data for median parietal patient and median control. Scores for each subject are mean numbers of letters correctly reported as a function of effective exposure duration, separately for left-field (left panel) and right-field (right panel) arrays. Calculation of effective exposure depends on a curve-fitting procedure described in Duncan *et al.* (in press), applied to data from masked (open squares) and unmasked (filled diamonds) displays. Solid curve is a fit to the data based on whole report theory of Bundesen 1990. (*b*) Patient with most severe impairment. The upper diagram shows the restricted inferior parietal lesion, drawn on standard slices from Gado *et al.* 1979. These slices show the right hemisphere on the left. Whole report data appear below. Adapted with permission from Duncan *et al.* (in press).

an array, letters were presented in a vertical column centred approximately 2.5° to left or right of fixation.

Example results are shown in figure 7.3. In *a* are shown data from the median patient in our right parietal group (left), compared with the median control subject (right). For each subject, separate panels show data from left- and right-field arrays. In each case, the number of letters reported increased roughly exponentially with increase in exposure duration. This increase, however, was substantially slower in the patient. The results are representative of the overall comparison between patients and controls; data from the worst patient are shown in *b*, along with a diagram showing this patient's restricted inferior parietal lesion. Importantly, the deficit in processing rate was typically bilateral in these right parietal patients. Although rate was somewhat lower in the left field (see examples in figure 7.3), the main result was decreased rate in both fields, implying a substantial non-lateralized component to the overall visual impairment (see Robertson 1989; Halligan and Marshall 1994; Husain *et al.* 1997).

Undoubtedly there is much more to be done to clarify the interpretation of these results. Figure 7.2 might suggest a stronger extinction tendency in parietal than in non-parietal patients, and this should be checked with larger patient groups. We have also observed deficits in overall processing rate in patients with lesions outside the parietal lobe. Additional, more specific deficits may be equally important in understanding the effects of parietal lesions, including perceptual minimization (Milner and Harvey 1995) or even active rejection (Mijovic-Prelec *et al.* 1994) of the neglected field. Already, however, it seems clear that the left sided difficulties of right parietal patients reflect a combination of deficits, including a general lateral bias, common to many unilateral brain injuries, and a gross overall reduction in the rate of visual processing.

7.5 Functional imaging

Control of the lateral focus of attention is also a basic question in our recent functional imaging studies. In these studies we have used positron emission tomography (PET) to measure regional cerebral bloodflow (rCBF) in normal subjects focusing attention to the left or right visual field.

In initial studies (Vandenberghe *et al.* 1997*b*), subjects were shown arrays consisting of two circular grating patches, one to each side of fixation. Each patch varied in two attributes, the orientation of the grating, and the precise location of the patch with respect to a surrounding frame. For each patch, both orientation and location varied randomly and independently from one trial to the next. Potentially, therefore, subjects could be asked to make discriminations of either orientation or spatial location in either left or right visual field, or any combination of these. A fixed task (e.g. orientation discrimination on the left) was performed throughout the period of each 40 s scan. Within this period, trials followed one another at a rate of approximately $36 \, \text{min}^{-1}$. For each trial, the display was flashed for 495 ms, and the subject reported the relevant judgement (e.g. left orientation) aloud. Central fixation was required throughout, and monitored by electrooculogram.

The first important results concern focused attention conditions. For these, the subject made only a single discrimination, either orientation or location on either left or right patch. For present purposes, the key contrast is between leftward and rightward attention, orientation and location tasks in fact giving rather similar results.

Results are shown in figure 7.4 (also see plate section). The figure shows regions of significant difference between leftward and rightward attention, based on mean data from orientation and location tasks. In each row, the brain is represented in five horizontal sections running from bottom (leftmost slice) to top (rightmost slice). The upper row shows regions of increased rCBF in leftward as compared to rightward attention; the lower row shows the reverse.

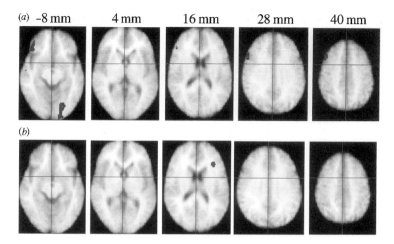

Fig. 7.4 Significant bloodflow differences ($p < 0.05$, corrected for multiple comparisons) between leftward and rightward attention. (*a*) Greater flow in leftward attention; (*b*) the reverse. Each series shows horizontal brain slices progressing from bottom (left) to top (right) of the brain, after averaging between subjects and normalization to the standard space of Talairach and Tournoux (1988). Standard z levels of each slice are shown at the top of the figure; within each slice, the left of the brain appears on the left. Significant differences are shown in red (see colour plate) on the mean of the 14 subjects' normalized magnetic resonance images (MRIs). Analyses conducted using standard SPM software (Friston *et al.* 1995). Adapted with permission from Vandenberghe *et al.* (1997*b*). (See colour plate section)

There are three results that are noteworthy. First, leftward attention was associated with increased bloodflow in the occipital cortex of the right hemisphere (upper row, first slice). In agreement with previous studies using both PET (Heinze *et al.* 1994) and event-related potentials (Van Voorhis and Hillyard 1977), such results suggest enhancement of visual processing on the side contralateral to attention. Given predominantly crossed representation in many early visual areas, this is very much the anticipated result. Although in our case the effect was restricted to the right hemisphere, subsequently we have observed symmetrical effects (Vandenberghe *et al.* 1997*a*), in agreement with others' results (for example, see Heinze *et al.* 1994).

Second, and somewhat striking, parietal lobe activity was entirely indifferent to the direction of attention. Instead, we observed substantial activation of the superior parietal lobule in all conditions, compared with a control task requiring no peripheral discriminations. As it was indifferent to the direction of attention, such activation is invisible in figure 7.4. In all conditions, parietal activation was stronger in the right hemisphere. Similar parietal activation has previously been reported in studies of peripheral attention (see, for example, Corbetta *et al.* 1993; Vandenberghe *et al.* 1996; Nobre *et al.* 1997). Although these studies have sometimes suggested stronger activity on the side contralateral to the attended focus, this has been at best a mild modulation occurring on a baseline of generally stronger activity on the right, and is certainly not visible in our results.

The third result is perhaps the most surprising. Attention to either side was associated with increased activity in the ipsilateral frontal lobe. Thus, leftward attention was associated with a broad band of activation of the left lateral frontal cortex (figure 7.4*a*, first and third to fifth slices). Rightward attention was associated with a more restricted activation of right lateral frontal cortex (figure 7.4*b*, third slice). The results suggest an intriguing hypothesis: on each side, one function of

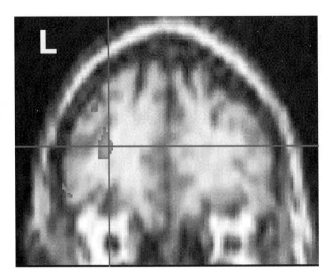

Fig. 7.5 Bloodflow differences ($p < 0.001$ uncorrected) between leftward and rightward attention for a single subject from the study of Vandenberghe *et al.* (1997*a*). Differences (orange–yellow; see colour plate section) shown on coronal slice from subject's individual MRI, normalized to standard space of Talairach and Tournoux (1988) and taken at $y = 42$ mm to show prefrontal cortex. Crosshair marks maximum activation in inferior frontal sulcus. Other details as in figure 7.4.

lateral frontal cortex may be to inhibit or accord a competitive disadvantage to the contralateral side of space. Indeed, frontal lesions are sometimes associated with disinhibition of unwanted activity on the opposite side, including reflexive eye movements (Butter *et al.* 1988; Paus *et al.* 1991). Neglect of the side ipsilateral to the lesion has also been reported (Kwon and Heilman 1991). Of course, frontal lesions can also be associated with contralateral neglect (Heilman and Valenstein 1972). In some cases, contralateral neglect may reverse as recovery progresses, producing a long-term ipsilateral deficit (Butter *et al.* 1988; Kwon and Heilman 1991).

Whatever its interpretation, we have found ipsilateral frontal activation to be a consistent result across three separate experiments, involving a variety of tasks and response modes. Illustrative results from our most recent study (Vandenberghe *et al.* 1997*a*) are shown in figure 7.5 (also see plate section). Here the data from one individual subject have been plotted on that subject's own magnetic resonance image to show in more detail the areas of left frontal activity associated with leftward attention. This subject's data illustrate three apparently separate activation foci, each of which is also seen in a number of other subjects. Two are on the lateral surface, one more dorsal, on the middle frontal gyrus, the other more ventral, on the inferior frontal gyrus. The third is buried within the depths of the inferior frontal sulcus. Although these are very preliminary results, they suggest the precision with which single-subject functional imaging may define regions of frontal involvement in controlling (or otherwise reflecting) the attentional focus.

A final set of results concerns divided attention. As we have seen, accuracy suffers when a person must identify properties of two different objects in a single, brief display. Properties of the same object, in contrast, can be identified together without accuracy loss. In a further experiment in our series (Vandenberghe *et al.* 1997), two discriminations were required for each display. In single-object tasks, subjects identified either orientation and location of the left patch, or orientation and location of the right patch. In dual-object tasks, subjects identified either orientation of the left patch and location of the right patch, or vice versa. The results suggest an interesting parallel to two-object performance cost. In both frontal and occipital lobes, extreme patterns of bloodflow were associated with exclusively leftward or rightward attention, while results were intermediate for the two-object case. In left lateral frontal and right occipital cortex, bloodflow was highest for attention to two properties of the left object, lowest for attention to two properties of the right object, and intermediate for attention to one property of each. A complementary pattern was seen in right frontal (although again not left occipital) cortex. The results seem directly to reflect competition between attentional foci, divided attention producing a compromise between the extreme states of cerebral activity associated with focused attention to either one side or the other (Van Voorhis and Hillyard 1977).

It is perhaps too soon to draw firm general conclusions from these functional imaging studies. Again, however, the results suggest that lateralized parietal activity may be at best a modest factor in directing attention to the contralateral field. A further consideration may be lateral frontal activity according a competitive disadvantage to contralateral space.

7.6 Single unit studies

The final studies to be considered measure attentional modulation of activity in single cells of the monkey brain. Only an outline of this work will be presented here; for more details see Desimone (this volume).

An illustrative study recorded the activity of single neurons in inferior temporal (IT) cortex during a simple version of visual search (Chelazzi *et al.* 1993, 1998). IT cortex is a high-level visual area whose neurons show selectivity for complex objects and their properties, e.g. complex combinations of colour and shape (Desimone and Ungerleider 1989). We asked how such neurons respond when an animal is instructed to select a specific target stimulus from a visual array.

For each neuron isolated, the experiment began by pre-testing with a selection of alternative stimuli. Given the complex preferences of IT units, the stimuli we used were digitized magazine pictures. Our aim was to identify two stimuli for use in the main experiment—one, the effective stimulus, producing a strong response from the cell, and a second, the ineffective stimulus, producing little or no response.

Once these stimuli had been identified, the cell's responses were recorded during several hundred trials of the main search task. Each trial began with a central dot on the screen, which the animal was required to fixate (see figure 7.6, top). Once fixation (measured by scleral search coil) was acquired, a 300 ms cue stimulus was presented, again at screen centre. On different trials this cue was either the effective or the ineffective stimulus. The cue was followed by a delay, during which the animal was simply to maintain central fixation. At the end of this delay, a search array was presented, containing both effective and ineffective stimuli in unpredictable locations within the visual field contralateral to the recording site. The task was to make an immediate saccade from the central fixation point to whichever search stimulus matched the preceding cue.

Mean responses in a population of 22 selective cells are shown at the bottom of figure 7.6. There are two trial types that can be distinguished, those in which the effective stimulus was cued, and so was the relevant or target stimulus for this trial (solid lines), and those in which it was uncued, and so was an irrelevant non-target (dashed lines). The distinction between effective and ineffective stimuli is shown in responses to the cue (first black bar on time axis). As intended, the effective stimulus produced a substantial response when presented as a cue, while the ineffective stimulus did not. Note, however, that once cues had been removed, subsequent visual input was exactly the same for the two types of trial. Any subsequent difference in neural activity was driven not by current visual input, but by behavioural context.

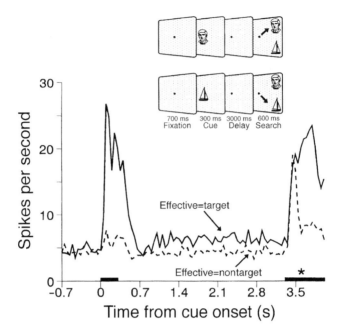

Fig. 7.6 Task and illustrative results from Chelazzi *et al.* (1993). Typical trial events are illustrated at upper right. Effective and ineffective stimuli (see text) are shown schematically as head and boat. Arrow on search display shows required saccade; no arrow was actually presented. Below is shown mean discharge rate (spikes per second) for 22 selective neurons as a function of time from cue onset. On the time axis, first bar marks cue presentation, second bar marks search array, asterisk marks mean time of saccade. Solid line: effective stimulus is cued and becomes target in search array. Dashed line: effective stimulus is uncued and becomes non-target. Adapted with permission from Desimone and Duncan (1994).

The first important result concerns activity in the delay interval, when only the fixation point was present on the screen. During this interval, cells fired more strongly when their effective stimulus was the relevant or target stimulus on this trial. Considering IT as a whole, one can conclude that, when a certain stimulus is defined as relevant to a current task, the population of cells responsive to that target shows enhanced or primed activity.

The second important result concerns responses to the search array (second black bar on time axis). Recall that this array always contained the cell's effective stimulus, and so was in principle capable of driving a positive response. Indeed, an initial positive response was always seen, whether or not the effective stimulus was the target. Beginning around 100 ms before the animal's saccade, however, responses on the two types of trial diverged. If the effective stimulus was the target, the response it produced was sustained into the period of the saccade. If the effective stimulus was a non-target, in contrast, the response it produced was rapidly suppressed. Considering IT as a whole, one can conclude that, by the time of the saccade, neural activity is dominated by responses to the relevant or target stimulus.

These results provide a direct motivation for our proposals concerning biased competition in extrastriate cortex. Competition between responses to target and non-target objects is biased by advance priming of the target neural population. The result is sustained response to targets, but suppressed response to non-targets.

The findings concerning selective delay activity have been amplified in a number of further studies. In the above task, behavioural relevance was defined by object identity: the animal was instructed to attend to a particular target object. Correspondingly, we observed selective delay activity in IT cortex, a region specialized for high-level object processing (see similarly Fuster *et al.* 1985; Miyashita and Chang 1988). In other tasks, the instruction is spatial: the animal must attend to whatever object is presented in a specified location. Corresponding spatial delay activity might be unexpected in IT, where receptive fields are large and spatial information correspondingly poor. Instead, it has been reported earlier in the visual system (regions V2, V4); here, cells show enhanced discharge when an animal is instructed to attend to a location lying within the receptive field (Luck *et al.* 1997). Somewhat analogous spatially selective delay activity has also been reported in other areas, including the parietal lobe (Gnadt and Andersen 1988). The results directly support our proposal that different forms of attentional cueing will be implemented by flexible, task-specific forms of neural priming in different extrastriate regions.

In both non-spatial (Fuster *et al.* 1985; Miller *et al.* 1996) and spatial (Niki and Watanabe 1976; Funahashi *et al.* 1989; di Pellegrino and Wise 1993) tasks, particularly strong and robust delay activity is observed in prefrontal cortex. Such results suggest a possible role for the frontal lobe in establishing and preserving top-down attentional bias (Desimone, this volume). Possible mechanisms would include priming of extrastriate cells responsive to current behavioural targets, and (consistent with our functional imaging findings) inhibition of cells responsive to non-targets. Such a role would be in line with the broad importance of the frontal lobe in both working memory function (Goldman-Rakic 1988) and behavioural control more generally (Luria 1966).

The findings concerning non-target suppression have also been amplified in other studies. Stronger responses to relevant than to irrelevant stimuli have been reported throughout much of extrastriate cortex, including areas V2, V4, MT, MST, IT, and area 7 of the parietal lobe (Bushnell *et al.* 1981; Moran and Desimone 1985; Motter 1994; Treue and Maunsell 1996; Luck *et al.* 1997), possibly extending back into striate cortex itself (Motter 1993). The extent to which non-target responses are suppressed—so that the network as a whole reflects only properties of the attended or target stimulus—depends very much on exact circumstances of the task and visual input, however. One important consideration is spatial separation of relevant and irrelevant inputs. Several studies have found far greater suppression of non-target responses when target and non-target both fall within the receptive field of the recorded cell (Moran and Desimone 1985; Treue and Maunsell 1996), implying that in many visual areas, much representation of non-targets remains across a whole cell population. Similarly, our IT results depend on the spatial layout of the display. If effective and ineffective stimuli lie on opposite sides of the visual meridian, we find that IT cells are driven not by the behaviourally relevant stimulus, but by whichever stimulus lies in the contralateral visual field (Chelazzi *et al.* 1998). A key consideration may be time. Early in the response, as we have seen, relevant and irrelevant inputs are equally represented in the neural signal (figure 7.6). The strongest suppression of non-target responses may take hundreds of milliseconds or more to develop (see, for example, Gottlieb *et al.* 1998; Motter 1994), as the appropriate selective state is established. An intriguing hypothesis is that factors such as spatial separation may be most important in an intermediate period between initial, strong non-target representation and final, substantial non-target suppression; a period that might be particularly important in studies whose stimuli last only a few hundred milliseconds.

7.7 Conclusion

Perhaps the key feature of the integrated competition hypothesis is its distributed view of attentional functions. Good examples are provided by several of the results I have described. Both our own lesion studies and others' results show how a lateral attentional imbalance arises from damage to many different brain areas. Our functional imaging studies suggest the joint involvement of prefrontal and occipital cortex in lateral attentional focus and competition. The single unit results suggest flexible involvement of several extrastriate systems in top-down attentional control by biased competition. More generally, 'attention' is seen as a widely distributed state, in which several brain systems converge to work on the different properties and action implications of the same, selected object.

Of course this framework has many points of uncertainty. In single unit studies, for example, it is clear that several factors influence competition for control of cellular responses, including proximity to the receptive field and side of visual space in addition to behavioural relevance. In a sense these factors reflect a failure of the network to integrate: when stimuli are widely separated, for example, different cells are dominated by different inputs. The strength of integration will also be a key factor in understanding the many reported dissociations in neglect, e.g. neglect restricted to one sensory modality (see, for example, Guariglia and Antonucci 1992). Although the tendency may be for different spatial systems to share a common dominant focus, this tendency is far from absolute. Already, however, we begin to see how three key concepts—competition, top-down control, and object integration—allow a coherent theoretical approach to the problem of visual attention from behavioural through to single unit levels.

Acknowledgements

Much of this work was supported by a grant from the Human Frontier Science Program. I thank my collaborators: C. Bundesen, R. Desimone, G. Humphreys, G. Orban and their many colleagues, for their contributions to all phases of the work, and for permission to cite published and unpublished results.

References

Bender, M. B. 1952 *Disorders in perception*. Springfield, IL: Charles C. Thomas.

Bisiach, E. and Vallar, G. 1988 Hemineglect in humans. In *Handbook of neuropsychology*, vol. 1 (eds F. Boller and J. Grafman), pp. 195–222. Amsterdam: Elsevier.

Broadbent, D. E. and Broadbent, M. H. P. 1987 From detection to identification: response to multiple targets in rapid serial visual presentation. *Percept. Psychophys.* **42**, 105–13.

Bundesen, C. 1990 A theory of visual attention. *Psychol. Rev.* **97**, 523–47.

Bundesen, C., Shibuya, H. and Larsen, A. 1985 Visual selection from multielement displays: a model for partial report. In *Attention and performance XI* (eds M. I. Posner and O. Marin), pp. 631–49. Hillsdale, NJ: Erlbaum.

Bushnell, M. C., Goldberg, M. E. and Robinson, D. L. 1981 Behavioral enhancement of visual responses in monkey cerebral cortex. I. Modulation in posterior parietal cortex related to selective visual attention. *J. Neurophysiol.* **46**, 755–72.

Butter, C. M., Rapcsak, S., Watson, R. J. and Heilman, K. M. 1988 Changes in sensory inattention, directional motor neglect and 'release' of the fixation reflex following a unilateral frontal lesion: a case report. *Neuropsychologia* **26**, 533–45.

Chelazzi, L., Miller, E. K., Duncan, J. and Desimone, R. 1993 A neural basis for visual search in inferior temporal cortex. *Nature* **363**, 345–7.

Chelazzi, L., Duncan, J., Miller, E. K. and Desimone, R. 1998 Responses of neurons in inferior temporal cortex during memory-guided visual search. *J. Neurophysiol.* **80**, 2918–40.

Corbetta, M., Miezin, F. M., Shulman, G. L. and Petersen, S. E. 1993 A PET study of visuospatial attention. *J. Neurosci.* **13**, 1202–26.

De Renzi, E. 1982 Disorders of space exploration and cognition. Chichester, UK: Wiley.

Desimone, R. and Duncan, J. 1995 Neural mechanisms of selective visual attention. *A. Rev. Neurosci.* **18**, 193–222.

Desimone, R. and Ungerleider, L. G. 1989 Neural mechanisms of visual processing in monkeys. In *Handbook of neuropsychology*, vol. 2 (eds F. Boller and J. Grafman), pp. 267–99. Amsterdam: Elsevier.

Desimone, R., Li, L., Lehky, S., Ungerleider, L. and Mishkin, M. 1990 Effects of V4 lesions on visual discrimination performance and on responses of neurons in inferior temporal cortex. *Soc. Neurosci. Abstr.* **16**, 621.

di Pellegrino, G. and Wise, S. P. 1993 Visuospatial versus visuomotor activity in the premotor and prefrontal cortex of a primate. *J. Neurosci.* **13**, 1227–43.

Driver, J. and Grossenbacher, P. G. 1996 Multimodal spatial constraints on tactile selective attention. In *Attention and Performance XVI* (eds T. Inui and J. L. McClelland), pp. 209–35. Cambridge, MA: MIT Press.

Driver, J. and Spence, C. J. 1994 Spatial synergies between auditory and visual attention. In *Attention and performance XV* (eds C. Umiltà and M. Moscovitch), pp. 311–31. Cambridge, MA: MIT Press.

Duncan, J. 1980 The locus of interference in the perception of simultaneous stimuli. *Psychol. Rev.* **87**, 272–300.

Duncan, J. 1983 Perceptual selection based on alphanumeric class: evidence from partial reports. *Percept. Psychophys.* **33**, 533–47.

Duncan, J. 1984 Selective attention and the organization of visual information. *J. Exp. Psychol. Gen.* **113**, 501–17.

Duncan, J. 1993*a* Coordination of what and where in visual attention. *Perception* **22**, 1261–70.

Duncan, J. 1993*b* Similarity between concurrent visual discriminations: dimensions and objects. *Percept. Psychophys.* **54**, 425–30.

Duncan, J. 1996 Cooperating brain systems in selective perception and action. In *Attention and performance XVI* (eds T. Inui and J. L. McClelland), pp. 549–78. Cambridge, MA: MIT Press.

Duncan, J. and Nimmo-Smith, M. I. 1996 Objects and attributes in divided attention: surface and boundary systems. *Percept. Psychophys.* **58**, 1076–84.

Duncan, J., Ward, R. and Shapiro, K. 1994 Direct measurement of attentional dwell time in human vision. *Nature* **369**, 313–15.

Duncan, J., Humphreys, G. W. and Ward, R. 1997*a* Competitive brain activity in visual attention. *Curr. Opin. Neurobiol.* **7**, 255–61.

Duncan, J., Martens, S. and Ward, R. 1997*b* Restricted attentional capacity within but not between sensory modalities. *Nature* **387**, 808–10.

Duncan, J., Bundesen, C., Olson, A., Humphreys, G., Chavda, S. and Shibuya, H. (in press) Systematic analysis of deficits in visual attention. *J. Exp. Psychol. Gen.*

Farah, M. J. 1990 Visual agnosia: disorders of object recognition and what they tell us about normal vision. Cambridge, MA: MIT Press.

Friston, K. J., Holmes, A., Worsley, K., Poline, J., Frith, C., Heather, J. and Frackowiak, R. S. J. 1995 Statistical parametric maps in functional imaging: a general approach. *Hum. Brain Mapp.* **2**, 189–210.

Funahashi, S., Bruce, C. J. and Goldman-Rakic, P. S. 1989 Mnemonic coding of visual space in the monkey's dorsolateral prefrontal cortex. *J. Neurophysiol.* **61**, 331–49.

Fuster, J. M., Bauer, R. H. and Jervey, J. P. 1985 Functional interactions between inferotemporal and prefrontal cortex in a cognitive task. *Brain Res.* **330**, 299–307.

Gado, M., Hanaway, J. and Frank, R. 1979 Functional anatomy of the cerebral cortex by computed tomography. *J. Comput. Assist. Tomogr.* **3**, 1–19.

Gnadt, J. W. and Andersen, R. A. 1988 Memory related motor planning activity in posterior parietal cortex of macaque. *Exp. Brain Res.* **70**, 216–20.

Goldman-Rakic, P. 1988 Topography of cognition: parallel distributed networks in primate association cortex. *A. Rev. Neurosci.* **11**, 137–56.

Gottlieb, J. P., Kusunoki, M. and Goldberg, M. E. 1998 The representation of visual salience in monkey parietal cortex. *Nature* **391**, 481–4.

Guariglia, C. and Antonucci, G. 1992 Personal and extrapersonal space: a case of neglect dissociation. *Neuropsychologia* **30**, 1001–9.

Halligan, P. W. and Marshall, J. C. 1994 Toward a principled explanation of unilateral neglect. *Cogn. Neuropsychol.* **11**, 167–206.

Harter, M. R. and Aine, C. J. 1984 Brain mechanisms of visual selective attention. In *Varieties of attention* (eds R. Parasuraman and D. R. Davies), pp. 293–321. Orlando, FL: Academic Press.

Heilman, K. M. and Valenstein, E. 1972 Frontal lobe neglect in man. *Neurology* **22**, 660–4.

Heinze, H. J. (and 11 others) 1994 Combined spatial and temporal imaging of brain activity during visual selective attention in humans. *Nature* **372**, 543–6.

Husain, M., Shapiro, K., Martin, J. and Kennard, C. 1997 Abnormal temporal dynamics of visual attention in spatial neglect patients. *Nature* **385**, 154–6.

Kahneman, D. and Henik, A. 1977 Effects of visual grouping on immediate recall and selective attention. In *Attention and performance VI* (ed. S. Dornic), pp. 307–32. Hillsdale, NJ: Lawrence Erlbaum.

Karnath, H.-O. 1988 Deficits of attention in acute and recovered visual hemi-neglect. *Neuropsychologia* **26**, 27–43.

Kinsbourne, M. 1987 Mechanisms of unilateral neglect. In *Neurophysiological and neuropsychological aspects of neglect* (ed. M. Jeannerod), pp. 69–86. Amsterdam: North-Holland.

Kwon, S. E. and Heilman, K. M. 1991 Ipsilateral neglect in a patient following a unilateral frontal lesion. *Neurology* **41**, 2001–4.

Lappin, J. S. 1967 Attention in the identification of stimuli in complex displays. *J. Exp. Psychol.* **75**, 321–8.

Luck, S. J., Chelazzi, L., Hillyard, S. A. and Desimone, R. 1997 Mechanisms of spatial selective attention in areas V1, V2, and V4 of macaque visual cortex. *J. Neurophysiol.* **77**, 24–42.

Luria, A. R. 1966 *Higher cortical functions in man*. London: Tavistock.

Merikle, P. M. 1980 Selection from visual persistence by perceptual groups and category membership. *J. Exp. Psychol. Gen.* **109**, 279–95.

Mesulam, M.-M. 1981 A cortical network for directed attention and unilateral neglect. *Ann. Neurol.* **10**, 309–25.

Mesulam, M.-M. 1990 Large-scale neurocognitive networks and distributed processing for attention, language, and memory. *Ann. Neurol.* **28**, 597–613.

Mijovic-Prelec, D., Shin, L. M., Chabris, C. F. and Kosslyn, S. M. 1994 When does 'no' really mean 'yes'? A case study in unilateral visual neglect. *Neuropsychologia* **32**, 151–8.

Miller, E. K., Erickson, C. A. and Desimone, R. 1996 Neural mechanisms of visual working memory in prefrontal cortex of the macaque. *J. Neurosci.* **16**, 5154–67.

Milner, A. D. and Harvey, M. 1995 Distortion of size perception in visuospatial neglect. *Curr. Biol.* **5**, 85–9.

Miyashita, Y. and Chang, H. S. 1988 Neuronal correlate of pictorial short-term memory in the primate temporal cortex. *Nature* **331**, 68–70.

Morais, J. 1978 Spatial constraints on attention to speech. In *Attention and performance VII* (ed J. Requin), pp. 245–260. Hillsdale, NJ: Lawrence Erlbaum.

Moran, J. and Desimone, R. 1985 Selective attention gates visual processing in the extrastriate cortex. *Science* **229**, 782–4.

Motter, B. C. 1993 Focal attention produces spatially selective processing in visual cortical areas V1, V2 and V4 in the presence of competing stimuli. *J. Neurophysiol.* **70**, 909–19.

Motter, B. C. 1994 Neural correlates of attentive selection for color or luminance in extrastriate area V4. *J. Neurosci.* **14**, 2178–89.

Niki, H. and Watanabe, M. 1976 Prefrontal unit activity and delayed response: relation to cue location versus direction of response. *Brain Res.* **105**, 79–88.

Nobre, A. C., Sebestyen, G. N., Gitelman, D. R., Mesulam, M.-M., Frackowiak, R. S. J. and Frith, C. D. 1997 Functional localization of the system for visuospatial attention using positron emission tomography. *Brain* **120**, 515–33.

Ostry, D., Moray, N. and Marks, G. 1976 Attention, practice, and semantic targets. *J. Exp. Psychol. Hum. Percept. Perf.* **2**, 326–36.

Pashler, H. 1994 Dual-task interference in simple tasks: data and theory. *Psychol. Bull.* **116**, 220–44.

Paus, T., Kalina, M., Patockova, L., Angerova, Y., Cerny, R., Mecir, P., Bauer, J. and Krabec, P. 1991 Medial vs. lateral frontal lobe lesions and differential impairment of central-gaze fixation maintenance in man. *Brain* **114**, 2051–68.

Phaf, R. H., van der Heijden, A. H. C. and Hudson, P. T. W. 1990 SLAM: a connectionist model for attention in visual selection tasks. *Cogn. Psychol.* **22**, 273–341.

Posner, M. I., Walker, J. A., Friedrich, F. and Rafal, R. D. 1984 Effects of parietal injury on covert orienting of attention. *J. Neurosci.* **4**, 1863–74.

Raymond, J. E., Shapiro, K. L. and Arnell, K. M. 1992 Temporary suppression of visual processing in an RSVP task: an attentional blink? *J. Exp. Psychol. Hum. Percept. Perf.* **18**, 849–60.

Robertson, I. H. 1989 Anomalies in the laterality of omissions in left unilateral visual field neglect: implications for an attentional theory of neglect. *Neuropsychologia* **27**, 157–65.

Robertson, I. H. and North, N. T. 1994 One hand is better than two: motor extinction of left hand advantage in unilateral neglect. *Neuropsychologia* **32**, 1–11.

Shibuya, H. 1993 Efficiency of visual selection in duplex and conjunction conditions in partial report. *Percept. Psychophys.* **54**, 716–32.

Sperling, G. 1960 The information available in brief visual presentations. *Psychol. Monogr.* **74** (11, Whole No. 498).

Talairach, J. and Tournoux, P. 1988 *Co-planar stereotaxic atlas of the human brain.* New York: Thieme.

Treisman, A. M. and Davies, A. 1973 Divided attention to ear and eye. In *Attention and performance IV* (ed. S. Kornblum), pp. 101–17. London: Academic.

Treisman, A. M. and Gelade, G. 1980 A feature integration theory of attention. *Cogn. Psychol.* **12**, 97–136.

Treisman, A. M., Kahneman, D. and Burkell, J. 1983 Perceptual objects and the cost of filtering. *Percept. Psychophys.* **33**, 527–32.

Treue, S. and Maunsell, J. H. R. 1996 Attentional modulation of visual motion processing in cortical areas MT and MST. *Nature* **382**, 539–41.

Vallar, G., Rusconi, M. L., Bignamini, L., Geminiani, G. and Perani, D. 1994 Anatomical correlates of visual and tactile extinction in humans: a clinical CT scan study. *J. Neurol. Neurosurg. Psych.* **57**, 464–70.

Vandenberghe, R., Dupont, P., De Bruyn, B., Bormans, G., Michiels, J., Mortelmans, L. and Orban, G. A. 1996 The influence of stimulus location on the brain activation pattern in detection and orientation discrimination. *Brain* **119**, 1263–76.

Vandenberghe, R., Duncan, J., Arnell, K., Herrod, N., Owen, A., Minhas, P. and Orban, G. A. 1997*a* Shifting or maintaining attention within left or right hemifield. *Soc. Neurosci. Abstr.* **23**, 300.

Vandenberghe, R., Duncan, J., Dupont, P., Ward, R., Poline, J. B., Bormans, G., Michiels, J., Mortelmans, L. and Orban, G. A. 1997*b* Attention to one or two features in left or right visual field: a positron emission tomography study. *J. Neurosci.* **17**, 3739–50.

Van Voorhis, S. and Hillyard, S. A. 1977 Visual evoked potentials and selective attention to points in space. *Percept. Psychophys.* **22**, 54–62.

Vecera, S. P. and Farah, M. J. 1994 Does visual attention select objects or locations? *J. Exp. Psychol. Gen.* **123**, 146–60.

von Wright, J. M. 1968 Selection in visual immediate memory. *Q. J. Exp. Psychol.* **20**, 62–8.

Walley, R. E. and Weiden, T. D. 1973 Lateral inhibition and cognitive masking: a neuropsychological theory of attention. *Psychol. Rev.* **80**, 284–302.

Zeki, S. M. 1978 Uniformity and diversity of structure and function in rhesus monkey prestriate visual cortex. *J. Physiol.* **277**, 273–90.

8

Cross-modal links in spatial attention

Jon Driver and Charles Spence

Abstract

A great deal is now known about the effects of spatial attention within individual sensory modalities, especially for vision and audition. However, there has been little previous study of possible crossmodal links in attention. Here we review recent findings from our own experiments on this topic, which reveal extensive spatial links between the modalities. An irrelevant but salient event presented within touch, audition, or vision, can attract covert spatial attention in the other modalities (with the one exception that visual events do not attract auditory attention when saccades are prevented). By shifting receptors in one modality relative to another, the spatial coordinates of these crossmodal interactions can be examined. For instance, when a hand is placed in a new position, stimulation of it now draws visual attention to a correspondingly different location, although some aspects of attention do not spatially remap in this way. Crossmodal links are also evident in voluntary shifts of attention. When a person strongly expects a target in one modality (e.g. audition) to appear in a particular location, their judgements improve at that location not only for the expected modality but also for other modalities (e.g. vision), even if events in the latter modality are somewhat more likely elsewhere. Finally, some of our experiments suggest that information from different sensory modalities may be integrated preattentively, to produce the multimodal internal spatial representations in which attention can be directed. Such preattentive crossmodal integration can, in some cases, produce helpful illusions that increase the efficiency of selective attention in complex scenes.

8.1 Introduction

More than 40 years of intensive study have produced an extensive body of research concerning the dramatic effects of selective attention on perception and action (see, for example, Driver and Mattingley 1995; Pashler 1998, for recent reviews; plus the other papers in this volume). The pioneering psychological studies of the 1950s and early 1960s (see, for example, Cherry 1953; Broadbent 1958; Treisman 1964) were primarily concerned with attentional effects on audition. From the 1970s onward, the focus shifted toward the study of attentional effects within vision (see, for example, Eriksen and Hoffman 1972; Neisser and Becklen 1975; Posner 1978; Treisman and Gelade 1980). This trend continued through the main development of the 1980s, namely the increasing study of neural responses from single cells in behaving animals as a function of their attentional state (see, for example, Wurtz *et al.* 1982; Moran and Desimone 1985). The emphasis on vision has largely remained in more recent work on selective attention, event-related potential (ERP), positron emission tomography (PET), and functional magnetic resonance imaging (fMRI) methods (see, for example, Corbetta *et al.* 1993; Hillyard *et al.* 1995). Despite substantial progress with all these approaches, we would argue that most work has overlooked one crucial question; namely, the extent to which selective attention operates cross-modally, rather than separately within each sensory modality.

It is customary for articles on selective attention to begin by noting that most everyday situations contain several stimuli, and that mechanisms of selective attention are therefore needed to pick out just the relevant sensory information for controlling current behaviour. However, the examples given typically refer to just a single sensory modality (e.g. to many objects in a visual scene all stimulating the retina at once; or to many sounds entering the ears simultaneously). Likewise, the experiments on attention that follow the opening remarks usually concern only a single sensory modality. Yet the fact is that most typical environments bombard all of our senses with numerous stimulations simultaneously. Even the textbook example of 'auditory' selective attention—listening to one conversation among many at a noisy party—turns out to be multi-modal on closer inspection. Listeners typically depend not only on auditory information, but also on visual cues from the lips, face, and other bodily gestures of the speaker. Furthermore, note that in such situations listeners must coordinate their visual and auditory attention appropriately, so that information from a common relevant source gets selected together across the different senses (e.g. both the sights and sounds produced by just the relevant person speaking). Such coordination poses a considerable computational challenge, because the stimulus properties signalling a common source across the modalities (e.g. the various cues to location in audition against vision) differ so greatly at the initial stages of sensory processing (e.g. vision is retinotopic, whereas audition is initially tonotopic and then head-centred).

In emphasizing the multimodal nature of everyday situations, by contrast with the unimodal nature of most previous attention experiments, we seek to highlight the point that many interesting and important questions are excluded when only unimodal situations are studied. These questions include some very fundamental issues about the psychological architecture of selective attention, such as: (i) the extent to which attention operates independently within each sensory modality in a strictly encapsulated modular fashion, as opposed to in a supramodal manner across all modalities; (ii) the nature of the spatial coordinates in which attention operates, and how these may depend on cross-modal integration; and (iii) the mechanisms by which attention is coordinated across modalities, allowing selection of a common source despite very different inputs to each sensory modality.

Finally, we note that many of the neural structures that have been particularly implicated in spatial attention (e.g. regions in the parietal and frontal lobes; and subcortical structures such as the superior colliculus) are known to be heavily involved in cross-modal interactions, and are thought by many investigators to subserve supramodal representations of space (see, for example, Stein 1992; Stein and Meredith 1993; Anderson *et al.* 1997). The study of cross-modal spatial interactions in such neural structures is a particularly active area in contemporary neuroscience. However, as yet the psychology of spatial attention has made little contact with this literature, beyond frequent assertions that the brain areas listed above play fundamental roles in spatial attention. We expect that the study of cross-modal spatial attention will prove to be a particularly fruitful area for interdisciplinary exchange. We also hope that its study will not only reveal new facts about selective attention, but may also provide a useful empirical handle on the mental representation of space. In this paper, we review recent studies with these aims in mind, concentrating primarily on just our own work with normal individuals, owing to length constraints (see Driver and Mattingley 1995; Driver *et al.* 1997; Mattingley *et al.* 1997; Driver 1998; for discussion of complementary work in brain-damaged patients with deficits of spatial attention, for whom many of the same cross-modal issues arise).

8.2   Cross-modal links in covert spatial attention: exogenous mechanisms

We begin with simple experiments that test whether shifts of spatial attention in one sensory modality tend to be accompanied by corresponding shifts in other modalities. Some standard terminology is helpful here. Overt shifts of attention involve the redirection of receptors (as in eye, head or hand movements) towards a region of interest. There is an interesting story to be told about cross-modal links in overt orienting (see, for example, Groh and Sparks 1996a; Jay and Sparks 1990; Yao and Peck 1997), but here we primarily restrict ourselves to considering internal covert mechanisms of spatial attention, when no receptor shifts are allowed. The spatial cueing paradigm (see, for example, Eriksen and Hoffman 1972; Posner 1978) has been widely used to study covert spatial attention, particularly in vision. In this paradigm, the experimenter attempts to direct the subject's attention to a particular location before the appearance of a single target event, by means of a cue.

Many studies have now found that a variety of visual discriminations can be performed better at the cued location than elsewhere, even though subjects are not allowed to shift their eyes (Spence and Driver 1996). This result is attributed to the cue shifting the spatial distribution of covert attention (sometimes referred to as covert orienting). The stimulus-driven ('exogenous') effects of spatially nonpredictive peripheral cues (i.e. cues whose location does not predict which position is most likely for the target, but which nevertheless sometimes appear at that position) have been distinguished from the strategic ('endogenous') effects of informative symbolic cues, which do predict the likely location of the upcoming target, but in an indirect manner (e.g. a central arrow indicating that participants should shift their attention to one particular side). The facilitatory effects of an exogenous cue on the side of the subsequent target tend to be smaller and more short-lived than the endogenous effects of a spatial expectancy. Further qualitative differences have now been observed between these two forms of cueing, and it is suspected that different neural substrates are involved (Spence and Driver 1994, 1996, 1997). Accordingly, when assessing any cross-modal links in spatial attention, it is important to distinguish links that affect exogenous–reflexive attention from those concerning endogenous–voluntary attention.

Fig. 8.1 Schematic view of the position of possible target loudspeakers (shown by ellipses) and target lights (shown as black circles), plus central fixation light, in Spence and Driver's (1996, 1997) studies of audiovisual links in covert spatial attention. The subject's head is cartooned, and the direction of steady fixation is indicated with dotted lines. A single target was presented on each trial, in hearing or vision, and the subject made a speeded response discriminating whether this target came from the upper or lower row, regardless of its side, and regardless of which side attention had been cued toward (either by an instruction about which side to expect targets on; or by a spatially nonpredictive peripheral event at an intermediate elevation between the two possible target locations on one side).

We have adapted the standard spatial-cueing paradigm to provide a measure for the distribution of attention in audition and touch, as well as in vision (Spence and Driver 1994, 1996, 1997; Driver 1998; Spence *et al.* 1998*a*). Our basic method is as follows: subjects are first cued by various means toward the left or right, and are then required to make a speeded elevation discrimination (up as opposed to down) for a subsequent target event, regardless of the side on which it appears (see figure 8.1 for an example of such a task). We repeatedly find that performance in the elevation discrimination task is better (i.e. faster and/or more accurate) for a target that appears on the cued rather than uncued side. Given that no shift in peripheral receptors is allowed (because we clamp the head and hands, and monitor gaze direction with infrared gaze monitors), this result presumably reflects covert rather than overt orienting mechanisms. Note also that as the lateral position indicated by the cue (i.e. left or right) is entirely orthogonal to the discrimination that must be made (i.e. up against down), the effect of the cue cannot be caused merely by it biasing responses in favour of one decision or another (as might happen if, say, a left–right discrimination was required following a left or right cue; see Kustov and Robinson (1996), and Ward (1994), for examples of this confound). Instead, our cueing effects must reflect a genuine improvement in localization in the cued region (Spence and Driver 1994, 1996, 1997), owing to the cue attracting covert attention there.

Having first demonstrated that this simple up–down task with lateral cueing is sensitive to the distribution of covert spatial attention within each of the modalities of vision, audition and touch, we can then use the task to examine any cross-modal links in covert attention. Here we first consider this cross-modal issue for the case of exogenous–reflexive attention. Will an irrelevant but salient event in one modality tend to attract covert attention toward it in other modalities? We find that the answer is clearly affirmative for most pairings of modalities (see, for example, Spence and Driver 1997; Spence *et al.* 1998*a*). A spatially nonpredictive, task-irrelevant abrupt sound on one side leads to better elevation judgements (on average, around 20–30 ms faster, and somewhat more accurate) for both visual and tactile events presented in the vicinity of the sound shortly (100–300 ms) after its onset. Thus, salient auditory events can evidently generate rapid cross-modal shifts of covert spatial attention. Similarly, spatially nonpredictive tactile events on one hand lead to better auditory and visual judgements on that side. So touch evidently generates cross-modal shifts of attention as well (Spence *et al.* 1998*a*). Finally, nonpredictive visual flashes lead to better tactile judgements in their vicinity; yet to our initial surprise, we have repeatedly found (see, for example, Spence and Driver 1997) that peripheral visual cues do not affect auditory judgements (at least, not when eye-movements are prevented; see Rorden and Driver 1998). This finding holds up across numerous variations in the physical properties of the particular visual and auditory stimuli used, and so seems to reflect a general rule about how the modalities relate to each other, rather than being merely caused by unintended differences in salience between the modalities for the particular stimuli used.

We are currently testing several possible accounts for the finding of no cross-modal exogenous influence from visual cues on auditory targets. Some of the potential explanations involve the neural properties of the colliculus, a subcortical structure that is thought by many investigators (Stein and Meredith 1993; Spence and Driver 1997) to be intimately involved in reflexive shifts of spatial attention, and in the cross-modal interactions which can influence such shifts. For now, we note only that the failure of visual events to attract auditory covert attention rules out the simplest explanation for all the many other cross-modal interactions we have found. It contradicts any proposal that exogenous covert orienting takes place within an entirely supramodal system (Farah *et al.* 1989). If a strictly supramodal system were shifted by sudden events in the periphery, then visual events which are demonstrably capable of attracting visual and tactile attention would necessarily attract auditory attention as well. Yet we find auditory attention to be unaffected by such visual events. Thus, although our experiments reveal extensive cross-modal links in the control of exogenous covert orienting (i.e. links between all possible pairings of cue modality with subsequent target modality, except for visual cues prior to auditory targets), the results also show that the underlying architecture is more complex than a strictly supramodal system.

8.3   Spatial coordinates of exogenous cross-modal attention

In all the experiments without saccades that we've described, the receptor systems for the various modalities were aligned in one particular 'default' posture. The subject's head and eyes were fixed straight ahead, with each hand resting on a table in its usual hemispace (i.e. left hand on the left, right hand on the right). However, in daily life we can adopt many different postures, and the important point is that these spatially realign the receptors from the different modalities. For instance, every time you move your eyes, retinotopic visual inputs are realigned relative to somatotopic tactile space, and to head-centred auditory space. Likewise, each movement of your hand can realign its tactile coordinates relative to vision and audition. Such considerations raise the computational problem of how the nervous system can represent the 'common' position of a particular external source across the different senses. This seems challenging given that the spatial organization of the senses is so different at input levels (vision is retinotopic, touch somatotopic, and audition first tonotopic and then head-centred). Furthermore, the mapping of which particular receptors in one modality (e.g. tactile receptors on a finger) correspond spatially with those in another modality (e.g. particular retinal positions) changes every time a new posture is adopted, because the eye, head and body parts do not move as one.

The means by which the brain derives useful representations of stimulus location across the senses, despite such complexities, has been intensively investigated at the single-cell level by recent physiological studies (see, for example, Graziano and Gross 1993; Anderson *et al.* 1997). Some neural structures (e.g. the superior colliculus) are known to code stimulation from several sensory modalities in approximate spatial register, such that cells tend to have spatially aligned receptive fields across the modalities (Stein and Meredith 1993). However, most of the initial single-cell recording studies on such cross-modal issues were done in anaesthetized animals, held in a fixed posture (typically with eyes, head and body all facing forward). A retinotopic visual map would of course appear to be in approximate alignment with a head-centred auditory map as long as the eyes faced forward within the head. Only when gaze is diverted would these spatial coordinate systems diverge. More recent single cell studies, often with behaving animals, have looked at spatial coding across modalities as the animals adopt different postures, which realign the receptors for different modalities. Several intriguing physiological results, from various different brain structures (e.g. colliculus, putamen, posterior parietal cortex, premotor cortex), have now shown that sensory responsiveness following stimulation at a particular location in one modality can depend on how the current posture spatially aligns the stimulated receptors with receptors from another modality (see, for example, Jay and Sparks 1984; Graziano and Gross 1993; Groh and Sparks 1996*b*; Anderson *et al.* 1997). For instance, the neural response to a sound or light can depend on how the eye is deviated in the head, and the response to tactile stimulation of a hand can depend on where that hand is located relative to the body or eye. Such findings may reveal how multimodal space is constructed at the level of individual neurons or cell populations. Our recent experiments have posed similar questions, but at the macroscopic functional level of where a person's attention gets directed in cross-modal situations, rather than at the microscopic level of how individual neurons behave.

8.4   Visual–tactile remapping

Recall our earlier finding that tactile stimulation of the left hand leads to faster up–down discrimination in the left rather than right visual field shortly afterwards (and vice versa for stimulation of the right hand). Does this pattern depend on some fixed mapping between touch and vision, such that particular somatotopic activations in touch always lower thresholds for particular retinal positions (perhaps owing to which hemisphere the stimuli initially project to; Kinsbourne 1993)? Or are the cross-modal links in exogenous spatial attention more complex in spatial terms, such that visual attention gets drawn to the current location of a stimulated hand, and hence to different positions in the external world (corresponding to different visual receptors) depending on the posture adopted? The latter arrangement would seem more adaptive. If an insect is suddenly felt crawling on your left hand, you presumably need your visual attention to be drawn to the external location of the insect, rather than to some fixed default location in left hemispace (your left hand might be located on the right when the touch is first felt). However, directing attention to the appropriate external location in one modality, based on stimulation in another, is quite demanding computationally, given that receptors for the different modalities can be spatially realigned against each other with every change in posture.

We have now done a number of studies where receptors in the three modalities of touch, vision and audition are shifted relative to one another, allowing us to determine the coordinates in which cross-modal exogenous attention operates, and thus how the modalities map into each other spatially. figure 8.2 illustrates one such study. In figure 8.2a, the hands lie in an uncrossed posture. As described earlier, a visual flash in the left visual field leads to faster tactile discriminations with the left rather than right hand shortly (100–300 ms) after the flash; whereas a right flash gives an advantage to the right hand. What happens if the hands are placed in a crossed posture

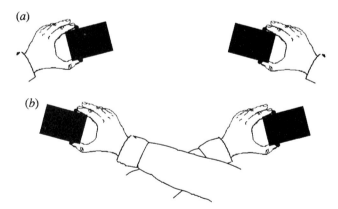

Fig. 8.2   Illustration of relative hand position in (a) the uncrossed and (b) crossed conditions in a visual–tactile or tactile–visual cueing experiment. Subjects gripped a sponge cube in each hand with thumb and index finger. Both cubes incorporated one vibrotactile device at the thumb (next to a small light, illustrated here by a black circle), and a separate vibrator at the index finger (next to another small light). In one series of experiments, visual stimulation (from both the lights near one or other hand) served as a spatially nonpredictive cue, that was task-irrelevant. Each such cue was followed by a target vibration from any one of the four possible vibrators, and subjects made a speeded tactile discrimination of whether this vibration came from an upper (index finger) or lower (thumb) position, regardless of which hand was stimulated. In another series of experiments, the roles of cue and target were reversed; a target light was presented for a speeded up–down discrimination following tactile stimulation of one or other hand.

(see figure 8.2*b*)? We find (Spence and Driver 1998*c*) that the results now completely reverse in terms of which parts of the eye and body have to be stimulated to produce better performance; although they remain unchanged when considered in terms of external space. In other words, a visual flash on the right still leads to faster tactile discriminations on that side of space (but now with the left hand), whereas a flash on the left now leads to faster tactile discriminations with the right hand (in left hemispace). Evidently, the spatial mapping from particular retinal activations in vision, to somatotopic activations in touch, gets updated when the hands adopt different postures. This is presumably owing to an influence from proprioceptive signals specifying the current hand positions (as confirmed in a later study). Thus, a third modality (here proprioception) can apparently influence the attentional interactions between two other modalities (here vision and touch).

In situations with the reverse roles for cue and target (i.e. with a spatially nonpredictive tactile cue preceding a visual target for elevation discrimination), we have examined the spatial precision of the cross-modal mapping more closely. In particular, we have tested (Driver 1998; S. Kennett and J. Driver, unpublished data) whether cross-modal attentional effects can apply to specific locations within one hemifield, rather than merely affecting the cued hemispace as a whole. In one such study, visual targets could be presented at any one of four possible eccentricities (outer left, inner left, inner right, outer right) for a speeded up–down elevation discrimination (there were thus eight possible visual target locations; four eccentricities, and two elevations at each). The uncrossed hands (i.e. left hand in left hemispace, right hand in right hemispace) could either be placed in alignment with the inner lights on each side, or with the outer lights. Stimulation of one hand led to faster visual elevation discriminations on that side at the visual eccentricity corresponding to the current hand position (i.e. cueing effects were bigger for the inner lights when the stimulated hand lay at the inner eccentricity on one side; but for the outer lights when the hands were placed further out).

This result once again demonstrates that the spatial mapping between modalities gets updated when different postures are adopted. Tactile stimulation can draw visual attention to the current location of the stimulated hand within a hemifield. The senses thus remain in useful register, with respect to each other and the outside world, despite changes in posture. However, to do so they must change the spatial mapping of which receptors in one modality (e.g. tactile receptors on the left hand) get linked to information from particular receptors in the other modalities (e.g. regions in the left or right visual field) to drive the attention shift. In the case of spatial cueing effects between touch and vision, this remapping presumably depends on proprioceptive (and/or visual) information about the current posture of the hands. The exact basis for the remapping can be tested. For instance, by occluding any view of the hands, or doing the study in total darkness, whether or not proprioception plays a critical role can be determined. In two studies we have confirmed that proprioception can indeed contribute to the spatial mapping between vision and touch that determines cross-modal exogenous cueing effects (Driver 1998).

8.5   When remapping fails

Thus far, even the reflexive aspects of cross-modal attention (i.e. shifts of attention that can be triggered within 100 ms of presenting a salient, but spatially nonpredictive, task-irrelevant event) have proved to be remarkably sophisticated, with the spatial mapping between the senses being sufficiently flexible to take into account how the current posture misaligns receptors across the modalities. However, a further covert orienting phenomenon reveals a more primitive level of the system. The studies described here all concerned the facilitatory effects found in discrimination tasks for targets presented near the location of a nonpredictive cue, shortly after its appearance.

These effects typically emerge very rapidly but are short-lived (e.g. being found for targets presented from around 50 ms after cue onset, but disappearing for targets presented 300 ms or more later; Spence and Driver 1994, 1997). It is well-known that an additional phenomenon often emerges at longer delays following a spatially nonpredictive cue, especially in speeded detection tasks. Although detection reaction times are typically faster for targets presented ipsilaterally rather than contralaterally to an immediately preceding cue, this pattern usually reverses at longer cue-target delays, so that targets on the cued side come to yield the slowest responses at delays of 300 ms or more. This robust finding has become known as 'inhibition of return' (IOR), reflecting Posner and Cohen's (1984) hypothesis that covert attention is first drawn to the cued position (thus producing the initial benefit there), and then moves on with a bias against returning to the location that has recently been attended (producing IOR). Most studies on IOR have been concerned only with vision, but we and others have recently found that a similar phenomenon can be found cross-modally (see, for example, Reuter-Lorenz et al. 1996; Tassinari and Campara 1996; Spence and Driver 1998a,b). For instance, visual detection can become slower at the location of a preceding auditory or tactile event than elsewhere, provided sufficient time has elapsed for the initial facilitatory effect in its vicinity to dissipate.

We have now begun to study the spatial coordinates in which cross-modal IOR arises. Surprisingly, our initial results suggest that tactile-visual IOR does not behave in the same manner as the earlier facilitatory cueing effect, when different postures are adopted (e.g. crossed compared with uncrossed hands, see figure 8.2). In other words, a tactile stimulation of the left hand can still produce IOR for a subsequent visual target in the left visual field, even when the hands are crossed, with the left hand lying in the right visual field. Unlike the initial facilitatory effects of cross-modal attention found near the cue shortly after its presentation, the later IOR phenomenon apparently does not remap spatially as a function of posture, thus revealing a more primitive level of the reflexive covert orienting system.

This primitive level, with no remapping, may also be revealed by eye-movements toward tactile events. Groh and Sparks (1996a) studied saccades towards tactile stimulation on an unseen hand. When the hands were crossed behind an occluding screen, saccades were accurate in their final landing position, but initially shot in the wrong direction (i.e. toward the uncrossed hemispace, where the crossed hand would usually lie; e.g. rightwards for the right hand even when it was located on the left). This initially erroneous saccadic response may relate to our finding that cross-modal IOR likewise applies to the hemispace where the stimulated hand would usually lie, rather than to its current position when crossed. Some relation seems plausible, given that several authors have previously proposed that IOR may be an after-effect of an initial saccadic program arising rapidly and reflexively in the superior colliculus (Rizzolatti et al. 1974; Wurtz et al. 1980; Spence and Driver 1998a,b). Note that while we did not allow any overt saccades to be executed in our own cueing studies of cross-modal IOR, this does not preclude some influence from internal saccade programmes generated automatically by peripheral events.

8.6   Audiovisual remapping

Changing the position of the hands is by no means the only way to study whether spatial remapping between the senses can influence exogenous cross-modal attention, across changes in posture. For instance, similar issues can be addressed simply by deviating gaze, while holding the head and body in a constant position. In recent audiovisual studies (Driver 1998; Driver and Spence 1998) we have tested whether spatially nonpredictive auditory cues can attract covert visual attention to specific locations within a hemifield; and also how this depends on gaze posture. Visual targets could be presented at any one of four possible eccentricities (outer left, inner left, inner right, outer right) for a speeded up–down elevation discrimination (there were thus eight possible light positions; see figure 8.3a). A spatially nonpredictive sound cue could precede each visual target from any one of the four eccentricities. When the subject faced and fixated straight ahead, the auditory cue drew facilitatory covert visual attention to its specific eccentricity within the cued hemifield, rather than merely to that entire hemifield compared with the other (e.g. a sound on the far left was a better cue for outer left visual targets than for inner left visual targets; whereas a sound on the near left was a better cue for inner visual targets on that side). We next tested a situation where the head of the subject still remained fixed in a forward-facing position, but with his or her gaze now directed off to one side rather than straight ahead (e.g. the subject might now fixate toward the left, between the previous inner left and outer left locations; see figure 8.3b). We shifted all the possible locations for the visual targets laterally along with the deviated gaze, so that the retinal stimulation remained as before; but kept the possible sound locations where they had been, so that the auditory stimulation also remained as before with respect to the craniotopic midline (as the head did not move).

Note that owing to the deviation in gaze, the correspondence of particular retinal locations with particular sounds in external space was changed (e.g. visual targets that were inner right on the retina now corresponded in external space to an inner left sound, when the subject fixated just past the location of the inner left sound-source; see figure 8.3b). If the cross-modal attention effects from sound cues on visual targets that we had previously found with eyes fixating straight ahead were caused by a fixed ear–retina mapping, then particular sounds should still benefit the same retinal positions as previously. If instead the relation between the modalities gets spatially remapped when gaze is deviated, then a sound from a particular location should benefit visual targets that are close to it in external space. Hence the sound would benefit different visual targets, in retinal terms, depending on how the eye is deviated. The results clearly supported the latter remapping hypothesis. For instance, with eyes straight ahead (figure 8.3a), an inner right sound benefited an inner right retinal position more than an inner left sound did. In contrast, when subjects held fixation to the left of the inner left sound (figure 8.3b), the inner left sound now became more beneficial for the same inner right retinal position. Sounds drew visual attention in the 'correct' direction with respect to external space even when the eyes were deviated in the head. This entails that the mapping between auditory locations and retinal locations, which directed exogenous cross-modal attention, must have changed, to keep vision and audition in register as regards external space. These psychological findings on audiovisual attention effects in people can be related to recent physiological findings on single cell activity in the parietal lobe and superior colliculus of monkeys, indicating that cells there change their coding of auditory location as a function of how the eyes are deviated in the head (Jay and Sparks 1984, 1990; Stricanne et al. 1996; Anderson et al. 1997).

To summarize the story so far, our studies with spatially nonpredictive peripheral cues have revealed many cross-modal links in the effects of exogenous covert attention. Indeed, such links were found for all pairings of modalities tested, except for auditory targets following visual cues (without saccades). The results also reveal that even these highly reflexive aspects of covert attention, triggered by salient but task-irrelevant events, are quite sophisticated in terms of the underlying spatial mappings between modalities. With the apparent exception of the mechanisms underlying cross-modal IOR, these mappings all change as a function of how the current posture realigns sensory receptors across the various modalities. Several of these findings indicate that the cross-modal interactions between two sensory modalities can be modulated by a third modality (e.g. proprioception), as when current hand position or eye position changes mappings between touch and vision, or between audition and vision.

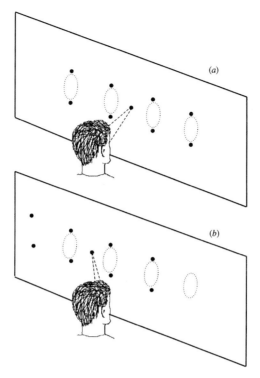

Fig. 8.3 Illustration of possible cue loudspeakers and possible target lights in an audiovisual cueing experiment (the loudspeakers are each marked by dashed lines, to indicate that they could not be seen in the darkened chamber). The subject's head is cartooned, and the direction of steady fixation shown with dotted lines. There were four possible positions for the spatially nonpredictive cue sound (outer left, inner left, inner right, outer right). The target light could appear from any one of eight positions (four eccentricities, with two elevations at each). The task was speeded discrimination of the elevation (up compared with down) of each target light, regardless of its side, and regardless of where the immediately preceding sound had been. In (*a*) the subject fixates directly ahead, between the aligned loudspeakers and possible light positions. Visual discriminations were best at the same eccentricity and side as the immediately preceding sound. In (*b*) the subject fixates between the outer- and inner-left loudspeaker (and note that all visual events have been laterally translated along with gaze). Visual discriminations were again best for lights at the same external location as the immediately preceding sound, but these now occupied different retinal locations as compared with *a*. See text for full explanation.

8.7   Cross-modal links in endogenous mechanisms of covert spatial attention

We now consider possible cross-modal links for the case of endogenous covert attention, which is directed in a voluntary manner on the basis of current spatial expectancies, rather than reflexively following a salient but task-irrelevant event (as in the preceding exogenous studies). Several pioneering authors (see, for example, Buchtel and Butter 1988; Butter *et al.* 1989) tested whether spatially informative peripheral cues in one modality, appearing at the probable location of a subsequent target in another modality, could influence performance in that second modality. Although positive findings from such studies are now common, we believe their method leads to an interpretative problem, and so may reveal little or nothing about the nature of any hard-wired links between the modalities. Informative cues by definition predict the likely location for events in the target modality. Hence any shift of attention may take place solely within only the latter modality, following interpretation of the informative cue. If so, the exact form of a predictive cue (be it visual, auditory, tactile, linguistic and so on) may scarcely matter, and so its modality in relation to the target modality becomes irrelevant to the underlying mechanisms.

Given these considerations, we have taken a different methodological approach when testing for any cross-modal links in endogenous spatial attention. Our general strategy has been to induce a strong spatial expectancy within only one sensory modality, and then test whether this has any influence on other modalities. For instance, Spence and Driver (1996) ran audiovisual experiments, with our usual elevation discrimination task (i.e. discriminating up compared with down, regardless of target side). In separate experiments, either audition or vision served as the more common primary modality (e.g. eight out of 11 targets in the pseudorandom sequence of trials would appear in this modality). Targets in another modality (termed secondary) were much rarer (e.g. only three out of 11 targets might appear in it). The subjects were given a strong spatial expectancy about the likely side for targets in the primary modality (e.g. seven out of eight targets in that common modality would appear on one specified side throughout a particular block of 96 trials). In contrast, they had no reason to expect targets on that side in the intermingled secondary modality (in fact two out of three targets in the rarer secondary modality appeared on the other side, to ensure that there was no strategic motivation to shift spatial attention to the same side across the two modalities).

The results revealed a substantial advantage in the efficiency of up–down discriminations for targets in the primary modality, on the side that was strongly expected for that modality. This is presumably owing to subjects directing their endogenous covert attention to the expected side within the primary modality (the spatial effect of such endogenous attention was typically two to three times larger than the exogenous effects described earlier). The more important result was that an advantage was also found on that same side for targets in the secondary modality, even though they were actually twice as likely on the other side! However, this spatial effect in the secondary modality was smaller (by about 50%) than that for the primary modality. This pattern of results held whether the primary modality was audition, with vision secondary, or vice versa. These findings suggest that when people have a strong spatial expectancy about the likely target side in only vision, or only audition, then their attention tends to shift in the same direction for the other modality as well, even when there is no strategic motivation for this to happen (indeed, even when the odds are somewhat stacked against it).

These findings demonstrate cross-modal links between audition and vision for covert endogenous attention. Note, however, that the results do not accord with a strictly supramodal system, contrary to Farah et al. (1989) and others; nor with averaging of probabilities across modalities by the subject, as the attentional effect was always larger in the primary modality (for which the strong spatial expectancy held) than in the secondary modality. Our findings therefore suggest that a strongly biased spatial distribution of endogenous attention in one modality tends to spread into other modalities as well, but at a reduced level. Recent evidence from audiovisual studies measuring neural activity via ERPs provides further support for this proposal (Hillyard et al. 1984; Eimer and Schröger 1998). Furthermore, we have recently extended the result to situations involving vision and touch (Spence et al. 1998b). We are currently testing various different accounts for how a spatial disposition might spread from the primary modality into the secondary modality, in attenuated form. For instance, on one account (Kinsbourne 1993) this may be owing to the relative activation of the two cortical hemispheres when attention is endogenously directed towards one hemifield in a particular modality.

Returning to our existing audiovisual study (Spence and Driver 1996), we next asked whether there were any circumstances in which endogenous covert attention could be simultaneously directed in opposite directions for audition and vision. Auditory and visual targets were now made equally common across blocks of 96 trials, but the subjects were told which side was more likely (by a ratio of 4 : 1) for targets within each modality. In common-side blocks, the two modalities were both more likely on the same side. In the opposite-side blocks that are of particular interest here, visual targets were more likely on one side, but auditory targets on the other. In the latter blocks, we found that auditory performance was better on the likely side for auditory targets, whereas visual performance was better on the opposite side, which was more likely for visual targets. Measures of the variability in performance suggested that this was owing to a true 'splitting' of spatial attention between the two modalities, rather than to any strategy of committing all attentional resources to only a single modality on each trial. Thus, endogenous covert attention can apparently be directed in opposite directions concurrently for audition and vision. On the other hand, the advantage on the expected side for a particular modality in these opposite-side blocks was significantly smaller (reduced by over 60%) than that found for the common-side blocks, suggesting that covert endogenous attention is more effectively focused on a common location across the modalities, even though it can be spatially split between the modalities to some extent. In an earlier study (Driver and Spence 1994), we had reached very similar conclusions from an entirely different method, namely continuous dual-task performance in audition and vision.

Finally, we have recently compared opposite-side and common-side blocks in the manner described here for elevation discriminations in vision and touch (Spence *et al.* 1998*b*). We find that it is difficult to direct endogenous attention toward one side in touch, while simultaneously attending to the other side in vision (e.g. to the right hand in right hemispace for touch, but to the left hemifield for vision). In contrast, directing visual and tactile endogenous attention to a common side does produce substantial advantages in elevation discrimination on that side for both modalities. When an uncrossed hand posture is compared with a crossed hand posture (see figure 8.2), the results reveal that it is easier to direct endogenous tactile and visual attention to a common external location, regardless of which particular visual and tactile receptors are involved. Thus, spatial remapping across different postures is evident in the cross-modal links for covert endogenous attention, as we had previously found for cross-modal exogenous attention.

8.8   Can cross-modal integration arise preattentively?

Thus far, our general approach has been to start by posing the simple question of whether a change in the spatial distribution of attention in one modality (be this an exogenous or endogenous change) tends to be accompanied by corresponding shifts in other modalities. Having found evidence for many such cross-modal links in spatial attention, we have then gone on to ask more detailed questions about the spatial mappings between the various sensory modalities that underlie such cross-modal shifts. Specifically, we have investigated whether these mappings may change as a function of how the current posture realigns sensory receptors in the various modalities (e.g. when the eyes are deviated relative to the head, or the hands placed in crossed hemispaces, and so on). On this spatial mapping issue, we have already encountered several situations where the effect of one modality upon another (e.g. of tactile or auditory cues upon response to visual targets) itself depends on inputs from a third modality (e.g. proprioceptive signals specifying the current location of unseen hands, or the current deviation of the eye in the head). Such results imply that cross-modal integration between the senses can itself contribute to cross-modal attentional interactions. For instance, proprioceptive information can evidently modify a tactile signal, so that the latter can indicate the true external location of a tactile event (rather than merely its somatotopic position on the body), and thus can direct visual and auditory attention to the appropriate external source of the tactile stimulation, whatever the current posture.

This general finding—that cross-modal integration can serve to direct cross-modal attention in an adaptive manner, by allowing the appropriate coding of space despite receptor misalignments— might be taken to suggest that cross-modal integration itself must precede attentional selection. The extent to which different types of sensory information can be integrated before attentional selection has, of course, attracted considerable research interest in purely visual attention research, under the framework of Treisman's influential feature integration theory (see Treisman, this volume). It may seem natural to ask whether the integration of sensory information from separate modalities requires focused attention to a particular location, in the same manner as was originally proposed by Treisman and her colleagues (see, for example, Treisman and Gelade 1980) for the integration of separate dimensions within the visual modality (e.g. colour, motion, shape and so on).

We suspect that it would be naive to assume that integration between the senses is directly analogous to the integration of different properties in one sense. Furthermore, we believe that it would be highly maladaptive for the nervous system to be incapable of integrating information from separate modalities without first focusing attention on a particular location (as previously claimed for the integration of separate visual features). This would seem especially problematic when one considers how the suggested 'location' that attention should be focused on could possibly be coded in a common manner across the senses, without some cross-modal integration already having taken place. In our view, extensive cross-modal integration is first required to construct a suitable representational space in which attention might be effectively directed. From this perspective, cross-modal integration would often tend to precede attentional selection, rather than the reverse arrangement.

However, the experiments described so far do not provide very direct evidence on this issue. At first glance, some of our cases of cross-modal exogenous orienting might seem to entail a degree of cross-modal integration prior to attentional selection. For instance, in several situations we found that the effect of a cue in one modality on a target in a second modality depended in turn on an influence from a third modality concerning the cue's location. This seems to entail that at least two of the modalities were integrated regarding the cue information, prior to the eventual influence of that cue on the subsequent target. One example of this is when proprioception influences the coding of a tactile signal, and thus changes which location visual attention gets drawn to by that tactile event. However, one might plausibly argue that the cue itself was attended in such cases (after all, it was always a salient and abrupt event, designed by an experimenter to attract attention). If so, cueing results of this kind need not entail that any cross-modal integration arose in a strictly preattentive manner.

In several recent studies, we have adopted a somewhat different experimental approach than the usual cueing paradigms, in an effort to tackle the issue of preattentive cross-modal integration more directly. This series of experiments differs in that a strictly irrelevant stream of distractor events is now always presented concurrently with the stream of relevant target events. We measure the extent to which the distractors can be ignored; and in particular whether the efficiency of ignoring distractors is ever influenced by factors that depend on cross-modal integration. Our idea is that if the ease of selecting targets from their distractors can be shown to depend on cross-modal integration, then this implies that some cross-modal integration must have taken place before attentional selection was completed. We shall illustrate this approach with two examples.

8.9 Tonic tactile–proprioceptive integration can influence tactile selection

Driver and Grossenbacher (1996) presented subjects with concurrent vibrotactile stimulation to each hand. The task was to discriminate the vibrations (two short pulses, versus one longer continuous pulse) presented to only one of the two hands, which was specified as the relevant hand throughout a block of trials. The vibrations on the other hand were entirely irrelevant, and should be ignored. We varied whether concurrent target and distractor vibrations were the same or different. In this way we could assess the efficiency with which vibrotactile distractors were ignored, by measuring the extent to which they impaired judgements of the concurrent target when different from it.

The critical manipulation was the relative position of the two hands in external space. The hands were either placed close together in one hemispace (i.e. both being held on the far right of the body, or both on the far left) or they were widely separated (i.e. the left hand on the far left of the body, the right hand on the far right). Note that this manipulation of hand separation does not in any way alter the vibrotactile stimulation that was applied to the finger pads (indeed, control conditions confirmed that the different postures did not affect the discriminability of the vibrations delivered to each hand). Nevertheless, hand separation had a dramatic effect on the efficiency of tactile selective attention. Incongruent distractor vibrations on the irrelevant hand (as compared with congruent distractors) substantially impaired judgements of target vibrations on the relevant hand when the hands were held close together. However, this distractor interference was substantially reduced when the hands were placed far apart, even though the tactile stimulation remained just the same.

We take these results to show that tactile endogenous spatial attention does not operate on a purely somatotopic representation of space. The somatotopic position of relevant and irrelevant vibrations remained identical across the hand postures, so the results cannot be explained in these terms. Instead, endogenous tactile attention seems to operate on a representation of space that captures the current layout of tactile receptors in external space; this representation changes as different postures are adopted, such as the various hand separations. Driver and Grossenbacher (1996) found their effects even for subjects wearing blindfolds, implying that somatotopic space gets recalibrated by proprioceptive inputs about current hand separation to produce the observed effect on tactile selection.

The effect of hand separation may seem counter-intuitive when one considers that only the vibrotactile stimulation was relevant to the required task, and that this stimulation was equivalent across the hand separation conditions. However, it makes better sense when one considers the usual function of touch in daily life. Touch does not serve merely to indicate the current stimulation on patches of skin, but instead uses this stimulation to derive felt properties of the external world. Tactile stimulation can only provide an indication of such external properties if it is integrated with proprioceptive and kinaesthetic information about the current spatial disposition of the tactile receptors as they move while exploring the world. Presumably, Driver and Grossenbacher's (1996) effect of hand separation on vibrotactile attention arises because tactile sensations are routinely recalibrated by proprioceptive inputs. In the case of their experiment, these inputs would indicate that the target and distractors vibrations were very far apart in the external world when the hands were widely separated, but were very close (so that they perhaps seemed more likely to stem from a common external source) when the hands were placed together.

From a theoretical perspective, the importance of this experiment is in demonstrating that some degree of cross-modal integration must have taken place (in this case, between proprioception and touch) before attentional selection was complete within one modality (in this case, within touch). How else could proprioceptive information about hand separation have influenced the ease with which tactile targets were attended and tactile distractors rejected? In this sense then, the study appears to demonstrate that some cross-modal integration can arise 'preattentively'. However, it should be noted that the separation of the hands was blocked in Driver and Grossenbacher's (1996) study, which means that fairly simple cross-modal interactions might be sufficient to explain the result. In particular, only a tonic influence from proprioception on touch (as opposed to phasic influences from kinaesthesia) would be required to explain the result. Proprioceptive inputs would only have to specify whether the hands were close together or far apart for an entire block of trials, and so this information did not need to be time-locked or integrated in any more specific fashion with particular tactile events. In other words, because the hands were held fixed, there were no transient kinaesthetic events to be integrated with concurrent tactile events stemming from a common external source (e.g. the shape of a felt object). This limitation of the study could be addressed in future experiments by applying similar techniques to dynamically moving hands, as they explore a real or virtual object in a haptic manner.

8.10 Dynamic audiovisual integration can influence auditory selection

The final study that we shall describe provides an initial demonstration that even phasic cross-modal integration, between concurrent dynamic events in separate modalities, can arise in an apparently 'preattentive' manner. This evidence stems from an audiovisual rather than a haptic situation. Driver (1996) presented subjects with two concurrent auditory messages. Each comprised three two-syllable words in random order (e.g. one message might comprise 'SUNSET–TULIP–HEADLINE' while the concurrent message might be 'MUSIC–FLOORING–PIGMENT'). As in the classic shadowing studies of auditory attention (Cherry 1953; Broadbent 1958; Treisman 1964), the task was to repeat one message (the target triplet of words) while ignoring the other concurrent message (the distractor triplet). Unlike standard shadowing situations, no auditory information specified which message was the target and which the distractor, because both messages were spoken by the same voice, on recordings played in synchrony from a single monosound source. Furthermore, both messages were random sequences of words. Which message was relevant was specified only visually. A screen displayed a continuous video of the face of the person who had recorded the two messages, showing her speaking the relevant words in perfect synchrony with the sounds she produced for that relevant message. The task was thus to repeat the words spoken on the video, with lip- and tongue-movements being available visually for the relevant message, but not for the irrelevant message.

It had previously been shown that adding visual lip-read information for just the relevant message can improve selective shadowing (Reisberg 1978). This would be expected, because even people with normal audition rely to a considerable extent on lip-read information during speech perception, as it can provide further phonological information about the heard speech-sounds (McGurk and McDonald 1976; Massaro 1987). The novel twist to Driver's (1996) study was to manipulate where the visual lip-read information was situated relative to the monosound source that presented the relevant and irrelevant sounds (see figure 8.4).

It is well-known that people tend to mislocate sounds toward their apparent visual source; the so-called 'ventriloquist' illusion (for a review, see Bertelson 1998). For instance, film audiences invariably hear a spoken soundtrack as emanating from actors appearing on the screen, even though

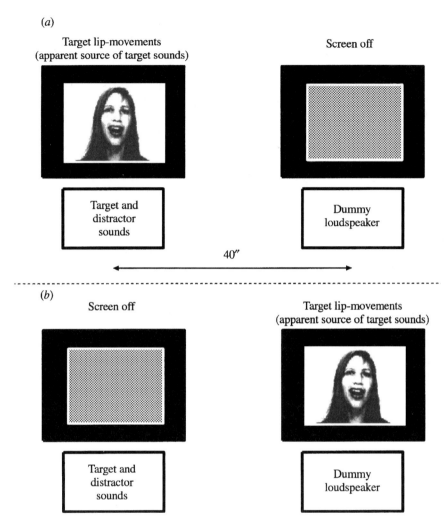

Fig. 8.4 Schematic illustration of the apparatus used by Driver (1996). Relevant and irrelevant words were played from a single loudspeaker (shown on the left in the illustration, but equally likely to be on the right), and spoken in the same voice. A video monitor on one side (left in *a*, right in *b*) showed lip-movements which matched the relevant auditory words that had to be repeated by the subject. Performance was better when the relevant lip-movements were displaced away from the true monosound source (as in *b*) because this produced an illusory separation between relevant and irrelevant sounds owing to ventriloquism.

the true sound source (i.e. the loudspeakers presenting the soundtrack) is located elsewhere. Driver (1996) aimed to determine the possible implications of this well-known illusion for selective attention. He varied the position of visual lip-read information for the relevant message, either presenting this on the same side as the true monosound source for both auditory messages (directly above the active loudspeaker, see figure 8.4*a*), or displaced to the opposite side (directly above a 'dummy' loudspeaker which, unknown to the subjects, did not present any sounds; see figure 8.4*b*).

Driver (1996) found better selective shadowing of the relevant message in the latter condition, when the visual lip-movements were displaced away from the true monosound source, rather than being presented at the same location as the sounds. He attributed this remarkable effect on objective performance to the subjective ventriloquist illusion. In the same-side condition, ventriloquism should scarcely affect performance, as the lips were presented very close to all of the speech sounds (figure 8.4a). However, in the displaced condition (figure 8.4b) any ventriloquism should pull the target sounds away from the distractor sounds, toward the side of the dummy loudspeaker where the lips appeared. Only the target sounds matched these lip-movements, and so only they should migrate towards the lips (as ventriloquism arises only for matching visual and auditory events; Bertelson 1998). Hence the distractor sounds would be effectively 'left behind' at the true sound source, as ventriloquism pulled the relevant sounds toward the displaced lips.

Thus, any ventriloquism should lead to an illusory spatial separation between the target and sounds in the displaced condition (figure 8.4b). The 17% benefit in performance that Driver observed for this displaced condition, relative to the same-side condition, implies that selective shadowing can be objectively improved by an illusory spatial separation between target and distractor sounds, just as previously found for real spatial separations (see, for example, Cherry 1953; Broadbent 1958). In this respect, the result is reminiscent of the well-known 'binaural masking difference' found in auditory psychophysical studies. When a monaural target signal is made to sound as though it comes from a different position to a masking signal in the same ear, by presenting an additional mask to the other ear, then target detection improves (Moore 1982). Driver's (1996) results likewise suggest that auditory attention can be usefully focused on the phenomenal rather than the physical location of a target sound. However, the crucial difference is that, in his case, the illusory position of the target sound depended on a cross-modal influence from vision.

The implication of Driver's (1996) results is therefore that some cross-modal integration can take place between audition and vision before auditory spatial selection is fully completed. The beneficial effect of ventriloquism on selective shadowing performance in the displaced condition (see figure 8.4b) could only arise if just the target sounds were illusorily pulled toward the matching moving lips, leaving the distractor sounds behind, to produce the apparent spatial separation in audition that proved so useful for selective listening. This effective separation of the target and distractor sounds could only happen after the system had already worked out to some extent which sounds matched the synchronous lip-movements (and as a result, should migrate toward them), and which sounds did not (and so should be left behind). As the illusory separation evidently benefited auditory selection, some of this cross-modal matching must have taken place before auditory selection was complete. In this sense, then, the results imply that cross-modal integration (i.e. the appropriate on-line matching of some speech sounds but not others with synchronous lip-movements) can arise 'preattentively'. Endogenous auditory attention does not operate solely on auditory information, in a strictly modular encapsulated fashion. Instead, attention operates on auditory information which has already been integrated to some extent with phasic visual information (note that only the dynamic correspondence between lip-movements and concurrent speech-sounds indicated which auditory message matched the lips, and so should migrate towards them).

Driver's (1996) study provides an unusual case of an illusion (namely, ventriloquism) actually aiding veridical perception (i.e. identification of the target words), which might at first appear to be a peculiar state of affairs. However, it is important to realize that, in real-world settings, ventriloquism should usually improve veridical perception of auditory locations, rather than producing illusory mislocalizations. Speech sounds usually do emanate from the moving lips which match them, and vision tends to provide more accurate location information than audition, especially in noisy situations. Hence, in many cases it will be adaptive to weight visual evidence for the location of a sound source more strongly than any competing auditory evidence. This will only lead to illusory mislocations in unusual cases, such as in cinemas or during experiments, where the true sound source is artificially displaced from its apparent visual source.

Thus, by means of visual ventriloquism, the listener can compensate for the relatively poor coding of location by audition that arises in noisy environments, such as the textbook 'cocktail party' situation of many competing conversations in a crowded room. However, note that this cross-modal mechanism for enhancing auditory localization, by means of the better spatial resolution available in vision, could not possibly help us to listen selectively in noisy settings (i.e. could not benefit auditory attention) if it arose only after auditory spatial selection was already completed. To aid selective listening, cross-modal ventriloquism would have to arise 'preattentively', precisely as Driver's (1996) study suggests.

We suspect that a similar logic will apply for many of the other forms of cross-modal integration considered in this paper. In order for attention to be adaptively directed with respect to external space, considerable cross-modal integration is first necessary to construct a suitable internal representation of space. Even in apparently unimodal situations, such as those investigated by researchers who only consider visual attention, the representational space in which attention gets directed will probably turn out to be determined by other modalities as well. Diffuse proprioceptive, kinaesthetic and vestibular inputs are already known to influence the mental representation of visual space, and can do so even for the perceived position of a single spot of light (see Driver and Grossenbacher 1996). However, the possible implications of these cross-modal influences for the nature of the 'space' in which visual attention gets directed has scarcely ever been considered (although see Ladavas 1987).

While the study of spatial attention seems well-advanced when single sensory modalities are considered (see the other papers in this volume), it is still in its infancy as regards cross-modal issues. Nevertheless, we hope that the studies described here may persuade the reader that the cross-modal questions we have posed merit further investigation, and that the senses should no longer be approached in strict isolation by attention researchers.

Acknowledgements

This research was supported by the Medical Research Council (UK), and the Wellcome Trust. We thank S. Kennett, E. Maculoso, F. Pavani and C. Rorden for helpful comments. Illustrations by Kennett Enterprises.

References

Anderson, R. A., Snyder, L. H., Bradley, D. C. and Xing, J. 1997 Multimodal representation of space in the posterior parietal cortex and its use in planning movements. *A. Rev. Neurosci.* **20**, 303–30.

Bertelson, P. 1998 Starting from the ventriloquist: the perception of multimodal events. In *Advances in psychological science. 1. Biological and cognitive aspects* (eds M. Sabourin, F. I. M. Craik and M. Robert). Hove, UK: Psychological Press. (In the press.)

Broadbent, D. E. 1958 *Perception and communication.* Elmsford, NJ: Pergamon.

Buchtel, H. A. and Butter, C. M. 1988 Spatial attention shifts: implications for the role of polysensory mechanisms. *Neuropsychologia* **26**, 499–509.

Butter, C. M., Buchtel, H. A. and Santucci, R. 1989 Spatial attentional shifts: further evidence for the role of polysensory mechanisms using visual and tactile stimuli. *Neuropsychologia* **27**, 1231–40.

Cherry, E. C. 1953 Some experiments upon the recognition of speech with one and two ears. *J. Acoustic. Soc. Am.* **25**, 975–9.

Corbetta, M., Miezin, F. M., Shulman, G. L. and Petersen, S. E. 1993 A PET study of visuospatial attention. *J. Neurosci.* **13**, 1202–26.

Driver, J. 1996 Enhancement of selective listening by illusory mislocation of speech sounds due to lip-reading. *Nature* **381**, 66–8.

Driver, J. 1998 Cross-modal links in spatial attention: the second EPS prize lecture. *Q. J. Exp. Psychol.* (In the press.)

Driver, J. and Grossenbacher, P. G. 1996 Multimodal spatial constraints on tactile selective attention. In *Attention and performance. XVI. Information integration in perception and communication* (eds T. Innui and J. L. McClelland), pp. 209–35. Cambridge, MA: MIT Press.

Driver, J. and Mattingley, J. B. 1995 Selective attention in humans: normality and pathology. *Curr. Opin. Neurobiol.* **5**, 191–7.

Driver, J. and Spence, C. J. 1994 Spatial synergies between auditory and visual attention. In *Attention and performance: conscious and nonconscious information processing*, vol. 15 (eds C. Umiltà and M. Moscovitch), pp. 311–31. Cambridge, MA: MIT Press.

Driver, J. and Spence, C. 1998 Pöppel's paradox partially resolved in people. (Submitted.)

Driver, J., Mattingley, J. B., Rorden, C. and Davis, G. 1997 Extinction as a paradigm measure of attentional bias and restricted capacity following brain injury. In *Parietal lobe contributions to orientation in 3D space* (eds P. Thier and H.-O. Karnath), pp. 401–29. Berlin: Springer.

Eimer, M. and Schröger, E. 1998 ERP effects of intermodal attention and cross-modal links in spatial attention. *Psychophysiology.* (In the press.)

Eriksen, B. A. and Hoffman, J. E. 1972 Some characteristics of selective attention in visual perception determined by vocal reaction time. *Percept. Psychophys.* **11**, 169–71.

Farah, M. J., Wong, A. B., Monheit, M. A. and Morrow, L. A. 1989 Parietal lobe mechanisms of spatial attention: modality-specific or supramodal? *Neuropsychologia* **27**, 461–70.

Graziano, M. S. A. and Gross, C. G. 1993 A bimodal map of space: somatosensory receptive fields in the macaque putamen with corresponding visual receptive fields. *Exp. Brain Res.* **97**, 96–109.

Groh, J. M. and Sparks, D. L. 1996a Saccades to somatosensory targets. 1. Behavioral characteristics. *J. Neurophysiol.* **75**, 412–27.

Groh, J. M. and Sparks, D. L. 1996b Saccades to somatosensory targets. 3. Eye-position dependent somatosensory activity in primate superior colliculus. *J. Neurophysiol.* **75**, 439–53.

Hillyard, S. A., Simpson, G. V., Woods, D. L., Van Voorhis, S. and Munte, T. F. 1984 Event-related brain potentials and selective attention to different modalities. In *Cortical integration* (eds F. Reinoso-Suarez and C. Ajmone-Marson), pp. 395–414. New York: Raven Press.

Hillyard, S. A., Mangun, G. R., Woldorff, M. G. and Luck, S. J. 1995 Neural systems mediating selective attention. In *The cognitive neurosciences* (ed. M. S. Gazzaniga), pp. 665–81. Cambridge, MA: MIT Press.

Jay, M. F. and Sparks, D. L. 1984 Auditory receptive fields in primate superior colliculus shift with changes in eye position. *Nature* **309**, 345–47.

Jay, M. F. and Sparks, D. L. 1990 Localization of auditory and visual targets for the initiation of saccadic eye movements. In *Comparative perception.* I. *Basic mechanisms* (eds M. A. Berkley and W. C. Stebbins), pp. 351–74. New York: Wiley.

Kinsbourne, M. 1993 Orientational bias model of unilateral neglect: evidence from attentional gradients within hemispace. In *Unilateral neglect: clinical and experimental studies* (eds I. H. Robertson and J. C. Marshall), pp. 63–86. Hillsdale, NJ: Lawrence Erlbaum.

Kustov, A. A. and Robinson, D. L. 1996 Shared neural control of attentional shifts and eye movements. *Nature* **384**, 74–7.

Ladavas, E. 1987 Is the hemispatial deficit produced by right parietal lobe damage associated with retinal or gravitational coordinates? *Brain* **110**, 167–80.

Massaro, D. M. 1987 *Speech perception by ear and eye.* Hillsdale, NJ: Lawrence Erlbaum.

Mattingley, J. B., Driver, J., Beschin, N. and Robertson, I. H. 1997 Attentional competition between modalities: extinction between touch and vision after right hemisphere damage. *Neuropsychologia* **35**, 867–80.

McGurk, H. and MacDonald, J. 1976 Hearing lips and seeing voices. *Nature* **264**, 746–8.

Moore, B. 1982 Introduction to the psychology of hearing. London: Academic.

Moran, J. and Desimone, R. 1985 Selective attention gates visual processing in the extrastriate cortex. *Science* **229**, 782–4.

Neisser, U. and Becklen, R. 1975 Selective looking: attending to visually specified events. *Cogn. Psychol.* **7**, 480–94.

Pashler, H. E. 1998 *The psychology of attention*. Cambridge, MA: MIT Press.

Posner, M. I. 1978 *Chronometric explorations of mind*. Hillsdale, NJ: Lawrence Erlbaum.

Posner, M. I. and Cohen, Y. 1984 Components of visual orienting. In *Attention and performance: control of language processes* Vol.10 (eds H. Bouma and D. G. Bouwhuis), pp. 531–56. Hillsdale, NJ: Lawrence Erlbaum.

Reisberg, D. 1978 Looking where you listen: visual cues and auditory attention. *Acta Psychol.* **42**, 331–41.

Reuter-Lorenz, P. A., Jha, A. P. and Rosenquist, J. N. 1996 What is inhibited in inhibition of return? *J. Exp. Psychol. Hum. Percept. Perf.* **22**, 367–78.

Rizzolatti, G., Camarda, R., Grupp, L. A. and Pisa, M. 1974 Inhibitory effect of remote visual stimuli on visual responses of cat superior colliculus: spatial and temporal factors. *J. Neurophysiol.* **37**, 1262–75.

Rorden, C. and Driver, J. 1998 Does saccade preparation affect auditory attention? *Neuropsychologia*. (In the press.)

Spence, C. J. and Driver, J. 1994 Covert spatial orienting in audition: exogenous and endogenous mechanisms facilitate sound localization. *J. Exp. Psychol. Hum. Percept. Perf.* **20**, 555–74.

Spence, C. and Driver, J. 1996 Audiovisual links in endogenous covert spatial attention. *J. Exp. Psychol. Hum. Percept. Perf.* **22**, 1005–30.

Spence, C. and Driver, J. 1997 Audiovisual links in exogenous covert spatial orienting. *Percept. Psychophys.* **59**, 1–22.

Spence, C. and Driver, J. 1998a Auditory and audiovisual inhibition of return. *Percept. Psychophys.* (In the press.)

Spence, C. and Driver, J. 1998b Inhibition of return following an auditory cue: the role of central reorienting events. *Exp. Brain Res.* **118**, 352–60.

Spence, C., Nicholls, M. E. R., Gillespie, N. and Driver, J. 1998a Cross-modal links in exogenous covert spatial orienting between touch, audition, and vision. *Percept. Psychophys.* **60**, 125–39.

Spence, C., Pavani, F. and Driver, J. 1998b Crossmodal links in spatial attention between vision and touch. (In preparation.)

Spence, C. and Driver, J. 1998c Integrated visuo-tactile representation of space revealed by crossmodal attention effects in normal humans. (Submitted.)

Stein, B. E. and Meredith, M. A. 1993 *The merging of the senses*. Cambridge, MA: MIT Press.

Stein, J. F. 1992 The representation of egocentric space in the posterior parietal cortex. *Behav. Brain Sci.* **15**, 691–700.

Stricanne, B., Anderson, R. A. and Mazzoni, P. 1996 Eye-centered, head-centered, and intermediate coding of remembered sound locations in area LIP. *J. Neurophysiol.* **76**, 2071–76.

Tassinari, G. and Campara, D. 1996 Consequences of covert orienting to non-informative stimuli of different modalities: a unitary mechanism? *Neuropsychologia* **34**, 235–45.

Treisman, A. 1964 The effects of irrelevant material on the efficiency of selective listening. *Am. J. Psychol.* **77**, 533–46.

Treisman, A. M. and Gelade, G. 1980 A feature-integration theory of attention. *Cogn. Psychol.* **12**, 97–136.

Ward, L. M. 1994 Supramodal and modality-specific mechanisms for stimulus-driven shifts of auditory and visual attention. *Can. J. Exp. Psychol.* **48**, 242–59.

Wurtz, R. H., Goldberg, M. E. and Robinson, D. L. 1982 Brain mechanisms of visual attention. *Sci. Am.* **246**, 100–7.

Wurtz, R. H., Richmond, B. J. and Judge, S. J. 1980 Vision during saccadic eye movements. III. Visual interactions in monkey superior colliculus. *J. Neurophysiol.* **43**, 1168–81.

Yao, L. and Peck, C. K. 1997 Saccadic eye movements to visual and auditory targets. *Exp. Brain Res.* **115**, 25–34.

Section 3

Spatial representation and attention

9

Place cells, navigational accuracy, and the human hippocampus

John O'Keefe, Neil Burgess, James G. Donnett,
Kathryn J. Jeffery and Eleanor A. Maguire

Abstract

The hippocampal formation in both rats and humans is involved in spatial navigation. In the rat, cells coding for places, directions, and speed of movement have been recorded from the hippocampus proper and/or the neighbouring subicular complex. Place fields of a group of the hippocampal pyramidal cells cover the surface of an environment but do not appear to do so in any systematic fashion. That is, there is no topographical relation between the anatomical location of the cells within the hippocampus and the place fields of these cells in an environment. Recent work shows that place cells are responding to the summation of two or more of gaussian curves, each of which is fixed at a given distance to two or more walls in the environment. The walls themselves are probably identified by their allocentric direction relative to the rat and this information may be provided by the head direction cells. The right human hippocampus retains its role in spatial mapping as demonstrated by its activation during accurate navigation in imaginary and virtual reality environments. In addition, it may have taken on wider memory functions, perhaps by the incorporation of a linear time tag which allows for the storage of the times of visits to particular locations. This extended system would serve as the basis for a spatio-temporal event or episodic memory system.

9.1 Introduction

Cells in the hippocampus of the rat signal the animal's location in an environment. Damage to this structure leads to severe spatial impairments in rats. These findings have provided support for the idea that the hippocampus in animals such as the rat operates like a cognitive map (O'Keefe and Nadel 1978). In this paper, we will discuss the way in which an environment is represented by the constellation of firing across a large number of hippocampal place cells, how the location and shape of the firing fields of the cells is controlled by environmental stimuli, how information about the animal's speed of movement through the environment is coded, and what our understanding of the rat hippocampus tells us about the functions of the human hippocampus.

9.2 Representation of an environment within the hippocampus

Cells in the CA1 field of the hippocampus code for an environment using a distributed representation. Neighbouring cells are as likely to code for distant regions of an environment as they are to code for nearby regions. Figure 9.1 shows the place fields of 15 CA1 pyramidal cells recorded simultaneously from a single tetrode while the animal moved around a 40 cm × 40 cm box, searching for small bits of rice. There was only a small lip on the box allowing the animal to search over

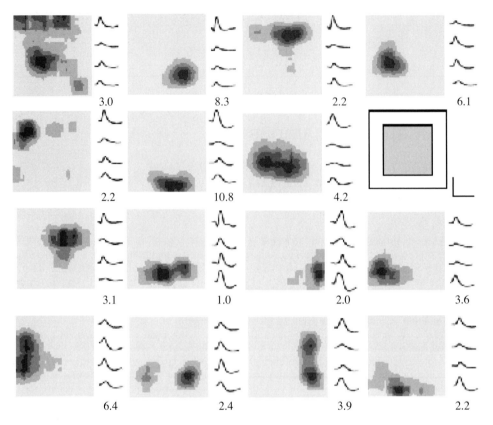

Fig. 9.1 Place fields of 15 complex-spike cells recorded simultaneously in the CA1 field of the hippocampus of a rat searching for grains of rice on a small 40 cm × 40 cm open platform. The surface area of the holding box relative to the overall camera view is shown in the inset. The waveform for each cell as recorded on the tetrode is shown to the right of the place field. Firing rates within the place fields are represented by four grey-scale levels, each reflecting 20% of the peak firing rate. Peak firing rate within each field is shown below the waveform. Calibrations for the spike waveform are 375, 250, 300 and 300 μV, respectively, from top to bottom and 1 ms.

the edge as well as on the floor of the box (see layout of the environment in figure 9.1). Each of the four electrodes in the tetrode has a diameter of 25 μM, approximately the size of a pyramidal cell body and can see action potentials from cells up to 100–150 μM away. If we assume that the amplitude of an action potential recorded by an extracellular electrode is a function of the distance of the spike generator from that electrode, then the tetrode allows us to get some idea of the topographical relation between the place fields of cells and their anatomical relation to each other. Cells that are anatomically closer to one electrode of the tetrode will have spikes of a larger amplitude on that tetrode. We can arrange the cells in a rough topographical ordering on the basis of the size of the potential on the different electrodes. In figure 9.1, cells whose amplitudes are relatively larger on electrode 1 are placed in the upper left-hand corner of the picture, those which are larger on electrode 2 are placed in the upper right-hand corner and so on.

We draw two conclusions from this picture. First, the fields of the 15 cells cover a considerable area of the environment and second, there does not appear to be any obvious topographical relation

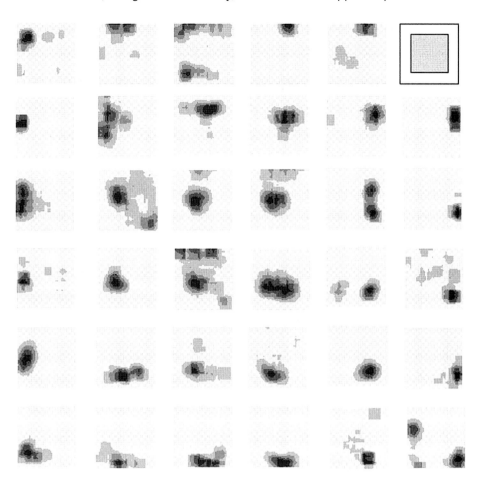

Fig. 9.2   Place fields of 35 simultaneously recorded hippocampal complex-spike cells arranged according to field location. Fields towards the northwest of the box are shown in the upper left part of the figure, those towards the northeast in the upper right and so on. Cells with double fields are placed with respect to the stronger field. Notice that the fields collectively cover a large proportion of the environment.

between the field locations and the anatomical locations of the cells relative to each other within the hippocampus. This lack of topography contrasts with a recent claim that there is a tendency for place fields recorded on the same electrode to show similar place fields in an environment (Shapiro *et al*. 1997). The conclusion that a small number of cells is adequate to represent the environment is strengthened by the inclusion of additional cells recorded on other tetrodes at the same time as those shown in figure 9.1. In all, 35 cells with place fields on the box were recorded at the same time and their fields are represented in figure 9.2. Here, the fields are represented by their relation to the environment and not to their anatomical location within the hippocampus. Cells with fields along the east side of the testing environment have been placed on the right-hand side of the figure; those with fields at the south side of the environment have been placed towards the bottom of the figure, and so on. Several aspects of the place field phenomenon can be seen from this figure.

First, the 35 cells cover a large proportion of the environment. On the basis of similar recordings, Wilson and McNaughton (1993) calculated that approximately 130 place cells would be sufficient to allow the hippocampus to compute the animal's location in an environment to an accuracy of 1 cm s^{-1} and about 380 cells for an accuracy of 1 cm per 0.1 s. Second, the fields towards the edge of the environment are smaller than those towards the centre. Notice that this change in field size occurs independently in the x and y directions. For example, as one moves from left to right along the bottom row of the figure, the fields sizes get larger and then smaller in the x dimension independently of their height in the y dimension. We will discuss these properties of place fields in §9.3 in the context of our model of place field formation. A second property of the place cells recorded in an open field environment is shown in figure 9.3. This picture shows the firing fields of four of the cells from figure 9.1. For each cell, the central panel shows the firing field without regard to the direction in which the animal is moving. In the surrounding panels are shown the same firing fields when the animal's direction of movement is taken into account. It is clear that the fields in the different directions are more or less equivalent. It was this property of omnidirectionality (see O'Keefe 1976; Muller *et al.* 1987) which originally suggested that these cells were not coding for simple sensory stimuli but were instead computing the more abstract concept of place or location. In §9.3 we will discuss experiments which provide information about the role that sensory information plays in the computation of the animal's location.

9.3 Sensory control over the location and shape of the hippocampal place cells

Why do the hippocampal place cells fire in particular locations in an environment? The way to answer this question is to study the types of modifications of the environment that lead to changes in the location of the place fields or in the shapes of those fields. In the first set of experiments of this kind, O'Keefe and Conway (1978) recorded place cells from the hippocampus of rats that had been trained on a place discrimination on a T-maze set in a cue-controlled environment. The only spatial cues available to the animal to guide its behaviour to the goal were a set of objects and stimuli around the periphery of the environment. Rotation of the constellation of spatial stimuli resulted in a concomitant rotation of the place fields. Similar results were reported by Muller and co-workers (1987). In their experiments, cells were recorded from animals that had been trained to forage for food pellets in a cylindrical environment where the only polarizing spatial cue was a white card attached to the wall of the cylinder. Despite the fact that the animals were not trained to pay attention to the cue card to solve the behavioural task, the fields rotated with rotation of the card in a manner strictly analogous to that found in the O'Keefe and Conway (1978) study. The difference between these two studies points to an important aspect of the property of place cells: the analysis of the sensory information which determines where in the environment each cell will fire is not dependent on the animal's attention to that set of stimuli.

It would be interesting to compare the place fields of cells recorded in two different conditions, one in which the animal was using a place strategy to solve the problem and therefore presumably attending to the spatial cues, and the other in which it was reaching the goal by a non-spatial strategy.

It appears then that cues at the periphery of an environment determine the angular orientation of the place fields. In a recent and important study, Cressant *et al.* (1997) have shown that prominent objects located towards the centre of an enclosure cannot provide this polarizing information but will readily do so when the same objects are moved to the periphery of the enclosure. As we shall see shortly, it is reasonable to suppose that the function of these polarizing cues in all of these experiments is to orient the head direction system and only indirectly to control the angular location of the place cell's fields.

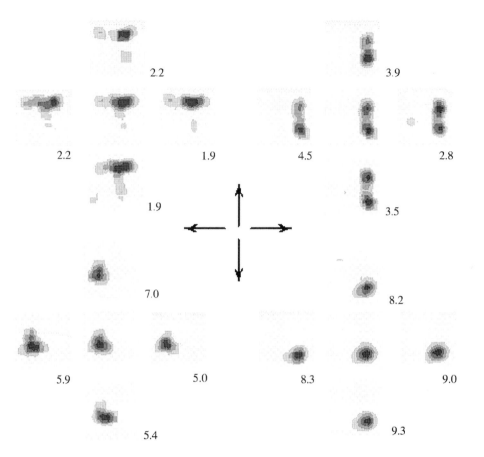

Fig. 9.3 Omnidirectional firing pattern in four hippocampal complex-spike cells. For each cell, the central panel shows the overall firing pattern irrespective of the direction of movement of the animal through the place field. In the surrounding panels, the firing fields have been separated according to the direction of movement. Northward direction is at the top, eastward to the right, southward at the bottom, and westward to the left. Peak firing rate is shown at the bottom right of each panel. Notice that each cell fires in the appropriate location irrespective of the animal's direction of movement.

A second geometrical manipulation of the environment which has provided information about the sensory control of the place cells has been environmental enlargement. Muller and Kubie (1987) have shown that some place cells increase their firing field when the size of a cylindrical or rectangular environment is doubled. Interestingly, the size of the field increase was not commensurate with the size of the increase in the environment. As we shall see in §9.4, this somewhat surprising result is explicable on the basis of the model we have generated for place cell construction.

The final type of environmental manipulation is one in which the size and the shape of the environment was modified. O'Keefe and Burgess (1996) recorded place cells in four rectangular boxes that varied in the length of one or both dimensions. The walls of each box were constructed from the same four planks of wood standing on edge (see figure 9.4a). These planks of wood were frequently interchanged as was the paper floor of the environment to eliminate local cues which could be used to identify position. Figure 9.4b,c shows two examples of cells recorded in this experiment. The place field of the cell in figure 9.4b signalled the animal's location in the bottom

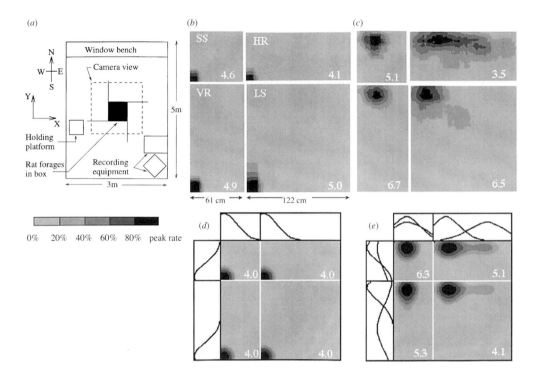

Fig. 9.4 (*a*) Layout of the experimental room as seen from above. The dashed area represents the camera view and the black-filled region represents the small-square (SS) testing box. The horizontally oriented (HR), vertically oriented (VR) rectangular boxes, and the large-square (LS) testing box were all created from the same wooden planks in different configurations. (*b*) Firing field of a simple place field in the four rectilinear environments. The cell fired in the southwest corner of each box irrespective of the overall box shape. (*c*) Firing field of a more complex place cell. The field centre maintained a fixed distance from the north and west walls but was stretched towards the east wall in the horizontal rectangle (*c*). (*d, e*) Computational models of the fields shown in *b* and *c*, respectively (after O'Keefe and Burgess 1996).

left corner of the box regardless of the shape and size of the box. In essence, the cell ignored both the top and right-hand walls. In contrast, the cell whose firing pattern is shown in figure 9.4*c* was influenced by both the left- and right-hand walls as well as the top wall. This is clearly shown by the firing pattern in the horizontal rectangle where the field becomes elongated along the long dimension of the box. These, and similar place field transformations, have led us to propose the model of place cell formation which is illustrated in figure 9.4*d,e*.

The essence of the model is that each place field comprises the summation of two or more Gaussians. The location of the centre, the amplitude and the width of each Gaussian is determined by its distance to a particular wall in a particular direction. Gaussians which are centred close to the wall which controls them are higher and more sharply peaked than ones centred further away. According to the model, the fields shown in figure 9.4*b* would be formed by the summation of one Gaussian fixed at a close distance to the left-hand wall of the box and a second Gaussian fixed to the bottom wall of the box (see figure 9.4*d*). The place field shown in figure 9.4*c* would comprise four Gaussians, each one fixed to one of the walls of the box. As one can see in figure 9.4*e*, stretching the box along the horizontal dimension results in a pulling apart of the Gaussian curves fixed to the left-hand and right-hand walls with the resultant flattening and stretching of their summed curve.

There are two notable features of this model which we would like to discuss here. The first is that the way in which the experiment was done meant that there was no distinctive sensory input intrinsic to a wall which the animal could use to differentiate any one wall from another. This is because the same four planks of wood were regularly interchanged to form the walls of the box. It follows that the animal must have been using some other source of information to identify each wall. The model suggests that this information consists of the direction of the wall from the animal and that this information is provided by the head direction cells found in the postsubiculum and the anterior thalamus. These are cells that signal the direction in which the animal's head is pointing in its environment regardless of its location in that environment (Taube *et al.* 1990). We will discuss evidence for this suggestion in §9.4. The sources of direction input in the experiments under discussion were not identified but were probably distant visual cues from the room external to the recording box and internal proprioceptive and vestibular (idiothetic) cues. The second aspect of the model which needs discussion is the means by which the animal determines its distance from the relevant wall. In our original paper, this was not specified. McNaughton (1996) has suggested that this is achieved primarily on the basis of self-motion cues. He suggests that the animal registers each contact with a wall that he bumps into and monitors the amount of movement from that wall as an indication of distance. We believe that this is too narrow a view and prefer to stick with the suggestion incorporated in the original cognitive map theory (O'Keefe and Nadel 1978) that several ways of measuring distance are available to an animal. In experimental paradigms in which there are many visual cues to distance, we believe that these are the primary source of distance information. For example, in our model of hippocampal control of navigation (Burgess and O'Keefe 1996), we suggested that the animal could calculate its distance to a wall on the basis of the vertical height, on its retina, of the line where the wall meets the floor. Under circumstances in which strong and salient visual cues are not available, the rat may use self-motion information as it moves away from identified features of the environment such as the walls of the box, but it also might use information from other modalities, for example, auditory or olfactory cues. The possibility that the animal uses self-motion cues to determine distance is strengthened by the existence of cells such as the one shown in figure 9.5. The firing rate of this cell was a linear function of the speed with which the animal moved through the environment. As shown in the figure, this relation between speed and firing rate was maintained irrespective of the direction in which the animal moved. Furthermore, requiring the animal to exert more force during the movement by pulling against a weight suspended from a pulley slowed its speed but had no effect on the speed–firing rate relation. These speed cells are only encountered rarely in the hippocampal formation and their waveform profiles suggest that they are recordings from axons. It seems likely that the cell bodies are located elsewhere, in one of the nuclei projecting to the hippocampus. As we shall see from the results of our experiments on functional imaging of the brain during human navigation (see §9.4), a candidate nucleus where the computation of speed through an environment might take place is the caudate nucleus.

9.4   Head directional control of the angular orientation of the hippocampal place fields

As we have seen, the hippocampal place fields can be rotated by the rotation of cues at or near the periphery of the environment. Furthermore, once the place fields have been rotated into a new location they remain in that orientation following the removal of the spatial polarizing cues at the periphery of the environment (Muller *et al.* 1987; O'Keefe and Speakman 1987). Appropriate orientation of the animal's sense of direction is maintained by both visual and self-motion cues (Sharp *et al.* 1995; Wiener *et al.* 1995). In the absence of salient visual cues, the

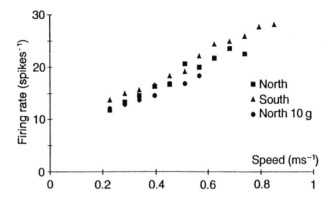

Fig. 9.5 Relation between firing rate of speed cell and speed of running on a linear track. Relation is maintained irrespective of direction of the movement and is not affected by increasing the effort required to reach any particular speed. In condition north 10 g, the rat was required to run in a northward direction while lifting a small 10 g weight attached to it via a string and pulley arrangement (J. O'Keefe, J. G. Donnett and P. Martin, unpublished results).

animal's sense of direction is continually updated on the basis of self-motion information. This has been demonstrated in experiments in our laboratory in which the rat's internal direction sense was altered by slowly rotating the animal in a small enclosed box outside of the environment (Jeffery *et al.* 1997). In this experiment, we assume the animal uses self-motion cues to continually update its sense of direction. In almost every case, the place fields rotated to maintain their alignment with the rat's internal direction sense. When the visual and idiothetic cues are both present but set in opposition to each other, the visual cues usually predominate unless they have been experienced as unreliable directional indicators (Jeffery 1998).

9.5 Role of the human hippocampus and spatial navigation

Ideas about the function of the human hippocampus have emphasized its role in memory and in particular in declarative or episodic memory. This stems primarily from the evidence that patients with damage to the hippocampal formation are severely amnesic (Scoville and Milner 1957). Patients such as H.M. have considerable difficulty recalling events of the past. Although H.M. has damage which extends beyond the narrowly defined hippocampus, other amnesic patients such as R.B. have histologically verified damage restricted to the hippocampus (Zola-Morgan *et al.* 1986). Recent work on three patients who sustained bilateral damage limited to the hippocampus early in life (Vargha-Khadem *et al.* 1997) suggests that such damage results in memory deficits for episodes and events but not for semantic or other factual material. It is particularly noteworthy in the present context that of the two formal recognition memory tasks on which these patients were impaired, one was an object-in-location task. These results raise several questions. Is there a special role for the human hippocampus in spatial navigation analogous to that in the rat? If there is, how does this tie into the more general episodic memory deficit characteristic of amnesic patients? In this section, we will present evidence which suggests that the answer to the first question is yes and then go on to suggest how the spatial system in humans might participate in the more general function of storing information about episodes and events.

Patients with damage to the right temporal lobe which includes the hippocampus have been shown to be selectively deficient in the memory for the location of objects. This was in the context of relatively preserved memory for the identity of the objects themselves (Smith and Milner 1982,

1989; but see Cave and Squire 1991). In a direct test of human cognitive mapping, Maguire *et al.* (1996*a*) studied the ability of normal subjects and patients with left or right temporal lobe damage to form spatial representations on the basis of viewing film footage of two routes through a small town. They showed the film footage several times until both groups were completely successful in recognizing scenes from the film when these were shown with appropriate foils in a forced-choice recognition task. The patients required slightly more trials than normals to reach and maintain perfect performance in scene recognition. Subsequent tests showed that the patients were particularly deficient in placing the scenes in the order in which they were encountered during the film, in estimating the distance between two scenes, and in drawing maps of the town. Of particular interest was the finding that patients with left temporal lobe damage were as impaired in many of these tasks as the right temporal patients. Maguire and her colleagues have argued that there is a role for both mesial temporal lobes in human navigation in large-scale environments.

Recent results from functional imaging experiments support a role for the medial temporal lobe in human navigation in large-scale environments. Positron emission tomography experiments in which subjects were scanned during the acquisition of spatial information provided by a film similar to that used in the Maguire *et al.* study showed activation in the right and left medial temporal lobe and in the right hippocampus (Maguire *et al.* 1996*b*). Furthermore, scanning of taxi drivers while they imagined driving along routes from one location to several others in London also showed activation of the right hippocampus and both parahippocampal gyri (Maguire *et al.* 1997). More recently, our group has used virtual reality techniques to allow subjects to learn about large-scale environments and to find their way from one location to another in these environments during scanning experiments. In our original experiments (Maguire *et al.* 1998*a*), we scanned volunteers while they were learning about two simple environments: one environment was relatively featureless while the other contained a set of distinctive objects which the subjects were asked to remember so that they could locate them subsequently. Learning the layout of the first environment did not engage temporal lobe structures while learning the second produced activation of the right parahippocampal gyrus. In our latest study (Maguire *et al.* 1998*b*), we have used a complex virtual environment measuring about 75×75 virtual metres and containing several main roads and in addition many shops and buildings which the subject could enter and navigate through. The subjects explored this environment for periods of 30–60 min until they felt they knew their way around reasonably well. At this point their brains were scanned during four conditions. In the first condition, they were instructed to go from their present location in the virtual world to a particular destination. In the second condition, they were asked to do the same except that now previously open doors were closed and a roadblock was moved across one of the main roads. These changes required the subject to take detours to reach their destinations. In a third condition, the subjects were asked to move through the environment following a trail of arrows on the floor. In this condition, therefore, they moved through the environment in a similar fashion to the first two conditions but without the requirement to use a spatial representation or a cognitive map to do so. In the fourth and final condition, subjects were asked to view static scenes from the environment and to decide whether a given scene contained a particular feature. The results enable us to map out the network of brain structures which co-operate to enable subjects to navigate through the virtual world and, we assume, the real world as well.

The network of brain areas revealed as participating in navigation includes both left and right hippocampi, the right inferior parietal lobe, the medial parietal lobes, the right caudate nucleus, and the prefrontal cortex. All movement conditions whether guided by a spatial representation (conditions 1 and 2) or by arrows (as in condition 3) when compared with the static scene condition activated the inferior parietal and the medial parietal cortices. To show activation in the hippocampus it was necessary to take each subject's performance into account. Subjects did not always successfully reach the target destinations and these trials were identified as incorrect navigation trials. Both left and right hippocampi were active when correct navigation was compared with incorrect navigation during condition 1. We considered next only those trials in which the subjects went to the correct location. Correct navigation in conditions 1 and 2 compared with movement through the environment following arrows (condition 3) activated the right hippocampus.

To examine in more detail the relation between navigation and bloodflow in the hippocampus, we constructed a measure of the accuracy of navigation. At regular intervals along a subject's path we measured the angular deviation from the direct heading towards the goal. The average of all these angular deviations over the entire path length gives a measure of inaccuracy of navigation. We subtracted this measure of inaccuracy from $180°$ to give a measure of accuracy and correlated the latter with the bloodflow in the brain. The highest correlation was found in the right hippocampus ($r = 0.56$) and the second highest in the right inferior parietal cortex ($r = 0.43$). We interpret this finding to mean that the output of the hippocampus on the right side is a vector which continuously points to the goal location, a finding consistent with our model of the hippocampus (see Burgess and O'Keefe 1996). The lower correlation in the parietal cortex may mean that the activity here reflects other variables in addition to the simple direction to the goal.

In contrast to the accuracy results, when we surveyed the brain for areas with bloodflow selectively correlated with the speed of movement through the environment we found a significant activation in the right caudate nucleus. This pinpoints the basal ganglia as a potential source of the information about speed which we had identified in our single-unit recording in the rat hippocampus. Alternatively, the basal ganglia might be an area which receives information from the hippocampal formation and which uses it to control movement through an environment.

It is not possible on the basis of these functional imaging results to determine how the hippocampal formation and the parietal cortex interact during human navigation. We believe that one difference between the two areas is the mode of representation of the spatial information contained in each. The bulk of evidence suggests that the spatial framework coded in the parietal cortex is an egocentric one whose origin is centred on the eye, head, and trunk in contrast to the allocentric representation of an environment in the hippocampal formation. This suggests that one mode of interaction might involve egocentric information contained in the parietal cortex being sent to parahippocampal regions and then to the hippocampus where it is transformed into an allocentric representation of the environment. Alternatively the parietal cortex might be on the output side of the circuit. Information about the heading direction from the current location to the goal location might be sent to the inferior parietal cortex. In the inferior parietal cortex this information would be used to control egocentric orientation within the local space to guide the subject's behaviour appropriately. From this point of view, the lower level of activation in the parietal cortex would reflect additional inputs such as the location of doors within egocentric body coordinates in addition to the allocentric goal from the hippocampus.

The left hippocampus was also active during successful navigation. However, unlike the right hippocampus, the left did not show a correlation with navigational accuracy. We interpret this to mean that it is involved in navigation but in a way different from the right hippocampus. Perhaps it stores representations of the goal location for use by the right hippocampus during navigation or alternatively, it provides episodic memories of trajectories which were experienced during the original exploration of the environment. These trajectories would be correct, but not necessarily optimal, ways of getting from a location to the destination.

9.6   Relation between the navigation system and episodic memory

If we assume that the human hippocampus provides the subject with a cognitive map which is similar to that of the rat, then the question arises as to why damage to this structure should result in an episodic memory deficit in addition to a purely spatial memory deficit. One possibility, suggested by O'Keefe and Nadel (1978), is that humans possess a sense of linear time which is not available to the rat. This sense of linear time when combined with a spatial system allows events to be located in both space and time and provides the basis for an episodic memory system. Damage to this system would have a double effect. On one hand, it would directly affect the storage of spatio-temporal event memories; on the other hand, it would indirectly prevent the use of the spatio-temporal context in which items were learned from being used as a spatio-temporal retrieval cue for the recall of this information. Further exploration of the role of a spatial mapping system as the basis for a spatio-temporal event memory may close the apparent gap between the role of the hippocampus in rats and humans.

References

Cave, C. B. and Squire, L. R. 1991 Equivalent impairment of spatial and nonspatial memory following hippocampal damage to the human hippocampus. *Hippocampus* **1**, 329–40.

Cressant, A., Muller, R. U. and Poucet, B. 1997 Failure of the centrally placed objects to control the firing fields of hippocampal place cells. *J. Neurosci.* **17**, 2531–42.

Jeffery, K. J. 1998 Learning of landmark stability and instability by hippocampal place cells. *Neuropharmacology.* (In press.)

Jeffery, K. J., Donnett, J. G., Burgess, N. and O'Keefe, J. 1997 Directional control of the orientation of hippocampal place fields. *Exp. Brain Res.* **117**, 131–42.

McNaughton, B. L. 1996 Cognitive cartography. *Nature* **381**, 368–9.

Maguire, E. A., Burke, T., Phillips, J. and Staunton, H. 1996*a* Topographical disorientation following unilateral temporal lobe lesions in humans. *Neuropsychologia* **34**, 993–1001.

Maguire, E. A., Frackowiak, R. S. J. and Frith, C. D. 1996*b* Learning to find your way—a role for the human hippocampal region. *Proc. R. Soc. Lond.* B **263**, 1745–50.

Maguire, E. A., Frackowiak, R. S. J. and Frith, C. D. 1997 Recalling routes around London: activation of the right hippocampus in taxi drivers. *J. Neurosci.* **17**, 7103–7110.

Maguire, E. A., Frith, C. D., Burgess, N., Donnett, J. G. and O'Keefe, J. 1998*a* Knowing where things are: parahippocampal involvement in encoding locations in virtual large-scale space. *J. Cogn. Neurosci.* **10**, 61–76.

Maguire, E. A., Burgess, N., Donnett, J. G., Frackowiak, R. S. J., Frith, C. D. and O'Keefe, J. 1998*b* Knowing where, and getting there: a human navigation network. *Science* **280**, 921–4.

Muller, R. U. and Kubie, J. L. 1987 The effects of changes in the environment on the spatial firing of hippocampal complex-spike cells in a fixed environment. *J. Neurosci.* **7**, 1951–68.

Muller, R. U., Kubie, J. L. and Ranck, J. B. 1987 Spatial firing patterns of hippocampal complex-spike cells in a fixed environment. *J. Neurosci.* **7**, 1935–50.

O'Keefe, J. 1976 Place units in the hippocampus of the freely-moving rat. *Exp. Neurol.* **51**, 78–109.

O'Keefe, J. and Burgess, N. 1996 Geometric determinants of the place fields of hippocampal neurons. *Nature* **381**, 425–8.

O'Keefe, J. and Conway, D. H. 1978 Hippocampal place units in the freely moving rat: why they fire where they fire. *Exp. Brain Res.* **31**, 573–90.

O'Keefe, J. and Nadel, L. 1978 *The hippocampus as a cognitive map*. Oxford: Clarendon Press.

O'Keefe, J. and Speakman, A. 1987 Single unit activity in the rat hippocampus during a spatial memory task. *Exp. Brain Res.* **68**, 1–27.

Scoville, W. B. and Milner, B. 1957 Loss of recent memory after bilateral hippocampal lesions. *J. Neurol. Neurosurg. Psychiat.* **20**, 11–21.

Shapiro, M. L., Tanila, H. and Eichenbaum, H. 1997 Cues that hippocampal place cells encode: dynamic and hierarchical representation of local and distal stimuli. *Hippocampus* **7**, 624–42.

Sharp, P. E., Blair, H. T., Etkin, D. and Tzanetos, D. B. 1995 Influences of vestibular and visual motion information on the spatial firing pattern of the hippocampal place cells. *J. Neurosci.* **15**, 173–89.

Smith, M. L. and Milner, B. 1982 The role of the right hippocampus and the recall of spatial location. *Neuropsychologia* **19**, 781–93.

Smith, M. L. and Milner, B. 1989 Right hippocampal impairment in the recall of spatial location: encoding deficit or rapid forgetting? *Neuropsychologia* **27**, 71–81.

Taube, J. S., Muller, R. U. and Ranck, J. B. 1990 Head—direction cells recorded from the postsubiculum in freely-moving rats. I. Description and quantitative analysis. *J. Neurosci.* **10**, 420–35.

Vargha-Khadem, F., Gadian, D. G., Watkins, K. E., Connelly, A., Van Paesschen, W. and Mishkin, M. 1997 Differential effects of early hippocampal pathology on episodic and semantic memory. *Science* **277**, 376–80.

Wiener, S. I., Korshunov, V. A., Garcia, R. and Berthoz, A. 1995 Inertial, substriatal and landmark cue control of the hippocampal CA1 place cell activity. *Euro. J. Neurosci.* **7**, 2206–19.

Wilson, M. A. and McNaughton, B. L. 1993 Dynamics of the hippocampal ensemble code for space. *Science* **261**, 1055–58.

Zola-Morgan, S., Squire, L. R. and Amaral, D. G. 1986 Human amnesia and the medial temporal region: enduring memory impairment following a bilateral lesion limited to field CA1 of the hippocampus. *J. Neurosci.* **6**, 2950–67.

10

Neural representation of objects in space: a dual coding account

Glyn W. Humphreys

Abstract

I present evidence on the nature of object coding in the brain and discuss the implications of this coding for models of visual selective attention. Neuropsychological studies of task-based constraints on: (i) visual neglect; and (ii) reading and counting tasks reveal the existence of parallel forms of spatial representation for objects: within-object representations, where elements are coded as parts of objects, and between-object representations, where elements are coded as independent objects. Aside from these spatial codes for objects, however, the coding of visual space is limited. We are extremely poor at remembering small spatial displacements across eye movements, indicating (at best) impoverished coding of spatial position *per se*. Also, effects of element separation on spatial extinction can be eliminated by filling the space with an occluding object, indicating that spatial effects on visual selection are moderated by object coding. Overall, there are separate limits on visual processing reflecting: (i) the competition to code parts within objects; (ii) the small number of independent objects that can be coded in parallel; and (iii) task-based selection of whether within- or between-object codes determine behaviour. Between-object coding may be linked to the dorsal visual system while parallel coding of parts within objects takes place in the ventral system, although there may additionally be some dorsal involvement either when attention must be shifted within objects or when explicit spatial coding of parts is necessary for object identification.

10.1 Introduction

Over the past 15 years or so, one of the most influential distinctions in the field of visual information processing has been that between 'object' and 'spatial' coding. This dichotomy, first introduced by Ungerleider and Mishkin (1982), holds that the neural areas supporting object recognition are separate from those supporting location coding, as are the computational processes involved in object and spatial coding in the brain. Indeed, to recognize the same object across different viewing positions and angles, it can be argued that the varying spatial information needs to be discarded so that recognition is based on the invariant 'object' information present (see Marr 1982, for one example). Nevertheless, to direct action to objects or to remember their location for future reference, spatial information needs to be encoded and maintained. The idea that there is parallel representation of objects and space meets with the independent requirements of object recognition and action (see also Milner and Goodale 1995).

The distinction, between object and spatial coding, has influenced work varying from computational modelling of pattern recognition (see, for example, Rueckl *et al.* 1989; Jacobs and Jordan 1992) to theories of selective visual attention (for reviews, see Humphreys and Bruce 1989; Styles 1997). Given the numerous stimuli that may be available in any scene, forms of selective attention are necessary both to ensure that recognition is successful (e.g. so that the parts of different objects are not linked together) and that action is directed to objects in a coherent way. Space-based theories propose that stimuli are selected for recognition and for action by attention being directed to their spatial locations (see, for example, Posner 1980; Eriksen and Yeh 1985; Treisman 1988). In contrast, object-based theories hold that the elements of objects are selected together, even when they overlap spatially with elements of other objects and when the elements of the object are no closer to one another than they are to the elements of other objects (Duncan 1984; Baylis and Driver 1993). These accounts are not mutually exclusive, however, and in some proposals spatial and object-based selection may be coupled by interactions between object- and space-based systems (see, for example, Farah *et al.* 1993; Humphreys and Riddoch 1993). For example, features coded during early stages of visual processing may be activated by both directed spatial attention and (top-down) by activated object representations, so that spatial attention affects object selection (biasing selection towards objects in the attended locations) and object properties affect spatial selection (so that spatial attention becomes locked onto objects). Such accounts allow for forms of interaction between 'object' and 'spatial' processing streams, so that coherent behaviour results (for similar arguments about coupling between brain areas, see Duncan 1996; Duncan *et al.* 1997).

Now, for coupling between the object and spatial systems to be effective, it may be useful for each system also to 'know' something about processing in the other stream: for some form of spatial information to be incorporated into object representations and for forms of object information to be incorporated into our representations of space. Top-down feedback from object to early visual representations may bias spatial selection most efficiently if the parts of objects are spatially coded; for example, without explicit coding of the spatial relations between parts, it may be difficult to facilitate selection for objects where parts are repeated (bodies, chairs, tables and so on). (An example of this can be found in connectionist models of visual recognition, where explicit coding of spatial information provides one way of representing multiple, repeated parts— as in the interactive activation model of reading (McClelland and Rumelhart 1981).) Likewise, all things being equal, it should be more effective to bias spatial attention to occupied rather than empty regions of space.

In this paper, I examine the nature of object and spatial coding in the brain and argue for the existence of at least two forms of visual representation: one in which elements are coded as parts of a single object (a within-object representation) and one in which elements are coded independently (a between-object representation). Both forms of representation can incorporate information about the spatial relations between visual elements, and I argue that the two forms of representation are realized in parallel by the visual system. The within-object representation serves object recognition, and so may be linked to the 'what' pathway, in Ungerleider and Mishkin's (1982) terms. Between-object representations may serve for spatial navigation and action, and so form part of the 'where' pathway suggested by Ungerleider and Mishkin. However, I also show that, aside from these forms of visual representation, the coding of visual space is extremely limited; there seems to be no representation of space devoid of objects. Thus 'where' codings itself involves forms of object representation. I discuss evidence for these arguments, and then review the implications of the suggestions for theories of selective visual attention.

10.2   The nature of object coding: parallel object representations

(a)   Bottom-up and top-down factors in object coding

Since the time of the Gestalt psychologists onwards, it has been clear that object descriptions can be derived in a bottom-up manner based on forms of grouping between visual elements (for a summary, see Bruce *et al.* 1996). Furthermore, grouped elements can be selected together for a response. For example, Donnelly and co-workers (1991) showed that response times to detect changes in part-elements were unaffected by the number of parts presented to subjects, provided the parts grouped into a familiar shape (for example, the corners making up a square; see also Baylis and Driver 1994; Humphreys *et al.* 1994*a*, for similar evidence). In contrast, if elements group into separate object descriptions there is serial selection of each description, even if discrimination of the same part-changes are required (Donnelly *et al.* 1991; Baylis and Driver 1998).

In addition, independent (ungrouped) visual elements can be selected together provided that the elements activate a single, stored object representation. For example, word naming times are relatively immune to increases in the numbers of letters present, for words up to about six letters long (see, for example, Frederiksen and Kroll 1976; see figure 10.3); this suggests that naming can be supported by parallel coding of the visual information within such stimuli. This parallel coding also seems to involve independent representation of the letters present. Thus, words do not necessarily show stronger effects of CaSe MiXiNg than pronounceable non-words, though this should disrupt word codes at a supra-letter level (McClelland 1976; Adams 1979; Mayall and Humphreys 1996). In such cases the visual elements (the letters) may be encoded and selected together not solely on the basis of low-level grouping but by parallel activation of a stored word representation. This parallel activation of a stored representation enables the independent parts to act as a single object description.

I conclude that, whether based on bottom-grouping or on activation of stored representations, parts within objects can be selected in a spatially parallel manner. This evidence for parallel selection of parts within objects indicates that object descriptions can be formed without the application of focal visual attention to each visual element. (Mack and co-workers (1992) have argued that visual elements do not group under conditions of complete inattention, although contrary data have been reported by Moore and Egeth (1997). Rather than straying onto this topic, I confine my discussion to cases where attention is paid to the general region of visual displays but in a distributed manner, and the discussion is focused on whether object descriptions are coded only when focal attention is paid to each display element.)

Some of the most striking evidence for object descriptions being coded without focal attention comes from neuropsychological studies, where patients who fail to attend to areas of space nevertheless show evidence that object coding in those regions has taken place. For instance, in the syndrome of unilateral neglect, patients fail to react to stimuli presented on the side of space contralateral to their lesion (Heilman and Valenstein 1979). Marshall and Halligan (1988) reported that right hemisphere lesioned patients with marked neglect of the left side of stimuli in same—different discrimination tasks revealed implicit left-side processing on preference judgements made to the same stimuli (see also Bisiach and Rusconi 1990). Other investigators (McGlinchey-Berroth *et al.* 1992; Ladavas *et al.* 1993) report semantic priming from objects in the neglected field, suggesting that unattended objects can even be processed to the level of meaning.

Experiments on the neuropsychological phenomenon of visual extinction further reveal the existence of both bottom-up and top-down factors in encoding object descriptions without focal attention. Extinction occurs when a patient is able to detect the presence of a single stimulus in the contralesional field, but fails to detect the same item when it is presented simultaneously with another item in the ipsilesional field (see, for example, Karnath 1988). This appears to be an attentional effect, because detection of the contralesional item fails only when it is placed under conditions of attentional competition with the ipsilesional stimulus. Ward and colleagues (1994) first reported that extinction could be reduced if the elements in the contralesional field grouped with items in the ipsilesional field. They used bracket stimuli, which could group by collinearity

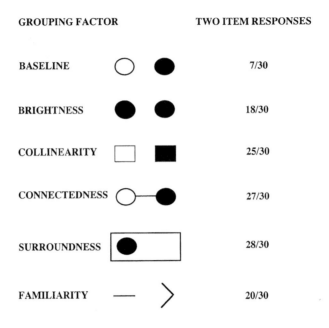

Patient GK

Fig. 10.1   Recovery from extinction. Results on a detection task from two-item displays. The task required discrimination between displays with none, one or two targets. Performance in no- and one-item trials was near ceiling.

between end segments or by symmetry. In addition, they showed that there was recovery from extinction for the elements of horizontal arrow stimuli, even when the line and angle components were widely separated in the field and unlikely to group by local Gestalt factors. In this last case, the elements may be recovered together by activating a stored object description. Similar converging data on extinction have been reported by Gilchrist and co-workers (1996) and by Mattingly and co-workers (1997). Gilchrist *et al.* showed that grouping effects were as strong between items presented in the contralesional field as between items in the ipsilesional field, although detection performance overall was better in the ipsilesional field. Thus, although patients may fail to attend to the contralesional field under conditions of attentional competition, grouping can be shown still to operate there.

Recent data from my laboratory on the variety of relations that can lead to recovery from extinction are presented in figure 10.1. Data here are from the patient, G.K. studied by Gilchrist and co-workers. G.K. suffered bilateral lesions, affecting the right parieto-occipital and parieto-temporal regions and the left tempero-parietal region, resulting in symptoms of Balint's syndrome in which he often fails to perceive more than one object at a time and shows mis-reaching under visual guidance (Balint 1909; for reports, see Humphreys *et al.* 1994*b*; Gilchrist *et al.* 1996). Due to the lesions in his right hemisphere being more severe, G.K. also manifests extinction to left-side targets. In this study, G.K. had to detect whether none, one or two stimuli were presented. Single stimuli appeared 1° of visual angle from fixation in either the left or right visual fields, and on two-stimulus trials, one item was in the left and the other in the right field. Performance in no- and one-item trials was near ceiling and data are presented only for two-item trials. In a baseline condition with minimal grouping, the items were circles of opposite contrast polarity (white and black) which were presented against a grey background. These items lack bottom-up support for grouping based on either collinearity common surface features. Reporting of two items was impaired (see also Gilchrist *et al.* 1996). However, the two-item report improved as cues were added to displays to enable the items in the ipsi- and contralesional fields to group. There was recovery from extinction if the elements had: the same brightness (two white or two black circles), collinear edges (with aligned squares, even though they had opposite contrast polarities, preventing grouping by common brightness), a connecting line (joining circles with opposite contrast polarities), and inside–outside relations (e.g. a left-field circle appearing within a surrounding rectangle). In addition to this, as reported by Ward and co-workers (1994), performance improved if the elements formed a familiar figure (an arrow), although there were then few bottom-cues to group the elements together. These results indicate that, within the same patient, both bottom-up grouping factors and stored knowledge can be used to recover elements within the contralesional field, even though the patient fails to attend to (and even detect items in) the contralesional field when items do not group (in the baseline condition).

(b) Parallel representations: a single case

Neuropsychological evidence not only indicates that object descriptions can be coded without focal attention, but also that separate forms of representation are generated in parallel—in the sense that one representation does not form the input for the other one. These separate forms of representation are revealed by dissociations in which patients seem impaired at using one but not the other form of representation. Patient J.R. was studied by myself and Jane Riddoch (Humphreys and Riddoch 1994, 1995). He had suffered bilateral lesions affecting the left parieto-occipital region and the right fronto-parietal regions. On a first screening he showed an unusual pattern of performance. When asked to read words and non-words scattered randomly around a page, he made substantial numbers of 'left neglect' errors when identifying each string (typically making letter substitution errors, such as pitch → ditch) but he also made 'right neglect' errors in which responses to strings on the right side of the page were omitted. These different patterns of spatial error did not reflect the positions of elements in the visual field, as they could be demonstrated with the same stimulus depending on the way in which it was coded for the task. We gave J.R. A4 sheets of paper with a large word or non-word written across each sheet. In one set of trials he was asked to read each string as a whole (light → light, nitch → nitch). In another set of trials his task was to read aloud each letter present (light → l, i, g, h, t; nitch → n, i, t, c, h). Marked differences emerged. When asked to read each string as a whole J.R. manifested left neglect (light → night; nitch → pitch). When asked to name each letter, right neglect was apparent. J.R. then read aloud the previously neglected left-side letters but he often omitted right-side letters that previously had been read (light → l, i, g, h, -; nitch → n, i, t, c, -). The left neglect errors in reading aloud the whole strings tended to occur more with non-words than with words. In contrast, there was no effect of the lexical status of the string on right neglect omissions when reading aloud each letter. The differential effects of lexical status provide converging evidence for the visual information being treated in different ways in the two tasks.

Similar results were also found in studies of shape perception. Donnelly and co-workers (1991) had used displays such as those used in figure 10.2 with normal subjects, with the task being to detect a target element that faced the opposite way with regards to fixation, relative to the other elements present. Fixation fell at the centre of each shape. In the grouped displays (figure 10.2*a*, where the elements had collinear ends and formed a closed shape), reaction times (RTs) were unaffected by the number of elements present, consistent with the parts being assimilated in parallel. In the non-grouped displays (when elements were reflected to no longer form a closed

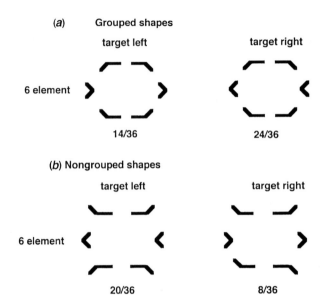

Fig. 10.2 Number of trials on which targets were detected by J.R. as a function of whether the target was on the left or right side of the display. (*a*) Grouped shapes; (*b*) non-grouped shapes. Performance was good when the target was absent.

figure; figure 10.2*b*), RTs increased as the number of elements increased. These results provide an operational definition of when object descriptions were formed (in grouped but not in non-grouped displays). When given the same task, J.R. made left neglect errors with grouped displays (missing left-side targets) and right-side errors with non-grouped displays (figure 10.2). Thus this contrast between left- and right-side neglect was not confined to reading tasks.

We (Humphreys and Riddoch 1994, 1995) proposed that J.R. manifested neglect on either the left or right side of space according to the way in which visual information was represented for the task. For example, when letter strings were read as wholes, the letters were coded as parts of each 'object' (the letter string). When they were named separately, the letters were treated as independent objects. Owing to his bilateral lesions, J.R. may have suffered two forms of neglect. There was left neglect within representations where parts were coded relative to the whole (within-object neglect) and right neglect when elements were coded as independent objects for response (between-object neglect). The evidence demonstrates that neither form of representation serves as input for the other; were that the case, then the earlier form of neglect would have been apparent even if a second form was subsequently added. For instance, consider what should have been the case if elements were first coded as separate objects and only subsequently as parts within objects. Then, when strings were read as wholes, there should have been left neglect on top of earlier right neglect of the end letters (e.g. reading light as nigh-); instead of this, right-end letters were fully represented in left neglect responses (light → night). This supports the argument for parallel coding of the two forms of representation.

In J.R.'s case, the anatomical evidence links within-object neglect to damage to the right hemisphere (producing left-side errors), and between-object neglect to damage to the left hemisphere (producing right-side omissions). It may be that the two forms of representation are selectively localized within each hemisphere and J.R. happened to have different forms of representation damaged on different sides. Alternatively, each hemisphere may be specialized for attention to a particular form of representation. This argument, for hemispheric specialization in attention to within- or between-object representations, is supported by group studies with patients with unilateral parietal lesions. Egly and co-workers (1994) found that right parietal patients were particularly impaired at switching attention from the ipsi- to the contralesional side of space but showed no extra cost when switches were made between objects on the left and right side. Left-hemisphere damage, however, produced additional costs in shifting attention between objects to detect contralesional targets (see also Buck *et al.* 1998, for converging evidence from SPECT analyses on patients with degenerative posterior atrophy).

(c) Parallel representations: a dissociative group study

J.R.'s case provides evidence that within- and between-object codes can dissociate within a single patient. Humphreys and Heinke (1998) demonstrate similar dissociations, but between rather than within patients. They used a dissociative approach in which patients were given sets of tasks in which they either had to attend to parts within objects or in which they had to attend to parts within each of two separate objects. All patients manifested unilateral neglect on simple drawing tasks. In one experimental test of within-object processing, patients received chimeric faces formed by aligning the left and right halves of two faces of either the same or opposite gender. The task was to decide whether each face was male, female or a mixture. In a test of between-object coding, sets of new, whole faces were presented onto piles placed either to the left or right of the patient's body. On each trial either a single new face was presented onto the left or right pile, or two faces were presented onto the left and right piles. The task was to decide if the new face on each trial was male, female or whether there was one male and one female face (on two item trials). With chimeric faces, patients had to discriminate the presence of different sexes within a single object (the face). Previous work suggests that neglect within objects can occur under these conditions, with patients failing to discriminate the left half of the face (Young *et al.* 1992). In the between-object task with separate whole faces, patients could respond correctly even if they attended only to the right side of each face, but they had to attend to each of the two faces present. We (Humphreys and Heinke 1998) found that some patients only neglected the chimerics but showed no neglect in the two-face task (showing neglect only within-objects); other patients demonstrated the opposite pattern (showing no neglect of the chimerics but failing to detect the left- or right-side face when two faces were present). These last patients manifested neglect between separate objects but not within each object (discriminating both sides of chimeric faces). There is thus a double dissociation between the two forms of neglect, consistent with there being two independent forms of representation.

(d) Parallel representations: reading and counting

It may be that the dissociation between neglect within and between objects itself reflects the hierarchical coding of visual stimuli for different tasks. For example, tasks of within-object coding, such as whole word reading, may rely on more global visual descriptions than tasks of between-object coding, such as reading the letters within words, where more local descriptions may be involved. Within-object neglect may occur in tasks such as whole word reading because patients are impaired at attending to one side of global representations. Between-object neglect may be linked to spatial biases when local spatial representations are used. This would be consistent with some of the evidence for hemispheric specialization linked to within- and between-object neglect. It has long been known that right hemisphere lesions (associated with within-object neglect) can impair attention to global visual descriptions; likewise, left hemisphere lesions (associated with neglect between objects) may disrupt attention to local visual descriptions (Robertson *et al.* 1988;

see Fink *et al.* 1996, for converging evidence using positron emission tomography). (One problem for this argument is that, in one of the patients documented by Humphreys and Heinke (1998), there was left neglect between objects (though right neglect would be expected if left hemisphere damage were crucial). However, this patient had bilateral lesions, making interpretation of the link between the lesion and side of neglect difficult.)

To test further the idea that there are separate within- and between-object representations, not simply differences in hierarchical representation of stimuli, Soren Kyllingsbaek, Andrew Olson and I assessed reading and counting in five patients with lesions affecting either posterior dorsal (parietal) or ventral (occipito-temporal) brain regions. It has long been known that damage to the posterior ventral cortex (particularly in the left hemisphere) can impair visual processing, leading to abnormal effects of the numbers of elements present in the field. Classically this has been associated with serial letter identification in reading (Dejerine 1892; see papers in Riddoch 1991), but it can also be found in other discrimination tasks with form elements (see Friedman and Alexander 1984; Rapp and Caramazza 1991; Humphreys *et al.* 1992). In contrast to this, the ability of the patients to count visual stimuli has been reported as good (see, for example, Kinsbourne and Warrington 1962)—although it has rarely been tested formally using reaction time (RT) measures (but see Humphreys *et al.* 1985). We reasoned that such patients may have difficulty encoding parts within objects in a parallel manner (for reading), but not in encoding separate objects for counting. The opposite pattern of performance may occur in patients with dorsal (parietal) lesions. Previous studies have shown deficits in visual counting tasks in patients with posterior dorsal lesions (see, for example, Dehaene and Cohen 1994), although the recognition of single objects may be intact (see, for example, Baylis *et al.* 1994). Here one might suspect that the patients are able to encode parts within-objects in a preserved (spatially parallel) manner but the lesion disrupts the ability to assemble or maintain spatial representations between-objects, disrupting counting. A failure specifically in assembling such representations may be assessed by testing a patient's ability to count small numbers of items (less than four), which normal observers seem able to enumerate in parallel (to 'subitize'), without requiring serial scanning or maintenance of previous counted items (see, for example, Trick and Pylyshyn 1993).

One dorsal patient was G.K., who, as noted here, had suffered bilateral parietal lesions. The other two patients, M.B. and M.P., had sustained unilateral right hemisphere damage affecting the parietal lobe. M.B. and M.P. both had mild neglect. Of the two ventral patients, one (D.M.) had unilateral left hemisphere damage affecting the medial occipito-temporal region (see Humphreys *et al.* 1997, for details of the lesion); the other (H.J.A.) had bilateral lesions affecting the occipito-temporal area (Humphreys and Riddoch 1987). Both D.M. and H.J.A. showed abnormally strong effects of string length on reading in clinical tests (a characteristic of letter-by-letter reading). We required patients to either name or count the letters in sets of frequency-matched words having from two to six letters (the conditions were presented in an ABBA design for each patient). In addition, a set of single letters was added, to provide data for string length one. Stimuli were presented on an IBM personal computer and responses triggered a voice key for RT recording. There was a minimum of 12 trials for each string length in each task. Note that the global shape of words does not alter with word length, so counting cannot be based on global shape information; rather it requires the individuation of the letters present.

The data for four patients, M.B. and M.P. (dorsal patients) and D.M. and H.J.A. (ventral patients) are given in figure 10.3. G.K. was unable to perform the counting task under unconstrained conditions (performing at chance level). Accordingly he was given a forced-choice version of both tasks in which he was given a choice between two stimuli on each trial, for both counting and reading. One alternative was correct, the other was another number either one more or one less than the target number (for the counting task; for example, light: four or five letters?) or a

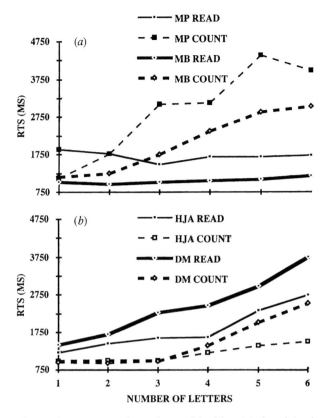

Fig. 10.3 Reading and counting responses by patients with either (*a*) dorsal (parietal) or (*b*) ventral (occipito-temporal) lesions. Very few errors were made.

word changed by one letter from the target (for the reading task; for example, light → light or night?).

The results revealed a form of double dissociation between reading and counting in the two sets of patients. The dorsal patients M.B. and M.P. were able to read and showed no effects of string length on naming times, consistent with there being parallel identification of the letters for word recognition. However, they showed effects of string length on counting, with counting times increasing directly as a function of the number of letters present. G.K. demonstrated a similar advantage and evidence for parallel word reading, although in his case an accuracy rather than a RT measure was used and reading was contrasted against an inability to count. He scored 32 and 28 out of 36 when asked to identify strings of one to three and four to six letters respectively (overall $\chi^2(1) = 16.53$, $p < 0.01$, relative to chance), but only 22 and 16 out of 36 when asked to count the numbers of letter present (no different from chance (18 out of 36) for string lengths one to three and four to six respectively.

The ventral patients showed the opposite pattern. For strings containing up to three letters there were no increases in counting time relative to the number of elements present, and R.T. increases for strings with more than three letters were relatively slight. The patients were able to enumerate a small number of items in a spatially parallel manner. However, reading times increased with string length, even for strings with few letters (less than three). Thus the ventral patients were impaired at assimilating in parallel the letters needed for word identification, although they were able to

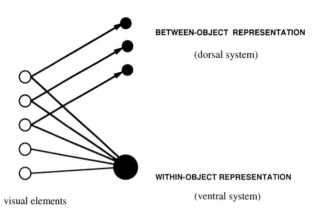

BETWEEN-OBJECT REPRESENTATION

(dorsal system)

WITHIN-OBJECT REPRESENTATION

visual elements   (ventral system)

Fig. 10.4   Schematic framework for a dual coding account of visual processing, illustrating independent forms of parallel processing supporting within- and between-object representations.

respond to information coded in parallel in counting. Interestingly, single-letter identification times were equally fast for the ventral and dorsally lesioned patients so the problem was not simply one of letter identification for the ventral patients. Humphreys *et al.* (1992) have reported converging evidence that parallel assimilation of form information for identification is impaired in patient H.J.A.

These data show for the first time a direct contrast between the effects of dorsal and ventral lesions on reading and counting tasks with the same stimuli and where the numbers of items have been varied to assess whether performance depends on parallel spatial coding of visual information. For both sets of patients, the preserved ability relies on spatially parallel coding, as there were no effects of string length on performance (on reading by the dorsal patients, and on counting small numbers of items by the ventral patients). There is, however, a breakdown in parallel coding for the affected task (counting, for the dorsal patients, and reading, for the ventral patients). The effects cannot easily be attributed to a contrast between local and global operations as performance in all cases relies on parallel spatial coding, which might be thought characteristic of 'global' visual processing. Instead the data fit with the proposal that there can be independent forms of visual coding: (i) parallel coding of parts within objects; and (ii) parallel coding of a small number of separate visual objects (between-object coding). These processes are limited by damage to different brain regions. Parallel coding of parts within objects is disrupted by ventral lesions; parallel coding of separate objects is affected by dorsal lesions (figure 10.4).

If parallel coding of parts within objects takes place within the ventral visual system, however, we are left with explaining why neglect within objects is associated with more dorsal lesions (e.g. in patients such as J.R.). I return to this point in §10.3.

10.3   Other forms of visual representation of space

I have argued that independent visual descriptions are coded in parallel with one another; there is one description in which stimuli are treated as parts within whole objects (within-object coding), and one in which they are treated as separate objects (between-object coding). Apart from these representations, however, is visual space coded in any other way? In particular, is visual space represented in some cartesian manner irrespective of whether objects are present or not? This is a kind of 'blackboard' view of vision, in which objects are depicted on a spatial canvas. On such a view it should be possible to represent the canvas even when objects are not present—for example, when we have to remember the location of where an object fell after it has been removed. Also, if object coding involves depiction on some form of internal blackboard, then effects of spatial distance on the blackboard should be primary and not modulated by factors to do with object coding. In fact, neither of these assertions seems to hold, casting doubt on any simple blackboard view. I will go on to argue that any coding of space devoid of objects is, at best, extremely limited.

(a) Coding empty space

To assess the question of whether spatial information can be coded even when objects are not present, Luis Fuentes, Derrick Watson, Kevin O'Regan and I evaluated memory for the location of a small target when subjects either maintained fixation on the location or made an eye movement between the presentations of the target. Previous studies have shown that memory for location can improve when visual landmarks are present in the environment (see, for example, Matin 1976), but they have not specified the nature of the visual codes that are employed. Here subjects saw for a variable duration an initial display containing randomly positioned white dots and one (target) green dot. The initial display then disappeared for a short interval (400 ms or longer, to minimize apparent movement) and was replaced by a match display, presented for an unlimited exposure. In the match display the green dot was either kept in the original location or it was shifted a small amount (0.25°). The task was to decide whether the green dot was in the same or a different location. In one condition, subjects were allowed to keep fixating on the target during the interval. In another, a small letter was presented 7° into the periphery during the interval; subjects had to make an eye movement to report this letter and then decide whether the target dot had moved when the match display was subsequently presented. In this condition, subjects had to maintain their memory for the target's location across an eye movement. There were also two variations in the density of the background (white) dots, which were either sparse (20 dots in the field) or dense (40 dots in the field). Data averaged over five subjects are shown in figure 10.5. The displacement of the target (on 'different location' trials) was set so that subjects scored about 62% correct even when the first display was presented for too brief a time to ensure that subjects could fixate the target dot.

When no eye movement was made during the inter-stimulus interval, memory for location improved as the exposure of the first display increased to about 300 ms and then it asymptoted close to ceiling. This held both for sparse and dense displays. The improvement in performance over the first 300 ms is likely to be owing to subjects taking some time to fixate the target dot in the initial display; but following its fixation, memory for the dot's location can be maintained across an interval and does not depend on the number (or proximity, given that the dots were presented within a limited area) of the background dots. In marked contrast to this are the data when an eye movement was made. For sparse displays there was then no improvement in memory no matter how long subjects were allowed to view the first display for. For dense displays there was an improvement over time.

These data suggest that memory for visual location can depend on several factors. First, a position memory can be maintained for a dot in an otherwise sparsely populated space, provided fixation does not shift from the location. Here performance depends either on a retinotopic code for the dot location or on some form of proprioceptive memory for eye position (e.g. subjects can judge whether the dot has shifted by keeping eye position constant and judging whether there is a change in acuity when the dot is re-presented—just as one might discriminate whether a shift has occurred by pointing a finger at the location and judging whether the dot reappears where the finger is). Second, a fine position memory for a single dot cannot be maintained across an eye movement (in the condition with sparse displays). Third, position memory across fixation is based on the coding of the relative locations of the dots—hence position memory is found with dense displays but not with sparse displays.

Our results indicate that it is extremely difficult to make fine spatial memory judgements across fixation in a sparsely coded visual world. The data are consistent with other studies on the integration (rather than memory, as here) of visual information across eye movements, which show the use of abstract information about the relative positions of visual elements rather than some form of buffer that codes visual space (see Irwin 1993). Hence we do not appear to encode some form of blackboard memory for empty space, which can be maintained when the eyes move. Across fixation, memory for location depends on coding the relative positions of objects. Given that the dots were randomly presented here, and so tended not to form any learned configuration, we suggest that performance was determined by a between-object spatial code.

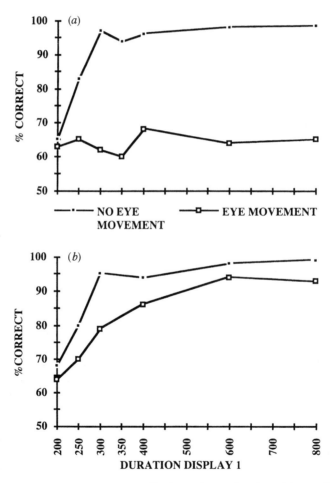

Fig. 10.5 Data from five subjects on the dot localization task, as a function of the number of dots present in the displays. (*a*) Sparse displays: one target, field 20, ISI 400 ms. (*b*) Dense displays: one target, field 40, ISI 400 ms.

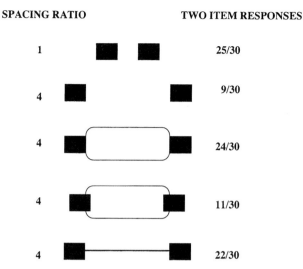

SPACING RATIO   **TWO ITEM RESPONSES**

Fig. 10.6 Data on extinction from patient G.K. The task required discrimination between displays with none, one or two items present; performance on no- and one-item displays was good and data are shown here only for two-item trials. There is extinction with two squares with a wide spacing ratio (size of spacing to size of elements) and when the squares maintain this ratio and occlude the background shape.

(b)   Spatial effects on visual selection are modulated by object coding

If visual elements are coded in terms of their positions on a spatial blackboard, then we would expect the distance between elements on the blackboard to affect both their coding into objects and how attention may then be applied to the elements. Certainly grouping by proximity should decrease as inter-element distance increases, as may other forms of grouping. Strong neuropsychological evidence for this comes again from studies of visual extinction. As we have already noted, Gilchrist *et al.* (1996) showed that extinction could be reduced when elements had both the same brightness and collinear edges (with collinearity producing an effect greater than that due to common brightness alone; figure 10.1). However, when the relative distance between the elements increased so that the distance was more than three times the size of each stimulus, extinction was restored (see figure 10.6). Now neither collinearity nor common brightness was sufficient to group the contra- and ipsilesional items together. Distance effects have also been shown to modulate selection in normal observers. For example, the time it takes normal subjects to switch attention from one object to another increases with their distance (Vecera 1994) and interference between incongruent items is larger when they are close than when they are distant, even when they are part of the same object (Kramer and Jacobson 1991).

Yet, other evidence from my laboratory shows that the coding of distance itself is modulated by grouping between stimuli. Again by using the extinction paradigm, we have found that the effects of distance on extinction can be eliminated if the space between elements is filled with an occluding figure. By using pairs of squares, we showed that there is re-grouping over distances that are otherwise sufficient to introduce extinction if the elements are coded to be grouped are separated by an occluder (figure 10.6)—an effect that may be owing to amodal completion. When the elements are moved slightly closer, so that they now occlude the background shape, extinction occurs again. Quite similar effects of occlusion on extinction have been reported by Mattingly *et al.* (1997). The present data extend them by showing that grouping between the occluded elements modulates distance effects in visual selection. Note that such effects run counter to a simple blackboard model of spatial coding; spatial representations deal with the relations between objects and are modulated by grouping between parts.

10.4 Spatial representation and attention

I have argued that: (i) independent representations of space within and between objects are encoded in parallel; (ii) the object representation that mediates performance can depend on the task; and (iii) forms of spatial representation other than those that code space within or between objects are limited.

(a) Implications for selective visual attention

These proposals have implications for understanding selective visual attention. I discuss three here.

1. The evidence indicates that both within- and between-object codes are assembled in a spatially parallel manner, without the need for focal attention to be paid to the elements. For example, consider studies of reading and counting. The data here demonstrate that each task can be unaffected by the number of elements present (i.e. each task is supported by parallel visual coding) at least up to a certain limit (three to four items, for counting), although the tasks also dissociate following different brain lesions (figure 10.3).

2. Although each representation is encoded in parallel, there are limits. For example, between-object codes seem constrained to just a small number of objects at a time, as indicated by the limit on subitization (four items or less). I suggest that the parallel coding of a small number of objects helps to provide useful information for future actions (for example, for navigation between separate objects, for bimanual actions and so on), without overloading the systems that control action. There are also limits on the number of within-object representations that can be used simultaneously for a response. Were there no limits at this level, we would be able to identify several stimuli presented simultaneously; however, there is considerable evidence against this (Duncan 1984; Baylis and Driver 1993). Elements encoded in parallel still need to be selected serially for identification, as one within-object description at a time. Interestingly, one consequence of preventing serial selection of numerous stimuli is that elements from each stimulus can be amalgamated into a single response (McClelland and Mozer 1986). Serial selection of within-object representations may thus be computationally useful to prevent cross-talk during the identification process. The neuropsychological phenomenon of extinction may also arise because of the limitation in the number of within-object codes that can selected at one time. The data on recovery from extinction by grouping indicates that elements can be processed in parallel even when they are subsequently extinguished—when grouping does not take place. Selection is limited by whether elements can be grouped into a single within-object spatial representation. However, if there is dual coding of within- and between-object representations, why do patients seem unable to use between-object codes to at least detect the presence of numerous items? This may be because the lesion, typically to the dorsal visual system, disrupts the use of between-object codes; this will make such patients reliant on within-object codes for detection and identification. We consider this point further.

3. There need to be forms of task-based selection, that determine whether within- or between-object codes guide responses (as in the reading and counting data). Task-based selection may operate by priming one form of coding so that it is selected before the other (cf. Chelazzi *et al.*

1993). Alternatively, within a system in which spatial attention and object recognition systems are coupled by re-entrant connections to early visual processing (cf. Humphreys and Riddoch 1993), attentional activation of one rather than another between-object representation could bias selection towards the within-object code at an associated location—much as envisaged by space-based theories of visual selection (Treisman, this volume). This may then control whether whole stimuli or their parts are selected for the response. What should be noted here, however, is that in such a model attention is not paid to empty space but only to an occupied location (signalled by the between-object code).

The account I have suggested differs from other current theories of visual selection in several respects. For example, unlike feature integration theory (Treisman, this volume), I propose that form elements are bound together without focal attention. On the account I have proposed, attention may be involved in selecting between several within-object descriptions for object identification, but it is not necessary either to encode the elements or to group them into within-object descriptions in the first place. This leaves to one side the question of how form descriptions are linked to surface properties of objects, which may require additional processes to those discussed here. Also, unlike the theory of visual attention (Bundesen, this volume), I suggest that there are dual forms of perceptual categorization, one to form within-object representations and one to form between-object representations. These dual forms of categorization can be dissociated after brain damage.

(b) Brain mechanisms

The evidence on reading and counting is consistent with the proposal that within-object codes are assimilated in parallel within the ventral visual system, whereas between-object codes are assimilated within the dorsal visual stream. Indeed, it may be the massive impairment of between-object codes in cases of bilateral parietal damage that causes the devastating loss of visual information for spatial guidance of action (see, for example, in Balint's syndrome; see also Treisman, this volume), although object recognition *per se* is relatively preserved (performed via the ventral stream). As I have already pointed out though, this still leaves unexplained why there is neglect within objects after putative dorsal lesions (Young *et al.* 1992; Humphreys and Riddoch 1994, 1995; Humphreys and Heinke 1998). There are two possibilities, as follows. It may be that the inferior parietal lobe actually forms part of a ventral or overlapping ventral-dorsal processing area that deals with aspects of object coding, and so lesions to this area affect object recognition (see Milner and Goodale 1995). Alternatively, dorsal processing areas may be recruited when attention needs to be switched from one part of an object to another (cf. Egly *et al.* 1994) or when the spatial relations between parts are important for identification (see Humphreys and Heinke 1998). Defining the brain regions mediating different forms of object representation constitutes only the first step in understanding how they may interact to determine behaviour across wide sets of circumstances.

Acknowledgements

This work was supported by grants from the Biological and Biotechnology Research Council and the Medical Research Council of the UK and from the Human Frontier Science Program. The research has benefitted from collaboration and discussion with a large number of friends and colleagues whom I thank: L. Alston, A. Cooper, L. Fuentes, I. Gilchrist, S. Kyllingsbaek,

A. Olson, K. O'Regan, J. Riddoch and D. Watson. Thanks also to A. Treisman and R. Ward for insightful comments on earlier drafts of the paper.

References

Adams, M. J. 1979 Models of word recognition. *Cogn. Psychol.* **11**, 133–76.

Balint, R. 1909 Seelenlahmung des 'Schauens', optische Ataxie, raumliche Storung der Aufmerksamkeit. *Manatsschr. Psychiatr. Neurol.* **25**, 51–81.

Baylis, G. C. and Driver, J. 1993 Visual attention and objects: evidence for hierarchical coding of location. *J. Exp. Psychol. Hum. Percept. Perf.* **19**, 451–70.

Baylis, G. C. and Driver, J. 1994 Parallel computation of symmetry but not repetition within single visual shapes. *Vis. Cogn.* **1**, 377–400.

Baylis, G. C. and Driver, J. 1998 Perception of symmetry and repetition within and across visual shapes: part-descriptions and object-based attention. *Vis. Cogn.* (In the press.)

Baylis, G. C., Driver, J., Baylis, L. L. and Rafal, R. D. 1994 Reading of letters and words in a patient with Balint's syndrome. *Neuropsychologia* **32**, 1273–86.

Bisiach, E. and Rusconi, M. L. 1990 Breakdown of perceptual awareness in unilateral neglect. *Cortex* **26**, 643–9.

Bruce, V., Green, P. and Georgeson, M. A. 1996 *Visual perception*, 3rd edn. London: Psychology Press.

Buck, B. H., Black, S. E., Behrmann, M., Caldwell, C. and Bronskill, M. J. 1998 Spatial- and object-based attentional deficits in Alzheimer's disease: relationship to HMPAOSPECT measures of parietal performance. *Brain.* (In the press.)

Chelazzi, L., Miller, E. K., Duncan, J. and Desimone, R. 1993 A neural basis for visual search in inferior temporal cortex. *Nature* **363**, 345–7.

Dehaene, S. and Cohen, L. 1994 Dissociable mechanisms of subitizing and counting: neuropsychological evidence from simultanagnosic patients. *J. Exp. Psychol. Hum. Percept. Perf.* **20**, 958–75.

Dejerine, J. 1892 Contribution a l'etude anatomoclinique et clinique des differentes varietes de cecite verbale. *Mem. Soc. Biol.* **4**, 61–90.

Donnelly, N., Humphreys, G. W. and Riddoch, M. J. 1991 Parallel computation of primitive shape descriptions. *J. Exp. Psychol. Hum. Percept. Perf.* **17**, 561–70.

Duncan, J. 1984 Selective attention and the organization of visual information. *J. Exp. Psychol. Gen.* **113**, 501–17.

Duncan, J. 1996 Co-operating brain systems in selective perception and action. In *Attention and performance XV* (eds T. Inui and J. L. McClelland), pp. 549–78. Cambridge, MA: MIT Press.

Duncan, J., Humphreys, G. W. and Ward, R. 1997 Integrated mechanisms of selective attention. *Curr. Opin. Biol.* **7**, 255–61.

Egly, R., Driver, J. and Rafal, R. D. 1994 Shifting visual attention between objects and locations: evidence from normal and parietal lesion subjects. *J. Exp. Psychol. Hum. Percept. Perf.* **123**, 161–77.

Eriksen, C. W. and Yeh, Y.-Y. 1985 Allocation of attention in the visual field. *J. Exp. Psychol. Hum. Percept. Perf.* **11**, 583–97.

Farah, M. J., Wallace, M. A. and Vecera, S. P. 1993 'What' and 'where' in visual attention: evidence from the neglect syndrome. In *Unilateral neglect: clinical and experimental studies* (eds I. H. Robertson and J. C. Marshall), pp. 123–38. London: Lawrence Erlbaum.

Fink, G. R., Halligan, P. W., Marshall, J. C., Frith, C. D., Frackowiak, R. S. J. and Dolan, R. J. 1996 Where in the brain does visual attention select the forest and the trees? *Nature* **382**, 626–8.

Frederiksen, J. R. and Kroll, J. F. 1976 Spelling and sound: approaches to the internal lexicon. *J. Exp. Psychol. Hum. Percept. Perf.* **2**, 361–79.

Friedman, R. B. and Alexander, M. P. 1984 Pictures, images and pure alexia: a case study. *Cogn. Neurol.* **1**, 9–23.

Gilchrist, I., Humphreys, G. W. and Riddoch, M. J. 1996 Grouping and extinction: evidence for low-level modulation of selection. *Cogn. Neurol.* **13**, 1223–56.

Heilman, K. and Valenstein, E. 1979 Mechanisms underlying hemispatial neglect. *Ann. Neurol.* **5**, 166–70.

Humphreys, G. W. and Bruce, V. 1989 Visual cognition: computational, experimental and neuropsycho-logical perspectives. London: Erlbaum.

Humphreys, G. W. and Heinke, D. 1998 Spatial representation and selection in the brain: neuropsycho-logical and computational constraints. *Vis. Cogn.* (In the press.)

Humphreys, G. W. and Riddoch, M. J. 1987 *To see but not to see: a case study of visual agnosia*. London: Erlbaum.

Humphreys, G. W. and Riddoch, M. J. 1993 Interactions between object and space systems revealed through neuropsychology. In *Attention and performance XIV* (eds D. E. Meyer and S. Kornblum), pp. 143–62. Cambridge, MA: MIT Press.

Humphreys, G. W. and Riddoch, M. J. 1994 Attention to within-object and between-object spatial repre-sentations: multiple sites for visual selection. *Cogn. Neurol.* **11**, 207–42.

Humphreys, G. W. and Riddoch, M. J. 1995 Separate coding of space within and between perceptual objects: evidence from unilateral visual neglect. *Cogn. Neurol.* **12**, 283–312.

Humphreys, G. W., Riddoch, M. J. and Quinlan, P. T. 1985 Interactive processes in perceptual organization: evidence from visual agnosia. In *Attention and performance XI* (eds M. I. Posner and O. S. M. Marin), pp. 301–18. Hillsdale, NJ: Erlbaum.

Humphreys, G. W., Riddoch, M. J., Quinlan, P. T., Price, C. J. and Donnelly, N. 1992 Parallel pattern processing in visual agnosia. *Can. J. Psychol.* **46**, 377–416.

Humphreys, G. W., Keulers, N. and Donnelly, N. 1994a Parallel visual coding in three dimensions. *Perception* **23**, 453–70.

Humphreys, G. W., Romani, C., Olson, A., Riddoch, M. J. and Duncan, J. 1994b Non-spatial extinction following lesions of the parietal lobe in humans. *Nature* **372**, 357–59.

Humphreys, G. W., Riddoch, M. J. and Price, C. J. 1997 Top-down processes in object identification: evidence from experimental psychology, neuropsychology and functional anatomy. *Phil. Trans. R. Soc. Lond.* B **352**, 1275–82.

Irwin, D. E. 1993 Perceiving an integrated world. In *Attention and performance XIV* (eds D. E. Meyer and S. Kornblum), pp. 121–43. Cambridge, MA: MIT Press.

Jacobs, R. A. and Jordan, M. I. 1992 Computational consequences of a bias towards short connections. *J. Cogn. Neurosci.* **4**, 323–36.

Karnath, H. O. 1988 Deficits of attention in acute and recovered visual hemi-neglect. *Neuropsychologia* **26**, 27–43.

Kinsbourne, M. and Warrington, E. K. 1962 A disorder of simultaneous form perception. *Brain* **85**, 461–86.

Kramer, A. F. and Jacobson, A. 1991 Perceptual organization and focused attention: the role of objects and proximity in visual processing. *Percept. Psychophysiol.* **50**, 267–84.

Ladavas, E., Paladini, R. and Cubelli, R. 1993 Implicit associative priming in a patient with left visual neglect. *Neuropsychologia* **31**, 1307–20.

McClelland, J. L. 1976 Preliminary letter recognition in the perception of words and nonwords. *J. Exp. Psychol. Hum. Percept. Perf.* **2**, 80–91.

McClelland, J. L. and Mozer, M. C. 1986 Perceptual interactions in two-word displays: familiarity and similarity effects. *J. Exp. Psychol. Hum. Percept. Perf.* **12**, 18–35.

McClelland, J. L. and Rumelhart, D. E. 1981 An interactive activation model of context effects in letter perception. 1. An account of basic findings. *Psychol. Rev.* **88**, 375–407.

McGlinchey-Beroth, R., Milberg, W. P., Verfaillie, M., Alexander, M. and Kilduff, P. T. 1992 Semantic processing in the neglected visual field: evidence from a lexical decision task. *Cogn. Neurol.* **10**, 79–108.

Mack, A., Tang, B., Tuma, R., Kahn, S. and Rock, I. 1992 Perceptual organization and attention. *Cogn. Psychol.* **24**, 475–501.

Marr, D. 1982 *Vision*. San Francisco: W. H. Freeman and Co.

Marshall, J. C. and Halligan, P. W. 1988 Blindsight and insight into visuo-spatial neglect. *Nature* **336**, 766–7.

Matin, L. 1976 Saccades and extraretinal signal for visual direction. In *Eye movements and psychological processes* (eds R. A. Monty and J. W. Sanders), pp. 205–19. Hillsdale, NJ: Lawrence Erlbaum.

Mattingly, J. B., Davis, G. and Driver, J. 1997 Pre-attentive filling-in of visual surfaces in parietal extinction. *Science* **275**, 671–4.

Mayall, K. A. and Humphreys, G. W. 1996 Case mixing and the task sensitive disruption of lexical processing. *J. Exp. Psychol. Learn. Mem. Cogn.* **22**, 278–94.

Milner, D. A. and Goodale, M. A. 1995 *The visual brain in action*. Oxford University Press.

Moore, C. M. and Egeth, H. 1997 Perception without attention: evidence of grouping under conditions of inattention. *J. Exp. Psychol. Hum. Percept. Perf.* **23**, 339–52.

Posner, M. I. 1980 Orienting of attention. *Q. J. Exp. Psychol.* **32**, 3–25.

Rapp, B. C. and Caramazza, A. 1991 Spatially determined deficits in letter and word processing. *Cogn. Neurol.* **8**, 275–311.

Riddoch, M. J. 1991 *Neglect and the peripheral dyslexias*. London: Erlbaum.

Robertson, L. C., Lamb, M. R. and Knight, R. T. 1988 Effects of lesions of temporal-parietal junction on perceptual and attentional processing in humans. *J. Neurosci.* **8**, 3757–69.

Rueckl, J. G., Cave, K. R. and Kosslyn, S. M. 1989 Why are 'what' and 'where' processed by separate cortical visual systems? A computational investigation. *J. Cogn. Neurosci.* **1**, 171–86.

Styles, E. 1997 *Attention*. London: Psychology Press.

Treisman, A. 1988 Features and objects: the Fourteenth Bartlett Memorial Lecture. *Q. J. Exp. Psychol.* A **40**, 201–37.

Trick, L. and Pylyshyn, Z. 1993 What enumeration studies can show us about spatial attention: evidence for limited capacity preattentive processing. *J. Exp. Psychol. Hum. Percept. Perf.* **101**, 80–102.

Ungerleider, L. G. and Mishkin, M. 1982 Two cortical visual systems. In *Analysis of visual behavior* (eds J. Ingle, M. A. Goodale and R. J. W. Mansfield), pp. 549–86. Cambridge, MA: MIT Press.

Vecera, S. P. 1994 Grouped locations and object-based attention: comment on Egly, Driver and Rafal 1994. *J. Exp. Psychol. Gen.* **123**, 316–20.

Ward, R., Goodrich, S. and Driver, J. 1994 Grouping reduces visual extinction: neuropsychological evidence for weight-linkage in visual selection. *Vis. Cogn.* **1**, 101–130.

Young, A. W., Hellawell, D. J. and Welch, J. 1992 Neglect and visual recognition. *Brain* **112**, 51–71.

11

Human cortical mechanisms of visual attention during orienting and search

Maurizio Corbetta and Gordon L. Shulman

Abstract

Functional anatomical studies indicate that a set of neural signals in parietal and frontal cortex mediates the covert allocation of attention to visual locations across a wide variety of visual tasks. This fronto-parietal network includes areas, such as the frontal eye field and supplementary eye field. This anatomical overlap suggests that shifts of attention to visual locations or objects recruit areas involved in oculomotor programming and execution. Finally, the fronto-parietal network may be the source of spatial attentional modulations in the ventral visual system during object recognition or discrimination.

11.1 Introduction

Any visual scene contains numerous objects, where each object comprises several features such as colour, shape, motion and location. Although we can select objects of interest based on any feature or combination of features, the selection of visual objects by location is a powerful way of selecting behaviourally relevant visual information. There are several lines of evidence indicating the importance of spatial selection in vision. First, many studies have shown that attending to a location (spatial cueing) enhances visual performance in a large variety of visual tasks, including threshold and suprathreshold detection of luminance increments, and discriminations involving shape and colour (Eriksen and Hoffman 1972; Posner *et al.* 1980; Prinzmetal *et al.* 1986; Downing 1988; Hawkins *et al.* 1990; Henderson 1996; Luck *et al.* 1996). The widespread effect of attending to location indicates that processes mediating spatial selection have wide access to visual processes specialized for feature and object analysis. Second, locations are also selected in the context of a large class of visuomotor behaviours including orienting to peripheral stimuli. Overt orienting refers to a set of processes by which stimuli of interest in a visual scene are detected in the periphery of the visual field and rapidly brought into the fovea, the retinal region of highest acuity, by means of rapid saccadic eye movements. Overt orienting tasks are dissociable in the laboratory from covert orienting tasks in which behaviourally relevant stimuli can be attended to in the absence of exploratory saccadic eye movements. Third, the role of visual locations is emphasized by several theories of higher vision. For instance, Ullman proposed that the computation of various spatial relations between objects requires the application of visual routines or processes to selected stimulus locations (Ullman 1984). However, because of computational limitations, visual routines can be applied only to one or two locations at any given time. The analysis of the whole visual scene therefore requires a mechanism for selecting and switching the focus of processing from one location to another. Similarly, Treisman's feature integration theory (Treisman and Gelade 1980; Treisman 1991) proposes that the perception of objects in cluttered visual scenes is critically dependent on an attentional mechanism that selects an object location and binds the features at that location into a unified object percept.

The neurophysiological mechanisms underlying spatial selection are under active investigation. Traditionally, failures of spatial attention have been associated with damage to parietal cortex (DeRenzi 1982; Heilman *et al.* 1985; Mesulam 1990; Vallar and Perani 1987). Similarly, single unit analyses in awake behaving monkeys have indicated that neuronal activity in parietal cortex is modulated by the direction of attention (Bushnell *et al.* 1981; Robinson *et al.* 1995; Steinmetz and Constantinidis 1995; Colby *et al.* 1996). Over the past five years, we have studied the neural basis of spatial selection in the normal human brain by combining psychophysics, neuroimaging, and recent image analysis methods for flattening the cortical mantle of the human brain. We have identified a network of parietal and frontal regions that is active whenever attention is directed towards peripheral stimuli, both during cued detection at several locations (Corbetta *et al.* 1993), and visual search of targets in cluttered visual displays (Corbetta *et al.* 1995). The same set of regions is also active during overt orienting to peripheral stimuli via saccadic eye movements (Corbetta 1998). The fronto-parietal cortical network may therefore represent a neural system for selecting spatial locations across a variety of tasks.

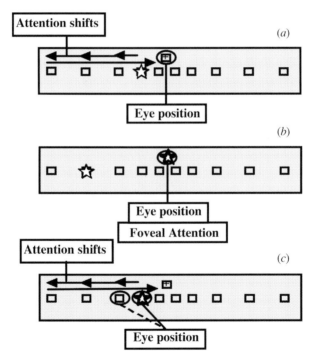

Fig. 11.1 Behavioural tasks for studying covert and overt orienting. (*a*) Shifting attention task. Subjects sequentially shifted attention (arrows) to successive boxes in a predetermined sequence to detect a briefly presented stimulus (star), while maintaining fixation on a central box. (*b*) Central detection with peripheral distractors task. The same sequence of peripheral stimuli was presented as in the shifting attention task, but subjects detected stimuli flashed in the central fixation box. (*c*) Saccadic eye movement task. The same sequence of peripheral stimuli was presented as in the shifting attention task, but before the onset of each stimulus, subjects moved their eyes to the expected location of the stimulus.

11.2 Functional anatomy of visuospatial attention in the human brain

Several functional anatomical studies have shown that a specific set of frontal and parietal regions is consistently recruited during covert orienting to simple unstructured peripheral visual stimuli. Corbetta and colleagues (Corbetta *et al.* 1993) measured regional cerebral blood flow with positron emission tomography (PET) in a group of 24 normal subjects during tasks designed to manipulate the direction of spatial attention. In one task, subjects shifted attention voluntarily along a series of locations positioned in the left or right visual field, while maintaining central fixation, to detect brief visual stimuli with a speeded key-press response (shifting attention task; figure 11.1*a*). In 80% of the trials, the peripheral visual stimuli occurred in a prespecified sequence (see figure 11.1*a*), allowing subjects to shift attention to the appropriate location before the stimulus appeared. In 20% of the trials, the stimuli were presented at unattended locations, i.e. locations that did not respect the prespecified sequence. For the duration of the actual PET scan (40 s), the percentage of stimuli at unattended locations was decreased to 5% to maximize shifts of attention in a given direction (the direction of attentional shifts was also manipulated in this experiment, but those findings will not be further discussed in this review). As expected, stimuli at attended locations were detected faster than stimuli at unattended locations. In a second task, subjects attended to and manually responded to stimuli in the fovea, while being presented with the same series of peripheral stimuli as in the shifting attention task (central detection with peripheral distractors task; figure 11.1*b*). Hence, this condition controlled for sensory stimulation of the peripheral visual field, arousal, and visuomotor processes (e.g. motor preparation–execution) recruited by a speeded visuomotor response. The central detection task mostly differed from the shifting attention task in the direction of attention, i.e. foveally maintained against peripherally shifted. In a third task, the same series of peripheral stimuli was presented as in the shifting attention and central detection task, but subjects were instructed to maintain central fixation without responding (passive task). This condition controlled for peripheral sensory stimulation in the absence of a motor response. Because the sudden onset of peripheral stimuli automatically captures attention to those locations (Yantis and Jonides 1990), the passive task also provides an opportunity to image processes related to sensory-driven or reflexive shifts of attention. Finally, in a fourth task (fixation task), no central or peripheral transients occurred and subjects simply maintained fixation. Eye movements were monitored in all conditions with an electro-oculogram (EOG) to ensure proper central fixation. Areas involved in covert orienting were localized by image subtractions between pairs of conditions. In particular, a subtraction image between the shifting attention and central detection task (shifting attention–central detection) controls for peripheral sensory stimulation, arousal, and motor demands, and hence reflects processes specifically involved in shifting attention. Significant blood flow changes were visualized in superior parietal and frontal cortex (figure 11.2; also see plate section). Interestingly, only the parietal region was active during the passive task, compared with the fixation task. Although we were not able to explicitly compare shifting attention and passive scans, the magnitude of parietal activations in the shifting task was comparable with the passive task (when both tasks were compared with the fixation task).

This pattern of results indicated that both superior parietal and frontal regions were related to endogenous shifts of attention. In both regions neural activity may reflect instruction signals for covertly (without change in eye fixation) shifting attention to peripheral locations. In parietal cortex, activity could also reflect a modulation (enhancement) of the sensory component of the peripheral visual stimuli, and/or sensory-driven shifts of attention induced by the sudden onset of those stimuli given the activation in the passive task (Yantis and Jonides 1990). In frontal cortex, activity could also reflect visuomotor processes, that are specifically related to the preparation–execution of a key-press response to peripheral visual stimuli, because no significant activity was

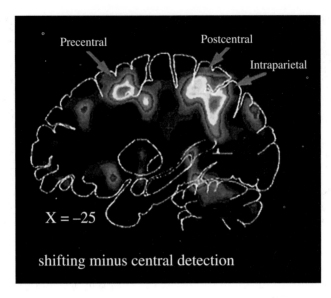

Fig. 11.2 Sagittal PET section, 25 mm left of midline, of group ($n = 24$) subtraction image between shifting attention and central detection with peripheral distractors tasks. (See colour plate section)

observed when subjects did not respond (passive task) or responded to central stimuli (central detection task).

To further investigate the relation between endogenous shifts of attention and the preparation–execution of a motor response, we have recently studied a 'no-response' version of the shifting attention task (Corbetta *et al.* 1998), in which subjects shifted attention voluntarily between peripheral locations and detected visual stimuli, but did not press a key to signal stimulus detection. Shifts of attention were therefore entirely decoupled from motor responses. To have some measure of performance, manual reaction times were measured in a prior psychophysical session in which subjects were trained to covertly shift attention to different locations in the periphery of the visual field. In addition to the shifting attention task, subjects were also scanned during a no-response central detection task, and a new no-response control task in which subjects detected foveal stimuli during central fixation (as in the central detection with peripheral distractors task), but no peripheral stimuli were simultaneously presented (central detection). This experiment was done by using functional magnetic resonance imaging (fMRI), which allows a more precise localization of functional activity in relation to the underlying anatomy in both single subjects and groups of subjects. The experiment was run as a blocked design in which each task was compared to a fixation control baseline. As in the PET experiment, regions in superior frontal and parietal cortex were strongly active when attention was directed toward the peripheral visual stimuli (figure 11.3, left; also see plate section), even in the absence of an overt motor response. Much weaker activations were evident in both frontal and parietal cortex during the central detection with peripheral distractors condition, i.e. when the same stimuli were unattended (figure 11.3, centre; also see plate section). Finally, only frontal cortex was weakly active during foveal attention without peripheral distractors (central detection, figure 11.3, right; also see plate section), suggesting that the parietal activity in the central detection with peripheral distractors task was related to the peripheral distractors. Although eye movements could not be recorded in the MR scanner, subjects were trained on these tasks in a prior behavioural session in which eye

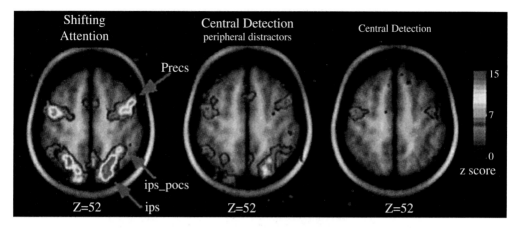

Fig. 11.3 Group fMRI activity superimposed on anatomical MRI during shifting attention, central detection with peripheral distractors, and central detection tasks in the left visual field. In the fixation control common to all tasks, the array of boxes was displayed, no stimuli were presented, and subjects maintained fixation on the central box. Transverse section, $z = 52$. Abbreviations: precs, precentral sulcus; ips_pocs, intraparietal sulcus–post-central sulcus; ips, intraparietal sulcus. (See colour plate section)

movements were monitored with EOG. Furthermore, the data from the fMRI experiment was very similar to the data from the PET experiment, in which eye movements were monitored during the scanning session. These fMRI findings confirm that activity in frontal and parietal cortex is unrelated to visuomotor manual processing *per se*, but is driven by the purely mental process of directing and shifting attention to different visual locations.

How general is the conclusion that a fronto-parietal cortical network is active during the allocation of attention to peripheral visual stimuli? To answer this question a meta-analysis of all published studies involving peripheral attention was done by using a new brain atlas (the Visible Man atlas) developed at Washington University by Heather Drury and David Van Essen. This atlas is based on the digital reconstruction of the anatomical sections of an adult male brain (Visible Human project, National Library of Medicine) (Drury *et al.* 1996; Van Essen and Drury 1997). The digital brain has been normalized to a standard 3D atlas space which is routinely used to localize responses in neuroimaging studies (Talairach and Tournoux 1988). The cerebral cortex has been flattened by using a reconstruction of layer 4 and foci of activation from all studies on peripheral attention have been plotted onto the 3D and 2D brain atlas representation. Each focus (indicated by a small sphere whose centre corresponds to x-, y-, z-coordinates of the activation in Talairach and Tournoux (1988) is surrounded by a 10-mm radius, which accounts for the variability in the mean location estimate (see Van Essen and Drury 1997). This variability has several sources: (i) imperfect registration of the functional data during the normalization to Talairach space; (ii) variability in the position of identified cortical areas in relation to nearby geographical landmarks; (iii) limited spatial resolution of the PET techniques; and (iv) variability in the anatomy of different groups of subjects.

This analysis involved studies that manipulated spatial attention in various ways: attention was dynamically shifted between different visual locations (Corbetta *et al.* 1993; Nobre *et al.* 1997), or maintained at a single peripheral location (Heinze *et al.* 1994; Woldorff *et al.* 1995; Vandenberghe *et al.* 1996, 1997), target locations were explicitly (spatial cueing) (Corbetta *et al.* 1993; Nobre *et al.* 1997), or implicitly cued (visual search) (Corbetta *et al.* 1995), and tasks required detection (Corbetta *et al.* 1993; Nobre *et al.* 1997) or discrimination (Heinze *et al.* 1994; Corbetta *et al.*

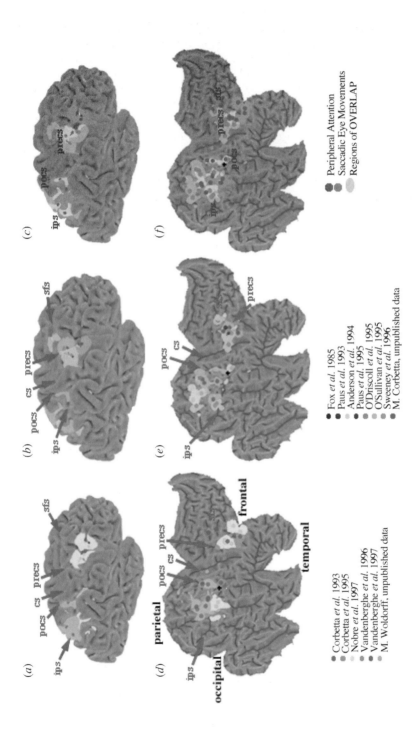

Fig. 11.4 3D rendering (*a–c*) and 2D flattened surface (*d–f*) of the Visible Man brain atlas, right hemisphere only. Lobes are indicated in 2D surface. Sulci are indicated as follows: sfs, superior frontal sulcus (s.); precs, precentral s.; cs represents central s.; pocs, postcentral s.; ips, intraparietal s. (*a, d*): areas of activation during peripheral attention. (*b, e*): areas of activation during saccadic eye movements. (*c, f*): anatomical overlap of areas active during peripheral attention and saccadic eye movements. (See colour plate section)

Corbetta *et al.* 1993
Corbetta *et al.* 1995
Nobre *et al.* 1997
Vandenberghe *et al.* 1996
Vandenberghe *et al.* 1997
M. Woldorff, unpublished data

Fox *et al.* 1985
Paus *et al.* 1993
Anderson *et al.* 1994
Paus *et al.* 1995
O'Driscoll *et al.* 1995
O'Sullivan *et al.* 1995
Sweeney *et al.* 1996
M. Corbetta, unpublished data

Peripheral Attention
Saccadic Eye Movements
Regions of OVERLAP

1995, 1996; Woldorff *et al.* 1995; Vandenberghe *et al.* 1996, 1997). All studies also differed in terms of the display characteristics and rate of stimulation. Overall, this analysis showed a very strong overlap in the pattern of cortical activation under all conditions (figure 11.4*a,d* also see plate section). In parietal cortex, activity localizes along post-central and intraparietal sulci. In frontal cortex, two distinct foci of activations are evident: one near the precentral sulcus–gyrus, the other near the posterior tip of the superior frontal sulcus. The similarity in the functional anatomy of shifting and tonic attention paradigms suggests that this fronto-parietal network controls the allocation of attention to peripheral locations. Furthermore, in experiments that involve object discrimination, the dorsal fronto-parietal network is active concurrently with ventral occipito-temporal regions involved in object analysis. Here, the direction of attention modulates both psychophysical performance and brain activity. Object targets presented at the attended location are discriminated more accurately, and produce stronger blood flow responses in ventral object-related regions, than targets presented at the unattended location (Heinze *et al.* 1994; Vandenberghe *et al.* 1996, 1997). Correspondingly, powerful neuronal enhancement of visual responses for the attended object have been recorded in occipital visual areas with scalp and single unit recordings in virtually the same paradigm (Hillyard and Picton 1987; Luck *et al.* 1997). We propose that attentional modulation in the ventral visual system reflects an interaction with a selective location signal from the fronto-parietal spatial network.

11.3   The relation between visuospatial attention and oculomotor processes

The existence of a set of psychological and neural processes for covertly (without changes in eye position) directing attention to locations raises the question of their relation to mechanisms responsible for saccadic generation, because under normal conditions attention and the eyes move together when peripheral targets are selected in the visual field. Early papers provided conflicting evidence on whether preparing an eye movement toward a location enhanced the visual processing of stimuli presented at the same location, and vice versa whether a shift of attention facilitated oculomotor execution (Klein 1980; Remington 1980). More recent work, however, has established that attention and eye movements are closely related. Shepherd and colleagues (Shepherd *et al.* 1986) separately manipulated the direction of spatial attention, by varying the probability that peripheral probe stimuli would appear in different positions, and the direction of saccades, by using a central arrow cue. They found that the preparation and execution of a saccadic eye movement enhanced the manual detection of stimuli presented at the saccadic target location, independently of probe probability. That is, even when attention and eye movements were cued to opposite locations, the effect of eye movement preparation–execution was predominant. Chelazzi and co-workers (Chelazzi *et al.* 1995) showed that the facilitation from saccadic preparation–execution extends to other locations in the same direction as the location of the saccade. Hoffman and Subramaniam (1995) confirmed in a dual task paradigm that target detection is superior at the saccade location regardless of the location at which attention was cued. Based on these new findings, the current view is that attention and saccadic systems are tightly related. For example, during the preparation of a saccade, the selection of a location is controlled by the oculomotor system, even when attempts are made to bias attention to different locations through experimental manipulations. It is still under discussion whether attentional processes may be separate when a saccade is planned but not performed, or when the eyes are fixated (Rafal *et al.* 1989; Klein 1994).

   Areas of the human brain involved in oculomotor processing have been identified by a variety of imaging studies that have used different types of oculomotor tasks including voluntary, visually guided, memory-guided and conditional saccades (Fox *et al.* 1985; Anderson *et al.* 1994; O'Sullivan *et al.* 1995; O'Driscoll *et al.* 1995; Sweeney *et al.* 1996; Bodis-Wallner *et al.* 1997; Darby *et al.* 1996; Lang *et al.* 1994; Law *et al.* 1997; Luna *et al.* 1998; Muri *et al.* 1996; Paus *et al.* 1993, 1995; Petit *et al.* 1993, 1996, 1997). Figure 11.4*b*,*e* summarizes selected studies from the early PET literature (until about mid-1996) that reported activations in Talairach atlas, plus those from our own laboratory that involved visually guided and memory-guided saccades. Preliminary analysis showed no consistent difference in the pattern of activation between different types of saccades. The only exception was the presence of prefrontal activity (not plotted) in some experiments that involved memory-guided saccades. In the frontal lobe activity centres on the precentral gyrus, extending from the central sulcus to the precentral sulcus. A second cluster is evident near the posterior tip of the superior frontal sulcus. Similar activations have been reported by PET studies that have not used Talairach based analysis (e.g. Petit *et al.* 1993), and more recent fMRI studies in single subjects (e.g. Luna *et al.* 1998; Petit *et al.* 1997). These regions are thought to contain the human homologue of the monkey's frontal eye field (FEF) (Paus 1996; Petit *et al.* 1997; Luna *et al.* 1998). Lesions in the FEF cause acutely an eye deviation toward the side of the lesion, and chronically the inability to suppress reflexive saccades (DeRenzi 1982; Henik *et al.* 1998). A third cluster (not shown) involves a region on the medial wall of the frontal lobe, probably corresponding to the supplementary eye field (SEF) (Shook *et al.* 1991; Schlag *et al.* 1992; Luna *et al.* 1998). In parietal cortex activity is again distributed near intraparietal and post-central sulci, and adjacent gyri, but extends also toward the precuneus.

To directly compare eye movement- and attention-related activations, foci for attention have been coloured in red, foci for eye movements in green, and areas of anatomical overlap in yellow. Areas of large overlap occur bilaterally in intraparietal and post-central regions, and frontally in the precentral region and superior frontal sulcus region. Exclusive eye movement activity is evident dorsally in the right precuneus, and left post-central gyrus. Exclusive attention activity is evident ventrally in the intraparietal sulcus. Overall, this analysis shows both overlap and segregation in the spatial distribution of cortical activity when attention- and eye movement-related foci are compared across PET experiments. The biological interpretation of these findings must be cautious given the presence of non-biological variability. Although the 10-mm radius of uncertainty associated with each focus should account for most of the methodological variability, differences in experimental variables across experiments (e.g. eccentricity of stimuli, rate of stimulus presentation) can also increase variability. However, if one emphasizes anatomical overlap, all three main sites of activation for attention (intraparietal, postcentral, and precentral) show convergent activation during eye movements. Vice versa, if one emphasizes anatomical segregation there appear to be large sections of parietal and frontal cortex that are uniquely active for each condition. For example, attention foci are more anteriorly located in frontal cortex than eye movement foci. In conclusion, this meta-analysis of PET experiments suggests that attention and eye movements share neural substrates. However, the variability in the data does not allow one to conclude that these two sets of processes involve identical cortical regions. As attention is generally shifted during an eye movement, some overlap is expected. It is unclear, however, whether making an eye movement adds any unique regions in parietal or frontal cortex.

A more precise test of the relation between saccadic eye movements and attention is provided by functional mapping experiments in which covert (attentional) and overt (saccadic) visual orienting mechanisms are compared in the same subject. Subjects were scanned with fMRI in separate blocks during the no-response shifting attention task, in which attention was shifted sequentially along a series of predictable locations and stimuli were covertly detected, and during an eye movement task (figure 11.1*c*) in which voluntary saccades were done along the same series of locations as in the no-response shifting attention task. In both tasks subjects shifted attention

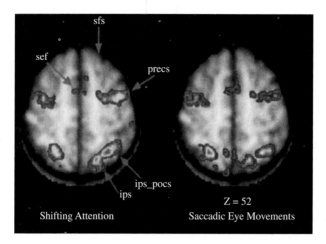

Fig. 11.5 Group ($n = 5$) fMRI activity superimposed on anatomical MRI during shifting attention and saccadic eye movement tasks in left visual field. A fixation control was common to both tasks. Anatomical regions as in figures 11.3 and 11.4. Abbreviations as in figure 11.3, and sef, supplementary eye field. (See colour plate section)

(shifting attention task), and attention and eye position (eye movement task) in anticipation of the sensory stimulus. Visual stimuli were therefore presented in the periphery of the visual field in the shifting attention task, and in the fovea in the eye movement task. The fixation task described earlier, in which no peripheral transients were presented and subjects maintained fixation, served as a control. Although eye movements could not be monitored in the MR scanner, subjects were trained on all tasks during a prior behavioural session in which eye movements were monitored via EOG, and behavioural effects measured in the shifting attention task. Subjects moved their eyes appropriately during the eye movement task and maintained fixation during the attention task. In the attention task, all subjects showed robust behavioural effects for attended against unattended stimuli. In this experiment, we found very similar activations during attention and eye movement shifts both in parietal and frontal cortex (figure 11.5; also see plate section). The frontal activation centred on the precentral region and extended to the posterior tip of the superior frontal sulcus, and probably involved several areas. The activation of the precentral region corresponds to the FEF activation found in other oculomotor tasks (see figure 11.4). A medial frontal focus probably corresponds to SEF (Shook *et al.* 1991; Schlag *et al.* 1992; Luna *et al.* 1998). The parietal activations may correspond to areas in macaque that contain both oculomotor and attentional signals (e.g. LIP and 7a) (Andersen *et al.* 1990; Andersen 1995; Colby *et al.* 1995, 1996). The eye movement condition also yielded several activations not found in the attention condition, including the medial cerebellum and occipital cortex. The cerebellar activations presumably reflected the presence of eye movements while the occipital activations presumably reflected the presence of foveal transients. Both results confirm that subjects were maintaining fixation during the attention condition.

   The extensive anatomical overlap of the neural systems for attention and eye movements is reminiscent of their tight functional relation at the behavioural level. In addition, the discovery of attention-related activity in the FEF suggest that covert attention processes involve oculomotor areas. The FEF is one of the cortical oculomotor centres of the brain. Neurons in the FEF are monosynaptically connected with the superior colliculus and pontine nuclei for eye movement control (Astruc 1971; Leichnetz *et al.* 1984). Microstimulation of the FEF with threshold electrical currents specifically produces contralateral saccades (Robinson and Fuchs 1969; Bruce and Goldberg 1985). A total of three populations of neurons have been described in the FEF: motor, visual, and visuomovement neurons (Bruce and Goldberg 1985). The motor neurons fire before and during a saccade, code target locations in motor parameters, i.e. direction and amplitude, and project to subcortical structures. Visual neurons respond to the onset of visual stimuli, and their response is enhanced when the visual stimulus is the target for a saccade. Visual neurons may provide sensory information about the target to motor neurons. Visuomovement neurons begin to discharge after the presentation of a visual stimulus, and remain active until a saccade is made into their movement field. Recently, Schall and colleagues have shown that during a pop-out visual search task, the activity of these neurons signals the location of a target before a saccade, or during a fixation task (Schall and Hanes 1993; Thompson *et al.* 1997). These modulations indicate that FEF may participate in target selection aside from motor programming.

Haemodynamic activity in the FEF during covert attention may reflect three separate neuronal signals. Shifts of attention may enhance visual responses of visual or visuomovement neurons. Alternatively, or in addition, shifts of attention may involve saccadic preparation that drives motor neurons in the FEF. This would imply that both saccades and attentional shifts are planned in motor coordinates (e.g. amplitude and direction from the current position) (Rizzolatti *et al.* 1987). A similar conclusion was reached by Kustov and Robinson (1996) who found that covert shifts of attention modify the vector of saccadic eye movements induced by the micro-electrical stimulation of the deep layer of the superior colliculus, the other oculomotor centre of the brain. Finally, FEF activity might reflect a fixation or suppression signal for preventing reflexive saccades to peripheral stimuli in the attention task. These latter possibilities are less likely as FEF activity is very weak in other tasks that require, as the shifting attention task, fixation during the presentation of peripheral stimuli (e.g. central detection or passive tasks in the PET experiment).

11.4   Fronto-parietal spatial network, visual search and the focus of processing

The functional link between shifts of visual attention and eye movements, and activity within a fronto-parietal cortical network provides important neurobiological constraints for unresolved issues in psychology and vision. We are referring in particular to the long-standing discussion about 'serial' and 'parallel' models of visual search. The basic phenomenon is well-known: while the search time for a high saliency target, e.g. a red triangle among green triangles (or feature search), is independent of the number of distractors, the search time for a low saliency target, e.g. a red triangle among green triangles and red squares (or conjunction search), increases with the number of distractors (Treisman and Gelade 1980; Duncan and Humphreys 1989; Wolfe *et al.* 1989). The biased competition model of Desimone and Duncan (1995) proposes that visual analysis proceeds in parallel (parallel search) across the field in both cases, but that its efficiency declines in conditions of low target discriminability when more noise (distractors) is added to the system. Other models, such as Treisman's feature integration theory propose that a spatial attention mechanism is recruited in conditions of low discriminability and serially inspects individual items or groups of items in the field, to discriminate between target and distractors (Treisman and Gelade 1980; Treisman and Gormican 1988). 'Pure' versions of these two competing models make different predictions about the underlying functional anatomy. Parallel models predict that feature and conjunction search should yield similar regions of activation, perhaps stronger in the conjunction search because of the longer time on task. As the target is defined by a non-spatial feature (e.g. colour) these models predict either no activation of the fronto-parietal network, or activation during both feature and conjunction tasks. In contrast, serial models predict a dissociated pattern of activation with the conjunction task uniquely recruiting a spatial selection mechanism. If the fronto-parietal network, active during visual orienting, also controls the focus of processing during visual search tasks, then this network should be preferentially recruited by the conjunction task.

To address this issue we compared blood flow (measured with PET) during visual search tasks involving either targets defined by colour or by motion, or targets defined by a conjunction of colour and motion (Corbetta *et al.* 1995). The visual display contained four square windows (4° eccentricity from fixation, 2° length), and each window contained coloured (red, orange), moving (fast, slow) dots. In the colour task subjects searched for a red window among orange windows. In the motion task subjects searched for the fast window among slow windows. In the conjunction task subjects searched for the red–fast window among orange–slow, orange–fast, and red–slow windows. All search tasks were compared with a common control condition, in which similar displays were passively viewed. In a separate behavioural session, the feature task yielded a flat search function relating response latencies to the number of items in the display, while the conjunction task yielded the expected increasing search function. Across the entire brain, feature and conjunction search were best distinguished by activity in posterior parietal cortex corresponding to regions that were also active for attentional and oculomotor shifts during the visual orienting tasks discussed here. Blood flow in posterior parietal cortex was strongly increased when subjects searched for conjunction targets of colour and motion, and was slightly decreased when they searched for feature targets of either colour or motion, as compared with a control condition that involved passive viewing of the same set of stimuli (see figure 11.6; also see plate section). This basic observation has been confirmed by other experiments involving the conjunction of colour and orientation (Hunton *et al.* 1995) and is further supported by recent transcranial magnetic stimulation (TMS) experiments. TMS is a relatively new technique in which radio frequency single pulses are applied through the skull via a magnetic stimulator to limited parts of the cortex. These magnetic pulses transiently disrupt neuronal activity in the stimulated brain region, and produce a transient functional deficit at different time points during the performance of a particular task. Ashbridge and co-workers (1997) stimulated posterior parietal cortex during various visual search tasks that involved either feature or conjunction targets. They showed that TMS stimulation of posterior parietal cortex significantly delayed search time for conjunction targets, whereas it did not influence search time for feature targets. The unique role of posterior parietal cortex during conjunction search, and its anatomical overlap with regions involved in shifting attention and eye movements to peripheral locations, is therefore consistent with models of search that predict the recruitment of a spatial attentional mechanism. It is important to note that this finding does not necessarily imply that subjects are serially shifting attention between all items in the display. For example, this finding is also consistent with hybrid parallel-serial models (Hoffman 1979; Wolfe *et al.* 1989), in which 'candidate targets' that pass an initial parallel screen are evaluated by a spatially selective, limited capacity mechanism.

Although the data indicate that the parietal component of the spatial attention network was selectively involved during the conjunction condition that yielded a serial search function, they do not indicate why this condition required spatial attention. Spatial attention may be required during any difficult search task that yields a serial search function (e.g. parietal activity might be present during a difficult feature search condition), and/or may be required to bind visual features at a certain spatial location. The greater PET activation in the conjunction task, for example, may reflect the 'binding' of colour and motion targets, which is not necessary when targets are defined by a single feature such as colour or motion alone. This view is consistent with a recent

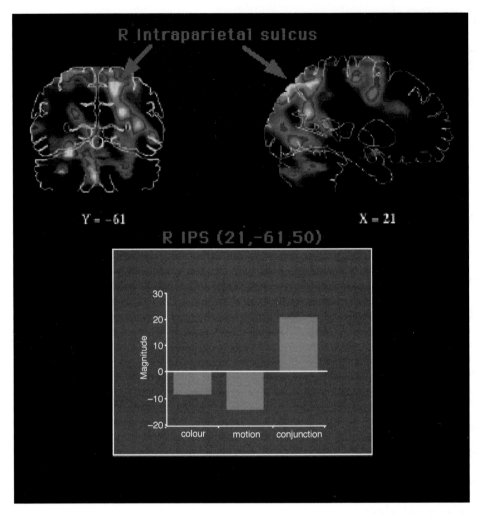

Fig. 11.6   Top: group ($n = 17$) PET activity from coronal (left) and sagittal (right) sections in the right intraparietal sulcus during visual search for targets defined by a conjunction of colour and motion speed. The control condition is passive viewing of the same display. Bottom: magnitude of blood flow responses (in PET counts) in the feature (colour, motion) and conjunction conditions for the intraparietal region maximally activated in the shifting attention task (figure 11.1). (See colour plate section)

behavioural analysis of a patient with bilateral occipital–parietal lesion and Balint's syndrome (Friedman-Hill *et al.* 1995). This patient showed profound deficits in encoding and using locations for visual behaviour, as well as problems in binding the features of simple visual objects, e.g. he might report seeing a green X when presented with a red X and a green O. Posterior parietal cortex may contain a spatial map, topographically connected (directly or indirectly through other structures, such as the pulvinar) to various feature maps (colour, motion, shape), which provides a location signal that is used during visual orienting tasks, difficult search tasks, or conjunction tasks involving the integration of several features at one location.

11.5 Conclusions

This review highlights psychological, functional anatomical, and cellular levels of the analysis of spatial visual selection. There are three main conclusions which can be derived from this body of results. First, there appears to be a robust set of neural signals in parietal and frontal cortex that reflect spatial attentional processes across a variety of detection and discrimination tasks. These signals occur during tonic and dynamic allocation of attention to a location, and during tasks that explicitly (cueing) and implicitly (search) direct attention to a location. Second, psychological and physiological data indicate that attentional processes are closely linked to oculomotor processes. Third, these selective spatial neural signals bias visual processing at selected locations in ventral visual areas related to object analysis.

Acknowledgements

This work was supported by grants NIH K08-EY00379-01, and the Charles A. Dana Foundation. We thank H. Drury and D. Van Essen for the use of the software Caret that contains the Visible Man brain atlas (for information, heather@v1.wustl.edu).

References

Andersen, R. A. 1995 Encoding of intention and spatial location in posterior parietal cortex. *Cerebr. Cortex* **5**, 457–69.

Andersen, R. A., Bracewell, R. M., Barash, S., Gnadt, J. W. and Fogassi, L. 1990 Eye position effects on visual, memory, and saccade-related activity in areas LIP and 7A of macaque. *J. Neurosci.* **10**, 1176–96.

Anderson, T. J., Jenkins, I. K., Brooks, D. J., Hawken, M. B., Frackoviack, R. S. J. and Kennard, C. 1994 Cortical control of saccades and fixation in man. *Brain* **117**, 1073–84.

Ashbridge, E., Walsh, V. and Cowey, A. 1997 Temporal aspects of visual search studied by transcranial magnetic stimulation. *Neuropsychologia* **35**, 1121–31.

Astruc, J. 1971 Corticofugal connections of area 8 (frontal eye field) in *Macaca mulatta. Brain Res.* **33**, 241–56.

Bodis-Wallner, I., Bucher, S. F., Seelos, K. C., Paulus, W., Reiser, M. and Oertel, W. H. 1997 Functional MRI mapping of occipital and frontal cortical activity during voluntary and imagined saccades. Neurology **49**, 416–20.

Bruce, C. J. and Goldberg, M. E. 1985 Primate frontal eye fields. I. Single neurons discharging before saccades. *J. Neurophysiol.* **53**, 603–35.

Bushnell, M. C., Goldberg, M. E. and Robinson, D. L. 1981 Behavioral enhancement of visual responses in monkey cerebral cortex. I. Modulation in posterior parietal cortex related to selective attention. *J. Neurophysiol.* **46**, 755–72.

Chelazzi, L., Biscaldi, M., Corbetta, M., Peru, A., Tassinari, G. and Berlucchi, G. 1995 Oculomotor activity and visual spatial attention. *Behav. Brain Res.* **71**, 81–8.

Colby, C., Duhamel, J. and Goldberg, M. 1995 Oculocentric spatial representation in parietal cortex. *Cerebr. Cortex* **5**, 470–82.

Colby, C. L., Duhamel, J. R. and Goldberg, M. E. 1996 Visual, presaccadic, and cognitive activation of single neurons in monkey lateral intraparietal area. *J. Neurophysiol.* **76**, 2841–52.

Corbetta, M. 1998 Frontoparietal cortical networks for directing attention and the eye to visual locations: identical, independent, or overlapping neural systems. *Proc. Natn. Acad. Sci. USA* **95**, 831–8.

Corbetta, M., Miezin, F. M., Shulman, G. L. and Petersen, S. E. 1993 A PET study of visuospatial attention. *J. Neurosci.* **13**, 1202–26.

Corbetta, M., Shulman, G. L., Miezin, F. M. and Petersen, S. E. 1995 Superior parietal cortex activation during spatial attention shifts and visual feature conjunction. *Science* **270**, 802–5.

Corbetta, M., Shulman, G. L., Conturo, T. E., Snyder, A. Z., Akbudak, E., Petersen, S. E. and Raichle, M. E. 1997 Functional magnetic resonance imaging (fMRI) of visuospatial attention: group and single subject analysis. *NeuroImage* **5**(suppl.), 85.

Darby, D. G., Nobre, A. C., Thangarai, V., Edelman, R., Mesulam, M. M. and Warach, S. 1996 Cortical activation of the human brain during lateral saccades using epistar functional magnetic resonance imaging. *NeuroImage* **3**, 53–62.

DeRenzi, E. 1982 Disorders of space exploration and cognition. New York: Wiley.

Desimone, R. and Duncan, J. 1995 Neural mechanisms of selective visual attention. *A. Rev. Neurosci.* **18**, 193–222.

Downing, C. J. 1988 Expectancy and visual–spatial attention effects on vision. *J. Exp. Psychol. Hum. Percept. Perf.* **14**, 188–97.

Drury, H. A., Van Essen, D. C., Anderson, C. H., Lee, C. W., Coogan, T. A. and Lewis, J. W. 1996 Computerized mappings of the cerebral cortex: a multiresolution flattening method and a surface-based coordinate system. *J. Cogn. Neurosci.* **8**, 1–28.

Duncan, J. and Humphreys, G. W. 1989 Visual search and stimulus similarity. *Psychol. Rev.* **96**, 433–58.

Eriksen, C. W. and Hoffman, J. E. 1972 Temporal and spatial characteristics of selective encoding from visual displays. *Percept. Psychophys.* **12**, 201–4.

Fox, P. T., Fox, J. M., Raichle, M. E. and Burde, R. M. 1985 The role of cerebral cortex in the generation of voluntary saccades: a positron emission tomographic study. *J. Neurophysiol.* **54**, 348–69.

Friedman-Hill, S. R., Robertson, L. C. and Treisman, A. 1995 Parietal contibutions to visual feature binding: evidence from a patient with bilateral lesions. *Science* **269**, 853–5.

Hawkins, H. L., Hillyard, S. A., Luck, S. J., Mouloua, M., Downing, C. J. and Woodward, D. P. 1990 Visual attention modulates signal detectability. *J. Exp. Psychol. Hum. Percept. Perf.* **16**, 802–11.

Heilman, K. M., Watson, R. T. and Valenstein, E. 1985 Neglect and related disorders. In *Clinical neuropsychology* (eds K. M. Heilman and E. Valenstein), pp. 243–93. New York: Oxford University Press.

Heinze, H. J. (and 11 others) 1994 Combined spatial and temporal imaging of brain activity during visual selective attention in humans. *Nature* **372**, 543–6.

Henderson, J. M. 1996 Spatial precues affect target discrimination in the absence of visual noise. *J. Exp. Psychol. Hum. Percept. Perf.* **22**, 780–7.

Henik, A., Rafal, R. and Rhodes, D. 1998 Endogenously generated and visually guided saccades after lesions of the human frontal eye fields. *J. Cogn. Neurosci.* (In the press.)

Hillyard, S. A. and Picton, T. W. 1987 Electrophysiology of cognition. In *The handbook of physiology. 1. The nervous system. V. Higher functions of the brain*, part 2 (eds F. Plum, V. B. Mountcastle and S. T. Geiger), pp. 519–84. Bethesda, MD: American Physiological Society.

Hoffman, J. E. 1979 A two-stage model of visual search. *Percept. Psychophys.* **57**, 787–95.

Hoffman, J. E. and Subramaniam, B. 1995 The role of visual attention in saccadic eye movements. *Percept. Psychophys.* **57**, 787–95.

Hunton, D. L., Corbetta, M., Shulman, G. L., Miezin, F. M. and Petersen, S. E. 1995 Common areas of parietal activations for shifts of spatial attention and tasks involving the conjunction of visual features. *Soc. Neurosci. Abstr.* **21**, 937.

Klein, R. 1980 Does oculomotor readiness mediate cognitive control of visual attention? In *Attention and performance VII* (ed. R. S. Nickerson), pp. 259–76. Hillsdale, NJ: Lawrence Erlbaum.

Klein, R. M. 1994 Perceptual-motor expectancies interact with covert visual orienting under conditions of endogenous but not exogenous control. *Can. J. Exp. Psychol.* **48**, 167–81.

Kustov, A. A. and Robinson, D. L. 1996 Shared neural control of attentional shifts and eye movements. *Nature* **384**, 74–7.

Lang, W., Petit, L., Hollinger, P., Pietrzyk, U., Tzourio, N., Mazoyer, B. and Berthoz, A. 1994 A positron emission tomography study of oculomotor imagery. *NeuroReport* **5**, 921–4.

Law, I., Svarer, C., Holm, S. and Paulson, O. B. 1997 The activation pattern in normal humans during suppression, imagination, and performance of saccadic eye movements. *Acta Physiol. Scand.* **161**, 419–34.

Leichnetz, G. R., Spencer, R. F. and Smith, D. J. 1984 Cortical projections to nuclei adjacent to the oculomotor complex in the medial dienmesencephalic tegmentum in the monkey. *J. Comp. Neurol.* **228**, 359–87.

Luck, S. J., Hillyard, S. A., Mouloua, M. and Hawkins, H. L. 1996 Mechanisms of visual-spatial attention—resource allocation of uncertainty reduction? *J. Exp. Psychol. Hum. Percept. Perf.* **22**, 725–37.

Luck, S. J., Chelazzi, L., Hillyard, S. A. and Desimone, R. 1997 Neuronal mechanisms of spatial selective attention in areas V1, V2, V4 of macaque visual cortex. *J. Neurophysiol.* **77**, 24–42.

Luna, B., Thulborn, K. R., Strojwas, M. H., McCurtain, B. J., Berman, R. A., Genovese, C. R. and Sweeney, J. A. 1998 Dorsal cortical regions subserving visually-guided saccades in humans: an fMRI study. *Cerebr. Cortex* **8**, 40–7.

Mesulam, M.-M. 1990 Large-scale neurocognitive networks and distributed processing for attention, language, and memory. *Ann. Neurol.* **28**, 597–613.

Muri, R. M., MT, I.-Z., Derosier, C., Cabanis, E. A. and Pierrot-Deseilligny 1996 Location of the human posterior eye field with functional magnetic resonance imaging. *J. Neurol. Neurosurg. Psychiat.* **60**, 445–8.

Nobre, A. C., Sebestyen, G. N., Gitelman, D. R., Mesulam, M. M., Frackowiack, R. S. J. and Frith, C. D. 1997 Functional localization of the system for visuospatial attention using positron emission tomography. *Brain* **120**, 515–33.

O'Driscoll, G. A., Alpert, N. M., Matthysse, S. W., Levy, D. L., Rauch, S. L. and Holzman, P. S. 1995 Functional neuroanatomy of amtisaccade eye movements investigated with positron emission tomography. *Proc. Natn. Acad. Sci. USA* **92**, 925–9.

O'Sullivan, E. P., Jenkins, I. H., Henderson, L., Kennard, C. and Brooks, D. J. 1995 The functional anatomy of remembered saccades: a PET study. *NeuroReport* **6**, 2141–4.

Paus, T. 1996 Location and function of the human frontal eye-field: a selective review. *Neuropsychologia* **34**, 475–83.

Paus, T., Petrides, M., Evans, A. C. and Meyer, E. 1993 Role of the human anterior cingulate cortex in the control of oculomotor, manual, and speech responses: a positron emission tomography study. *J. Neurophysiol.* **70**, 453–69.

Paus, T., Marrett, S., Worsley, K. J. and Evans, A. C. 1995 Extraretinal modulation of cerebral blood flow in the human visual cortex: implications for saccadic suppression. *J. Neurophysiol.* **74**, 2179–83.

Petit, L., Orrsaud, C., Tzourio, N., Crivello, F., Berthoz, A. and Mazoyer, B. 1996 Functional anatomy of a prelearned sequence of horizontal saccades in man. *J. Neurosci.* **16**, 3714–26.

Petit, L., Orrsaud, C., Tzourio, N., Salamon, G., Mazoyer, B. and Berthoz, A. 1993 PET study of voluntary saccadic eye movements in humans: basal ganglia–thalamocortical system and cingulate cortex involvement. *J. Neurophysiol.* **69**, 1009–17.

Petit, L., Clark, V. P., Ingeholm, J. and Haxby, J. V. 1997 Dissociation of saccade-related and pursuit-related activation in human frontal eye fields as revealed by fMRI. *J. Neurophysiol.* **77**, 3386–90.

Posner, M. I., Snyder, C. R. R. and Davidson, B. J. 1980 Attention and the detection of signals. *J. Exp. Psychol. Gen.* **109**, 160–74.

Prinzmetal, W., Presti, D. and Posner, M. I. 1986 Does attention affect visual feature integration? *J. Exp. Psychol. Hum. Percept. Perf.* **12**, 361–70.

Rafal, R. D., Calabresi, P. A., Brennan, C. W. and Sciolto, T. K. 1989 Saccade preparation inhibits reorienting to recently attended locations. *J. Exp. Psychol. Hum. Percept. Perf.* **15**, 673–85.

Remington, R. 1980 Attention and saccadic eye movements. *J. Exp. Psychol. Hum. Percept. Perf.* **6**, 726–44.

Rizzolatti, G., Riggio, L., Dascola, I. and Umiltá, C. 1987 Reorienting attention across the horizontal and vertical meridians: evidence in favor of a premotor theory of attention. *Neuropsychologia* **25**, 31–40.

Robinson, D. A. and Fuchs, A. F. 1969 Eye movements evoked by stimulation of frontal eye fields. *J. Neurophysiol.* **32**, 637–48.

Robinson, D. L., Bowman, E. M. and Kertzman, C. 1995 Covert orienting of attention in macaques. II. Contributions of parietal cortex. *J. Neurophysiol.* **74**, 698–721.

Schall, J. D. and Hanes, D. P. 1993 Neural basis of saccade target selection in frontal eye field during visual search. *Nature* **366**, 467–8.

Schlag, J., Schlag-Rey, M. and Pigarev, I. 1992 Supplementary eye field: influence of eye position on neural signals of fixation. *Exp. Brain Res.* **90**, 302–6.

Shepherd, M., Findlay, J. M. and Hockey, R. J. 1986 The relationship between eye movements and spatial attention. *Q. J. Exp. Psychol.* **38**, 475–91.

Shook, B. L., Schlag-Rey, M. and Schlag, J. 1991 Primate supplementary eye field. II. Comparative aspects of connections with the thalamus, corpus striatum, and related forebrain nuclei. *J. Comp. Neurol.* **307**, 562–83.

Steinmetz, M. A. and Constantinidis, C. 1995 Neurophysiological evidence for a role of posterior parietal cortex in redirecting visual attention. *Cerebr. Cortex* **5**, 448–56.

Sweeney, J. A., Mintum, M. A., Kwee, S., Wiseman, M. B., Brown, D. L., Rosenberg, D. R. and Carl, J. R. 1996 Positron emission tomography study of voluntary saccadic eye movement and spatial working memory. *J. Neurophysiol.* **75**, 454–68.

Talairach, J. and Tournoux, P. 1988 *Co-planar stereotaxic atlas of the human brain* (Rayport, Mark, Trans.). New York: Thieme Medical Publishers, Inc.

Thompson, K. G., Bichot, N. P. and Schall, J. D. 1997 Dissociation of visual discrimination from saccade programming in macaque frontal eye field. *J. Neurophysiol.* **77**, 1046–50.

Treisman, A. 1991 Search, similarity, and integration of features between and within dimensions. *J. Exp. Psychol. Hum. Percept. Perf.* **17**, 652–76.

Treisman, A. M. and Gelade, G. 1980 A feature-integration of theory of attention. *Cogn. Psychol.* **12**, 97–136.

Treisman, A. M. and Gormican, S. 1988 Feature analysis in early vision: evidence from search asymmetries. *Psychol. Rev.* **95**, 15–48.

Ullman, S. 1984 Visual routines. *Cognition* **18**, 97–159.

Vallar, G. and Perani, D. 1987 The anatomy of spatial neglect in humans. In *Neurophysiological and neuropsychological aspects of spatial neglect* (ed. M. Jeannerod), pp. 235–58. North-Holland and Elsevier Science Publishers.

Vandenberghe, R., Duncan, J., Dupont, P., Ward, R., Poline, J.-B., Bormans, G., Michiels, J., Mortelmans, L. and Orban, G. A. 1997 Attention to one or two features in left and right visual field: a positron emission tomography study. *J. Neurosci.* **17**, 3739–50.

Vandenberghe, R., Dupont, P., Debruyn, B., Bormans, G., Michiels, J., Mortelmans, L. and Orban, G. A. 1996 The influence of stimulus location on the brain activation pattern in detection and orientation discrimination—a PET study of visual attention. *Brain* **119**, 1263–76.

Van Essen, D. C. and Drury, H. A. 1997 Structural and functional analyses of human cerebral cortex using a surface-based atlas. *J. Neurosci.* **17**, 7079–102.

Woldorff, M., Fox, T., Matzke, M., Veeraswamy, S., Jerabek, P. and Martin, C. 1995 Combined PET and REP study of sustained visual spatial attention and visual target detection. *Hum. Brain Mapp.* **1**, 49.

Wolfe, J. M., Cave, K. R. and Franzel, S. L. 1989 Guided search: an alternative to the feature integration model for visual search. *J. Exp. Psychol.* **15**, 419–33.

Yantis, S. and Jonides, J. 1990 Abrupt visual onsets and selective attention: voluntary versus automatic allocation. *J. Exp. Psychol. Hum. Percept. Perf.* **16**, 121–34.

Section 4

Visual attention and action

12

Neural coding of 3D features of objects for hand action in the parietal cortex of the monkey

Hideo Sakata, Masato Taira, Makoto Kusunoki,
Akira Murata, Yuji Tanaka and Ken-ichiro Tsutsui

Abstract

In our previous studies of hand manipulation task-related neurons, we found many neurons of the parietal association cortex which responded to the sight of three-dimensional (3D) objects. Most of the task-related neurons in the AIP area (the lateral bank of the anterior intraparietal sulcus) were visually responsive and half of them responded to objects for manipulation. Most of these neurons were selective for the 3D features of the objects. More recently, we have found binocular visual neurons in the lateral bank of the caudal intraparietal sulcus (c-IPS area) that preferentially respond to a luminous bar or plate at a particular orientation in space. We studied the responses of axis-orientation selective (AOS) neurons and surface orientation selective (SOS) neurons in this area with stimuli presented on a 3D computer graphics display. The AOS neurons showed a stronger response to elongated stimuli and showed tuning to the orientation of the longitudinal axis. Many of them preferred a tilted stimulus in depth and appeared to be sensitive to orientation disparity and/or width disparity. The SOS neurons showed a stronger response to a flat than to an elongated stimulus and showed tuning to the 3D orientation of the surface. Their responses increased with the width or length of the stimulus. A considerable number of SOS neurons responded to a square in a random dot stereogram and were tuned to orientation in depth, suggesting their sensitivity to the gradient of disparity. We also found several SOS neurons that responded to a square with tilted or slanted contours, suggesting their sensitivity to orientation disparity and/or width disparity. Area c-IPS is likely to send visual signals of the 3D features of an object to area AIP for the visual guidance of hand actions.

12.1 Introduction

Binocular stereopsis is one of the principal characteristics of primates, and is essential for the visual guidance of skilled hand movements. It was Charles Wheatstone who invented the stereoscope and discovered the psychophysical mechanisms of stereopsis. He said in his paper in the *Philosophical Transactions* in 1838 'the mind perceives an object of three dimensions by means of the dissimilar pictures projected by it on the two retinae'. He demonstrated with his mirror stereoscope, that if the two perspective projections of the same solid object are presented simultaneously to each eye, the observer will perceive a figure in three dimensions. He stated that 'the determination of the points which appear single seems to depend on previous knowledge of the form we are regarding'.

This hypothesis was challenged by Bela Julesz (1971) with his random dot stereogram. He demonstrated beyond any doubt that the detection of binocular disparity happens at an early stage of visual information processing before the process of form perception. David Marr (1982) proposed in his comprehensive theory of vision that surface orientation, a necessary form of information, the representation of 3D shape, can be computed from changes of binocular disparity. Figure 12.1 shows how a slanted surface produces a gradual change of disparity. However, the disparity gradient is not the only cue for surface orientation in depth. There are several kinds of disparities on inclined or slanted surfaces other than horizontal positional disparity included in

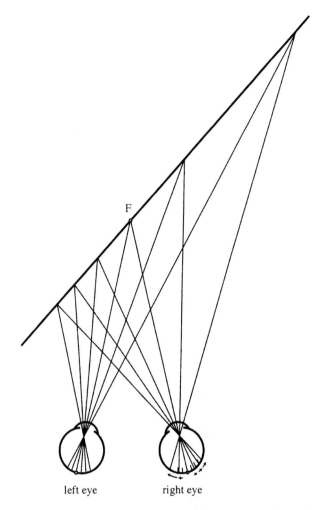

left eye   right eye

Fig. 12.1 Diagram to show the gradient of disparity produced by a slanted surface. A total of six points on the surface are projected on the retina of the left eye at equal intervals and, in the right eye, the difference between the corresponding points indicated with tics and the projected points increases gradually from the fovea to the periphery as indicated by the small arrows.

the random dot stereogram (for a review, see Howard and Rogers 1995). Among these, orientation disparities and width disparities are the most important. It is interesting that the original figures of line drawings for the stereoscope by Wheatstone (1838) contained these two disparities for inclination and slant. Figure 12.2 shows how an inclined line produces an orientation disparity and a slanted line produces width disparity.

Neurophysiological studies of the mechanisms of binocular stereopsis have been limited to the striate cortex (V1) (Barlow *et al.* 1967; Nikara *et al.* 1968; Poggio and Fischer 1977) and adjacent prestriate cortical areas, thick cytochrome oxidase stripes of V2 (Hubel and Livingstone 1987), V3 and V3A (Zeki 1978; Poggio *et al.* 1988). Neurons in these areas were sensitive to simple horizontal positional disparity. Therefore, their activity did not correspond directly to the perception of the 3D features of objects. Our recent studies of the manipulation-related

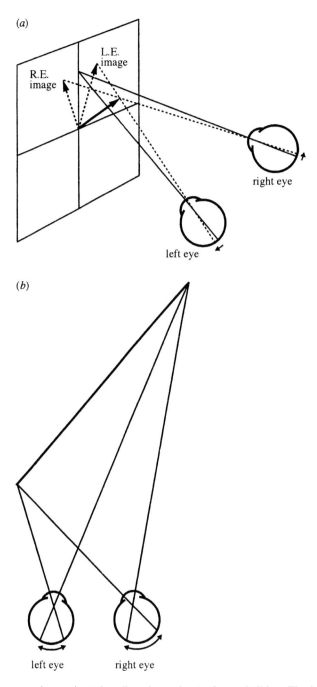

Fig. 12.2 (*a*) Diagram to show orientation disparity owing to forward tilting. The image of the tilted arrow in the right eye is tilted on the screen toward the left (contralateral) side (right eye arrow with broken line) and that in the left eye is tilted toward the right side (left eye arrow with broken line). Crossed disparity of the tip of the arrow is indicated with a small arrow on the back of each eye. (*b*) Diagram to show the width disparity due to the slant of the line in the horizontal plane. The retinal image of the slanted line is longer in the right eye than in the left eye.

neurons in the anterior part of the lateral bank of the intraparietal sulcus (IPS) (AIP area) of alert monkeys have demonstrated that many of them were visually sensitive to the shape, orientation or size of geometric objects for manipulation (Sakata *et al.* 1995; Murata *et al.* 1996). These findings suggested the possibility that some visual neurons in the posterior parietal cortex may be specialized to code the 3D features of objects in a way that is useful for the visual guidance of hand action (Sakata *et al.* 1997*a*). In our search for such visual neurons in the parietal cortex we found binocular visual neurons in the lateral bank of the caudal intraparietal sulcus (c-IPS area) that preferentially respond to a bar, plate or solid object at a particular orientation in space. We studied the visual properties of c-IPS neurons by using a 3D computer graphics display (Kusunoki *et al.* 1996; Shikata *et al.* 1996; Tsutsui *et al.* 1997). The results suggest that the c-IPS area is a higher centre of stereopsis for the extraction of spatial features of objects from sets of binocular disparity signals. It may also incorporate monocular signals for shape discrimination.

12.2 Visual responses of hand manipulation-related neurons

The cortical neurons that are involved in visually guided hand movement were first recorded in the inferior parietal lobule by Mountcastle *et al.* (1975) and Hyvärinen and Poranen (1974). They designated these neurons as 'hand manipulation' neurons. More recently, neurons that are involved in hand movement were found to be concentrated in the AIP area (Sakata *et al.* 1995). This area is strongly interconnected with area F5 of the inferior (ventral) premotor cortex (Matelli *et al.* 1986), in which Rizzolatti *et al.* (1988) recorded 'grasping-with-the-hand neurons'. We recorded the activity of neurons in this area from monkeys that had been trained to manipulate various types of switch (Taira *et al.* 1990; Sakata *et al.* 1995). Many of these hand manipulation task-related neurons were highly selective and were preferentially activated during the manipulation of one of four routinely used objects (push button, pull lever, pull knob and pull knob in groove).

The task-related neurons were classified into three groups according to the difference between the level of neuronal activity during manipulation of the objects in light and that during manipulation of objects in the dark: 'motor-dominant' neurons, 'visual-and-motor' neurons and 'visual-dominant' neurons. Many of the latter two types of visually responsive neurons were activated by the sight of objects during fixation without grasping (object type), although other neurons were not activated during object fixation (non-object type).

(a)   Orientation selectivity of visual-dominant neurons

About one-quarter of the cells were found to be highly selective; the activity of these cells for a particular object was significantly stronger than that for any other objects. The activity profile of one highly selective 'visual-dominant' neuron is shown in figure 12.3. This cell was most strongly activated during manipulation of the pull lever in the light (figure 12.3*a*, left). However, no significant activation occurred during manipulation in the dark (figure 12.3*a*, centre). The cell was fully active during fixation of the lever in the light (figure 12.3*a*, right). The sustained activity during manipulation of the pull lever was smaller than that during object fixation, probably owing to the occlusion of the object by the grasping hand. Most of the cells that showed a stronger response to the pull lever showed selectivity in the orientation of the axis of the lever. This cell showed a stronger response to the upright vertical lever and was sharply tuned to this orientation; the lever in any other orientation did not activate the cell (figure 12.3*b*). However, it was not clear in this series of experiments whether or not the visual-dominant neurons were discriminating the

3D shape of the manipulanda because these objects were selected primarily in terms of the pattern of hand movement.

(b) Selectivity for the 3D shape of objects

In more recent experiments on hand manipulation task-related neurons (Murata *et al*. 1996) we used six different objects of simple geometric shape: sphere, cone, cylinder, cube, ring and square plate. We used three sets of six shapes at different sizes: small, medium and large. These objects were connected to microswitches and set in six sectors of a turntable which presented them in a random order one at a time. As the objects were painted white, they stood out against the black background. The animal was required to grasp and pull the object to turn the microswitch on or fixate on the spot reflected on a half mirror that was superimposed on the object. More than one-quarter of the hand manipulation task-related neurons (32 out of 112) were highly selective for one particular object. The activity profile of one highly selective object-type visual-dominant neuron during the object fixation task is shown in figure 12.4. This cell showed the strongest response to the view of the square plate among the six objects. The square plate and circular ring were the most commonly preferred objects, and many of the cells that preferred these two objects showed selectivity to the orientation of the plate or ring. We also found moderately selective neurons that responded to two or more objects equally well (55 out of 112). Some of these moderately selective neurons showed preference for a certain category of geometric shapes such as round objects (sphere, cone and cylinder), angular objects (cube and square plate), or flat objects (plate and ring). By using a cluster analysis of the response profiles across the six objects, cone, sphere and cylinder were grouped in the same category, and plate, ring and cube were grouped in another category in which plate and ring were the closest. These results suggested that the visually responsive neurons in area AIP may represent spatial characteristics of objects for manipulation, and at least some of these neurons may be involved with recognition of the 3D shape of an object, categorized into a limited number of simple geometric shapes. However, it is not clear where and how the visual signals are processed in the cortical visual pathways to encode 3D shapes.

12.3   Axis-orientation selective neurons

Discrimination of axis-orientation in egocentric space or a viewer-centred coordinate system is important for the manipulation of objects to match the hand orientation with that of the object and may be dissociated from visual axis perception (Perenin and Vighetto 1988; Goodale *et al*. 1991; Milner *et al*. 1991). Indeed, we found that most of the cells that preferred the pull lever were selective for the axis-orientation of the metal rod (see figure 12.3). During further investigation, we found a group of neurons in the lateral bank of the caudal part of the intraparietal sulcus (c-IPS area) that showed selectivity to the orientation of a luminous bar (Kusunoki *et al*. 1993; Sakata and Taira 1994). We recorded the axis orientation selective (AOS) neurons that preferred either vertical, horizontal or sagittal bars or bars tilted to the left or to the right in the frontal plane, tilted either forward or backward in the sagittal plane, and one that responded most strongly to a diagonal bar in between the two planes. It was clear that these neurons had orientation selectivity in 3D space in a viewer-centred coordinate system. The discharge rate of AOS neurons increased monotonically with increasing length of the stimulus. Most of these AOS neurons were binocular visual neurons that responded much less strongly under monocular viewing conditions.

   Therefore, in more recent experiments (Kusunoki *et al*. 1996) we used a 3D computer graphics display to present stimuli with binocular disparity at various orientations, sizes and positions. A back-projection stereoscopic display with a screen size of 105 cm × 150 cm was used.

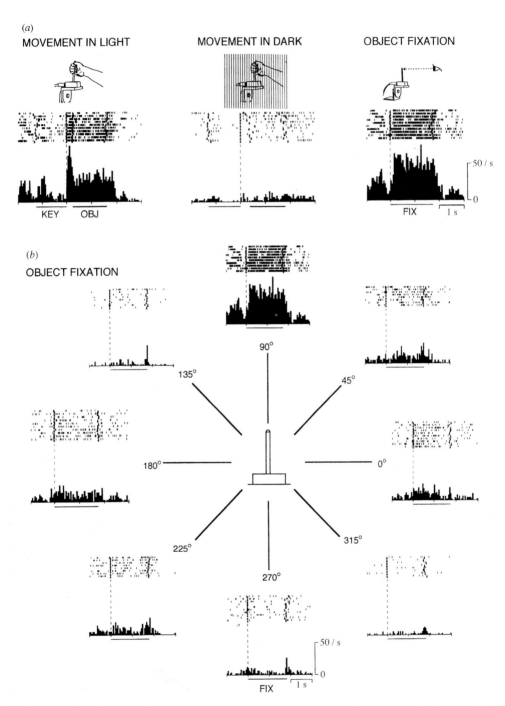

Fig. 12.3 (*a*) Activity of an object-type visual-dominant neuron in area AIP, during manipulation of the pull lever in the light and in the dark as well as during object fixation, shown with rasters and histograms. The cell was not activated during manipulation in the dark. (*b*) Activity of the same neuron during fixation of the lever in various orientations, recorded at intervals of 45° in the frontal plane.

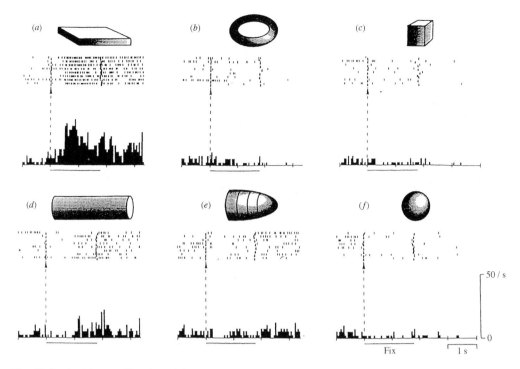

Fig. 12.4 Activity profile of an object-type visual-dominant neuron during object fixation (*Fix*) in the light for six objects of simple geometric shape: (*a*) square plate, (*b*) ring, (*c*) cube, (*d*) cylinder, (*e*) cone and (*f*) sphere (from Murata *et al*. 1996).

Polarizing filters were set in front of the projector and a pair of images with horizontal disparity were presented alternatively (refresh rate: 60 Hz each). The monkey, wearing polarized glasses, fixated on a small spot in the centre of the screen placed at a distance of 100 cm. Figure 12.5 shows an example of an AOS neuron that responded strongly to the diagonal cylinder on the stereoscopic display. An initial survey of orientation tuning for this neuron showed that the preferred orientation was between vertical and 45° backward in the sagittal plane, and between vertical and 45° in the frontal plane. Thus, the best orientation as tilted 22° backward and 22° leftward, and a far stimulus (50 cm from the screen) was better than a near stimulus (figure 12.5*a*). When the polarized glasses were removed and double images were seen, the response to the best stimulus was reduced and the difference due to the distance (far compared with near) was lost (figure 12.5*b*). Response to the monocular stimulus either to the left or the right eye was smaller than that to the binocular stimulus (figure 12.5*c*).

We examined the effect of a change of thickness on the response of the same AOS neuron to a square column in vertical orientation. The response to the square column decreased as the thickness of the column increased and no response was obtained when the width was equal to the length (figure 12.6). Thus, the width response curve showed a monotonic decreasing function within the range of 2–32 cm (figure 12.6, lower graph). This is a general feature of AOS neurons, although the response reached a plateau with intermediate thickness of 10 cm in some AOS neurons. We also examined the effect of changing the length of the stimulus on the screen on the responses of AOS neurons. The discharge rate of the AOS neurons increased monotonically with increasing length of the stimulus. In some neurons the maximum response was obtained with a length as long as 70 cm or more on the screen at 57 cm from the eyes (subtending 50° or more).

These results suggest that AOS neurons represent the orientation of the longitudinal axes of objects in 3D space. The most likely cue for orientation of a line in the sagittal plane is orientation disparity as initially demonstrated by Wheatstone (1838) (see figure 12.2*a*). Blakemore *et al.* (1972) reported that some neurons in the cat striate cortex showed a slight difference in preferred orientation between the two eyes. Hänny and co-workers (1980) also reported a few neurons in the monkey striate cortex that showed tuning to orientation disparity. In the present study, the AOS neurons that showed orientation tuning in the sagittal plane reduced their response drastically when the polarized glasses were removed or the stimulus was presented binocularly with zero disparity, suggesting their sensitivity to orientation disparity. The most likely cue for the slant of the axis in the horizontal plane is width disparity (Howard and Rogers 1995). Although we have not found, so far, any AOS neurons that were tuned to a slanted axis in the horizontal plane, a few neurons showed tuning to a diagonal axis, suggesting their sensitivity to width disparity as well as orientation disparity.

In human patients with parietal lobe lesions, a considerable shift of the vertical and horizontal axes toward the contralesional side was reported by Bender and Jung (1948). McFie and colleagues (1950) described a similar symptom in several patients with a right occipitoparietal lesion. Similar deficits in the perception of line orientation owing to a parietal lobe lesion were reported recently by von Cramon and Kerkhoff (1993). De Renzi and co-workers (1971) reported that patients with right parieto-occipital lesions showed significantly larger errors than the other brain-damaged groups in the task of placing a rod, fixed on a support by a hinged joint, in the same orientation

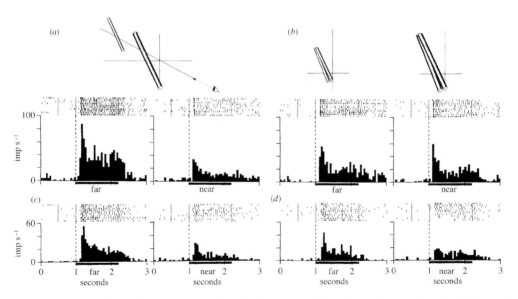

Fig. 12.5 Comparison of the responses of an AOS neuron to binocular and monocular stimulation and the effect of removal of the polarized glasses. (*a*) Response to the best stimulus: a diagonal cylinder (20 cm × 2 cm) tilted 22° backward and 22° leftward at the distance of +50 cm from the screen (150 cm from the eye) compared with the response to the same stimulus at a distance of 50 cm from the eye. (*b*) Response to the same set of stimuli without polarized glasses. (*c*, *d*) Responses to the monocular stimuli of the same parameters.

in space as a model. Therefore, the discrimination of axis orientation is one of the prominent functions of the parietal cortex in the domain of space perception.

12.4 Surface-orientation selective neurons

According to Marr's theory of vision (Marr 1982), the main purpose of vision is object-centred representation of the 3D shape and spatial arrangement of an object. The main stepping stone toward this goal is representing the geometry of the visible surface. Therefore, if 3D shape is to be represented somewhere in the cerebral cortex, there should be an area in the visual cortical pathways that represents surface orientation and curvature.

Discrimination of viewer-centred surface orientation is also important on its own for manipulation of objects. We found that the hand manipulation-related neurons that responded to the view of a square plate showed selectivity to the orientation of the plane. This suggested that some of the parietal visual neurons can discriminate surface orientation. We found that some neurons in the c-IPS area, where we identified AOS neurons, responded preferentially to flat objects such as the square plate or circular disk. We used the 3D computer graphics display to present a solid plate or checkerboard at various orientations and distances and changed stimulus parameters such as width and thickness. The following description is based on a study of 36 parietal visual neurons recorded in three hemispheres of two Japanese monkeys (*Macaca fuscata*; Shikata *et al.* 1996).

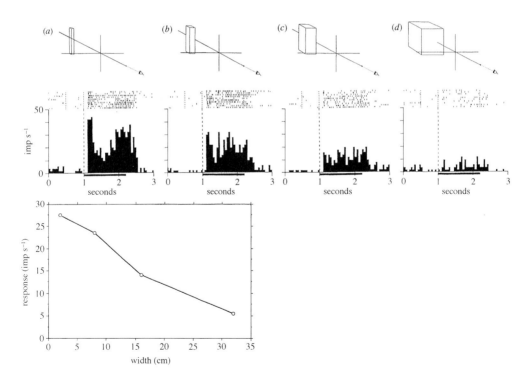

Fig. 12.6 Response of an AOS neuron to a square column of various widths. The maximum response was obtained with a thin column with a width of 2 cm. (*a*) 2 cm × 2 cm × 30 cm; (*b*) 8 cm × 8 cm × 30 cm; (*c*) 16 cm × 16 cm × 30 cm; (*d*) 32 cm × 32 cm × 30 cm. The width response curve is shown below.

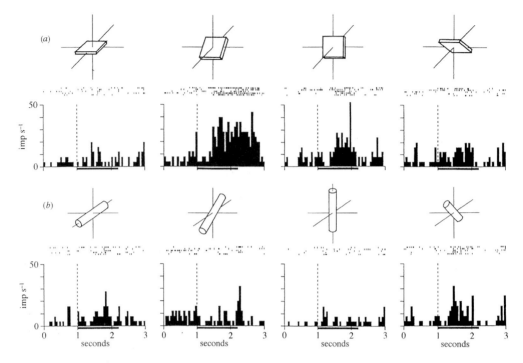

Fig. 12.7 Responses of an SOS neuron that preferred a square plate (15 cm × 15 cm × 2 cm) tilted: (*a*) backward to a cylinder (20 cm × 4 cm); (*b*) in the same orientation to the cylinder.

We first compared the responses of cells to a flat stimulus with responses to an elongated stimulus. A total of 17 cells that preferred the flat to the elongated stimulus (17 out of 32) showed selectivity to the surface orientation of the stimulus presented on the screen of the stereoscopic display. A total of 13 of these cells (13 out of 17) were defined as surface-orientation selective (SOS) neurons with a criterion of high orientation index (O.I. ≥ 2), with O.I. response to optimal surface–response to orthogonal surface. Figure 12.7 shows an example of an SOS neuron that responded preferentially to a square plate tilted 45° backward (figure 12.7*a*). No response was obtained when a cylinder was presented at the same orientation (figure 12.7*b*). Almost all SOS neurons responded more strongly to a binocular than to a monocular stimulus. The responses of all of the SOS neurons tested ($n = 6$) changed with the depth on the stereoscopic display (we changed disparity while keeping the size of the stimulus on the screen constant). Half of these SOS neurons responded to near stimuli, and the other half responded to far stimuli. None of these neurons showed as sharp a tuning in depth as tuned excitatory cells, but their depth-tuning curves showed a plateau, similar to a near cell that responds over a range of crossed disparities or a far cell that responds over a range of uncrossed disparities as defined by Poggio and Fischer (1977), except that the range of disparity for the excitatory response was larger than that in the case of the disparity-selective neurons in V1 and V3A (Poggio *et al.* 1988).

To verify that the SOS neurons responded to an extended surface rather than an edge or corner, we studied the effect of changing the width of the stimulus. In contrast to the AOS neurons, the magnitude of the response of SOS neurons to the stimulus decreased gradually as the width was reduced and the stimulus changed from a square to a narrow rectangular plate or bar as shown in figure 12.8, although the response reached a plateau or peak at some intermediate width. Most

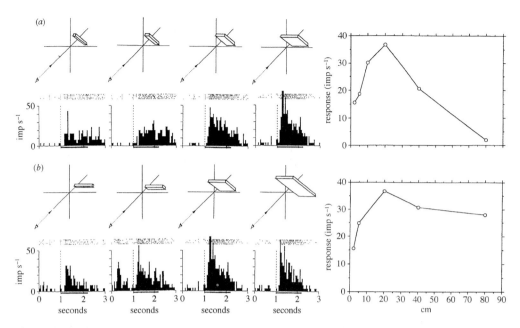

Fig. 12.8 Responses of an SOS neuron to a plate of various widths and lengths. (*a*) Responses of the cell to a plate of various widths ranging from 2–20 cm and the width response curve up to 80 cm. (*b*) Responses of the cell to a plate of various lengths ranging from 2–40 cm and the length response curve up to 80 cm (from Shikata *et al.* 1996).

of the SOS neurons showed no change in response intensity with a change in stimulus shape (for example, disc compared with square plate) or even thickness, suggesting that they represented the orientation of the flat surface in space independently of shape. However, some of them preferred a thin to a thick plate, and a square plate to a disc, showing selectivity to both the shape and stimulus orientation.

More recently, we trained a monkey on a delayed match-to-sample (DMS) task discriminating surface orientation of the stereoscopic stimuli in a random dot stereogram (RDS) as well as in a solid figure stereogram (SFS) with binocular contour disparity, to discover whether SOS neurons respond to a square at various orientations embedded in the RDS (Tsutsui *et al.* 1997). We identified 27 SOS neurons in the c-IPS area and examined 18 of them for their response to RDS and SFS. All of these 18 cells showed tuning in surface orientation in the routine test of nine orientations; frontal, backward and forward tilt (45°) leftward and rightward slant (45°), and four diagonal orientations of combined tilt and slant.

A total of 11 SOS neurons responded to RDS stimuli and showed orientation tuning. A total of five of these 11 cells showed orientation tuning even when the stimulus did not have any perspective cues at its edges, suggesting that the cells discriminated the surface orientation purely from disparity gradient as Marr (1982) predicted in his theory of vision. A total of nine out of 13 SOS neurons that responded to SFS with disparate contours showed orientation tuning even when the contours of the square did not have any perspective cues for orientation in depth, suggesting that the cells discriminated the surface orientation of the square using orientation disparity and/or width disparity.

There has not been much clinical evidence that the parietal cortex is involved in the perception of surface orientation, except for the confusion of planes in drawings by patients with right parieto-occipital lesions (Paterson and Zangwill 1944; McFie *et al.* 1950; Ettlinger *et al.* 1957), for example, the frame of a bicycle was drawn in the frontal plane while the wheels were drawn in the sagittal plane. However, disturbances in the ability to draw 3D shapes such as houses (Piercy and de Ajuriaguerra 1960) or copy block designs (Critchley 1953) may be partly owing to a disturbance in the ability to perceive surface orientation. Recently, the performance of a visual agnosia patient with relatively intact parieto-frontal cortical function was studied in a task of matching the orientation of a plate held in the hand to that of a plate presented visually in front of the body (Dijkerman *et al.* 1996). The patient performed very poorly in this task under monocular viewing conditions, suggesting that the parietal cortex depends on binocular input for the discrimination of surface orientation when information from the ventral visual pathways is unavailable.

12.5 Selectivity in 3D shape

During the study of AOS neurons and SOS neurons, we found cells in the same area that preferred a solid stimulus to a flat or thin stimulus. Figure 12.9 shows the responses of one such cell that was classified as an AOS neuron. When we examined the effect of changes in thickness, we found that the cell responded most strongly to a cylinder of intermediate thickness (10 cm diameter). The length–response curve peaked at an intermediate length (20 cm), and a dramatic change was observed when we changed the shape of the stimulus (figure 12.9*a*). The cell responded most strongly to a cylinder (10 cm × 20 cm) tilted backward and to the right, but a square column of the same size and orientation elicited only a weak response, and a square plate (20 cm × 20 cm) in the same orientation was even less effective than the square column. The cell was strongly binocular, showing almost no response to monocular stimulation, and was activated only by stimuli nearer than the fixation point. Thus, the cell was likely to discriminate a cylinder from a square column on the basis of surface curvature. This supports the hypothesis that there is a class of binocular stereoscopic neurons in the lateral bank of the caudal IPS that discriminates the 3D shape of objects using stereopsis.

There is no direct clinical neuropsychological evidence that the parietal cortex is involved in the perception of 3D shape. However, if one examines the drawings by a patient with a right parietal lobe lesion, disturbances in the ability to draw 3D objects such as a cube or a house may be seen clearly (for example, see Hécaen *et al.* 1956). The results of a number of studies on constructional apraxia owing to parieto-occipital lesion suggest that the right hemisphere supplies a perceptual component and the left hemisphere an executive component to visuoconstructional tasks (Warrington 1969). Therefore, the symptom of constructional apraxia owing to parietal lesion may be indirect evidence that the parietal cortex is involved in the perception of 3D shape.

12.6 Discussion

One of the most surprising findings from our study of hand manipulation task-related neurons in area AIP was that a number of task-related neurons showed selectivity for 3D shape, as visual form perception has previously been attributed to the ventral visual pathway and the inferotemporal cortex according to the concept of two cortical visual systems (Ungerleider and Mishkin 1982). However, our finding fits with the idea that the visual projection system to the parietal cortex provides action-relevant information about the structure and orientation of objects (Goodale and Milner 1992). Information about 3D shape is necessary to guide preshaping of the hand that is disturbed by posterior parietal lesions (Jeannerod *et al.* 1994). To manipulate objects, it is necessary to construct their 3D representations in viewer-centred coordinates (Sutherland 1979), and binocular stereopsis is essential for that purpose. The neurons of area c-IPS that were sensitive to binocular disparity and selective for the 3D orientation of the longitudinal axis or surface together with the neurons that were selective for 3D shape are likely to meet these requirements.

The most interesting finding from our studies of the functional properties of c-IPS neurons by using a 3D computer graphics display was that many of the SOS neurons responded to squares embedded in random dot stereograms, and showed orientation tuning in depth. This provided us with clear evidence that at least some of the SOS neurons discriminated surface orientation on the basis of the change of binocular disparity, as postulated by David Marr (1982) in his theory of vision. As shown in figure 12.1 a slanted surface produces a gradual increase of disparity from the fovea to the periphery along the horizontal meridian, and an inclined surface produces a similar gradient of binocular disparity along the vertical meridian. If one postulates that the SOS neurons integrate the signals of a set of disparity-sensitive neurons with different optimal disparities, neural

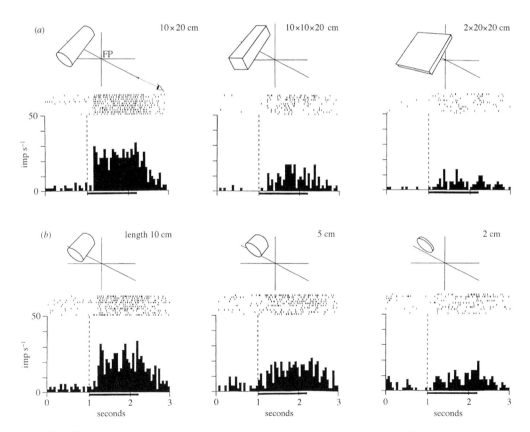

Fig. 12.9 Responses of an AOS neuron that showed a stronger response to a cylinder of intermediate length and thickness. (*a*) Responses of the cell to a stimulus of different shapes in the same orientation, from the left, cylinder, square column and square plate. (*b*) Responses of the cell to a cylinder of various lengths ranging from 2–10 cm. (From Sakata et al. 1997*b*.)

computation of the surface orientation in depth is feasible. Equally important was the finding that some of the SOS neurons responded to squares with contours with orientation disparity and/or width disparity, without any monocular cues for depth such as linear perspective, texture gradient or shading. These disparities of contours are even more important for the discrimination of axis orientation in depth. As shown in figure 12.2, tilted and slanted lines in the sagittal and horizontal planes produce orientation disparity and width disparity, respectively. If one postulates that AOS neurons combine the signals from a pair of monocular neurons with slightly different preferred orientations or preferred lengths, the cell will be tuned to axis orientation in depth. The fact that AOS neurons and SOS neurons coexist in the c-IPS area suggests that the main processing site of these disparities is not at the level of the striate and prestriate cortex, but at the level of the association cortex. It also implies that integration of orientation and width disparity may not happen at an early stage of vision, as postulated by Julesz (1971), but may happen at a later stage after some integration of line orientation. Thus, the present results have led us to a reappraisal of Wheatstone's original idea that the combination of slightly different perspective images from the two eyes results in the perception of the 3D features of objects.

The present results also provide some evidence that c-IPS neurons may be concerned with the discrimination of 3D shape on the basis of binocular disparity. However, further investigation is necessary to elucidate the mechanism of discrimination of surface curvature and surface boundary to get solid evidence that the representation of 3D shape is constructed in this area. It is also important to investigate how monocular cues of depth are integrated with binocular disparity cues in the parietal cortex, as there are reciprocal connections between the posterolateral bank of the IPS and inferotemporal cortex that may convey monocular cues for shape (Webster *et al.* 1994). It may be concluded from the present investigation that area c-IPS adjacent to area V3A is a higher centre of stereopsis that integrates various binocular disparity signals to represent neural codes of 3D features of objects and sends them to area AIP for the visual guidance of hand movement.

Acknowledgements

We gratefully acknowledge the support from the Ministry of Education, Science and Culture of Japan (05267105, 07244103 and 04NP0101) and the research grant from the Human Frontier Science Program (1990–92 and 1993–95).

References

Barlow, H. B., Blakemore, C. and Pettigrew, J. D. 1967 The neural mechanism of binocular depth discrimination. *J. Physiol.* **193**, 327–42.

Bender, M. B. and Jung, R. 1948 Abweichungen der subjektiven optischen Vertikalen und Horizontalen bei Gesunden und Hirnverletzten. *Arch. Psychiat. Nervenkr.* **181**, 193–212.

Blakemore, C., Fiorentini, A. and Maffei, L. 1972 A second neural mechanism of binocular depth discrimination. *J. Physiol.* **226**, 725–49.

Critchley, M. 1953 *The parietal lobes*. London: Arnold.

De Renzi, E., Faglioni, P. and Scotti, G. 1971 Judgement of spatial orientation in patients with focal brain damage. *J. Neurol. Neurosurg. Psychiatr.* **34**, 489–95.

Dijkerman, H. C., Milner, A. D. and Carey, D. P. 1996 The perception and prehension of objects oriented in the depth plane. I. Effects of visual form agnosia. *Exp. Brain Res.* **112**, 442–51.

Ettlinger, G., Warrington, E. and Zangwill, O. L. 1957 A further study of visual-spatial agnosia. *Brain* **80**, 335–61.

Goodale, M. A. and Milner, A. D. 1992 Separate visual pathways for perception and action. *Trends Neurosci.* **15**, 20–25.

Goodale, M. A., Milner, A. D., Jakobson, L. S. and Carey, D. P. 1991 A neurological dissociation between perceiving objects and grasping them. *Nature* **349**, 154–6.

Hänny, P., von der Heydt, R. and Poggio, G. F. 1980 Binocular neuron responses to tilt in depth in the monkey visual cortex. Evidence for orientation disparity processing. *Exp. Brain Res.* A **41**, 26.

Hécaen, H., Penfield, W., Bertrand, C. and Malmo, R. 1956 The syndrome of apractognosia due to lesions of the minor cerebral hemisphere. *Arch. Neurol. Psychiatr.* **75**, 400–34.

Howard, I. P. and Rogers, B. J. 1995 *Binocular vision and stereopsis.* Oxford University Press.

Hubel, D. H. and Livingstone, M. S. 1987 Segregation of form, color and stereopsis in primate area 18. *J. Neurosci.* **7**, 3378–415.

Hyvärinen, J. and Poranen, A. 1974 Function of the parietal associative area 7 as revealed from cellular discharge in alert monkeys. *Brain* **97**, 673–92.

Jeannerod, M., Decety, J. and Michel, F. 1994 Impairment of grasping movements following a bilateral posterior parietal lesion. *Neuropsychologia* **32**, 369–80.

Julesz, B. 1971 *Foundations of cyclopean perception.* University of Chicago Press.

Kusunoki, M., Tanaka, Y., Ohtsuka, H., Ishiyama, K. and Sakata, H. 1993 Selectivity of the parietal visual neurons in the axis orientation of objects in space. *Soc. Neurosci. Abstr.* **19**, 770.

Kusunoki, M., Tanaka, Y., Shikata, E., Nakamura, H. and Sakata, H. 1996 Response properties of axis-orientation of surface of stereoscopic stimuli. *Soc. Neurosci. Abstr.* **22**, 398.

McFie, J., Piercy, M. F. and Zangwill, O. L. 1950 Visual-spatial agnosia associated with lesions of the right cerebral hemisphere. *Brain* **73**, 167–90.

Marr, D. 1982 *Vision.* San Francisco: Freeman.

Matelli, M., Camarda, R., Glickstein, M. and Rizzolatti, G. 1986 Afferent and efferent projections of the inferior area 6 in the macaque monkey. *J. Comp. Neurol.* **251**, 281–98.

Milner, A. D. (and 10 others) 1991 Perception and action in 'visual form agnosia'. *Brain* **114**, 405–428.

Mountcastle, V. B., Lynch, J. C., Georgopoulos, A., Sakata, H. and Acuna, C. 1975 Posterior parietal association cortex of the monkey: command functions for operations within extrapersonal space. *J. Neurophysiol.* **38**, 871–908.

Murata, A., Gallese, V., Kaseda, M. and Sakata, H. 1996 Parietal neurons related to memory-guided hand manipulation. *J. Neurophysiol.* **75**, 2180–6.

Nikara, T., Bishop, P. O. and Pettigrew, J. D. 1968 Analysis of retinal correspondence by studying receptive fields of binocular single units in cat striate cortex. *Exp. Brain Res.* **6**, 353–72.

Paterson, A. and Zangwill, O. L. 1944 Disorders of visual space perception associated with lesions of the right cerebral hemisphere. *Brain* **67**, 331–58.

Perenin, M. T. and Vighetto, A. 1988 Optic ataxia: a specific disruption in visuo-motor mechanism. I. Different aspects of the deficit in reaching for objects. *Brain* **111**, 643–74.

Piercy, M. H. and de Ajuriaguerra, J. 1960 Constructional apraxia associated with unilateral cerebral lesions; left and right sided cases compared. *Brain* **83**, 225–42.

Poggio, G. F. and Fischer, B. 1977 Binocular interaction and depth sensitivity in striate and prestriate cortex of behaving rhesus monkeys. *J. Neurophysiol.* **40**, 1392–405.

Poggio, G. F., Gonzalaz, F. and Krause, F. 1988 Stereoscopic mechanisms in monkey visual cortex: binocular correlation and disparity selectivity. *J. Neurosci.* **8**, 4531–50.

Rizzolatti, G., Camarda, R., Fogassi, L., Gentilucci, M., Luppino, G. and Matelli, M. 1988 Functional organization of inferior area 6 in the macaque monkey. II. Area F5 and the control of distal movement. *Exp. Brain Res.* **71**, 491–507.

Sakata, H. and Taira, M. 1994 Parietal control of hand action. *Curr. Opin. Neurobiol.* **4**, 847–56.

Sakata, H., Taira, M., Murata, A. and Mine, S. 1995 Neural mechanisms of visual guidance of hand action in the parietal cortex of the monkey. *Cerebr. Cortex* **5**, 429–38.

Sakata, H., Taira, M., Kusunoki, M., Murata, A. and Tanaka, Y. 1997*a* The parietal association cortex in depth perception and visual control of hand action. *Trends Neurosci.* **20**, 350–7.

Sakata, H., Taira, M., Murata, A., Gallese, V., Tanaka, Y., Shikata, E. and Kusunoki, M. 1997*b* Parietal visual neurons coding 3D characteristics of objects and their relation to hand action. In *Parietal lobe* *contributions to orientation in 3D-space* (eds P. Thier and H. O. Karnath), pp. 237–54. *Exp. Brain Res. Suppl. Series*. Berlin and New York: Springer.

Shikata, E., Tanaka, Y., Nakamura, H., Taira, M. and Sakata, H. 1996 Selectivity of the parietal visual neurons in 3D orientation of surface of stereoscopic stimuli. *NeuroReport* **7**, 2385–94.

Sutherland, N. S. 1979 The representation of three-dimensional objects. *Nature* **278**, 395–98.

Taira, M., Mine, S., Georgopoulos, A. P., Murata, A. and Sakata, H. 1990 Parietal cortex neurons of the monkey related to the visual guidance of hand movement. *Exp. Brain Res.* **83**, 29–36.

Tsutsui, K., Taira, M., Jiang, M. and Sakata, H. 1997 Processing of 3D visual features by neurons in monkey caudal intraparietal sulcus. *Soc. Neurosci. Abstr.* **23**, 1546.

Ungerleider, L. G. and Mishkin, M. 1982 Two cortical visual systems. In *Analysis of visual behavior* (eds D. J. Ingle, M. A. Goodale and R. J. W. Mansfield), pp. 549–86. Cambridge, MA: MIT Press.

Warrington, E. K. 1969 Constructional apraxia. In *Handbook of clinical neurology*, vol. 4 (eds P. J. Vinken and G. W. Bruyn). Amsterdam: North-Holland.

Webster, M. J., Bachevalier, J. and Ungerleider, L. G. 1994 Connections of inferior temporal areas TEO and TE with parietal and frontal cortex in macaque monkey. *Cerebr. Cortex* **5**, 470–83.

Wheatstone, C. 1838 Contributions to the physiology of vision part the first on some remarkable and hitherto unobserved phenomena of binocular vision. *Phil. Trans. R. Soc. Lond.* B **128**, 371–84.

von Cramon, D. Y. and Kerkhoff, G. 1993 On the cerebral organization of elementary visuo-spatial perception. In *Functional organization of the human visual cortex* (eds B. Gulyas, D. Ottoson and P. E. Roland). Oxford: Pergamon Press.

Zeki, S. M. 1978 The third visual complex of rhesus monkey prestriate cortex. *J. Physiol.* **277**, 245–72.

13

Neuropsychological studies of perception and visuomotor control

A. D. Milner

Abstract

According to recent conceptualizations, there are two separate cortical visual systems—each with its own distinctive cortical and subcortical links—and these two systems respectively serve the functions of perception and of motor control. These ideas have been arrived at through a confluence of neuroanatomical, electrophysiological, behavioural, and neuropsychological research. It is proposed that this distinction between two broad purposes of vision and their neural bases can provide useful working procedures for analysing both (i) the nature of visuomotor processing in the normal brain and also (ii) the abnormal patterns of visual processing that are seen in certain neurological conditions.

13.1 Introduction

The human brain appears to have two somewhat distinct visual systems operating in parallel within it (Milner and Goodale 1995). One system provides the visual contents of our perceptual experience, and codes information in an abstract form suitable for storage and for deploying in cognitive processes like imagining, recognizing, and planning. The other visual system serves the much more immediate function of guiding our actions from moment to moment, and therefore needs to code information in a quick, ephemeral and view-specific form. Its contents are probably not accessible for cognitive elaboration or conscious monitoring.

An important part of the evidence that has led to these conclusions has been provided by neuropsychology. It has been known for over 100 years that bilateral damage to the posterior parietal cortex in monkeys causes severe visuomotor difficulties in reaching for and grasping food objects (Ferrier and Yeo 1884), and it has been known for nearly 90 years that comparable damage in humans results in closely similar difficulties (Bálint 1909; see Harvey 1995). Bálint's patient had great difficulty in reaching out to take hold of objects under visual guidance; yet this was not due to a purely visual difficulty, because he only reached inaccurately when he used his right hand. Presumably, therefore, his more successful left hand must have had access to the necessary visuospatial information. In addition, Bálint's patient could touch parts of his own body quite accurately even with his right hand, showing that his difficulties were not simply motor. Bálint thus concluded that the disorder must be *visuomotor*, and he coined the term 'optic ataxia' to refer to it.

We now know that optic ataxia not only affects the visuomotor control of actions within the spatial domain, but also prevents patients from accurately forming their grip size in anticipation of grasping objects of different sizes (Jeannerod 1986; Jakobson *et al.* 1991; Jeannerod *et al.* 1994). We also know that optic ataxia causes gross visual errors in guiding the orientation of the wrist. This was first shown by asking patients to extricate a small object lodged in a groove that was presented at different angles from trial to trial (Tzavaras and Masure 1976), and later by asking similar patients to pass the hand through a large oriented slot (Perenin and Vighetto 1988). Complementary studies have shown that the visual perception of size (Jeannerod *et al.* 1994), as well as of location and orientation (Perenin and Vighetto 1988) can remain largely intact in these same patients.

Of course these findings alone would not force us to conclude that there were two separate visual processing systems, one mediating perception, and the other motor control. It was, in fact, generally inferred from the results that optic ataxia resulted from a disconnection between an intact perceptual system and an intact system for motor control. Thus perception could remain intact while visuomotor control was lost. But that hypothesis, which assumes that the visual control of action is achieved through a serial linkage between perceptual and motor systems, would not be able to explain a converse pattern of dissociations from those described by Jeannerod *et al.* (1994) and Perenin and Vighetto (1988). That is, it would not be able to account for a pattern in which perception was lost yet visuomotor control remained intact.

Yet this opposite pattern is exactly what we found a few years ago (Milner *et al.* 1991) in a patient suffering from a remarkably pure form of the condition known as 'visual form agnosia' (Benson and Greenberg 1969). Our patient, D.F., has a profound difficulty in perceiving and discriminating simple shapes, or even their size or orientation, much like previously described cases of this disorder (Goldstein and Gelb 1918; Efron 1969; Abadi *et al.* 1981). But she is far from being severely impaired in visuomotor control, as the serial processing hypothesis would predict. Instead, she is indistinguishable from normal control subjects in her ability to orient her wrist when reaching to pass her hand or 'post' a hand-held plaque through a slot placed at different orientations (Goodale *et al.* 1991; Milner *et al.* 1991). Similarly she is quite normal in her ability to tailor her grip size during reaching movements to grasp blocks of different sizes (Goodale *et al.* 1991).

This clear double dissociation between perception and visuomotor control is difficult to account for except on the assumption that the two visual functions are mediated by separate visual processing systems. And this assumption is strengthened by a host of neuroanatomical and neurophysiological evidence which has identified two broad groupings of visual areas in the primate cerebral cortex with quite distinct neural outputs and quite distinct functional correlates (Milner and Goodale 1995). These two visual systems were first unambiguously identified by Ungerleider and Mishkin (1982), who traced a 'dorsal pathway' from primary visual cortex (V1) to posterior parietal cortex (PPC) and a 'ventral pathway' from V1 to inferior temporal cortex (ITC). Although many more cortical visual areas have since been discovered, this broad division has been bolstered by more recent studies of the cortico-cortical anatomy (Morel and Bullier 1990; Baizer *et al.* 1991; Felleman and Van Essen 1991; Young 1992).

Ungerleider and Mishkin (1982) reviewed the contrasting effects of experimental lesions to these two systems, and also the contrasting physiological properties of single neurons in the two systems. They took the evidence overall as supporting their working hypothesis that the two pathways processed different aspects of the visual array, specifically that 'the ventral or occipitotemporal pathway is specialized for object perception (identifying *what* an object is) whereas the dorsal or occipitoparietal pathway is specialized for spatial perception (locating *where* an object is)' (p. 549). But in that same year, Glickstein and May (1982) also wrote an important review, starting with a different emphasis and reaching a rather different conclusion as to the functions of the two systems. Instead of contrasting the visual inputs the ventral and dorsal areas received, they contrasted the output connections of the two systems. They reported that several dorsal visual areas send profuse neuronal projections to the superior colliculus and to motor nuclei in the pons, while none of the ventral visual areas do this. These brainstem target structures in turn supply visual information to the cerebellum (the superior colliculus doing so via the pontine nuclei). Glickstein and May therefore proposed that 'The behavioural, anatomical, and physiological evidence suggests that the parietal lobe visual areas are especially concerned with the visual guidance of movement' (1982, p. 136).

More recent evidence confirms the differential outputs of the two systems and thereby gives further clues to their respective functions. It transpires that areas in the dorsal system project not only to sensorimotor areas in the brainstem, but also to specific premotor areas in the frontal lobe, each related to different action domains such as saccadic eye movements, arm reaching movements, and hand grasping movements (Cavada and Goldman-Rakic 1989; Boussaoud et al. 1996; Wise et al. 1997). On the other hand, the ITC has strong reciprocal connections with the amygdala (see, for example, Baizer et al. 1993), a structure with which the PPC in contrast has very few if any interconnections. The amygdala is implicated in processes of learning to associate visual stimuli with reward (see, for example, Mishkin 1982; Gaffan et al. 1988) and also with social and emotional cues (Kling and Brothers 1992; Brothers and Ring 1993). Thus, whereas the dorsal system has direct and rapid access to motor-related systems, the ventral stream seems to provide the visual route to associative learning, and can thereby mediate more flexible and long-term visual effects on behaviour.

Recent neurophysiological evidence also favours Glickstein and May's (1982) interpretation, and at the same time allows us to extend the scope of their hypothesis. Although their emphasis was on visuomotor control rather than on visuospatial perception, nevertheless they saw the main role of the dorsal system as supplying visual information for the guidance of actions in space. At that time it was already known from the work of Hyvärinen and Poranen (1974), Mountcastle et al. (1975), and others, that out of six categories of visually driven neurons in the monkey's PPC, five would require visual coding of the egocentric spatial location of the stimulus: (i) visual saccade neurons; (ii) visual tracking neurons; (iii) arm-projection neurons; (iv) visual fixation neurons; and (v) light-sensitive neurons (cells that did not appear to have any selective association with a particular kind of behaviour on the part of the animal). None of these categories of cells seemed to have any selectivity for stimulus shape or orientation. But Mountcastle et al. (1975) did identify a sixth group of visual neurons, albeit without exploring them in detail: 'manipulation' neurons. It was not until 1990 that Sakata, one of the original co-authors in the Mountcastle et al. (1975) paper, began to publish more detailed studies of these cells (see Sakata et al., this volume).

The first of these reports from Sakata's laboratory was by Taira et al. (1990). By showing that many neurons in the anterior part of the intraparietal sulcus (an area now known as AIP) are not only selectively associated with specific visual stimuli, but are very non-selective with regard to the location of those stimuli, these authors refuted the notion that visual processing in PPC is restricted to an analysis of visual space. Most of the cells they recorded from were associated with particular motor acts (grasping, pulling, pushing, and so on), rather like a group of neurons that Rizzolatti et al. (1988) had previously found in area F5 of the premotor cortex. It is surely not coincidental that areas F5 and AIP are heavily and reciprocally interconnected (Godschalk et al. 1984; Matelli et al. 1986). Sakata and his colleagues have recently gone further, revealing neurons in a more posterior part of the intraparietal sulcus selective for visual object properties such as stimulus orientation in three dimensions, and the height : width ratio of elongated shapes (Shikata et al. 1996).

In short, the balance of evidence from both electrophysiological and neuropsychological sources has now shifted decisively in favour of viewing the dorsal visual stream as dedicated to the guidance of movements rather than to the analysis of space (Milner and Goodale 1995). Furthermore, although visual space clearly does have to be analysed to provide guidance for movements of the eyes, head, arm, wrist, and the body as a whole, it is now quite certain that this spatial analysis is not done by a single all-purpose system in the PPC. There is a growing range of evidence from monkey electrophysiology (see, for example, Colby and Duhamel 1997; Andersen *et al.* 1997; Snyder *et al.* 1997) for several visuospatial coding systems in PPC, each associated with a different response modality (e.g. saccades versus arm reaches). Neuroimaging studies show that the same is true in the human posterior parietal cortex: there are separate visual representations for guiding eye and hand movements towards the same stimulus locations (Kawashima *et al.* 1996). In the case of stimulus motion, the neuronal signals are beginning to be analysed separately for different oculomotor purposes even within the monkey's 'purely visual' area MT (V5). As would be expected, microstimulation at a given locus within MT generally influences pursuit and saccadic eye movements in consistent ways, as if there was a real perturbation of the visual stimulus velocity (Gruh *et al.* 1997). But occasionally such stimulation affects the two oculomotor responses in quite different, inconsistent, ways. Presumably therefore, different outputs regarding visual motion are already being processed in MT for transmission on to separate saccadic and tracking systems in such areas as 7a and LIP.

13.2 The dorsal stream uncovered

A felicitous coherence between recent electrophysiological and neuropsychological findings has thus allowed us to decide between two equally promising interpretations of (at that time) ambiguous data on dorsal stream function (Glickstein and May 1982; Ungerleider and Mishkin 1982). Remarkably, in fact, the visuomotor function discovered in patient D.F. matches very closely what one would expect from a person with an intact but isolated dorsal system, given the physiological evidence from neurons in the monkey PPC. For example, Shikata *et al.* (1996) have observed that the selectivity of neurons in the monkey intraparietal sulcus to the orientation of a surface lying in depth is very sensitive to binocular input. When one eye is covered, most of the neurons lose their orientation selectivity. In precisely the same way, we have found that although D.F. is qualitatively and quantitatively indistinguishable from normal controls when reaching to grasp a 5 cm^2 plaque that is tilted in the sagittal plane when she uses binocular vision, her performance declines dramatically when she views the shape monocularly (Dijkerman *et al.* 1996; Milner 1997*b*).

In another set of experiments, D.F. has been tested with a variety of patterns presented on sheets of paper at different orientations, and asked to 'stamp' them with an inked elongated block, as if 'posting' the block into a slot. From this it has been possible to explore the cues to contour that she can use to guide the orientation of her manual responses. As one might expect, D.F.'s accuracy when responding to oriented luminance contours is good (Goodale *et al.* 1994*a*). She can respond well above chance to the 'columns' in a dot matrix whose column–row dot spacing has a ratio of 1 : 6 or 1 : 4, thus exploiting the Gestalt principle of 'grouping by proximity' (E. Ashbridge and D. I. Perrett, unpublished data). D.F.'s responses, however, were not improved by the addition of 'grouping by similarity' cues such as colour (alternating red and green columns of dots). Furthermore, for displays eliminating proximity cues (i.e. with a column–row ratio of 1 : 1), she was unable to use grouping by colour similarity to guide her responses. Yet D.F. is not achromatopsic: she could identify verbally, and point to, individual coloured spots among an array of spots of different colours. She was also well able to direct her stamping responses to the orientation of patterns of abutting bars alternating in colour (E. Ashbridge and D. I. Perrett, unpublished data). These results fit well with what is known of colour coding in the dorsal stream: whereas MT neurons are unselective for particular wavelengths, many of them continue nevertheless to respond to the orientation of a wavelength defined boundary, even at equiluminance (Saito *et al.* 1989).

The extent to which D.F.'s visuomotor control in everyday situations resembles that of normal control subjects encourages us to treat her as an 'experiment of nature' which might help us to delineate the visual limits of the human dorsal visual system. This approach gains still further encouragement from the two described instances where her performance breaks down under conditions where, from our knowledge of primate electrophysiology, we would expect the system to break down. We have therefore examined the limits of D.F.'s visual processing for motor control in a variety of other task situations, with a view to erecting hypotheses as to the operating characteristics of the normal human dorsal stream. These hypotheses would be difficult, of course, to test directly in humans, but they would make falsifiable predictions as to the upper-limit properties of neurons within the monkey dorsal stream.

Previous demonstrations of both temporal and spatial limits on D.F.'s visuomotor control have been summarized in a previous paper (Milner 1997*b*). Thus she is able to scale her grip size appropriately to grasp blocks of different sizes when they are immediately present to her eyes, but her grip scaling falls to chance when a delay of 2 s or more is imposed on her response. This indicates that a short visual 'memory' is characteristic of the visuomotor system underlying D.F.'s grasping.

In more recent studies, we have found that delays of a few seconds also severely reduce the spatial accuracy of both D.F.'s saccadic eye movements (Dijkerman *et al.* 1997), and her manual reaching movements (Milner *et al.* 1998*b*). Yet her immediate saccades and immediate reaches to the identical visual targets are both of normal accuracy. These new results indicate that there are low limits on the time for which useful visuospatial information is retained within the posterior parietal systems governing both saccadic eye movements and manual reaches in D.F. Future work may allow us to determine whether the time constants are the same in these three domains of visuomotor control (grasping, reaching and saccades).

The *spatial* limits on D.F.'s visuomotor system are obvious from her poor performance in copying or matching tasks. A response made at a site shifted away from the stimulus loses its accuracy quite dramatically. For example, if she is shown a single line drawn on a piece of paper she is initially unable to copy its orientation on a separate piece of paper (Dijkerman and Milner 1997). Yet she is able to trace over a single oriented line, and even 'cheat' in the copying task by tracing the presented line 'in the air' before then promptly drawing her copy. In fact, she can even deploy the strategy of imagining herself tracing over the line while holding the pencil to the paper and then transform this imagined movement into a fairly successful copying response (Dijkerman and Milner 1997). Interestingly, D.F.'s introspection when doing this is that if she delays more than a second or two before committing the pencil to paper when using this motor imagery strategy, then she 'loses it'.

Other limits on D.F.'s spared visual coding have become apparent by exploring in various ways her ability to process visual form. For example, we have extended the 'posting task' mentioned earlier to see whether she could post a T-shaped object into a T-shaped aperture presented in the frontal plane in front of her. We found that she divided her responses almost 50 : 50 between two kinds of hand orientation: one in which the shape correctly corresponded to the orientation of the T-shaped aperture, and the other in which the orientation was approximately 90° away from the target orientation (Goodale *et al.* 1994*a*). In other words, she was able to rotate her wrist correctly with respect to one of the two orientations of the T-shaped aperture, but was not able to take the orientations of both segments of the T into account in turning her wrist.

In another attempt to explore the shape processing capacity of D.F.'s visuomotor system, we used a grasping task. She was presented with a solid cross shape in the frontal plane, the two bars of the cross being 7.5 cm in length and 1.6 cm in width. We found in this task that normal control subjects consistently reached out to grasp the cross using the thumb and three middle fingers, tailoring the orientation of the wrist such that each of the four digits engaged with the spaces between the arms of the cross. Thus, for example, the orientation of the forefinger–thumb axis immediately prior to contact changed in a linear relation as a function of the orientation of the cross. In contrast, D.F. maintained the same default orientation of the hand whatever the orientation of the cross (Carey *et al*. 1996).

Clearly, although her behaviour was different in the two experiments, D.F. showed no evidence in either of these experiments for an appreciation of the shape formed by two oriented contours presented in combination. But of course the nature of 'shape' or 'form' is not easy to define in a universally agreed way, and the idea that it requires an appreciation of the orientation of two or more contours in combination is only one possible conceptualization.

Informally, we have been aware for some time that D.F. has no difficulty in combining more than one feature from different domains in guiding her actions: for example, she can catch a ball (requiring an integration of space, size and motion-in-depth). Those observations are perhaps not surprising given that Sakata and co-workers (1997) have recently described visual-fixation neurons in monkey PPC that are specifically active during tracking of a target moving in depth. But D.F. can even catch a thrown lightweight $35\,cm \times 1.5\,cm$ wooden dowel quite competently, a feat requiring an integration of space, size, orientation, and motion-in-depth (Carey *et al*. 1996). In a formal experimental test, we examined whether D.F. was able to combine the width and orientation of singly presented rectangular blocks of different width (but all with identical surface area). We found that her visual control of grip size and also of the orientation of her hand were both completely normal when reaching out to grasp the blocks (Carey *et al*. 1996).

What was more interesting, from the point of view of shape processing, was that D.F. distributed her grasps between the long and the short dimensions of these rectangular blocks in a completely normal way. That is, she did what all normal subjects do quite unconsciously, which is to grasp the narrower of the two dimensions of an elongated block; and again like normal subjects, the more elongated the block, the higher her ratio of 'narrow' grasps to 'wide' grasps (though even the longest block could be grasped either way). This simple observation indicates that like some of the neurons described by Shikata *et al*. (1996) in the monkey's PPC, D.F.'s visuomotor system is able to compute the aspect ratio of rectangular shapes (and act accordingly). Independent evidence confirms that D.F. can extract the gross shape of an object to determine her grasp points when picking it up. Goodale *et al*. (1994*b*) tested her with randomly contoured smooth flat shapes that permitted only two or three stable precision grasp locations for the opposed forefinger and thumb. D.F. performed well on this task, selecting grasp points similar to those chosen by normal control subjects. Yet she performed at chance level, of course, when asked to match pairs of the shapes as 'same' or 'different'. D.F.'s choice of stable grasp points in this task may indicate that her visual system is able to compute relative curvature at different points around the circumference of the shapes used in the study.

We are beginning to discern from studies such as these some of the visual coding limitations of D.F.'s visuomotor system, and accordingly to construct hypotheses as to the limitations built in to the normal human dorsal stream. So far the results are consistent with the work of Sakata and his colleagues on the properties of individual neurons in the monkey's PPC. But we can go further, and make certain predictions from what we have found in D.F.—such as that it is unlikely that visual neurons will be found in PPC that are selective for two-component shapes like T or X. On the other hand, neurons that can compute and discriminate the curvature of object contours would be predicted to exist.

13.3 Covert vision: actions speak louder than words

In normal clinical practice, as in normal visual psychophysics, it is tacitly assumed that people's visual capacities can be assessed by asking them to say what they can or cannot see. It is assumed that if brain damage causes a visual problem, then patients should be able to introspect about it, and what they say they can or cannot see should correspond with their level of visual functioning in everyday active life. D.F. gave the lie to this, when she startled us with her excellent visuo-motor control despite the most profound perceptual disability. The converse dissociation between perception and visuomotor control, while not quite so sharp, had already been reported by using similar visual tests of perception and motor control in patients with optic ataxia (Perenin and Vighetto 1988; Jeannerod *et al*. 1994). If we (Milner and Goodale 1995) are right in our argument that this striking double dissociation can be reified with reference to the human homologues of the dorsal and ventral cortical streams of visual processing, then the tasks that reveal the dissociations should provide us with a diagnostic tool for trying to understand other neurological disorders of vision. While the conventional approach may tell us a great deal about the deficits that follow disruption of the ventral stream and its input channels, the use of visuomotor tasks may tell us not only whether there is a disruption of the dorsal stream, but also may reveal unexpected covert visual function, as seen in D.F.

(a) Hemianopia

The first and best known example of 'covert' visual capacity was of course provided by certain patients with hemianopic field defects following damage to the primary visual cortex (V1) or to the optic radiations passing from the LGNd to V1. The phenomenon of 'blindsight' was first studied in detail by Weiskrantz and his colleagues (see Weiskrantz *et al*. 1974; Weiskrantz 1986, 1997), and the tasks they first used to demonstrate it were visuomotor tasks. It is now generally accepted that although hemianopic patients (by definition) are unable to perceive a light in the affected parts of the contralesional visual hemifield, some of them are nonetheless able to surprise themselves by directing their gaze or their hand at well-above chance levels towards the location of the light.

The usual interpretation of these preserved saccadic and pointing abilities (see, for example, Weiskrantz 1986) has been that in the absence of a viable geniculostriate visual pathway, the patient has to rely on the older colliculo-pulvinar route from the eye to the brain. The superior colliculus in itself is an ancient sensorimotor structure that appears to have the machinery necessary to guide shifts of gaze in response to visual stimuli (Robinson and McClurkin 1989; Sparks and Hartwich-Young 1989) and even to guide arm reaching responses to visual stimuli (Werner 1993; Werner *et al*. 1997). In a recent functional MRI experiment, Sahraie and co-workers (1997) have found that there is an increased level of activation in the superior colliculus during unconscious detection of motion (i.e. in blindsight) as compared with conscious detection of motion (obtained by using different stimulus parameters) in the same patient's impaired field.

But on the other hand, it is possible that the visuomotor structures of the cortical dorsal stream are necessary for blindsight as well, and indeed it would be difficult to explain why the extent and nature of blindsight varies so much from one hemianopic patient to another if extrastriate visual cortex played no role. In addition, electrophysiological studies have shown that dorsal stream structures maintain neuronal activity in response to visual stimuli following the ablation or inactivation of V1, whereas this is not the case for ventral stream areas (Gross 1991; Bullier *et al*. 1994). This preserved cortical activity in dorsal stream areas may thus plausibly be proposed as a critical physiological correlate of blindsight.

Recent research with hemispherectomized patients is consistent with such a proposal. In contrast with earlier studies, it now seems that if cortical damage is not restricted to primary visual cortex but also includes the rest of the cerebral hemisphere, then there is no true blindsight (King *et al*. 1996; Stoerig *et al*. 1996). It seems that any residual detection in the contralesional visual field following hemispherectomy can be attributed to the use by the patients of scattered light spreading within the ocular medium into the good hemifield, where it can of course be detected consciously by the patient (see Stoerig and Cowey 1997, for review).

If then, extrastriate cortex is necessary for blindsight, can we go further and argue that the dorsal stream in particular has a crucial role? Perenin and Rossetti (1996) have now provided good evidence for this idea, by using the same tasks that revealed covert visual function in patient D.F. They have reported that a V1-damaged patient shows qualitatively just the same dissociation between perception and visuomotor control as D.F. When asked to post a card into a slot presented at different orientations in the hemianopic field, the patient performed significantly above chance (though his spatial accuracy was not sufficient for him to actually insert the card), and when asked to reach out and grasp blocks of different sizes, the patient calibrated his grip at statistically above-chance levels. In contrast, however, he performed randomly when asked to indicate the orientation of the slot or the size of the blocks, either manually or verbally. The same result has now been found with another patient. Her spatial accuracy was better, allowing her to post the card successfully on several trials (Rossetti 1998). Interestingly, Rossetti found that this second patient suffered severe interference with her posting behaviour when asked to make simultaneous verbal guesses of the orientation of the slot while making her reaches.

This work confirms that blindsight is demonstrable for intrinsic as well as extrinsic (location and motion) visual properties of objects, and the clear contrast between the perceptual and motor versions of the tasks strongly suggests that blindsight patients are able to use the same visuomotor structures as D.F. Of course, D.F. has the additional advantage of a functioning area V1 (as shown by her good acuity and relatively intact visual fields, as well as by structural MRI). This presumably provides her with a much higher-resolution visual input into the dorsal stream structures mediating these visuomotor functions.

Of course, it must be conceded that not all blindsight can be comprehended in terms of dorsal stream function, although we have argued (Milner and Goodale 1995) that most of it can. In particular, the unconscious discrimination of wavelength that has been recorded in a number of patients requires a different account, most probably in terms of intact LGN neurons projecting through an extrastriate route direct to cortical areas V2 and/or V4 (Cowey and Stoerig 1992).

(b) Visuospatial neglect

A tendency to ignore stimulus items in the left half of extrapersonal space is not unusual after right middle cerebral artery strokes that affect the region of the parietal lobe bordering the temporal lobe (Bisiach and Vallar 1988). Curiously, such leftward neglect is not restricted to purely retinocentric, or even head-centred visual coordinates, as quite often items even on the right side of space will be neglected if they fall on the left side of objects or other perceptually segregated regions of the visual field (Walker 1996).

One of the more intriguing, and most easily demonstrated, features of visuospatial neglect is the tendency of patients to make rightward errors when asked to bisect a horizontal line at its midpoint. These errors can often be of several centimetres in magnitude. We have investigated the cause of these errors by showing patients lines that have been pre-bisected at various points, and asking them to point to whichever end of the line appears to be closer to the bisection mark. We have found that most patients who make bisection errors show a leftward bias when asked to point in this way, even when the prebisection mark is located at the exact midpoint of the line (Milner et al. 1993; Harvey et al. 1995). This suggests that most neglect patients make bisection errors because they misperceive the line, rather than because they have a motor bias to respond rightwards (in which case they should point rightwards, if anything, in our prebisected-lines task, an outcome that we have seen only in rare cases).

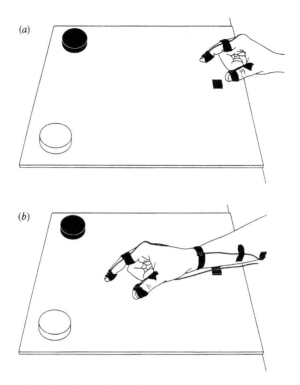

Fig. 13.1 Visual neglect: size estimation and grasping tasks. (*a*) In the size estimation task, the subject did not reach out, but merely opened his or her finger and thumb to indicate how wide one of two identical-size cylinders (the white one) was judged to be. In some trials the white cylinder was on the right, in others it was on the left. (*b*) In the grasping task, the subject reached for the white cylinder in each trial and picked it up.

We have explored directly this apparent tendency in neglect patients to perceive the left half of lines as shorter than the right half, by presenting pairs of stimuli of the same or different length for them to make larger–smaller judgements. We have found that the most of the neglect patients judge the leftward of two horizontal lines or rectangles to be shorter than an identical stimulus on the right (Milner and Harvey 1995; Pritchard *et al.* 1998). This tendency is not present in right-hemisphere patients without neglect, nor in healthy controls.

One possibility is that there is a rather high-level visual representational system located in the right parieto-temporal lobe region which when damaged gives rise to these perceptual distortions. We have therefore begun to investigate which cortical stream provides this putative system with its visual inputs. We have tested a neglect patient (E.C.) by using an arrangement whereby she is presented with two plastic cylinders of identical size, one white and one black (figure 13.1), varying the location of the white stimulus between left and right from trial to trial (Pritchard *et al.* 1997). The patient was asked in one test condition to reach out and grasp the white object in each trial using her forefinger–thumb precision grip, and in the other condition not to reach out, but instead to show us how big the white object is simply by opening her finger and thumb. In the grasping task, we measured the maximum grip size achieved during the reach, which typically occurs about two-thirds of the way along the trajectory. In both tasks, an Optotrak 3020 system was used to measure the vectored distance between infrared markers attached to the finger and thumb.

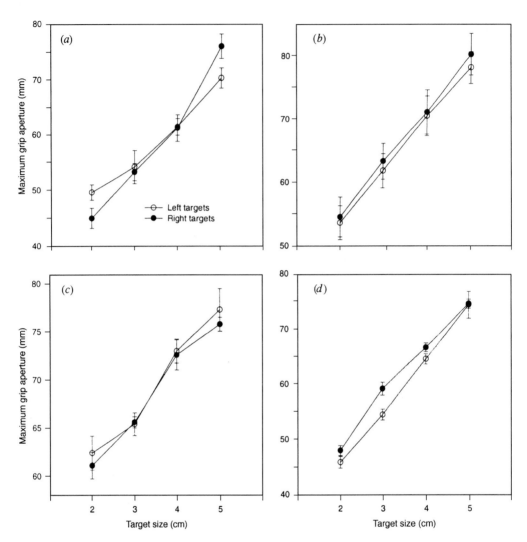

Fig. 13.2 Grip scaling during grasping, in a patient with visuospatial neglect (*a*, E.C.), along with data for two right-hemisphere lesion controls (*c*, RCVA control JM; *d*, RCVA control WR) and a group of eight healthy controls (*b*). The diameter of the target cylinder is shown on the abscissa. The ordinate represents the maximum separation in millimetres between two infrared-emitting diodes (IREDs), one attached to the forefinger and the other to the thumb, attained during reaches. E.C. scaled her grip size accurately when reaching out to grasp a cylinder, with no consistent under-scaling on the left relative to the right. (From Pritchard *et al.* 1997.)

We found that E.C. was able to grasp the target stimulus skilfully, whichever side it was placed on. She always opened her finger–thumb grip in proportion to the size of the object ahead of time when reaching to grasp it. Indeed E.C.'s finger–thumb aperture showed a highly significant linear relationship with the actual size of the object, whichever side it was presented on. Furthermore, as shown in figure 13.2, there was no significant difference between the maximum grip apertures attained when reaching to the left and when reaching to the right. Her grasps were similar, for a given size object, whichever side the object appeared on. (Although there was a slight tendency

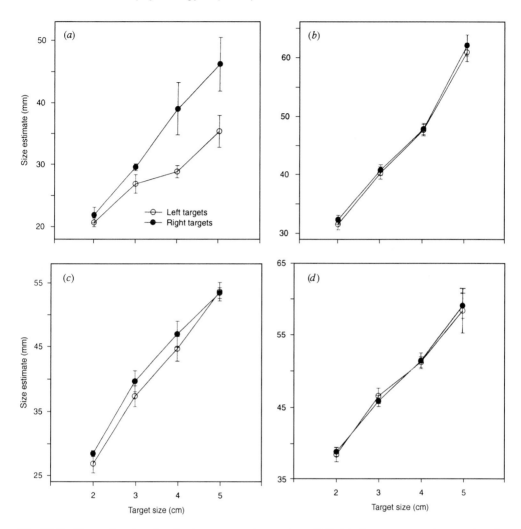

Fig. 13.3 Size estimation data in the same neglect patient, E.C. (*a*). In contrast to the grasping data shown in figure 13.2, she under-estimated the size of cylinders presented on her left (open circles), relative to the same cylinders when presented on her right (closed circles). The ordinate represents the mean asymptotic separation in millimetres between IREDs attached to the forefinger and the thumb while the subject attempted to match the diameter of a cylinder. Conventions as in figure 13.2. (From Pritchard *et al.* 1997.)

for the gain to be higher on the right side of space, the interaction did not approach statistical significance.)

In contrast, when E.C. was asked to estimate the size of the target objects, it is clear from figure 13.3 that her judgements were very different on the two sides. Although once again her finger–thumb aperture correlated highly significantly with the actual size of the object, on either side of space, there was nonetheless a consistent difference between the two sides. In agreement with her size-matching data, she underestimated the size of the target cylinders when they were placed on her left, often by as much as 1 cm relative to the right. This left–right difference was highly significant, a result never yet found in any of the control subjects (brain-damaged or healthy) we have tested.

We conclude that the use of comparable tests of visual perception and visuomotor control can reveal something about neglect, just it has done about other conditions such as visual form agnosia and hemianopia. In particular, it appears that neglect can influence the visual perception of size without affecting visuomotor control in relation to the very same stimuli. We conclude that neglect is a perceptual phenomenon rather than one which relates all-pervasively to visual processing. We believe that our finding lends indirect support therefore to the view that the representational system that is damaged in neglect is probably much more closely linked to the ventral stream of processing than to the dorsal (Milner 1995, 1997a; Milner *et al.* 1998a).

(c) Williams' syndrome

Another recent example where investigators have contrasted performance on tests of perception and action to help clarify the nature of a neurological disorder is the work of Atkinson and her collaborators (1997) with children suffering from Williams' syndrome. In this congenital disorder, children have a severe deficit in spatial cognition, but relatively spared visual perception. To investigate the possible visual pathways that might be compromised in this condition, Atkinson and co-workers tested a group of affected individuals first on their thresholds for seeing coherent motion in patterns of dots. As would be predicted if the dorsal stream area MT (V5) was damaged, elevated thresholds were found. But in addition, they tested the children on posting a card into an oriented slot, and showed that there was a selective deficit in this task relative to a perceptual matching version of the task. This would suggest that dorsal stream areas well within posterior parietal cortex are compromised, as well as area MT (which lies more postero-ventrally in the human brain than in the monkey).

It appears that like adults (and children: H. C. Dijkerman, E. Isaacs, S. R. Jackson, A. D. Milner, R. Newport and A. Shaw, unpublished data) with damage to the dorsal stream, Williams' syndrome children have a visuomotor impairment that cannot be explained in perceptual terms. Thus, as well as helping to further our understanding of a particular disorder, these results add further support to the idea of separate visual processing systems in the brain.

13.4 Conclusions

The view has developed from electrophysiological and behavioural studies in the monkey, as well as from studies of optic ataxia and normal visually guided behaviour in humans, that there are two rather separate visual processing systems in the cortex, each with different functional endpoints and operating characteristics, and that they correspond to the monkey's dorsal and ventral streams. An intensive series of studies of one particular patient with pure visual form agnosia (D.F.) is strongly consistent with this idea, and seems to provide a rather pure example of a selective disruption of the ventral (perceptual) system without serious damage to the dorsal system.

One can work backwards from this proposition in two ways. First, one can determine the limits of D.F.'s visual skills in guiding her motor acts, to construct hypotheses about the parameters of the normal human dorsal system. Second, one can apply tasks that have been developed to establish these neuropsychological dissociations to try to understand the visual pathways that are disrupted in other forms of neurological disorder.

Acknowledgements

I thank the Wellcome Trust for financial support of the research described here, and C. L. Pritchard for allowing me to reproduce her data on patient E.C.

References

Abadi, R. V., Kulikowski, J. J. and Meudell, P. 1981 Visual performance in a case of visual agnosia. In *Functional recovery from brain damage. Developments in neuroscience*, vol. 13 (eds M. W. Van Hof and G. Mohn), pp. 275–86. Amsterdam: Elsevier.

Andersen, R. A., Snyder, L. H., Bradley, D. C. and Xing, J. 1997 Multimodal representation of space in the posterior parietal cortex and its use in planning movements. *A. Rev. Neurosci.* **20**, 303–30.

Atkinson, J., King, J., Braddick, O., Nokes, L., Anker, S. and Braddick, F. 1997 A specific deficit of dorsal stream function in Williams' syndrome. *NeuroReport* **8**, 1919–22.

Baizer, J. S., Ungerleider, L. G. and Desimone, R. 1991 Organization of visual inputs to the inferior temporal and posterior parietal cortex in macaques. *J. Neurosci.* **11**, 168–90.

Baizer, J. S., Desimone, R. and Ungerleider, L. G. 1993 Comparison of subcortical connections of inferior temporal and posterior parietal cortex in monkeys. *Vis. Neurosci.* **10**, 59–72.

Benson, D. F. and Greenberg, J. P. 1969 Visual form agnosia: a specific deficit in visual discrimination. *Arch. Neurol.* **20**, 82–9.

Bisiach, E. and Vallar, G. 1988 Hemineglect in humans. In *Handbook of neuropsychology*, vol. 1 (eds F. Boller and J. Grafman), pp. 195–222. Amsterdam: Elsevier.

Boussaoud, D., Di Pellegrino, G. and Wise, S. P. 1996 Frontal lobe mechanisms subserving vision-for-action versus vision-for-perception. *Behav. Brain Res.* **72**, 1–15.

Brothers, L. and Ring, B. 1993 Mesial temporal neurons in the macaque monkey with responses selective for aspects of social stimuli. *Behav. Brain Res.* **57**, 53–61.

Bullier, J., Girard, P. and Salin, P.-A. 1994 The role of area 17 in the transfer of information to extrastriate visual cortex. In *Cerebral cortex. 10. Primary visual cortex in primates* (eds A. Peters and K. S. Rockland), pp. 301–30. New York: Plenum Press.

Carey, D. P., Harvey, M. and Milner, A. D. 1996 Visuomotor sensitivity for shape and orientation in a patient with visual form agnosia. *Neuropsychologia* **34**, 329–38.

Cavada, C. and Goldman-Rakic, P. S. 1989 Posterior parietal cortex in rhesus monkey. II. Evidence for segregated corticocortical networks linking sensory and limbic areas with the frontal lobe. *J. Comp. Neurol.* **287**, 422–45.

Colby, C. L. and Duhamel, J. R. 1997 Spatial representations for action in parietal cortex. *Cogn. Brain Res.* **5**, 105–15.

Cowey, A. and Stoerig, P. 1992 Reflections on blindsight. In *The neuropsychology of consciousness* (eds A. D. Milner and M. D. Rugg), pp. 11–38. London: Academic Press.

Dijkerman, H. C. and Milner, A. D. 1997 Copying without perceiving: motor imagery in visual form agnosia. *NeuroReport* **8**, 729–32.

Dijkerman, H. C., Milner, A. D. and Carey, D. P. 1996 The perception and prehension of objects oriented in the depth plane. I. Effects of visual form agnosia. *Exp. Brain Res.* **112**, 442–51.

Dijkerman, H. C., Milner, A. D. and Carey, D. P. 1997 Impaired delayed and anti-saccades in a visual form agnosic. *Exp. Brain Res.* **117**(Suppl.), 66 (abstract).

Efron, R. 1969 What is perception? *Boston Stud. Phil. Sci.* **4**, 137–73.

Felleman, D. J. and Van Essen, D. C. 1991 Distributed hierarchical processing in the primate cerebral cortex. *Cerebr. Cortex* **1**, 1–47.

Ferrier, D. and Yeo, G. F. 1884 A record of experiments on the effects of lesion of different regions of the cerebral hemispheres. *Phil. Trans. R. Soc. Lond.* B **175**, 479–564.

Gaffan, E. A., Gaffan, D. and Harrison, S. 1988 Disconnection of the amygdala from visual association cortex impairs visual reward-association learning in monkeys. *J. Neurosci.* **8**, 3144–59.

Glickstein, M. and May, J. G. 1982 Visual control of movement: the circuits which link visual to motor areas of the brain with special reference to the visual input to the pons and cerebellum. In *Contributions to sensory physiology*, vol. 7 (ed W. D. Neff), pp. 103–45. New York: Academic Press.

Godschalk, M., Lemon, R. N., Kuypers, H. G. J. M. and Ronday, H. K. 1984 Cortical afferents and efferents of monkey postarcuate area: an anatomical and electrophysiological study. *Exp. Brain Res.* **56**, 410–24.

Goldstein, K. and Gelb, A. 1918 Psychologische Grundlagen hirnpathologischer Fälle auf Grund von Untersuchungen Hirnverletzter. *Z. Neurol. Psychiatr.* **41**, 1–142.

Goodale, M. A., Milner, A. D., Jakobson, L. S. and Carey, D. P. 1991 A neurological dissociation between perceiving objects and grasping them. *Nature* **349**, 154–6.

Goodale, M. A., Jakobson, L. S., Milner, A. D., Perrett, D. I., Benson, P. J. and Hietanen, J. K. 1994*a* The nature and limits of orientation and pattern processing supporting visuomotor control in a visual form agnosic. *J. Cogn. Neurosci.* **6**, 46–6.

Goodale, M. A., Meenan, J. P., Bandülthoff, H. H., Nicolle, D. A., Murphy, K. J. and Racicot, C. I. 1994*b* Separate neural pathways for the visual analysis of object shape in perception and prehension. *Curr. Biol.* **4**, 604–10.

Gross, C. G. 1991 Contribution of striate cortex and the superior colliculus to visual function in area MT, the superior temporal polysensory area and inferior temporal cortex. *Neuropsychologia* **29**, 497–515.

Gruh, J. M., Born, R. T. and Newsome, W. T. 1997 How is a sensory map read out? Effects of microstimulation in visual area MT on saccades and smooth pursuit eye movements. *J. Neurosci.* **17**, 4312–30.

Harvey, M. 1995 Translation of 'Psychic paralysis of gaze, optic ataxia, and spatial disorder of attention' by Rudolph Bálint. *Cogn. Neuropsychol.* **12**, 265–82.

Harvey, M., Milner, A. D. and Roberts, R. C. 1995 An investigation of hemispatial neglect using the landmark task. *Brain Cogn.* **27**, 59–8.

Hyvärinen, J. and Poranen, A. 1974 Function of the parietal associative area 7 as revealed from cellular discharges in alert monkeys. *Brain* **97**, 673–92.

Jakobson, L. S., Archibald, Y. M., Carey, D. P. and Goodale, M. A. 1991 A kinematic analysis of reaching and grasping movements in a patient recovering from optic ataxia. *Neuropsychologia* **29**, 803–9.

Jeannerod, M. 1986 The formation of finger grip during prehension: a cortically mediated visuomotor pattern. *Behav. Brain Res.* **19**, 99–116.

Jeannerod, M., Decety, J. and Michel, F. 1994 Impairment of grasping movements following bilateral posterior parietal lesion. *Neuropsychologia* **32**, 369–80.

Kawashima, R. (and 11 others) 1996 Topographic representation in human intraparietal sulcus of reaching and saccade. *NeuroReport* **7**, 1253–6.

King, S. M., Azzopardi, P., Cowey, A., Oxbury, J. and Oxbury, S. 1996 The role of light scatter in the residual visual sensitivity of patients with complete cerebral hemispherectomy. *Vis. Neurosci.* **13**, 1–13.

Kling, A. and Brothers, L. 1992 The amygdala and social behavior. In *The amygdala: neurobiological aspects of emotion, memory, and mental dysfunction* (ed. J. Aggleton), pp. 353–77. New York: Wiley–Liss.

Matelli, M., Camarda, R., Glickstein, M. and Rizzolatti, G. 1986 Afferent and efferent projections of the inferior area-6 in the macaque monkey. *J. Comp. Neurol.* **251**, 281–98.

Milner, A. D. 1995 Cerebral correlates of visual awareness. *Neuropsychologia* **33**, 1117–30.

Milner, A. D. 1997*a* Neglect, extinction, and the cortical streams of visual processing. In *Parietal lobe contributions to orientation in 3D space* (eds P. Thier and H.-O. Karnath), pp. 3–22. Heidelberg: Springer.

Milner, A. D. 1997*b* Vision without knowledge. *Phil. Trans. R. Soc. Lond.* B **352**, 1249–56.

Milner, A. D. and Goodale, M. A. 1995 *The visual brain in action*. Oxford University Press.

Milner, A. D. and Harvey, M. 1995 Distortion of size perception in visuospatial neglect. *Curr. Biol.* **5**, 85–9.

Milner, A. D. (and 11 others) 1991 Perception and action in 'visual form agnosia'. *Brain* **114**, 405–28.

Milner, A. D., Harvey, M., Roberts, R. C. and Forster, S. V. 1993 Line bisection errors in visual neglect: misguided action or size distortion? *Neuropsychologia* **31**, 39–49.

Milner, A. D., Harvey, M. and Pritchard, C. L. 1998*a* Visual size processing in spatial neglect. *Exp. Brain Res.* (In the press.)

Milner, A. D., Dijkerman, H. C. and Carey, D. P. 1998*b* Visuospatial processing in a pure case of visual-form agnosia. In *Spatial functions of the hippocampal formation and the parietal cortex* (eds N. Burgess, K. Jeffery and J. O'Keefe). Oxford University Press. (In the press.)

Mishkin, M. 1982 A memory system in the monkey. *Phil. Trans. R. Soc. Lond.* B **298**, 85–95.

Morel, A. and Bullier, J. 1990 Anatomical segregation of two cortical visual pathways in the macaque monkey. *Vis. Neurosci.* **4**, 555–78.

Mountcastle, V. B., Lynch, J. C., Georgopoulos, A. P., Sakata, H. and Acuña, C. 1975 Posterior parietal association cortex of the monkey: command function of operations within extrapersonal space. *J. Neurophysiol.* **38**, 871–908.

Perenin, M. T. and Rossetti, Y. 1996 Grasping without form discrimination in a hemianopic field. *NeuroReport* **7**, 793–7.

Perenin, M.-T. and Vighetto, A. 1988 Optic ataxia: a specific disruption in visuomotor mechanisms. I. Different aspects of the deficit in reaching for objects. *Brain* **111**, 643–74.

Pritchard, C. L., Milner, A. D., Dijkerman, H. C. and MacWalter, R. S. 1997 Visuospatial neglect: veridical coding of size for grasping but not for perception. *Neurocase* **3**, 437–43.

Pritchard, C. L., Harvey, M., Beschin, N. and Milner, A. D. 1998 Visual size matching in spatial neglect. (In preparation.)

Robinson, D. L. and McClurkin, J. W. 1989 The visual superior colliculus and pulvinar. In *The neurobiology of saccadic eye movements* (eds R. H. Wurtz and M. E. Goldberg), pp. 337–60. Amsterdam: Elsevier.

Rossetti, Y. 1998 Implicit perception in action: short-lived motor representations of space. In *Finding consciousness in the brain: a neurocognitive approach* (ed P. G. Grossenbacher). New York: Benjamins. (In the press.)

Sahraie, A., Weiskrantz, L., Barbur, J. L., Simmons, A., Williams, S. C. R. and Brammer, M. J. 1997 Pattern of neuronal activity associated with conscious and unconscious processing of visual signals. *Proc. Natn. Acad. Sci. USA* **94**, 9406–11.

Saito, H., Tanaka, K., Isono, H., Yasuda, M. and Mikami, A. 1989 Directionally selective response of cells in the middle temporal area (MT) of the macaque monkey to the movement of equiluminous opponent color stimuli. *Exp. Brain Res.* **75**, 1–14.

Sakata, H., Taira, M., Kusunoki, M., Murata, A. and Tanaka, Y. 1997 The parietal association cortex in depth perception and visual control of hand action. *Trends Neurosci.* **20**, 350–7.

Shikata, E., Tanaka, Y., Nakamura, H., Taira, M. and Sakata, H. 1996 Selectivity of the parietal visual neurones in 3D orientation of surface of stereoscopic stimuli. *NeuroReport* **7**, 2389–94.

Snyder, L. H., Batista, A. P. and Andersen, R. A. 1997 Coding of intention in the posterior parietal cortex. *Nature* **386**, 167–70.

Sparks, D. L. and Hartwich-Young, R. 1989 The deep layers of the superior colliculus. In *The neurobiology of saccadic eye movements* (eds R. H. Wurtz and M. E. Goldberg), pp. 213–55. Amsterdam: Elsevier.

Stoerig, P. and Cowey, A. 1997 Blindsight in man and monkey. *Brain* **120**, 535–59.

Stoerig, P., Faubert, J., Ptito, M., Diaconu, V. and Ptito, A. 1996 No blindsight following hemidecortication in human subjects? *NeuroReport* **7**, 1990–4.

Taira, M., Mine, S., Georgopoulos, A. P., Mutara, A. and Sakata, H. 1990 Parietal cortex neurons of the monkey related to the visual guidance of hand movements. *Exp. Brain Res.* **83**, 29–36.

Tzavaras, A. and Masure, M. C. 1976 Aspects différents de l'ataxie optique selon la latéralisation hémisphérique de la lésion. *Lyon Méd.* **236**, 673–83.

Ungerleider, L. G. and Mishkin, M. 1982 Two cortical visual systems. In *Analysis of visual behavior* (eds D. J. Ingle, M. A. Goodale and R. J. W. Mansfield), pp. 549–86. Cambridge, MA: MIT Press.

Walker, R. 1996 Spatial and object-based neglect. *Neurocase* **1**, 371–83.

Weiskrantz, L. 1986 *Blindsight: a case study and implications*. Oxford University Press.

Weiskrantz, L. 1997 *Consciousness lost and found: a neuropsychological exploration*. Oxford University Press.

Weiskrantz, L., Warrington, E. K., Sanders, M. D. and Marshall, J. 1974 Visual capacity in the hemianopic field following a restricted occipital ablation. *Brain* **97**, 709–28.

Werner, W. 1993 Neurons in the primate superior colliculus are active before and during arm movements to visual targets. *Eur. J. Neurosci.* **5**, 335–40.

Werner, W., Dannenberg, S. and Hoffmann, K.-P. 1997 Arm-movement-related neurons in the primate superior colliculus and underlying reticular formation: comparison of neuronal activity with EMGs of muscles of the shoulder, arm and trunk during reaching. *Exp. Brain Res.* **115**, 191–205.

Wise, S. P., Boussaoud, D., Johnson, P. B. and Caminiti, R. 1997 Premotor and parietal cortex: cortico-cortical connectivity and combinatorial computations. *A. Rev. Neurosci.* **20**, 25–42.

Young, M. P. 1992 Objective analysis of the topological organization of the primate cortical visual system. *Nature* **358**, 152–5.

14

Action-based mechanisms of attention

Steven P. Tipper, Louise A. Howard and George Houghton

Abstract

Actions, which have effects in the external world, must be spatiotopically represented in the brain. The brain is capable of representing space in many different forms (e.g. retinotopic, environment-, head-, or shoulder-centred), but we maintain that actions are represented in action-centred space, meaning that, at the cellular level, the direction of movement is defined by the activity of cells. In reaching, for example, object location is defined as the direction and distance between the origin of the hand and the target. Most importantly, we argue that more than one task-relevant action can be evoked at any moment in time. Therefore, highly efficient selection processes that accurately link vision and action have had to evolve. Research is reviewed which supports the notion of action-based inhibitory mechanisms that select the target from competing distractor.

14.1 Introduction

It is apparent that vision and action systems evolved together to enable successful interactions with the environment, and that highly efficient vision–action systems have evolved in humans (see, for example, Gibson 1979). There is now abundant evidence that visual processes can flow automatically into actions, such that the latter can be evoked with little or no conscious intention to act (see, for example, Simon 1969; Bridgeman *et al.* 1979; Reason 1979; Duncan-Johnson and Koppell 1981; Norman 1981; Lhermitte 1983; Coles *et al.* 1985; Weiskrantz 1986; Goldberg and Segraves 1987; Gratton *et al.* 1988; Miller and Hackley 1992).

One of the drawbacks to such efficient vision–action systems is that, unrestrained, they would result in chaotic behaviour that is unrelated to behavioural goals. Under conditions of disinhibition, such as can occur with damage to the frontal lobes of the brain, the great propensity to respond to stimuli is released (see, for example, Lhermitte 1983). That is, the most dominant perceptual input captures action, and this varies haphazardly over time. Clearly, therefore, to exercise free choice and control it is essential that organisms have the capacity to resist the strongest response of the moment (Diamond 1990). Paradoxically, the best definition of voluntary action is those actions that can be suppressed.

Of course, one of the most striking features of the actual behaviour of higher mammals is its selectivity. Such selective behaviour is achieved because the many actions that are evoked by visual inputs are not released (and as we discuss here, it is also unlikely that all visual inputs in extremely complex environments are simultaneously processed to a point that they evoke action). Consider an apparently trivial task such as picking up a glass of beer from a table containing several other glasses, for example (see Tipper *et al.* 1992). How does the hand consistently reach one particular glass, given that each of the other glasses evokes a similar action? Extremely efficient mechanisms to achieve goals such as these have had to evolve. These selection mechanisms have been associated with the subjective phenomenon of attention, in which the mind selects from a multitude of available perceptual inputs, one for deeper contemplation and action (James 1890).

In psychologists' attempts to understand attention disparate issues have been addressed, such as the way in which attention can be moved from one spatial location to another to facilitate or inhibit perceptual processes (see, for example, Posner 1980), or how it searches complex environments for target objects (see, for example, Treisman and Gelade 1980). Our concern in this paper is with another specific issue: the medium of attention. That is, within which kinds of internal representation do selection processes occur (see Tipper and Weaver 1998)?

The experimental measures described here provide insights into both the medium of attention, and the mechanisms by which selection is achieved. There are three kinds of dependent measure that are taken. First, the interference effects caused by the presence of a distracting to-be-ignored object can be used to infer the kinds of internal representation achieved by the ignored object, and the medium or frame of reference within which selection takes place. The second measure of negative priming also enables us to infer the frame of reference of selection, and in addition, reveals which of a distractor's representations are associated with inhibition during selection. The third measure arises from ideas based on distributed neural representations for reaching behaviours. That is, ignored objects should influence the path of the hand as it reaches to a target.

There is increasing evidence that, depending on the behavioural goals of an organism, mechanisms of attention have access to different frames of reference. For example, when the task requires a saccade to a specific locus, inhibition is associated with a retinotopic frame of reference (Abrams and Pratt 1998). When the task requires detection of stimulus onset, the frame of reference in which inhibitory selection mechanisms are observed is environment-based (see, for example, Posner and Cohen 1984). When mobile objects are encountered, object-based frames are active, and inhibition can move with the object (Tipper *et al.* 1990, 1991, 1994).

The research to be reviewed here demonstrates that when the behavioural goal is to reach for an object, the frame of reference in which the objects are represented and on which selective inhibition mechanisms act, is hand-centred. This means that the location of an object is specified at the neuronal level in respect of the current location of the hand, and the movement required to apprehend the object from that location. The findings are incompatible with other frames of reference that might theoretically determine reaching behaviour, such as retinotopic-, environment-, head-, or shoulder-centred frames. Rather, it appears that within the constraints of a particular behavioural goal (e.g. picking up a glass) the actions which different objects evoke (afford) can automatically be encoded in parallel, and that competition and selection take place between these action-based representations.

14.2   Interference effects

Figure 14.1 represents the stimuli used by Tipper and co-workers (1992). Participants were required to reach from the start location and depress the key adjacent to the red target light. The critical variable manipulated in this experiment was the location of interfering irrelevant yellow distractor lights. By examining the pattern of interference and negative priming produced by distractors it was possible to infer which internal representations guide selective behaviour in this task.

Although targets could appear in any location, we only discuss data for reaches to the middle row. When the starting position of the reaching hand was at the front of the display adjacent to the participant's hand (figure 14.1a) distractors in the front row produced significantly greater interference (23 ms) than those in the back row (4 ms). However, when the starting position of the hand was at the back of the board, the pattern of interference was completely reversed. Now distractors at the back of the board (near the participant's hand) produced greater interference (26 ms) than those at the front (2 ms) (figure 14.1b).

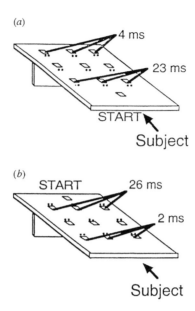

Fig. 14.1 Stimulus board with keys, each accompanied by two light-emitting diodes (LEDs), used by Tipper *et al.* (1992). (*a*) Shows the start key close to the participant, (*b*) shows the start key far from the participant. (Not drawn to scale.)

These results confirm that stimuli which are irrelevant to the participants' behaviour are automatically encoded in terms of the actions they evoke in a hand-centred frame of reference. The data cannot be explained in terms of visual frames of reference, such as retinal (Eriksen and Eriksen 1974) or viewer-centred frames (Downing and Pinker 1985), because visual input was held constant by maintaining fixation at the centre of the display. Similarly, the distractor interference effects cannot be explained in terms of other body-centred frames, such as head-centred (Andersen and Zipser 1988) or shoulder-centred (Soechting and Flanders 1989), because these body parts remained in essentially the same loci relative to the display whether the hand was at the front or the back of the board.

We therefore interpret our data in terms of a hand-centred race model. Reaches to near objects are initiated faster than to far objects. This advantage for more proximate movements has previously been demonstrated by Fitts and Peterson (1964), Glencross (1973) and Rosenbaum (1980) in adult subjects, and in infants who prefer to reach for the closer of two objects which subtend the same visual angle (Bower 1972). Faster responses are interpreted as reflecting quicker processing of the stimulus and its associated response.

The mechanisms that enable action to be directed to one object in the presence of other objects which evoke competing responses have been extensively debated. Our account suggests that there are dual mechanisms of attention (see, for example, Houghton and Tipper 1994). That is, as well as excitatory processes directed towards the target, there are also inhibitory processes directed towards the distractor. Houghton and Tipper (1994) and Houghton *et al.* (1996) have argued that the inhibition mechanism is reactive, responding to the relative activation level of the distractor. In the present reaching tasks distractors close to the hand have greater levels of activation than those far from the hand, which is the reason for their greater interference with responses to the target. Hence, in this experiment, distractors closer to the responding hand than the target would be expected to cause high levels of interference because they win the race for the control of action, and so are harder to ignore, requiring greater levels of inhibition than distractors further from the hand than the target.

14.3 Negative priming effects

Negative priming effects are thought to be one means by which the aforementioned inhibitory processes can be observed (see, for example, Neill 1977; Tipper 1985). The logic of the procedure is as follows: if the internal representations of a distractor are associated with inhibition during selection of the target, then processing of subsequent stimuli that gain access to or retrieve the same representations will be impaired. For example, if a picture of a dog is ignored while the participant attends to a picture of a table, processing the picture of the dog shortly afterwards will be impaired if the prior inhibitory processing is retrieved. In line with Houghton and Tipper (1994), inhibition reacts to the distractors' levels of excitation. Thus, distractors near to the responding hand will be associated with greater levels of inhibition, and hence negative priming will be greater for near than for far items.

The anticipated pattern of data was confirmed in a series of experiments by using a stimulus board similar to that shown in figure 14.1, and examples of the prime-probe sequence of trials are shown in figure 14.2. In the prime display of each trial, participants reached for a key adjacent to a red target light-emitting diode (LED), in the presence of a yellow distractor LED which they ignored. On the immediately subsequent probe display, participants again reached for the red target and ignored the yellow distractor. Comparisons were drawn between the time taken to reach for targets in probe displays which were in the same location as the prime distractor, and those in which the probe target was in a completely different location from any items in the prime

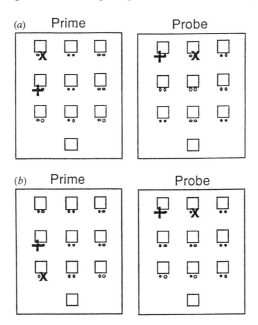

Fig. 14.2 Negative priming procedure. Trials consist of prime and probe displays, each incorporating a red target (+) and yellow distractor (×). In the example, identical sequences of reach are shown (left, centre row in prime, and left, back row in probe). In (a) the ignored-repetition trials, however, the probe target is in the same location as the prime distractor, whereas in (b) the control trials it is not.

display (see Tipper *et al.* 1992). Response time was longer in the former than the latter condition, which is the negative priming effect. Importantly, negative priming was greater for distractors closer to the responding hand (32 ms against 15 ms when the hand was at the front of the board, and 22 ms against 12 ms when the hand was at the back of the board).

Therefore the negative priming effects confirm the interference effects. The distractors compete and are inhibited in a hand-centred frame. All other frames (for example, retinal-, viewer-, head- and shoulder-centred) were held constant whether the hand was at the front or back of the board. Hence these frames cannot account for the dramatic changes in interference and negative priming that occur with different starting positions of the hand.

14.4 Further evidence for hand-centred frames

As discussed, distractors between the responding hand and target object produce most interference effects and require substantial levels of inhibition for successful action. There are two possible reasons why such results are observed. First, it could be that interference is caused because the distractor is in the reach path as the hand moves towards the target. Hence the problem is one of preventing action being captured by the distractor as the hand approaches and passes it (Tipper *et al.* 1992; Pratt and Abrams 1994). Alternatively, the proximity of the distractor to the action path may not be the main source of the interference effects. Rather, all the effects could be determined simply by the initial distance between the distractor and the responding hand. The closer the distractor to the hand, the greater the interference effects produced by it when reaching for a more distant target. As discussed, the action-based model described predicts that the distance between object and hand is the main factor determining the size of the interference effects produced by the object.

Experiments by Meegan and Tipper (1998*a*) have investigated this issue in displays similar to that of figure 14.3. Consider reaching for the far-left target. If interference is caused because the distractor is close to the path the hand takes to the target, then particular patterns of interference are predicted. For example, a distractor adjacent to the target on the reach path (middle row, left side) should produce greater interference than a distractor that is close to the starting position of the hand, but not on the reach path (near-right key). This is because the former distractor is spatially close to the target, and the hand passes closer as it approaches the target. In contrast, the hand never approaches the distractor at the near-right location, and in fact it moves away from this key throughout most of the reach.

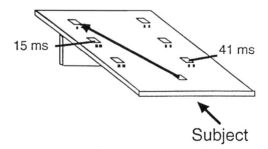

Fig. 14.3 Interference effects of a distractor on the hand path (15 ms) and of one close to the start point of the hand (41 ms) in reaches to the far-left target.

However, if distractor interference effects are caused by the initial spatial proximity of the distractor to the responding hand, then the opposite pattern of interference effects are predicted. That is, the near-right distractor is closer to the start point of the hand than the distractor on the reach path, and hence the near-right distractor should interfere most. Across a range of similar contrasts, the data clearly supported the distance hypothesis (see figure 14.3) (near-right distractor: 41 ms interference; middle-left distractor: 15 ms interference). Thus, interference effects were greater when the initial locus of the distractor was close to the responding hand, and this was little affected by whether or not the distractor was within the response path towards the target. Furthermore, these results cannot be accounted for by spotlight models which involve a spatiotopic map. This is because the distractor on the reach path is much closer to the far-left target than is the near-right distractor. The extensive literature demonstrating that distractors closer to the target interfere more than distant distractors (see, for example, Eriksen and Eriksen 1974; Eriksen and Schultz 1979) predicts results opposite to those obtained here.

In the experiments described here, although eye, trunk, head and shoulder position could largely be controlled, the focus of covert attention could not. Therefore one explanation of the observed results could be that because the target location could not be known in advance, participants did not attend to the visual display. Rather, as the task required participants to move their hands from the start point to the target, covert visual attention was focused on the reaching hand. If this were the case, the patterns of distractor interference effects that were obtained could have been produced because distractors close to the hand were also close to the focus of covert attention, and they therefore received preferential processing. To dissociate explanations based on the focus of visual attention from those based on action-centred frames, a task was required which held constant the locus of the hand–attention, while varying the nature of the action.

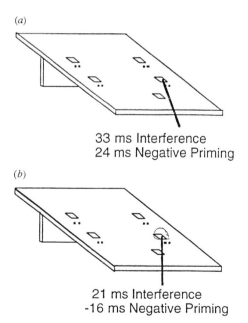

(a)

33 ms Interference
24 ms Negative Priming

(b)

21 ms Interference
-16 ms Negative Priming

Fig. 14.4 Stimulus board with four target–distractor keys. Mean interference from, and negative priming effects at the near-right location are shown. In (b), when the near-right key is occluded, there is less interference, and priming becomes facilitatory.

A considerable body of evidence has shown that the time taken to prepare a motor programme is a direct reflection of the complexity of the action to be produced, both in simple (see Keele 1981, for review) and choice (see Klapp 1978, for review) reaction time tasks (see also Henry and Rogers (1960) and Sternberg *et al.* (1978), for other 'response complexity' effects). Therefore Meegan and Tipper (1998*b*) varied the ease with which an action could be evoked by a stimulus while holding its spatial location constant.

In the near-right stimulus location is of most importance. In figure 14.4*a* this location is equivalent to that used in the first series of studies. Participants can efficiently reach out and depress the target key. Because the location of this stimulus is near and ipsilateral to the responding right hand, actions are fast. Therefore, when this stimulus is ignored it produces substantial interference because the processing associated with it tends to win the race against the other stimuli, which are processed more slowly. Because inhibition is reactive to the level of activation (Houghton and Tipper 1994), high levels of inhibition are associated with this stimulus, as observed via negative priming effects.

In figure 14.4*b* the near-right stimulus now includes a transparent occluding surface. The visual information available concerning the critical key and stimulus lights is equivalent in figure 14.4*a,b*: the actions required, however, are very different. In figure 14.4*b* participants have to reach around the occluding surface to depress the key. This action is substantially more complex and takes significantly longer to complete. Therefore, according to an action-based race model, in competition with the other stimuli, the occluded stimulus should now lose the race for the control of action, and hence interference from it, and inhibition associated with it, should be markedly reduced.

In contrast, the alternative account explains distractor interference effects in terms of the locus of covert attention, which may be directed towards the responding hand at the start of experimental trials. In this experiment, of course, the hand always starts from the same location. Therefore, the spatial spotlight account predicts that there should be no change in the pattern or size of distractor interference and negative priming effects.

The results clearly support the action-centred account, in which stimuli are encoded in terms of the actions they evoke, not in terms of visuospatial frames. Thus, when the action towards the near-right distractor can be rapidly programmed (figure 14.4*a*), interference (33 ms) and negative priming (24 ms) effects associated with this stimulus are large. In contrast, when the action to this same location in space is made more complex (figure 14.4*b*), interference declines (21 ms), and most interestingly, negative priming is not observed. In fact, a small facilitatory priming effect is produced (-16 ms). It is difficult to interpret this facilitation with the spatial spotlight account. However, in action-centred terms, it could be argued that the occluded stimulus does not require any inhibition as a distractor in the prime display, and therefore the residual activation leads to a repetition priming effect.

14.5 Investigations of reach kinematics

So far our investigations of selective reaching behaviour have relied entirely on temporal measures. Either the total response time from target onset to response completion has been reported; or this has been subdivided into reaction time (RT) to begin the movement, and movement time to complete the action. Of course reaching behaviour is played out throughout space as well as time, and hence our more recent work has begun to investigate the kinematic properties of the hand as it moves through 3D space. Consideration of the physiological processes known to mediate reaching behaviour motivates our search for other means of investigating selective reaching.

Georgopoulos (1990), Kalaska (1988), and Kalaska *et al.* (1983) have investigated neural responses associated with reaching behaviour in area 5 of the parietal cortex and in the motor cortex. They observed distributed neural activity in which a particular reach is represented by the activity of a population of cells. Each individual neuron's level of activity is broadly tuned to various reach directions, which are centred on its particular preferred direction of reach, in which highest activity is evoked. Accordingly a given cell will contribute, to a greater or lesser extent, to reaching movements in various directions. The direction of the reach is determined by the sum of the single cell contributions to the population vector.

To try to understand and predict attentional effects on reach kinematics in more detail we have been developing a computational model which aims to integrate our previous modelling work on the strategic use of inhibition in attention (Houghton and Tipper 1994) with such current ideas concerning the nature of the representations controlling reaching actions. In doing so, we also hope to give more substance to the idea of 'action-centred' attentional processes.

In the model, representations guiding reaching are: (i) hand-centred, in that directions of objects are represented dynamically with respect to the (moving) hand; and (ii) action-centred, in that direction of reach (for example, away against towards the body) affects the salience of objects (Tipper *et al.* 1992). The model represents, in parallel, the directions of two objects with respect to the current hand position. Direction is coded by the distributed activity of a population of cells, as discussed already in this paper. This can be computed from the differences in position of the hand and object with respect to some other frame of reference, for example, the body. Hand movement direction is derived from the resultant of the direction cell population vector. As the simulated hand moves, the position of objects with respect to it changes, and the directional representation changes moment by moment. The amplitude of the cell responses is also affected by the distance of an object from the hand.

We suggest that when attention is fixed on a target object, inhibition acts on the representation of a potential distractor, but in a way that is dependent on the action (Tipper *et al.* 1992). In particular, objects lying ahead in the direction of movement, and in the space between the current hand position and the target (i.e. closer to the hand) can produce strong interfering activation in the direction cell population. In the model, if this interfering activation is not suppressed the hand path will deviate significantly in the direction of the distractor, and the reach may even be 'captured' by the distractor. This may, in fact, reflect one source of the 'slips of action' which have been investigated in other realms (see, for example, Reason 1979). Objects beyond the attended target produce less interfering activation, and path deviations of the reach are less significant, even without distractor suppression. Combined with the use of the distributed population vector to determine reach direction, this has interesting consequences, depending on the relative locations of target and distractor and direction of movement.

Figure 14.5*a* shows the magnitude of activation in cells tuned to make an action at a particular angle; across the cells, this forms a distributed representation of a reach to a target near to the hand on the left of the participant's midline. However, we have argued that at least two reaches can be encoded at the same time, and figure 14.5*b* shows the distributed representation in the same population of cells for a reach to a distractor further from the hand on the right. Because of the distributed nature of these representations, it is likely that some activated cells are common to both the target and distractor representations (cells 10–14 in this example). The overall population of neural activity for the target and distractor is shown in figure 14.5*c*. In the absence of any inhibitory mechanisms acting on this distributed representation, the reach, as shown by the resultant of the population vector (signified by the arrow), would pass between the two objects.

Although such behaviour has been observed in eye movement systems when two stimuli have been presented (centre of gravity effects: Findlay 1982), they are not typically observed in reaching

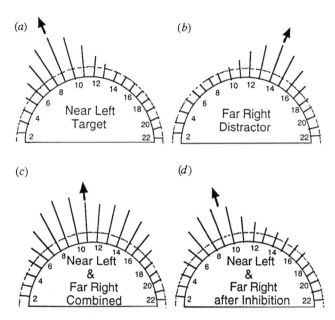

Fig. 14.5 Simulation of neural activity representing a reach to a near-left target and far-right distractor (Tipper *et al.* 1997). The length of each line represents the level of cell activity. The dotted semi-circle represents baseline activity levels. The arrow in each panel represents the mean of the distribution, which is the resultant reach direction. Activation is normally distributed with s.d. $= 1.35$. $M = 9$ and the maximum activity level is set at 5 for the near-left reach (*a*). $M = 14$ and the maximum activity level is set at 4 for the far-right reach (*b*). (*c*) Shows the combined activation when these two reaches are simultaneously activated, $M = 03$. The distribution shown in (*d*) represents the near-left target after inhibition of the far-right non-target, $M = 41$. Inhibition is normally distributed, centred on the direction of the distractor (i.e. cell 14), and s.d. $= 2.00$. The extent of inhibition is determined by the relative level of activation between target and distractor, expressed as a percentage of 78% (at which level path is not affected). Thus, to create the activation levels shown in *d*, the maximum inhibition is 62.4% (4–5 of 78%) which is applied to the distribution in *c*. The mean of the resultant distribution has shifted rightward, slightly towards the far-right non-target.

behaviour. Therefore, we propose that inhibitory mechanisms, centred on the population vector of the distractor, suppress neural activity. At the present time it is not known how the selection dimension of colour (select red, ignore yellow), which is encoded in the ventral stream (V4) is integrated with the parietal–frontal system mediating reaching.

It can be seen in figure 14.5*d* that as a result of the inhibitory selection processes, the population vector has shifted slightly to the right, towards the distractor, as compared with reaches in which the target is presented alone (figure 14.5*a*). Under other circumstances, it is possible for inhibition to result in a shift away from the distractor. Recall that inhibition is reactive to the relative activation level between target and distractor. That is, the greater the activation of the distractor representation, the greater is the inhibition feeding back on to it. When the distractor is less salient than the target (for example, it is further away from the reaching hand), less inhibition will feedback on to it, and hence reach path will deviate towards the distractor, as in the present example. However, this model also predicts that distractors that are more salient than the target will receive greater reactive inhibition, and in extreme cases this will result in paths deviating away from the distractor. This latter situation is shown in figure 14.6*a,d*, where the target is in

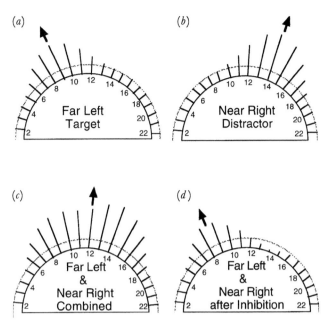

Fig. 14.6 Simulation of neural activity representing a reach to a far-left target and near-right distractor (Tipper *et al.* 1997). The figure shows the activity of the same cells as figure 14.5 under these different conditions. (*a*) Shows activation levels associated with the far-left target, with maximum activity set at 4, $M = 9$. (*b*) Shows activation levels associated with the near-right reach, and maximum activity is set at 5. (*c*) Shows the combined activity of cells involved in both reaches, in which the activity of cells involved in both reaches (cells 8 to 15) has been summed, $M = 11.97$. (*d*) Represents reach direction after inhibition of the distractor, $M = 8.66$. For the far-left target with a near-right non-target, the maximum level of inhibition is 97.5% (5–4 of 78%), and reduces the activity of cells 13 to 17 below baseline levels. The mean of the distribution remaining above baseline has shifted to the left, away from the near-right distractor.

the far-left and the distractor is in the near-right loci. Note that in figures 14.5 and 14.6 we have represented stimulus salience by the level of neural activity. That is, objects near to the hand are represented by more intense firing than those far from the hand. This increased intensity may result from an increased rate of firing, or from increased numbers of cells firing synchronously. At this point, however, there is little experimental evidence that proximity to the hand affects the intensity of neural firing.

The idea that different stimuli are represented by overlapping neural populations, and that the distribution of neural activity can be effected by inhibition or fatigue, has been previously demonstrated in vision. For example, consider the tilt after-effect shown in figure 14.7. Perception of lines of a particular orientation (for example, vertical) is believed to be determined by a population of cells (figure 14.7a). When adapting to a second orientation (figure 14.7b) many of the same cells are activated, and after extensive viewing these cells become fatigued. Hence when viewing the vertical stimulus again (figure 14.7c), the underlying population of cells has a different distribution as compared with that of initial viewing (figure 14.7a), and hence the lines in this stimulus are actually perceived as being tilted to the left.

Experiments by Tipper and co-workers (1997) have analysed reach paths to test these ideas. In line with the mentioned reactive inhibition model, the reach path does deviate when a distractor is present, as compared with trials in which the target is presented alone. This deviation can

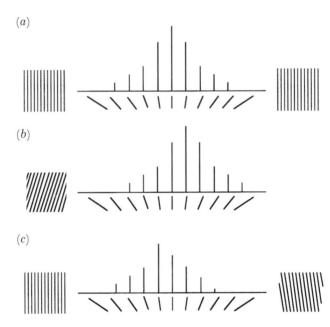

Fig. 14.7 Explanation of the tilt after-effect. The stimuli are shown on the left, cellular distributions are in the middle, and resultant perceptions are shown on the right. In (*a*), vertical lines are perceived correctly in accordance with the pattern of activation over the relevant cells. (*b*) Shows the cell activation levels at the beginning of adaptation. When the vertical lines are subsequently viewed (*c*), the fatigued cells can no longer respond as in *a*, and until they recover, the lines are perceived as being tilted in the opposite direction to those of the previous stimulus.

be towards or away from the distractor. For example, when reaching for a near-left target the hand veers towards a far-right distractor (figure 14.8*a*) as predicted by the neural activity shown in figure 14.5 (at the midpoint, the distance between the reach paths was 7 mm ($p < 0.05$)). In contrast, when reaching towards a far-left target while ignoring a near-right distractor, the hand veers away from the distractor (figure 14.8*b*: distance between the reach paths at their midpoint = 14 mm ($p < 0.05$)). This supports the notion represented in figure 14.6, that more salient distractors receive proportionally greater inhibitory feedback.

Finally, a serious concern in the interpretation of such path effects is that they could be produced by distractors being encoded as obstacles. Specifically, hand deviations away from distractors may not reflect inhibitory mechanisms so much as the avoidance of a collision between the reaching hand and the distractor. Various control experiments were undertaken in our original research (Tipper *et al.* 1997) which eliminated obstacle collisions as the sole explanation of our path deviation effects.

14.6 Inhibition of return (IOR) effects

More recently, we have begun to investigate other inhibitory attention mechanisms by analysing the reach path. To successfully search an environment it is critical that attention is not immediately returned to previously examined loci. One means by which movement of attention to novel loci may be achieved is by inhibition of previously attended loci. Posner and Cohen (1984)

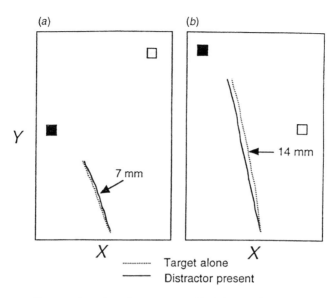

Fig. 14.8 Mean *xy* coordinates of reach paths to targets (black boxes) in the presence and absence of a distractor (shaded boxes). (*a*) Shows a near-left reach with a far-right distractor. Compared with the target alone condition (dotted line) the hand path deviates slightly towards the distractor. (*b*) Shows a far-left reach with a near-right distractor, and in this case, the hand path clearly deviates away from the distractor.

demonstrated inhibition of the return of attention (IOR) in the following simple procedure. Initially a peripheral cue was briefly flashed on a computer screen. Participants were informed that this cue was irrelevant and to be ignored. Nevertheless, responses to a subsequent target were affected by cue location: responses to targets at the same location as the cue were slower than responses to those at new locations. It was hypothesized that the sudden onset of the cue triggered automatic exogenous orienting of attention to the cued location, which was then inhibited as attention was withdrawn. Processing of targets subsequently appearing at the cued location was impaired because attention was inhibited from returning to that recently attended place.

  We examined such IOR in a reaching task by using two measures. The first was the traditional RT measure. Consider figure 14.9*a*, which represents the to-be-ignored red cue. This cue, which is presented in all trials, and equally often in all locations, does not predict the locus of the subsequent target. It was predicted that detection of the green target 500 ms after the cue would be slower when the target was in the cued location (figure 14.9*b*) than in an uncued location (figure 14.9*c*). What is novel in this work was that IOR could also be observed in the path of the reaching hand when responding in uncued trials. For example, in figure 14.9*c* the reach is directed towards the far-left target after cueing of the near-right location. If the cue and subsequent target activate populations of cells in motor systems, as described already in this paper, then any residual activity in the network associated with the cue would affect the reach path to the uncued target (figure 14.9*d*).

  Potentially, three forms of reach path can be produced, depending on the level of reactive inhibition. In each case it is assumed that the cue evokes a hand-centred representation, meaning that reaching actions are evoked and have to be suppressed. If the amount of reactive inhibition is low, then there may be residual activation in the cell population associated with the cue which

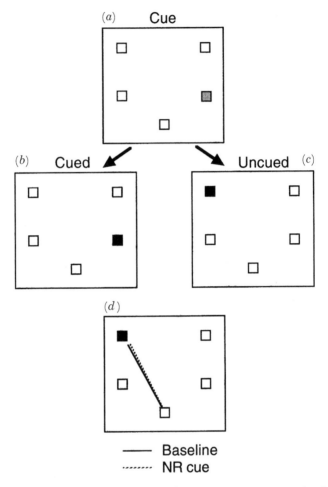

Fig. 14.9 IOR procedure. A cue (near-right in (*a*)) is followed by a target appearing in the cued (*b*) or uncued location (far-left in (*c*)). IOR is seen in the delayed response to a cued location. It is predicted that inhibition might also be seen in path deviations during uncued reaches (*d*).

may bias the population vector that controls the target reach towards the cued location. This is similar to the ideas described in figure 14.5. In contrast, if the amount of inhibition of the neural population activated by the cue is high, then the hand may veer away from the cued location, similar to figure 14.6. Finally, the level of inhibition may be such that no changes in hand path are observed compared with baseline. In fact, as can be seen in figure 14.10*a*, there is a tendency for the hand to veer very slightly towards the cued location, suggestive of a low level of inhibition.

We suspect that reach path reveals hand-centred internal representations; whereas the traditional RT measure accesses visual frames of reference, whether they be retinotopic-, location-, or object-based. One reason for supposing the RT and path measures arise from different representations is that they appear to be dissociable. For example, the proportion of trials with and without cues affects path, but not RT. Figure 14.10 shows the results of an experiment in which the proportion of trials in which a cue was presented was manipulated. In figure 14.10*a*, a cue preceded the target on 100% of trials, producing an IOR effect in an RT of 47 ms, and a small significant deviation

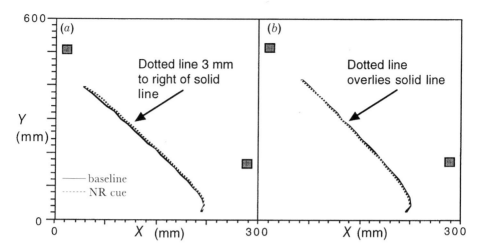

Fig. 14.10 Hand path and RT effects in an IOR experiment for reaches to a far-left target. (*a*) Shows a small deviation in hand path towards the near-right cue (cue presented in 100% of trials); (*b*) (Cue presented in 80% of trials) shows no deviation for the same reach, although the RT effect remains comparable (47 ms against 50 ms).

in hand path towards the cue (3 mm at the midpoint). Figure 14.10*b* shows results from the same conditions when no cue was presented on 20% of the trials in the experiment. The RT measure is little affected, being 50 ms, but in sharp contrast, there is no significant effect on the path (1.2 mm).

It is likely that in the IOR procedure, when a cue precedes targets in 100% of trials, little stimulus processing is required, because participants can simply respond to the second (target) event. However, if no cue appears in 20% of trials, participants must process stimulus colour (by which cue and target are discriminated) if they are to perform the task correctly. In this latter version of the task, cues are processed more thoroughly than in the first version, and according to the reactive inhibition model, will require greater inhibitory feedback. In this experiment, that amount of inhibition was enough to obscure the path deviation effect towards the cue which is otherwise apparent (figure 14.10) but was not enough to make the path deviate away from the cue. However, the IOR effect in RT remains at the same level in both versions of the task, which we therefore assume arises from a frame of reference in which stimulus selection is unaffected by the probability of a cue.

14.7 Conclusion

We have argued for a view of visuomotor processes in which information flows continuously into action-based representations. These representations are highly flexible, being determined by the behavioural goals of the task. In the current work they have been hand-centred frames, but in a task where a foot response was required, as when kicking a ball for example, the frame of reference would shift to this body part. It is important to note that we are not proposing that extremely large numbers of objects can all activate their associated responses in parallel independent of task context. Rather, a small number of task relevant objects, such as glasses of beer when about to reach for one's own glass, are able to evoke actions independent of the individual's intention to reach for a specific glass. A corollary of such efficient visuomotor processes, is that highly effective selection mechanisms have evolved, to prevent what would otherwise be chaotic behaviour, driven by the dominant action representation of the moment. Our research suggests that an important component of this selection system is an inhibitory mechanism acting on the competing hand-centred representations of the distractor object.

Acknowledgements

This research was supported by a grant awarded to S.P.T. from the ESRC (UK 000235573). We thank C. Lortie, G. Baylis, D. Meegan and J. Lupiáñez for assistance with this research programme.

References

Abrams, R. A. and Pratt, J. 1998 Retinal coding of inhibited eye movements to recently attended locations. (Submitted.)

Andersen, R. A. and Zipser, D. 1988 The role of the posterior parietal cortex in co-ordinate transformations for visual-motor integration. *Can. J. Physiol. Pharmacol.* **66**, 488–501.

Bower, G. H. 1972 Object perception in infants. *Perception* **1**, 15–30.

Bridgeman, B., Lewis, S., Heit, G. and Nagle, M. 1979 Relation between cognitive and motor-oriented systems of visual position perception. *J. Exp. Psychol. Hum. Percept. Perf.* **5**, 692–700.

Coles, M. G., Gratton, G., Bashore, T. R., Eriksen, C. W. and Donchin, E. 1985 A psychophysiological investigation of the continuous flow model of human information processing. *J. Exp. Psychol. Hum. Percept. Perf.* **11**, 529–53.

Diamond, A. 1990 Developmental time course in human infants and infant monkeys, and the neural bases of, inhibitory control in reaching. *Ann. NY Acad. Sci.* **608**, 637–76.

Downing, C. J. and Pinker, S. 1985 The spatial structure of visual attention. In *Attention and performance XI* (eds M. I. Posner and O. S. M. Marin), pp. 171–87. Hillsdale, NJ: Lawrence Erlbaum.

Duncan-Johnson, C. C. and Koppell, B. S. 1981 The Stroop effect: brain potentials localize the source of interference. *Science* **214**, 938–40.

Eriksen, B. A. and Eriksen, C. W. 1974 Effects of noise letters upon the identification of a target letter in a non-search task. *Percept. Psychophys.* **16**, 143–9.

Eriksen, C. W. and Schultz, D. W. 1979 Information processing in visual search: a continuous flow conception and experimental results. *Percept. Psychophys.* **25**, 249–63.

Findlay, J. M. 1982 Global visual processing for saccadic eye movements. *Vis. Res.* **22**, 1033–45.

Fitts, P. M. and Peterson, J. R. 1964 Information capacity of discrete motor responses. *J. Exp. Psychol.* **67**, 103–12.

Georgopoulos, A. P. 1990 Neurophysiology of reaching. In *Attention and performance XIII* (ed. M. Jeannerod), pp. 849–59. Hillsdale, NJ: Lawrence Erlbaum.

Gibson, J. J. 1979 *The ecological approach to visual perception.* Boston, MA: Houghton Mifflin.

Goldberg, M. E. and Segraves, M. A. 1987 Visuospatial and motor attention in the monkey. *Neuropsychologia* **25**, 107–18.

Gratton, G., Coles, M. G., Sirevaag, E. J., Eriksen, C. W. and Donchin, E. 1988 Pre- and post-stimulus activation of response channels: a psychophysiological analysis. *J. Exp. Psychol. Hum. Percept. Perf.* **14**, 331–44.

Henry, F. M. and Rogers, E. E. 1960 Increased response latency for complicated movements in a 'memory drum' theory of neuromotor reaction. *Res. Q.* **31**, 448–58.

Houghton, G. and Tipper, S. P. 1994 A model of inhibitory mechanisms in selective attention. In *Inhibitory mechanisms in attention, memory and language* (eds D. Dagenbach and T. Carr), pp. 53–112. Orlando, FL: Academic Press.

Houghton, G., Tipper, S. P., Weaver, B. and Shore, D. I. 1996 Inhibition and interference in selective attention: some tests of a neural network model. *Vis. Cogn.* **3**, 119–64.

James, W. 1890 *The principles of psychology.* New York: Holt.

Kalaska, J. F. 1988 The representation of arm movements in postcentral and parietal cortex. *Can. J. Physiol. Pharm.* **66**, 455–63.

Kalaska, J. F., Caminiti, R. and Georgopoulos, A. P. 1983 Cortical mechanisms related to the direction of two-dimensional arm movements: relations in parietal area 5 and comparison with motor cortex. *Exp. Brain Res.* **51**, 247–60.

Keele, S. W. 1981 Behavioural analysis of movement. In *Handbook of physiology. 1*, vol. II, part 2 (ed. V. B. Brooks), pp. 1391–414. Baltimore, MD: American Physiological Society.

Klapp, S. T. 1978 Reaction time analysis of programmed control. In *Exercise and sport sciences reviews*, vol. 5 (ed. R. Hutton), pp. 231–53. Santa Barbara, CA: Journal Publishing Affiliates.

Lhermitte, F. 1983 'Utilization behavior' and its relation to lesions of the frontal lobes. *Brain* **106**, 237–55.

Meegan, D. V. and Tipper, S. P. 1998*a* Reaching into cluttered visual environments: spatial and temporal influences of distracting objects. *Q. J. Exp. Psychol.* A **5**, 225–49.

Meegan, D. V. and Tipper, S. P. 1998*b* Visual search and target-directed action. (Submitted.)

Miller, J. and Hackley, S. A. 1992 Electrophysiological evidence for temporal overlap among contingent mental processes. *J. Exp. Psychol. Gen.* **121**, 195–209.

Neill, W. T. 1977 Inhibition and facilitation processes in selective attention. *J. Exp. Psychol. Hum. Percept. Perf.* **3**, 444–50.

Norman, D. A. 1981 Categorization of action slips. *Psychol. Rev.* **88**, 1–15.

Posner, M. I. 1980 Orienting of attention. The VIIth Sir Frederick Bartlett Lecture. *Q. J. Exp. Psychol.* A **32**, 3–25.

Posner, M. I. and Cohen, Y. A. 1984 Components of visual orienting. In *Attention and performance* (eds H. Bouma and G. G. Bouwhuis), pp. 531–54. Hillsdale, NJ: Lawrence Erlbaum.

Pratt, J. and Abrams, R. A. 1994 Action-centred inhibition: effects of distractors on movement planning and execution. *Hum. Movement. Sci.* **13**, 245–54.

Reason, J. T. 1979 Actions not as planned. In *Aspects of consciousness*, vol. 1 (eds G. Underwood and R. Stevens), pp. 51–74. London: Academic Press.

Rosenbaum, D. A. 1980 Human movement initiation: specification of arm, direction, and extent. *J. Exp. Psychol. Gen.* **109**, 444–74.

Simon, H. A. 1969 Reactions toward the source of stimulation. *J. Exp. Psychol.* **78**, 344–6.

Soechting, J. F. and Flanders, M. 1989 Sensorimotor representations for pointing to targets in three-dimensional space. *J. Neurophysiol.* **62**, 582–94.

Sternberg, S., Monsell, S., Knoll, R. and Wright, C. E. 1978 The latency and duration of rapid movement sequence: comparisons of speech and typewriting. In *Information processing in motor control and learning* (ed. G. Stelmach), pp. 117–52. New York: Academic Press.

Tipper, S. P. 1985 The negative priming effect: inhibitory priming by ignored objects. *Q. J. Exp. Psychol.* A **37**, 571–90.

Tipper, S. P. and Weaver, B. 1999 The medium of attention: location-based, object-centred or scene-based? In *Visual attention* (ed. R. Wright). Oxford University Press.

Tipper, S. P., Brehaut, J. C. and Driver, J. 1990 Selection of moving and static objects for the control of spatially directed action. *J. Exp. Psychol. Hum. Percept. Perf.* **16**, 492–504.

Tipper, S. P., Driver, J. and Weaver, B. 1991 Object-centred inhibition of return of visual attention. *Q. J. Exp. Psychol.* A **37**, 591–611.

Tipper, S. P., Lortie, C. and Baylis, G. C. 1992 Selective reaching: evidence for action-centred attention. *J. Exp. Psychol. Hum. Percept. Perf.* **18**, 891–905.

Tipper, S. P., Weaver, B., Jerreat, L. M. and Burak, A. L. 1994 Object-based and environment-based inhibition of return of visual attention. *J. Exp. Psychol. Hum. Percept. Perf.* **20**, 478–99.

Tipper, S. P., Howard, L. A. and Jackson, S. R. 1997 Selective reaching to grasp: evidence for distractor interference effects. *Vis. Cogn.* **4**, 1–38.

Treisman, A. and Gelade, G. 1980 A feature integration theory of attention. *Cogn. Psychol.* **12**, 97–136.

Weiskrantz, K. 1986 *Blindsight: a case study and implications.* Oxford: Clarendon Press.

Section 5

The control of attention

15

Prefrontal cortex and the neural basis of executive functions

Earl K. Miller

Abstract

Complex, intelligent behaviour depends on both 'executive' functions that plan and control behaviour and 'slave' functions that maintain relevant information 'on line' and available for processing. Most neurophysiological studies of the prefrontal (PF) cortex have focused on maintenance functions. Here, I review recent work in monkeys that demonstrates that PF neurons also have properties consistent with executive functions. They can select behaviourally relevant information from sensory inputs and from long-term memory, integrate diverse information to serve common behavioural goals, and represent information about behavioural context. The latter property may reflect the role of the PF cortex in representing the abstract rules that guide complex thoughts and actions.

15.1 Introduction

Much of the work on the functions of the prefrontal (PF) cortex stems from the widely held belief that it mediates complex mental processes. It has long been known that humans with PF damage exhibit a 'dysexecutive syndrome', a loss of the ability to coordinate and control behaviour (Baddeley 1986). This is exemplified by their profound impairment on the Wisconsin Card Sort Task, which requires subjects to sort cards by a changing set of abstract rules such as 'sort by colour' or 'sort by shape' (Milner 1963). In general, PF damage in humans is associated with dysfunctions in planning behaviour, in selecting one action when there are many available options, and in keeping 'on task', i.e., in ignoring distractions and persisting in the task at hand.

Such operations have been captured in models of human cognition that posit both executive functions that control and plan behaviour and 'slave' functions that maintain information online and available to the executive functions (Baddeley 1986; Norman and Shallice 1986; Johnson and Hirst 1991). Models based on animal studies have likewise suggested both executive-like functions that acquire and select among behaviour-guiding rules (Passingham 1993; Fuster 1995; Wise *et al.* 1996) as well as maintenance functions (Fuster 1989, 1995; Goldman-Rakic 1990; Goldman-Rakic *et al.* 1990). Neurophysiological studies have primarily focused on maintenance. They have employed delay tasks in which a single stimulus is presented as a cue and then, after a delay, monkeys make a response based on that cue. During the delay, many PF neurons show high levels of often cue-specific activity (Fuster and Alexander 1971; Kubota and Niki 1971; Fuster 1973; Funahashi *et al.* 1989; di Pellegrino and Wise 1991; Wilson *et al.* 1993; Miller *et al.* 1996; Cohen *et al.* 1997; Courtney *et al.* 1997; Rao *et al.* 1997; Rainer *et al.* 1998b). Thus, this 'delay activity' appears to maintain cue-related information online while monkeys wait to make a decision or execute an action. Temporary maintenance of sensory inputs is fundamental to a wide range of cognitive operations (Goldman-Rakic 1987).

By contrast, much less is known about the neural basis of the executive functions that guide complex rule-guided behaviour, the functions that select and coordinate sensory information and stored knowledge and map them to behaviour. In this chapter, I will summarize our recent work in non-human primates that is beginning to explore the neural basis of these mechanisms.

15.2 Selection

The ability to select only that information which is currently relevant is central to cognition. It is well established that the high-level mechanisms that underlie our conscious intentions are severely limited in capacity; we can 'think about' just a few items simultaneously (Miller 1956; Luck and Vogel 1997). Selection, then, is an important executive function.

Selecting sensory inputs

At any given moment we are bombarded with a wide variety of sensory information, any of which could potentially be represented in working memory, reach our awareness, and guide our actions. Yet, only a small fraction can and does. In vision, selection of relevant sensory inputs is evident throughout much of the visual cortex. The activity of many neurons reflects attended visual field items while unattended items are largely filtered out (Fischer and Boch 1985; Moran and Desimone 1985; Chelazzi et al. 1993; Motter 1993; Gottlieb et al. 1998). Which visual inputs are attended and reach awareness can be determined automatically, such as when an unexpected event grabs our attention or when objects seem to 'pop out' because they are different from their surroundings. Often, though, we need to purposefully direct our attention to items that are currently relevant for behaviour. The PF cortex is thought to play a central role in this process (Owen et al. 1991; Desimone and Duncan 1995; Dias et al. 1997). Gregor Rainer, Wael Asaad, and I explored its role during a visual search task that required monkeys to view a cluttered scene and remember only one object from that display (Rainer et al. 1998b).

At the start of each block of trials, monkeys were cued to a relevant object with 'cue trials' (figure 15.1, bottom). On cue trials, a relevant object appeared alone; otherwise the task require-ments were the same as during the array trials. On 'array trials', a sample array of three objects was simultaneously and briefly presented, one at each of three extrafoveal locations (figure 15.1, top) while monkeys maintained central gaze. One of the objects was the relevant object and had to be remembered. This was followed by a 1500 ms delay, and then by an array of three test objects. The monkeys were required to release a lever if the relevant object appeared in the same location as it had in the sample array. While each of the three objects was relevant, in turn, for a block of trials, its location in the sample array was chosen randomly on each trial. Thus, when the sample array appeared, the monkeys had to find the relevant object and remember its location. We tested whether PF neurons could selectively communicate information about only the relevant object.

Behavioural relevance had a very strong influence on PF activity. For most of the PF neurons studied (81/97, or 84%) activity to physically identical sample arrays varied significantly depend-ing on which object in the array was currently relevant. This is illustrated in figure 15.2. This neuron showed a high level of activity both during the sample period and the subsequent delay when one of the objects in the display was relevant, and a low level of activity to the same array when either of the other objects was relevant. A detailed analysis of this neuron's properties revealed it was selective for the relevant object, but not its location. Other neurons were sensitive to which object was relevant and its location whereas others were sensitive to the location of the relevant object only.

These results suggested to us that PF neurons were selectively encoding information about the relevant object. In other words, information about the irrelevant objects was filtered out from

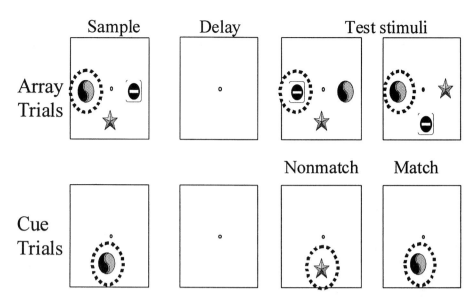

Fig. 15.1   Sequence of trial events. On array trials, (top) three sample objects were presented simultaneously for 750 msec. Only one of the objects was relevant on each block and thus only that object and its location (indicated by the dotted circle) needed to be remembered. There was then a 1500 msec delay followed by presentation of a test array in which the same three objects appeared, but not necessarily in the same locations as they had in the sample array. If the relevant object was in the same location as in the sample array, then the test array was considered a 'match' and the monkey released the lever within 750 msec to receive a juice reward. Otherwise, the monkey continued to hold the lever and, after another delay, a match array appeared which required a lever release. We directed the monkey to the relevant object with cue trials (bottom) in which only the relevant object was used but otherwise task requirements were the same.

activity. We confirmed this by comparing neural activity during array trials and cue trials. As can be seen in figure 15.2, for this neuron as for many others, activity to an array when a given object was relevant was indistinguishable from activity on the corresponding cue trials when that object appeared alone in the same location. Thus, many PF neurons responded as if the irrelevant objects were simply not presented. Selection of the relevant object occurred very early in the PF cortex; its location was evident in activity beginning as soon as 140 msec after array onset.

The ability to select which information is processed and remembered is a defining feature of focal attention. It thus seemed likely that the effects we observed reflected the monkeys focusing their attention on the relevant object. We confirmed this in separate behavioural experiments. The fixation requirement was removed and monkeys were allowed to freely examine the sample array. Under free gaze conditions, eye movements and focal attention are closely coupled. We found that during sample array presentations, monkeys spent 71% of the time looking at the relevant object. On a typical trial, monkeys made a direct saccade to the relevant object and maintained gaze there for the duration of the array. Thus, the requirement to remember only the relevant object resulted in the monkeys selectively attending to it.

To direct attention to the relevant object, however, the monkeys needed to remember which object was currently relevant. In other words, they needed an 'attentional template', a memory of a sought-after relevant object, used to select it from the sample array. PF activity seemed to provide this as well. Many PF neurons showed a chronic change in activity, evident within and

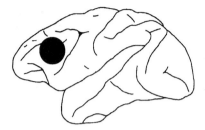

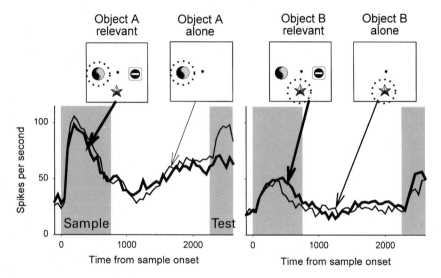

Fig. 15.2 Example of a single PF neuron whose activity depended on which object in the array was currently relevant. The grey bar on the left of each histogram indicates time of sample presentation while the grey bar on the right indicates presentation of the test array. The thick lines show activity on array trials while the thin lines show activity on corresponding cue trials (i.e., when the relevant object appeared alone in the same location). Note that activity on array trials to physically identical arrays is different depending on which object in the array the monkey needed to attend and retain in memory. Also note that activity on array and corresponding cue trials was remarkably similar. Thus, on array trials the irrelevant objects had little or no influence on activity. The brain figure shows the location of recording sites in this experiment. Bin width, 50 msec.

between trials, depending on which object was currently relevant. A given object was the target for an entire block of trials and this presumably reflects its maintained memory.

Biased competition models of attention (Desimone and Duncan 1995; Duncan *et al.* 1997) (Desimone, this volume; Duncan, this volume), suggest that the PF cortex provides an attentional template to the visual cortex. This activity is thought to bias competitive interactions in visual cortex in favour of a stimulus or visual field location that is currently relevant for behaviour. Indeed, PF activity seems ideal for this role. PF neurons can maintain information about a sought-after object across intervening sensory inputs (Miller *et al.* 1996) while activity in the inferior temporal cortex (Miller *et al.* 1993, 1996) and the posterior parietal cortex (Constantinidis and Steinmetz 1996) is labile and easily disrupted. Likewise, brain imaging studies in humans indicate that PF activation is more closely linked with sustained mnemonic activity while extrastriate visual cortex activity is more closely linked with visual stimulation (Cohen *et al.* 1997; Courtney *et al.* 1997). More direct evidence for an interaction was provided by Fuster *et al.* (1985) who found that cooling the PF cortex reduces neuronal activity in the inferior temporal cortex. Interestingly, selection of an object during visual search tasks occurs in inferior temporal cortex about 175 msec after the object is available (Chelazzi *et al.* 1993), which is much later than the selection observed in our study (140 msec). This is consistent with the view that the PF cortex is the source of the signals that mediate selection.

Selection of stored information

Intelligent behaviour depends on more than selecting sensory inputs, it also depends on selecting information from long-term memory, where we store the knowledge gleaned from our experiences. Indeed, in models of cognition, recall is a critical executive function (Baddeley 1986; Johnson 1992). Consistent with this role is the large number of interconnections between the PF cortex and limbic system structures involved in laying down long-term memories (Pandya and Barnes 1987; Pandya and Yeterian 1990).

To study whether PF neurons can reflect recalled memories, Gregor Rainer, S. Chenchal Rao, and I trained monkeys on a symbolic delayed match-to-sample (SDMS) task (Rainer *et al.* 1997). A sample object was briefly presented at the centre of gaze. This was followed by a brief delay and then by presentation of a test object. SDMS differs from standard, or identity DMS (IDMS) in that the correct test object is different from the sample object. The monkey learned through extensive training that when, for example, object A was the sample, they must choose object 1. When object B was the sample, object 2 must be chosen. Monkeys were required to release a response lever if a test object was the correct choice for that sample. We used six objects to form three pairs of sample-correct choice objects.

In principle, selective activity observed during the delay could reflect either the object the animal just saw (e.g., object A) or the object the animal anticipated choosing at the end of the delay (e.g., object 1). To distinguish between these possibilities, we also trained the monkeys on a standard, IDMS task. In the IDMS task, the monkey chose the test object that matched the sample (e.g., if object 1 was the sample, it was also the correct choice). By comparing delay activity during the SDMS task to that during the IDMS task, we could determine whether delay activity during the SDMS task conveyed the sample or its anticipated associate. The latter would reflect information about the paired associate recalled from long-term memory.

Many PF neurons showed activity consistent with a role in recall. That is, their delay activity reflected the anticipated choice object regardless of whether the monkey had been cued with its paired associate (SDMS task) or with the object itself (IDMS task). For example, the neuron shown in figure 15.3*a* showed a high level of delay activity on IDMS trials when a specific object ('object 1') needed to be retained in memory and a low level of delay activity when any of the other objects was the sample. On SDMS trials, there was a similar high level of delay activity when the paired associate of object 1 was the sample ('object A'). This suggests that on SDMS trials, PF neurons were maintaining a representation of the paired associate, which needed to be recalled from long-term memory. Note that this neuron did not exhibit selectivity during the sample presentation. This independence of sensory and mnemonic activity is common in the PF cortex (di Pellegrino and Wise 1991; Miller *et al.* 1996).

These neural results suggested that monkeys were recalling the paired associate of the sample early in the delay and maintaining it in working memory. The monkeys' pattern of behavioural

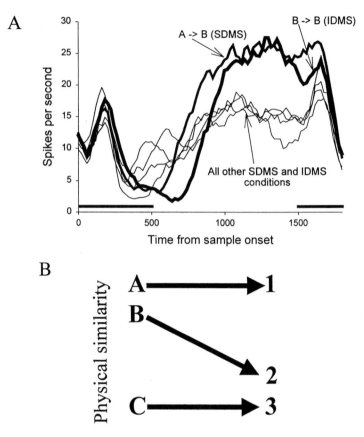

Fig. 15.3 (a) Activity of a single PF neuron involved in recall of a long-term memory. The figure shows activity during performance of a symbolic delayed matching to sample (SDMS) task and an identity delayed match-to-sample (IDMS) task. The small horizontal line on the left of the histogram shows the time of sample presentation and the small horizontal line on the right shows when the choice objects were presented. Note that this neuron showed a high level of delay activity on IDMS trials when the monkey remembered 'object 1' over the delay. It showed a similar level of delay activity when, on SDMS trials, the sample was object 1's paired associate ('object A'). Thus, on SDMS trials delay activity seemed to reflect the object anticipated at the end of the delay ('1'), which needed to be recalled from long-term memory. (b) Schematic diagram of the confusion matrix design. The vertical distance indicates relative physical similarity of the objects. Objects A and B were similar and different from C and objects 2 and 3 were similar and different from 1. The arrows indicate the associative pairings between the objects (e.g., if the monkey was cued with object A, it was required to select object 1 after the delay).

errors also suggested this. We employed a 'confusion matrix' design, which is illustrated schematically in figure 15.3b. Of the three sample objects, two were similar and one sample was dissimilar. The three choice objects associated with the samples also included two that were similar and one that was dissimilar. The two similar sample stimuli were associated with two dissimilar choice stimuli and two dissimilar sample objects were associated with similar choice objects. We found that behavioural errors were based on the similarity of the anticipated objects, not on the similarity of the recently seen sample objects. This suggests that during the delay monkeys held the anticipated choice object 'in mind' (i.e., in working memory), not the recently seen sample stimulus. That is, monkeys adopted a 'prospective' strategy of representing in working memory the information needed in the near future (the choice object) not the now irrelevant past event (Honig and Thompson 1982). Other experiments in monkeys (Gaffan 1977) and a variety of other animals also indicate that animals tend to solve delay tasks by adopting a prospective coding strategy. The role of the PF neurons in prospective coding is not limited to objects; Watanabe has recently demonstrated that they can convey information about expected rewards (Watanabe 1996). Quintana and Fuster (1992) found that neurons in the prefrontal cortex can code the probability of a forthcoming spatially-directed behavioural response. Nor is the PF cortex the only area likely to be involved. A few neurons that appeared to reflect the recall of an object from long-term memory have been found in inferior temporal regions mediating object recognition (Sakai and Miyashita 1991).

The ability to prospectively code information recalled from long-term memory is important for planning complex behaviour (Cohen and O'Reilly 1996). It is also critical for visual search. Most studies of the neural basis of visual search have employed tasks that only required short-term storage of the sought-after target; animals were cued with the target shortly before search commences. By contrast, visual search in the 'real world' typically begins with recall of the target from long-term memory. If we search for a lost set of keys, for example, we begin by recalling what they look like from long-term memory. Thus, the ability of PF neurons to use long-term memory to generate representations of targets further suggests a central role in directing attention and selecting what reaches awareness and guides behaviour. In the following sections, we will examine some of the operations that PF neurons can perform on selected information.

15.3 Integration

Neural processing is highly fragmented. Information about the outside world streams into, and is processed by, largely separate neural systems. However, we often use diverse information for a common behavioural purpose and our subjective experiences, arguably the 'output' of all this sensory processing and the raw materials of thought, are typically that of a seamless world in which multiple sensory attributes are experienced together. Ultimately, then, some neurons must have access to diverse neural information. Given the role of PF cortex in executive functions, it seems a likely region where integrated information might be evident. To explore this issue, we decided to use the well-known bifurcation of visual information processing, the separation of information about an object's form and colour (*what*) from information about its spatial location (*where*).

The primate visual system contains a network of at least 30 cortical areas that appear to be organized into two major processing streams or pathways (Ungerleider and Mishkin 1982; Maunsell and Newsome 1987). The ventral pathway, extending from area V1 to the inferior temporal cortex, emphasizes processing stimulus attributes such as form or colour. The dorsal pathway extends from V1 to the posterior parietal cortex and emphasizes processing of visuospatial information. This is thought to reflect a separation of processing of the form and colour information needed to identify objects (*what* information) from that of the information needed to localize objects (*where* information) into the ventral and dorsal pathways, respectively (Ungerleider and Mishkin 1982; Maunsell and Newsome 1987). It has also been proposed to reflect a separation of the computations needed for conscious perception (ventral pathway) from those needed to direct action (Goodale and Haffenden 1998). In any case, here we will refer to the dichotomy as *what* versus *where*.

The lateral prefrontal cortex is well positioned to play a role in integrating diverse visual information and linking it to behaviour. It is interconnected with much of the visual system and with cortical and subcortical systems critical for voluntary behaviour. Whether or not object and spatial information is integrated within the PF cortex, however, has not been clear. Below, I review some relevant work and a recent experiment from our laboratory that was designed to explore whether single PF neurons can integrate information about objects and their locations.

Anatomy

Visual neocortical inputs to the lateral PF cortex are largely organized by pathway. The ventrolateral (VL) PF cortex (areas 12 and 45) receives highly processed information about object identity from the inferior temporal (IT) cortex and other ventral (*what*) visual pathway areas (Ungerleider *et al.* 1989; Webster *et al.* 1994). The dorsolateral (DL) PF cortex (areas 46 and 9), by contrast, receives highly processed spatial information from posterior parietal cortex and other dorsal (*where*) visual pathway areas (Petrides and Pandya 1984; Cavada and Goldman-Rakic 1989*a*). The dissociation is not complete, however. VL area 45 receives inputs from both object and spatial visual areas (Webster *et al.* 1994; Bullier *et al.* 1996). More importantly, there are extensive interconnections between VL and DL PF cortex that could mediate integration of *what* and *where*. For example, area 12 (VL) has interconnections with both areas 46 and 9 (DL). It is important to note that there are opportunities for integration of *what* and *where* within the visual cortex as well.

Behavioural studies

The behavioural effects of PF damage tend to mirror the pattern of inputs described above. They have been studied primarily using delay tasks that emphasize maintenance working memory functions. DL PF lesions, especially those restricted to the principal sulcus region (area 46) impair spatial delay, but not object delay tasks whereas VL PF lesions can impair some object delay tasks (Mishkin 1957; Gross and Weiskrantz 1962; Goldman *et al.* 1971; Passingham 1975; Mishkin and Manning 1978; Funahashi *et al.* 1993). Again, however, the dissociation is not complete. Spatial reversal tasks can show little or no impairment after DL PF lesions (Goldman *et al.* 1971; Passingham 1975; Gaffan and Harrison 1989), dorsal PF lesions can impair certain types of object tasks, such as those requiring memory for the order of a sequence of objects (Petrides 1995), and VL lesions can impair some spatial tasks (Mishkin *et al.* 1969; Passingham 1975).

The pattern of behavioural deficits resulting from PF damage does suggest some preferential involvement of the VL or DL PF cortex in object and spatial processing, respectively. It is important to note, though, that these results could reflect the pattern of inputs to the PF cortex; they do not necessarily mean that object and spatial information are not integrated within the PF cortex. As Petrides (1994) has pointed out, VL and DL lesions may tend to produce deficits on object or spatial tasks, not because they are specialized for processing *what* or *where*, but because they deprive the entire PF cortex of highly processed object and spatial information, respectively. A lesion restricted to the DL PF cortex, for example, would deprive the entire lateral PF cortex of spatial information because of the DL PF cortex's preferential connections with the *where* visual system pathway. To determine whether *what* and *where* can be integrated in the PF cortex, we can examine the neurophysiological properties of its neurons.

Neurophysiology

Only a few neurophysiological studies have examined whether PF neurons can represent both spatial and object information. Fuster and colleagues recorded from neurons throughout the DL and VL PF cortex using an object task and a spatial task (Fuster *et al.* 1982). The object task was delayed-match-to-sample. Monkeys were briefly shown a sample colour and then, after a delay, had to choose that colour from a number of test colours. The spatial task was delayed response. A location was cued and then, after a delay, monkeys made a reaching motion to the cued location. They found that cells with object-selective delay activity and cells with spatially selective delay activity were intermixed throughout the lateral PF cortex, which was suggestive of integration of the segregated what and where inputs to the PF cortex. However, no single cells were found to process both attributes. Watanabe (1981) also found that PF cells tuned for *what* or *where* were intermixed in the lateral PF cortex. Furthermore, he found a few cells that appeared to process both. However, his experiment used a conditional paradigm in which a sequence of two patterns cued a particular location and, as he acknowledged, single cells with apparent tuning for both what and where could have been coding this pattern sequence rather than what and where *per se.* Hasegawa *et al.* (1998), recently found examples of single lateral PF cells whose activity was influenced by both the direction of a forthcoming saccade and the pattern used to cue that saccade direction.

Some investigators have emphasized regional specialization of object and spatial processing that mirror visual system inputs to the PF cortex. Wilson *et al.* (1993) conducted a study in which monkeys made either a rightward or leftward saccade depending on which of two cues were seen before a delay. In the object task, monkeys made the rightward saccade if one object was the sample and a leftward saccade if the other object was the sample (e.g., A → 'go right'; B → 'go left'). In the spatial task, the saccade location was explicitly cued by flashing a spot to the right or left of fixation. They found that the majority of VL PF neurons were selectively activated during the object task but not during the spatial task. This, of course, does not mean that there are no PF neurons that integrate *what* and *where*. Even with the relatively small number of cells studied, Wilson and colleagues found a few neurons that were engaged by both tasks. Further, it is important to note that the object task used by Wilson *et al.* (1993) employed conditional associations between objects and spatially-directed saccades (e.g., A → 'go right'; B → 'go left'). It is possible that the VL PF neurons could have been coding these *what–where* associations. Recent studies suggest that the lateral PF cortex, in particular the VL portion, plays a role in acquiring and representing such associations (Murray and Wise 1997; Asaad *et al.* 1998) and see below.

Thus, previous studies have yielded different views of the topography of object and spatial processing in the PF cortex. It is important to note that topography is a somewhat separate issue from integration. Even if some lateral PF regions tend to be more involved in object or spatial processing (Wilson *et al.* 1993; Goldman-Rakic 1996), it does not preclude the existence of neurons in each region that can integrate both attributes. Thus far, few studies have reported such neurons. For the most part, however, previous studies have explored the representation of object and space in the PF cortex by training monkeys to perform separate object and spatial tasks. Because the PF cortex plays a central role in learning complex behaviour, it may be that separate *what* and *where* tasks foster distinct task-related representations in the PF cortex; that is, the task demands may have 'tuned' the PF cortex away from integration. Further, previous studies used object and spatial tasks that employed very different types of stimuli. The spatial tasks have used only simple stimuli such as spots of light. No studies have tested responses of PF neurons to complex objects appearing at multiple visual field locations. Thus, it is not known if object-selective PF neurons can also convey spatial information. To test whether PF neurons can integrate *what* and *where*, then, we need a task that requires monkeys to link objects with their visual field locations.

S. Chenchal Rao, Gregor Rainer, and I employed such a task (Rao *et al.* 1997). On each trial, while the monkey maintained fixation of a central fixation spot, a sample object was presented briefly at the centre of gaze. After a delay of one second, two test objects were briefly presented at two of four possible extrafoveal locations. One of the objects matched the sample, the other was a non-match. After another delay, the monkey made a saccade to the remembered location of the match. Thus, this task required that the monkey remember the sample object over the first delay (the *what* delay) and then remember the location of the match over the second delay (the *where* delay). Note that this task requires a within-trial linking of *what* with *where*. The monkeys were forced to use information about what the sample object looked like to find the match and its location. Because this engages mechanisms that direct an action to an object's location, it is a more 'natural' test of whether *what* is integrated with *where* than an experiment using separate tasks.

We recorded from 166 neurons with delay activity in the DL and VL PF cortex of two monkeys. While some neurons were specialized for either *what* working memory (figure 15.4a) or *where* working memory (figure 15.4b), many were not specialized and were engaged by both. Almost half (45%, or 74/166) of the cells with delay activity showed significantly different levels of *what* delay activity depending on which object the monkey was cued to remember, and significantly different levels of *where* delay activity depending on which location was cued (figure 15.4c). A population of neurons with access to information about both an object's features and its spatial location (we called them '*what-and-where* cells') could provide a neural substrate for linking information about objects and their locations. Imaging studies in human PF cortex have shown that there is overlap of the representations of object and spatial information (Owen *et al*. 1996a,b, 1998; Oster *et al*. 1997; Cullen *et al*. 1998; Postle and D'Esposito 1998). Even studies that report some separation of these attributes also find regions of overlap (Courtney *et al*. 1998). These results are also consistent with the finding that humans hold in working memory, not independent representations for the different features of an object, but coherent representations that integrate different object features (Luck and Vogel 1997).

The large proportion of *what-and-where* neurons found in this study may reflect the PF cortex becoming 'tuned' to task demand during training (Rao *et al*. 1997). Indeed, functional plasticity is evident in many of the neocortical areas interconnected with the PF cortex (Mitz *et al*. 1991; Chen and Wise 1995, 1996; Recanzone *et al*. 1992a,b,c; Karni 1996; Bichot *et al*. 1996). A particularly relevant example was recently provided by Bichot *et al*. (1996), who recorded in the frontal eye fields (FEF) of monkeys trained to saccade to the unique stimulus in an array (e.g., to the one green stimulus among several red). The FEF receives major inputs from the PF cortex and controls purposeful eye movements (Schiller *et al*. 1979; Bruce and Goldberg 1985; Schiller *et al*. 1987). Its neurons tend to be spatially selective; they typically do not show colour-selectivity. However, FEF neurons in monkeys trained to saccade to a particular colour showed selectivity for that colour, which suggests experience-dependent plasticity.

In any event, our results do not necessarily imply that different regions of the PF cortex are functionally uniform, even with regard to *what* and *where* processing. We did not record throughout the entire PF cortex and therefore cannot determine whether or not there is some regional emphasis of *what* and *where*. Rather, our results indicate that when monkeys need to link objects and their locations 'in mind', there are a large number of PF neurons that reflect that demand. Even simple behaviour such as reaching for an object requires that, ultimately, *what* and *where* have access to the same neurons. These neurons are evident in the PF cortex, a region that plays a central role in guiding voluntary, intentioned behaviour.

Many cognitive functions require simultaneous representation of *what* and *where*. Take searching for a coffee cup. We have in mind not only what the cup looks like but also where it is likely to be (e.g., on the desk rather than floating in the air above it). Thus, while we search for it we keep both *what* and *where* in mind simultaneously. Rainer, Asaad and Miller (1998a) recently demonstrated that many PF neurons can do just that. Monkeys were trained on a go/no-go delayed

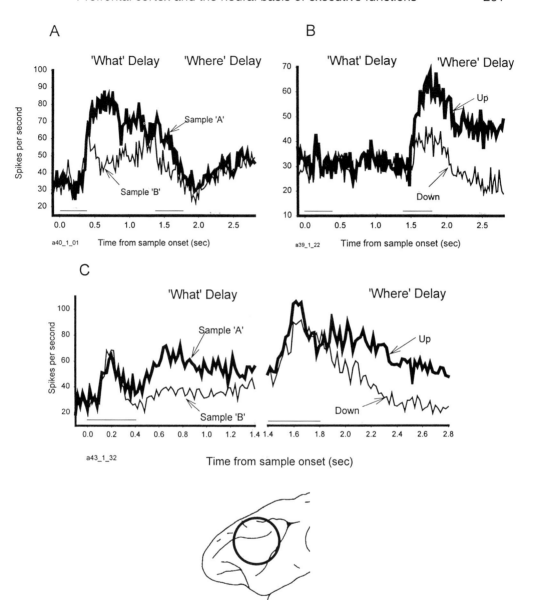

Fig. 15.4 Histograms of single prefrontal neurons specialized for object working memory (a), spatial working memory (b), and a single neuron involved in both object and spatial working memory (c). The small line on the left of each histogram shows when the sample object was presented. The small line to the right shows when the test objects were presented. Note that the neuron specialized for *what* (a) and the neuron specialized for *where* (b) were selectively activated during the *what* or *where* phase of the task. By contrast, the neuron shown in figure 15.4c was activated during both the *what* and *where* task phases. It showed different levels of delay activity depending on which object or which location needed to be remembered. Bin width, 20 msec. The brain figure at the bottom shows the locations of the recording sites from this experiment.

match-to-object-place task that required them to remember, over a brief delay, which of 2–5 sample objects had appeared in which of 25 visual field locations. They released a lever when a test object matched a sample in both identity and location. During the delay, about half of the neurons simultaneously conveyed information about the object and its precise location. In fact, the average diameter of the 'memory field' (MF) of the *what-and-where* neurons was only about 9°. Further, unlike inferior temporal neurons, object-selective PF delay activity did not emphasize central vision. Rather, it seemed well suited to the task demand to remember an object throughout a wide portion of the visual field. Many *what-and-where* neurons had MFs that were entirely extrafoveal and some were maximally activated by peripheral locations. Thus, across the population, these neurons could both identify and localize objects throughout a wide area of the visual field, both near the fovea and in the periphery.

Integration of *what* and *where* is unlikely to occur solely with the PF cortex. There are anatomical interconnections between the ventral and dorsal pathways within the visual system that could bring disparate attributes together (Maunsell and Van Essen 1983; Desimone and Ungerleider 1986; Boussaoud *et al.* 1990; Van Essen *et al.* 1992). In fact, studies indicate that such 'cross-talk' does occur. For example, area V4, an early station in the *what* visual system pathway, contains many neurons whose activity is modulated when monkeys must select a stimulus whose direction of motion (thought to be analysed in the *where* pathway) matches one held in memory (Ferrera *et al.* 1994). Similarly, neurons in area V4 and the inferior temporal cortex (the final *what* area) are strongly modulated by spatial attention (Moran, Desimone 1985; McAdams, Maunsell 1997). It should also be noted that *what* and *where* processing may not be completely separate to begin with. The differences between the pathways may be relative, not absolute. Inferior temporal neurons' receptive fields, for example, are not uniform and thus can convey spatial information (Gross *et al.* 1972; Desimone *et al.* 1984). In fact, during object and spatial memory tasks, many neurons in the inferior temporal cortex show spatial selectivity while many neurons in the posterior parietal (PP) cortex (*where* pathway) show object selectivity (Sereno and Maunsell 1995). Also, as noted above, the two cortical visual streams may separate, not object from spatial information, but perceptual information from information needed for action (Goodale and Haffenden 1998). In this model, the object and spatial information used for perception are not separate. Instead, they are integrated within the ventral visual pathway. The relative contribution of the PF cortex to the integration of *what* and *where* remains to be determined.

In any event, many PF neurons have access to information about both object identity and location and thus can play a role in integrating these attributes. They are likely to play a role in integrating even more diverse information as well. The lateral PF cortex contains zones that receive overlapping projections from visual, auditory, and somatosensory cortex (Pandya and Barnes 1987). Further, Watanabe (1992) has shown that when monkeys perform tasks in which both visual and auditory cues are behaviourally significant, many lateral PF neurons respond to both modalities. The extent to which PF neurons can participate in cross-modal integration needs further investigation.

The ability of PF neurons to select relevant information was also evident in our study. Many PF neurons selectively represented *what* or *where* attributes of a stimulus depending on which needed to be remembered at that moment. *What-and-where* cells were highly selective for sample objects during the *what* delay when monkeys needed to remember the sample. However, once an object's identity was no longer important (during the *where* delay), many of the *what-and-where* cells were no longer object-selective. They instead conveyed only information about the object's location, which was then relevant (Rao *et al.* 1997). Thus, these neurons appeared to 'switch modes' from being highly object-selective in the first half of the trial to being purely location-selective in the second half, a transformation that mirrored task requirements. A similar effect was observed by Sakagami and Niki (1994*a*), who showed that many PF neurons selectively encode the dimension of a stimulus (e.g., colour vs. shape) that is currently relevant for behaviour. This dependence on task demands of which stimulus dimension is encoded suggests a more dynamic view of PF representations than that of a system with specific neurons dedicated to processing a specific type of information. Indeed, this ability to adapt to current task demands is what we would expect from a region important for the flexible guidance of behaviour.

15.4 Mapping information to action: rule-learning

Complex behaviour is typically rule-based. Our previous experiences arm us with sets of behaviour-guiding scripts, or rules, that relate events to possible outcomes and consequences. They specify the conditions and behaviours needed for achieving a goal (Abbott *et al.* 1985; Barsalou and Sewell 1985; Norman and Shallice 1986). We can use these rules in difficult or novel situations. Take, for example, using the subway in an unfamiliar city. Based on our experiences in other cities we can attend to important information (e.g., the fare chart, the token booth, etc.) and enact routines that coordinate our actions and get us to our final destination. Behaviour-guiding rules not only dictate what behaviours are likely to be rewarding or appropriate, but also which visual features are likely to be important and worth attending.

Studies of brain-damaged humans and other animals have suggested that the PF cortex plays a major role in rule-guided behaviour. For example, Grafman (1994) suggests that the PF cortex contains managerial knowledge units (MKUs) that describe related events, possible actions, and consequences. An MKU may describe the expected events and appropriate responses for dining in a restaurant, for example. PF dysfunction is thought to result in a loss of MKUs or in an inability to access them. Similarly, Cohen and colleagues suggest a major role for the PF cortex in providing representations of context information needed to guide behaviour (Cohen and Servan-Schreiber 1992; Cohen *et al.* 1992). In their view, the PF cortex conveys the constellation of behaviourally relevant context information associated with a given stimulus. For example, in the classic Stroop test, subjects must either read a word or report the colour in which the word is printed. Sometimes these attributes are in conflict, such as when the word 'green' is printed in red ink. According to Cohen and colleagues, the job of the PF cortex is to maintain a representation of which attribute is currently relevant. Like MKUs, PF representations of behavioural context can include a wide variety of multi-modal information. As we will see below, there is evidence from neurophysiological studies that PF neurons do convey information about behavioural context.

Based on animal studies, Wise *et al.* (1996) and Passingham (1993) argue that rule learning is a cardinal PF function. In this view, abstract rules guide response selection when there are multiple response options and/or when well-learned, automatic responses cannot be used. A similar view is suggested by Fuster's (1985, 1989) conjecture that the PF cortex is important for representing 'cross-temporal contingencies' of events and actions. Others have found that the PF cortex is important for switching attention to and from different rules and/or in inhibiting automatic, prepotent responses from interfering with execution of less dominant, but behaviourally appropriate, action (Diamond and Goldman-Rakic 1989; Diamond 1990; Owen *et al.* 1991; Cohen and Servan-Schreiber 1992; Cohen *et al.* 1996; Dias *et al.* 1997). PF mechanisms for acquiring and representing information about behavioural rules and context may correspond to the executive functions of Baddeley's model of working memory (1986) and with Norman and Shallice's notion of a supervisory attention system (thought to be located in the PF cortex), that plans and guides voluntary, non-automatic behaviour (Shallice 1982; Norman and Shallice 1986).

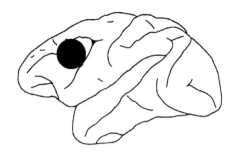

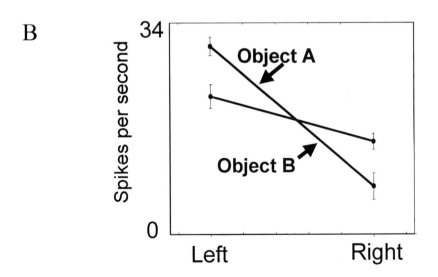

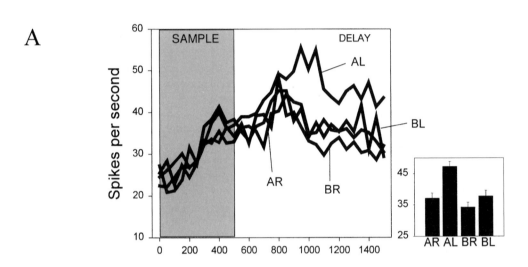

Fig. 15.5 PF neurons tuned for object–spatial associations. (a) Histogram of the activity of a single PF neuron. AR – Object 'A' was associated with 'go right' (i.e., 'A → go right'), AL – 'A → go left', BR – 'B → go right', BL – 'B → go left'. The small bar graph shows the average activity in the delay for each

A laboratory task used to study rule learning is the conditional association task. In this task, there are a set number of responses the monkey can perform (e.g., a saccade to one of a small number of locations). Which response is correct depends on which cue is presented on that trial. Thus, no single response leads invariably to a reward. Instead, monkeys must learn an arbitrary association between a cue and a response, a rule that maps a stimulus to an action.

Damage to the lateral PF cortex has long been known to disrupt conditional learning. Lesions of the lateral PF cortex or damage that disconnects the lateral PF cortex from IT cortex cause deficits in conditional object-spatial learning (Gaffan and Harrison 1988; Murray and Wise 1997). Wael Asaad, Gregor Rainer and I decided to begin exploring the role of PF neurons in coding rules (Asaad *et al.* 1998).

We used a conditional visuomotor task in which the monkeys learned to associate each of 2 initially novel objects with either a saccade to the left or a saccade to the right (e.g., A → go right; B → go left). While the monkey maintained fixation of a fixation target, one of the objects was presented at the centre of gaze. Then, after a one second delay, the fixation point was extinguished and two choice dots were presented to the left and right of fixation. Monkeys made a saccade to one of the dots depending on which object had been the sample. After learning the initial object-direction pairings, the associations were reversed (now A → go left; B → go right). Once the reversals were learned, the associations were again reversed and then again for up to 9 reversals after the initial learning. The reversals allowed us to avoid confounding object and spatial information, i.e., exclusively associating a specific object with a specific saccade direction. Thus, the relative effects of object and spatial information on neural activity can be determined.

Reversals also allowed us to explore the capability to use feedback from the environment to quickly adjust behaviour, something at which humans with PF damage are remarkably impaired. In tasks such as the Wisconsin Card Sort, they continue to follow a previously successful strategy even when it is clear that the rules of the task have changed and that strategy is no longer successful. Use of an explicit cue greatly improves performance by PF patients in similar circumstances. To this end, we did not provide the monkeys with an explicit cue to signal the reversal. Rather, by monitoring the consequences of their actions, they had to deduce that the rules had changed and modify their behaviour accordingly.

Monkeys learned the associations rapidly, learning the initial associations and the reversals in an average of 15 trials. The first question we asked was whether PF delay activity represented these object–spatial associations. Many PF neurons seemed to; almost 60% (120/202) showed activity that depended on both the sample object and the currently associated saccade direction. A few cells exhibited a straightforward, linear combination of object and spatial information. For most of these cells, however, object and spatial information combined in a non-linear fashion. For example, the neuron depicted in figure 15.5*a* showed a relatively high level of activity in the second half of the delay whenever sample object 'B' was associated with a saccade to the rightward location, but a low level of activity to all other associations of objects and saccade locations. This neuron was not merely tuned to object 'B' because B → go left did not elicit the same level of activity as B

---

of the conditions. The error bars show the standard error of the mean. Note that this neuron shows a high level of delay activity when sample object B is associated with a saccade to the right. By contrast, its delay activity is lower when same object is associated with a saccade to the left or when another object ('A') is associated with a saccade to the left or to the right. Thus, this neuron appears to be tuned for 'B → go right'. (b) Example of another single PF neuron. Plotted on the figure is the average delay activity when either object A or B is associated with either a saccade to the right or a saccade to the left. The error bars show the standard error of the mean. Note that this neuron also showed a non-linear interaction between object and spatial information. It was highly spatially selective when object A cued a rightward or leftward saccade, but showed little spatial selectivity when B was the sample. The brain figure shows the location of recording sites in this experiment.

→ go right. Nor was it merely tuned to 'go right' because A → go right also did not produce the same activity as B → go right. Thus, this neuron seemed to be tuned to the combination of 'B' and 'go right'. Figure 15.5*b* shows another type of 'non-linear' neuron. Plotted on this figure is the average activity in the delay to two different sample objects when they were each associated with either a saccade to the right or a saccade to the left. Note that this neuron showed different degrees of spatial selectivity depending on which object was the sample. There was a larger difference in activity between 'go right' and 'go left' when object 'A' was associated with these directions than when object 'B' was associated with them. Such non-linear interactions between object and spatial information suggest that PF activity is not merely reflecting a simple addition of pre-existing object and saccade direction preferences; rather they may be explicitly coding the learned associations.

These results show that during an associative learning task, many PF neurons coded both the object and the currently associated saccade direction. The majority encoded non-linear combinations of object and spatial information, which suggests a representation of the rules that mapped the objects to their currently associated directional responses. Such rule-based tuning appears to be very common in the PF cortex. For example, responses of lateral PF neurons to a sensory stimulus can vary dramatically depending on the behavioural significance of the stimulus (Watanabe 1990, 1992; Sakagami and Niki 1994*b*). Sakagami and Niki (1994*b*) found that many of the neurons studied responded differently to a visual stimulus depending on whether that stimulus currently required an immediate or delayed release of a response lever. Watanabe (1990, 1992) found many neurons that responded differentially to a sensory stimulus depending on whether it signalled that a reward would or would not be delivered on that trial. In fact, many single PF neurons were tuned to the associative significance of both visual and auditory cues (Watanabe 1992). White and Wise (1997) recently found that the activity of many PF neurons reflected whether monkeys used a spatial rule (attend to the location where a cue had appeared) or a conditional rule (attend to the location associated with the cue, e.g., 'object A→attend right').

Further, there are a wide variety of behavioural studies suggesting that animals retain in working memory not only simple stimulus representations but also the rules and behavioural context associated with the stimulus. For example, delay tasks can be acquired more rapidly if each of the distinct sample stimulus–correct response pairings is associated with a unique reward (Peterson 1984), and changing reinforcers after a task is learned can interfere with performance (Peterson, Trapold 1980). This suggests that working memory representations include information about the different sample–choice pairings and their outcomes, much as the PF neurons in our study convey information about sample–saccade pairings. Also, animals who have learned identity delayed-matching-to-sample with one set of stimuli typically show incomplete transfer to a new set of stimuli; their performance can drop dramatically (Cumming and Berryman 1965) (E. K. Miller, unpublished observations). Even when they have been explicitly trained to generalize by varying the training stimuli, they typically perform better with the stimuli with which they have had the most experience (E. K. Miller, unpublished observation). This suggests that animals do not acquire these tasks by learning to apply a generalized 'matching rule' to a simple sensory representation held in working memory. Rather, they seem to acquire delay tasks by learning a set of conditional rules (e.g., a set of 'if-then' rules) for the different sample stimulus–choice stimuli contingencies (Cumming, Berryman 1965; Carter, Werner 1978). All said, the pattern of neurophysiological and behavioural results do not fit well with 'copy/trace models' in which working memory (and PF delay activity) simply acts as a temporary buffer for sensory inputs and maintains simple stimulus representations. Rather, they fit nicely with 'multiple rule' accounts of working memory, which suggests that working memory (and PF) representations include information about the behavioural rules and context in which the stimulus is imbedded (e.g., see Grant 1993).

15.5 Conclusions

Prefrontal neurons have properties consistent with a role in the executive functions that guide complex thought and action. They can select necessary information from available sensory inputs and from long-term storage. They can integrate information from diverse sources to serve a common behavioural goal. They can map relevant information to action. As might be expected from a region so closely associated with complex behaviour, PF neurons are strongly influenced by task demands. They preferentially represent the stimulus information relevant to behaviour and the information about behavioural context needed to form the abstract rules that guide complex behaviour and mediate executive functions.

The ability to acquire and represent behavioural context presumably depends on a malleable cognitive system. It may be that the PF cortex, which reaches its developmental apex in primates, exhibits functional plasticity. In fact, given its role in the flexible guidance of behaviour, it would seem to be one brain region in which plasticity is essential. Functional plasticity is evident in the sensory and motor cortical areas interconnected with the PF cortex (Mitz *et al.* 1991; Recanzone *et al.* 1992*a,b,c*; Chen and Wise 1995, 1996; Karni 1996; Bichot *et al.* 1996). Indeed, when monkeys are highly trained on a task, the large portion of task-related neurons suggests that the PF cortex has become 'tuned' to task demands (Rao *et al.* 1997). Of course the PF cortex will not be wholly changeable. It has a finely detailed anatomy that must have important functional significance and constrain plasticity (Goldman-Rakic 1987; Cavada and Goldman-Rakic 1989*a, b*). It may be that within this infrastructure, PF networks are modifiable and acquire the information about stimuli and their behavioural context needed to generate the models and abstractions of behaviour, that is, the 'blueprints' that govern our thoughts and actions.

Acknowledgements

I wish to thank Wael Asaad, David Freedman, Mark Histed, Cynthia Kiddoo, Gregor Rainer, S, Chenchal Rao, and Richard Wehby for valuable discussions and Kathleen Anderson, James Mazer, Richard Wehby, and Marlene Wicherski for their comments on this manuscript. This work was supported by funding from the National Institute of Neurological Disorders and Stroke, The Pew Charitable Trusts, The McKnight Foundation, The John Merck Fund, and The Whitehall Foundation.

References

Abbott, V., Black, J. B. and Smith, E. E. 1985 The representation of scripts in memory. *J. Memory and Lang.* **24**, 179–99.

Asaad, W. F., Rainer, G. and Miller, E. K. 1998 Neural activity in the primate prefrontal cortex during associative learning. *Neuron* **21**, 1399–407.

Baddeley, A. 1986 Working Memory. Oxford: Clarendon Press.

Barsalou, L. W. and Sewell, D. R. 1985 Contrasting the representation of scripts and categories. *J. Memory and Lang.* **24**, 646–65.

Bichot, N. P., Schall, J. D. and Thompson, K. G. 1996 Visual feature selectivity in frontal eye fields induced by experience in mature macaques. *Nature* **381**, 697–699.

Boussaoud, D., Ungerleider, L. G. and Desimone, R. 1990 Pathways for motion analysis: cortical connections of the medial superior temporal and fundus of the superior temporal visual areas in the macaque. *J. Comp. Neurol.* **296**, 462–95.

Bruce, C. J. and Goldberg, M. E. 1985 Primate frontal eye fields: I. Single neurones discharging before saccades. *J. Neurophysiol.* **53**, 607–35.

Bullier, J., Schall, J. D. and Morel, A. 1996 Functional streams in occipito-frontal connections in the monkey. *Behav. Brain Res.* **76**, 89–97.

Carter, D. E. and Werner, T. J. 1978 Complex learning and information processing by pigeons: A critical analysis. *J. Exp. Anal. Behav.* **29**, 565–601.

Cavada, C. and Goldman-Rakic, P. S. 1989*a* Posterior parietal cortex in rhesus monkey: I. Parcellation of areas based on distinctive limbic and sensory corticocortical connections. *J. Comp. Neurol.* **287**, 393–421.

Cavada, C. and Goldman-Rakic, P. S. 1989*b* Posterior parietal cortex in rhesus monkey: II. Evidence for segregated corticocortical networks linking sensory and limbic areas with the frontal lobe. *J. Comp. Neurol.* **287**, 422–45.

Chelazzi, L., Miller, E. K., Duncan, J. and Desimone, R. 1993 A neural basis for visual search in inferior temporal cortex [see comments]. *Nature* **363**, 345–7.

Chen, L. L. and Wise, S. P. 1995 Supplementary eye field contrasted with the frontal eye field during acquisition of conditional oculomotor associations. *J. Neurosci.* **73**, 1122–34.

Chen, L. L. and Wise, S. P. 1996 Evolution of directional preferences in the supplementary eye field during acquisition of conditional oculomotor associations. *J. Neurosci.* **16**, 3067–81.

Cohen, J. D. and O'Reilly, R. C. 1996 A preliminary theory of the interactions between prefrontal cortex and hippocampus that contribute to planning and prospective memory. In *Prospective Memory: Theories and Applications* (eds M. Brandimonte, G. O. Einstein and M. A. McDaniel), pp. 267–95. Mahwah, NJ.: Lawrence Erlbaum.

Cohen, J. D. and Servan-Schreiber, D. 1992 Context, cortex, and dopamine: A connectionist approach to behavior and biology in schizophrenia. *Psychol. Rev.* **99**, 45–77.

Cohen, J. D., Servan-Schreiber, D. and McClelland, J. L. 1992 A parallel distributed processing approach to automaticity. *Am. J. Psychol.* **105**, 239–69.

Cohen, J. D., Dunbar, K. and McClelland, J. L. 1996 On the control of automatic processes: A parallel distributed processing model of the Stroop effect. *Psychol. Rev.* **97**, 332–61.

Cohen, J. D., Perlstein, W. M., Braver, T. S., Nystrom, L. E., Noll, D. C., Jonides, J. and Smith, E. E. 1997 Temporal dynamics of brain activation during a working memory task. *Nature* **386**, 604–8.

Constantinidis, C. and Steinmetz, M. A. 1996 Neuronal activity in posterior parietal area 7a during the delay periods of a spatial memory task. *J. Neurophysiol.* **76**, 1352–5.

Courtney, S. M., Ungerleider, B. G., Keil, K. and Haxby, J. V. 1997 Transient and sustained activity in a distributed neural system for human working memory. *Nature* **386**, 608–11.

Courtney, S. M., Petit, L., Maisog, J. M., Ungerleider, L. G. and Haxby, J. V. 1998 An area specialized for spatial working memory in human frontal cortex. *Science* **279**, 1347–51.

Cullen, C. M., Bucci, J., Snow, M., Miller, E. K. and Corkin, S. 1998 FMRI activation during performance on object and spatial components of a working memory task. *NeuroImage* **8**, S867.

Cumming, W. W. and Berryman, R. 1965 The complex discriminated operant: Studies of matching to sample and related problems. In *Stimulus Generalization* (ed. D. I. Mostofsky), pp. 284–330. Stanford: Stanford University Press.

Desimone, R. and Duncan, J. 1995 Neural mechanisms of selective visual attention. *Annu. Rev. Neurosci.* **18**, 193–222.

Desimone, R. and Ungerleider, L. G. 1986 Multiple visual areas in the caudal superior temporal sulcus of the macaque. *J. Comp. Neurol.* **248**, 164–89.

Desimone, R., Albright, T. D., Gross, C. G. and Bruce, C. 1984 Stimulus-selective properties of inferior temporal neurons in the macaque. *J. Neurosci.* **4**, 2051–62.

di Pellegrino, G. and Wise, S. P. 1991 A neurophysiological comparison of three distinct regions of the primate frontal lobe. *Brain* **114**, 951–78.

Diamond, A. 1990 The development and neural bases of memory function as indexed by the AB and delayed response tasks in human infants and infant monkeys. In *The Development and Neural Bases of Higher Cognitive Functions* (ed. A. Diamond), pp. 267–317. New York: NY Academy of Science Press.

Diamond, A. and Goldman-Rakic, P. S. 1989 Comparison of human infants and rhesus monkeys on Piaget's AB task: evidence for dependence on dorsolateral prefrontal cortex. *Exp. Brain Res.* **74**, 24–40.

Dias, R., Robbins, T. W. and Roberts A. C. 1997 Dissociable forms of inhibitory control within prefrontal cortex with an analog of the Wisconsin Card Sort Test: restriction to novel situations and independence from 'on-line' processing. *J. Neurosci.* **17**, 9285–97.

Duncan, J., Humphreys, G. and Ward, R. 1997 Competitive brain activity in visual attention. *Current Opinion in Neurobiology* **7**, 255–261.

Ferrera, V. P., Rudolph, K. K. and Maunsell, J. H. 1994 Responses of neurons in the parietal and temporal visual pathways during a motion task. *J. Neurosci.* **14**, 6171–86.

Fischer, B. and Boch, R. 1985 Peripheral attention versus central fixation: modulation of the visual activity of prelunate cortical cells of the rhesus monkey. *Brain Res.* **345**, 111–123.

Funahashi, S., Bruce, C. J. and Goldman-Rakic, P. S. 1989 Mnemonic coding of visual space in the monkey's dorsolateral prefrontal cortex. *J. Neurophysiol.* **61**, 331–49.

Funahashi, S., Bruce, C. J. and Goldman-Rakic, P. S. 1993 Dorsolateral prefrontal lesions and oculomotor delayed-response performance—evidence for mnemonic scotomas. *J. Neurosci.* **13**, 1479–97.

Fuster, J. M. 1973 Unit activity in prefrontal cortex during delayed-response performance: neuronal correlates of transient memory. *J. Neurophysiol.* **36**, 61–78.

Fuster, J. M. 1985 The prefrontal cortex, mediator of cross-temporal contingencies. *Hum. Neurobiol.* **4**, 169–79.

Fuster, J. M. 1989 The Prefrontal Cortex. New York: Raven Press.

Fuster, J. M. 1995 Memory in the Cerebral Cortex. Cambridge, MA: MIT Press.

Fuster, J. M. and Alexander, G. E. 1971 Neuron activity related to short-term memory. *Science* **173**, 652–4.

Fuster, J. M., Bauer, R. H. and Jervey, J. P. 1982 Cellular discharge in the dorsolateral prefrontal cortex of the monkey in cognitive tasks. *Exp. Neurol.* **77**, 679–94.

Fuster, J. M., Bauer, R. H. and Jervey, J. P. 1985 Functional interactions between inferotemporal and prefrontal cortex in a cognitive task. *Brain Res.* **330**, 299–307.

Gaffan, D. 1977 Response coding in recall of colours by monkeys. *Q. J. Exp. Psychol.* **29**, 597–605.

Gaffan, D. and Harrison, S. 1988 Inferotemporal-frontal disconnection and fornix transection in visuomotor conditional learning by monkeys. *Behav. Brain Res.* **31**, 149–63.

Gaffan, D. and Harrison, S. 1989 A comparison of the effects of fornix transection and sulcus principalis ablation upon spatial learning by monkeys. *Behav. Brain Res.* **31**, 207.

Goldman-Rakic, P. S. 1987 Circuitry of primate prefrontal cortex and regulation of behavior by representational memory. In *Handbook of Physiology: The Nervous System* (ed. F. Plum), pp. 373–417. Bethesda: *Am. Physio. Soc.*

Goldman-Rakic, P. S. 1990 Cellular and circuit basis of working memory in prefrontal cortex of nonhuman primates. *Prog. Brain Res.* **85**, 325–35; discus.

Goldman-Rakic, P. S. 1996 Prefrontal cortex revisited: a multiple-memory domain model of human cognition. In: *Vision and Movement Mechanisms in the Cerebral Cortex* (eds R. Caminiti, K. P. Hoffman, F. Lacquaniti and J. Altman), pp. 162–72. Strasbourg: HFSP.

Goldman, P. S., Rosvold, H. E., Vest, B. and Galkin, T. W. 1971 Analysis of the delayed-alternation deficit produced by dorsolateral prefrontal lesions in the rhesus monkey. *J. Comp. Physiol. Psychol.* **77**, 212–20.

Goldman-Rakic, P. S., Funahashi, S. and Bruce, C. J. 1990 Neocortical memory circuits. *Cold Spring Harb. Symp. Quant. Biol.* **55**, 1025–38.

Goodale, M. A. and Haffenden, A. 1998 Frames of reference for perception and action in the human visual system. *Neurosci. Biobehav. Rev.* **22**, 161–72.

Gottlieb, J. P., Kusunoki, M. and Goldberg, M. E. 1998 The representation of visual salience in monkey parietal cortex. *Nature* **391**, 481–4.

Grafman, J. 1994 Alternative frameworks for the conceptualization of prefrontal functions. In *Handbook of Neuropsychology* (eds F. Boller and J. Grafman), pp. 187–202. Amsterdam: Elsevier.

Grant, D. S. 1993 Coding processes in pigeons. In *Animal Cognition* (ed. T. R. Zentall), pp. 193–216. Hillsdale: Elsevier.

Gross, C. G. and Weiskrantz, L. 1962 Evidence for dissociation of impairment on auditory discrimination and delayed response following lateral frontal lesions in monkeys. *Exp. Neurol.* **5**, 453–76.

Gross, C. G., Rocha-Miranda, C. E. and Bender, D. B. 1972 Visual properties of neurons in inferotemporal cortex of the Macaque. *J. Neurophysiol.* **35**, 96–111.

Hasegawa, R., Sawaguchi, T. and Kubota, K. 1998 Monkey prefrontal neuronal activity coding the forth-coming saccade in an oculomotor delayed matching-to-sample task. *J. Neurophysiol.* **79**, 322–333.

Honig, W. and Thompson, R. K. R. 1982 Retrospective and prospective processing in animal working memory. In *The Psychology of Learning and Motivation: Advances in Research and Theory* (ed. G. H. Bower), pp. 239–83. New York: Academic Press.

Johnson, M. K. 1992 MEM: Recollections of memory. *J. Cog. Neurosci.* **4**, 268–80.

Johnson, M. K. and Hirst, W. 1991 Processing subsystems of memory. In *Perspectives in Cognitive Neuroscience* (eds R. G. Lister and H. J. Weingartner), pp. 3–16. New York: Oxford University Press.

Karni, A. 1996 The acquisition of perceptual and motor skills: A memory system in the adult human cortex. *Cognit. Brain Res.* **5**, 39–48.

Kubota, K. and Niki, H. 1971 Prefrontal cortical unit activity and delayed alternation performance in monkeys. *J. Neurophysiol.* **34**, 337–47.

Luck, S. J. and Vogel, E. K. 1997 The capacity of visual working memory for features and conjunctions. *Nature* **390**, 279–281.

Maunsell, J. H. and Newsome, W. T. 1987 Visual processing in monkey extrastriate cortex. *Annu. Rev. Neurosci.* **10**, 363–401.

Maunsell, J. H. and Van Essen, D. C. 1983 The connections of the middle temporal visual area (MT) and their relationship to a cortical hierarchy in the macaque monkey. *J. Neurosci.* **3**, 2563–86.

McAdams, C. J. and Maunsell, J. H. R 1997 Spatial attention and feature-directed attention can both modulate responses in macaque area V4. *Soc. Neurosci. Abstr.* **23**, 2062.

Miller, E. K., Li, L. and Desimone, R. 1993 Activity of neurons in anterior inferior temporal cortex during a short-term memory task. *J. Neurosci.* **13**, 1460–78.

Miller, E. K., Erickson, C. A. and Desimone, R. 1996 Neural mechanisms of visual working memory in prefrontal cortex of the macaque. *J. Neurosci.* **16**, 5154–67.

Miller, G. A. 1956 The magic number seven plus or minus two: some limits on capacity for processing information. *Psychol. Rev.* **63**, 81–97.

Milner, B. 1963 Effects of different brain lesions on card sorting. *Arch. Neurol.* **9**, 90.

Mishkin, M. 1957 Effects of small frontal lesions on delayed alternation in monkeys. *J. Neurophysiol.* **20**, 615–22.

Mishkin, M. and Manning, F. J. 1978 Non-spatial memory after selective prefrontal lesions in monkeys. *Brain Res.* **143**, 313–23.

Mishkin, M., Vest, B., Waxler, M. and Rosvold, H. E. 1969 A re-examination of the effects of frontal lesions on object alternation. *Neuropsychol.* **7**, 357–64.

Mitz, A. R., Godschalk, M., Wise, S. P. 1991 Learning-dependent neuronal activity in the premotor cortex: activity during the acquisition of conditional motor associations. *J. Neurosci.* **11**, 1855–72.

Moran, J. and Desimone, R. 1985 Selective attention gates visual processing in the extrastriate cortex. *Science* **229**, 782–4.

Motter, B. C. 1993 Focal attention produces spatially selective processing in visual cortical areas V1, V2, and V4 in the presence of competing stimuli. *J. Neurophysiol.* **70**, 909–19.

Murray, E. A. and Wise, S. P. 1997 Role of the orbitoventral prefrontal cortex in conditional motor learning. *Soc. Neurosci. Abstr.* **27**, 12.1.

Norman, D. A., Shallice, T. 1986 Attention to action: willed and automatic control of behavior. In *Consciousness and Self-Regulation: Advances in Research and Theory* (eds R. J. Davidson, G. E. Schwartz and D. Shapiro), pp. 1–18. New York: Plenum.

Oster, M. N., Snow, M., Miller, E. K. and Corkin, S. 1997 FMRI activation during performance on object and spatial components of a working memory task. *Soc. Neurosci. Abstr.* **23**, 2110.

Owen, A. M., Roberts, A. C., Polkey, C. E., Sahakian, B. J. and Robbins, T. W. 1991 Extra-dimensional versus intra-dimensional set shifting performance following frontal lobe excisions, temporal lobe excisions, or amygdalo-hippocampectomy in man. *Neuropsychologia* **29**, 993.

Owen, A. M., Evans, A. C. and Petrides, M. 1996*a* Evidence for a two-stage model of spatial working memory processing within the lateral frontal cortex: A positron emission tomography study. *Cereb. Cortex* **6**, 31–8.

Owen, A. M., Milner, B., Petrides, M. and Evans, A. C. 1996*b* Memory for object features versus memory for object location: a positron-emission tomography study of encoding and retrieval processes. *Proc. Natl. Acad. Sci. USA* **93**, 9212–7.

Owen, A. M., Stern, C. E., Look, R. B., Tracey, I., Rosen, B. R. and Petrides, M. 1998 Functional organization of spatial and nonspatial working memory processing within the human lateral frontal cortex. *Proc. Natl. Acad. Sci. USA* **95**, 7721–6.

Pandya, D. N. and Barnes, C. L. 1987 Architecture and connections of the frontal lobe. In *The Frontal Lobes Revisited* (ed. E. Perecman), pp. 41–72. New York: The IRBN Press.

Pandya, D. N. and Yeterian, E. H. 1990 Prefrontal cortex in relation to other cortical areas in rhesus monkey—architecture and connections. *Prefrontal. Cortex.* **85**, 63–94.

Passingham, R. 1975 Delayed matching after selective prefrontal lesions in monkeys (*macaca mulatta*). *Brain Res.* **92**, 89–102.

Passingham, R. 1993 The Frontal Lobes and Voluntary Action. Oxford: Oxford University Press.

Peterson, G. B. 1984 How expectancies guide behavior. In *Animal Cognition* (eds H. L. Roitblat, T. G. Bever and H. S. Terrace), pp. 135–48. Hillsdale: Lawrence Erlbaum.

Peterson, G. B. and Trapold, M. A. 1980 Effects of altering outcome expectancies in pigeons' delayed conditional discrimination performance. *Learning and Motivation* **11**, 267–88.

Petrides, M. 1994 Frontal lobes and working memory: Evidence from investigations of the effects of cortical excisions in nonhuman primates. In *Handbook of Neuropsychology*, Vol. 9 (eds F. Boller and J. Grafman), pp. 59–82. Amsterdam: Elsevier.

Petrides, M. 1995 Impairments on nonspatial self-ordered and externally ordered working memory tasks after lesions of the mid-dorsal part of the lateral frontal cortex of the monkey. *J. Neurosci.* **15**, 359–75.

Petrides, M. and Pandya, D. N. 1984 Projections to the frontal cortex from the posterior parietal region in the rhesus monkey. *J. Comp. Neurol.* **228**, 105–16.

Postle, B. R. and D'Esposito, M. 1998 Analysis of spatial and object delayed response with event-related fMRI. *Proc. Cog. Neuro. Soc.* **5**, 85.

Quintana, J. and Fuster, J. M. 1992 Mnemonic and predictive functions of cortical neurons in a memory task. *Neuroreport.* **3**, 721–4.

Rainer, G., Rao, S. C. and Miller, E. K. 1997 Prospective memory for objects in the monkey prefrontal cortex. *Soc. Neurosci. Abstr.* **23**, 1965.

Rainer, G., Asaad, W. F. and Miller, E. K. 1998*a* Memory fields of neurons in the primate prefrontal cortex. *Proc. Natl. Acad. Sci. USA* **95**, 15008–13.

Rainer, G., Asaad, W. F. and Miller, E. K. 1998*b* Selective representation of relevant information by neurons in the primate prefrontal cortex. *Nature* **393**, 577–9.

Rao, S. C., Rainer, G. and Miller, E. K. 1997 Integration of what and where in the primate prefrontal cortex. *Science* **276**, 821–4.

Recanzone, G. H., Merzenich, M. M. and Dinse, H. R. 1992*a* Expansion of the cortical representation of a specific skin field in primary somatosensory cortex by intracortical microstimulation. *Cereb. Cortex.* **2**, 181–196.

Recanzone, G. H., Merzenich, M. M., Jenkins, W. M., Grajski, K. A. and Dinse, H. R. 1992*b* Topographic reorganization of the hand representation in cortical area 3b owl monkeys trained in a frequency-discrimination task. *J. Neurophysiol.* **67**, 1031–56.

Recanzone, G. H., Merzenich, M. M. and Schreiner, C. E. 1992*c* Changes in the distributed temporal response properties of SI cortical neurons reflect improvements in performance on a temporally based tactile discrimination task. *J. Neurophysiol.* **67**, 1071–91.

Sakagami, M. and Niki, H. 1994*a* Encoding of behavioral significance of visual stimuli by primate prefrontal neurons: relation to relevant task conditions. *Exp. Brain Res.* **97**, 423–36.

Sakagami, M. and Niki, H. 1994*b* Spatial selectivity of go/no-go neurons in monkey prefrontal cortex. *Exp. Brain Res.* **100**, 165–9.

Sakai, K. and Miyashita, Y. 1991 Neural organization for the long-term memory of paired associates. *Nature* **354**, 152–5.

Schiller, P. H., True, S. D. and Conway, J. L. 1979 Effects of frontal eye field and superior colliculus ablations on eye movements. *Science* **206**, 590–2.

Schiller, P. H., Sandell, J. H. and Maunsell, J. H. 1987 The effect of frontal eye field and superior colliculus lesions on saccadic latencies in the rhesus monkey. *J. Neurophysiol.* **57**, 1033–49.

Sereno, A. B. and Maunsell, J. H. R. 1995 Spatial and shape selective sensory and attentional effects in neurons in the macaque lateral intraparietal cortex (LIP). *Invest. Ophthalmol. Vis. Sci.* **36**, 692 (Abstract).

Shallice, T. 1982 Specific impairments of planning. *Philos. Trans. R. Soc. Lond. [Biol.]* **298**, 199–209.

Ungerleider, L. G. and Mishkin, M. 1982 Two cortical visual systems. In *Analysis of Visual Behavior* (eds J. Ingle, M. A. Goodale and R. J. W. Mansfield), pp. 549–86. Cambridge, MA: MIT Press.

Ungerleider, L. G., Gaffan, D. and Pelak, V. S. 1989 Projections from inferior temporal cortex to prefrontal cortex via the uncinate fascicle in rhesus monkeys. *Exp. Brain Res.* **76**, 473–84.

Van Essen, D. C., Anderson, C. H. and Felleman, D. J. 1992 Information processing in the primate visual system: an integrated systems perspective. *Science* **255**, 419–23.

Watanabe, M. 1981 Prefrontal unit activity during delayed conditional discriminations in the monkey. *Brain Res.* **225**, 51–65.

Watanabe, M. 1990 Prefrontal unit activity during associative learning in the monkey. *Exp. Brain Res.* **80**, 296–309.

Watanabe, M. 1992 Frontal units of the monkey coding the associative significance of visual and auditory stimuli. *Exp. Brain Res.* **89**, 233–47.

Watanabe, M. 1996 Reward expectancy in primate prefrontal neurons. *Nature* **382**, 629–32.

Webster, M. J., Bachevalier, J. and Ungerleider, L. G. 1994 Connections of inferior temporal areas TEO and TE with parietal and frontal cortex in macaque monkeys. *Cereb. Cortex* **4**, 470–83.

White, I. M. and Wise, S. P. 1997 Rule-dependent neuronal activity in the prefrontal cortex. *Soc. Neurosci. Abstr.* **23**, 1303.

Wilson, F. A. W, O Scalaidhe, S. P. and Goldman-Rakic, P. S. 1993 Dissociation of object and spatial processing domains in primate prefrontal cortex. *Science* **260**, 1955–8.

Wise, S. P., Murray, E. A. and Gerfen, C. R. 1996 The frontal-basal ganglia system in primates. *Crit. Rev. Neurobiol.* **10**, 317–56.

16

Task-switching: positive and negative priming of task-set

Alan Allport and Glenn Wylie

Abstract

The first half of this chapter provides a critical review of experiments on task-switching, with reference to the theoretical interpretation of behavioural 'switch-costs'. Our review focusses on intrinsically competing pairs of tasks, such as object naming in either of two languages; competing arithmetic operations; and Stroop colour-naming vs. word-reading. We argue that the behavioural costs of switching between competing tasks of this kind result from components of the task-set for the *preceding* task(s), which can remain primed involuntarily ('task-set inertia').

The second half of the chapter describes some new experiments, designed to test the hypothesis of higher-order priming at the level of task control. Three experiments, using existing task-switching paradigms, confirm the prediction that it is control characteristics of the *preceding* task (the task FROM which a switch is made) that primarily determine switch-costs between competing tasks, rather than characteristics of the upcoming task. The results also challenge the assumption that task-set is fully reconfigured on 'non-switch' trials, in current task-switching paradigms. Two further experiments explore a new experimental procedure, designed to exploit the phenomenon of higher-order priming of task control-states, to investigate properties of task-set. The results permit the functional separation of positive and negative components of task-set in competing (Stroop-like) tasks: activation or facilitation of constituents of one task, and inhibition of the competitor task. Following a switch to the competitor task, these components of the previous control state appear, respectively, in the form of competitor priming and negative priming of the current task.

16.1 Introduction

Item specific priming and priming of higher-order task-set

Item-specific priming has been studied in many different stimulus domains. Repetition of the same item-type (e.g., a face, a visual object, a spoken or written word) can facilitate recognition of that item-type on a second or later occasion, over considerable intervals of time, in spite of changes to particular, 'episodic' features of the stimulus, such as its size, orientation, letter-case, speaker's voice, change from part-to-whole view, etc. (e.g., Biederman and Cooper 1992; Brunas *et al.* 1990; Evett and Humphreys 1981; Kirsner *et al.* 1986; Scarborough *et al.* 1977; Schacter and Church 1992). Repetition priming of stimulus-type has been found to be unaffected by changes of the task, or of the external environment, between prime and test (e.g., Ellis *et al.* 1990; Monsell 1985); moreover, the underlying effect apparently remains constant over manipulations of attention and of 'levels of processing' (Jacoby and Dallas 1981; Jacoby 1994).

A striking general property of these type-specific repetition-priming effects is thus their substantial independence of strategic or volitional factors. For this reason, repetition priming offers a powerful and attractive set of methods for studying the underlying cognitive representations (structural descriptions), unconfounded by strategic effects of the subject's intentional set. They have been fruitfully exploited for this purpose in a variety of different cognitive domains (e.g.,

Biederman and Cooper 1992; Bruce *et al.* 1994; Monsell 1985; Taft 1991; Kirsner and Speelman 1993; and others). In contrast, priming between semantically associated stimulus-categories shows very different properties, being generally short-lasting (but see Becker *et al.* 1997), and subject to extensive strategic effects of expectancy, encoding task, etc. See Neely (1991) for review.

Negative priming effects from previously ignored distractors have also provided a valuable methodology for studying processes of selective attention (e.g., Driver and Tipper 1989; DeSchepper and Treisman 1996). (See Fox (1995); May *et al.* (1995); Milliken and Tipper (1998), for reviews.) Again, unlike long-term repetition priming, repetition of a previously ignored distractor, occurring as the target in a subsequent, selective probe trial, can result in delay of probe response or in net facilitation, depending on the attentional conditions during the probe trial, the time interval between prime and probe, intervening events, stimulus novelty, and other factors. Of particular relevance to the topic of the present paper, negative priming effects have been shown to depend strongly on the subject's task at the time of encoding (Tipper *et al.* 1994).

The varieties of priming effect referred to above have all been interpreted as reflecting either temporary or long-term changes at the level of individual cognitive representations, either of types or tokens. However, involuntary priming effects are not confined to item-specific cognitive representations, but apply also to stimulus–response (or, more generally, condition–action) mapping rules and other higher-order task variables. There were several empirical demonstrations of such effects in the 1970s. Rabbitt and Vyas (1973, 1979) and Duncan (1977, 1978), established the existence of facilitation effects in speeded choice-response tasks, when the same mapping 'rules', relating stimuli and responses, were repeated, independently of the repetition of individual stimulus or response items. However, to our knowledge, these effects have not been systematically studied since then.

The proposal that we explore in this paper is that involuntary priming (both positive and negative) of task-specific condition–action rules is the principle determinant of performance costs in switching between competing tasks. We further propose that the study of these higher-order priming effects, across tasks, may provide a comparably powerful set of methods for studying the nature of selective task-set.

Priming of higher-order 'control' variables across tasks

Priming at the level of higher-order task variables has received little recent attention. Empirically, therefore, we have relatively little basis on which to make predictions concerning the characteristics of such effects: e.g., their duration, their susceptibility to intervening events, to strategic or volitional manipulations, etc. The literature on item-specific priming effects, referred to above, includes effects with widely differing time-courses; some of these item-specific priming effects are massively affected by strategic factors and by intervening events; others appear immune to manipulations of the subject's explicit intention. A similar heterogeneity may be true of priming effects pertaining to S–R mappings and higher-order 'control' variables. What we need is a methodology. Then we can start to find out.

A particularly powerful method for probing priming effects is distractor- or competitor-priming. An early example is Warren (1972, 1974). Warren used a Stroop colour-naming task to study priming of the distractor or 'base' word that the subject was attempting to ignore. The greater the priming of that word, the harder it is to ignore, hence the longer the response time (RT) to name the ink colour. Our current approach to the priming of task-set, to be described here, uses a similar competitor-priming method.

In this general approach, it is contrived for a subject first to adopt one task-set (the prime), and then later a second, potentially competing task-set (the probe). Increased response time (RT) and/or errors in the execution of the probe task provide the principal index of continued priming of the prior, prime task. Accordingly, competitor priming between tasks is naturally studied in situations in which the subjects are required to shift from one task to another. They may do so repeatedly or, in the limit, just once.

Our current approach developed out of some earlier studies of task-switching, in the course of our attempts to understand the behavioural costs that can be associated with a shift of task (Allport *et al.* 1994; Hsieh and Allport 1994; Meuter and Allport, in press). In order to explain the motivation for our more recent experiments, we shall need to review, first, some of these earlier task-switching studies, from our own and other laboratories. This is the subject of §16.2 of this chapter. In §16.3 we describe some more recent studies, which prompt a partial reappraisal of our earlier ideas.

16.2 Task-switching and priming of task-set: a critical review

Task-switching with and without time-costs

Some of the earliest studies of task-switching (Jersild 1927; Spector and Biederman 1976) compared performance at each of two tasks, A and B, in self-paced series of trials at the same, repeated task, AAAA . . . and BBBB . . . ('pure' blocks), against other series in which the subjects alternated regularly between the two tasks, ABABAB . . . , on successive trials ('alternating' blocks). For example, in one experiment, subjects were asked to work down lists of two-digit numbers, as fast as possible, adding 3 to each number, and saying the result aloud (task A). In task B, they worked down other lists, but now subtracting 3s. The mean completion time for pure tasks A and B was then compared to the time taken in alternating blocks, i.e., adding 3 to the first number, subtracting 3 from the next, and so on. In these (and other) pairs of tasks, large time costs were found for task alternation, amounting to several hundred ms per item. Spector and Biederman found that adding an *extrinsic* reminder-cue to the task to be performed (e.g., a 'plus' or 'minus' sign beside each number) reduced the time cost of task alternation, but that a substantial time cost still remained.

However, following Jersild (1927), the same authors also reported an important, and arguably fundamental boundary-condition on the occurrence of task-alternation costs, in their paradigm. Task A was adding 3s, as before; task B was giving the opposite of common antonyms (happy, dark, old, etc.). In this case, there was no time cost for alternating between the two tasks. Spector and Biederman proposed that the critical feature in eliminating the shift cost was the degree to which each task was 'unambiguously cued by the stimuli'; however, they did not elaborate further on this proposal.

Clearly, the 'plus' and 'minus' signs, in the previous study, also 'unambiguously' cued the respective tasks of adding and subtracting, but it appears that *extrinsic* cueing of each task was not sufficient, in this case, to remove the cost of task-switching. The numbers themselves—the 'intrinsic' task-stimuli to which the response is computed—still afforded both tasks. In contrast, in alternating between adding 3s and naming opposites, there was no overlap in the two sets of task-stimuli, nor in their responses; there is also no possibility of applying either task operation to the set of stimuli for the other task. One cannot add 3 to the word 'dark', nor do two-digit numbers have verbal 'opposites'. It is thus plausible to suppose that, in the alternating condition, the task-sets for *both* of these tasks can be kept in a state of readiness, to be triggered by the appropriate stimuli, trial by trial, without mutual conflict.

On the other hand, adding 3s or giving opposites are certainly not the only such tasks that these stimuli afford. Even if we consider only very well learned operations and oral responses, it is obvious that two-digit numbers afford a whole range of similar tasks, from simple naming, to adding (or subtracting) any other integers (besides 3), to categorising the number as odd or even, etc., etc. Written words, likewise, afford many other, familiar tasks such as reading aloud, giving synonyms, associates, and so on. In this respect, Spector and Biederman's tasks were far from uniquely or 'unambiguously' cued by the task-stimuli themselves. Hence, the evidence suggests, efficient, cost-free switching between tasks requires only that the intrinsic task-stimuli uniquely afford one or other (but not both) of the tasks *currently active* in working memory. Other, equally, or even more familiar task-sets, that are *not currently active*, appear to have no effect on task-alternation costs. The 'bottom-up' cueing of even highly overlearned tasks, it appears, is dependent on the current state of stimulus-to-task mappings in working memory.

The question is: *What determines the set of currently active tasks in procedural working memory?* How is task-set activation related to the subject's explicit intentions? And what are the consequences of task-set activation for the performance of *other*, potentially competing tasks? We believe these questions to be of fundamental importance for our understanding of working memory and the intentional control of tasks.

Task-switching and the activation of intended and unintended tasks in procedural working memory

Allport *et al.* (1994, Experiment 4) set out to address this question, using task-stimuli with an explicitly built-in ambiguity of task cueing, or task affordance, namely 'Stroop' stimuli. For one group of participants, task A was the 'Stroop' colour-naming task (MacLeod 1991). In this task, colour-words are written in incongruent ink-colours, and the task is to name the ink-colour, ignoring the word; e.g., the word GREEN might be written in red ink, and the correct response is to say 'red'. Task B was an analogous number-numerosity 'Stroop' task, in which groups of one to nine identical numerals were presented, and the task was to name the size of the group—its numerosity—ignoring the (incongruent) numeral value. Clearly, there is no overlap between either stimuli or responses in these two tasks, A and B; furthermore, the set of stimuli for one task does not afford the mental operations demanded by the other. Accordingly, it should be possible for *both* task-sets (colour-naming, numerosity-naming) to remain active in the alternating condition, to be triggered selectively by the alternating stimulus-types, without switching costs. In fact, as this account would predict, after a small amount of practice our participants were able to alternate between these two tasks without additional time cost. Another group of participants was given the identical stimulus-set to the first group, but carried out the complementary (and much easier) tasks, respectively, of reading aloud the colour-words (in the colour-word display) and naming the numerals (in the number-numerosity displays). Like the first group, after a few practice lists, they too were able to alternate between these two tasks, trial by trial, without any additional time-cost compared to the pure lists.

Thus far, the results are consistent with the proposal that task-alternation costs can be eliminated when each set of task-stimuli uniquely affords just one of the currently intended (or currently designated) tasks. (The corollary of this proposal would appear to be that the cost of task-alternating represents the time taken to remember, trial by trial, which of the current tasks is the one I should be doing now. When this ambiguity is removed, the results discussed so far suggest, there may be no further source of time-costs in task alternation.)

Note that the task-stimuli may still afford *other* possible, and even very familiar tasks, outside the set of tasks assigned to the participants in the experimental context. Our task-stimuli were selected precisely to test this. Thus, for the participants in the first group, who named the *colour* of the Stroop colour-word stimuli and the *numerosity* of the numeral-groups, the two sets of stimuli undoubtedly provided highly compatible cues for the complementary (and potentially dominant or 'prepotent') tasks of word-reading and numeral-naming, respectively. (Evidence that the incongruent stimulus-dimensions do in fact cue these 'prepotent' competing tasks is provided by over 50 years of research on the Stroop effect (MacLeod 1991)). Yet alternation between these two *non*-dominant, 'Stroop' tasks (colour-naming; numerosity-naming) showed performance with zero costs of task-switching, compared to the pure task baseline.

However, this was not the end of the experiment. The participants were now asked to forget their previous tasks. The group that had previously named colours and numerosities was now instructed to read the words and to name the numerals, still with the same two types of 'Stroop' stimuli; and the group that had started off with word-reading and numeral-naming was switched to colour- and numerosity-naming, also with the same stimuli as before. This time, however, there were large time-costs of task alternation. Over the first three lists of the new tasks, for example, the group now doing the 'non-Stroop' tasks of word-reading and numeral-naming showed a mean task-alternation cost of about 300 ms per item (over and above a pure task baseline of about 500 ms per item). Over the next three lists, the alternation-cost dropped to around 125 ms, with a further drop over the next three lists. However, even for the last 15 lists of the block, there was still a highly significant alternation-cost ($p < 0.0001$) which showed no tendency to diminish further over the remainder of the block.

In a third and final block of the experiment, the participants were switched back once again to their original pairs of tasks, still with the same stimuli. Again there were large time costs in the alternating conditions. Thus, at the start of this third block, the group who reverted to their original tasks of word-reading and numeral-naming now had an alternation-cost of over 300 ms; this dropped steeply over the next few lists, but persisted as a small but highly significant effect for the remainder of the experiment. Interestingly, list times for the two *pure* or non-alternating tasks (reading, numeral-naming) were also slower over the first few lists of block 3 than they had been in the first block. We shall describe further experiments directed to this phenomenon (task-switching costs on 'non-switch' trials) in §16.3.

We can now return to the question that this experiment was designed to address. We asked: What determines the set of *currently active tasks* in procedural working memory? And how is this related to the subject's explicit intentions? The results provide some very clear answers. They tell us, first, that activated task-sets are not confined simply to those tasks currently designated for execution by the experimenter—and which the subject is explicitly engaged in performing. They can include also other tasks in which the subject was recently or formerly engaged, even though these tasks are no longer explicitly intended by the subject. Second, once they have been engaged, facilitation of these *no-longer-intended* but competing task-sets can apparently persist over many successive trials of the new tasks. (Thus, in the experiment just described, participants performed seven trials in sequence (one 'list') at each of the two new tasks, as pure tasks, even before the first set of alternating trials.) Third, however, the competing task-set activations evidently declined over the next few sequences of trials at the new tasks (in our experiment, over some 20 to 40 trials). Nevertheless, residual competition from the earlier tasks, in the form of significant alternation costs, appeared to persist over an entire block (of 168 trials, in 24 lists) of the new tasks.

We have described the results of this experiment at some length, as they provide the starting point for some of our more recent experiments, which we review below. What they show, we suggest, is a new form (or forms) of *priming*, at the level of competing condition–action rules in procedural working memory. Such rules, together with related Goal activations, we assume, are constitutive of intentional task control, or task-set. A striking implication of these results, as regards the traditional distinction between 'controlled' and 'automatic' processes, is thus that task-set, the prototypical constituent of 'control', is itself subject to 'automatic' priming effects.

Task-set inertia (TSI): competitor-priming and negative priming of task-set

As described above, when the task-stimuli themselves do not cue unequivocally the task to be performed, within the currently active set of tasks, task-alternation (or task-switching) shows a characteristic pattern of costs in the speed and accuracy of performance. An intuitive interpretation of these 'task-switching costs' is that they reflect, directly, the time taken to reconfigure the processing system in readiness for the upcoming task. Allport *et al.* (1994), however, suggested an alternative interpretation, in terms of proactive interference between competing task-sets. They proposed that the task-alternation costs resulted from the involuntary persistence of stimulus-to-task mappings for the preceding trial(s) into the processing of the next (switch) trial. The alternation costs, they suggested, were thus an interference, or response conflict effect between competing S–R mappings or condition–action rules.

Allport *et al.* presented four principal, empirical arguments for this interpretation. The first was the demonstration of relatively long-lasting competitor priming effects from preceding, but no longer valid or intended tasks, described above, which they referred to as 'task-set inertia' (TSI). The second was the finding that an unfilled preparation interval many times longer than the switch-cost, with a fully predictable shift of task, was not sufficient to eliminate the RT switch-cost on the next trial, even though the subject knew that a switch of set was required and was requested to do his or her best to prepare for it. They inferred from this that the RT switch-costs *as a whole* could not simply represent the time needed to execute an anticipatory 'shift of set', in advance of the next trial.

The third piece of evidence in favour of their interpretation was a reversed asymmetry that they reported in the switch-costs between certain pairs of tasks. In a further experiment, on successive trials, participants switched directly between competing versions of the classic Stroop colour-word task, using incongruent Stroop stimuli (Stroop 1935), i.e., they switched between naming the colour and reading the word. With these stimuli—in the more usual, repeated-task conditions—colour-naming shows interference from the incongruent colour-word, whereas word-reading typically shows *no* interference from the incongruent ink-colour (MacLeod 1991). This well known asymmetry in interference effects has been attributed to differences in the learned 'strength of processing' in the competing pathways (MacLeod and Dunbar 1988; Cohen *et al.* 1990). However, with these two tasks, Allport *et al.* found asymmetric switch-costs in the *opposite* direction: that is, larger costs in switching to the dominant word-reading task than to the 'weaker' task of colour-naming. This result appears paradoxical if the switch-cost is taken to represent the time needed for a control operation to prepare for the upcoming task. If this were the principal origin of the switch-cost, why should it take longer to prepare for the easier, better-learned task of word-reading than for the weaker, non-dominant task of colour-naming? On the other hand, if the switch-cost is determined primarily by the characteristics of the *preceding* task-set, as we argue below, this pattern of results becomes readily intelligible.

The critical assumption is this. For the 'weaker' of the two competing tasks (i.e., here, colour-naming) to be performed, not only must the task-set for colour-naming be activated, but the competing (and normally dominant) task-set for word-reading must be actively suppressed or inhibited. Note that this analysis applies, in principle, to any pairing of mutually competing tasks, A and B, potentially elicited by the same (composite or overlapping) stimulus ensembles, with divergent S–R mappings. According to the TSI hypothesis, the S–R mapping established on preceding trial(s) tends to persist, involuntarily. Suppose that A is the weaker of two divergent S–R tasks, A and B. When the task-demand shifts from task A to task B (still with the same set of stimuli), persisting facilitation of the prior task, A, becomes a form of *competitor priming*, interfering with the execution of B; persisting suppression of the previous competitor-task, B, across the same shift of task, now becomes a form of *negative priming* of task B.

The 'paradoxical' (reversed) asymmetry in the switch-costs between Stroop colour-naming and word-reading is now easily understood, in terms of the TSI hypothesis. Consider first a switch of task from Stroop colour-naming ('Colour') to word-reading ('Word'). When stimulus processing on the switch trial begins, the task-set for Colour—now the competitor task—remains partially activated while the (now intended) Word task is still suppressed. Hence a very slow response; that is, a large 'switch-cost' from Colour to Word. Now consider a switch of task in the other direction, from Word to Colour. In contrast to Colour, the Word task should require little or no suppression of colour-naming. Thus, on a switch from Word, there is little or no suppression of colour-naming to carry over into, and compete with, the complementary task. Hence a relatively small switch-cost from Word to Colour.

The fourth and last piece of evidence, put forward by Allport *et al.* for their interpretation of switch-costs, came from the same experiment. On the switch trials from colour-naming to word-reading, they found large (c. 150 ms) 'reverse Stroop' interference effects. That is, unlike word-reading in the usual, pure task condition, on task-switching trials the incongruent colour now interfered dramatically with word-reading. Furthermore, this reverse Stroop effect remained present (with little or no reduction in magnitude) after a preparation interval for the word task of a second or more. If the task-set for normal word-reading had been engaged *prior* to stimulus processing on the switch trial, this result would appear entirely unaccountable. On the other hand, if the task-set established on the preceding, colour-naming trial (colour-task activation, word-task suppression) persisted involuntarily into the next, word-reading trial, this is exactly the result we should expect.

TSI and the active disengagement of task-set

One clarification of the TSI hypothesis is needed. Allport *et al.* proposed that their task-alternation costs resulted from the involuntary persistence of a prior, competing, or conflicting, task-set. However, this hypothesis emphatically does not presuppose that the persisting task-set activations must remain, necessarily, unaffected by any other, subsequent processes, other than passive decay. It is most unlikely that any neuro-cognitive activation/inhibition functions should remain encapsulated from other ongoing processes in this way. (Clearly, the item-specific negative and associative priming effects referred to in the Introduction are affected by subsequent, related processing.) Allport *et al.* explicitly proposed that disengagement from the prior task-set can be triggered by task-relevant stimuli for the upcoming task, in conjunction with an instruction (or intention) to shift tasks. ('Active disengagement from the task set of preceding trials, it appears, must wait until triggered by the imperative stimulus for the following trial.' Allport *et al.* 1994, p. 441.)

Apparently, this (to its authors, obvious) feature of the TSI hypothesis was not clearly understood. In a series of elegant experiments on task-switching, Rogers and Monsell (1995) reported that, with a predictable switch of task every fourth trial, the cost of a task-switch (defined as the difference in performance between switch and non-switch trials) did not dissipate gradually over the four trials but was carried entirely by the first trial of a run (the 'switch' trial). This is an important and interesting result, to which we shall return later. However, Rogers and Monsell claimed that this outcome was incompatible with the TSI account, 'as it is essential to the explanatory adequacy of TSI . . . that it persist over many intervening trials.' We are puzzled by this statement. If the correct stimulus–response mapping is in fact executed on the switch trial (as it generally is), how could this leave unchanged the pattern of task-set activation/inhibition for subsequent trials? Clearly, according to the principle of task-set inertia, the new task-set—implemented correctly (although slowly) on the switch trial—should now, in turn, affect the immediately following trial(s); just as the previous task-set, in turn, must have been engaged by control processes on an earlier trial. (If not, where could the TSI come from in the first place?) On the other hand, the question of how far, or under what conditions, the reconfiguration of S–R mappings is *complete* after a single 'switch' trial, is an empirical question, to which we return in §16.3.

Undoubtedly, additional control processes are brought to bear on the pre-existing task-set, on a 'switch' trial. If not, the previous task would continue to be executed. (See also the following section, *Anticipatory preparation of task-set*.) How this occurs; what forms of task-relevant cueing can facilitate or impede it; how the appropriate condition–action rules—mediating an externally and/or internally cued shift of stimulus-to-task mappings—are represented in procedural working memory; and how such rules are initially compiled or acquired; these are all fundamental questions for a theory of task control. They constitute a major agenda for future research. In this paper, however, we are concerned primarily with the nature of the resulting control states, and their consequences, once they have been engaged. Nevertheless, in concluding this brief review of current, experimental studies of task-switching, some questions about anticipatory task-preparation need to be addressed.

Anticipatory preparation of task-set

Our more recent experiments, to be described below, strongly support the TSI analysis. However, in one respect at least, Allport *et al.* (1994) were clearly, empirically mistaken. Finding no compelling evidence in their own data for active preparation of the upcoming task, or 'task-set reconfiguration', *in advance* of the imperative stimulus for a switch trial, they were tempted to infer that such anticipatory task-preparation might simply not be observable in task-switching paradigms of this kind. (They suggested that 'perhaps other, quite different experimental paradigms will be more successful in this respect.') In this they overlooked an important and pioneering study by Sudevan and Taylor (1987). Since then, a number of other authors have provided clear evidence of anticipatory task-preparation, using task-switching paradigms with variable preparation interval (Rogers and Monsell 1995; Meiran 1996; Meiran *et al.*, submitted; De Jong 1996; De Jong *et al.*, submitted). Using competing (divergent) S–R tasks, either with a predictable switch of task (Rogers and Monsell 1995) and/or with explicit cueing of the upcoming task (Meiran 1996, Meiran *et al.*, submitted; De Jong 1996), these authors showed that mean RT and accuracy of response on the switch trials can improve dramatically over the course of a preparation interval (PI). Much of this improvement appears to be made in the first 600 ms or so of task preparation, but can continue over intervals of several seconds.

However, even after a PI of one to three seconds, large, residual 'switch-costs' in mean RT (relative to the 'non-switch' trials) remain, in practically all reported studies. To date we know of only one exception. In this one case, De Jong *et al.* (submitted) found that the switch-cost in a two-alternative classification task was reduced to near zero over a PI of 1.5 s, for their young (though not for old) participants. The experiment required subjects to switch between response to letter-shape (X vs O) and response to colour (red vs blue). The task pre-cue conditions of this experiment appear critical. A precue displayed, in advance, the two possible values of the current, task-relevant stimulus dimension, viz. a pair of Xs and Os, or a pair of red and blue colour patches. We offer the conjecture that participants prepare for the upcoming task by *imagining* executing one or more trials with the intended S–R mapping. Presentation of a task-relevant stimulus as a precue presumably facilitates this. In the absence of a task-stimulus preview like that used by De Jong *et al.*, voluntary task preparation leaves a substantial residual 'switch-cost', compared to performance on the 'non-switch' trials. This is the case in all other reported cases known to us (using divergent S–R tasks).

Nevertheless, anticipatory task-preparation undoubtedly occurs. Task-cueing in advance of the imperative stimulus clearly facilitates a shift of set. Its effect appears to be to reduce or antagonise the previous task-priming (TSI). Covert execution of an instance of the intended task would provide a possible mechanism for this effect.

We have three further comments to make.

- First, the reduction in switch-costs is generally much smaller than the corresponding preparation interval. For example, participants in Rogers and Monsell's (1995) Experiment 3 were able to reduce their switch-costs by about 90 ms over a PI of 1.2 s. Hence, as Allport *et al.* (1994) suggested, it is clear that the size of the RT switch-cost cannot be taken to measure *the time taken to execute a 'shift of set', in advance* of processing the switch-trial stimulus. Emphatically, the size of the so-called 'preparatory' or 'endogenous' component—that is, that portion of the RT switch-cost that declines over a PI—cannot be interpreted in this way. A moment's reflection makes this clear. The process of anticipatory preparation evidently can continue over several seconds, i.e., over a period that can be an order of magnitude longer than the size of the 'shift cost' itself. (Thus, in Rogers and Monsell's experiment, just cited, the 'endogenous' switch-cost was 90 ms, but the *time taken* to achieve this much preparation-benefit was 1.2 s.) The time-course of the relevant, anticipatory control operation bears no currently known relation to the magnitude of the RT 'switch-cost', nor to any component of it.

- Second, it is by no means clear what, precisely, has been 'reconfigured' during the course of the preparation interval. In the studies referred to above, participants switched between two competing task-relevant stimulus attributes or stimulus dimensions. In such cases, as De Jong *et al.* suggest, 'configuration of the correct task set . . . might thus be thought to involve preparing the perceptual system for selective processing of the relevant stimulus dimension and loading the appropriate stimulus–response mapping.' Meiran (1996) and Meiran *et al.* (submitted) put forward a similar proposal. Clearly, if task preparation (over a switch of task-relevant stimulus type) had such an effect on selective processing of task-relevant vs -irrelevant stimulus dimensions, a direct consequence should be the gradual reduction of crosstalk interference effects from the previously relevant (but now irrelevant) stimulus dimension, as the switch-costs progressively declined over increasing PI. However, this is not what these authors observed. They found large interference effects on switch trials from the previously relevant stimulus attribute (task congruity effects). The interference effects were generally smaller on non-switch trials (e.g., De Jong *et al.*, submitted, Experiments 1 and 3; Meiran 1996, Experiments 1–4; Meiran *et al.*, submitted, Experiment 4; Rogers and Monsell 1995, Experiments 1 and 3, etc.), and were smaller still in pure task blocks (e.g., De Jong *et al.*, submitted, Experiment 3). However, in none of these experiments which manipulated the duration of a task-preparation interval did RT interference (from stimulus attributes relevant to the other task) decrease over PI, nor did it enter into a reliable third-order interaction involving preparation interval and switch vs non-switch. Consequently, whatever anticipatory reconfiguration occurred in these experiments over the course of a 1-sec (or 3-sec) PI, there is no evidence that it affected the relative perceptual pertinence (i.e. the attentional weight, Bundesen 1990) of task-relevant vs irrelevant stimulus attributes.[1]

- Our third comment concerns the appropriate baseline for measuring performance under optimum task preparation. Rogers and Monsell (1995) argued that the difference between performance in alternating and pure blocks of trials (Jersild's method for studying task-switch-costs) confounded at least two factors: task-set reconfiguration and having two, rather than one, task-sets 'active' or 'available' in procedural working memory. They also suggested that the alternating blocks were likely to result in greater arousal, effort, etc., than pure-task blocks.[2] Motivated by these considerations, Rogers and Monsell introduced an ingenious experimental method, which they named the 'alternating runs paradigm'. Participants made a predictable switch of task every second trial (in one experiment, referred to above, every fourth trial). Within the same block there were thus 'switch' trials and 'non-switch' trials. Rogers and Monsell then estimated the 'cost of task-switching' as the difference in mean RT—and error-rate—between switch and non-switch trials. The basic assumption here is explicitly that task-set reconfiguration is 'completed' over the course of a single switch trial; or at least, that it is completed prior to the immediately next 'non-switch' trial. Complete task-set reconfiguration presumably includes not only full engagement of the current task-set, but also full disengagement from any prior, competing task-sets. All studies of task-switching (like those referred to above), in which the 'switch-cost' is defined as the difference between 'switch' and 'non-switch' trials within the same block, rest on the same assumption. This is the assumption that optimum or 'complete' task-set reconfiguration is achieved after a single switch trial, within a task-switching block.

We doubt the validity of this assumption. In the remainder of this chapter we describe evidence showing that task-set reconfiguration—in particular, disengagement from a previous, competing task-set—is not necessarily completed by the first 'non-switch' trial. Using the 'alternating runs' method, we demonstrate that the 'non-switch' trials may still show massive competitor priming from the alternating task. Then, using a new method, we show that activation of a prior, but no longer relevant task-set, and negative priming of the current task, can persist over a number of 'non-switch' (pure task) trials, after a switch of task. Moreover, competing stimulus-to-task mappings from a prior task-set can be re-evoked, at the start of a new block of trials, with no further switch of task, even after several blocks of 'pure task' trials at the new task.

16.3 New experiments

'Switch-costs': (1) Engagement vs disengagement of task-set?

According to the TSI hypothesis, the cost of switching between mutually competing tasks is determined primarily by the task-set in the *preceding* task. This accounts for the between-task interference effects described above (e.g., the 'reverse Stroop' effects) on task alternation; it accounts also for the reversed or 'paradoxical' asymmetry of the switch-costs between Stroop word-reading and colour-naming (above). Another example of a 'paradoxical' asymmetry in switch-costs was reported by Meuter and Allport (in press). Bilingual subjects named numerals in either their first or second language, L1 or L2. The cost of a switch of language from the preceding trial was consistently larger when switching to L1 from the weaker L2, than vice versa. That is, switching to L1, their dominant language, was harder than a switch to the less well-learned L2. The result seems paradoxical, if switch-costs depend on the characteristics of the task (or language) TO which the switch is made. The result no longer appears paradoxical, however, if the switch-cost results from the facilitation/suppression pattern of the *preceding* task. Naming in the weaker L2, on the preceding trial(s), should be able to win the competition for control of spoken production, against the stronger L1, only if L1 is actively suppressed. On the following switch trial from L2 to L1, when processing begins, L1 is still suppressed, by TSI. In contrast, naming in L1 should normally require relatively little (if any) active suppression of L2. Hence a less costly subsequent transition, on a switch from L1 to L2.

A more recent study in our laboratory (Loasby 1998) examined whether similar effects of the relative 'processing strength' of two competing languages could be manipulated on an item-by-item basis. Proficient bilinguals named line drawings of objects in a predictable language-switching paradigm, using Rogers and Monsell's (1995) 'alternating runs' method and 500 ms

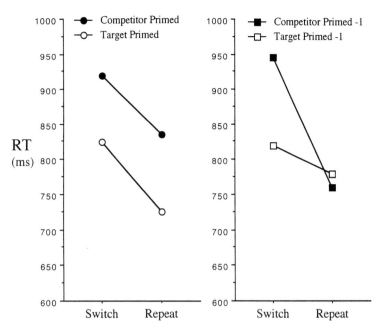

Fig. 16.1 Effects of item-specific practice (priming) on picture naming in a language-switching task. Bilinguals switched between two proficient languages. Panel A (left) shows mean naming latency (RT) on primed trials. Primed items were to be named either in the language in which the item had been practised ('target primed') or in the other, competing language ('competitor primed'). Panel B (right) shows RT on unprimed (neutral) trials immediately *following* target primed or competitor primed trials, respectively.

response-to-stimulus interval (RSI). Prior to the experiment (and also between trial blocks), participants practised speeded naming of selected vocabulary items, some items in one language, a different subset of items in the other language. Other items were left unpractised. Different vocabulary subsets were counterbalanced across participants. In the switching task, half the practised items were presented for naming in the language in which they had been practised ('target-primed' items); the other set of primed items was presented for naming in the other, competing language ('competitor-primed' items). All primed trials were preceded and followed by unprimed (Neutral) trials. Priming had large effects on naming latency, but, as predicted, this manipulation did not interact with the cost of switching (figure 16.1a). This is because the trial immediately *preceding* the primed trial was, by design, always a neutral trial. (Possible longer-term priming effects from more remote, preceding trials should not differ—i.e., should cancel out—between target primed and competitor primed trials.) If asymmetric switch-costs are determined by the preceding trial, as the TSI hypothesis asserts, we should predict no asymmetry in switch-cost on the primed trials. On the contrary, if switch-costs reflect the difficulty of configuring task-set for the *current* trial, as most other accounts of task-switching assume, the absence of any interaction between language priming and switch-cost, on the current trial, is problematic.

However, the main purpose of the experiment was to examine the cost of language-switching on trials immediately *following* a primed trial. The results are shown in figure 16.1, Panel B (right). Following a 'target-primed' trial, on which the conflict between the competing name-responses in the two languages should be more easily resolved in favour of the target language, with minimal suppression of the competitor, the mean cost of a language switch was less than

40 ms. In contrast, following a 'competitor-primed' trial, the mean switch-cost was over 180 ms. In the latter case, on the competitor-primed trial, competition from the primed name-response in the unwanted language would presumably have required strong suppression. By hypothesis, this suppression should then persist into the processing of the next trial; hence a large cost on a switch to the suppressed language. Note that this result is predicted, provided that, in language switching, suppression of the primed competitor-item results in suppression not only of that item but of the competing language vocabulary *as a whole*. This is an important demonstration that TSI can apply to a task ensemble—in this case, to a language-set—as a whole, and not simply to individual items.

A related study in our laboratory explored the effects of differential practice at one or other of two simple arithmetic operations (Yeung 1997). Participants switched between adding 3s and subtracting 2s, with single digits, again using the 'alternating runs' method. After a short period of practice at one of these operations, say operation A, the cost of a switch to A (the practised operation), with the same stimulus set, *increased*, while the cost of a switch to B was dramatically reduced. When the complementary operation, B, was practised, the switch-costs reversed again (see figure 16.2). Detailed analyses subject by subject showed, as predicted, that the larger the effect of practice on differential proficiency at either operation, the larger the corresponding, reversed or 'paradoxical' asymmetry in the switch-costs. An interesting follow-on experiment would be to practise individual arithmetic items ($7 - 2 = 5$), rather than all 'subtract-2' operations.

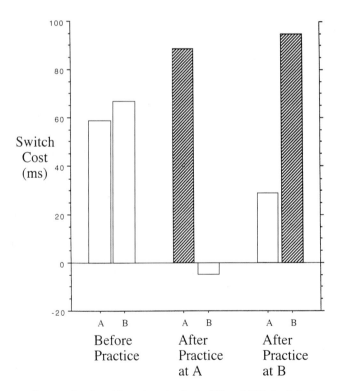

Fig. 16.2 Switch-costs for two simple arithmetic tasks (tasks 'A' and 'B'). Left: before practice at either task; middle: after practice at task 'A'; right: after practice at task 'B'.

The results should be important in differentiating item-specific, stimulus-to-task priming from practice effects on the task operations of a more general kind.

Notice that, in each of these cases, the stimulus ensemble (pictures, numerals) was the same for both tasks. Hence both sets of S–R mappings, if active, are liable to be triggered by the stimuli. The same applies to the other recent studies of task-switching, referred to above, in which different stimulus dimensions (or attributes) were relevant to one or other task, but both dimensions were present in the composite imperative stimulus for *both* tasks (as in switching between different versions of Stroop tasks).

'Switch-costs': (2) Switching TO or switching FROM?

The results of all of these studies are consistent with the TSI hypothesis, which asserts that the costs of switching between intrinsically competing tasks, with 'divergent' stimulus–response (S–R) mappings, are determined primarily by competitor-priming and negative priming effects from the *preceding* task-set.

An even stronger test of the TSI hypothesis would be to examine switch-costs with only partially divergent—asymmetrically overlapping—S–R mappings, as follows. Consider alternation between two tasks, A and B. For A, the task stimuli afford the set of S–R mappings for A, but *not for B*. According to Spector and Biederman's (1976) classification, therefore, task A is 'unambiguously cued' by the task-stimuli themselves. For task B, on the other hand, the task-stimuli afford both task A and B. In other words, the task-stimuli for B afford divergent, competing S–R mappings; the stimuli for task A do not. If what matters, as regards switch-costs, is the divergence of (active) S–R mappings in the task TO which a task-switch is made, switching to task B should show substantial switch-costs. According to the same principle, the cost of switching to task A, on the contrary, should be minimal.

The TSI hypothesis predicts exactly the opposite. The primary determinant of switch-costs, according to this account, is the competitive divergence of (related) S–R mappings *preceding* the switch. Hence task B, because preceded by the neutral or non-competing task, A, should be subject to minimal competitor-priming and negative priming from A. Hence, according to the TSI hypothesis, a switch from A to B should show no greater cost than between non-overlapping tasks. On the other hand, a switch from B to A, because it is a switch FROM the divergent task, should show a relatively large cost.

Experiment 1. We set out to test these competing predictions, as follows (Wylie and Allport, submitted). The tasks selected were colour-naming (A) and word-reading (B). This choice was guided, in part, by our earlier findings, described above, (1) of asymmetrical performance costs in switching between these two tasks, with incongruent Stroop stimuli for both tasks; and (2) of 'reverse' Stroop interference effects on switching from colour-naming to word-reading (Allport *et al.* 1994). As outlined above, this observed pattern of results is consistent with substantial negative priming of word-reading, and positive priming ('competitor-priming') of colour-naming, persisting involuntarily from the task-set needed for (Stroop) colour-naming on preceding trials. We again made use of Rogers and Monsell's (1995) 'alternating runs' paradigm.

In the critical condition, participants switched, every second trial, between colour-naming (task A) with *neutral* stimuli, consisting of a row of coloured Xs, and word-reading (task B), with incongruent Stroop stimuli. We refer to this as the ColourNeutral/WordStroop condition. Task A is 'unambiguously cued' by the intrinsic task-stimuli; task B is not. There were two other, control conditions. These were designed to establish switch-costs (i) when *both* tasks used neutral stimuli, specific to each individual task (coloured Xs for colour-naming, uniform black words for word-reading)—referred to as the Allneutral condition; and (ii) when both colour and word tasks used the same, overlapping set of incongruent Stroop stimuli—the AllStroop condition. The three conditions were tested in a fixed order: (1) Allneutral first; then (2) the critical

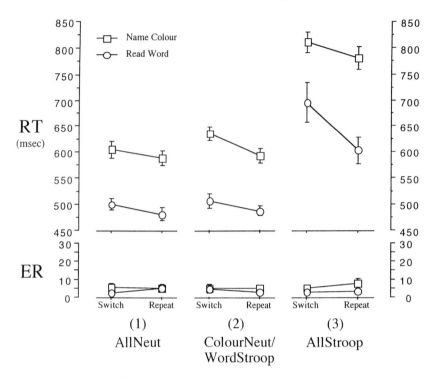

Fig. 16.3 Switching between Colour-naming and word-reading (Experiment 1). Mean response time (RT) and error-rate (ER) in three different stimulus conditions: (1) in which both Colour and Word stimuli are Neutral; (2) in which Colour stimuli remain Neutral but Words are incongruent Stroop stimuli; (3) in which stimuli for both tasks are incongruent Stroop stimuli.

ColourNeutral/WordStroop condition; and lastly (3) the AllStroop condition. The rationale for this fixed sequence of conditions was to avoid the possibility of long-lasting priming, in particular, negative priming, from task-sets required in earlier conditions. Thus, in the critical condition, participants had yet to encounter the colour-naming task in response to incongruent (Stroop) colour-word stimuli. At this stage in the experiment, therefore, they would have had no need to suppress word-reading responses to these stimuli.

The principal results, in terms of mean RT and error probabilities, are shown in figure 16.3. Consider first the two control conditions, Allneutral (1) and AllStroop (3). In condition (1) the mean RT switch-costs were small (under 20 ms) and symmetrical for the two tasks. Colour-naming RTs were about 110 ms slower than word-reading. In condition (3), switch-costs were somewhat larger, and markedly asymmetrical (30 ms for colour-naming, 92 ms for word-reading). RTs were also much slower than in condition (1), for both tasks. This is to be expected for colour-naming, since responses in condition (3) were made to incongruent Stroop stimuli: compared to condition (1), colour-naming RTs showed a net Stroop interference effect of around 190 to 205 ms on non-switch and switch trials, respectively. However, in condition (3) *word-reading* RTs were also much slower than in condition (1); in other words, there was a large 'reverse' Stroop effect, on the order of 125 ms on non-switch trials, and as much as 190 ms on switch trials. The data for condition (3) thus replicate the pattern of results reported by Allport *et al.* (1994, Experiment 5), with AllStroop stimuli, showing (a) asymmetrical switch-costs, larger for the dominant (word-reading) task than for the weaker colour-naming task; and (b) 'reverse' Stroop interference on word-reading, in task-alternating conditions, present also on the 'non-switch' trials.

Now consider the ColourNeutral/WordStroop condition (2). The critical test case concerns the word-reading task. If switch-costs are determined by the characteristics (potentially conflicting S–R mappings, etc.) of the task TO which a switch is made, then the cost of switching to the word-reading task should be about the same in condition (2) and condition (3), since both require response to the same, incongruent Stroop stimuli. On the other hand, if switch-costs are determined largely by the character of the *previous* task-set (where this conflicts with the intended task), that is, by the task FROM which the switch is made, as asserted by the TSI hypothesis, then the cost of switching to word-reading should be about the same in condition (2) and condition (1), since both require a switch from neutral colour-naming. The results are unambiguous. The cost of switching to the word-reading task was essentially identical in conditions (1) and (2), and smaller by a factor of five than that in condition (3). The switch-costs in this case appear to be determined overwhelmingly by the task-set FROM which the shift is required, rather than by the task that is switched TO.

Switch-costs for the colour-naming task are also of interest, although the experiment was not designed to compare these symmetrically in the same way. (Moreover, as predicted, the difference in switch-costs between Allneutral and AllStroop conditions is much less marked for colour-naming than it is for word-reading.) The most straightforward comparison is between conditions (1) and (2). In both of these, the imperative stimulus for colour-naming is a row of coloured Xs. If switch-costs depend on the ambiguity or uniqueness of S–R mappings in the task TO which the switch is made, they should not differ between these two conditions. On the other hand, if they depend on conflicting S–R mappings in the preceding task, they should be larger for colour-naming in condition (2) than condition (1). In fact, the switch-costs were significantly larger in condition (2), by a factor of nearly three.

RT distributions: the status of 'non-switch' trials

Figure 16.4 shows the averaged cumulative distribution function (CDF) of RT in Experiment 1, for the two critical Word task conditions (conditions 2 and 3), in which the stimuli for word-reading were incongruent Stroop stimuli. To compute these functions, the rank-ordered RTs for each participant were divided into quintiles (20% bins) in each condition, Vincentized (Ratcliff 1979), and the results then averaged over participants for each quintile. The data are shown as a function of trial type ('switch' vs 'non-switch'), for conditions (2) and (3).

Two features of these RT distributions are of particular interest. First, in condition (2) the difference between 'switch' and 'non-switch' Word RTs remains approximately constant, at around 20 ms, over most of the RT distribution, diverging only in the slowest quintile. The principal effect of a 'switch' trial, in condition (2), is thus to shift the entire RT distribution upwards by this small amount. In contrast, in condition (3), in which Stroop stimuli are used for the Colour task also, the difference between 'switch' and 'non-switch' RTs is only about 40 ms in the fastest RT quintile, but increases monotonically to around 150 ms at the slow end of the distribution. Thus, in condition (3), as well as a shift of the RT distribution upwards, 'switch' trials show a larger dispersion of RT than 'non-switch' trials. De Jong (1996) proposed that the latter pattern of results reflects a partial (i.e., intermittent) failure of anticipatory reconfiguration of task-set. Some 'switch' trials are prepared in advance, others remain unprepared. In De Jong's analysis, as in the analyses by Rogers and Monsell (1995), and Meiran (1996), the baseline for estimating the fully prepared state is provided by the 'non-switch' or 'repetition' trials, within the same switching block. That is, it is a basic working assumption of their analyses (and of these authors' measure of switch-cost) that task-set on the 'non-switch' trials is fully, or optimally, reconfigured.

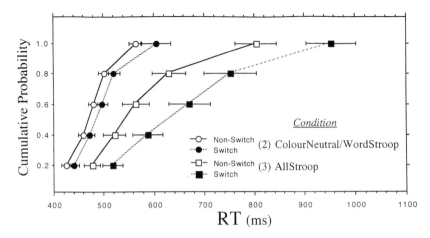

Fig. 16.4 Cumulative distribution functions for reaction time (RT) in the word-reading task (Experiment 1). The figure shows data for 'non-switch' and 'switch' trials in conditions (2) and (3): solid line, 'non-switch'; broken line, 'switch'.

However, the second striking feature of the RT distributions in figure 16.4 is the dramatic difference between the '*non-switch*' (repeat) trials in conditions (2), and (3), respectively. On the basis of this comparison, we are constrained to infer that 'non-switch' word-reading trials, in condition (3), represent a radically *incomplete* state of preparedness (reconfiguration of task-set) for the word-reading task, compared to condition (2). 'Non-switch' word-reading RTs in conditions (2) and (3) were elicited in response to the identical stimuli with the identical S–R mappings. Yet even the fastest RT quintile, for non-switch trials, is slower by about 50 ms in condition (3) than in condition (2), and this difference increases monotonically over the RT distribution to around 240 ms for the slowest quintile. (In percentage terms, this is an RT difference of about 13%, for the fastest quintile, and around 43% for the slowest quintile.) In other words, as figure 16.4 makes clear, the difference in the degree of task-set preparation (or 'reconfiguration') for the Word task is even greater between the '*non-switch*' trials in these two conditions, with identical S–R mappings, than it is between the '*switch*' and '*non-switch*' trials within condition (3).

Contrary to the working assumption made by Rogers and Monsell (1995), De Jong (1996) and others, task-set reconfiguration is not necessarily 'completed' in the course of a single switch trial.

Positive and negative priming of task-set after a single switch of tasks

The experiments that we have described, so far, consistently show up the impact of previous, competing task-sets, whose persisting pattern of task facilitation and suppression conflicts with the next (switch) task. Moreover, the results just described suggest that performance on the '*non-switch*' trials, in these task-alternation paradigms, can also be very considerably affected by residual activation/inhibition of a previous competitor task. It is possible that the 'non-switch' trials are affected, also, by the readiness for an anticipated, future switch to the competing task, in both predictable and unpredictable task-switching paradigms. For both of these reasons, we may question whether the 'non-switch' trials in a switching block represent a condition of anything like complete or optimum reconfiguration for the current task.

These considerations suggest two modifications to current task-switching paradigms that it might be useful to explore.

- First, it would be instructive to have, as a further baseline, a well practised sample of performance at task A *prior* to any exposure to the competing task, B, in the experimental context. These data could then be compared with task A performance *after* a switch from B to A. (Note that possible, further practice benefits on A in the course of the experiment are liable to reduce the difference between these two sets of data, if anything; hence the comparison is conservative in this respect. If required, a control group can be used to monitor for possible time-order effects on task A, in the experiment, in the absence of exposure to task B.)

- Second, it would be useful to study the switch to a block of task A trials (following one or more trials of task B) when the participants know that no further trials of task B will be required. Again, performance could be compared with the initial baseline performance of A. Note that task A is performed as a 'pure' task, both before and after exposure to task B. In both cases, only one task has to be kept 'available', or held intentionally in working memory, namely task A. In this comparison there is therefore no confound between intentional 'working memory load' and switching.

The 'Before and After' paradigm

Together, these modifications suggest a simple experimental design, which we call the 'Before and After' paradigm. The experiment is run in three successive phases. In phase 1, participants practise task A over successive blocks of trials, as a 'pure' task, to provide a stable baseline of performance. In phase 2, they perform one or more blocks of trials at the competing task B. Then, in phase 3, they return to task A for one (or more) further blocks of trials, again as a pure task. There are thus just two switches of task in the experiment. A control group performs the identical sequence of task A trials, but they do not perform the competing task B in phase 2. (Additionally, if the effects of task A on task B are of interest, two further groups of participants could perform the same two tasks in the reverse order: first B, then A, then B again, in an *experimental* group; and B, then some other, unrelated activity, then B, in a *control* group.) In principle, the paradigm could be adapted for many different exemplars of 'divergent', competing tasks, A and B.

In our explorations of this procedure, to date, we have confined ourselves to studying a single, very well practised 'task A', namely oral word-reading, before and after exposure to a competing task, viz., Stroop colour-naming or picture-naming. We describe here the results of two exploratory 'Before and After' experiments of this kind. (Details of experimental procedure, etc., are given in Wylie and Allport, in preparation.) Oral word-reading is tested, both before and after exposure to the competing task, with incongruent 'Stroop' stimuli as well as with Neutral word stimuli. We report here an experiment with Stroop colour-naming as the competing task.[3]

Experiment 2. Three groups of participants were recruited from the Oxford University subject panel, 10 subjects per group, mean age 26.4 years. For all participants, task A was speeded oral word-reading (the Word task), with the words RED, GREEN, BLUE, PURPLE, PINK, and ORANGE as stimuli. The words appeared in large (30 point), upper case, OUTLINE style. 'Neutral' word stimuli were presented with the background screen colour (grey) filling in the outline letters. The word shapes for the incongruent Stroop stimuli were filled in, uniformly, with any one of the six colours, other than the colour named by the word. For the two experimental groups, task B was Stroop colour naming (the Colour task), using the same incongruent Stroop stimuli as for the word-reading task. For the third (control) group, task B was omitted. The screen was bisected by a bold horizontal line. For half the participants, stimuli for the Word task appeared above the line, in the upper half of the screen, and stimuli for the Colour task (where relevant) appeared in the lower half; for the other participants, this was reversed.

Prior to the main experiment, all participants received 30 trials of practice at a speeded, perceptual comparison task, designed to differ as far as possible (in terms of stimuli, responses, and cognitive operations) from oral word-reading and colour-naming. This was used as a filler task, in phase 3 of the experiment, to study possible residual priming effects from colour-naming, persisting over an interval occupied by an unrelated task. In this ('Unrelated') task, participants judged which of two circles, presented side by side, was (a) the larger or (b) the brighter of the two, and indicated their response by pressing a right or left key. Subjects were randomly assigned to one or other version, (a) or (b), of the Unrelated keypress task.

There were three main phases in the experiment. In *phase 1*, participants in all three groups practised reading Stroop and Neutral words (30 trials of each), followed by four short blocks of 10 trials each, alternate blocks with Stroop and Neutral stimuli, as the word-reading baseline. In *phase 2*, participants in the two experimental groups were instructed that incongruent Stroop stimuli would now be presented in the other half of the screen, and they would be asked to name the colour (of the 'ink') of these stimuli. After 10 trials of practice at colour-naming, they paused for further instructions, which included a small financial incentive for fast and accurate performance on the Colour task. They were told that they would perform just 20 further trials of the Colour task, followed by two blocks of 10 trials of word-reading (*phase 3*). At the end of the block of 20 Colour trials, there was a brief pause (2 sec) during which the instruction 'READ WORDS' appeared on the screen for 1 sec; this was followed by the horizontal line, against a blank background, for a further 1 sec, followed by the first Word stimulus, in the same location on the screen in which Word stimuli appeared in phase 1. For one experimental group ('Neutral First') the first block of 10 Word trials consisted of Neutral word stimuli, the second block consisted of Stroop stimuli; for the other group ('Stroop First') the order of stimulus blocks was reversed. The two blocks of 10 Word trials were separated by a further 2 sec pause, with the prompt to 'READ WORDS' presented on the screen for the first 1 sec. Finally, in *phase 3B*, all participants performed a sequence of three blocks of 10 trials, as follows. The first block of 10 trials was the Unrelated task, practised at the start of the experiment, followed, after a 2 sec pause and the prompt, 'READ WORDS', by two further blocks of the Word task, as before. This sequence of three blocks was then repeated six times.

The control group (10 subjects) proceeded through the identical sequence except that they never experienced colour-naming.

The mean RT and error rates for the Word task (phases 1 and 3) and for the Colour task (in phase 2) are shown in figure 16.5. Each block of trials is divided into three bins: trial 1 (the 'switch' trial), trials 2–5, and the remainder of the block.

First, some preliminaries: (1) In phase 1, prior to colour-naming, there were no differences in mean RT or accuracy due to either stimulus-type or subject-group. That is, the three subject groups were well matched in terms of word-reading performance, and there was no sign of 'reverse' Stroop interference.

(2) In each block of 10 Word trials, RT on trial 1 was systematically slower than in the remainder of the block, by the order of 100 ms or more. This 'restart' effect was highly reliable ($p < 0.0001$) over both the baseline (phase 1) and later (phase 3b) Word trials. Evidently, some component of task-set configuration is impaired, even over a 2 s pause, with no change of task. (In a follow-up experiment, we have established that this effect cannot be attributed to the change from Neutral to Stroop stimuli, or vice versa; we obtained a similar, or even larger, first-trial delay when the word-reading task continued with the identical stimuli, after a 2 s pause. De Jong *et al.* (submitted, Experiment 3) report a similar finding on the first trial of pure task blocks, with a 2-choice keypress task. The first-trial delay was even larger (approaching 400 ms) in old subjects.) In our data, there were also fewer errors on trial 1 ($p < 0.0005$ over phase 1; $p < 0.005$ over phase 3b). We discuss

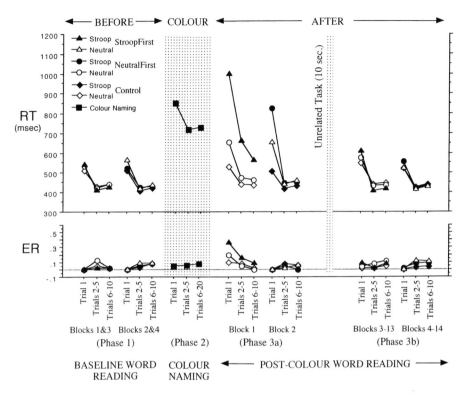

Fig. 16.5 Experiment 2: 'Before and After' paradigm. The figure shows mean response time (RT) and error-rate (ER) for the word-reading task (in phases 1 and 3), and for the Colour-naming task (in phase 2), as a function of stimulus-type (Stroop or Neutral) and serial position in each trial block. Phase 3b (the Unrelated task, then two blocks of word-reading) was repeated 10 times. Results are shown for two experimental groups, who performed Colour-naming in phase 2, and for a control group who did no Colour-naming.

some implications of these first-trial, 'restart' effects in another paper (Allport and Wylie, in press).

Now the main findings. In the Word trials immediately following colour-naming (phase 3a, blocks 1 and 2), there were massive after-effects of the competing Colour task, affecting both RT and errors ($p < 0.0001$). These can be divided into negative priming effects on word processing, detectable on *Neutral* word-reading trials; and positive priming effects of the prior, competing Colour task ('competitor priming'), detectable as a large, additional interference on the incongruent *Stroop* trials. These effects were largest on trial 1 of block 1. (Relative to the controls, StroopFirst subjects showed a 'reverse Stroop' effect of about 450 ms on trial 1.) But the competitor priming effect on Stroop trials was still large on trials 2–5 ($p < 0.01$) and can still be seen even on trials 6–10 in figure 16.5 ($p = 0.05$). Furthermore, similar RT effects reappeared dramatically on the first trial of block 2. (Note: in block 2, participants who had encountered only Neutral words in block 1—the NeutralFirst group—now had to read incongruent Stroop stimuli. Relative to the controls, on the first trial of block 2 they showed a 'reverse Stroop' effect of around 300 ms. Evidently, 10 trials of word-reading with Neutral words, in block 1, was not sufficient to eliminate (to 'reconfigure') the previous Colour task activation.)

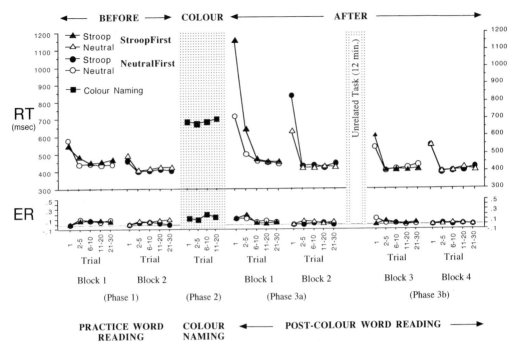

Fig. 16.6 Experiment 3: Replication of Experiment 2, with minor modifications. All participants performed Colour-naming in phase 2. Before phase 3b, they performed an unrelated task for 12 min.

Finally, in phase 3b, after-effects of the Colour task in phase 2 could still be detected on the first trials of these later word-reading blocks ($p < 0.0005$ for the interaction of stimulus-type (Stroop vs Neutral) with trial-order and group), but not on the later trials of each block. That is, on trial 1 there was still a small 'reverse Stroop' effect, which diminished gradually over successive iterations of the Word task and the Unrelated task, and was no longer detectable by the last iteration (blocks 13 and 14).

Experiment 3. The striking effects just described were replicated in Experiment 3, with some secondary modifications in the experimental design, as follows. The Word task was presented in 30-trial blocks; the Unrelated task was continued for a much longer period (12 min) in phase 3b, with only two subsequent blocks of Word trials; and participants received a smaller amount of initial practice at word-reading. There was no control group in Experiment 3. Performance on the Word task in phase 3a, following colour-naming, was compared with the same subjects' performance in phase 1 and in the later phase 3b. RTs and errors on the Word and Colour tasks in Experiment 3 are shown in figure 16.6.

The negative priming and competitor priming effects on trial 1 of the Word task, immediately following colour-naming, were even larger than in Experiment 2, perhaps as a result of the smaller amount of initial practice at the Word task in Experiment 3. Moreover, even on trials 6 to 30 of the first post-Colour block, RTs were reliably slower ($p < 0.01$) than in any other Word block. (Trials 6–30 did not differ significantly from one another, over the remainder of this block. Note that, contrary to Rogers and Monsell's (1995) argument, this pattern of consistent, asymptotic RTs within a run of 'non-switch' trials does not guarantee complete task reconfiguration to baseline efficiency.) Unlike Experiment 2, however, the difference between Stroop and Neutral stimuli had disappeared in these later trials of the first post-Colour block. The very large post-Colour priming effects on the first trial of the *next* block (post-Colour, block 2) were also replicated. Participants in the NeutralFirst group, for whom block 2 was their first encounter with Stroop stimuli in the post-Colour word-reading task, showed a mean RT approximately double their previous baseline ($p < 0.0001$), with 'reverse Stroop' effects of about 300 ms on the first trial (relative to block 2 of their practice Word performance before Colour naming). However, in phase 3b, after 12 min of the unrelated filler task, no reliable priming effects from the Colour task could be detected, although there is a suggestion of a small 'reverse' Stroop effect on trial 1.

Experiments 2 and 3 establish the usefulness of these simple 'Before and After' comparisons of task (re)configuration, showing negative priming and competitor priming effects from the task-set required in the intervening task, even when *all* trial blocks involve 'pure' tasks. They demonstrate that continued task-priming from a previous (but no longer valid), competing task-set can persist over relatively long time intervals, and (in some conditions at least) over many successive 'non-switch' trials of a subsequent divergent task. Moreover, even after 10 trials (Experiment 2) or 30 trials (Experiment 3) of the Word task, a short (2 sec) interval and 'restart' is sufficient to reinstate residual task uncertainty, and massive interference from the prior, competing task on the initial trial of a new block.

An important implication of these results (as also of Experiments 1 and 2) is that the true behavioural costs of a switch of tasks may not be appropriately estimated, simply as the difference between 'switch' and 'non-switch' trials in a switching block. Even though there may, in some conditions, be no further improvement over a series of 'non-switch' trials, as Rogers and Monsell (1995, Experiment 6) reported, this does not necessarily imply that task-set reconfiguration is 'complete' on the 'non-switch' trials. Priming effects of prior, competing tasks (and perhaps anticipation of engaging in them in the future) can have massive effects on 'non-switch' trial performance, as we have shown.

Many variables (and many task-combinations) remain to be explored, using modifications of this simple 'Before and After' paradigm. One very obvious factor is the effect of practice at repeated switching (cf. Sudevan and Taylor 1987). Suppose that phases 2 and 3 are iterated for a number of cycles. In our preliminary explorations of this issue, to date, we find that the negative priming and competitor priming effects on trial 1 are considerably reduced, but remain qualitatively similar to those reported in Experiments 2 and 3. Later trials in a block, however, may show minimal task-priming effects. Another variable that we have begun to explore is the number of trials of the inducing task ('task B') in phase 2, prior to switching back to task 'A'. Preliminary results suggest that the performance costs of a switch from task B back to A are sensitive to the relative frequency, as well as recency, of task B trials, relative to A.

16.4 Conclusions

The experiments reported here, together with our earlier experiments (Allport *et al.* 1994; Meuter and Allport, in press), establish the role of involuntary priming, both positive and negative, operating at the level of higher-order 'control' variables, in effective task readiness or task-set. Intentional shift to a competing (divergent) S–R task reveals task-switching costs, in the form of continued priming of the previous task (competitor-priming) and suppression (negative priming) of the currently intended task. These effects, we believe, result from control states (stimulus-to-task bindings) imposed on preceding trials, and thus provide a method for studying those control states directly.

The task-set that we selected as our 'inducing' task (in Experiments 1, 2 and 3, above) was (Stroop) Colour-naming. Our data provide a new form of evidence that the task-set for this much-studied task involves both *facilitation* of condition–action rules pertaining to the Colour task and *suppression* of constituents of the competing Word task. Our data also reflect the radically different control state—and radically different, resulting task-priming effects—induced by Neutral colour-naming (Experiment 1, condition 2).

In a later paper (Allport and Wylie, in press) we attempt to develop a more specific character-isation of task control states and their persisting after-effects. In particular, the reinstatement of positive and negative priming effects on a 'restart' trial (Block 2 of Post-colour word-reading, in Experiments 2 and 3) suggests a somewhat different conception of 'task-set inertia' than that pro-posed by Allport *et al.* (1994). What persists from a prior task-set, these data suggest, is the learned, competitive weighting of stimulus types, or stimulus attributes, as associative retrieval cues for the task operations to be performed. Explicit, behavioural response to a stimulus, we suppose, requires some kind of 'binding' of stimulus attributes to the task operations and to the resulting response. A 'restart', even after as little as a 2 sec interrupt, with repeated task instructions, may trigger renewed retrieval/binding of competing stimulus-attributes to tasks, with resulting rein-statement of task interference effects. TSI would thus include the biased weighting of learned, individual stimulus-to-task associations, biased according to the relative frequency and recency of their use.

It is perhaps necessary to reiterate here that our proposals about involuntary priming at the level of constituents of task-set ('Task-Set Inertia') are not in opposition to, or an alternative to, the idea of control processes. On the contrary, we believe that the priming effects result directly from interactive (both top down and bottom up) control processes imposed by current and (in particular) previous task demands.

Priming effects in other domains provide the basis for some of the most effective behavioural methods available to study underlying cognitive representations. Priming of task-set, or compon-ents of task-set, we believe, may offer the exciting prospect of comparably effective methods for the study of higher-order cognitive structures in procedural working memory.

Notes

1. Sudevan and Taylor (1987) trained their participants in the use of two different task pre-cues, over 20 one-hour sessions. The two tasks were numeral-classification (odd/even vs high/low). Unfortunately, they did not report their data in terms of 'switch' and 'non-switch' trials. They found anticipatory preparation effects continuing over some 4.0 s of PI. Over the first 4 days of training, task-incongruity (interference) effects showed no interaction with PI benefits. Data from later sessions, however, showed a progressive reduction in the (asymmetrical) task-interference with increasing PI. By days 17–20, a PI of 2 s was sufficient to eliminate all crosstalk interference between tasks (Sudevan and Taylor, Fig. 3). The effect of extended practice on task-cueing deserves further study.

2. Clearly, the requirement to keep two task-sets 'active', in a task-alternating condition, does not *neces-sarily* result in performance costs, relative to the corresponding pure task (or single task) conditions. An example is the experiment by Spector and Biederman (1976), described above, in which partici-pants alternated between two non-overlapping tasks without any behavioural costs of alternation, compared to their pure task baseline.

   Furthermore, arousal, effort, etc., can vary trial by trial, as well as between blocks of trials. Our own experience as participants in the alternating runs paradigm is that switch trials receive much greater 'effort' than non-switch trials. This is particularly salient with longer inter-trial preparation intervals.

3. J. R. Stroop (1935) used a similar design in his landmark paper, Experiment 3. He included a phase of extended practice at 'Stroop' colour-naming, over 1,600 trials, before his participants returned to a period of 'Stroop' word-reading. Word-reading speed was recorded in terms of 50-item list-completion times; and Neutral word-reading was not tested in the final test-phase. In other respects, his experiment closely resembles ours. To our knowledge, Stroop's Experiment 3 has not been followed

up in the intervening 60-year period. We became aware of this resemblance only after completing the experiments described here, causing us a mixture of embarrassment (having not previously read Stroop's original paper!) and delight.

References

Allport, A. and Wylie, G. (in press). Task switching, stimulus-response bindings, and negative priming. In S. Monsell and J. Driver (eds), *Control of cognitive processes. Attention and Performance, XVIII*.

Allport, D. A., Styles, E. A. and Hsieh, S. 1994 Shifting intentional set: Exploring the dynamic control of tasks. In C. Umilta and M. Moscovitch (eds), *Attention and Performance XV* (pp. 421–52) . Cambridge MA: MIT Press.

Becker, S., Moscovitch, M., Behrmann, M. and Joordens, S. 1997 Long-term semantic priming: A computational account and empirical evidence. *Journal of Experimental Psychology: Learning, Memory, and Cognition* 23, 1059–82.

Biederman, I. and Cooper, E. E. 1992 Size invariance in visual object priming. *Journal of Experimental Psychology: Human Perception and Performance* 18, 121–33.

Bruce, V., Burton, M., Carson, D., Hanna, E. and Mason, O. 1994 Repetition priming of face recognition. In C. Umilta and M. Moscovitch (eds), *Attention and Performance XV* (pp. 179– 201). Cambridge MA: MIT Press.

Brunas, J., Young, A. W. and Ellis, A. W. 1990 Repetition priming from incomplete faces: Evidence for part to whole completion. *British Journal of Psychology* 81, 43–56.

Bundesen, C. 1990 A theory of visual attention. *Psychological Review* 97, 523–47.

Cohen, J. D., Dunbar, K. and McClelland, J. L. 1990 On the control of automatic processes: A parallel distributed processing account of the Stroop effect. *Psychological Review* 97, 332–61.

De Jong, R. 1996 Cognitive and motivational determinants of switching costs in the task-switching paradigm. Paper presented at the IX ESCOP Conference, Wurzburg, Germany, September 1996.

De Jong, R., Emans, B., Eenshuistra, R. and Wagenmakers, E.-J. (submitted). Strategies and intrinsic limitations in intentional task control.

DeSchepper, B. and Treisman, A. 1996 Visual memory for novel shapes: Implicit coding without attention. *Journal of Experimental Psychology: Learning Memory and Cognition* 22, 27–47.

Driver, J. and Tipper, S. P. 1989 On the nonselectivity of 'selective' seeing: Contrasts between interference and priming in selective attention. *Journal of Experimental Psychology: Human Perception and Performance* 15, 304–14.

Duncan, J. 1977 Response selection rules in spatial choice reaction tasks. In S. Dornic (ed.), *Attention and Performance VI* pp. 49–61. Hillsdale, NJ: Lawrence Erlbaum.

Duncan, J. 1978 Response selection in spatial choice reaction: Further evidence against associative models. *Quarterly Journal of Experimental Psychology* 30, 429–40.

Ellis, A. W., Young, A. W. and Flude, B. M. 1990 Repetition priming and face processing: Priming occurs within the system that responds to the identity of a face. *Quarterly Journal of Experimental Psychology* 42A, 495–512.

Evett, L. J. and Humphreys, G. 1981 The use of abstract graphemic information in lexical access. *Quarterly Journal of Experimental Psychology* 33A, 325–50.

Fox, E. 1995 Negative priming from ignored distractors in visual selection: A review. *Psychonomic Bulletin and Review* 2, 145–73.

Hsieh, S. and Allport, A. 1994 Shifting attention in a rapid visual search paradigm. *Perceptual and Motor Skills* 79, 315–35.

Jacoby, L. L. 1994 Measuring recollection: Strategic versus automatic influences of associative context. In C. Umilta and M. Moscovitch (eds), *Attention and Performance XV* (pp. 661–79) . Cambridge MA: MIT Press.

Jacoby, L. L. and Dallas, M. 1981 On the relationship between autobiographical memory and perceptual learning. *Journal of Experimental Psychology: General* 3, 306–40.

Jersild, A. T. 1927 Mental set and shift. *Archives of Psychology, Whole No. 89.*

Kirsner, K. and Speelman, C. 1993 Is lexical processing just an 'ACT'? In A. F. Collins, S. E. Gathercole, M. A. Conway and P. E. Morris (eds), *Theories of Memory* pp. 303–26. Hove, UK: Lawrence Erlbaum.

Kirsner, K., Milech, D. and Stumpfel, V. 1986 Word and picture recognition: Is representational parsimony possible? *Memory and Cognition* **14**, 398–408.

Loasby, H. 1998 The effects of language switching and priming in a picture naming task. Unpublished MS, University of Oxford.

MacLeod, C. M. 1991 Half a century of research on the Stroop effect: An integrative review. *Psychological Bulletin* **109**, 163–203.

MacLeod, C. M. and Dunbar, K. 1988 Training and Stroop-like interference: Evidence for a continuum of automaticity. *Journal of Experimental Psychology: Learning Memory and Cognition* **14**, 126–35.

May, C. P., Kane, M. J. and Hasher, L. 1995 Determinants of negative priming. *Psychological Bulletin* **118**, 35–54.

Meiran, N. 1996 Reconfiguration of processing mode prior to task performance. *Journal of Experimental Psychology: Learning Memory and Cognition* **22**, 1423–42.

Meiran, N., Chorev, Z., Marciano, H., Sapir, A. and Yona, L. (submitted). Component processes in task-shifting.

Meuter, R. F. I. and Allport, A. (in press). Bilingual language switching and naming: Asymmetrical costs of language selection. *Journal of Memory and Language.*

Milliken, B. and Tipper, S. P. 1998 Attention and inhibition. In H. Pashler (ed.), *Attention* pp. 191–221. Hove, UK: Psychology Press.

Monsell, S. 1985 Repetition and the lexicon. In A. W. Ellis (ed.), *Progress in the Psychology of Language*, Vol. 2 pp. 147–95. London: Lawrence Erlbaum.

Neely, J. H. 1991 Semantic priming effects in visual word recognition: A selective review of current findings and theories. In D. Besner and G. W. Humphreys (eds), *Basic Processes in Reading: Visual Word Recognition* (pp. 264–336). Hillsdale, NJ: Lawrence Erlbaum.

Rabbitt, P. M. A. and Vyas, S. 1973 What is repeated in the 'repetition effect'? In S. Kornblum (Ed.), *Attention and Performance, IV* (pp. 327–42). London and New York: Academic Press.

Rabbitt, P. M. A and Vyas, S. 1979 Memory and data-driven control of selective attention in continuous tasks. *Canadian Journal of Psychology* **33**, 71–87.

Ratcliff, R. 1979 Group reaction time distributions and an analysis of distribution statistics. *Psychological Bulletin* **86**, 446–61.

Rogers, R. D. and Monsell, S. 1995 The cost of a predictable switch between simple cognitive tasks. *Journal of Experimental Psychology: General* **124**, 207–31.

Scarborough, D. L., Cortese, C. and Scarborough, H. S. 1977 Frequency and repetition effects in lexical memory. *Journal of Experimental Psychology: Human Perception and Performance* **3**, 1–17.

Schacter, D. L. and Church, B. A. 1992 Auditory priming: Implicit and explicit memory for words and voices. *Journal of Experimental Psychology: Learning Memory and Cognition* **18**, 915–30.

Spector, A. and Biederman, I. 1976 Mental set and shift revisited. *American Journal of Psychology* **89**, 669–79.

Stroop, J. R. 1935 Studies of interference in serial verbal reactions. *Journal of Experimental Psychology* **18**, 643–62.

Sudevan, P. and Taylor, D. A. 1987 The cueing and priming of cognitive operations. *Journal of Experimental Psychology: Human Perception and Performance* **13**, 89–103.

Taft, M. 1991 *Reading and the Mental Lexicon.* Hove, UK: Lawrence Erlbaum.

Tipper, S. P., Weaver, B. and Houghton, G. 1994 Behavioural goals determine inhibitory mechanisms of selective attention. *Quarterly Journal of Experimental Psychology* **47A**, 809–40.

Warren, R. E. 1972 Stimulus encoding and memory. *Journal of Experimental Psychology* **94**, 90–100.

Warren, R. E. 1974 Association, directionality and stimulus encoding. *Journal of Experimental Psychology* **102**, 151–8.

Wylie, G. and Allport, A. (submitted). Task switching and the measurement of 'switch costs'.

Wylie, G. and Allport, A. (in preparation). Task switching and priming.

Yeung, N. 1997 The effect of practice on task switching. Paper presented at meeting of the Experimental Psychology Society, Oxford, March 1997.

17

Sustained attention deficits in time and space

Ian H. Robertson and Tom Manly

Abstract

We review critically the influential framework of attentional systems developed by Posner and Petersen (1990). Their proposal that three independent supramodal attentional control systems exist in the brain—selection, alertness and spatial attention respectively—is examined in the light of evidence accumulated over the last decade. We conclude that while evidence for differentiable supramodal selection and alertness systems is quite strong, the notion of a posterior supramodal spatial attention system centred in the parietal lobes is much weaker. We review evidence showing that unilateral neglect consequent on parietal lesions is both strongly associated with non-lateralized attentional deficits, and strongly modifiable by manipulation of these non-spatial variables. Spatial selective attention may be better conceived of as an emergent property of competition between distributed but integrated representations of objects and space between the two hemispheres. The role of the parietal lobes in spatial selection may be related to the integration of cross-modal representations and motor preparation in the organisation of responses towards the environment. But the parietal lobe of the right hemisphere appears to have an additional, but as yet inadequately specified role, in the maintenance of the alert state over time and other non-lateralized aspects of attention.

17.1 Introduction

Sustained attention is as widely used a term as it is poorly defined. One purpose of this chapter is to try to help characterize a concept which has become increasingly used in the last decade in lesion, functional imaging, and electrophysiological studies. In particular we would like to examine the inter-relationship between this phenomenon and other aspects of behaviour broadly characterised as 'attentional'. In so doing, we hope to critically evaluate the explanatory value of 'attention' and its putative subtypes as useful concepts. First, however, it is important to set the concept of sustained attention in its historical roots.

In the psychological literature the concept of sustained attention is sometimes encountered as a 'nuisance' variable obscuring other factors in long testing sessions. When it has been considered in its own right, however, it is usually studied in the context of performance on vigilance tasks of the 'watchkeeping' variety (Mackworth 1968; Parasuraman 1983). So strong is the link between this type of task and the construct of sustained attention that in many cases, the terms are often used synonymously (See 1995). Vigilance tasks were not, however, originally designed to investigate an underlying and potentially unitary attentional system but rather were developed as an applied tool to assess human performance under a particular and arguably rare set of circumstances. It became apparent that in tasks such as monitoring a radar screen, despite the adequate functioning of the equipment, important signals were nevertheless missed by their human operators. N. H. Mackworth developed a task designed to simulate the conditions a radar operator was exposed to. Over a 2-hour period, participants were asked to detect rare and temporally unpredictable targets which occurred at the oppressively slow rate of approximately 24 per hour. Increases in the rate of omissions were noted in each subsequent half-hour block. This pattern of performance was characterized as the vigilance decrement (Mackworth 1950).

With the parameters of such tasks under the experimenter's control, this human limitation and factors which modulated it were available for investigation. Much research was conducted in the 1950s and '60s on these tasks, again often with applied aims. Models of performance were expressed in various terms from variation in arousal levels (Deese 1955) to changes in signal detection parameters (Broadbent and Gregory 1963; Egan *et al.* 1961). It was an initial finding of the signal detection approach that a decline in performance with time was primarily related to shifts in criteria towards a more conservative response strategy, that is both 'hits' and 'false positives' declined (Broadbent 1971). However as the range of studied task parameters increased it became apparent that under different conditions, different reasons, including shifts in target sensitivity, may underlie decrement. Reviewing these studies Parasuraman and Davies argued for a vigilance taxonomy classifying tasks on the basis of event rate, the nature of target/non-target discrimination, sensory modality and source complexity on the basis of these differential patterns of performance decline (Davies and Parasuraman 1982).

An important further distinction was made by Fisk and Schneider (1981) who considered vigilance performance under conditions where target detection was vulnerable to becoming 'automatic' compared with tasks requiring constant, 'controlled' attention. Using this distinction from Schneider and Shiffrin's influential work (Schneider and Shiffrin 1977; Shiffrin and Schneider 1977) they found, perhaps not surprisingly, that when there was a constant and simple relationship between target and response, detection became rather automatic and a decline in performance over time was relatively slight. When however, target-response pairings shifted from block to block, significantly steeper declines were apparent (Fisk and Schneider 1981). A study by Paus and colleagues (Paus *et al.* 1997) suggests the neural changes which could underlie such shifts from active attentional to more automatic engagement. Healthy participants were asked to perform a simple vigilance task for around 60 min. Every 10 min, regional cerebral blood flow and EEG were measured. Significant reductions in blood flow were observed in subcortical structures, the thalamus, substantia innominata and putamen, and in right hemisphere cortical areas, including frontal and parietal cortex. These were interpreted by the authors as a subcortical arousal system and right cortical attentional system, respectively. Increases in low theta activity, associated with reduction in arousal, were also observed on the EEG as the task progressed. Despite the reduction in blood flow in the right hemisphere based 'attentional' and subcortical 'arousal' networks, the number of successful target detections did not significantly decline over the hour of the task. This was interpreted as reflecting a need for active attentional engagement early on in the task which declined as target detection became increasingly automatic. Results such as these suggest that the term 'sustained attention' may be somewhat inappropriately applied to situations which clearly require sustained *performance* but which may actually make relatively limited demands on what might be termed attention. This distinction is perhaps best captured by consideration of whether 'maintaining' responsivity to an arbitrary but overlearned stimulus such as one's own name requires anything approaching an active maintenance of attention at all.

These results point to the most commonly accepted paradigmatic definition of sustained attention being built on conceptually quite distinct tasks united only by a common time-on-task analysis. This does not, in itself, mean that common underlying factors may not have some utility in accounting for performance declines in different situations; for example, the decrements in the very different tasks of digging the garden and running a marathon may be both accounted for by muscular fatigue—but it does urge caution. There is a danger in reifying one aspect of performance such as decline, especially one which is apparently so variable, into a unitary construct thought to resist it.

Sustained attention, selective attention, divided attention, spatial attention, and their ilk are essentially descriptions of *task demands* or the final products of cognitive processes rather than of specific *brain systems*. Making the link between task demands and neural systems requires neuropsychological evidence, evidence from animal models, and, over recent years, evidence from functional imaging studies. The extent to which this evidence has supported the existence of functionally distinct attentional networks is considered in the next section.

17.2 Are there dissociable and supramodal attentional control systems in the brain?

The issue as to whether 'attention' has explanatory value as a concept has still not been resolved. One commonly held view is that attention is simply an early form of motor preparation, and that rather than attention having the status of a controller dictating what we do and perceive, attention is simply another way of describing the preparation to act (Allport 1993; Rizzolatti and Berti 1993). One alternative view is that there are indeed control systems which can be termed 'attentional', which are supramodal, and whose job it is to 'create' sensory inputs which have been selected as relevant, as well as to select appropriate responses. In the context of the aforegoing discussion of vigilance, attentional control systems have also been invoked, whose job it is to sustain attention over time, particularly under circumstances where attention is not modulated by novel, challenging or otherwise arousing external stimuli.

Posner and Petersen's (1990) paper was extremely influential in arguing the 'supramodal control system' approach to attention. This paper was heavily influenced by the functional imaging studies which had emerged in the 1980s. According to these authors, three inter-related mechanisms, operating semi-autonomously, underlie attention in humans. These are orienting, selection, and alerting/sustained attention. Orienting, it is argued, is controlled by a 'posterior attention system' based in the posterior parietal lobe, the superior colliculus and the lateral pulvinar nucleus of the posterolateral thalamus, among other areas. Selection involves the focal or conscious attention system which is strongly connected, functionally and anatomically, to the posterior attention system. It is related to target selection and recognition (other than automatic recognition—say of automatically detected word forms) and its anatomical basis is possibly the anterior cingulate and supplementary motor areas. Alerting or sustained attention is a system for sustaining a preparation to respond in the absence of salient or novel external stimuli which engage attention automatically; the right hemisphere—possibly particularly the right prefrontal cortex—appears, according to Posner and Petersen, to be specialized for this.

The fortunes of this typology have been mixed in the decade that has passed since the publication of this influential paper. As shall be seen later in this chapter, scientific fate, for instance, has not been kind to the idea that each parietal lobe is the basis for attention to contralateral space. An alternative view is that spatial attention may be the end product of a process of competition for selection of objects (see Duncan, this volume). This competition for selection can be biased, however, by top-down inputs, and there is accumulating evidence that the source of some such 'gating' inputs is in the frontal cortex (Büchel and Friston 1997). Posner and Petersen's suggestion that the anterior cingulate is the site of selective attention control has also been controversial, with some studies suggesting more general roles for this part of the brain, ranging from basic arousal (Paus *et al.* 1997), to more general initiation, motivation, and goal-directed behaviours (Devinsky *et al.* 1995).

While research continues into the nature and substrate of attentional systems, there is no doubt that these broad categorizations have proved useful in developing the clinical assessment of attention. The processes of standardizing clinical measures also allows for the analysis of statistical clusterings in large samples of the normal population. A factor analysis of the Test of Everyday

Attention in fact provided support for a separation between selective and sustained attention abilities and a factor characterized as 'attentional switching' or more generally 'attentional control' (Robertson *et al.* 1996). The post-hoc nature of standard factor analysis makes this a rather weak test of Posner and Petersen's proposals, however. A stronger test is to carry out a confirmatory factor analysis prospectively on an independent population sample, using often quite different test materials.

Recently, we had this opportunity in developing the Test of Everyday Attention for Children (Manly *et al.* 1998). The aim in developing this measure was to help bridge the gap between the conceptual shifts in the study of attention, which had been made largely with adult populations, and the intense but largely clinical interest which has been paid to children's attention, most particularly, of course, concerning varieties of attentional deficit/hyperactivity disorder (ADHD). Following on from the adult version, those measures which had significant loadings on the three non-spatial attentional factors from the adult test were adapted for children between the ages of 6 and 16. In addition, a task requiring the withholding of a response to rare targets based on the adult Sustained Attention to Response Test (Robertson *et al.* 1997a), a measure putatively of verbal inhibition and an auditory dual task (monitoring speech for an animal while simultaneously counting tones), were included. Using structural equation modelling, the three factors from the adult test were entered as latent variables to account for the observed pattern of variance in the normal performance of 293 children. These three factors did indeed form a very neat and parsimonious fit to the data. The spread of the tests on the factors suggests that more superficial reasons for clustering such as shared modality or response type, the requirement for speed and so forth are very unlikely to account for the pattern. That the predicted broad three-way split of attentional function should emerge above the noise of development in a normal population suggests that there is some validity to these distinctions.

17.3 Sustained attention and the right hemisphere

Of Posner and Petersen's postulated structure–function relationships, evidence for the involvement of the right hemisphere—and particularly the right dorsolateral prefrontal cortex—in tasks which demand prolonged attentive processing in the absence of strong environmental facilitation, has been relatively strong. An enhanced capacity for maintaining a readiness to respond in the right hemisphere was suggested as early as 1973. A study of split-brain patients showed that, following sectioning of the corpus callosum, target detection accuracy and response latencies were superior when temporally spaced visual stimuli were presented to the isolated right hemisphere than when they were presented to the isolated left (Dimond and Beaumont 1973).

A measure which is sensitive to a capacity to *self*-sustain attention is that of maintaining a count of rather monotonous stimuli. Wilkins *et al.* (1987) asked patients with focal neurological lesions to count a series of tones and a series of tactile stimuli. At longer interstimulus intervals (ISIs), patients with lesions to the right frontal lobe were particularly impaired relative to left frontal and posterior patients. At shorter intervals, this difference disappeared. This interval duration effect can be seen in other contexts such as the gap between a warning and target in a reaction time task. Right hemisphere patients, relative to left hemisphere patients, for example, benefit disproportionately from a cue to attend shortly before stimulus presentation (Posner *et al.* 1987) and facilitation of subsequent response times has been shown to be greater if warnings of between 1 and 2 s are presented to the right hemisphere in normal subjects (Heilman and Van Den Abell 1979).

The relationship between the demands of maintaining a monotonous count and right cortical function has been supported in a PET imaging study. Pardo *et al.* (1991) asked normal participants to count brief interruptions in somatosensory stimulation over a 40-s period. Relative to rest, significant activation was seen in right frontal and parietal cortex independent of the laterality of the stimulation. No change in left frontal activity was observed. A similar pattern of activation was seen on a second visual task leading the authors to conclude that these regions supported a cross-modal system for sustaining attention. As discussed, Paus *et al.*'s auditory vigilance task also produced right and not left frontal and parietal activation relative to a passive listening baseline, supporting earlier findings by Cohen and colleagues using a similar measure (Cohen *et al.* 1988; Cohen *et al.* 1992; Paus *et al.* 1997). Coull *et al.* (1996) obtained a compatible PET result using a quite different type of sustained attention task. This task involved detecting sequences of visually presented digits embedded within an ongoing rapidly presented series. Compared to an eyes-closed control, this task also produced significant activation in the right frontal cortex—specifically in the superior frontal gyrus rostrally.

Common to these diverse paradigms is the requirement to maintain active a simple goal (e.g. keeping count) under circumstances where the stimuli attended lack the characteristics known to trigger orientation and alertness. That is, these stimuli lack novelty, emotionality, sensory salience, and unpredictability: in other words, they are monotonous. Furthermore, the tasks involved in these paradigms offer no significant cognitive, motoric, sensory, or emotional challenge to the subject for their successful completion. All that is required for such tasks is the simple sustaining of attention over periods of seconds to a simple goal. It seems that this is far from being a trivially easy task for the human brain. Our working definition of sustained attention, therefore, is the endogenous maintenance of a goal-related behaviour (preparing a response, maintaining a count, and so forth) under conditions where external events on the one hand, and challenge of task demands on the other, do not exogenously engage them.

In line with this definition we have investigated performance under conditions where the goal that needs to be kept in mind is pitted directly against more automatic, task-driven behaviour. In the Sustained Attention to Response Test (SART) participants are asked to make a key-press response for every number they see appear on a computer screen. Because of the temporally pre-dictable, rhythmic presentation of the digits every 1.15 s, this aspect of the task is trivially easy and vulnerable to rapid automation—that is it requires little moment-to-moment attentional control. The catch is that periodically and unpredictably a target digit is presented to which no response should be given. Success in not pressing to these rare targets requires that attentive supervision of the response process is maintained. Most subjects do this imperfectly and make a few errors. Patients with traumatic brain injuries in whom frontal damage is likely and patients with right hemisphere strokes have significantly greater difficulty (Robertson *et al.* 1997a). If, however, the task is adjusted such that the intervals between targets—and hence the period over which a readiness to withhold must be *self*-maintained—are reduced, performance is significantly improved (Manly *et al.*, under review). Similarly if an auditory cue is periodically presented to remind participants of their goal, despite long inter-target intervals, performance is also significantly enhanced. The comparison of performance under these conditions which require more or less endogenous attentional maintenance provides one route to better characterising these capacities.

17.4 Arousal

A wide range of lesions to the right hemisphere produce impairments of sustained attention. This is also true of arousal, a concept often linked to sustained attention function. Certainly, as indicated in the working definition above, the emotional or motivational salience of events appear to influence our capacity to maintain our attention upon them. In a series of papers in the 1970s and early '80s, Heilman and colleagues showed the predominance of the right hemisphere in mediating this generalized enhanced responsivity/activation to stimuli (Coslett *et al.* 1987; Heilman *et al.* 1978; Heilman and Valenstein 1979). Patients with right hemisphere lesions were hypoaroused relative to left hemisphere lesioned patients, for example, showing virtually absent galvanic skin response (GSR) to pictures of emotionally arousing scenes (such as of mutilated hands and battles) (Morrow *et al.* 1981). Similar results were obtained from painful stimuli; again, right temporo-parietal lesioned patients showed greatly reduced GSR responses in comparison to either left brain damaged patients or controls.

Unilateral right temporal lobectomy patients also show basic hypoarousal when compared to left temporal lobectomy patients, as measured by GSR (Davidson *et al.* 1992). In a subsequent study, these authors showed, however, that these differences occur only under passive, non-evaluative stimulus conditions. When performance feedback was given, right temporal lobe patients showed normal arousal as measured by GSR and reaction time following success feedback. In other words, with this patient group, the right hemisphere lesion-induced low arousal was reversible by appropriate exogenous input.

The right hemisphere dominance for both arousal and sustained attention has, as will be discussed further, led to the development of models which incorporate the two concepts into a functional network (Heilman *et al.* 1987). Other studies, for example those of Paus *et al.* (1997), highlight the need to maintain a conceptual separation between subcortical arousal structures and cortical 'attentional' networks.

To summarize, then: though Posner and Petersen's formulation of 1990 requires substantial reworking, particularly in considering the suggested anatomical basis of its proposed attentional subsystems, the basic framework of the approach is supported. That is, the data lead us to accept the view that there may be more than one supramodal attentional control system. One such system may bias or gate perceptual selection in a range of posterior regions (Knight *et al.* 1989; Woldorff *et al.* 1993; Yamaguchi and Knight 1990), while another may help sustain selected representations over time (Cohen *et al.* 1992; Pardo *et al.* 1991). (Whether another system should be invoked to account for attentional switching is a matter which will not be dealt with here.) One way of testing the usefulness of this typology is to examine how one of these systems—that for sustaining over time—behaves in relation to spatial behaviour. That is the issue we turn to now.

17.5 Sustained attention in space

One of the most dramatic examples of the breakdown of spatial attention following brain lesion is unilateral spatial neglect, where people demonstrate a lack of responsiveness to, or even awareness of, one side of space—usually the left. It is now widely agreed that this syndrome is not unitary, with many dissociations, including personal- versus extra-personal (Guariglia and Antonucci 1992), within- versus between-object neglect (Humphreys and Riddoch 1994) and many others. The purpose of the present chapter is to return to an association which has been described for the last 20 or 30 years, but which so far does not have a satisfactory theoretical explanation. This is the association between spatial attention deficits on the one hand, and disorders of a constellation of phenomena variously termed 'arousal', 'alertness', 'sustained attention', and 'vigilance' on the other.

Heilman and his group have been at the forefront of research exploring this relationship. In a review of the behavioural and neural mechanisms of attention, Heilman *et al.* argue that 'the right hemisphere may have a special role in mediating the arousal response as well as in selective attention.' (1987, p. 475). They argue that the greater incidence and severity of neglect from right hemisphere lesions in humans is due to the asymmetry of the receptive fields for novel or significant stimuli. They propose that the temporal–parietal cortex in the right hemisphere may have receptive fields for novel stimuli for both left and right hemispaces, whereas the equivalent area in the left hemisphere has receptive fields for novel or significant stimuli only in right hemispace. By this argument, left hemisphere damage can relatively easily be compensated for by a right hemisphere capable of responding to novel and significant stimuli in both hemispaces. Heilman and colleagues therefore make a distinction between hypoarousal associated with right temporal parietal damage on the one hand, and spatial selective attention on the other. But a clear formulation of the precise relationship between these two systems remains elusive.

17.6 Correlational evidence for a link between unilateral spatial inattention and arousal problems

Sufferers from both left and right stroke are equally likely to suffer distortions of spatial attention in the immediate post-stroke period. Quite rapidly, however, the pattern becomes unbalanced with right hemisphere patients forming the overwhelming majority of those who show chronic spatial deficits (Stone *et al.* 1991, 1992, 1993). Various reasons for this pattern have been proposed, including the possibility that the right parietal cortex controls attention to both hemifields, while the left parietal cortex controls spatial selective attention to the right hemifield only.

In considering the possible influence of more generalized attentional deficits in accounting for this, Robertson *et al.* (1997*b*) examined the performance of a large number of right hemisphere stroke patients on a non-spatial sustained attention measure. Despite reasonable equity between groups on indices of functional severity, such as motor function, right hemisphere patients who showed neglect were significantly more likely to have problems with this task than those who had no obvious neglect. Indeed, the discriminative power of this sustained attention measure which consists simply of maintaining a count of tones was greater than a conventional measure of visual neglect, namely line bisection.

Hjaltason *et al.* (1996) have also shown a strong relationship between the presence of sustained attention deficits on the one hand, and severity of neglect on the other. They studied 17 patients suffering from unilateral left visuospatial neglect. To measure sustained attention, they used a 7-min continuous performance test requiring the detection of an auditorally presented letter *E* ($N = 53$ targets) among other letter distractors ($N = 259$ distractors). The group was then divided into two groups, one of nine subjects with normal and the other of eight subjects with abnormal sustained attention (based on the performance of a control group). These two groups did not differ in lesion size, but they did differ significantly in the degree of unilateral spatial neglect shown. The authors concluded that persisting unilateral neglect is related to an impairment in sustained attention.

Recently, Duncan *et al.* have clearly shown this in a series of patients with unilateral neglect and right parietal lesions. They found that these patients had severely reduced perceptual capacity on both left and right hemispaces (Duncan *et al.*, in press). A number of other studies report similar non-spatial attentional capacity limitations in this group including a much extended dwell time on a non-lateralized 'attentional blink' task (Husain *et al.* 1997). From being considered a deficit which is specific to space, therefore, the evidence is growing that chronic neglect in adults is likely to be seen within a context of more widespread non-spatial attentional difficulties. Given the apparent specialization of the right hemisphere in mediating a number of non-spatial attentional functions and the pattern of recovery from neglect between right and left hemisphere patients and within right hemisphere patient groups, it is therefore plausible that such co-existing non-spatial deficits act to at least modulate and perpetuate the spatial aspects of the disorder.

Samuelsson *et al.* (1997) have also found that non-lateralized attentional deficits are extremely strong predictors of persisting unilateral neglect. Their measure of attention was an auditory reaction time task, with a warning foreperiod of 2–7 s. (We argue that bridging temporal gaps even of this length in this task meets the criteria for sustained attention specified above: patients have to maintain the goal state in a simple task in the absence of salient, attentionally modulating, external events.) Both responses and auditory stimuli appeared ipsilateral to the lesion. Extended reaction times to the auditory stimuli were strongly predictive of the presence of unilateral neglect, and indeed the strongest correlate of persisting slow reactions involved lesions to the same area as predicted persisting unilateral neglect, namely the paraventricular white matter in the temporal lobe (see below).

There is also increasing evidence that such a relationship between lateralized and non-lateralized attentional deficits may not be limited to adults. Manly *et al.* (1997) reported the case of AC, a 9-year-old child who showed many aspects of spatial bias characteristic of the adult disorder despite no obvious neurological precursor or abnormality on MRI examination. When tested with a non-spatial tone-counting paradigm, the SCORE sustained attention measure from the Test of Everyday Attention for Children (Manly *et al.* 1998), a robust and reliable impairment was apparent. This deficit, many standard deviations below the control mean, was all the more striking in the context of AC's generally high levels of abilities including a verbal IQ of 123. Assessment with other measures in the TEACh battery and on parent checklists showed that AC also displayed a constellation of attentional problems which were consistent with a DSM IV diagnosis of an attentional deficit/hyperactivity disorder.

A previous indication that children who experienced such difficulties may also have spatial biases had been reported by Voeller and Heilman (1988). They found a disproportionate number of left-sided omissions on a simple cancellation task made by a group of seven ADHD boys relative to age controls. While the largely behavioural diagnostic criteria for ADHD form no guarantee that children who share the diagnosis will necessarily share cognitive difficulties or aetiology, at a group level a number of neurological abnormalities in areas known to support attentional function have been observed. For example, reduced corpus callosum volume measured by MRI has been reported (Hynd *et al.* 1991), as has reduced cerebral blood flow in frontal regions (Zametkin *et al.* 1990). The prevalence and form of any neurochemical abnormalities in ADHD children, perhaps surprisingly given the frequency of pharmacological intervention, remains controversial (Swanson *et al.* 1998).

Additional support for at least some children with this diagnosis showing abnormalities in spatial attention has recently come from Nigg and colleagues (Nigg *et al.* 1997). They showed that ADHD-diagnosed boys were significantly slower in responding to left-sided stimuli in a speeded computer administered task, a feature which was also observed, though to a lesser extent, in their parents.

17.7 Experimental evidence for a causal link between unilateral spatial inattention and arousal problems

Robertson *et al.* (in press) tested the hypothesis, originally suggested by Posner (1993), that the right hemisphere arousal system should directly and specifically modulate the spatial selection system. The prediction was that phasically increasing the patients' alertness should transiently ameliorate the spatial bias in perceptual awareness, and indeed the results provided the first direct confirmation of this proposal. The task required right hemisphere neglect patients to judge whether a left visual event preceded a comparable right event, or vice versa. Neglect patients became aware of left events half a second slower than right events, on average. This dramatic spatial imbalance in the timecourse of visual awareness could be reversed if a warning sound alerted the patients phasically. Even a sound on the right dramatically accelerated the perception of left visual events in this way. A non-spatial alerting intervention can thus overcome disabling spatial biases in perceptual awareness after brain injury.

In a clinical–experimental corollary of the above study, we attempted directly to rehabilitate sustained attention in a group of patients with unilateral left neglect following right hemisphere lesions. These patients were trained while doing a variety of tasks with no lateralized scanning component: periodically the patients had their attention drawn to a routine task—for example a sorting task—by combining a loud noise with an instruction to attend. Patients were then gradually taught to 'take over' this alerting procedure using a self-generated verbal cue so that eventually it became a self-alerting procedure. Among this group of eight patients, not only were there improvements in sustained attention, but there were also very significant improvements on spatial neglect over and above those expected by natural recovery. This study shows that the spatial bias in unilateral neglect can be briefly reduced using exogenous alerting stimuli, but that it may also be possible to reduce this bias endogenously, using self-initiated alerting mechanisms.

The brain's right hemisphere appears to play a role in sustaining a tonic level of alertness. Lesions to the right hemisphere, as was shown earlier, lead to quite widespread under-arousal, and associated lack of basic psychophysiological responsiveness to stimuli, including novel, emotionally arousing ones. In a tachistoscopic study of lateralized presentation of dual stimuli to normal subjects, Whitehead (1991) studied the effects of presenting a salient auditory alerting stimulus simultaneously to the visual stimuli. In the absence of such alerting stimuli, there was a left visual field advantage in reaction times to the visual stimulus under conditions of sustained visual attention—as defined earlier. This asymmetry was, however, eliminated when the auditory stimulus appeared simultaneously with the target. In other words, external alerting appeared to boost left hemisphere performance to a level equivalent to that shown by the unaided right hemisphere. It seems therefore that there may be a certain functional equivalence between voluntary sustained alerting on the one hand, and the more automatic exogenous alerting on the other, as suggested in the previous section.

Strong supportive evidence for Whitehead's conclusions comes from an ERP study of normal subjects (Yamaguchi *et al.* 1994). As part of a series of experiments, subjects carried out a standard Posner-type spatial attention task, requiring the detection of peripheral targets. Central arrow cues predicted target side onset with 80% validity, and these cues were presented at varying cue-target intervals, namely 200, 500, or 800 ms. ERP recordings were made during these intervals. This study found that central cues induced a negative ERP shift at around 240 ms after cue onset over the contralateral posterior scalp to the cued visual field, with this effect spreading to anterior sites with time. Later, however, between 500 and 800 ms, the right temporal-parietal areas showed sustained negativities, regardless of visual field. The authors concluded that the right hemisphere temporal-parietal regions 'may be more important for maintaining sustained attention than for phasic attention shifts in adults' (p. 560).

Duncan (this volume) has also reviewed evidence from functional imaging studies to show that the parietal lobe is indifferent to the direction of attention in tasks involving leftward and rightward visual discrimination. He reports substantial activation of the superior parietal lobule in all task conditions, irrespective of visual field, compared with a control task requiring no peripheral discriminations. Furthermore, in all conditions, parietal activation was stronger in the right hemisphere.

The right parietal cortex is of course precisely the region commonly implicated in unilateral neglect (Vallar 1993), and the neglect of the left side of space manifested in this disorder has commonly been attributed to the role of that cortical region in deploying attention to that region of space. Yet here we have growing evidence that the most salient role of this region may be non-spatial.

Several studies converge to suggest that the right parietal cortex has a particularly strong role in sustaining attention irrespective of the spatial locus of that attention. This being the case, it is plausible from a neuroanatomical point of view to suggest that a fundamental deficit in unilateral neglect is a deficit in this ability to sustain attention independently of spatial location. Such a conclusion ties in closely with the experimental evidence reviewed in the previous section showing indeed that manipulating sustained attention dramatically influences unilateral neglect, as well as with the correlational studies reviewed in the first section showing an intimate link between spatial neglect and sustained attention deficits. But what is the nature of this 'sustained' capacity, which we are attributing to the right posterior cortex? That brings us on to the final section of this chapter.

17.8 Exogenous and endogenous processes in sustaining attention over time

Heilman has argued for the existence of neuroanatomical circuits which would correspond to two different mechanisms for modulating alertness in the brain (Heilman *et al.* 1987). One mechanism increases arousal in a 'bottom-up' way, via the mesencephalic reticular formation and the thalamic relay nuclei. According to Heilman, the cortical projections of this system are particularly strong in the frontal and parietal cortex, and represent the ability of the brain to be aroused or alerted by novel, important, or emotionally arousing stimuli. Heilman and colleagues argue that the mid-brain alerting system can also be activated in a 'top-down' fashion, particularly from the right dorsolateral prefrontal cortex. This type of system would be needed in tasks where the external environment provides no intrinsically arousing stimulation, but where, nevertheless, an alert readiness to respond must be maintained endogenously. These mid-brain structures also seem to be closely involved in circadian fluctuations in arousal (Braun *et al.* 1997), as well as showing significant increases in activation from a relaxed state to one required for an attentionally demanding reaction time task (Kinomura *et al.* 1996).

In the case of unilateral neglect following right hemisphere damage, it would appear plausible that one or both of these systems may be significantly impaired. Evidence that the exogenous bottom-up system can be impaired comes from Heilman's group showing that basic emotional and arousing stimuli produce significantly lower psychophysiological responding in neglect patients. Evidence on the other hand, that the top-down, endogenous systems may also be impaired, comes for instance from the study described above showing that voluntary sustained attention impairment is a marker of the presence of unilateral visual neglect (Robertson *et al.* 1997b). As previously described, Samuelsson *et al.* (1997) have shown that the persistence of unilateral neglect into a chronic stage is predicted strongly by the presence of damage to the paraventricular white matter in the temporal lobe, combined with damage to the temporo-parietal lobe. These ascending white matter bundles would be precisely those anatomical structures implicated in the exogenous bottom-up system proposed by Heilman, through which external stimuli would have their arousing effects on the cortex. Other recent research has also confirmed a strong role for damage to the white matter underlying the temporo-parietal-junction in determining the presence of neglect (Leibovitch *et al.* 1998).

17.9 Conclusions

Posner and Petersen's view that there are separable supramodal attention systems for selection, sustaining, and spatial orientation requires some revision. Evidence for the existence of frontal systems whose role is top-down modulation of perceptual, spatial, and language systems in the posterior regions of the brain is strong. So is there good evidence for a separate system responsible for sustaining attention and modulating the alert state. Whether spatial selection can be considered as a supramodal control system, rather than the emergent property of competing systems and representations, is less clear. The possibility that a system for attentional switching exists must also be considered, but the evidence for this is largely correlational. (A recent study, however, suggests that spatial shifts in attention involve activation of an anterior right frontal region quite distinct from the dorsolateral area associated with sustained attention (Macaluso *et al.* 1998).)

Posner's suggestion that the spatial orientation and sustained attention systems should interact intimately has been supported by experimental and correlation evidence, but quite how they interact is less clear. Part of the problem here is that the unitary system for maintaining alertness proposed by Posner now appears to have at least two components. One of these is a rather low-level, probably mid-brain-located arousal system, and the other is a right hemisphere dominant system whose role is partly to modulate the level of alertness of the brain in response to task and motivational demands. These two systems interact reciprocally, and can be influenced both by exogenous events in the environment, as well as by symbolic, endogenous events.

Posner and Petersen suggested that the right hemisphere alertness system was a diffuse, low-level system related to a putative right hemisphere dominant norepinephrine (NE) neurotransmitter system. There is some evidence that this system is right hemisphere dominant (Oke *et al.* 1978), and the literature on attention deficit disorder shows that the noradrenergic agonist methylphenidate does indeed reverse the spatial orientation bias found in some ADHD children. Nevertheless, all the evidence reviewed above suggests that a more complex model of sustained attention is needed to account for the range of phenomena in this area. Such a model should incorporate top-down and bottom-up influences between the two hypothetical interacting systems described above.

Unilateral neglect has been considered by many as the paradigmatic manifestation of a spatial attention deficit, yet the evidence reviewed in this chapter suggests that, in fact, the spatial aspect of this syndrome may be overshadowed by questions of slowed temporal processing (Husain *et al.* 1997), impaired arousal (Robertson *et al.*, in press), reduced bilateral perceptual capacity (Duncan *et al.*, in press; Robertson 1989) and impaired sustained attention (Robertson *et al.* 1997b). If we were to discard as no longer useful the concept of a supramodal spatial attention system, then this would suggest the need to re-interpret a large number of studies which have suggested that the right parietal cortex has a dominant role for spatial selective attention (Corbetta *et al.* 1993; Corbetta *et al.* 1995; Gitelman *et al.* 1996), an interpretation that has not been borne out in recent functional imaging studies (see Duncan, this volume). The default hypothesis to be addressed, therefore, would be that the primary role of the parietal cortex of the right hemisphere is not one of supramodal spatial selection. Rather, its spatial role may be confined to integration of perceptuo-motor responses (see Milner, this volume, and also Mattingley *et al.* 1998). Furthermore, another important role of the right parietal cortex may be some other as yet poorly-defined role related to perceptual capacity, sustained attention, or some other aspect of non-lateralized attention. One strength of this latter hypothesis is that it would more comfortably offer a springboard towards interpreting the growing evidence for an intimate link between sustained attention over time on the one hand and distributed attention to space on the other.

References

Allport, A. 1993 Attention and control—Have we been asking the wrong questions: A critical review of 25 years. In D. E. Meyer and S. Kornblum (eds), *Attention and performance XIV: Synergies in experimental psychology, artificial intelligence and cognitive neuroscience* (pp. 183–218). Cambridge, MA.: MIT Press.

Braun, A. R., Balkin, T. J., Wesensten, N. J., Carson, R. E., Varga, M., Baldwin, P., Selbie, S., Belenky, G. and Herscovitch, P. 1997 Regional cerebral blood flow throughout the sleep-wake cycle. An H215O PET study. *Brain* **120**, 1173–97.

Broadbent, D. E. 1971 *Decision and stress*. London: Academic Press.

Broadbent, D. E. and Gregory, M. 1963 Vigilance considered as a statistical decision. *British Journal of Psychology* **54**, 309–23.

Büchel, C. and Friston, K. J. 1997 Modulation of connectivity in visual pathways by attention: Cortical interactions evaluated with structural equation modelling and fMRI. *Cerebral Cortex* **7**, 768–78.

Cohen, R. M., Semple, W. E., Gross, M., Holcomb, H. J., Dowling, S. and Nordahl, T. E. 1988 Functional localization of sustained attention. *Neuropsychiatry, Neuropsychology and Behavioural Neurology* **1**, 3–20.

Cohen, R. M., Semple, W. E., Gross, M., King, A. C. and Nordahl, T. E. 1992 Metabolic brain pattern of sustained auditory discrimination. *Experimental Brain Research* **92**, 165–72.

Corbetta, M., Miezin, F. M., Schulman, G. L. and Petersen, S. E. 1993 A PET study of visuospatial attention. *The Journal of Neuroscience* **13**, 1202–6.

Corbetta, M., Shulman, G. L., Miezin, F. M. and Petersen, S. E. 1995 Superior parietal cortex activation during spatial attention shifts and visual feature conjunction. *Science* **270**, 802–5.

Coslett, H. B., Bowers, D. and Heilman, K. M. 1987 Reduction in cerebral activation after right hemisphere stroke. *Neurology* **37**, 957–62.

Coull, J. T., Frith, C. D., Frackowiak, R. S. J. and Grasby, P. M. 1996 A fronto-parietal network for rapid visual information-processing: A pet study of sustained attention and working memory. *Neuropsychologia* **34**, 1085–95.

Davidson, R. A., Fedio, P., Smith, B. D., Aureille, E., and Martin, A. 1992 Lateralised mediation of arousal and habituation: Differential bilateral electrodermal activity in unilateral temporal lobectomy patients. *Neuropsychologia* **30**, 1053–63.

Davies, D. R. and Parasuraman, R. 1982 *The psychology of vigilance*. New York: Academic Press.

Deese, J. 1955 Some problems in the theory of vigilance. *Psychological Review* **62**, 217–23.

Devinsky, O., Morrell, M. J. and Vogt, B. A. 1995 Contributions of anterior cingulate cortex to behaviour. *Brain* **118**, 279–306.

Dimond, J. J. and Beaumont, J. G. 1973 Differences in the vigilance performance of the right and left hemispheres. *Cortex* **9**, 259–66.

Duncan, J., Bundesen, C., Olson, A., Humphreys, G., Chavda, S. and Shibuya, H. (in press). Systematic analysis of deficits in visual attention. *Journal of Experimental Psychology: General.*

Egan, J. P., Greenberg, G. Z. and Schulman, A. I. 1961 Operating characteristics, signal detectability and the method of free response. *Journal of the Acoustical Society of America* **33**, 993–1007.

Fisk, A. D. and Schneider, W. 1981 Control and automatic processing during tasks requiring sustained attention: A new approach to vigilance. *Human Factors* **23**, 737–50.

Gitelman, D. R., Alpert, N. M., Kosslyn, S., Daffner, K., Scinto, L., Thompson, W. and Mesulam, M. M. 1996 Functional imaging of human right hemispheric activation for exploratory movements. *Annals of Neurology* **39**, 174–9.

Guariglia, C. and Antonucci, G. 1992 Personal and extrapersonal space: A case of neglect dissociation. *Neuropsychologia* **30**, 1001–9.

Heilman, K. M., Schwartz, H. D. and Watson, R. T. 1978 Hypoarousal in patients with the neglect syndrome and emotional indifference. *Neurology* **28**, 229–32.

Heilman, K. M. and Valenstein, E. 1979 Mechanisms underlying hemispatial neglect. *Annals of Neurology* **5**, 166–70.

Heilman, K. M. and Van Den Abell, T. 1979 Right hemisphere dominance for mediating cerebral activation. *Neuropsychologia* **17**, 315–21.

Heilman, K. M., Watson, R. T., Valenstein, E. and Goldberg, M. E. 1987 Attention: Behavior and neural mechanisms. In F. Plum (ed.), *Handbook of physiology, Section 1: The nervous system* (Vol. 5, pp. 461–81). Bethesda, MD: American Physiological Society.

Hjaltason, H., Tegnér, R., Tham, K., Levander, M. and Ericson, K. 1996 Sustained attention and awareness of disability in chronic neglect. *Neuropsychologia* **34**, 1229–33.

Humphreys, G. W. and Riddoch, M. J. 1994 Attention to within-object and between-object spatial representations: Multiple sites for visual selection. *Cognitive Neuropsychology* **11**, 207–41.

Husain, M., Shapiro, K., Martin, J. and Kennard, C. 1997 Abnormal temporal dynamics of visual attention in spatial neglect patients. *Nature* **385**, 154–6.

Hynd, G. W., Semrud-Clikeman, M., Lorys, A. R., Novey, E. S., Eliopulos, D. and Lyytinen, H. 1991 Corpus callosum morphology in attention deficit-hyperactivity disorder: Morphometric analysis of MRI. *Journal of Learning Disabilities* **24**, 141–6.

Kinomura, S., Larsson, J., Gulyas, B. and Roland, P. E. 1996 Activation by attention of the human reticular formation and thalamic intralaminar nuclei. *Science* **271**, 512–5.

Knight, R. T., Scabini, D. and Woods, D. L. 1989 Prefrontal gating of auditory cortex transmissions in humans. *Brain Research* **504**, 338–42.

Leibovitch, F. S., Black, S. E., Caldwell, C. B., Ebert, P. L., Ehrlich, L. E. and Szalai, J. P. 1998 Brain-behavior correlations in hemispatial neglect using CT and SPECT: The Sunnybrook Stroke Study. *Neurology* **50**, 901–8.

Macaluso, E., Driver, J. and Frith, C. D. 1998 Differential activation of anterior and posterior brain regions during spatial covert orienting. *Journal of Cognitive Neuroscience* (Suppl. S), p. 72 (abstract).

Mackworth, J. F. 1968 Vigilance, arousal and habituation. *Psychological Review* **75**, 308–22.

Mackworth, N. H. 1950 *Researches in the measurement of human performance*. Medical Research Council Special Report No. 268. London: HM Stationery Office. Reprinted in H. W. Sinaiko (ed.), *Selected papers on human factors in the design and use of control systems* (pp. 174–331). New York: Dover, 1961.

Manly, T., Robertson, I. H., Anderson, V. and Nimmo-Smith, I. 1998 *Test of Everyday Attention for Children (TEAch)*. Bury St Edmunds: Thames Valley Test Company.

Manly, T., Robertson, I. H. and Galloway, M. 1998 *The absent mind*. Manuscript under review.

Manly, T., Robertson, I. H. and Verity, C. 1997 Developmental unilateral neglect: A single case study. *Neurocase* **3**, 19–30.

Mattingley, J. B., Husain, M., Rorden, C., Kennard, C. and Driver, J. 1998 Motor role of human inferior parietal lobe revealed in unilateral neglect. *Nature* **392**, 179–82.

Morrow, L., Vrtunski, K., Kim, Y. and Boller, F. 1981 Arousal responses to emotional stimuli and laterality of lesion. *Neuropsychologia* **19**, 65–71.

Nigg, J. T., Swanson, J. M. and Hinshaw, S. P. 1997 Covert visual spatial attention in boys with attention deficit hyperactivity disorder: Lateral effects, methylphenidate response and results for parents. *Neuropsychologia* **35**, 165–76.

Oke, A., Keller, R., Mefford, I. and Adams, R. 1978 Lateralization of norepinephrine in human thalamus. *Science* **200**, 1411–3.

Parasuraman, R. 1983 Vigilance, arousal and the brain. In A. Gale and J. A. Edwards (eds), *Physiological correlates of human behaviour* (pp. 35–55). London: Academic Press.

Pardo, J. V., Fox, P. T. and Raichle, M. E. 1991 Localization of a human system for sustained attention by positron emission tomography. *Nature* **349**, 61–4.

Paus, T., Zatorre, R. J., Hofle, N., Caramanos, Z., Gotman, J., Petrides, M. and Evans, A. C. 1997 Time-related changes in neural systems underlying attention and arousal during the performance of an auditory vigilance task. *Journal of Cognitive Neuroscience* **9**, 392–408.

Posner, M. I. 1987 Isolating attentional systems: A cognitive-anatomical analysis. *Psychobiology* **15**, 107–21.

Posner, M. I. 1993 Interaction of arousal and selection in the posterior attention network. In A. D. Baddeley and L. Weiskrantz (eds), *Attention: Selection, awareness and control* (pp. 390–405). Oxford: Clarendon Press.

Posner, M. I. and Petersen, S. E. 1990 The attention system of the human brain. *Annual Review of Neuroscience* **13**, 25–42.

Rizzolatti, G. and Berti, A. 1993 Neural mechanisms of unilateral neglect. In I. H. Robertson and J. C. Marshall (eds), *Unilateral neglect: Clinical and experimental studies.* Hove, Sussex: Lawrence Erlbaum.

Robertson, I. H. 1989 Anomalies in the lateralisation of omissions in unilateral left neglect. *Neuropsychologia* **27**, 157–65.

Robertson, I. H., Ward, T., Ridgeway, V. and Nimmo-Smith, I. 1996 The structure of normal human attention: The Test of Everyday Attention. *Journal of the International Neuropsychological Society* **2**, 525–34.

Robertson, I. H., Manly, T., Andrade, J., Baddeley, B. T. and Yiend, J. (1997*a*). Oops!: Performance correlates of everyday attentional failures in traumatic brain injured and normal subjects: The Sustained Attention to Response Task (SART). *Neuropsychologia* **35**, 747–58.

Robertson, I. H., Manly, T., Beschin, N., Daini, R., Haeske-Dewick, H., Hömberg, V., Jehkonen, M., Pizzamiglio, L., Shiel, A. and Weber, E. (1997*b*). Auditory sustained attention is a marker of unilateral spatial neglect. *Neuropsychologia* **35**, 1527–32.

Robertson, I. H., Mattingley, J. B., Rorden, C. and Driver, J. (in press). Phasic alerting of right-hemisphere neglect patients overcomes their spatial deficit in visual awareness. *Nature.*

Samuelsson, H., Jensen, C., Ekholm, S., Naver, H. and Blomstrand, C. 1997 Anatomical and neurological correlates of acute and chronic visuospatial neglect following right hemisphere stroke. *Cortex* **33**, 271–85.

Schneider, W. and Shiffrin, R. M. 1977 Controlled and automatic human information processing: 1. Detection, search and attention. *Psychological Review* **84**, 1–66.

See, J. 1995 Meta-analysis of the sensitivity decrement in vigilance. *Psychological Bulletin* **117**, 230–49.

Shiffrin, R. M. and Schneider, W. 1977 Controlled and automatic human information processing: II. Perceptual learning, automatic attending, and a general theory. *Psychological Review* **84**, 127–90.

Stone, S. P., Wilson, B. A., Wroot, A., Halligan, P. W., Lange, L. S., Marshall, J. C. and Greenwood, R. J. 1991 The assessment of visuo-spatial neglect after acute stroke. *Journal of Neurology, Neurosurgery and Psychiatry* **54**, 345–50.

Stone, S. P., Patel, P., Greenwood, R. J. and Halligan, P. W. 1992 Measuring visual neglect in acute stroke and predicting its recovery: The visual neglect recovery index. *Journal of Neurology, Neurosurgery and Psychiatry* **55**, 431–6.

Stone, S. P., Halligan, P. W. and Greenwood, R. J. 1993 The incidence of neglect phenomena and related disorders in patients with an acute right or left hemisphere stroke. *Age and Ageing* **22**, 46–52.

Swanson, J., Castellanos, F. X., Murias, M., LaHoste, G., and Kennedy, J. 1998 Cognitive neuroscience of attention deficit hyperactivity disorder and hyperkinetic disorder. *Current Opinion in Neurobiology* **8**, 263–71.

Vallar, G. 1993 The anatomical basis of spatial neglect in humans. In I. H. Robertson and J. C. Marshall (eds), *Unilateral neglect: Clinical and experimental studies* (pp. 27–59). Hove, Sussex: Lawrence Erlbaum.

Voeller, K. K. S. and Heilman, K. M. 1988 Attention deficit disorder in children: A neglect syndrome? *Neurology* **38**, 806–8.

Whitehead, R. 1991 Right hemisphere processing superiority during sustained visual attention. *Journal of Cognitive Neuroscience* **3**, 329–35.

Wilkins, A. J., Shallice, T. and McCarthy, R. 1987 Frontal lesions and sustained attention. *Neuropsychologia* **25**, 359–65.

Woldorff, M. G., Gallen, C. C., Hampson, S. A., Hillyard, S. R., Pantev, C., Sobel, D. and Bloom, F. E. 1993 Modulation of early sensory processing in human auditory cortex during auditory selective attention. *Proceedings of the National Academy of Science, USA* **90**, 8722–6.

Yamaguchi, S. and Knight, R. T. 1990 Gating of somatosensory input by human prefrontal cortex. *Brain Research* **521**, 281–8.

Yamaguchi, S., Tsuchiya, H. and Kobayashi, S. 1994 Electoencephalographic activity associated with shifts of visual attention. *Brain* **117**, 553–562.

Zametkin, A., Notdahl, T. and Gross, M. 1990 Cerebral glucose metabolism in adults with hyperactivity of childhood onset. *The New England Journal of Medicine* **20**, 1361–6.

18

Interactions between perception and action systems: a model for selective action

Robert Ward

Abstract

A model of selective processing in vision and action is described. The selective action network is an alternative to traditional accounts describing the relationship between visual processing and action. Standard one-way models assume that action is the terminal output stage of processing, with no impact on previous processes of visual perception and attention. In contrast, the selective action model proposes simultaneous influence among many systems, processing spatial and non-spatial visual attributes of objects, spatial and non-spatial components of action, and intention or goals. In the model, plans for location serve to bias selective perceptual processing towards relevant objects, in much the same way that visual processing can be biased towards particular locations or particular object features. Selective processing in the network emerges in a gradual and coordinated way, so that representations of a single object and its implications for action comes to dominate across multiple systems of perception and action.

18.1 Introduction

What is the relationship between systems for visual perception and systems for action? Some early information-processing models of selective visual processing, such as Sternberg's (1969) account of visual search, are quite explicit in suggesting that perception is necessarily prior to action processing. Sternberg (1969) found additive effects of target quality and probability on visual search reaction times, and hypothesized discrete processing stages, arranged to form a one-way channel of information flow: visual input first passed through a stage of stimulus encoding; after the input was conclusively analysed, the results were passed to subsequent stages of response organization and execution. In this one-way model, task demands can affect perceptual processing—for example, by selecting search targets on the basis of colour rather than shape—but the planning or execution of an action in itself can not.

Very powerful implications can be drawn from a generalization of Sternberg's (1969) one-way model, in which action is contingent on perception. In principle, since the terminal output stage of response can not affect earlier stages of perception, perceptual processing can be examined independently of the responses measured. That is, whether we measure key presses, verbal responses, lever throws, foot switches, or reaches, our conclusions about the underlying perceptual mechanisms should be the same. This notion of action strictly contingent on perception is still widely held, at least implicitly, and the dominance of this model might even explain some of the generally limited exchange between researchers in visual attention and in motor control.

But is this widely held model correct? Is perception necessarily prior to a terminal, output-stage, of action? The suggestion seems compelling, and maybe even logically necessary. However, there is nothing in the architecture of the primate brain suggesting a terminal stage of processing. As summarized by Young (1995), over 80% of the connections between cortical regions in the macaque investigated to that date were found to be reciprocal; the remainder of one-way connections are dispersed such that there are one or more indirect efferent paths from any one region to any other. In particular, areas associated with the initiation and control of action, such as premotor and frontal regions, project to areas important in the control of visual processing, such as parietal cortex (e.g. Matelli *et al.* 1994), and temporal areas (Jones and Powell 1970). The functional significance of these 'backward' projections is still unclear, but they do suggest a general principle of mutual influence between components of a cognitive processing stream. If perceptual systems can direct or influence the output of action systems, then we might also expect action systems to influence the output of perceptual ones.

Such reciprocal influence suggests a very different status for action systems, compared to the one-way model. In general, coordinated plans for action require the integration of a number of information sources. For example, the act of reaching for a coin must synthesize data describing the intention of the reach (e.g. whether to pick it up or cover it up), the location of the coin (within a variety of spatial frames), as well as other non-spatial attributes of the coin, for now referred to as object 'features' (e.g. its size, shape, estimates of probable weight, etc.). In an interactive system of reciprocal influences, not only would information concerning intention, object location, and object features be feeding into the action system, but there would be a corresponding flow back out, from action to this variety of other systems. By this conception, far from being the terminal output stage with no possible impact on previous processing, systems for action planning and execution can be seen as a central influence within a distributed processing system: a common junction through which intention, spatial, and non-spatial perceptual systems interact and potentially influence one another.

The model proposed here takes seriously this constraint of reciprocal connectivity between perception and action systems. It describes how selective processing can emerge in a distributed network, so that responses to important, task-relevant stimuli are made at the expense of responses to distracting or irrelevant items. In this sense, it is a model of selective visual attention, describing the allocation of limited visual-processing capacity to objects in the environment. However, the network is called a model of *selective action*, to emphasise that its scope is wider than selection of relevant objects. For effective action, it is as important to select the right parameters for action as it is to select the right object for action. In the network, selection of action attributes, such the correct shape for grasp, or the correct location for a reach, proceeds in parallel with selection of object attributes, such as target shape and location. The selective action model attempts to formulate a clear alternative to one-way models of vision and action, and to develop a minimal framework for considering how action and perceptual processes may interact in the control of behaviour.

18.2 Architecture and operation of the network

There are three fundamental assumptions of the selective action model.

1. There are specialized systems for processing the different attributes necessary for visually selected action. In particular, there are systems representing object form, location, the intention or goal of action, as well as systems coding pairwise conjunctions between these attributes.
2. Within each system, there is competition; between processing systems, there is reciprocal support for mutually consistent states.
3. Visual selection for action consists of the stable state of activity arising across the entire network of processing systems.

The model shares important assumptions of the integrated competition hypothesis (Duncan 1996; Duncan *et al.* 1997*a*), in particular the notion of coordinated and selective processing emerging as the result of interactions among many systems (see also Cohen and Huston 1994; Phaf *et al.* 1990). The most obvious difference between the selective action model and most other models of visual attention is the explicit integration of action systems into a model describing selective visual processing.

The network is an interactive activation and competition (IAC) model, as described by McClelland and Rumelhart (1981), using the same activation rules, parameters (although not parameter values), software (McClelland and Rumelhart 1988), and so on. Readers interested in detailed accounts of an IAC model's operation are referred to McClelland and Rumelhart (1981, 1988). Simply put, the model consists of simple processing units, with weighted connections between them. Each unit has an activation value, which can change with time. For each time slice, or cycle, in a run of the model, the change in a unit's activation is computed by a non-linear integration of the weighted excitatory and inhibitory inputs currently arriving at the unit. Included in this calculation is a constant 'decay' term, which tends to move a unit's activity to the baseline, sub-threshold value. If activation exceeds the unit's threshold value, the unit transmits this activity to other units, again weighted by connections. For each cycle of a simulation, all changes in activation are computed and then later applied simultaneously to all units. Although effects of noise can be easily incorporated into an IAC model, this is somewhat tangential to the current concerns, and in the present case the entire process is deterministic (as in McClelland and Rumelhart 1981).

Connections in the network are reciprocal, so that the weight from unit *i* to unit *j* is the same as that from unit *j* to unit *i*. This reciprocity means that two connected units will be either mutually inhibitory or mutually excitatory. Mutually inhibitory units compete with each other: as the activation of one unit goes up, it will tend to force down the activity of competing units. Mutual inhibition promotes a 'winner take all' result by amplifying differences in activation with time. As a unit gains an activation advantage, it will inhibit its neighbour more than its neighbour will inhibit it. On the next cycle of the simulation (all other inputs being equal), the activation advantage will then be even greater. In contrast, mutually excitatory units support one another: if one of a pair of mutually excitatory units is active, both units will tend to become active, and afterwards maintain each other's activation.

Processing in this IAC network continues until the network has entered a *stable state*, that is, until the pattern of activity in the network is stable with time. For example, consider a network consisting of only two mutually excitatory units. One stable state of this network would have both units below threshold activation. At sub-threshold activation, neither unit can send an output to activate the other, and so both will remain at this level. By contrast, an unstable state would be one where only the first of the two units was active. In this case, one of two things will happen. If the activity of the first unit, and the weighting between the units, is sufficiently high, the network will 'settle' or 'relax' into a stable state in which both units are active. Otherwise, the activation of the first unit will decay towards sub-threshold baseline levels, and the stable state will be reached where neither unit is active. Such a stable state of activation can be considered a locally optimal solution to a problem of weak constraint satisfaction, as in Rumelhart (1986).

A central concern of the model is how multiple sources of information can be used together to specify objects of most relevance in the environment. These multiple information sources are organized into specialized processing systems, as illustrated in figure 18.1. There are three invariant 'global' representations: the What, Where, and How systems. Each of these systems is connected to the others through a mediating conjunctive code. These conjunctive codes are

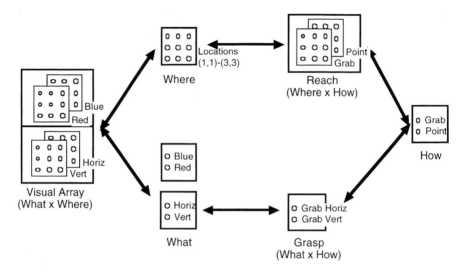

Fig. 18.1 Schematic of the selective action model, an interactive network of specialized visual and action processing systems. Invariant codes for What, Where, and How are connected to each other by appropriate conjunctive codes. All connections within the network are reciprocal. Within a system, all connections are mutually inhibitory (with the exception of shape and colour representations in the Visual Array and What systems). Groups of mutually inhibitory units are denoted by the square outlines. Between systems are mutually excitatory connections for units which may reflect consistent states. Excitatory links are indicated by arrows. For example, the 'Grab' unit of the How system projects and receives excitatory connections to the 'Grab Horizontal' and 'Grab Vertical' units of the Grasp system. See text for details.

represented in the Visual Array, Reach, and Grasp systems. The content of each system is described below.

What. Activity within the What system indicates the presence of the designated visual feature somewhere in the visual environment, but not where the feature occurs, or what action it may be associated with. Such a 'global' representation of feature activity establishes an invariant code that would be useful for object recognition. The model has separate encodings for horizontal and vertical shapes, which would affect actions such as grasping, as well as for red and blue colours, which would be irrelevant to the mechanics of action. Representations of colour and shape are independent, for example, an activated shape will inhibit other shape representations, but not ones for colour. A unit in the What system supports the activity of all units within the corresponding feature map of the Visual Array. In addition, shape features which potentially affect the mechanics of action support the activation of corresponding units in the Grasp system.

Where. Activity within the Where system indicates the presence of an object at a specific location within the Visual Array, but gives no information itself as to the visual features of that object. Units in this system each represent a separate location in a small grid. Each unit within the Where system supports activity at the corresponding location of all feature maps in the Visual Array, and likewise all action maps of the Reach system. For example, the unit representing the upper left location in the Where system has excitatory connections to the upper left unit of all the feature and action maps.

How. The units within the How system represent different intentions for action, but not a plan of execution. That is, units here do not specify how a particular reaching or grasping movement will be carried out. In the model, two possible actions are represented: intentions can be made either to point to or grab an object. Both pointing and grabbing actions must be made to a specific location.

Units in the How system therefore support the activity of all units in the appropriate action map of the Reach system (described below). In addition, a plan for grabbing must specify both the location of the target and the way the target will be grasped. Therefore, the unit representing the grab intention supports the activity of units in the Grasp system.

Visual Array. The conjunctive code of Where and What representations produces a set of 'feature maps'. Activity within these feature maps indicates both the presence of a particular visual feature, and the location of that feature. Units within the same feature map compete. To a lesser degree there is competition between feature maps encoding shape, and between feature maps encoding colour. Again, colour and shape are represented independently, so there is no inhibition between feature maps for shape and those for colour. Feature map units support activity in the What and Where systems, has described above.

Grasp. This system provides a conjunctive code of What and How representations. Units in the Grasp system correspond to the different ways an action may be carried out, as a function of the visual affordances offered by the target object. Many actions to a visual target must be adjusted to non-spatial properties of the object. For example, the action of grabbing a rectangle will be carried out differently depending upon the rectangle's orientation. Other actions, like pointing to a visually defined target, are carried out independently of the object's affordances. Here we have separate units for representing a plan to grasp a horizontal and a vertical object. There are no units representing the conjunction of pointing actions and target shape; pointing to targets is executed in the same way, regardless of shape.

Reach. Units in the Reach system represent the ways in which the action plan must be modified as a function of the target location. For example, a grabbing action to the left will involve different limb mechanics than one to the right. Different actions towards the same location may also involve different limb mechanics. The conjunctive code in the Reach system provides the required versatility. Units here are organized into 'action maps', with separate maps for each action. Unit activity represents a plan for a particular action to be directed towards a particular location.

Having described the representations in the network, it is now easier to describe how connections within and between modules are determined. Each unit in the network can be taken to reflect a hypothesis about the current state of the visual world and the action to take within it (e.g. Rumelhart 1986). For example, activity within the What system reflects hypotheses about the shapes of target objects, and the Where system the target locations. In general, whether two units share an excitatory, inhibitory, or null connection depends upon the consistency between the hypotheses they represent. If two units represent independent attributes of an object or action, then activation of one should not predict whether to expect activation of the other. For example, in the model's world, the colour of an object predicts nothing about its shape, so units representing colour share a null connection of weight zero to units representing shape. Often the hypotheses represented by different units are not independent. In these cases, if two units might potentially represent the attributes of a single object and its associated action, they are consistent and share an excitatory connection; units representing inconsistent properties share an inhibitory connection. For example, in the model, objects occupy only a single location. Therefore all units within the Where system are mutually inhibitory, as are all units within the same feature map of the Visual Array. However, activity within any location of the red feature map is consistent with the activation of the Red unit in the What system. All units in the red feature map therefore both project and receive an excitatory connection to the Red unit. The general rule of consistency is applied to the model, such that there is competition within systems, and support between them.

Although it is tempting in some ways, no strong claims are being made about the mapping of the functional representations in the model to anatomical regions of the brain. Admittedly, the representational schemes in the model are not sophisticated. Single units represent complicated concepts, such as the intention to grab something. These rather improbable representations are used to simplify analysis of the network's performance, by emphasizing the role of its architecture, rather than the internal structure of its concepts, in determining the final states of the network.

It may not be obvious that the network illustrated in figure 18.1 can do anything useful. What will coordinate the activity of this variety of systems, operating in parallel within a circular network structure? For example, what ensures that shape representations selected in the What system can be used to guide selection within the Grasp system? Or the Where system?

18.3   Simulation 1. The timecourse of selective action

The first simulation demonstrates how the selection of a single object and action emerge from processes of competition and support across many specialized systems. The network is asked to construct a plan for grabbing the red object. The visual world consists of a red vertical bar on the left (the target), and a blue horizontal bar on the right (the distractor). To successfully complete the task, the network must determine the shape of the red object, its location, and a corresponding reach and grasp. Within the confines of the network's representation, this means that the network must selectively activate the units in the What, Where, Reach, and Grasp units which correspond to the target's visual attributes and the task specification.

The visual world and task are specified by external inputs provided by the experimenter, and applied continuously through the course of the simulations. The visual world is represented by activation of the appropriate units within the feature maps of the Visual Array—that is, the middle left unit of the vertical map and the red map, and the middle right unit of the horizontal map and the blue map. External inputs to these units represent effects of the visual stimulation provided by the presentation of the red and blue bars. The task is specified by external input to both the 'grab' unit of the How system (hereafter simply the Grab unit), and the 'red' unit in the What system (Red unit). The former can be considered a general intention for action, and the latter a 'template' for the desired target object. In this case, the external inputs are meant to result from decisions, made outside the scope of the model, about current behavioural goals. As described later, these external inputs will act to bias the competition occurring within systems.

How does the model react to this environment and task specification? As an illustrative example, we can first consider how the model will determine the shape and location of the red item. As a result of external input, activity propagates from the two occupied positions of the Visual Array to the corresponding locations in the Where system, and also to all the feature units within the What system. If this were the only input to the network, then competition within the Visual Array, What, and Where systems would be perfectly balanced, and there would be no selective processing; attributes of both the target and distractor would be represented to an equal degree in all systems. However, the biasing influence provided by external input to the Red unit changes the situation dramatically, resulting in a chain reaction of propagating bias. External input to the Red unit gives it a competitive advantage over the Blue one, an advantage which becomes magnified with time. This progressive advantage means that the red feature map receives more input from the What system than the blue feature map, so that, in turn, a competitive advantage for the red feature map emerges in the Visual Array. In turn, this advantage propagates to the Where system. The middle left unit of the Where system (Left unit) receives more activation from the red feature map than the Right unit receives from the blue feature map. The competitive advantage of the Left over the Right unit indicates that the network has successfully located the red object, and is now selectively representing its location over the distractor location.

And the biases continue to propagate! Now units representing the middle left location of feature maps in the Visual Array receive more support from the Where system than those for the middle right. This means that the units in both the red feature map and the vertical feature map now have a competitive advantage over units in the blue and horizontal maps, respectively. The developing advantage for the vertical map means that the vertical unit of the What system (Vertical unit) receives more activation support from the Visual Array than the horizontal one. The eventual advantage for the Vertical unit over the Horizontal one indicates selective processing of the target shape in preference to the distractor shape.

This description illustrates a general process, of bias in one system propagating throughout a network of other competitive systems. Hopefully this example demonstrates that the model's underlying principles of competition and support are not arbitrary; together these processes ensure a stable state of activation will develop, in which a single object, perhaps one with a previously established competitive advantage, will dominate. The example is simplified, of course, since it ignores concurrent activity in the How, Reach, and Grasp systems, where similar processes are also occurring. We now take a broader look at the emergence of selective processing throughout the network.

Figure 18.2 illustrates the development of selectivity in different systems of the network. The figure compares the timecourse of activation for units representing properties of the target to those for the distractor, including both their visual properties and properties related to the desired grab action. In each case, we see an initial period in which target and distractor items are at an equal activation level, near or below threshold levels. At some point, the activation trajectories separate, such that target activation rises very quickly to an asymptotic level while distractor activity is simultaneously inhibited to the minimum possible. This separation of trajectories marks the emergence of selective target processing. Figure 18.3 plots selectivity across systems in a slightly different way, as a type of ratio between target and distractor activation (see figure caption for details). The figure illustrates the propagation of selective bias for the target across systems. In this case, selectivity is first seen for target location, followed by reach location, target shape, and finally grasp shape. The stable state of this network is characterized by the dominance of the target object and its associated action over the distractor, across all systems.

What determines the timecourse of selectivity seen in figure 18.3? The pattern of results is robust with changes in network parameters. Is it then a basic property of the network that selectivity in location precedes selectivity in shape? The best answer is probably yes and no. For the 'yes' answer, consider that in the current model, objects have only three visual properties, a colour, a shape, and a location. Colour and shape are completely independent, so that colour does not predict shape nor vice versa. In the model as presented, the only thing to indicate that a colour and a shape belong to the same object is their shared location. Accessing one object property from another, for example, shape from colour, must therefore be done through the shared location code. In this sense, location serves to bind the features together. As we would expect, given a template for target colour, the network in the current simulations selectively processes target location before selectively processing target shape.

For the 'no' answer, we must question the cartoonish nature of the representations used in these simulations. In the real world, familiar objects are not simply bundles of otherwise independent features linked only by a shared 'location', but are frequently composed of spatially distributed parts assembled in a structured manner. This structure might be represented in part by supposing units which encode conjunctions of features within the What system, or more realistically, representations which encode the possible structural relationships between features which frequently co-occur. For example, in the IAC model of word reading (McClelland and Rumelhart 1981), word-level units, encoding the structure of words from letters, allow a letter in one position of the display to support the activity of a different letter in another part of the display. In this case, a common structure (the word), serves to bind together a number of component features. A more sophisticated representation of objects might therefore allow activation of one part of an object to provide a competitive advantage for parts of the same object, compared to unrelated components of a different object. This would suggest that, with structured representations of objects and their parts, selectivity in location need not necessarily precede selectivity in other systems.

The simulation demonstrates how, given an initial state resulting from external input describing the visual world and the task to be performed, the interactive network of figure 18.1 gradually settles into a stable state in which all systems reflect properties of the target action. Several general, inter-related properties of the network are illustrated in this example. First, we have seen how a selective bias induced in one or more systems, in this case primed by external inputs to the What and How systems, can be propagated throughout the network, even to systems processing attributes

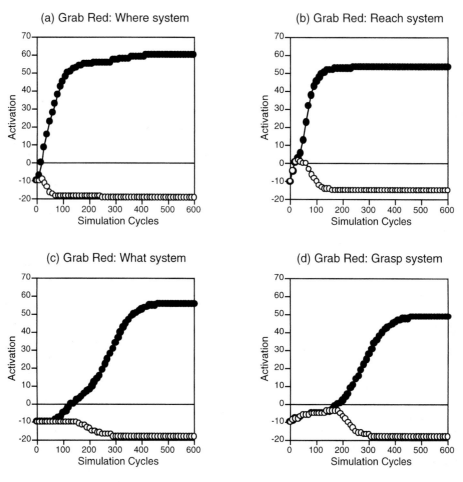

Fig. 18.2 Timecourse of activations in Simulation 1. Figures plot activation values as a function of time (simulation cycles). The activation pattern corresponding to the target object is shown in filled circles; the distractor shown in open circles. Threshold activity is marked at 0; baseline activation level is −10. (*a*) activity within the Where system (left target location and right distractor location); (*b*) activity within the Reach system (plotting activation within the grab action map for target and distractor locations); (*c*) activity within the What system (vertical target shape vs horizontal distractor shape); and (*d*) activity within the Grasp system (grab vertical target vs grab horizontal distractor).

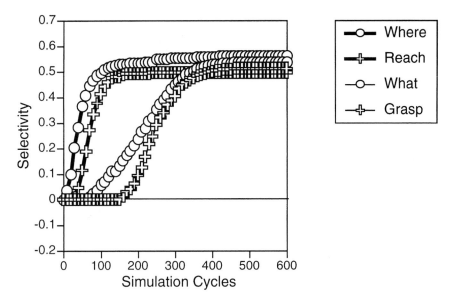

Fig. 18.3 Timecourse of selectivity in Simulation 1, in the form of relative activation of target and distractor, plotted for the What, Where, Reach, and Grasp systems. Selectivity at each cycle is calculated as the difference between target and distractor activation, divided by one plus their sum. The figure shows selectivity occurring first in the Where system, followed by the Reach, What, and Grasp systems.

which are completely independent to those primed. Units which have established a competitive edge in one system induce competitive biases in neighbouring systems, by selectively activating particular units in those systems. In this way, the network solves the problem of coordinating the activity of concurrent, parallel systems.

Second, these results illustrate the double-edged sword of competition. An obvious effect of competition within a system is that the representational capacity of that system is limited. In a winner-take-all network of mutually inhibitory units, only the properties represented by a single unit are able to sustain their activation. However, another effect of competition, at least within a coordinated network like this one, is to ensures that attributes of the selected target, and only those of the target, are represented throughout the network. Without competition, attributes from multiple objects might be represented in each system. Such a situation would create binding problems in deciding, for instance, which of the active units in the Where system should be associated with which of the active units in the What system. As demonstrated here, competition within a coordinated network addresses binding problems by focusing separate processing systems onto the same, single, target. Representational capacity is therefore limited, but tied to the properties of a single object. Similar qualities are found in behaviour, where concurrent identification of two properties from different objects produces interference, but not identification of two properties of one object (e.g. Duncan 1980, 1993; Ostry *et al.* 1976; Shiffrin and Grantham 1974).

Finally, the simulation demonstrates how selective processing can emerge both gradually with time, and broadly, across a distributed network of many different interacting systems.

18.4 Simulation 2. Competition and extinction

Many theories of normal visual attention view selective attention as a competition between visual objects for limited capacity processing (for example, Bundesen 1990; Cave and Wolfe 1990;

Duncan 1985). Strong competitors engage processing resources and response mechanisms in preference to weaker ones. Competitive advantages might result from low-level perceptual salience or as a result of goal-directed behaviour towards a desired target. For example, in a simple search for the letter Z, curved letters like D and O might be very weak competitors and produce no interference on target detection, while letters like M and X may be very strong competitors and hinder or prevent the target from being found (e.g. Neisser 1967).

This competitive account of normal attentional function can be extended to explain deficits of visuospatial attention, such as the deficit of visual extinction. Visual extinction is a relatively common disorder following unilateral brain damage to a number of areas, in particular, the right parietal lobe (Bender 1952; see Bisiach and Vallar 1988 for a review). Extinction is a deficit in detecting the more contralesional of two events, which cannot be attributed to any deficit in detecting the contralesional event on its own. Patients demonstrating visual extinction are able to detect a single stimulus in either visual field. However, when two stimuli are presented simultaneously, only the more ipsilesional stimulus is detected; in effect, the contralesional item is 'extinguished' by the ipsilesional one.

By a competitive account, visual extinction is simply a spatially specific bias of a normal attentional limitation (Ward et al. 1994; Ward and Goodrich 1996). Unilateral parietal damage weakens the competitive strength of contralesional stimuli relative to ipsilesional ones. When a contra- and ipsilesional stimulus are presented simultaneously, the ipsilesional stimulus is selected at the expense of the weak contralesional one. When the contralesional stimulus appears alone, it is still a weak potential target; but in this case, since there are no other competitors within the display, the contralesional stimulus can engage limited-capacity processes. In this way, the processing disadvantage for the contralesional stimulus only emerges under simultaneous presentation of ipsi- and contralesional stimuli. The second simulation demonstrates the different effects of bias on single- and multi-item displays.

Effects of competition between items in visual extinction emerge naturally from the selective action model. The effects of damage to a connectionist network can be simulated in a variety of ways, for example, by increasing noise or eliminating units (e.g. Humphreys et al. 1992). In the current simulations, bias against left targets following right parietal damage is simulated by applying a constant inhibitory input to units on the left side of the Where system. These 'damaged' units have effectively had their activation functions altered so that more input will be required to reach any given activation level. They will therefore be at a competitive disadvantage to units on the right side. In these simulations, no task or template is specified. Activations in the network are initially driven 'bottom-up' from the input to the Visual Array. In this simulation, the Visual Array will contain either a single item: a red vertical bar on either the left or right of the array, or two competing items as in Simulation 1, with the red vertical bar on the left and the blue horizontal one on the right.

Figure 18.4 compares the timecourse of selectivity in the damaged Where system for single targets appearing on either the left or right. For these displays containing an isolated target, moderate levels of rightward bias have very little effect. There is an advantage for right targets, but both targets show substantial levels of selectivity. By contrast, as shown in figure 18.5 when left and right items are in competition, as in the two-object displays, there is a marked disadvantage for the left target. In this case, the left target is quickly suppressed by the right, and never rises above threshold levels. The competitive bias against the left object in the Where system extends to all other systems as well: attributes of the extinguished left object and its associated reach and grasping components for action never rise above threshold.

These results show how damage to a spatial representation in the network, in the form of an inhibitory bias, can emulate the effects of visual extinction. As such, they provide a working

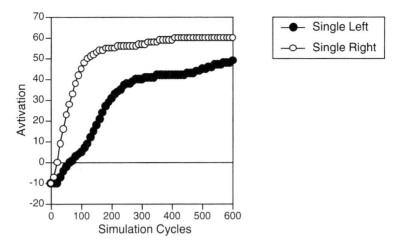

Fig. 18.4 Processing of isolated items following unilateral 'damage'. A constant inhibitory input is applied to all units representing left locations of the Where system. A single stimulus is presented either on the left (filled circles) or right (open circles). Timecourse of activity within the Where system is plotted. Despite the bias against left locations, there is substantial activation for isolated stimuli presented either to the left or right.

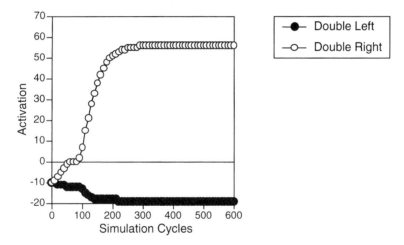

Fig. 18.5 Timecourse of activation following unilateral 'damage' to the Where system. A constant inhibitory input is applied to all units representing left locations of the Where system. Stimuli are simultaneously presented both to the left (filled circles) AND right (open circles). Competition now prevents activation on the left side.

demonstration of a competitive account of visual extinction, as outlined in Ward *et al.* (1994). The model extends previous network models of extinction (e.g. Cohen *et al.* 1994), by demonstrating how all attributes of the extinguished item, including non-spatial features and associated action, can be suppressed following damage to spatial representations. Finally, these results illustrate a pervasive effect in this competitive network: the effects of a small bias are dramatically amplified when multiple items compete.

18.5   Simulation 3. Integration and modularity

If cognitive function is not entirely modular, it is at least true that many processes are largely dissociable. This dissociability can be demonstrated in several ways. The dual-task paradigm rests on the assumption that cognitive processes share resources to varying degrees, so that the degree of interference between tasks reflects their degree of overlap (e.g. Baddeley and Hitch 1974). Dissociations of attentional function can be demonstrated in this way; for example, attention to visual and auditory stimuli appears to depend upon at least partially separate resource pools, although more central limitations can be observed (Duncan *et al.* 1997*b*). Dissociations of attentional function are also observed following brain damage in man. Visual and motoric neglect appear dissociable (e.g. Karnath 1997). Neglect for visual, auditory, and tactile stimulation are all separable disorders (e.g. Bisiach 1990; Beschin *et al.* 1996; DeRenzi *et al.* 1984), although there is also integration between them (e.g. Mattingley *et al.* 1997). Even different measures of visual neglect are dissociable (Halligan and Marshall 1992). It seems quite likely that selective attention results from the operation of numerous processes which are separable at least to some extent.

A reasonable question is whether dissociations frequently seen in selective attention would be expected in the sort of well-integrated network considered here. In the selective action model, processing is integrated, so that biases in one system propagate throughout the network. Previous analysis of interactive network models suggests dissociations should be possible. Shallice's (1988) analysis of double dissociations includes consideration of 'coupled systems' analogous to the selective action network described here. It is clear that for two interacting systems, for example, the Where and Reach systems, loss of one system would not strictly prevent the other from operating. For Shallice, the issue was therefore not whether double dissociations could be observed within coupled systems, but how to best characterize the processing of a coupled system: as a single, or as multiple, functional units? Shallice concluded that it is probably inappropriate to consider the components of a coupled system as wholly independent or as wholly integrated. He suggested the term *partially isolable*, to reflect the possibility of graded influence within an interactive system. The next simulation provides concrete support for this analysis.

As a simple demonstration of dissociability, two separate versions of the network were prepared, using the same parameters and inputs as in Simulation 1. In addition, external inhibitory input was applied to units in either the Where or Reach system encoding the location of the red target. As in Simulation 2, the immediate effect of the biasing input is to shift processing in the affected systems away from the target location and towards the distractor. In these simulations, damage was purposefully not so severe as to completely prevent target processing, but only enough to slow and impede it. Figure 18.6 plots the resulting timecourse of selectivity in the Where and Reach systems. As might be expected, bias against a target exerts its strongest effects in the system where the bias is applied. So, selectivity in the Where system is slower to resolve as a result of damage to the Where system than equivalent damage to the Reach system, and the reverse is also true.

Despite the pattern of double dissociation seen in figure 18.6, there is also evidence of integration between the damaged and undamaged systems. Figure 18.7 plots results from the damaged networks of figure 18.6 and the undamaged network of figure 18.3. The figure shows that while effects of damage are greatest in the lesioned system, they have smaller but still evident impact throughout the network. Damage to the Where system results in a slower rise to asymptotic selectivity within the undamaged Reach system (figure 18.7*b*). Such a result might be expected within a stage model, if disrupted information from the affected system were passed downstream to subsequent ones. However, that is not a sufficient explanation in this case, since damage to the Reach system results in lower asymptotic selectivity within the undamaged Where system (figure 18.7*a*).

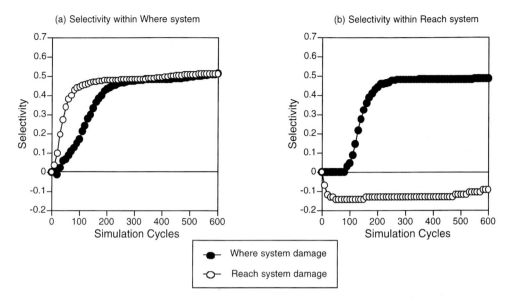

Fig. 18.6 Double dissociation following selective damage. Units representing the left side of space were damaged in either the Reach system (open circles) or the Where system (filled circles). The input consists of a target on the left and a distractor on the right. Timecourse of selectivity is plotted for (*a*) the Where system, and (*b*) the Reach system. A form of double dissociation is seen, such that effects of bias are most clearly seen in the system where the bias is applied. Note that in (*b*) there is selectivity for the wrong item.

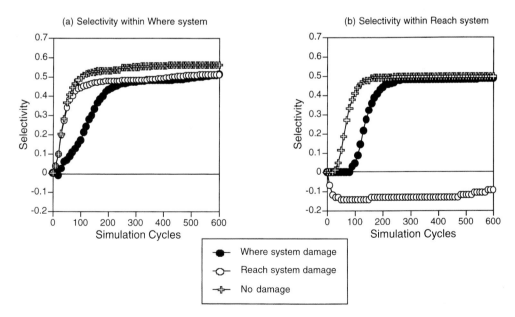

Fig. 18.7 Effects of integration following damage. Effects of damage to the Where system (filled circles) and Reach system (open circles) are compared to processing in an undamaged system (crosses). Selectivity is plotted for (*a*) the Where system, and (*b*) the Reach system. Effects of damage can be seen even outside the damaged system.

Instead, bias against the target representation in one system reduces the support that can be provided to target attributes in other systems. We therefore see effects of both modularity, in the pattern of double dissociation of figure 18.6, and simultaneously, effects of integration, as shown by effects of lesions on processing in undamaged systems.

18.6 Simulation 4. Effects of action on perception

The structure of the network suggests that each processing system has at least an indirect influence on all other systems. In particular, unlike stage models of visual attention, the interactive account suggests that action systems should influence visual processing systems. This suggestion can be questioned on two grounds. First, is there any evidence that the model actually demonstrates these action-based effects? The results from Simulation 1 show action selectivity arising in action systems only *after* selectivity in associated perceptual systems. This single aspect of the results might be compatible with one-way models. A second question is, even if action-based effects can be found in the model, is there any reason to believe that effects of action can be observed on the human perceptual system?

Whether or not it is worth answering the first question may depend on the answer to the second. It does appear that action can influence perceptual and attentional processes. This influence has been demonstrated most frequently in unilateral neglect patients with parietal damage, where neglect can be mitigated by some types of motor activity and postural adjustments. For example, neglect of the left side is reduced if subjects orient their trunk and/or head towards the left, even when eye fixation is maintained centrally. Studies by Robertson and colleagues have found that contralesional visual and spatial deficits in unilateral visual neglect can be reduced by appropriate forms of action or 'limb activation' (e.g. Robertson and North 1992; Robertson *et al.* 1992). In general, benefits come from directing action towards contralesional space, for example, by clinching the contralesional hand during cancellation (Robertson and North 1994) or walking (Robertson *et al.* 1994). Activation of prehensive control systems also appears to reduce manifestations of neglect: Robertson *et al.* (1995) found that bisection errors to a horizontal rod were reduced when patients reached to grab the middle of the rod, as opposed to pointing towards the middle. Another form of bias in selective visual processing might therefore be spatial and affordance-based compatibilities between visual stimuli and concurrent actions. One way to summarize these findings would be to say that directed action towards an object induces a bias to attend the object. This action-based bias may be sufficient to override a bias induced by damage to parietal areas.

This suggestion was tested in a simulation comparing the effects of pointing and grabbing actions on perceptual performance within the network. As described earlier, the 'grab' action of the How system supports activity in both the Reach and the Grasp systems. This bidirectional support is necessary because a coordinated grab must take into account both the location of the target and its shape (as well as its size, weight, etc.). A pointing action need not vary with object shape, and therefore neither supports nor receives support from units in the Grasp system. This difference in connectivity predicts differences in network activation: a grab action can potentially promote selectivity of the target, via support of target shape, in a way that a pointing action cannot.

The simulation offers an analogue to the Robertson *et al.* (1995) study comparing bisection errors with pointing and grabbing tasks. In this case, the network is given the usual visual display with a red vertical target on the left and a blue horizontal distractor on the right. Similar to Simulation 2, an inhibitory bias is applied to units on the left side of the Where system. The network is instructed, through activation of the Red unit and appropriate How units, to select the red object, either for a pointing or grabbing action. In these simulations, we compare the timecourse of activation within the damaged Where system as a function of the action specified.

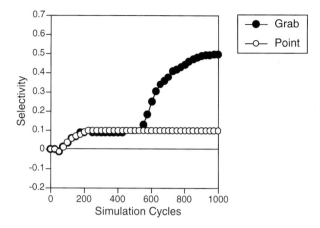

Fig. 18.8 Comparison of grabbing and pointing effects following damage to the Where system. A constant inhibitory input is applied to all units representing left locations of the Where system. The visual input consists of a red target on the left and a blue distractor on the right. The figure compares selectivity in the damaged Where system following instructions to grab the target (filled circles), or point to the target (open circles).

These results are shown in figure 18.8. The grab action is clearly less sensitive to damage within the Where system than the pointing action. This effect must be attributed to extra support for the target as a result of the mutual support between the grabbing action and units within the Grasp system. The mechanisms within the network responsible for this effect are detailed below; at present we can see that this result is similar to the findings of Robertson *et al.* (1995), and consistent with their account of 'leakage' from an undamaged processing stream required for the grasping task.

A similar account based on action-based facilitation of perception might be applied to the case of DF (Goodale *et al.* 1991). Following carbon monoxide poisoning and bilateral damage to ventro-occipital areas, DF demonstrated profound perceptual loss. She was unable to do simple same–different judgments based on line orientation, and was unable to estimate the size of graspable objects. Despite this impairment, DF was little different from controls in more active tasks requiring orientation judgment and size discrimination. For example, she could post a card through a slot of variable orientation, and her grip aperture varied in a consistent manner with the size of the target object. Goodale and Milner suggest that DF's good performance on active tasks reflects the integrity of her dorsal pathway.

According to the Goodale and Milner account, visual information reflecting shape information would be represented in two places. Ventrally, shape information would be used for object recognition and categorization. Dorsally, there would be a separate system including representations of shape and other object properties necessary for grasping. By this account, DF would have lost the ventral pathway and the ability to perform overt object recognition; however, the undamaged shape representations available dorsally would allow good performance on grasping tasks.

A second possibility is that there is only a single representation of object shape available, but that directed action to a target can facilitate processing of object shape. In the selective action model, this claim can be examined by comparing grabbing actions, which both require and support representations of object shape, to pointing actions, which do not actively support shape representations. The simulations illustrated in figure 18.9 were set up in much the same

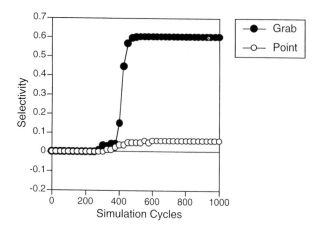

Fig. 18.9 Comparison of grabbing and pointing effects following damage to the What system. A constant inhibitory input is applied to all units in the What system. The visual input consists of a red target on the left and a blue distractor on the right. The figure compares selectivity in the damaged What system following instructions to grab the target (filled circles), or point to the target (open circles).

way as for figure 18.8. However, in this case, rather than implementing a spatial bias within the Where system, both the horizontal and vertical shape representations in the What system receive inhibitory external input. This inhibition is meant to reflect the effects of pervasive damage to shape representations, as in the case of DF. The effects of this damage are severe with the pointing task, as seen in figure 18.9. In this case, there is little selective processing of target shape possible within the damaged What system. However, selective processing of shape is possible if the task is to grab rather than point to the target, as shown in figure 18.9. With the grabbing action, the What system receives support from activated representations in the Grasp system, to counteract opposing, non-specific inhibitory effects of damage within the What system.

How do these action-based effects arise? How is it that the activation of a plan such as grab, which in itself is not specific to attributes of either the target or distractor, mitigates specific effects of damage? Although not apparent in figures 18.8 and 18.9, these benefits of action rely on differences in sub-threshold levels of target and distractor representation within the damaged system. In these simulations, the negative bias induced by damage is more than sufficient to prevent activation of target attributes from rising above threshold, but can not completely negate influences from other systems, such as input from the Visual Array, and the selective effects of activating a desired visual 'template' in the What system. The result is that in the absence of additional inputs, there remain small differences between the sub-threshold activations of target and distractor. Consider a non-specific input which provides an equal boost to both target and distractor activations, so that the activation difference is the same, but now above threshold. At such a point, competition between representations would mean that the initial advantage of the target is amplified at the expense of the distractor, so that selectivity would develop much as in Simulation 1. Essentially, the grab action provides this non-specific boost.

Because the grabbing action has mutually excitatory connections with the Grasp system, which the pointing action does not, grabbing produces two non-specific effects which eventually serve to amplify sub-threshold differences elsewhere in the network. First, mutual support between the grab unit and the Grasp system means that, for a given external input to the How system, a grab will result in slightly higher asymptotic activation within the How system than a point. This higher asymptotic activation provides greater non-specific support for units in the Reach system, and one link later, to the Where system. In the simulation analogous to Robertson *et al.* (1995), illustrated in figure 18.8, differences between target and distractor in the Where system, at sub-threshold levels due to effects of damage, are amplified by this activation flow. Second, non-specific activation of the Grasp system from the grab unit promotes non-specific activation of graspable features in the What system. In the simulation analogous to the DF case study, illustrated in figure 18.9, this would amplify the sub-threshold advantage for the target shape.

It appears that results from both brain-damaged populations and the selective action model support the notion of action-based influences on perception. In the selective action model, biases induced by action serve to focus processing on objects in exactly the same manner as biases induced by templates for target colour, shape, or location.

18.7 General discussion

The selective action model simulates the emergence of capacity-limited selective processing in an interactive network of visual and action systems. The architecture of the model is derived from a few simple principles. In particular, systems processing global representations of shape, location, and intention for action are reciprocally connected to each other through mediating conjunctive codes. Objects and actions compete within separate processing systems, but between systems, consistent states support one another. The end result is that biases induced in one system, whether as a result of damage, stimulation from the environment, or strategic goals, propagate both gradually and broadly throughout the entire network, so that a single object and its associated action come to dominate all systems.

The simulations reported here demonstrate the emergence of selective action, given a representation of the visual world and a specification of the task; extinction-like effects produced through bias and competition; dissociations and integration occurring simultaneously within the network; and action-based effects on perceptual processing. In addition to issues raised in the discussion of each of these results, it is worth highlighting two of the more general properties of these simulations. First, there is no devoted mechanism for visual or action selection within the network. Selectivity develops as a result of competitive and cooperative interactions in a distributed network. Second, any system within the distributed network of the model has the potential to influence processing within any other system. In this regard, the point given the most emphasis here has been on the link between action and perception, and the way that selectivity for object and action attributes can develop in a mutually influential way. But a number of other predictions can be made: that selectivity in the Where system aids selectivity in the What system, that selectivity in Grasp aids Where, and so on. For example, if there is a bias in the What system to process objects over non-objects (e.g. Ward and Goodrich 1996), then the model would predict correspondingly better localization in the Where system for objects over non-objects. The model therefore offers a framework for considering the general question of how multiple information sources influence one another in selection.

How does the operation of the selective action model compare to other models of selective attention? Current models of visual attention share a number of important qualities. Many otherwise disparate theories of visual attention (e.g. Bundesen 1990; Duncan 1996; Humphreys and Müller 1993; Treisman and Gormican 1988; Wolfe 1994), and including this one, suggest that attention can be directed on the basis of many attributes (at least perceptual attributes); that selection is a competitive process in which some candidates are given a higher weighting than others; and that selection of an object gives access to all (or at least many) of its properties. Differences between the selective action model and other models of selective processing seem to fall along two main lines, concerning the basic mechanisms for producing selective processing, and the status of action-based processing in the control of selectivity.

Many qualities of the model's selective processing are a function of its interactive network architecture. In some respects, the operation of the selective action model is similar, or at least consistent with, other interactive accounts of attention (e.g. Duncan 1996; Farah *et al.* 1993; Cohen and Huston 1994; Humphreys and Riddoch 1994; Phaf *et al.* 1990), but can be contrasted with more traditional serial models, in which selectivity is produced by moving attention from one object in the display to the next (e.g. Posner 1980; Sternberg 1969; Treisman and Gelade 1980; Treisman and Gormican 1988; Wolfe 1994). In the selective action model there is no explicit 'attention' system, separate from the processes computing representations of object shape, location, grasp, and so on. There is, for example, no machinery to move a 'spotlight' of attention from one object to another, or to track which items have been previously attended. Selection mechanisms cannot be localized to any anatomical focus, such as the anterior and posterior attention systems of Posner and Dehaene (1994). Each system interacts with all the others, so that there is no terminal, output stage of processing. Instead of distinguishing between 'preattentive', 'attentional', or 'post-attentional' processes, there is a continual and developing selectivity, beginning with parallel processing for all objects across all systems, and converging in a stable state in which a single object and action are dominant throughout.

But are such distinctions from more traditional models a good thing or a bad thing? There are at least some reasons to prefer parallel, interactive models like the selective action network. Traditional serial models typically assume that attention is moved at relatively high rates, of approximately 50 ms per item. However, studies which measure the timecourse of attention directly suggest that the reallocation of attention from one item to another is a slow process, lasting a half-second or more (e.g. Duncan *et al.* 1994; Raymond *et al.* 1992; Ward *et al.* 1996). This extended dwell time of attention is consistent with the gradual development of the network's stable selective state. But while predicting long dwell times of attention, the model also predicts differences between conjunctive and feature search performance (e.g. Treisman and Gelade 1980), typically used in support of high-speed models. Greater competition within a feature map than between feature maps produces the desired effect. In conjunctive search, but not feature search, there is inhibition from non-targets on all target features. Simulations show increasing numbers of non-targets in conjunctive search conditions increase target inhibition, and slow selective target processing at a roughly linear rate. Increasing non-targets in feature search has little to no effect on selective target processing. This result is not necessarily surprising, as it is well known that parallel systems can mimic many of the outputs of serial ones (Townsend and Ashby 1982), and other models of attention assuming parallel processing of display items have captured distinctions between conjunctive and feature search (e.g. Bundesen 1990; Humphreys and Müller 1993; Ward and McClelland 1989). Nevertheless, these results do demonstrate some of the wider applications of the model.

Experiments examining the relationship between grouping and spatial selectivity also support interactive models. It is often assumed that spatially parallel 'preattentive' processes group and segment the visual world, and then pass their results on to spatial attention systems (Treisman 1988; Wolfe 1994). Many experiments demonstrate such effects of grouping on spatial selection (e.g. Prinzmetal 1981; Prinzmetal and Millis-Wright 1984; Ward *et al.* 1994). However, the reverse outcome may also be possible. Recent findings suggest that grouping based on bottom-up similarity can be modulated by spatial attention (Ben-Av *et al.* 1992; Mack *et al.* 1992; but see Moore and Egeth 1998). Such results argue against a stage of 'preattentive' processing, separate and prior to 'attentional' processes. However, mutual influence between specialized processing systems is the heart of interactive models like the selective action network. Other results have found that overt response to 'preattentive features' is an attention-demanding process; for example, pop-out orientation targets are not be detected during the period of the attentional blink (Joseph *et al.* 1997). Joseph *et al.* question the notion of preattentive representations distinct from attention. An alternative would be an interactive network like the selective action model: once an object has gained control of the network's stable state, even simple feature representations of other objects will be inhibited (e.g. within the What system). In these ways, the selective action model offers a different way to characterise the transition from early, spatially parallel processing, to the later selective focus on the properties of a single object.

The selective action model is probably unique in its assertion that selection of object and action attributes occur in a mutually influential way. However, the model does share important qualities with the premotor theory of attention, developed by Rizzolatti and colleagues (e.g. Rizzolatti *et al.* 1987). According to premotor theory, spatial attention is driven by the same mechanisms responsible for movement in space. For example, covert attention to the left-most of two objects would be driven by a suppressed motor plan to fixate the left object. The selective action model shares this important characteristic of the premotor theory, on the role of action-based representations in the development of the selective states. However, premotor theory provides no role for non-spatial influences in the development of selective spatial attention. In this respect, premotor theory is the converse of many traditional models, which have been developed primarily as models of processes involved in object recognition. Just as these models afford no role for action-based systems in selective processing of object attributes, premotor theory suggests no influence of non-spatial object attributes in the selection of action-based, spatial representations. In the absence of a computational version of premotor theory, it is unclear whether such separation of object and action attributes would work effectively in practice. The selective action model is explicit in suggesting that both spatial and non-spatial systems, specialized for both vision and action, play mutually influential roles in the control of selective processing.

The current model has numerous shortcomings. We have already seen limitations arising from the lack of structure in the model's representation of visual objects. Tighter mapping to brain structures might also be potentially valuable. Perhaps a more serious concern is that the model predicts that action may enhance, but should never inhibit, the perception of objects whose attributes and affordances are consistent with the action. As described earlier, facilitation from action has been found in neglect patients (e.g. Robertson *et al.* 1995), but evidence from healthy adults on this point is divided. Some studies have found that planning for lateralized eye-movements biases attention towards the planned fixation (Sheliga *et al.* 1994, Duebel and Schneider 1996). More recently, Duebel and Schneider (1998) have shown similar results for prepared lateralized reaching movements, such that visual attention appears biased towards the location of the reach. Other evidence consistent with action-based enhancement would include effects reported by Tipper *et al.* (1992; see Chapter 14, this volume). Using a large display board, Tipper *et al.* asked participants to reach for a target (red) LED light in the presence of a distractor (yellow) light. Interference from the distractor, as measured by response latency, was a function of distractor distance from the responding hand, rather than distance from the head, body, or target LED. Tipper *et al.* suggest that objects automatically evoke plans for action which compete for execution. In this case, competition between objects is biased by the location of the acting hand.

However, there are other demonstrations showing that action can interfere with the visual processing of objects consistent with the action. Fischer (1997) found a discrimination advantage for visual targets appearing contralateral to the cued reach location. Müsseler and Hommel have discovered a form of 'action-blindness', such that execution of lateralized movement interferes with the identification (Müsseler and Hommel 1997*a*) and detection (Müsseler and Hommel 1997*b*) of items semantically related to the response. For example, a left key press interfered with the detection of left-pointing arrows. Müsseler and Hommel (1997*a*) suggest their findings of 'action blindness' may be similar to difficulties in binding multiple tokens to a single type, as in studies of repetition blindness (Kanwisher 1987). In this case, preparation for action may bind a global type representation so that it is unavailable for the subsequent visual stimulus. Inhibitory effects of action may then be based on effects arising from successive stimulus presentations, which are currently not modelled by the selective action network. However, even this conclusion may be premature. At present the database describing the effects of action on perception is too limited to allow the principled distinctions one would like when classifying studies showing facilitatory and inhibitory effects. More research on this topic is deserved.

It is too bad, but the odds of any theory being 'correct' approach zero. The simple assumptions used to keep the model's behaviour understandable are surely too simple, or perhaps just wrong. Despite this, the selective action model may offer a different way to think about selective states of attention, how they arise, and the variety of processing systems that may be involved. Ultimately, the selective action model's most general prediction is of a gradual and broad selectivity, occurring simultaneously over interacting systems for perception and action. Hopefully, this general approach provides a minimal framework for considering integrated systems of perception and action.

References

Baddeley, A. D. and Hitch, G. J. 1974 Working memory. In G. H. Bower (ed.), *The Psychology of Learning and Motivation*: Vol 8 (pp. 47–89). New York: Academic Press.

Ben-Av, M. B., Sagi, D. and Braun, J. 1992 Visual-attention and perceptual grouping. *Perception and Psychophysics* **52**, 277–94.

Bender, M. B. 1952 *Disorders in Perception*. Springfield, Illinois: Charles C. Thomas.

Beschin, N., Cazzani, M., Della Sala, S. and Spinazzola, L. 1996 Ignoring left and far: An investigation of tactile neglect. *Neuropsychologia* **34**, 41–9.

Bisiach, E. 1991 Extinction and neglect. In J. Paillard (ed.), *Brain and Space* (pp. 251–7). Oxford: Oxford University Press.

Bisiach, E. and Vallar, G. 1988 Hemineglect in humans. In F. Boller and J. Grafman (eds), *Handbook of Neuropsychology*: Vol. 1 (pp. 195–222). Amsterdam: Elsevier.

Brunn, J. L. and Farah, M. J. 1991 The relation between spatial attention and reading: Evidence from the neglect syndrome. *Cognitive Neuropsychology* **8**, 59–75.

Bundesen, C. 1990 A theory of visual attention. *Psychological Review* **97**, 523–47.

Cave, K. R. and Wolfe, J. M. 1990 Modeling the role of parallel processing in visual search. *Cognitive Psychology* **22**, 225–71.

Cohen, J. D. and Huston, T. A. 1994 Progress in the use of interactive models for understanding attention and performance. In T. Inui and J. L. McClelland (eds), *Attention and Performance*, Vol XV (pp. 453–76). Cambridge, MA: MIT Press.

Cohen, J. D., Romero, R. D., Servan-Schreiber, D. and Farah, M. J. 1994 Mechanisms of spatial attention: The relation of macrostructure to microstructure in parietal neglect. *Journal of Cognitive Neuroscience* **6**, 377–87.

DeRenzi, E., Gentilini, M. and Pattacini, F. 1984 Auditory extinction following hemisphere damage. *Neuropsychologia* **22**, 733–44.

Deubel, H. and Schneider, W. X. 1996 Saccade target selection and object recognition: Evidence for a common attentional mechanism. *Vision Research* **36**, 1827–37.

Deubel, H. and Schneider, W. X. 1998 Selective dorsal and ventral processing: Evidence for a common attentional mechanism in reaching and perception. *Visual Cognition*, in press.

Duncan, J. 1980 The locus of interference in the perception of simultaneous stimuli. *Psychological Review* **87**, 272–300.

Duncan, J. 1993 Similarity between concurrent visual discriminations: Dimensions and objects. *Perception and Psychophysics* **54**, 425–30.

Duncan, J. 1996 Cooperating brain systems in selective perception and action. In T. Inui and J. L. McClelland (eds), *Attention and Performance*, Vol XVI (pp. 549–78). Cambridge, MA: MIT Press.

Duncan, J., Ward, R. and Shapiro, K. 1994 Direct measurement of attentional dwell time in human vision. *Nature* **369**, 313–15.

Duncan, J., Humphreys, G. W. and Ward, R. 1997*a*. Competitive brain activity in visual attention. *Current Opinion in Neurobiology* **7**, 255–61.

Duncan, J., Martens, S. and Ward, R. 1997*b*. Restricted attentional capacity within but not between sensory modalities. *Nature* **387**, 808–10.

Farah, M. J., Wallace, M. A. and Vecera, S. P. 1993 'What' and 'where' in visual attention: Evidence from the neglect syndrome. In I. H. Robertson and J. C. Marshall (eds), *Unilateral Neglect: Clinical and Experimental Studies* (pp. 123–37). New York: Lawrence Erlbaum.

Fischer, M. 1997 Attention allocation during manual movement preparation and execution. *European Journal of Cognitive Psychology* **9**, 17–51.

Goodale, M. A., Milner, A. D., Jakobson, L. S. and Carey, D. P. 1991 A neurological dissociation between perceiving objects and grasping them. *Nature* **349**, 154–6.

Halligan, P. W. and Marshall, J. C. 1992 Left visuospatial neglect: A meaningless entity? *Cortex* **4**, 525–35.

Humphreys, G. W. and Müller, H. J. 1993 Search via recursive rejection (SERR): A connectionist model of visual search. *Cognitive Psychology* **25**, 43–110.

Humphreys, G. W. and Riddoch, M. J. 1994 Attention to within-object and between-object spatial representations: Multiple sites for visual selection. *Cognitive Neuropsychology* **11**, 207–42.

Humphreys, G. W., Freeman, T. A. C. and Müller, H. J. 1992 Lesioning a connectionist model of visual search: Selective effects of distractor grouping. *Canadian Journal of Psychology* **46**, 417–60.

Jones, E. G. and Powell, T. P. 1970 An anatomical study of converging sensory pathways within the cerebral cortex of the monkey. *Brain* **93**, 793–820.

Joseph, J. S., Chun, M. M. and Nakayama, K. 1997 Attentional requirements in a 'preattentive' feature search task. *Nature* **387**, 805–7.

Kanwisher, N. 1987 Repetition blindness: Type recognition without token individuation. *Cognition* **27**, 117–43.

Karnath, H. O. 1997 Spatial orientation and the representation of space with parietal lobe lesions. *Philosophical Transactions of the Royal Society of London, Series B: Biological Sciences* **352**, 1411–19.

Mack, A., Tang, B., Tuma, R., Kahn, S. and Rock, I. 1992 Perceptual organization and attention. *Cognitive Psychology* **24**, 475–501.

Matelli, M., Luppino, G., Murata, A. and Sakata, H. 1994 Independent anatomical circuits for reaching and grasping linking the inferior parietal sulcus and inferior area 6 in macaque monkey. *Society for Neuroscience Abstracts* **20**, 404.4.

Mattingley, J. B., Driver, J., Beschin, N. and Robertson, I. H. 1997 Attentional competition between modalities: Extinction between touch and vision after right hemisphere damage. *Neuropsychologia* **35**, 867–80.

McClelland, J. L. and Rumelhart, D. E. 1981 An interactive activation model of context effects in letter perception: Part 1. An account of basic findings. *Psychological Review* **88**, 375–407.

McClelland, J. L. and Rumelhart, D. E. 1988 Explorations in Parallel Distributed Processing: A Handbook of Models, Programs, and Exercises. Cambridge, MA : Bradford.

Moore, C. M. and Egeth, H. 1997 Perception without attention: Evidence of grouping under conditions of inattention. *Journal of Experimental Psychology: Human Perception and Performance* **23**, 339–52.

Müsseler, J. and Hommel, B. 1997*a* Blindness to response-compatible stimuli. *Journal of Experimental Psychology: Human Perception and Performance* **23**, 861–72.

Müsseler, J. and Hommel, B. 1997*b* Detecting and identifying response compatible stimuli. *Psychonomic Bulletin and Review* **4**, 125–9.

Neisser, U. 1967 *Cognitive Psychology*. New York: Appleton-Century-Crofts.

Ostry, D., Moray, N. and Marks, G. 1976 Attention, practice, and semantic targets. *Journal of Experimental Psychology: Human Perception and Performance* **2**, 326–36.

Phaf, R. H., van der Heijden, A. H. C. and Hudson, P. T. W. 1990 SLAM: A connectionist model for attention in visual selection tasks. *Cognitive Psychology* **22**, 273–341.

Posner, M. I. and Dehaene, S. 1994 Attentional networks. *Trends in Neurosciences* **17**, 75–9.

Posner, M. I. 1980 Orienting of attention. *Quarterly Journal of Experimental Psychology* **32**, 3–25.

Prinzmetal, W. 1981 Principles of feature integration in visual perception. *Perception and Psychophysics* **30**, 330–40.

Prinzmetal, W. and Millis-Wright, M. 1984 Cognitive and linguistic factors affect visual feature integration. *Cognitive Psychology* **16**, 305–40.

Raymond, J. E., Shapiro, K. L. and Arnell, K. M. 1992 Temporary suppression of visual processing in an RSVP task: An attentional blink? *Journal of Experimental Psychology: Human Perception and Performance* **18**, 849–60.

Rizzolatti, G., Riggio, L., Dascola, I. and Umita, C. 1987 Reorienting attention across the horizontal and vertical meridians: Evidence in favor of a premotor theory of attention. *Neuropsychologia* **25**, 31–40.

Robertson, I. H. and North, N. T. 1992 Spatio-motor cueing in unilateral left neglect: The role of hemispace, hand and motor activation. *Neuropsychologia* **30**, 553–63.

Robertson, I. H. and North, N. T. 1994 One hand is better than 2: Motor extinction of left hand advantage in unilateral neglect. *Neuropsychologia* **32**, 1–11.

Robertson, I. H., North, N. T. and Geggie, C. 1992 Spatiomotor cueing in unilateral left neglect: Three case studies of its therapeutic effects. *Journal of Neurology, Neurosurgery, and Psychiatry* **55**, 799–805.

Robertson, I. H., Tegner, R., Goodrich, S. J. and Wilson, C. 1994 Walking trajectory and hand movements in unilateral left neglect: A vestibular hypothesis. *Neuropsychologia* **32**, 1495–501.

Rumelhart, D. E. 1986 Schemata and sequential thought. In J. L. McClelland and D. E. Rumelhart (eds), *Parallel Distributed Processing: Explorations in the Microstructure of Cognition*, Vol. 2 (pp. 7–57), Cambridge, MA: Bradford.

Shallice, T. 1988 *From Neuropsychology to Mental Structure*. New York: Cambridge University Press.

Sheliga, B. M., Riggio, L. and Rizzolatti, G. 1994 Spatial attention and eye movements. *Experimental Brain Research* **105**, 261–75.

Shiffrin, R. M. and Grantham, D. W. 1974 Can attention be allocated to a sensory modality? *Perception and Psychophysics* **15**, 460–74.

Sternberg, S. 1969 The discovery of processing stages: Extensions of Donders' method. In W. G. Koster (ed.), *Attention and Performance II*. Amsterdam: North-Holland. (Reprinted from *Acta Psychologia* 1969, **30**, 276–315.)

Tipper, S. P., Lortie, C. and Baylis, G. C. 1992 Selective reaching: Evidence for action-centered attention. *Journal of Experimental Psychology: Human Perception and Performance* **18**, 891–905.

Townsend, J. T. and Ashby, F. G. 1983 *Stochastic modelling of elementary psychological processes*. Cambridge UK: Cambridge University Press.

Treisman, A. 1988 Features and objects: The fourteenth Bartlett Memorial Lecture. *Quarterly Journal of Experimental Psychology* **40A**, 201–37.

Treisman, A. and Gelade, G. 1980 A feature integration theory of attention. *Cognitive Psychology* **12**, 97–136.

Treisman, A. M. and Gormican, S. 1988 Feature analysis in early vision: evidence from search asymmetries. *Psychological Review* **95**, 15–48.

Ward, R. and Goodrich, S. J. 1996 Differences between objects and non-objects in visual extinction: A competition for attention. *Psychological Science* **7**, 177–80.

Ward, R. and McClelland, J. L. 1989 Conjunctive search for one and two identical targets. *Journal of Experimental Psychology: Human Perception and Performance* **15**, 664–72.

Ward, R., Goodrich, S. J., and Driver, J. 1994 Grouping reduces visual extinction: Neuropsychological evidence for weight-linkage in visual selection. *Visual Cognition* **1**, 101–29.

Ward, R., Duncan, J. and Shapiro, K. 1996 The slow time-course of visual attention. *Cognitive Psychology*, **30**, 79–109.

Wolfe, J. M. 1994 Guided search 2.0: A revised model of visual-search. *Psychonomic Bulletin and Review* **1**, 202–38.

Young, M. P. 1995 Open questions about the neural mechanisms of visual pattern recognition. In M. S. Gazzaniga (ed.), *The Cognitive Neurosciences*. Cambridge, MA: Bradford.

Index

The main treatment of a given topic is indicated in bold